SPRINGER PUBLISHING

MW00838050

GET THE MOST FROM YOUR BOOK

SPRINGER PUBLISHING
C⦁NNECT™

VOUCHER CODE:
FWAG294J

Online Access

Your print purchase of *Trauma Counseling: Theories and Interventions for Managing Trauma, Stress, Crisis, and Disaster, Second Edition*, includes **online access via Springer Publishing Connect**™ to increase accessibility, portability, and searchability.

Insert the code at http://connect.springerpub.com/content/book/978-0-8261-5085-1 today!

Having trouble? Contact our customer service department at cs@springerpub.com

Instructor Resource Access for Adopters

Let us do some of the heavy lifting to create an engaging classroom experience with a variety of instructor resources included in most textbooks SUCH AS:

INSTRUCTOR'S MANUAL

POWERPOINTS

TEST BANK

Visit **https://connect.springerpub.com/** and look for the **"Show Supplementary"** button on your **book homepage** to see what is available to instructors! First time using Springer Publishing Connect?

Email **textbook@springerpub.com** to create an account and start unlocking valuable resources.

Trauma Counseling

Lisa López Levers, PhD, LPCC-S, LPC, CRC, NCC, is Professor Emeritus of Counselor Education and Human Development in the Department of Educational Foundations and Leadership at Duquesne University, Pittsburgh, PA. She is a Licensed Professional Clinical Counselor (LPCC-S, endorsed supervisor, Ohio), Licensed Professional Counselor (LPC, Pennsylvania), Certified Rehabilitation Counselor (CRC), and National Certified Counselor (NCC). She has worked clinically with survivors of trauma and offered crisis intervention counseling since 1974. She regularly has taught several trauma-related graduate courses over the last three decades, and she has provided trauma and crisis intervention training to such diverse groups as mental health professionals, police officers, teachers, and medical personnel. Levers was awarded as a Fulbright Scholar (2003–2004, Botswana) and held the Endowed Chair of African Studies (2012–2017, Duquesne University). With international recognition for her work with traumatized populations, she has provided extensive trauma counseling, training, and research throughout the southern region of Africa as well as in Rwanda, 12 years after the genocide, through a research-based collaboration with the Rwandan Ministry of Health. She worked with a team of mental health professionals in Russia, shortly after the end of the Soviet era, to initiate and develop a system of community-based foster care for vulnerable children there. She has continued to work with local community organizations, offering trauma-informed services in response to specific events as well as when the need arises for community-based advocacy. She was elected to serve as the president-elect (2022–2023) of the *International Association for Resilience and Trauma Counseling*, an affiliate of the *American Counseling Association*.

Trauma Counseling

Theories and Interventions for Managing Trauma, Stress, Crisis, and Disaster

Second Edition

LISA LÓPEZ LEVERS, PHD, LPCC-S, LPC, CRC, NCC

 SPRINGER PUBLISHING

Springer Publishing Company, LLC
11 West 42nd Street, New York, NY 10036

www.springerpub.com
connect.springerpub.com/

Acquisitions Editor: Rhonda Dearborn
Senior Content Development Editor: Lucia Gunzel
Compositor: Transforma

ISBN: 978-0-8261-5084-4
ebook ISBN: 978-0-8261-5085-1
DOI: 10.1891/9780826150851

 A robust set of instructor resources designed to supplement this text is located at http://connect.springerpub.com/content/book/978-0-8261-5085-1. Qualifying instructors may request access by emailing textbook@springerpub.com.

Instructor's Manual ISBN: 978-0-8261-5086-8
Instructor's PowerPoint ISBN: 978-0-8261-5087-5
Transition Guide From First Edition to Second Edition ISBN: 978-0-8261-5088-2

22 23 24 25 / 5 4 3 2 1

The author and the publisher of this Work have made every effort to use sources believed to be reliable to provide information that is accurate and compatible with the standards generally accepted at the time of publication. The author and publisher shall not be liable for any special, consequential, or exemplary damages resulting, in whole or in part, from the readers' use of, or reliance on, the information contained in this book. The publisher has no responsibility for the persistence or accuracy of URLs for external or third-party Internet websites referred to in this publication and does not guarantee that any content on such websites is, or will remain, accurate or appropriate.

Library of Congress Cataloging-in-Publication Data

Names: Levers, Lisa López, editor.
Title: Trauma counseling: theories and interventions for managing trauma, stress, crisis, and disaster /
    Lisa López Levers, PhD, LPCC-S, LPC, CRC, NCC, editor.
Description: Second Edition. | New York, NY : Springer Publishing Company, 2022. | Includes bibliographical references and index.
Identifiers: LCCN 2021970067 | ISBN 9780826150844 (paperback) | ISBN 9780826150851 (ebook)
Subjects: LCSH: Psychic trauma–Treatment. | Wounds and injuries–Psychological aspects.
Classification: LCC RC552.P67 L475 2022 | DDC 616.85/21–dc23/eng/20220114
LC record available at https://lccn.loc.gov/2021970067

Levers, Lisa López: https://orcid.org/0000-0002-7723-6893

Publisher's Note: **New and used products purchased from third-party sellers are not guaranteed for quality, authenticity, or access to any included digital components.**

Printed in the United States of America by Gasch Printing.

This book is dedicated to my daughter,

Koketso Sheebah K. Letsatsi.

Sheebah, you are the joy of my life; you light my world!

Contents

Contributors

Reverend Paul T. Abernathy, MPIA, M. Div CEO, Neighborhood Resilience Project, Pittsburgh, Pennsylvania

Amy E. Alexander, PhD, School Counselor, Penn Hills Senior High School, Penn Hills School District, Pittsburgh, Pennsylvania; Founder and CEO of LegAAcy, Culturally Aware Advising and Consulting

Fatemah S. Alghamdi, PhD, NCC, CCTP, Assistant Professor of Psychology, Psychology Department, King Abdulaziz University; Owner and Clinical Mental Health Counselor at Roshd for Psychotherapy and Supervision, Jeddah, Saudi Arabia

Demond E. Bledsoe, PhD, LPC, Senior Program Director, UPMC Western Psychiatric Hospital; Owner-Resolutions Counseling and Behavioral Health Services, Pittsburgh, Pennsylvania

Jayna Bonfini, PhD, LPC, NCC, MAC, ACS, Associate Professor, Department of Counseling, University of the Cumberlands, Williamsburg, Kentucky

Roger P. Buck, PhD, LPCC, DAC, Retired, Former Military

R. Joseph Charette II, PhD Candidate, MSEd, LPC, NCC, Counselor Education and Supervision, Duquesne University, Pittsburgh, Pennsylvania; Assistant Professor, Mental Health Counseling, Philadelphia College of Osteopathic Medicine, Philadelphia, Pennsylvania

Laura Hensley Choate, EdD, Jo Ellen Levy Yates Professor, Counselor Education, School of Education, College of Human Sciences and Education, Louisiana State University, Baton Rouge, Louisiana

Andrea Doyle, LICSW, PhD, Assistant Professor, Behavioral Medicine and Psychiatry Department, West Virginia University School of Medicine, Morgantown, West Virginia

Natalie A. Drozda, PhD, LPC, Assistant Professor of Counselor Education, Department of Counseling and Development, College of Education, Slippery Rock University, Slippery Rock, Pennsylvania

Amy Ellis, PhD, Interim Director, Trauma Resolution and Integration Program, Nova Southeastern University, Fort Lauderdale, Florida

F. Barton Evans, PhD, Clinical Professor of Psychiatry and Behavioral Sciences, Retired, George Washington University School of Medicine, Washington, DC

Nancy N. Fair, PhD, Private Practice, Pittsburgh, Pennsylvania

Misty M. Ginicola, PhD, Professor, Counseling and School Psychology, Southern Connecticut State University, West Haven, Connecticut

Tom R. Hanauer, PhD Candidate, University of California–Riverside, Riverside, California

Shannon Hodges, PhD, LMHC, NCC, ACS, Professor of Clinical Mental Health Counseling, Niagara University, Niagara University, New York

Jo Ann Jankoski, EdD, Associate Professor, Human Development and Family Studies, Pennsylvania State University, Lemont Furnace, Pennsylvania

Kenya Johns, PhD, LPC, NCC, CAADC, CCTP, ACS, Assistant Professor of Counselor Education, Coordinator of the School Counseling Program, Geneva College, Beaver Falls, Pennsylvania

Sara P. Johnston, PhD, MPH, CRC, Associate Professor, Department of Occupational Therapy, Drake University, Des Moines, Iowa

Carole Justice, BA, BS, MEd, JD, Justice Consulting Services Retired Tribal Prosecutor, Shoshone and Arapaho Tribe; Member in Good Standing, the Wind River Bar, Wind River Tribal Court, Wind River Indian Reservation (1994–present), Wyoming

Ali Khadivi, PhD, ABAP, Chief of Psychology, Department of Psychiatry, BronxCare Health System; Professor of Psychiatry and Behavioral Sciences, Albert Einstein College of Medicine, Bronx, New York

Lisa López Levers, PhD, LPCC-S, LPC, CRC, NCC, Professor Emeritus, Counselor Education and Human Development, Department of Educational Foundations and Leadership, School of Education, Duquesne University, Pittsburgh, Pennsylvania

Tumani Malinga, MSW, PhD, Senior Lecturer, Department of Social Work, University of Botswana, Gaborone, Botswana

J. Barry Mascari, EdD, Deceased

Tapologo Maundeni, MSW, PhD, Professor, Department of Social Work, University of Botswana, Gaborone, Botswana

Judith L. M. McCoyd, PhD, Associate Professor, Rutgers University School of Social Work, New Brunswick, New Jersey

Bradley McDaniels, PhD, CRC, Assistant Professor, Department of Rehabilitation and Health Services, College of Health and Public Service, University of North Texas, Denton, Texas

Laurence Miller, PhD, PA Independent Practice in Clinical and Forensic Psychology, Boca Raton, Florida

Robert G. Moering, PsyD, VA Southern Nevada Health Care System, Clinical and Forensic Psychologist, Local Recovery Coordinator, Associate Director of Psychology Training, Las Vegas, Nevada

Elias Mpofu, PhD, CRC, Professor, Department of Rehabilitation and Health Services, College of Health and Public Service, University of North Texas, Denton, Texas

Frank M. Ochberg, MD, Clinical Professor, Department of Psychiatry, Michigan State University, East Lansing, Michigan

Kirrily Pells, PhD, Associate Professor of Childhood, Social Research Institute, University College London, London, United Kingdom

Staci Perlman, MSW, PhD, Deceased

Abeer Ali Rasheed, PhD, Assistant Professor of Self-Development Department, Vice Dean of Students' Affairs, Head of Self-Development Department, Deanship of Preparatory Year, Professional Counselor and Clinical Supervisor at the University Counseling Center, Imam Abdulrahman bin Faisal University, Dammam, Saudi Arabia

Carol M. Smith, MACE, PhD, Professor, and Coordinator of Violence, Loss, and Trauma Certificate; Marshall University, South Charleston, West Virginia

Vilia M. Tarvydas, PhD, CRC, Retired, Professor Emerita, Faculty Director, I-SERVE, Department of Rehabilitation and Counselor Education, University of Iowa, Iowa City, Iowa

John R. Tomko, PharmD, BCPP, Associate Professor, Duquesne University, School of Pharmacy, Division of Pharmacy Practice, Pittsburgh, Pennsylvania

Scott L. Tracy, PhD, Associate Professor, Counselor Education and Student Affairs, Kutztown University of Pennsylvania, Kutztown, Pennsylvania

Chaste Uwihoreye, PhD, Clinical Psychologist and Country Director, Uyisenga Ni Imanzi, Kigali, Rwanda

Cory Viehl, PhD, LPC, NCC, ACS, CORE Faculty, School of Counseling, College of Social and Behavioral Sciences, Walden University, Minneapolis, Minnesota

Matthew J. Walsh, PhD, LPC, NCC, Chief Clinical Officer, Oasis Mental Health Applications, Greensburg, Pennsylvania; Adjunct Professor, Department of Counseling, Psychology, and Special Education, Duquesne University, Pittsburgh, Pennsylvania

Justin Watts, PhD, NCC, Assistant Professor, Department of Rehabilitation and Health Services, College of Health and Public Service, University of North Texas, Denton, Texas

Jane M. Webber, PhD, LPC, Assistant Professor of Counselor Education and Doctoral Program Coordinator, Kean University, Union, New Jersey

Rachel Wurzman, PhD, MSSA, LCSW-A, Affiliate Faculty, Neuroethics Studies Program, Georgetown University School of Medicine, Washington, DC

Waganesh A. Zeleke, EdD, LPC, NCC, LCPC, Associate Professor, Department of Counseling, Psychology and Special Education, Duquesne University, Pittsburgh, Pennsylvania

Foreword

"It was the best of times, it was the worst of times, it was the age of wisdom, it was the age of foolishness, it was the epoch of belief, it was the epoch of incredulity, it was the season of light, it was the season of darkness, it was the spring of hope, it was the winter of despair."

Charles Dickens

The prophetic words of Dickens seem more relevant today than ever before. We live in an extraordinary time—a time of significant change and great awakening. The global pandemic has ripped open the very nature of society and humanity and exposed the best and worst of our circumstances and selves. We have walked headlong into a clarion moment, where the trauma of our pasts and the wounds of our circumstances collide. Now, perhaps more than at any other time in our modern history—we need a trauma-informed worldview.

Dr. Lisa López Levers, a distinguished academic and seasoned mental health professional, carefully lays out a roadmap for university students, helping professionals, and all of us to follow. In *Trauma Counseling: Theories and Interventions for Managing Trauma, Stress, Crisis, and Disaster,* Second Edition, Levers offers a carefully researched review of the evidence, compelling narrative, and practical interventions for trauma counseling and trauma support. The text provides the reader with a go-to manual for understanding not only the neurobiological impact of early childhood adverse experiences, but an in-depth review of the sociological and cultural implications of untreated and underrecognized trauma.

I have had the privilege of working with Dr. Levers on a number of projects. Her deep experience as a clinician, writer, researcher, and educator is evident in how she applies a trauma-informed approach to all her life work. From her international efforts in the child welfare sector to her academic writings and classroom teaching, Levers fully embodies trauma-informed counseling's central tenet, authenticity. This honesty and compassion are evident through the writing and language of *Trauma Counseling.*

Levers brings impeccable credentials and a deep understanding of brain science and the interconnected role of social-cultural-political-economic influences. This connected narrative of cause-and-effect is evident throughout the text. Through an integrated approach to writing about and teaching trauma counseling, Levers and her co-authors bring a refreshing approach to discussing one of the most important and seminal aspects of modern life—trauma. The refreshing emphasis on practical, evidence-based applications for therapy and treatment mean students and clinicians can use the text as not only a reference—but a complete methodology.

In my work as a physician, public health professional, and global health steward, the central reoccurring theme of everything we do is understanding the deep and anastomosing connection of trauma in the lives of the people we serve. For over 30 years I have worked at the nexus of health and disease with people living in the experience of profound multidimensional poverty, homelessness, and complex sociopolitical challenges. I have witnessed the impacts of deep trauma in the lives of many of the people. The most important lesson we have learned in our work is to lead with trauma sensitivity and awareness. Incorporating a trauma-informed worldview means training ourselves to look past the apparent and seek holistic levels of understanding. Leading with a trauma-informed lens allows us to work in an integrated, whole-person approach and to connect in a more meaningful way.

For over 25 years, researchers, scientists, clinicians, and academics have known about the biggest little secret. We have known that trauma and adverse childhood experiences are not the exceptions but the norm. For years, we have known that nearly a quarter of children starting their first year of school have lived through an adverse childhood event. We have known that exponentially, as we grow and mature in this human experience, a very high percentage (>60%) of us are shaped by trauma. This connection is known. It is rigorously studied and deeply embedded in evidence-based practice.

Nevertheless, how many of us receive training on having difficult conversations, trauma-informed practices and principles, or motivational interviewing? How many of us receive a course in trauma stewardship or nonviolent communication? How many professional counseling programs talk about the intersectionality of trauma, race, culture, society, justice, and learning? Levers brings the story together in a meaningful and compelling way. Together with her co-authors, Levers offers a clarion call for a world reeling from the impact of a global pandemic and a baseline of trauma.

The next generation of change agents and world leaders will need to take this holistic, trauma-informed worldview to a deeper level. In the context of a planet upended by a pandemic, social inequity, economic disparity, and racial and ethnic injustice, future leaders will need to understand how to use trauma awareness to craft evidence-based interventions and person-first policies and practices. They will be called to lead a paradigm shift that seeks to understand and connect the profound experiences and challenges of our past with our future opportunities. They will be asked to find a new way forward.

In clear, accessible writing, Levers provides the structure and methodology for all of us to find the way forward, creating a way of healing and hope.

Wayne A. Centrone, MD, MPH
Health Bridges International, Inc.
Founder and Executive Director

Preface

The first edition of *Trauma Counseling* found a home in counseling and psychology departments across the nation, as well as in national and local training programs around the world. I am honored that I have been able to contribute, by assembling materials that cover a wide array of trauma, stress, crisis, and disaster issues and by presenting them in a meaningful way, for students and clinicians alike. However, our understandings of trauma and related experiences have evolved so much since the publication of the first edition, in 2012, that now seemed like the right time for a second edition.

I have been working professionally with trauma, both clinically and instructionally, for nearly 50 years. The inspiration for the first edition of this book came perhaps as early as late 1975. It was toward the end of my master's degree, when I was an idealistic 23-year-old counselor intern, also volunteering my services for nearly 2 years at a crisis intervention agency, *Townhall II*, located in Kent, Ohio. I received incredible preservice training and experience there, and I always have considered *Townhall II* to be the place where I began to get my "real-world" education. I remember learning in a graduate class, during that same time, not to worry about incest abuse; according to the authoritative wisdom at the time, we would never see a case of incest, and *if* we were to see one, it would occur only one time in a million cases. I recall finding this odd at the time, considering the strength of the universal cultural taboo regarding incest. I thought it strange that the incest taboo would be so profound and so enduring in the face of one-in-a-million odds. But what did I know? I was just a kid from a small town in Ohio, lucky enough to be able to work my way through undergraduate and master's degrees at a state university. Therefore, I humbly accepted the knowledge of experts who told me to believe something that seemed so counterintuitive.

Shortly after finishing my master's degree in December 1975, in January 1976, I turned 24 and left on a backpacking journey to various countries in Europe. I also served as one of the few American delegates at the *International Tribunal on Crimes Against Women*, held in March 1976, in Brussels (the Tribunal was orchestrated by feminist scholar Dr. Diana E. H. Russell, who passed away on July 28, 2020). At the Tribunal, I learned about multiple cases of incest, along with many other types of gender-based and political violence against women. Regarding the incest, I reasoned that the numbers were possible because of the international presence at the Tribunal. There were thousands of women from nearly two hundred countries, representing millions of people around the world—narratives of multiple incidences could have been attributable to global scale alone, but I remained unsettled about the statistical accuracy of what the experts had said and what our professors had taught us at that time. Regarding the other types of violence, I recall being very stunned and feeling so woefully unprepared to process many of the horrible firsthand accounts of atrocities that were reported at the Tribunal as well as what I learned from some of the other women in casual conversation. For example, I met Aboriginal women from Australia who had experienced severe cultural oppression; I bunked with women from South Africa who provided personal details about the horrors of apartheid. I learned more at the Tribunal than my young mind even could absorb on a conscious level. In retrospect, I have come to regard this experience as profoundly relevant training for what were my next 13 years of community mental health work and my ensuing three-decade career as an academic.

After returning from the Tribunal and my travels, I did an initial 6-month stint as the first professional counselor on a female maximum security ward at a large state psychiatric facility, at the very beginning of that state's implementation of its newly enacted client rights and deinstitutionalization legislation. I then made my transition to the community mental health sector, where I spent the next 12.5 years of my career. It did not take long for me to see how wrong the experts actually were regarding incest abuse as well as other types of sexual assault. I had read the files of the women on my ward at the state facility, and I listened to the narratives of my clients at the community mental health center. Certainly not all client reports are absolutely accurate, but at the same time, clients' reports of personal events should not be disregarded or dismissed automatically. Not only were my clients teaching me about incest abuse, I also was witness to the psychosocial aftermath of all sorts of traumatic events. Some of these events were more unspeakable than others, and many of them were beyond the ability of a young clinician to process, especially at a time (beginning in the mid-to-late 1970s) when so little in the professional literature addressed trauma.

Due to the location of the first community mental health center, where I worked for 10 years, in a poor predominantly African American neighborhood in a large urban area, I began to learn about historical trauma, before Maria Yellow Horse Braveheart coined the term and before the term became popularized. I have carried with me the many stories of trauma, which were shared with me by Black elders, about the horrors that they had experienced during the Jim Crow era. I actually felt a bit "shell shocked," to use an old term, by what I had learned at the Tribunal, and this sense of shock continued, as I continued my professional journey in clinical mental health and rehabilitation counseling. I suspect that many early-stage clinicians also have felt a bit "shell shocked," or overwhelmed, when they first are exposed to clients' traumatic experiences. This is one of the reasons that it is so important to have preservice training related to trauma issues, as well as the availability of trauma-informed clinical supervision, and this is one of my original reasons for preparing this type of broad-spectrum textbook.

Eventually, I began to see clients with increasingly more complex trauma histories. I already had become one of the few go-to therapists whenever the local, newly established rape crisis centers and domestic violence shelters had a client who needed immediate counseling services— again, it was the mid-to-late 1970s, centers dealing with sexual assault and intimate partner abuse were just developing, and these grass-roots organizations did not have funding for in-house counselors. I had gained the trust of the agencies, having a reputation for being willing to rearrange my schedule to see someone, usually a female victim of interpersonal violence, who was in immediate crisis.

The clinical challenges were great, and there was a point at which I had to search throughout the city to acquire the advanced trauma-specific clinical supervision that was not available at the community mental health center where I worked. This led to connecting with a psychiatrist and group of therapists who had formed a trauma study group, which provided a format for us to support one another in our clinical work with survivors of complex trauma and dissociative disorders. This also hints at some of the systemic challenges during this same period. An example of such a challenge occurred in the late 1970s, when the director of one of the rape crisis agencies (where I was a board member at the time) and I compared notes about trends we had been observing with clients at our respective agencies. Both being master's-level mental health clinicians, we decided to initiate the first incest survivor support group in a large metropolitan area in northeastern Ohio. When word got out regarding recruitment for the group, both of our agencies began to receive hostile and threatening calls from members of the mental health establishment, attributing all sorts of catastrophic outcomes to such a support group, including the patronizing accusation that we would be "feeding the delusions of these poor women."

The satisfying ending to this story was that the administrator of my agency was a feminist who insisted that we proceed with our plans, and the rape crisis center had a supportive board of directors (that obviously included me), enabling its director to move forward as well. We conducted the support group, to the benefit of the clients involved, and, indeed, there were no associated catastrophes.

After providing 15 years of community mental health services and engaging in trauma-focused private practice, I made a transition to the professoriate, teaching graduate courses in counselor education as well as in research and educational leadership. Part of the motivation for my move was that *of course* the university environment would be more intellectually progressive, and *of course* I would be able to put into instructional practice all that I had learned on the front lines of community mental health and working with traumatized clients. What a surprise it was to engage a whole new set of systemic and administrative challenges, along with a recapitulation of the *unease* with which issues of trauma have been regarded, even by academicians who are knowledgeable about clinical mental health matters. In fact, it has been a relatively recent phenomenon for any of the accrediting bodies of preservice academic programs for the helping professions to include at least some language in their standards regarding trauma, crisis, and disaster issues.

As a young professor, I learned quickly that I would need to acquire new sets of skills to navigate the academic system of getting new trauma-related courses approved. At that time, it seemed that the academy was not ready for graduate courses that focused on issues of interpersonal violence and other traumatic events. I preferred to take this on as an advocacy project rather than as a fight. Of the four academic institutions where I have taught, there was only one at which I did not need to advocate strongly and vociferously to be able to teach an elective course associated with issues of trauma. However, attitudes about trauma and violence have begun to change; the current public climate has shifted, and there is greater support for *hearing* the voices of survivors rather than *silencing* them. Preservice programs more recently have begun to require at least some course work that focuses on trauma issues.

At many junctures in the current textbook, as in the previous edition, the authors of the chapters highlight a variety of the controversies that have arisen throughout the decades, and which have surrounded the clinical issues associated with trauma. I feel like I have survived some of the battle zones of these controversies, in both my clinical and academic work, in terms of advocating for the clinical needs of traumatized clients as well as for the instructional needs of counseling students. All of this brings us to the present landscape, in which the human services field finally has recognized the overwhelming presence of everyday trauma and crisis in the lives of many people, along with increasingly more frequent highly publicized global disasters—and with more immediate media exposure than ever before. Just as the #*MeToo* and the *Black Lives Matter* movements have begun to acknowledge and amplify the voices of those affected by interpersonal violence and systemic racism, we also are grappling with the disaster-causing results of anthropogenic climate change and the exponential effects of the global COVID-19 pandemic. In fact, the COVID-19 pandemic certainly has pushed the boundaries of the trauma discourse, with so many people experiencing a sense of isolation, fear, and trauma due to their pandemic experiences.

Preservice academic programs, especially those training entry-level master's clinicians who arguably provide the bulk of direct psychosocial services, need to catch up with what our graduates are certain to see once they enter the field—indeed, what our students already are seeing, and for which many are unprepared, in their pre-graduation practica, internships, and other field-based experiences. I have had the privilege of teaching several different courses, across institutions, on counseling survivors of trauma, for over three decades now. Although more and more published books are devoted to issues of trauma, crisis, and disaster, I have not yet found a textbook that serves as an adequate source for grounding students and clinicians in these areas. I believe that clinicians need a strong introduction to the theories and practices associated with trauma, stress, crisis, and disaster while also preparing them for the emotional intensity of this type of work. I finally decided, humbly, that perhaps I should take on the responsibility of preparing such a textbook. It was rewarding to embrace this challenge, and I have learned a lot from the feedback that I have received concerning the first edition. It also is apparent, with the relatively recent emergence of Polyvagal Theory, as well as other recent brain science findings, that the present time is right for this second edition.

The Relevance of This Textbook

Those of us who have done clinical work for any length of time know that trauma is as ubiquitous as the many other psychosocial issues that we consider pervasive, for example, issues like alcoholism and substance abuse. Many of us have dealt with clinical cases, in which clients present with a plethora of *other* issues. But once we scratch the surface of the situation, we then often learn that the real problem is not solely the alcoholism or the substance abuse—or the depression, or the anger, or the shame, or any number of other clinical issues—that permeate the problems bringing people to seek mental health assistance. Rather, it is the underlying experience of trauma that needs to be addressed. Still, it has taken the helping professions some time to grapple with the ubiquity of trauma and to understand the effects of traumatic events on the people who experience them. However, now, with recent advances in technology and neurobiology, we are able to understand, better than ever, the extent to which the human brain responds physiologically to trauma.

The major purpose of this book is to provide a much-needed text for a trauma-specific course in the preservice training of master's level professional counselors, social workers, psychologists, and other human service clinicians. Trauma and its attendant dynamics represent pervasive and overwhelming phenomena, and because there are so many mental health clinicians practicing today without the advantage of having had trauma-, crisis-, or disaster-related course work or supervision as a part of their respective curricula, such a text is relevant to and much needed by a variety of practicing human service clinicians. Perhaps the intersections of trauma, crisis, and disaster issues that have unfolded during the past year or so, with the promise of even longer-term effects, makes the book's relevance even more poignant.

This textbook offers a relatively comprehensive review of various types of traumatic experiences; of the human vulnerability for experiencing and witnessing trauma, stress, crisis, and disaster situations across the life-span; and of the intersections among trauma, crisis, and disaster events. It discusses pertinent diagnostic and case conceptualization issues as well as presenting individual and systems interventions and collaborations. This textbook was conceptualized and organized from a perspective that is anchored in an ecological and systemic view of people's psychosocial needs and interactions. The second edition includes relevant updates concerning new findings in neuroscience and the importance of Polyvagal Theory to our understanding of how trauma affects the brain. A unique feature of this textbook is that, at the end of each chapter, access is provided, via a URL, to online-only resources for use by students, instructors, and clinicians. These resources are specific to the trauma-related topic of the chapter and include suggested websites, manuals, films, instructional videos, and a variety of other useful tools. In addition, most of the chapters offer a case study or explicate an important field-based clinical detail to assist readers in understanding the relevance of the chapter topic. An Instructor's Manual and chapter-based PowerPoint presentations are available online from Springer for qualified instructors (see request access information at the end of the Preface); the Instructor's Manual includes sample syllabi for a semester-long course as well as an intensive seminar, along with discussion questions and activities for each chapter.

The Content of This Textbook

Trauma Counseling: Theories and Interventions for Managing Trauma, Stress, Crisis, and Disaster, Second Edition, is a much-needed update that offers an in-depth and comprehensive exploration of the variety of relevant issues concerning clients' traumatic, crisis-related, and disaster events that commonly are encountered by professional counselors and other mental health professionals.

The textbook is framed, theoretically, within a systemic paradigm, including important recent physiological and neurobiological understandings of the impact of trauma on individuals. In the chapters in Section I, "Trauma, Crisis, and Context," the aim is to offer a foundation for understanding the various trauma-associated issues in this textbook. In fact, I have tried, with a great deal of intentionality, in the first four chapters to construct a *trauma scaffold* of foundational knowledge, upon which students can build increasingly more complex conceptualizations of more nuanced clinical issues associated with trauma. Chapter 1, by Lisa López Levers, introduces an historical context for how we have come to regard trauma-related issues, explicating a number of the controversies surrounding the development of a clinical understanding of trauma, stress, crisis, and disaster. In Chapter 2, Lisa López Levers provides theoretical contexts for understanding the effects of trauma, stress, crisis, and disaster, thus establishing a tone and perspective for the rest of the book. Lisa López Levers offers an introduction to stress management and crisis intervention in Chapter 3. John R. Tomko details the neurobiological effects of trauma and psychopharmacology in Chapter 4. Together, these four chapters provide a strong foundation for considering contextual, theoretical, and neurobiological aspects of trauma.

In Section II, "Trauma and Crisis of Loss, Vulnerability, and Interpersonal Violence," relevant constructs are explicated, such as loss and grief; these constructs continue to build upon and expand the trauma scaffolding of the first section. Section II also offers information about the traumatic events that may be experienced by specific age groups, people who are vulnerable, and other particular populations. Judith L. M. McCoyd and Lisa López Levers discuss important psychosocial constructs associated with loss and grief in Chapter 5. In Chapter 6, Laura Hensley Choate emphasizes an ecological approach to conceptualizing and treating sexual trauma. Andrea Doyle and Lisa López Levers explicate the nature of traumatic experiences of early childhood in Chapter 7; in Chapter 8, Andrea Doyle and Staci Perlman describe the developmental aspects of trauma that may be experienced in adolescence. In Chapter 9, Carol M. Smith discusses treating adults with complex trauma or a complexity of traumas. Intimate partner violence is the focus of Chapter 10, by Carole Justice, Frank M. Ochberg, Lisa López Levers, and Nancy N. Fair. In Chapter 11, Elias Mpofu, Bradley McDaniels, and Justin Watts discuss issues of trauma survivorship and disability. Elias Mpofu offers information about older adults' health resourcing in Chapter 12. In Chapter 13, Rachel Wurzman describes addictions and psychological trauma as well as their implications for counseling strategies. In Chapter 14, Laurence Miller describes the traumatic experiences associated with criminal victimization. Jayna Bonfini details the specific traumatic aftermath of homicide and suicide in Chapter 15. The 11 chapters in Section II identify and examine many of the psychosocial constructs, neurobiological impacts, and other relevant issues associated with personal trauma and interpersonal violence.

The focus of Section III is on "Intolerance and the Trauma of Hate." Tom R. Hanauer begins the section with his explication, in Chapter 16, of the moral psychology of evil. In Chapter 17, Waganesh A. Zeleke and Lisa López Levers highlight how racial, ethnic, and immigration intolerance serve as a framework for violence and trauma. In Chapter 18, Cory Viehl, Misty M. Ginicola, Amy Ellis, and R. Joseph Charette II discuss issues relevant to understanding and responding to affectional and transgender prejudice and victimization. These three chapters emphasize the personal and social dynamics of *othering* in an attempt to unravel some of the *dark side* tendencies of humanity.

In Section IV, the emphasis on "Community Violence, Mass Violence, Crisis, and Large-Scale Disaster" presents a broader systemic context for understanding the effects of trauma on groups of people. Matthew J. Walsh, Reverend Paul T. Abernathy, and Lisa López Levers detail the contextual issues of historical trauma and trauma-affected communities in Chapter 19. In Chapter 20, Kenya Johns, Tumani Malinga, Tapologo Maundeni, and Lisa López Levers discuss the effects of mass violence. In Chapter 21, Amy E. Alexander and Lisa López Levers focus on the traumatic effects of school violence. Scott L. Tracy explains the impact of natural disasters in Chapter 22, addressing important mental health issues related to first responders. In Chapter 23, Kirrily Pells and Chaste Uwihoreye consider the community and personal effects of genocide, war, and political violence. Lisa López Levers and Natalie A. Drozda enumerate a confluence of crises in Chapter 24, outlining the trauma-related effects of migration, anthropogenic climate change, mass casualties, war, and civil unrest. Concluding this section, in Chapter 25, Robert G. Moering, Roger P. Buck, and Lisa López Levers examine the impact of war on military veterans. These seven chapters illuminate the profound impact that large-scale violence and natural and human-made disasters can have on individuals, families, communities, and nations.

The focus of Section V involves "Clinical Assessment and Treatment Issues." In Chapter 26, F. Barton Evans and Ali Khadivi analyze assessment methods and interventions associated with psychological trauma. Lisa López Levers, Jane M. Webber, J. Barry Mascari, and Carol M. Smith identify and discuss the larger scope of integrative approaches to trauma, crisis, and disaster intervention in Chapter 27, thus emphasizing the importance of more systemic models. In Chapter 28, Jane M. Webber, Carol M. Smith, and J. Barry Mascari detail selected strategies and techniques for counseling survivors of trauma. These three chapters offer a framework for beginning to consider the nature of clinical work with clients who have experienced trauma, crisis, and disaster events.

Section VI highlights "Professional Concerns for Trauma, Crisis, and Disaster Counselors." Sara P. Johnston and Vilia M. Tarvydas begin the section by presenting ethical perspectives on trauma work in Chapter 29. Jo Ann Jankoski explicates vicarious traumatization in Chapter 30, highlighting the need for counselor self-awareness. In Chapter 31, Shannon Hodges focuses on the importance of mindfulness-based self-care for counselors, encouraging clinicians to be healing counselors rather than wounded healers. In Chapter 32, Demond E. Bledsoe, Abeer Ali Rasheed, Fatemah S. Alghamdi, and Lisa López Levers emphasize the absolute necessity of trauma-informed and trauma-specific clinical supervision when working with survivors of trauma. Lisa López Levers concludes this section and the book, with Chapter 33, by asserting the need for continued development of ecological applications and offering a conceptual framework for an integrative systemic approach to trauma (ISAT) model. The focus of these five chapters is on the critical juncture between the personhood of the clinicians and their professional conduct. This juncture promotes a kind of *collaborative work ethos*, which refers to the interconnection of ethical behavior, acute self-awareness and self-reflection, responsible supervision, and advocacy for a systemic approach that brings all of these collaborative endeavors back to the best interests of clients who have experienced traumatic events, excessive stress, crises, or disasters.

The six sections of this book are interrelated in many ways. First, the various sections underscore the pervasiveness of traumatic experiences, along with crisis and disaster, across societies, in general, and specifically within mental health populations. Second, the authors of each of the chapters attest to the ultimate importance of therapists being able to recognize the effects of trauma in their clients and knowing how to assess and treat survivors of trauma, crisis, and disaster events. Third, the content for each chapter reflects our continuing understanding of the neurobiological effects of trauma and toxic stress. Fourth, the connections between individual experiences of trauma and resilience and larger contextual issues are highlighted. Finally, bearing clinical witness to the lived experiences of trauma survivors is emphasized across the sections of this textbook as part of a larger systemic process. We need to view clients who have been affected by traumatic events as whole people, we need to acknowledge our own roles and responses in the therapeutic relationship, and we need to engage the contextual and systemic aspects of trauma work if we are going to assist our clients in healing and growing. *Trauma Counseling: Theories and Interventions for Managing Trauma, Stress, Crisis, and Disaster,* Second Edition, is a textbook that aims to provide a basis—a trauma scaffold—for doing this important work.

Acknowledgments

I wish to acknowledge all of the people on the planet who have been affected by the COVID-19 pandemic, which is pretty much all of us. The totality of our losses has been tragic, and our lives have been altered in previously unimaginable ways. Within the small circle of authors of this book, we have lost two dear friends to the virus: Fambaineni Innocent Magweva and J. Barry Mascari. Other contributing authors of this book have lost partners, parents, other family members, and friends to the pandemic. We also lost Staci Perlman in 2015. We continue to grieve our losses. I also wish to acknowledge the power of resilience and recovery, and I wish a healing pathway for everyone, in emerging from the dire effects of this pandemic.

Instructor Resources

 A robust set of instructor resources designed to supplement this text is located at http://connect.springerpub.com/content/book/978-0-8261-5085-1. Qualifying instructors may request access by emailing textbook@springerpub.com.

Available resources include:

- **Instructor's Manual:**
  - Discussion Questions
  - Activities and Exercises
  - Out-of-Class Assignments
  - Practice-Based Resources

- **Chapter-Based PowerPoint Presentations**

CHAPTER 1

An Introduction to Counseling Survivors of Trauma: Beginning to Understand the Historical and Psychosocial Implications of Trauma, Stress, Crisis, and Disaster

LISA LÓPEZ LEVERS

CHAPTER OVERVIEW

This chapter introduces foundational knowledge necessary for understanding the effects of psychosocial trauma, stress, crisis, and disaster. It offers brief discussions about the historical implications of how psychosocial trauma has come to be defined as well as how the related diagnostic categories have developed. Finally, the importance of recognizing the human capacity for resilience and growth, in the face of trauma, is emphasized.

LEARNING OBJECTIVES

After reading this chapter, the reader should be able to:

1. Identify basic concepts regarding trauma and the effects of trauma;
2. Discern the history of professional understandings about trauma;
3. Develop awareness of how the developing constructs of trauma and posttraumatic stress disorder (PTSD) have evolved into diagnostic criteria in the various iterations of the *Diagnostic and Statistical Manuals*; and,
4. Recognize that, in spite of stressful and traumatic experiences, individuals have the capacity to build resilience, to make meaning and derive purpose from what has happened to them, and to grow and develop as a result.

INTRODUCTION

Traumatic events are a part of life. The types of lived experiences of trauma that result from human violence, medical crises, natural disasters, and other disruptive circumstances have had repeated histories that span millennia. Scientific, religious, literary, and artistic traditions have captured and represented this history, and contemporary media continue to replay the effects of trauma on a daily basis. Perhaps the first narrative of interpersonal violence resides in the account of the offspring of Adam and Eve. Cain killed his brother Abel, thus committing the first homicide, as recorded in the Old Testament as well as in the Holy Quran. Adam and Eve not only had to deal with the existential consequences of "the fall," but two of their children set the stage for the primordial discourse on the traumatic effects of homicide. Modern archaeological discoveries have revealed early evidence of killing and warfare (e.g., Handwerk, 2016; University of Wyoming, 2021). Representations of trauma continue to be depicted in contemporary art (e.g., Kulasekara, 2016; Pollock, 2009); film (e.g., Elm et al., 2014; Koehne & Kabalek, 2014; Levers, 2001; Lowenstein, 2005; Spallacci, 2019); and literary discourses (e.g., Heidarizadeh, 2015; Mambrol, 2018; Stringer, 2009). With 24/7 cable news, horrific traumatic images are aired in our living rooms and on our personal devices, sometimes in real time or only moments after an event has occurred.

The reality is that there always have been, and, unfortunately, there most likely always will be, perpetrators who prey on the vulnerable, as well as natural disasters and accidents that decimate populations and dramatically alter the lives of individuals and families. In other words, the experience of trauma is a long-lived human dilemma, and in spite of everything that we have learned over the millennia, we continue to deal with the overwhelming consequences of trauma and associated elements of stress, crisis, and disaster. Most mental health-related training programs have seemed relatively reluctant to include issues of trauma as a part of preservice training, at least until very recently (Courtois & Gold, 2009; Kumar et al., 2019; Levers, 2020). The Council for the Accreditation of Counseling and Related Educational Programs (CACREP, 2016) requires that counselors receive preservice training on the effects of crisis, disasters, and trauma on clients, but without further specificity (Tarvydas et al., 2017, 2018). The American Psychological Association (APA, 2015) has published guidelines on trauma competencies for education and training but does not mention trauma in its accreditation manual for health service psychology. Likewise, the accreditation manual for the Council on Social Work Education (CSWE, 2015) also does not mention trauma. Major mental health-related preservice training programs have been slow to design and offer trauma-informed curricula to students, while at the same time, based upon the actual needs of the field, it is essential for all mental health professionals to have received preservice training in areas related to working with trauma. It is important for all mental health professionals to grasp just how ubiquitous trauma is among the clients who see us, and how the stressors of trauma, crisis, disaster, and modern life affect both the psyche and the body. In fact, recent brain science continues to illuminate the powerful physiological effects of trauma on our bodies (e.g., Gerge, 2020; Porges, 2011; Portwood et al., 2021), which has moved the trauma–response paradigm, significantly, from talk-only therapy to modalities that incorporate relevant somatic work with clients.

People experience and live through traumatic events in many different ways. This textbook aims to explore these variations in a manner that can help social science and human service students and clinicians to understand trauma from neurobiological, psychosocial, systemic, and contextual perspectives. It also aims to illuminate the best-practice theories and interventions for managing trauma as well as managing stress, crisis, and disaster. The first section of this book, particularly the first three chapters, establishes an important foundation for understanding stress, crisis, and trauma, what I am referring to as a *trauma scaffold*—such a scaffolding process builds upon basic knowledge about trauma, in order to prepare for understanding increasingly more complex issues that are presented throughout the book. This foundation also provides the groundwork for understanding human responses to disaster and larger scale violence, issues that are discussed in later sections of the book. This first chapter offers an introduction to counseling survivors of trauma as well as a beginning reference point for a professional understanding of the historical and psychosocial implications of trauma; theories that ground the practice of trauma counseling are presented in the next chapter, along with important foundational information drawn from recent neuroscience regarding how trauma affects the brain. Stress management and crisis intervention are discussed in Chapter 3.

The purpose of this chapter is to provide a basic professional understanding of psychosocial trauma and associated issues. This is accomplished in discussions in the following sections:

Basic Understanding of Trauma, Historical Implications of Trauma, Modernity and the Conceptualization of Trauma, Posttraumatic Stress Disorder and the *Diagnostic and Statistical Manuals*, and Resilience. Following the discussions in these sections, counseling implications are identified, and the content of the chapter is summarized. The chapter concludes by offering helpful resources for instructors, students, and clinicians.

BASIC UNDERSTANDING OF TRAUMA

The Dalai Lama has stated that "pain is inevitable, suffering is optional." I find this to be a helpful beginning point in understanding trauma. Life can be challenging and difficult; even in ideal circumstances, some painful experiences are a part of human existence, so in this sense, emotional pain is inevitable. However, getting stuck in pain and continuing to suffer is not a necessary consequence of psychosocial pain. In fact, one of the reasons that it is important for mental health professionals to understand the implications of stress, crisis, trauma, and disaster is so that we are able to assist people who are experiencing psychological distress, thus helping them to make meaningful transformations. The purpose of this brief section, then, is to offer operational definitions of key terms, in order to become conversant with more advanced concepts that are detailed and further discussed in chapters throughout this textbook.

A first important part of this conversation is to highlight the role of stress, both as a motivational force and in dealing with uncomfortable situations. A second aspect of this discussion is to make a distinction among the terms "crisis," "trauma," and "disaster." Briefly, not all crisis situations are traumatizing; however, all traumatic events involve some element of crisis. All disaster events involve some element of crisis and may very well be traumatizing, but not necessarily. It is important to establish, early in this textbook, that not every individual exposed to trauma necessarily feels traumatized. In fact, many individuals either are resilient or are able to develop greater resilience, thus mitigating negative effects that may occur under difficult circumstances; many individuals are able to experience interpersonal growth as they make meaning of whatever traumatic event has occurred. These are issues that are discussed, from various angles, later in this chapter and in other chapters throughout the book.

Stress and Crisis

Stress is a natural part of our biological functioning and is a normal part of life; everyone experiences stress (Levers, 2020). In fact, some stress, originally called "eustress" (Selye, 1956), is productive. An example of "eustress" may involve a student who wants to earn a good grade preparing a presentation for class. This small amount of positive stress is enough to motivate the student to conduct the requisite research, in order to construct a PowerPoint and prepare for the presentation. Without a burst of eustress, the person might succumb to the temptation to procrastinate, which would not facilitate the kind of work that the student wants to do for the class. However, the complexities of modern life produce many stressors that, cumulatively, can be harmful. Too much stress can lead to surges of hormones, like adrenaline and cortisol, which in excess then upset the natural balance of the body (Mayo Clinic, 2019). Individuals may experience acute stress, which is short-term stress, or chronic stress, which is long-term stress.

Not all stress leads to trauma, although a particular stressor or set of stressors can become traumatizing. The concept of adverse life experiences helps us to understand that there is a continuum from normal stress to trauma, with varying degrees of adversity occurring at various points between stress and trauma. Prolonged stress eventually can lead to anxiety. Clients may seek help after recognizing that a stressor or adversity has affected them negatively; counselors then can assist with managing the stress in ways that may prevent stressors and adversity from producing anxiety or even becoming traumatizing. The issue of stress is discussed more fully in Chapters 2 and 3 of this textbook, as well as its connections to larger physiological processes in the body and particularly in the brain.

A crisis can precipitate both danger and opportunity. Crisis is defined in a number of ways, and people experience many differing types of crises. Chapter 3 of this textbook provides a full discussion of crisis and crisis intervention. However, as a foundation for beginning to understand crisis in relationship to the broader issue of trauma, a brief definition is offered here. A crisis is an event that a person perceives as threatening or potentially harmful; this leads to distress that may interrupt or impair the individual's usual coping mechanisms (Kanel, 2019).

Trauma

Stated simply, "trauma is an emotional response to a terrible event" (American Psychological [APA], 2019, "Trauma," para. 1). However, as detailed in Chapter 2 of this textbook, when we unpack the term "emotional," in reference to the impact of trauma, the matter becomes more complex, because what we call an emotional response to trauma actually entails physiological processes that involve the brain and other major organs in the body. There are many types of traumatic events, and different people experience trauma in different ways. Common trauma events include some of the following examples (this is not intended to be an exhaustive list):

- Sexual assault;
- Physical abuse;
- Domestic or intimate partner violence;
- Community, workplace, and school violence;
- Medical and health-related trauma;
- Mass public health concerns, such as the COVID-19 pandemic;
- Motor vehicle accidents;
- Acts of terrorism;
- War experiences;
- Natural and human-made disasters;
- Anthropogenic climate change and resulting weather disasters;
- Homicides and suicides; and,
- Other traumatic losses.

People typically suffer when they experience these types of events. However, we can mitigate the effects of traumatic experiences through trauma counseling and other types of therapeutic interventions. While individuals may not forget the trauma that they have experienced, trauma survivors can learn to manage the effects and resume productive lives. In this sense, trauma may disrupt—or even severely disrupt—the lives of those affected, but recovery is always possible; it is thereby imperative that traumatized individuals receive some type of clinical intervention sooner rather than later. The longer that treatment is delayed, the possibility increases that a traumatized person may develop posttraumatic stress disorder (PTSD). Mental health professionals help clients to deal with trauma in its early stages as well as to deal with PTSD. Several important dynamics, often associated with psychosocial trauma, are discussed here; the issues are foundational to understanding trauma, and the discussions are intended to be brief, as these facets are examined more fully in later chapters of this textbook.

Attachment

The concept of attachment, originally proposed by Bowlby (1958), is highly relevant to the discussion of early childhood trauma. The term has referenced the emotionally close and important social relationships that people have with each other. Bowlby's (1958) work provided the framework for identifying four basic characteristics of attachment that have assisted professionals in understanding bonding—or the lack thereof—in relationships between children and their caregivers: having a safe haven, having a secure base, engaging in proximity maintenance, and showing separation distress. It is widely thought that if attachment is seriously interrupted, as is often the case with early childhood trauma, significant developmental problems may result, and attachment disruptions can affect people across the life-span. Recent neurobiological research regarding the effects of trauma on the brain has assisted us in understanding more about the integrative effects of a particular individual's attachment and neurobiology (e.g., Newman et al., 2015).

Loss, Grief, and Suffering

"Loss is at the heart of life and growth," according to Walter and McCoyd (2009, p. 1). A similar sentiment concerns the experience of trauma: loss, grief, and suffering are at the center of experiencing trauma. Not all experiences of loss, grief, and suffering necessarily involve trauma. However, loss, grief, and suffering are implicit aspects of trauma across the varying circumstances that may manifest as traumatic experience (Levers, 2020). This point underscores the importance of these constructs and illuminates their centrality to the experience of trauma.

Kübler-Ross (1969) wrote *On Death and Dying: What the Dying Have to Teach Doctors, Nurses, Clergy and Their Own Families*, the source of the now widely accepted and reified stages of grief: (a) Denial and Isolation, (b) Anger, (c) Bargaining, (d) Depression, and (e) Acceptance. At the time of the original publication, professional helpers were eager to view these concepts as linear stages through which clients would progress. However, this was never Kübler-Ross's intention. The book was the result of her interviews with clients facing death; the aim was to understand their experiences and to illuminate the phenomena. Eventually, clinicians learned that clients facing loss and grief issues do not necessarily experience any or all of these, and further, individuals may not experience these stages sequentially. Bowlby later (1980/1998) postulated these stages of loss:

- Numbness (defined as being shocked and stunned, not as denial);
- Separation Anxiety (viewed as yearning/searching);
- Despair and Disorganization (as the loss sinks in, the person attempts to recognize the loss and to develop a "new normal" without the object of the loss); and,
- Acquisition of New Roles/Reorganization (the bereaved begins to relinquish efforts aimed at preparing for the deceased's return, like getting rid of the loved one's clothing; this movement toward new aspects of life and relationships with others is seen as moving through reorganization).

More recently, Worden (2008) has offered his task-based grief theory and intervention framework. This theory emerged in response to some of the stage- and phase-based models of the late 1960s through the early 1990s, thereby providing clinicians with a more behavioral and process-oriented perspective to make clinical intervention decisions. Worden's model includes the following steps: (a) accept the reality of the loss; (b) experience the pain of the grief; and (c) adjust to a world without the deceased.

Shame

Although survivors of trauma may experience a myriad of emotions following a traumatic event, a sense of shame can be particularly insidious. Shame is a self-conscious feeling of painfulness and humiliation. It is important to distinguish between shame and guilt (Tull, 2020); shame is a negative judgment or evaluation of one's entire being as less worthy, whereas guilt is the consequence of a negative behavior. One can alleviate guilt by making amends and repairing relationships, but absolving a sense of shame is much more difficult. Studies have shown that trauma survivors' shame can lead to greater self-isolation and other types of avoidance behaviors (Saraiya & Lopez-Castro, 2016) and is linked to a sense of betrayal, based on the emotional proximity of the perpetrator (e.g., proximal family member versus distal stranger) (Platt &

Freyd, 2015). Shame can be debilitating for some trauma survivors and can serve as an impediment to recovery, at least until fully processed.

Disaster

A disaster is any catastrophic event that causes or has the potential to cause serious and widespread material damage and loss of life. In the context of mental health services, disaster situations usually are divided into two types: natural disasters and human-made disasters. Natural disasters include events like tornados, hurricanes, floods, earthquakes, and fires and require special response training for intervention; these issues are discussed in detail in Chapter 22 of this textbook. A variety of human-made disasters are examined across several chapters in this book and include the following: accidents (Chapter 11), mass violence (Chapter 20), war (Chapters 23 and 25), and anthropogenic climate change (Chapter 24).

HISTORICAL IMPLICATIONS OF TRAUMA

People long have recognized the profound impact that trauma can have upon the psychological well-being of those who encounter it (Herman, 1992b; Sexton, 1999; van der Kolk, 2014). However, it only has been since 1980 that the formal diagnosis of the trauma-related disorder PTSD has been included in the *Diagnostic and Statistical Manual of Mental Disorders*, the diagnostic nosology published by the American Psychiatric Association (APA). PTSD specifically was introduced in the *DSM-III* (APA, 1980). Following that pivotal event, acute stress disorder (ASD) was added to a later revision of the manual, the *DSM-IV* (APA, 1994) in 1994. These inclusions constituted the first criteria-based clinical distinctions between shorter-term responses to trauma, that is, those lasting for less than a month (ASD), and longer-term responses of over 1 month (PTSD).

The presentation of a full history of the evolving perceptions and understandings of psychosocial trauma is not possible here, yet some understanding of the historical context is important, especially for students who are new to the mental health field. Contemporary understandings of trauma are perhaps more relevant than recapitulations of long-ago historical events, so the focus here is primarily on relatively more recent clinical landscapes; however, at least a brief discussion of high-impact past events can be instructional, especially as this might illuminate the often-violent past treatment of those with psychiatric disorders. This discussion also forecasts important information detailed in other chapters in this volume, particularly those chapters that deal with gender and age-related issues (Chapters 7, 8, 9, and 12), scapegoating and "othering" (Chapter 16), racial and ethnic intolerance (Chapters 17 and 19), gender orientation (Chapter 18), and massive ethnic and political violence and genocide (Chapter 23). Discussion of historical events, social injustice, and the role of the scapegoat naturally leads to the discussion of a relatively new concept in traumatology, that of historical trauma, which Chapters 2 and 19 examine more fully. Therefore, the remaining parts of this section deal with these important issues: The Role of Social Scapegoat as Victim and The Abuse of Power.

The Role of Social Scapegoat as Victim

We often may find ourselves wondering, especially in the face of daily catastrophic news coverage, how one human being (or group of humans) can treat another human being (or group of humans—or any other sentient being, for that matter) in such a violent manner. Our perceptions about trauma are culturally and historically determined, and yet inflicting violence is highly personal. The effects of interpersonal violence, social violence, warfare, and natural disaster have marked ancient societies, just as they have modern ones. Although we could learn much from an examination of the Greek and Roman empires, along with non-Western civilizations, such a full historical examination is beyond the scope of this textbook. It suffices to note that the norms of civilization tend to oppose violent practices, while tending to endorse acts that assist others, especially in times of crisis or disaster. It seems that historical events, over at least the last several centuries (spanning the Dark/Middle Ages and the Age of Reason/ Enlightenment), have influenced how our contemporary psychiatric paradigm has come to conceptualize the impact of traumatic events on the human psyche.

Psychosocial stressors and their aftermath often have led to the institutionalization and marginalization of those who have mental health problems, and, by extension, those who have experienced trauma. Indeed, the history of institutionalizing people for medical and psychiatric reasons in Western society offers rich illustrations of scapegoating. This information is an important backdrop for trying to make sense of how victims of violence so often have been— and continue to be, even now—cast as scapegoats. Understanding this offers insight regarding how it is that the mental health professions came to take so long to address trauma issues in *helpful* rather than *victim-blaming* ways. Many survivors of sexual assault, as an example, end up being victimized further, not only by mental health and legal systems, but also by other citizens for even reporting the crime. Box 1.1 presents a brief historical account of some particular types of social scapegoating.

BOX 1.1

A Lesson From History: The "Other" as Scapegoat

In his book, *Madness and Civilization: A History of Insanity in the Age of Reason*, Foucault (1973) traced the origins of the mental asylum in Western civilization to the leprosy epidemic in the Middle Ages. He illuminated how the number of leprosaria, the asylums in which lepers were institutionalized, grew in proportion to the number of cases of leprosy that were diagnosed. Foucault posited that as the need for the leprosaria declined, the centers originally built for the seclusion of lepers began to be filled with paupers, "incurables," the "mentally ill," and others perceived as socially deviant. Foucault (1973) suggested that although leprosy disappeared, the residential structures remained, and "the formulas of exclusion would be repeated, strangely similar 2 or 3 centuries later. Poor vagabonds, criminals, and 'deranged minds' would take the part played by the leper" (p. 7). The "part" referenced by Foucault was the social role played by groups of people who have been marginalized; these disenfranchised persons have represented the social "other," thereby enabling societal institutions to justify, in far too many cases, brutal treatment.

Foucault outlined the history of the leprosaria, or lazar houses, as they came to be known, through their transformation to asylums for the "insane" throughout Western Europe; he cited this as the birth of the classical experience of "madness." In the introduction to Foucault's book, Jose Barchilon, MD, pointed out that "as leprosy vanished, in part because of segregation, a void was created and the moral values attached to the leper had to find another scapegoat" (Foucault, 1973, p. vi). Cast in a parallel fashion by Berger and Luckmann (1967) is an assertion of the institutional world as being of human construction, one that does not have "ontological status apart from the human activity that produced it" (pp. 60–61). Foucault also noted that, although it was common knowledge that, in the 17th century, large hospitals/houses of confinement were created, it was not commonly known that "more than one out of every hundred inhabitants of Paris found themselves confined there within several months" (p. 38). This legacy continued and gave birth to the "mental asylum"; even well into the 20th century, "insane" people were placed into abhorrent conditions and exposed to horrendous treatments. In an attempt to redress this situation, the clients' rights movement of the 1970s and 1980s led to deinstitutionalizing psychiatric clients and returning them to their "home" communities; unfortunately, communities did not have sufficient resources, and an entire set of additional community-based problems surfaced.

(continued)

Foucault (1973) offered an astute inquiry of the architectural confinement of the scapegoat. Thomas Szasz (1970/1997) illustrated how the myth of "mental illness," in his view, has been manufactured by a society in need of a scapegoat, thus providing social sanction and cultural legitimacy to the persecution of certain people. In his book, *The Manufacture of Madness*, Szasz examined the powerful metaphoric constructions of "mental illness," suggesting parallels between the Inquisition and some of the consequences of modern psychiatry. Szasz clearly delineated the persecution of witches, the persecution of Jewish people, and ultimately the persecution of people with psychiatric disorders as artifacts of the Inquisition. In doing so, he illuminated the ways in which multiple strands of human behavior, belief, or status can become encoded as violations of the ideology of those in power, thereby assisting the powerful to maintain control. Throughout history, we have seen many instances in which the maintenance of power has involved violence against those without power. According to Szasz, the transformation of the role of social scapegoat to witches, heretics, Jewish people, and "the insane" paralleled the moralistic transformation of dogmas from religion to science: "The metamorphosis of the medieval into the modern mind entailed a vast ideological conversion from the perspective of theology to that of science" (p. 137). He concluded that the evolving construct of mental illness is an artifact of this paradigm shift. This is not intended to cast doubt upon legitimate principles of science, but rather to comment on the misrepresentation of dogma as science. In a public health crisis, science reigns; when socially constructed metaphors are used to castigate the "other" into further marginalization, then such dogma needs to be questioned and analyzed.

As the role of one social scapegoat declined, new scapegoats emerged (Thurston, 2007). The Inquisition, initiated by the politically powerful Roman Catholic Church in the 12th century, was aimed at the persecution of heretics. People were tortured and killed in gruesome ways during the centuries that spanned the Inquisition. Some groups of people were affected more than others, and this included the persecution of anyone thought to be a witch and anyone thought to be of Jewish ancestry. For the first time in history, in 1215, by decree of Pope Innocent III, Jewish people were ordered to wear yellow badges in order to identify themselves (Szasz, 1970/1997). The roots of anti-Semitism were embedded in European culture long before the expulsion of Jews from Spain in 1492 and long before the 20th century Holocaust; unthinkably, we are witnessing a horrific reemergence of anti-Semitism in the 21st century.

Misfortunes of all sorts were blamed on witches and Jewish people, who were massacred for such events as epidemics and poor crops. During the Inquisition, witches—or at least those accused of witchcraft—also took on the role of societal scapegoat. Thousands, and by some estimates hundreds of thousands, of (mostly) women, were executed throughout Europe from the 14th to the 17th centuries (Ehrenreich & English, 1973; Thurston, 2007). Intended to systematize the persecution of witches, Pope Innocent VIII's papal bull was implemented in 1486, along with the publication of the infamous manual for witch-hunters, the *Malleus Maleficarum* (*The Hammer of Witches*); the manual detailed how to identify the so-called witches and prescribed ensuing treatments of heinous and unspeakable natures. Not surprisingly, the publication of the nosology was followed by an "epidemic" of witchcraft (Szasz, 1970/1997). Szasz explained that

> the incidence of witches increased, as the authorities charged with their suppression covertly demanded that it should; and a corresponding increase of interest in methods aimed at combating witchcraft developed. For centuries, the Church struggled to maintain its dominant role in society. For centuries, the witch played her appointed role as society's scapegoat. (p. 7)

Szasz (1970/1997) affirmed that in the 17th century, as the power of the Church and its religious worldview began to decline, an "inquisitor-witch complex disappeared" and was replaced by an "alienist-madman complex" (p. 13). In this new secular and scientific order,

(continued)

parallel conformity was still demanded; Szasz cited this shift in the social order as a move from a worldview, conceptualized in terms of "divine grace," to one cast more in terms of health.

In reference to institutional psychiatry ("forced" psychiatry, in contrast with what he regarded as a less imposing contractual psychiatry), Szasz (1970/1997) asserted that violence always has been, and remains to be, the key problem. This violence dialectic involves, on the one hand, the feared or perceived violence of the "madman," and, on the other hand, what Szasz refers to as the "actual counter-violence of society and the psychiatrist against him" (p. xvii). If we were to cast these dynamics in a more contemporary landscape, we perhaps would be discussing the feared violence of the "other" and the counterviolence of society against the marginalized "other."

The Abuse of Power

One may or may not agree with Szasz's (1970/1997) position regarding institutional psychiatry and its historical implications. However, this type of "official" projective dynamic arguably has been at play in myriad ways across societies and social structures; it unfortunately has been linked with peoples around the world, representing various types of societal needs for scapegoats and also representing the ways in which individuals are willing to act, uncritically, in accordance with institutional demands that equate with evil. For instance, the "good Nazi soldier" has constituted an example of this, as have the results of social psychology experiments in the 1960s and 1970s (e.g., the Milgram experiment and the Stanford Prison experiment), which have served to underscore the dynamics. Such power-related links between Inquisition-era violence and social scapegoats perhaps have become clearer in some of the more recent atrocities spanning the last several centuries. These include the near-extermination of indigenous peoples in the Americas and other parts of the world, the brutal abduction and enslavement of Africans, the Jewish Holocaust, genocides in Rwanda and Sudan, the high-profile genocide of the Rohingya in Myanmar, and the horrifying treatment of asylum seekers at the southern border of the United States, especially during 2016 to 2020 and especially concerning the separation of children from their families. These examples represent manifestations of a psychology of exclusion or marginalization, of othering, in ways that are marked by an abuse of power and serve as an antecedent lack of morality, and in ways that have had egregious consequences.

The perpetration of violence has presumed the ability to instill fear, and ultimately to control or to take power over others; indeed, it has presumed the role of a more or less passive victim. In many ways, early conceptualizations of trauma were linked to sin, to a fall from grace, or to moral weakness on the part of the victim who somehow "deserved" punishment or persecution. Later conceptualizations of trauma, beginning with the rise of the psychiatric asylum, were subordinate to a diagnosis of mental illness; in fact, some sequelae of PTSD often were misinterpreted, and clients, usually women, were misdiagnosed as having hysteria or schizophrenia and placed in psychiatric hospitals, where they were traumatized further.

These historical examples have indicated as much about the perpetrators of violence—and the abusive power of the institutions that they have represented—as about the cultural assumptions regarding how experiences of trauma have been viewed. The effects of such brutal behaviors do not necessarily go away; they can continue to resonate, for many generations, among the offspring and in the family systems of people who have been brutalized and victimized. This raises the issue of historical trauma and its effects on marginalized groups of people. The field has developed a greater understanding of the effects of historical or racial trauma and consequential epigenetic changes; a fuller discussion of this is presented in Chapters 2 and 19 of this textbook. The field also has identified the impact of adverse childhood experiences (ACEs), which are expounded in Chapter 2. We do not fully understand as yet the social and cultural effects on the people who perpetrate such actions or who allow such conduct to occur in their midst, and this would seem to be an important area for further research.

MODERNITY AND THE CONCEPTUALIZATION OF TRAUMA

The modern study of how trauma affects the human condition is rooted in the genesis of modern psychiatry. In the mid-1800s, Jean-Martin Charcot studied young Parisian women who were hospitalized at the Salpêtrière. In his consideration of "neurosis," Charcot examined the repercussions of lives filled with sexual assault, poverty, and violence. Charcot recognized that these women were acting out of their subjective realities and that their conditions were psychological in nature (Herman, 1992b). Charcot's students, Sigmund Freud, Joseph Breuer, and Pierre Janet, expanded upon his exploration of hysteria and neurosis and further hypothesized that these conditions were caused by exposure to psychological trauma (Bogousslavsky & Dieguez, 2014). Freud, Janet, and Breuer's conceptualization of what constituted psychological trauma was initially quite narrow and was constrained to the idea that hysteria and neuroses were caused by psychosexual events. However, by 1917, extensive exploration of the subject of traumatic conditions had created an expanded definition of psychological trauma.

Freud's classical psychoanalytic approach emphasized the process of repression, replacing earlier notions of dissociation (Diamond, 2020). His contributions served as a launching pad for various contemporary approaches, which interestingly evolved to re-emphasize the process of dissociation (dissociation is discussed further in Chapter 2 of this book). In his *Introductory Lectures on Psychoanalysis*, Freud proposed a broadened concept of psychological trauma that included "war, railway collisions, and other alarming accidents involving fatal risks" (Freud & Strachey, 1966/1977, p. 274). This more inclusive definition later served as a foundation for delineating and classifying trauma-related disorders within the APA's *DSMs*. The remaining parts of this section outline the emergent understanding of trauma in World Wars I and II as well as the growing awareness of the impact of trauma in recent decades (the effects of trauma on war veterans are detailed in Chapter 25 of this textbook).

World War I and World War II

Initial investigations into the psychological consequences of traumatic exposure were not limited to hysterical women. The advent of World War I, with its proliferation of what were viewed as emotionally disturbed soldiers, brought the psychological devastation that often resulted from combat to the attention of the field of psychology. Charles Myers, a pioneering psychologist in the study of combat-related disturbance, recognized that the soldiers' symptoms appeared to be similar to behaviors that Freud observed in women who suffered from hysteria. Myers originally hypothesized that the behaviors had a physical cause and attributed the behaviors to the intensity of the concussions resulting from explosive weapons (Herman, 1992b). Because of his hypothesis, Myers labeled the syndrome "shell shock." Probably to the dismay of the military, further study showed that many soldiers exhibited the characteristic symptoms of the syndrome, even without exposure to the physical trauma of concussive force (Herman, 1992b). Eventually, the soldiers' neurosis was acknowledged to be the result of the psychological trauma and stress of combat, with its constant state of violence, threats to life, and horrific images (Herman, 1992b; van der Kolk, 1996, 2000, 2014).

By the end of World War I, psychiatric professionals had adopted the position that combat fatigue, or "war hysteria" as it became known, was a disease created by a lack of "will to be well" on the part of the affected soldier (van der Kolk, 1996). This view, especially prevalent among professionals serving in the military or in positions with connection to the armed services, followed a course of development similar to the earlier studies of hysteria in women. Soldiers were expected to be brave, heroic, and stoic in their adaptation to the rigors of their war experiences. Those who succumbed to psychological distress were categorized as being of poor moral character or of weak temperament (Herman, 1992b; van der Kolk, 1996). This view mirrored initial interpretations of women who exhibited neurotic symptoms as being internally weak and flawed.

Some psychiatrists of the time, most notably W. H. R. Rivers, viewed combat neurosis, or war hysteria, as a pathological, traumatic syndrome that was a result of the severity of the stressors of combat and not a weakness of character (Herman, 1992b; van der Kolk, 1996, 2014). Rivers, who based his treatment interventions upon psychoanalytic principles, strongly believed that combat-related hysteria could affect any soldier, regardless of moral character or capacity for bravery (van der Kolk, 1996). After the war ended, veterans' hospitals continued to serve the psychiatric needs of soldiers who experienced persistent disabilities resulting from their combat experiences. However, these veterans garnered little attention from the medical community, which seemingly adopted the view that the horrors of war and the lasting consequences either could be forgotten or erased, if only they were ignored (Herman, 1992b).

During the time of peace between World War I and World War II, there was little scientific interest in the field of traumatic study. However, the issue of traumatic exposure remained of interest to a few professionals within the arena of psychology. After a career in psychoanalysis and anthropology, American psychiatrist Abram Kardiner began to study combat-related disorders and psychological trauma (van der Kolk, 2001, 2014). Kardiner explored past assessments, theoretical frameworks, and studies on combat-related hysteria, synthesizing his findings in his 1941 work, *The Traumatic Neuroses of War*. Kardiner decried the use of the label "hysterical" in reference to suffering soldiers, as he felt that it promulgated the impression that the experienced disturbance was a result of character weakness or internal flaws (Herman, 1992b).

Growing Awareness of the Impact of Trauma

Social awareness of PTSD evolved concomitantly within the psychiatric community and the public (Friedman et al., 2007; Jones & Wessely, 2006). As an example of emerging public awareness, the symptoms of PTSD were portrayed in Hollywood *film noir* in the 1940s, more than 30 years before the diagnosis first was included in the *DSM-III* (Miller, as cited in Levers, 2001). Earlier war-related investigations of trauma eventually piqued the interest of the civilian sector, and conditions born from noncombat-related trauma began to be examined. As televised atrocities routinely aired in living rooms across the globe, the social movements of the 1960s and 1970s spawned an expansion of examining traumatic experiences and their impact. The experiences certainly were traumatic for those involved, but the news-consuming public also experienced the trauma, vicariously, vis-à-vis newspaper accounts and television news footage. Several of these movements relevant to this conversation are discussed in the following text.

Civil Rights Movement

The Tulsa Massacre occurred on May 31 and June 1, 1921, and its 100-year anniversary recently was commemorated, instructing a large swath of the population about a sordid incident in American history that had been covered up. This massacre was an extreme example of the many savage attacks on African American communities post emancipation (*Smithsonian Magazine* offers a vivid account of this atrocity at: www.smithsonianmag.com/history/tulsa-race-massacre -century-later-180977145/). The civil rights movement in the United States, during the 1950s and 1960s, unveiled the violence long associated with racism. Even though slavery had been abolished in the previous century, Jim Crow laws legalized segregation, continuing from after the Civil War through the end of the 1960s (Chapter 17 of this textbook offers more information about this). The fight for civil rights, led mostly by African Americans, but having some allies of other races, had a vicious backlash then, similar to what we are witnessing now (Glickman, 2020). Emmet Till, a 14-year-old African American male, was brutally murdered in Mississippi. Lynching of African Americans still was occurring in the United States through the late 1960s (NAACP, 2021). These types of events were traumatizing, and they were used by certain White Americans to terrorize and attempt to control Black Americans (Lartey & Morris, 2018). These types of events galvanized the civil rights movement.

Federal civil rights legislation was proposed in the early 1960s, first by President John F. Kennedy and then by President Lyndon B. Johnson. The response to the proposed legislation was vile and led to many instances of violence against African Americans, including murder. Groups of mostly African American civil rights activists formed, and they were called Freedom Riders (History.com Editors, 2021); the groups included both Black and White activists, and those who wished to deny the civil rights of African Americans targeted both. The late John R. Lewis, former U.S. Representative, was a youth activist and a Freedom Rider during the civil rights movement of the 1960s, continuing until his death in 2020. Although televised news coverage was not yet available to capture earlier atrocities, such as the Tulsa Race Massacre in 1921, people watched their television news programs in horror in 1965, as Mr. Lewis and other young activists were beaten, savagely, on the Edmund Pettus Bridge. It was on this bridge that state troopers attacked peaceful protesters, who were exercising their rights to free speech and to protest peacefully against racism; this day became etched in the memory of the public as "Bloody Sunday." It is not surprising, then, that racism, along with its tantamount historical trauma, have contributed to and constituted the serious public health problem that we continue to face today (Cardarelli et al., 2021; Wamsley, 2021).

Vietnam

As the men and women who served in combat in Vietnam returned to the United States, interest arose, again, concerning the effects of combat upon the human psyche. The tensions related to the social discourse surrounding the war brought the issue to the forefront of the national media. Television news programs broadcast images of longhaired, wild-eyed soldiers into the homes of unsuspecting Americans, who were forced to consider the negative psychological results of war upon the nation's sons and daughters. The images of the conquering hero, which had been the theme of the returning World War II soldier, were replaced with a more disturbing reality. American men and women were returning home with trauma-related mental health conditions that seriously affected their ability to function in all of the domains of their lives. This new breed of veteran often felt guilt-ridden, angry, and emotionally volatile, which had serious implications for their spouses and children (Z. Solomon et al., 1987). The general population was drawn into an emerging awareness of combat-related trauma conditions.

Violence Against Women and the Rape Crisis Movement

Professional and popular conceptualizations of trauma continued to expand through the end of the 20th century. With the advent of the second wave of the women's liberation movement, issues related to the "tyranny of private life" for women began to be examined (Herman, 1992b). Early exercises of consciousness-raising groups, in the 1960s and 1970s, soon led to open, and heretofore unprecedented, discussions of the psychological impact of rape, sexual assault, incest, and the sexual subjugation of women for political purposes (Herman, 1992b; Lating & Everly, 1995; Sinha et al., 2017). The field of psychiatry then acknowledged that sexual assault led to psychological distress that substantially mimicked combat neurosis in its symptom presentation. Psychiatric nurses Lynda Holmstrom and Ann Burgess observed a pattern of numbing, increased startle response, nightmares, dissociative symptoms, nausea, and insomnia in rape victims who came to Boston Hospital for treatment (Burgess & Holmstrom, 1974). They labeled this pattern of symptom presentation as "Rape Trauma Syndrome," thus pushing the field to consider an even broader definition of traumatic victimization that later was incorporated into the formal diagnostic criteria for PTSD.

Violence Against Children and the Child Protective Movement

As traumatic exposure in noncombat-related situations became more widely recognized as a source of emotional distress and disturbance, issues related to children emerged as a particular area of focus. It long had been acknowledged that children are equally susceptible to the stressors of traumatic events as are their adult counterparts, but it was thought that the reactions of children were of a less severe nature and shorter lived than for adults (Yule, 1998). Prior to 1987, little research existed to define or delineate the differences in stress responses between adults and children. Since the 1990s, differential diagnosis of PTSD in children has included refinements of symptom presentation that may manifest in children. Some significant differences have included developmentally sensitive displays of disorganized or agitated behavior in children, as well as generalized nightmares and traumatic play (APA, 2000, 2013). The *DSM-5* (APA, 2013) has included a new subtype of PTSD that is specific to children under the age of 6 years (Substance Abuse and Mental Health Services Administration [SAMHSA], 2016).

Statistics have suggested that children experience rape, robbery, assault, and physical violence at a greater rate than do adults (Finkelhor et al., 2013). According to a 1990 study by the U.S. Department of Justice, adolescents were 2.5 times more likely to be the victim of a violent crime than adults, although this trend has decreased since the mid-1990s to a little over one-sixth of what it had been (e.g., Child Trends, 2018; Wordes & Nunez, 2002). However, it has been alarming that these experiences often occur within the child's own family system.

One relatively recent development in the study of PTSD in children has been increased research regarding exposure to family and domestic violence as a catalyst for the development of children's stress-related disorders. Further confounding studies of family violence and PTSD, is the disturbing fact that children who experience trauma at home also are more likely to experience violence in their community, with their peers, and in their personal relationships (Margolin & Vickerman, 2007). Often these exposures are of a chronic nature, presenting challenges to accepted definitions of trauma and trauma experience. These challenges, referenced as complex trauma, are addressed later in this chapter and examined more fully in Chapter 9 of this textbook. It is widely accepted that PTSD appears to be one of the most common psychiatric disorders in children and young adults (SAMHSA, 2014).

POSTTRAUMATIC STRESS DISORDER AND THE *DIAGNOSTIC AND STATISTICAL MANUALS*

The construct of psychological trauma has changed over time. Especially pertinent to this discussion is how the construct has changed in relationship to mental health diagnostics, which has not been without controversy (Carvajal, 2018). This section briefly explores the evolution of trauma-related conceptualizations in the *Diagnostic and Statistical Manuals*, the relatively recent discussion of complex trauma, and the interface of trauma with multiple diagnostic categories.

The Articulation of Trauma in the *Diagnostic and Statistical Manuals*

In 1952, the American Psychiatric Association released the first *Diagnostic and Statistical Manual of Mental Disorders* as a means to mitigate some of the limitations found in using nomenclature from the *International Statistical Classification of Diseases, Injuries, and Causes of Death* (ICD-6). The ICD has been the World Health Organization's (WHO) diagnostic nosology, used globally since its inception. In the *ICD-6*, stress-related reactions were labeled as "acute situational maladjustment" (WHO, 1949). The *DSM-I* labeled stress-related conditions under the heading of "Transient Situational Personality Disturbance" (APA, 1952). The diagnosis of gross stress reaction was included under this heading and defined psychic disturbance related to combat or civilian catastrophe. Under the same heading, other stress-related conditions were given the labels of adult situational reaction as well as adjustment reaction of infancy, of childhood, of adolescence, or of late life (APA, 1952).

A revised edition of the *DSM* was released in 1968; the *DSM-II* (APA, 1968) reclassified traumatic experience into a category called "Adjustment Reaction of Adult Life." There was no longer a description of the diagnosis, and criteria were explained through the provision of three examples of qualifying experiences. These experiences were unwanted pregnancy, military combat, and being sentenced to death (APA, 1968). There was an asterisk next to the category, which directed the reader to the appendices, where additional examples of similarly qualifying stressful events could be found. These events included railway, car, boat, and plane accidents (Wilson, 1995). One might wonder about the lack of explication of the various types of trauma and the resultant psychological manifestations, but clearly, the intent of the authors was to provide an inclusive category within which to place reactions related to all traumatic experiences that resulted in anxiety, fear, and feelings of overwhelming loss of control (van der Kolk et al., 2007; Wilson, 1995).

In 1980, the third edition of the manual, the *DSM-III* (APA, 1980), offered another reclassification of trauma-related syndromes, locating it within the anxiety disorder section of the manual. The manual contained a new diagnosis, PTSD, which encompassed combat neurosis, rape trauma syndrome, and battered women syndrome. Based substantially upon Kardiner's (1941) work, the diagnosis was a compendium of symptoms culled from clinical records, research, and literary explorations of those working with various trauma-related syndromes (van der Kolk, 1996, 2000). The symptoms of PTSD were clustered into three distinct categories, from which an individual needed to exhibit four symptoms in order to meet the criteria for diagnosis. These clusters encompassed symptoms of re-experiencing the trauma, a display of the effects of numbing and detachment, and changes in personality. In order to meet the diagnostic criteria, the manual further specified that a stressor of relatively universal concern or suffering must be present (APA, 1980). The requirement to identify a recognizable stressor replaced the previously provided list of examples of qualifying traumatic events that were present in earlier editions of the manual. Although there appeared to be a tacit understanding that certain types of events would be particularly distressing, there was neither a discussion of etiology nor an examination of how individual perceptions of events as being traumatic can vary from person to person (Everly & Lating, 1995). The notion of the variability of human perception of events as traumatic became a salient feature for the diagnosis of PTSD in future iterations of the *DSM* and is discussed at a later point in this chapter.

In 1987, the *DSM-III-R* (APA, 1987) was published, with further revisions to the diagnosis of PTSD. In an attempt to provide clarification of what constituted a traumatic event or recognizable stressor, the phraseology "outside of the range of normal human experience . . . that would be markedly distressing to almost anyone" was added to the criteria (APA, 1987, p. 250). Further, a list of examples of qualifying events was provided again. These examples included serious harm or threats of serious harm to self, children, spouse, or other loved ones; seeing another person killed or seriously injured as a result of violence or accident; and experiencing the sudden destruction of one's home (APA, 1987). Of note, traumatic events that were within the realm of normal human experience, such as being the victim of a violent crime or experiencing or witnessing a serious automobile accident, and that we now view as highly traumatic and as potential triggers for PTSD, were *not* included in the description (Spitzer et al., 2007). Additionally, the list of symptoms was expanded to 17, and the number of symptoms necessary for diagnosis was increased to six. The final significant change in the *DSM-III-R* diagnostic criteria for PTSD was the extension of special qualifiers that related to the manifestation of the disorder in children. Prior to this point, the field promulgated an assumption that children experienced, processed, and exhibited symptoms of traumatic exposure in much the same way as adults, if at all. The *DSM-III-R* clarified that children may display disorganized or agitated behavior instead of the fear, helplessness, or horror listed as adult symptoms under criterion A of the diagnostic category (APA, 1987). According to criterion B, children may demonstrate repetitive play with themes related to the trauma instead of having intrusive recollections, and further, children's dreams may be frightening but occur without recognizable content of the trauma, as would be present in adult experiences (APA, 1987). Although the revisions were intended to provide clarity and to refocus on PTSD as a disorder, debate continued well into the preparation of the *DSM-IV*.

The 1994 revision of the manual, *DSM-IV* (APA, 1994), again brought substantial changes to the PTSD diagnosis. The previously noted statements regarding the need for the stressor to cause distress for most people and to be beyond the normal range of human experience were removed from the criteria in an effort to define trauma more explicitly and to address the problem of common, yet clearly traumatic, events being excluded from the criteria. Some clinical experts suggested that the stressor be defined in terms that are more subjective. Among the experts, most notably, were S. D. Solomon and Canino (1990), who advocated for defining the qualifying circumstances or traumas in a more general manner, such as an "extremely shocking event," that would speak to the subjective perception of the individual and provide for broad inclusion of experiences. Others advocated for a more objective classification that further would delineate the symptom and response presentation necessary for differential diagnosis (Lasiuk & Hegadoren, 2006; van der Kolk et al., 2007). Eventually, a combination of subjective and objective measures was included within criterion A.

Criterion A1 addressed the subjective nature of traumatic exposure by defining a qualifying event in which the individual "experienced, witnessed, or was confronted with an event or events that involved actual or threatened death or serious injury, or a threat to the physical integrity of self or others" (APA, 1994, p. 427). The addition of criterion A1 mitigated the previous omission of considering the subjective or perceptual reality of the individual who experienced the event. The external nature of the event sustained the notion that the etiology of the disorder is external to the individual. Criterion A2 addressed the need for an objective component of the definition by describing the individual's response as one that demonstrated "intense fear, helplessness, or horror" (APA, 1994, p. 428). These changes propagated the controversy surrounding the diagnosis, perhaps going too far with the notion of perception by using the words "confronted with" in criterion A1 (APA, 1994, p. 427). As a broad concept, open for significant interpretation, the addition of this wording substantially expanded the number of individuals who met the criteria for the disorder and allowed for conceptual bracket creep, or a stretching of the boundaries of the diagnosis, beyond the categorical limitations of earlier definitions (McNally, 2003). The last substantive change to the diagnostic criteria of PTSD in the *DSM-IV* was the addition of specifications regarding the duration of symptoms. The following delimitations primarily affected time frames: (a) acute, which was defined as duration of symptoms of less than 3 months; (b) chronic, with duration of symptom presentation of 3 months or more; and (c) delayed onset, with a symptom presentation that did not appear until 6 months or more after exposure to the stressor (APA, 1994).

In an attempt to separate what could be viewed as an early, simple reaction to traumatic exposure from the more chronic, debilitating sequelae of PTSD, a new trauma-related disorder was included in the *DSM-IV*. Placed within the anxiety disorder category, ASD had many of the same diagnostic criteria as PTSD but had an onset of occurrence of symptom presentation within 1 month of the traumatic exposure and was described as lasting for at least 2 days and for a maximum of 4 weeks (APA, 1994). Additionally, ASD criteria included the presence of three or more dissociative symptoms from a list of five that was provided (APA, 1994). Some have argued that the high rates of individuals who progress from ASD to PTSD and the shared symptom profile of the two disorders strongly pointed to ASD as an early form of PTSD, not a separate condition (Classen et al., 1996; Marshall et al., 1999).

In 2000, the APA released the *DSM-IV-TR*. There were no substantive changes to the trauma-related diagnostic criteria in this edition. Rather, as the last edition was published some 16 years prior, and the next full revision was not expected until 2012 at the earliest, changes in the descriptive text were made to reflect the current state of research and empirical literature. Debate regarding trauma-related disorders continued, with many changes proposed for the *DSM-5* (with the fifth edition, the American Psychiatric Association switched from using a Roman numeral to using an Arabic numeral in the sequencing of the volumes). A number of dramatic events, in the first decade of the new millennium, compelled a renewed social science examination of human response to extraordinary circumstances. Some of these events of mass violence (further detailed in Chapter 20 of this book) and natural disaster (further detailed in Chapter 22 of this book) included the terrorist attacks of September 11, 2001; the Oklahoma City bombing; the shootings at Columbine High School and Virginia Tech; the shootings and bombing in Norway; the 2010 earthquakes in Haiti and Chile; and the 2011 earthquake/tsunami/nuclear disaster in Japan.

The APA released the much-anticipated *DSM-5* in 2013. In this most recent revision, PTSD was removed from its previous category as an anxiety disorder in *DSM-IV-TR* (APA, 2000), and has been placed in the chapter on Trauma- and Stressor-Related Disorders in the *DSM-5*. However, the very location of the chapter has been significant, in that it immediately follows chapters on Anxiety Disorders and Obsessive-Compulsive and Related Disorders and appears right before the chapter on Dissociative Disorders. The introduction to the Trauma- and Stressor-Related Disorders chapter importantly notes that the sequencing of the chapter indicates a close relationship among these sets of diagnoses (APA, 2013). An understanding of the relationships among these diagnostic categories is essential for ruling out unsuitable diagnoses and for making accurate diagnoses (Tehrani & Levers, 2016). Other changes to the diagnostic criteria, from the *DSM-IV* to *DSM-5*, have included the following modifications: eliminating the subjective component in defining trauma, explaining and narrowing the definitions of trauma and exposure to it, increasing and rearranging the symptoms criteria, and alterations in additional criteria and specifiers (Pai et al., 2017).

Further revisions that are specific to the diagnostic criteria for PTSD in *DSM-5* (APA, 2013) have involved the addition of new items such as experiencing exaggerated negative expectations, having a distorted sense of self-blame, and experiencing persistent negative emotions. In addition, some of the revisions have offered clarification of what constitutes "experiencing a traumatic event" as well as a redefinition of the symptom presentation of dissociative reactions and the concept of avoidance. A number of scholars and clinicians have suggested that perhaps the best and most efficacious approach is to reconceptualize the diagnosis as a spectrum disorder rather than a single entity, with resilience at one end and severe symptomology at the other (e.g., Goodman, 2012; Lasiuk & Hegadoren, 2006; Wolf et al., 2018). The trauma- and stressor-related disorders included in the current *DSM-5* (APA, 2013) comprise the following:

- Reactive Attachment Disorder (RAD)
- Disinhibited Social Engagement Disorder (DSED)
- Posttraumatic Stress Disorder (PTSD)
- Acute Stress Disorder (ASD)
- Adjustment Disorders
- Other Specified Trauma- and Stressor-Related Disorder
- Unspecified Trauma- and Stressor-Related Disorder

The changes in the *DSM-5* (APA, 2013) have not gone without criticisms, which began significantly prior to publication (e.g., Rosen et al., 2008). It goes beyond the scope of this chapter to detail all of the controversies that surround the latest articulation of PTSD, but it is important to highlight some of the more widely discussed areas of concern. First, a number of experts consider criterion A to be too limiting—it requires actual exposure to a traumatic event as a specific benchmark, to the possible exclusion of those who have experienced other trauma-related clusters of symptoms. Second, many experts advocated for the inclusion of a complex posttraumatic stress disorder (CPTSD) diagnosis in *DSM-IV* (e.g., Courtois, 2008; Herman, 1992a) and, subsequently, in *DSM-5*. Other scholars (e.g., Resick et al., 2012; Rosen et al., 2008) have argued, conversely, that while the discussion magnifies the complexity of multiple traumatic events, the actual evidence has not supported the classification of a new diagnostic category. Finally, some experts have expressed concerns about referencing "disorder" as a descriptor for the trauma that people experience in the event of danger and potential or real harm. Ochberg (2012) has suggested the term "posttraumatic stress injury" (PTSI) as a less stigmatizing and more suitable designation. However, similar to the momentum for inducting CPTSD into the new manual, the drive simply did not gain adequate support for inclusion in the *DSM-5* (Tehrani & Levers, 2016). In the face of all of these changes over the decades since PTSD first was included in the *DSM-III*, it is likely that the criteria will remain under scrutiny and that experts will continue to examine the nature of trauma and its effects. Whether CPTSD finds a designation in a future version of the *DSM* is anyone's guess, but the construct remains a useful one for clinicians (e.g., Ford, 2020; John et al., 2019; Kumar et al., 2019; Yearwood et al., 2019) and warrants a brief discussion here.

Posttraumatic Stress Disorder and the Effects of Complex Trauma

The diagnostic criteria for PTSD have undergone revisions, as research regarding the phenomena of traumatic experience has continued to elucidate its effect on the human condition. By the early 1990s, clinicians and researchers, who were exploring PTSD in people who had experienced domestic violence, child abuse, and other long-term exposures, began to identify that the symptom pattern produced by these types of exposures was not defined adequately by the prevailing diagnostic criteria (Briere, 1987; Courtois, 2008; Herman, 1992b). At issue seemed to be what were classified as "comorbid" conditions that, arguably, appeared to be a result of traumatic exposures of a more complex nature (Courtois, 2008). For example, children who have been exposed to family violence, child abuse, or other ongoing maltreatment have experienced trauma over extended periods. These experiences have occurred during different phases of the children's emotional development, and at the hands of their family members or other significant caregivers, which makes their experiences substantially different from those of combat veterans or individuals who experience acute types of trauma like accidents or natural disasters. Although the effects of such exposure were found to be similar in nature to the prevailing understanding of PTSD, there were significant differences (Herman, 1992b; John et al., 2019; Kliethermes et al., 2014; McCormack & Thomson, 2017; Yearwood et al., 2019). These differences seemed especially pronounced in relationship to the developmental trajectories of children experiencing maltreatment early in childhood, at the hands of the very caregivers whom the children *ought* to be able to trust. In evidence were psychological disturbances not incorporated within the *DSM-III* diagnostic criteria for PTSD, such as medical and somatic complaints, depression, anxiety, dissociative disorders, substance abuse issues, and interpersonal relationship problems (Courtois, 2008).

Because of research regarding the experience of complex exposure to trauma, experts in the field proposed that the PTSD committee, which had been empaneled to explore stress disorders for the *DSM-IV*, also conduct field trials regarding complex exposure to trauma. The committee set out to investigate the possibility of including a diagnosis of complex PTSD, as well as a constellation of trauma-related symptoms not under the umbrella of trauma-related conditions at the time, which could be classified as "Disorders of Extreme Stress Not Otherwise Specified (DESNOS)" (Roth et al., 1997). The DESNOS designation was intended to focus primarily on the effects of early interpersonal trauma. The DESNOS category would consist of the following seven additional criteria, which may result from chronic victimization: (a) changes in emotional regulation, including difficulty with modulation of anger and self-destructive behavior; (b) alterations in consciousness, including amnesias and dissociative episodes; (c) alterations in self-perception such as shame, guilt, and stigmatization; (d) changes in relationship to others, including a lack of trust or loss of intimacy; (e) somatic complaints; (f) changes in one's sense of meaning such as loss of faith or despair; and, (g) changes in perceptions about the perpetrator (Herman, 1992b; Pelcovitz et al., 1997; van der Kolk, 2001).

The *DSM-IV* field trial, conducted between 1991 and 1992, found 92% comorbidity between DESNOS and PTSD and, as such, a separate diagnosis was not included in the revision of the manual; however, the symptom pattern was incorporated as an associated feature of PTSD (APA, 1994). Since those first field trials, interest in the impact of early and repetitive exposure to relational trauma has continued to increase, and based on continuing research, support for a separate diagnosis has continued to grow (e.g., Ford, 2017; John et al., 2019; Kliethermes et al., 2014; McCormack & Thomson, 2017). Ford (1999, 2017, 2020) found that DESNOS could, in fact, occur in the absence of PTSD, despite the substantial overlap. He further found that PTSD and DESNOS were substantially different in terms of symptoms and functional impairment features (Ford, 1999, 2017, 2020). Research continues to examine whether these conditions are, indeed, separate conditions that frequently may be comorbid but are patently unique.

A primary issue has arisen with the growing awareness that treatment interventions between individuals with PTSD and with DESNOS may need to be significantly different in order to intervene, safely and effectively, with those having complex trauma histories (Ford, 1999, 2017, 2020; John et al., 2019; Kliethermes et al., 2014; McCormack & Thomson, 2017; van der Kolk, 2001). Although the case that was made for complex trauma seemingly was not sufficient for inclusion in the *DSM-5*, the WHO has included complex posttraumatic stress disorder (C-PTSD) in its final draft of the 11th edition of the *International Statistical Classification of Diseases and Related Health Problems (ICD-11)* (Rosenfield et al., 2018). As previously suggested, while complex trauma is not officially recognized in the *DSM-5*, it is nonetheless a useful construct for clinicians in understanding the rippled effect that multiple and complex traumas may have on an individual client. The utility of understanding complex trauma is elaborated more fully in Chapter 9 of this textbook.

The Interface of Trauma With Multiple Diagnostic Categories

As previously discussed, the notion that traumatic exposure and stress can create psychiatric illness in "normal" individuals has had a long and well-researched history. By definition, the diagnosis of PTSD remains unique in that its etiology stems from an outside stressor. Demonstrated in an earlier study, although exposure rates of traumatic events among the general population ranged from 36% to 81%, only 7% to 10% of exposed individuals developed PTSD (Breslau et al., 1998). In a later study, Kilpatrick et al. (2013, p. 537) found that "Traumatic event exposure using *DSM-5* criteria was high (89.7%), and exposure to multiple traumatic event types was the norm." What has continued to confound those in the field is the prevalence of comorbid conditions, which suggest that, perhaps, there is a combination of factors at work (Yehuda & McFarlane, 1995). Although any real consensus among experts has remained elusive, an existing body of PTSD research seems to describe a spectrum of disorders that often are present in those who have survived traumatic exposure.

An abundance of evidence has suggested that traumatic exposure can lead to a wide array of psychological disturbances that meet the diagnostic criteria within the *DSM*. The disorders vary in severity from adjustment disorders to more lasting and grave manifestations. Traumatic exposure has shown a strong correlation with anxiety disorders (Spinhoven et al., 2014), substance abuse disorders (Killeen et al., 2015), dissociative disorders (McDowell et al., 1999; Swart et al., 2020), major depression (Flory & Yehuda, 2015; Spinhoven et al., 2014), and eating disorders (Brewerton, 2007; Rijkers et al., 2019). Additionally, borderline personality disorder (BPD) displays commonality with the symptom cluster of complex PTSD and shares, at its core, a high frequency of interpersonal trauma (Cloitre et al., 2014; Harned et al., 2018; Yen et al., 2002). When a broad definition of trauma is applied to the life experiences of people seeking treatment for psychological disorders, most are found to have experienced at least one traumatic exposure across the life-span.

Given the statistical probability that individuals will experience traumatic exposure during their lifetimes, it is the expectation rather than the exception that mental health clients will present with trauma histories. Indeed, a significant percentage of clients who are diagnosed with serious mental disorders such as psychotic disorders, schizophrenia, and bipolar disorder detail extensive trauma backgrounds (Goodman et al., 1997; SAMHSA, 2014). Further, individuals with extensive trauma histories often present with complex symptom patterns that involve multiple disorders, making differential diagnosis difficult. Najavits et al. (2009) describe this as a "central paradox," stating that "comorbidity with PTSD is the norm, yet treatment outcome studies routinely exclude clients with significant comorbid conditions and fail to assess for them" (p. 508).

RESILIENCE

An introductory discussion of trauma would not be complete without emphasizing the courage and resilience shown by survivors of trauma. It is important that mental health professionals bear in mind that not everyone who experiences trauma develops PTSD. For a variety of reasons, many individuals possess or are able to develop greater resilience and then can cope better with the immediate or aftereffects of traumatic experiences. The U.S. Department of Veterans Affairs (USDVA, 2018) has reported that about 60% of men and 50% of women experience a traumatic event in their lifetimes. Epidemiological research (Benjet et al., 2016) has indicated that about 70% of people, worldwide, have been exposed to at least one traumatic incident in their lives. About 7% to 8% of the population qualifies for a diagnosis of PTSD at some point in life (USDVA). So, as ubiquitous and terrifying as trauma may be, it appears that human beings have a real capacity for resilience in the face of traumatic events; the human spirit seems to have an innate ability to transcend adversity. In fact, research has suggested that between 30% to 70% of individuals who experience trauma also report positive change and growth emerging from the traumatic experience (Joseph & Butler, 2010).

Calhoun and Tedeschi (1998) have initiated the concept of posttraumatic growth (PTG), although the construct has remained somewhat controversial. PTG may account for the positive psychological change that results from an individual's engagement with a traumatic event. Tedeschi and Calhoun (2004) have defined PTG as representing

> the experience of individuals whose development, at least in some areas has surpassed what was present before the struggle with crises occurred. The individual has not only survived, but has experienced changes that are viewed as important, and that go beyond the status quo. Posttraumatic growth is not simply a return to baseline—it is an experience of improvement that for some persons is deeply profound. (p. 4)

Posttraumatic growth has been associated with a number of interrelated constructs, including resilience, hardiness, and a sense of coherence (Almedom, 2005). However, even though PTG has been reported in an array of samples, it remains controversial due to measurement challenges (Park & Lechner, 2006). Typically, PTG is assessed by self-report, through interviews, or in questionnaires, and sceptics question the validity of the construct (e.g., Frazier & Kaler, 2006; Park & Sinnott, 2018; Steger et al., 2006). A web-based study of 1,739 adults concluded that growth, following trauma, might entail the strengthening of character (Peterson et al., 2008). PTG should not be perceived as a consequence of trauma; rather, it is one possible outcome of the process of working through the aftermath of trauma (Levers, 2020). The discussion of growth after trauma does not discount, in any way, the negative effects of trauma. Rather, attention to growth-promoting therapeutic strategies can facilitate a meaning-making process that potentially enhances a survivor's sense of purpose and promotes personal growth and change (Altmaier, 2017). It is essential to understand how the various risk factors and protective factors existing in a person's life at the time of a trauma event and immediately after may contribute to the degree to which the trauma has a lesser or greater impact. Clinicians need to consider the resilience and hardiness of their clients and to maintain a growth-oriented and meaning-making perspective when working with clients who have been traumatized.

According to a publication by Harvard University's Center on the Developing Child (n.d., pp. 1–2), the following elements are important considerations regarding resilience:

- Resilience requires supportive relationships and opportunities for skillbuilding.
- Resilience results from a dynamic interaction between internal predispositions and external experiences.
- Learning to cope with manageable threats to our physical and social well-being is critical for the development of resilience.

▪ Some children respond in more extreme ways to both negative and positive experiences.
▪ Individuals never completely lose their ability to improve their coping skills, and they often learn how to adapt to new challenges.

COUNSELING IMPLICATIONS

As suggested by the rates of exposure to traumatic events among the general population, trauma is a factor that clinicians need to consider when they embark upon a course of treatment with any client. Although most mental health agencies and clinicians routinely obtain information regarding medical and psychosocial histories, it is not nearly as routine to ask about a history of trauma. This, in fact, should be a standard line of inquiry that is a part of any routine intake process, and the information should be requested in as normalized a fashion as possible—in other words, it should be posed as a simple and nonthreatening question that is a part of the larger intake protocol.

Diagnoses are not dogma; by reviewing the history of how the effects of traumatic events have been viewed through the ages, we can see that the psychosocial notion of trauma is one that has been constructed by humans, over time, and that is connected to the cultural ethos in which people pay attention to those affected by traumatic events. At the same time, we now understand that a traumatic event triggers a cascade of neurochemical responses that account for many trauma-related reactions (this is discussed further in Chapters 2, 3, and 4). Clinicians need to *listen* to the narratives of clients describing the effects of traumatic events and to pay attention both to interpersonal and to family dynamics. Statistically speaking, the potential is high that most therapists are likely to counsel clients who have trauma histories. It also is likely that any practicing clinician may see the effects of racial or transgenerational trauma.

One of the most robust implications across the various clinical fields is the need for more preservice training around issues pertaining to the effects of traumatic events. We need to assist students in understanding the evaluation and treatment of persons who have been exposed to trauma as well as to the effects of stress, crises, and disasters. I am hopeful that, by presenting related foundational knowledge as a trauma scaffold, students and clinicians alike can build upon this scaffold, incorporating other foundational practice and treatment information as we continue to understand increasingly more advanced and complex issues regarding trauma. Along these lines, more research is needed regarding assessment, treatment, and pedagogical issues associated with the effects of trauma.

CONCLUSION

In this chapter, we have explored the historical context of the way in which we have come to view the effects of traumatic events and how we have arrived at several trauma-related diagnostic categories. Although trauma has been a part of the human experience, probably since the beginning of time, an awareness of the impact of trauma on the lives of affected people has developed slowly and only within recent history. We have seen how, in certain historical eras, specific groups of people have been marginalized and actually targeted for violence. In these instances, the abuse of institutional power seems to be linked with the willingness of some members of society to perpetrate violence against the targeted groups. We also have seen how an interest in the experience of psychological trauma emerged with the advent of psychoanalysis and continued through the lens of war and particular social movements. A brief discussion regarding resilience has emphasized the importance of growth-oriented and meaning-making recovery processes, especially in an effort to mitigate diagnostic tendencies toward viewing trauma as necessarily psychopathological. Finally, I have identified some of the implications for understanding the historical and psychosocial contexts of trauma. I believe that an awareness of the historical context of certain traumatic events and an understanding of societal responses can help those mental health professionals working with trauma, stress, crisis, and disaster to be more effective in their practice.

Author's Note

This chapter is a complete revision of a chapter that appeared in the first edition of this textbook: Hyatt-Burkhart, D., & Levers, L. L. (2012). Historical contexts of trauma. In L. L. Levers (Ed.), *Trauma counseling: Theories and interventions* (pp. 23–46). Springer Publishing Company.

ADDITIONAL RESOURCES

 | A robust set of instructor resources designed to supplement this text is located at http://connect.springerpub.com/content/book/978-0-8261-5085-1. Qualifying instructors may request access by emailing textbook@springerpub.com.

PRACTICE-BASED RESOURCES AND REFERENCES

To view a list of resources and all the references, please visit connect.springerpub.com via the following url: http://connect.springerpub.com/content/book/978-0-8261-5085-1/part/part01/chapter/ch01

Theoretical Contexts of Trauma Counseling: Understanding the Effects of Trauma, Stress, Crisis, and Disaster

LISA LÓPEZ LEVERS

CHAPTER OVERVIEW

This chapter introduces multiple theoretical contexts for understanding the impact of trauma. Building upon the foundational information presented in Chapter 1, the current chapter examines how the construct of trauma evolved from primarily life-span and psychological understandings, to a more systems and psychosocial perspective, to our current neurobiological realizations about the effects of trauma. The connections among facets of trauma, which are described in Chapters 1 and 2, offer a foundational scaffold upon which to understand the profound effects of traumatic experiences.

LEARNING OBJECTIVES

After reading this chapter, the reader should be able to:

1. Begin to identify a larger context for understanding the often interconnected issues of stress, crisis, trauma, and disaster;
2. Begin to understand developmental, bioecological, and neurobiological theories regarding the effects of trauma;
3. Define trauma from clinical, phenomenological, and systemic perspectives; and,
4. Develop perceptions about the scaffold of intersecting constructs related to stress, crisis, disaster, and trauma.

INTRODUCTION

The world can be a violent and dangerous place, thus making people vulnerable to all sorts of traumatic experiences. Emotional trauma has the potential to inflict severe harm to a person's psyche and biological systems; unabated trauma and toxic stress also can cause physiological damage. Traumatic events can have profound effects on the individuals who experience them, and the impact of such stressful events or circumstances often results in people feeling fearful, overwhelmed, vulnerable, confused, angry, betrayed, helpless, frightened, alone, or any combination of these emotions. As already indicated in Chapter 1, the American Psychological Association (APA) briefly defines trauma as "an emotional response to a terrible event" (APA, 2020, p. 1); however, there is a lot to unpack in this succinct statement. The influences of trauma may manifest in many ways; some may be unique to the individual, whereas others appear to be more culture based, and yet others may be relatively universal. Some traumatic experiences are so unspeakable that victims go without verbalizing the cruelty or assault inflicted upon them. The symptoms of trauma, as clinically defined by the psychiatric profession at the current time, represent only one dimension of the lived experience of trauma; people experience and live through traumatic events in a variety of ways.

Traumatic experiences can cause not only physical and psychological wounds, but deep spiritual or existential wounds as well. For many survivors, the notion of reliving the trauma is agonizingly unthinkable; yet, with great courage, many come forward and seek trauma counseling or some means of recovery or meaning making. The request for trauma counseling often also serves as a request to engage in what needs to be a healing journey for the client. By definition, then, for therapists working with traumatized clients, "trauma counseling" inherently involves a focus on the client's healing process, and this necessitates a holistic view of the person. In order to understand the *whole person* who has experienced trauma, clinicians need to grapple with the ubiquity and the ugliness of traumatic events as well as to engage with the complexity of trauma-associated responses. The aftermath of a traumatic event is profoundly personal; at the same time, the lives of individuals intricately intersect with the lives of other people as well as with pets, places, time, social institutions, and cultural systems. Therefore, many clinical and treatment questions emerge that concern the nature of the person's lived experience of a traumatic event, and the answer frequently is, "it depends." It depends on the developmental stage at the time of the trauma event; it depends on whether the trauma event was of a personal nature or a large-scale disaster; if personal, it depends on whether the perpetrator was a trusted family member/friend or a stranger; it depends on the extent of the person's support system; it depends on gender and cultural perspectives; and it depends on numerous variables that are not always evident immediately, including health status and responses by the autonomic nervous system (ANS). For these reasons, and precisely because so much about working with a trauma survivor depends on the person's circumstances, this book offers a comprehensive view of trauma, stress, crisis, and disaster events, one that is situated within a systemic understanding of the whole person and one that incorporates our most recent understandings about what happens in the brain when someone is experiencing a traumatic event.

Of necessity, once a survivor of trauma seeks counseling, this person's support system extends to the therapeutic milieu, thereby including the therapist, clinical supervisors, the treating agency, and any larger arenas of the treatment system. Survivors of trauma need the clinical world to be more aligned and harmonized in this matter. Once we make the decision to work with traumatized clients, we owe them this level of respect. This kind of integrative approach requires a holistic and systemic perspective of trauma; it requires looking at trauma through a particular contextual lens. I intend for this chapter to offer such a lens, one that enables the reader to begin to understand the impact of traumatic experience from multiple personal and systemic perspectives as well as to make important connections with the evolving historical understandings of trauma, as presented in Chapter 1. The purpose of this chapter is to ground the construct of psychosocial trauma within its various phenomenological, clinical, neurobiological, and sociocultural contexts. My aim is to offer a scaffold that enables readers to see readily and to understand clearly the connections between the personal and the systemic impacts of trauma, within historical context. This aim is accomplished by addressing relevant contextual issues in the following major sections of this chapter: (a) Context for Thinking About Trauma, (b) Defining Trauma, and (c) Counseling Implications. These sections are followed by a brief summary of the chapter and relevant resources for instructors, students, and clinicians.

CONTEXT FOR THINKING ABOUT TRAUMA

Since the earliest days of psychoanalysis in the late 19th century, professional discussions about the construct of trauma have been fraught with controversy. Even Sigmund Freud recanted some of the trauma-related parts of his theory in response to the furor that it caused in affluent Viennese society. As seen in Chapter 1 of this text, the historical details and nuances are important, as they relate to how the international psychotherapeutic establishment has come to comprehend and deal with issues of trauma. Having established this historical understanding, it is essential, in this chapter, to address the variety of meanings, controversies, and contexts associated with the discourse on trauma, especially as these forecast fuller discussions of specific constructs in chapters that appear later in this text. In many ways, Chapters 1, 2, 3, and 4 together are intended to offer a scaffold that firmly supports and readies the reader for the nuanced comprehensions of more complex issues of trauma in later chapters of the book.

Clinicians from the various helping disciplines—professional counselors, psychiatric nurses, psychiatrists, psychologists, social workers, and other behavioral scientists, along with religious helpers and other spiritual guides—have recognized the profound impact that traumatic experiences can have on individuals' psyches. This has been ongoing, long before the more or less recent wave of related research and theory building of the last several decades and leading up to the most contemporary neurobiological understandings of trauma. Psychotherapists working with trauma survivors have realized that the resulting effects of trauma range from acute stress disorder (ASD), posttraumatic stress disorder (PTSD), and other serious psychopathological responses, to existential crises, to post-trauma resilience, growth, and development (McEwen et al., 2015). Those working in the field have learned from clients that the causes of trauma differ widely and include interpersonal violence, sexual assault, physical maltreatment, political- or community-scale violence, war, various crisis situations, large-scale disasters, the effects of anthropogenic climate change, and witnessing or vicariously experiencing any of these. Yet controversies, along with exciting new scientific findings, continue to abound concerning the etiology, diagnosis, and treatment of trauma-related experiences, sequelae, and disorders.

Some of the controversies relate directly to systemic failures that impede rather than assist traumatized people in acquiring access to needed help. In many ways, the controversies may reflect an elementary psychodynamic about helping professionals and about the very nature of trauma. It may be much easier to intellectualize about abstract diagnostic constructs than to grasp and to engage with the perverse reality of a parent raping or sodomizing their child or of a child soldier who has been trained to kill family members and neighbors. Offering counseling to survivors of trauma can be emotionally intense work for the counselor and thus requires a strong self-reflective orientation. Some clinicians may feel that they are bearing witness to the effects of pure evil, whereas others elect to refer traumatized clients elsewhere.

Understanding the effects of traumatic events is a complex endeavor. Trauma affects people on multiple levels, including in the most intimately personal, as well as in relational, social, and cultural ways. Relatively recent findings in brain science, particularly Polyvagal Theory (PVT; Porges, 2007, 2011, 2020), have extended, exponentially, our knowledge about the physiological effects of trauma. Examining some of the various theories of human development can offer a base upon which to build understandings concerning the effects of trauma and the potential for attachment interruptions. For this reason, I believe that it is helpful to revisit, briefly, some of the relevant models of human growth and development before moving on to trauma theory. In this section, I focus on relevant issues of life-span development and the importance of a bioecological perspective, thus providing the background for the next sections of this chapter on defining trauma and on examining various systemic perspectives about trauma, including a brief and basic account of recent neurobiological findings about trauma.

Life-Span Development

Numerous theories and models exist to help us in understanding how people grow and develop across the life-span. Several relevant psychological models have influenced our knowledge of human development and motivation, including Maslow's hierarchy of needs and the developmental theories of Freud, Erikson, and Piaget. However, although these theories are necessary to our understanding, they are not sufficient in addressing the concerns of individuals who have been traumatized. They do not lay out an adequate foundation for grappling with some of the fundamental questions of development, especially child development, as these concern traumatic experiences, for example: How does a traumatic event or ongoing trauma interrupt or delay developmental tasks? What developmental trajectories might we expect when abnormal events occur in the lives of ordinary people? How do these alternative developmental trajectories reflect individuals' environmental conditions, especially concerning relative levels of risk, security, and attachment? In spite of their inadequacy to answer questions of trauma fully, these models offer important background information—they contribute to the scaffold of knowledge that is necessary to understand trauma and are discussed briefly in the following text.

Maslow

Although more of a motivational theory, Maslow's (1998) widely recognized model has some utility in considering certain aspects of trauma. The model has posited that the categorical needs of human beings are hierarchical; these needs are represented in the figure of a pyramid (see Figure 2.1). The base of the pyramid represents *physiological needs*, those involving such basic necessities as food, water, and shelter. The rungs of the pyramid, in ascending order above physiological needs, include the following: *safety needs*, composed of such features as security, law, order, and stability; *love and belonging*, composed of such elements as affiliation and friendships; *esteem*, composed of such attributes as confidence, respect, and status; and, at the very top of the pyramid, *self-actualization*, or the ability to realize one's full potential. It is important to note that each of these need levels can be interrupted and affected by violent or traumatic events. One practice limitation of this model is that it often is engaged by professionals at the esteem level, without much consideration of the important foundational needs at the base of the model. An example of this would be a school counselor or a school psychologist who focuses on a child's self-esteem without understanding that the child might have walked to school from a local domestic violence shelter where their mother sought safety the night before, or that the child might not have had dinner the night before or breakfast that morning. The child potentially would have difficulty focusing on self-esteem issues when more basic and immediate needs have not been addressed. This model is one that offers necessary constructs about basic needs, but it is not sufficient in explaining the needs of at-risk individuals or those who have experienced a traumatic event.

Freud, Erikson, and Piaget

Important pioneers in theories of human development, Freud, Erikson, and Piaget have presented their developmental theories as stage models. A comparison of these stages can be seen in Table 2.1.

Freud's theory of psychosexual development includes five sequential stages: oral, anal, phallic, latency, and genital. However, these stages, like much of Freudian theory, long have been criticized for many reasons, and further elaboration goes beyond the scope of this chapter. For our purposes here, it suffices to say that beyond noting their historical importance, these stages tend to be less relevant to the contemporary discourse on developmental issues, at least outside of a psychoanalytic context.

Influenced by Freud, Erikson's sequential eight-stage developmental theory has involved the completion of stage-specific tasks and resulting alternative consequences or crises when these tasks are not completed in stage-salient ways. Although Erikson's model was designed with the healthy individual in mind, it is helpful to see, especially in the initial stages, how early childhood maltreatment potentially can establish pathways of development that may deviate from a healthy norm and even initiate a developmental trajectory eventually marked

Figure 2.1

Maslow's Hierarchy of Needs

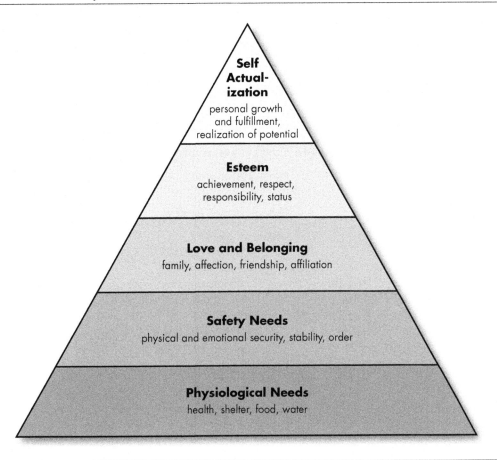

Data for the diagram are based on Hierarchy of Needs from "A Theory of Human Motivation," in *Motivation and Personality* (2nd ed.) by A. H. Maslow. Copyright 1970 by Abraham H. Maslow. Copyright 1991 by Wm. C. Brown Publishers. Adapted with permission.

by developmental psychopathology. For example, let us consider the case of a child who is so severely abused or neglected during the first year of life that this child is not able to engage in a trusting relationship with a primary caregiver. Instead, the child learns to mistrust the world around them. This has serious implications for the child's developmental pathway, from both psychological and biological perspectives, as well as for attachment issues, at the time and in the future (child and adolescent attachment issues are discussed more fully in Chapters 7 and 8 of this book).

Piaget's sequential sensorimotor and operational periods have relevance to physical and neurocognitive development. As we have continued to learn more about brain function (Institute of Medicine & National Research Council, 2015; National Research Council and Institute of Medicine, 2000; Thompson, 2016), it becomes clearer how early childhood deprivation and maltreatment can affect the developing child (neurochemical issues related to trauma also are discussed in Chapters 4 and 9 of this book). In fact, recent research has suggested that the effects of such early neglect can persist and be associated with adult brain structure and its functioning (Mackes et al., 2020; Thompson, 2016). However, concerning the developmental theories at hand, some may argue that such age- or stage-dependent theories are somewhat deterministic

Table 2.1

Comparison of Freud, Erikson, and Piaget's Stage Theories

Stages (approximate age ranges)	Freud	Erikson	Piaget
Infancy (birth to around 18 months)	Oral	Trust vs. mistrust	Sensorimotor period
18 months to 3 years	Anal	Autonomy vs. shame and doubt	Preoperational thought
3–5 years	Phallic	Initiative vs. guilt	Preoperational thought
6–12 years	Latency	Industry vs. inferiority	Concrete operations
12–18 years	Genital	Identity vs. role confusion	Formal operations
Young adulthood (around 19–40 years)		Intimacy vs. isolation	Formal operations
Middle adulthood (40–65 years)		Generativity vs. stagnation	
Maturity (65 years to death)		Integrity vs. despair	

and reductionist. Far too often, purely psychological approaches may ignore other factors in the environment and may place the onus of developmental deviations on the individual. For these reasons, I argue that these historically important theories allow us to understand necessary information about individuals, but that they are not sufficient in helping us to understand the full needs of trauma survivors.

Other Relevant Models

Purely mechanistic models do little to assist our understanding of peoples' lived experiences and worldviews. So in contrast to the aforementioned more linear and more or less purely psychological models, other theoretical models, which also have influenced our understanding, perhaps better account for individuals' worldviews and their interface with social influences. These theories include Bowlby's (1969/1982, 1973, 1980, 1988) attachment theory, Bandura's (1977) social learning theory, Vygotsky's (1978, 1986, 1997) social development theory, and Deci and Ryan's (2012) self-determination theory (SDT). It is not my purpose in this chapter to analyze the corpus of these substantive works. Rather, I raise these pertinent and pervasive theories of human development and social learning to remind us of concepts that are necessary in understanding human development but perhaps are not sufficient for understanding the impact of traumatic experiences on the developing and growing individual. Earlier professional discussions have emphasized the centrality of the nature versus nurture (genetic vs. environmental/contextual influences) discourse, along with the interplay of continuity and discontinuity dynamics throughout the life-span (e.g., Durwin & Reese-Weber, 2020; Lerner, 2002). Thompson (2016, p. 23) has reported that recent research demonstrates that "biology and environment are each important and indissociable." On this note, I turn the conversation to more systemic and biological perspectives.

A Bioecological Perspective

Bronfenbrenner (1979, 1981, 1994) has offered an elegant model for understanding the comprehensive influence of multiple systems on children's development. Simply put, ontogenic (individual) development is nested within larger systems that affect the person's development (see Figure 2.2). From proximal (closer) to distal (at a greater distance), these systemic influences include the *microsystem* (immediate environment, including family), the *mesosystem* (situations in which two or more microsystems come together to have some effect on the individual's life), the *exosystem* (community and neighborhood), the *macrosystem* (broad cultural values and beliefs), and the *chronosystem* (denoting sociohistorical time as well as the real-time personal events and developmental transitions in an individual's life since birth). Environmental factors, along with genetic predispositions, influence the child, and continual reciprocal transactions within the environment, or ecology, determine risk and protective factors. After the initial development of his *ecological model*, Bronfenbrenner later renamed the model, changing it from the former ecological model to the more newly termed *bioecological model*, thus reemphasizing the interactions between heredity and environment. This is significant, particularly in light of the more recent neurobiological research concerning the physiological effects of trauma on the brain and on other systems of the body (the recent neuroscience research is discussed later in this section and detailed more fully in Chapter 4).

Figure 2.2

Bronfenbrenner's Bioecological Model of Human Development

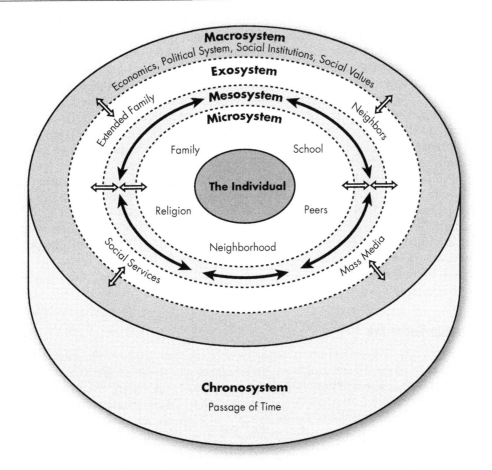

From Bronfenbrenner, U. (1979). *The ecology of human development: Experiments by nature and design.* Harvard University Press.

Most contemporary theories of development have acknowledged the roles of both heredity and environment, and many have suggested the importance of a systemic perspective. Lerner's (2002, 2006) notion of developmental contextualism, for example, has offered a framework for integrating important developmental theories and for arriving at a developmental systems theory. The literature on developmental psychopathology (e.g., Cicchetti, 2013; Cicchetti & Lynch, 1993, 1995; Toth & Cicchetti, 2013) has provided a developmental–ecological framework for understanding the profound interplay between normal development and abnormal events, especially in the form of child maltreatment. Developmental psychopathology has emphasized the role of attachment in children's lives (Belsky et al., 1996), seeking to assess connections between the quality of attachment and the impact of maltreatment. This perspective has offered a baseline for comprehending the effects of chronic violence on children—and by extension, some of the trauma-related sequelae of adults who experienced severe maltreatment in early childhood.

Drawing from Bronfenbrenner's (1979, 1981, 1994) bioecological model, developmental psychopathology examines the risk factors, as well as the compensatory or protective factors, which exist across the multiple and interactive environments in which we all live. The arrows in Figure 2.2 represent the potential for both risk and protective factors, across and within the systemic levels. The arrows also represent the reciprocity of the model; the environment has an impact on the individual, just as, in reciprocal nature, the individual has an impact on the environment. From this theoretical paradigm, Cicchetti and Lynch (1993) have detailed a related ecological–transactional model that offers an avenue for understanding, in a comprehensive way, the influence of multiple factors—at multiple levels—on children's development. Such an articulation of the transactional nature of development is paramount to understanding the complex, sometimes paradoxical, effects of maltreatment on children at multiple systemic levels.

An understanding of the bioecological model, its transactional and systemic nature, and the role of attachment across the life-span is an essential aspect of understanding the impact of trauma. An ecological–transactional perspective allows us to situate the lived experiences of traumatized persons within the time and space of a relevant ecology in order to understand the trauma event as well as personal meaning making. Lynch and Levers (2007) have suggested the compatibility of ecological, transactional, and motivational perspectives in applying developmental theories to trauma counseling. Also compatible with these perspectives, and as an extension of the biological dimension of the individual, seen as nested within the microsystem and other systemic levels of the bioecological model (represented in Figure 2.2), is Polyvagal Theory (PVT, Porges, 2007, 2011). Introduced by Stephen Porges in 1994, PVT has assisted clinicians in understanding the effects of trauma on the ANS and its interaction with brain activity and the activity of other major organs in the body before, during, and after a traumatic event. In many ways, PVT offers a portal through which mental health clinicians, who may not be brain experts, have an avenue for better understanding the neurobiological perspective of trauma.

A Neurobiological Perspective

Over the last couple of decades, the broader field of mental healthcare has arrived at better understandings of physiological and hormonal responses to stress, crisis, anxiety, and trauma; this, in turn, has led to increased knowledge about how the brain is involved in the physiological effects of trauma (Children's Bureau, 2015; Newman et al., 2015). Trauma affects the brain, and it even has the ability to change the brain. In scans of a healthy brain, shown beside the brain of someone who has experienced traumatic abuse (Perry, 2002), the differences in the scans are readily evident, even to nonneurologists. Neurobiological research also has helped in cultivating a better apprehension of the ways in which the brain affects social relationships (e.g., Cozolino, 2006; Fishbane, 2007; Goleman, 2006; Siegel, 2007). Recent advances in neuroscience have helped us in understanding why some people are more susceptible to developing symptoms of PTSD, while others remain more resilient, in the face of traumatic events (Rattel et al., 2019).

The Vagus Nerve

As indicated in the previous subsection, PVT is perhaps one of the most intriguing and promising contributions to the field of traumatology in recent years. PVT relies on an understanding of the vagus nerve, which may be the most important cranial nerve that most people probably do not know that they have. The vagus nerve, actually the tenth pair of the 12 cranial nerves, is like the body's superhighway, carrying sensory information between the brain and various other internal organs (Gould, 2019; Seymour, 2017). Sometimes referred to as the "gut-brain axis," it is key in understanding mind–body connections (Forsythe et al., 2014). The vagus nerve extends from the brain, branching out toward the neck and the torso, to reach the body's organs and tissues. The word "vagus" derives from the Latin term that means "wandering" (Seymour, 2017).

The functions and mechanisms of the vagus nerve have important implications for how we respond to, experience, and process stress, crisis, anxiety, and trauma. As previously indicated, the vagus nerve has important links to the brain, heart, lungs, and other major organs. The auricular branch of the vagus nerve even links to the ear, so that vibrations in the ear ultimately can have a calming effect on the vagus nerve, which accounts for the soothing reaction to certain types of music or the body-calming effect of ancient syllables (e.g., "Om") used in meditation and chanting. The practice of mindfulness, for example, has been successful in its use with anxiety- and trauma-related conditions, and its efficacy can be explained in reference to the functions of the vagus nerve (Forner, 2019).

The Autonomic Nervous System

The vagus nerve is the longest and most complex nerve in the ANS and interacts with two major parts of the ANS: the parasympathetic nervous system (PNS) and the sympathetic nervous system (SNS). According to PVT, these two nervous systems have three circuits or functions that are instrumental in understanding not just the brain's response to trauma, but also the whole body's response to stress, crisis, anxiety, and trauma:

- Social-communicative engagement (ability to interpret facial and social cues)
- Mobilization (fight or flight)
- Immobilization ("shut-down"—inability to fight or flee)

The ANS regulates body functions that generally are beyond conscious awareness, for example, breathing and heartbeat. The PNS is responsible for the *rest and digest* system; it *conserves energy* by slowing the heart rate, increasing intestinal and gland activity, and relaxing sphincter muscles in the gastrointestinal tract. Conversely, the SNS is responsible for what commonly is referred to as the *fight or flight response*, which is when the body panics, due to a lack of safety or to danger cues in the environment. The SNS *energizes* or *activates* body mechanisms by increasing muscle blood flow and tension, dilating the pupils, accelerating heart rate and respiration, and increasing perspiration and arterial blood pressure.

The ANS essentially scans the environment for safety and for danger. The ANS continually picks up and assesses information in the environment, and the responses to this information are not voluntary (Porges, 2011). In other words, this processing is not conscious or intentional, but rather, it is happening at the neural level. "Perception" is not quite the right word to use, because the process is not a cognitive one; therefore, Porges coined the term "neuroception" (cited in Dana, 2018). Neuroception allows the body to define risk or threat, at the autonomic neural level, in these three essential ways: (a) threat perception, (b) threat sensitivity, and (c) self-image. At the neuroception level, the ANS detects safety or danger, and then engages the PNS or the SNS, depending upon the neurocepted environmental cues. An individual's response to a stressor, to danger, or to a potentially threatening or traumatizing event is beyond conscious control and therefore is not processed at a cognitive level—it is happening at the neuroceptive ANS level.

This explains why two people experiencing the same incident may have very different responses to the incident. It also offers evidence for refuting some of the intense and persistent victim blaming that occurs, even in light of scientific findings (e.g., Bob, 2019; Gravelin et al., 2018).

Dissociation

Over the decades, the construct of dissociation has returned to an increasingly more dominant point in the discussion of trauma, in general; its prominence in the *Diagnostic and Statistical Manual of Mental Disorders* (5th ed.; *DSM-5*; American Psychiatric Association, 2013) discussion of PTSD, specifically, has called greater attention to the significance of dissociation in the trauma-response process. It also is an instrumental concept within the framework of PVT. Dissociation is an altered state of consciousness and actually serves as a biological protection mechanism. While in this state, conscious awareness splits apart from feelings or memories that may be scary or terrifying to the person (Huntjens et al., 2019). A continuum of symptoms may be experienced, from relatively mild sensations of fogginess, sleepiness, or difficulty concentrating to a feeling of numbness or being separated from others, from the world, or even from parts of oneself (Levers, 2020). In extreme altered states, a person may even "lose time" or experience amnesia; this is called dissociative amnesia, and it is classified within the dissociative disorders section of the *DSM-5* (APA, 2013).

Fight, Flight, and More

An understanding of the fight-or-flight response originated in the early 20th century (Cannon, 1915), and its implications have been examined and better understood since that time. However, PVT accounts for a broader range of responses that actually match the wider scope of trauma experiences (Porges, 2011; Porges & Dana, 2018). Rather than focusing on only fight or flight, PVT acknowledges a more inclusive continuum of responses to potentially traumatizing experiences, among them dissociative responses. Therefore, it may be helpful to think of the neurobiology of trauma as manifesting in stages, with greater degrees of dissociation occurring in later stages (Levers, 2020). Schauer and Elbert (2010) refer to these stages as the *6 'Fs' of Trauma Response*, and these are:

- Freeze
- Flight
- Fight
- Fright
- Flag
- Faint

Freeze is an orienting response, which involves the initial neuroception of danger—the *deer-in-the-headlights* phenomenon. With hormones shooting throughout the body and the SNS activating, the person under threat prepares either to take flight or to fight. Mild stages of dissociation mediate these first three defensive responses. It is within the activation of the final three responses that dissociation becomes increasingly stronger. According to Schauer and Elbert (2010), fright involves unresponsive immobility; the person is beginning to feel overwhelmed by the threat. In the flag stage, the threat has become so extreme that the SNS's arousal is beginning to shut down, and the PNS starts to engage. Schauer and Elbert (2010, p. 117) state that this stage "of the defense armament encompasses forms of dissociation and is characterized by reduced sympathetic arousal and passivity or a 'shut-down' peripherally dominated by vagal activity." If the threat or danger continues unabated, a full shutdown may occur in the final, faint stage, and the person literally may faint, experiencing vasovagal syncope (Schauer & Elbert, 2010). If we think about what happens during a faint, we get a glimpse of how incredibly elegant our body systems are. When a person faints, the person falls to the ground, the floor, or some other surface, usually stretched out; it is being in this prone position, then, that facilitates physiological functions like breathing and heart rate to begin to return to normal. This ability to recalibrate or rebalance, after exposure to fear, is an illustration of our capacity for resilience.

DEFINING TRAUMA

Beginning to define trauma and its encompassing emotional and physiological effects is a daunting task. The effects of traumatic events are complex, reflecting the intricacy of the human beings who are exposed to trauma. Traumatic events involve objective or factual situations, and *DSM*-related criteria attempt to quantify symptoms in an objective fashion. However, the way in which people experience traumatic events is highly subjective, and trauma theories must allow for the reality that people construct personal meanings from their traumatic experiences.

Current theories about trauma offer a framework for understanding the various types of trauma, such as single-event versus complex trauma, and the different ways in which people respond, such as being completely overwhelmed and stuck there, versus making meaning of the trauma in a way that eventually may produce growth and transformation. Although many discussions of PTSD appear in the chapters that follow in this textbook, the diagnostic category of PTSD is only one facet of defining trauma. Laurence J. Kirmayer, MD, James McGill professor and director of the Division of Social and Transcultural Psychiatry at McGill University, offers the following comment regarding PTSD:

> Diagnostic constructs also work as metaphors, both in terms of their explicit use as conceptual models and their implicit connotations as labels that affect social relations between people. The construct of PTSD, which has dominated discussions of the treatment of trauma in recent years, emphasizes the enduring effects of fear conditioning on subsequent adjustment and response to later stressors. But PTSD is a limited construct that captures only part of the impact of violence, ignoring issues of loss, injustice, meaning and identity that may be of greater concern to traumatized individuals and their families and children or later generations. (2007, p. vi)

The various discussions in this textbook acknowledge PTSD as an important but limited construct. Indeed, as explicated in Chapter 1, the history of the *DSM* illustrates the extent to which the notion of PTSD is socially constructed and ever changing, even within the psychiatric model.

One powerful tool in understanding the effects of trauma is through interdisciplinary means. For example, during my initial exposure to clinical trauma narratives, early in my career as a young clinician, I recall thinking about the cubist paintings that I had seen in European museums, perceiving the trauma experience through the disciplinary lens of my undergraduate work in literature and art history. Focusing on the deconstructed images in the cubist paintings, like those of Picasso, for example, assisted me to comprehend, even in a limited fashion, the fragmentation that traumatized clients had experienced and tried to share with me. Psychiatry and psychology are not the only professional fields of endeavor that enhance understandings of trauma. Rather, not only do other social and behavioral sciences focus on issues of trauma, for example, professional counseling, sociology, social work, anthropology, nursing, and other allied health professions, but those pursuits involving the arts and humanities and fields such as technology and journalism also contribute to illuminating the effects of trauma. In this section, continuing to build upon the scaffold that we began to construct in Chapter 1, I emphasize some of the multiple facets of how people experience trauma. This is accomplished through the following discussions: Trauma as a Clinical Issue; Phenomenology of Trauma; Trauma as a Systemic Issue; and Intersection of Constructs Related to Stress, Crisis, Disaster, and Trauma.

Trauma as a Clinical Issue

The word "trauma" has been popularized and often is used to indicate almost any stressor experienced by an individual. However, in its clinical sense, trauma refers to events that are extremely difficult and overwhelming for individuals (Briere & Scott, 2006; Substance Abuse and Mental Health Services Administration [SAMHSA], 2014). Understanding the clinical presentation of trauma can be complex. As discussed in Chapter 1 of this textbook, the definition of trauma has continued to change and evolve across the various iterations of the *DSM* and has reflected our continuing understandings of the effects of trauma. As delineated in Chapter 1, the trauma- and stressor-related disorders articulated in the current *DSM*-5 (APA, 2013) span multiple diagnostic categories and include reactive attachment disorder (RAD), disinhibited social engagement disorder (DSED), PTSD, ASD, adjustment disorder, other specified trauma- and stressor-related disorders, and unspecified trauma- and stressor-related disorders. Importantly, the location of the chapter presenting these diagnoses, *Trauma- and Stressor-Related Disorders*, is relevant. The chapters regarding *Anxiety Disorders* and *Obsessive-Compulsive and Related Disorders* precede that chapter, and the chapter is followed by the chapter on *Dissociative Disorders*. As noted in the introduction to the *Trauma- and Stressor-Related Disorders* chapter, the sequencing of the chapters indicates a close relationship among these sets of diagnoses (APA, 2013).

A clinical understanding of the separate trauma-related diagnoses, along with an understanding of the relationships among these diagnostic categories, is essential for making accurate diagnoses (Tehrani & Levers, 2016). It also is important for clinicians to be well versed with all of the trauma-related diagnoses, as pertinent client issues, such as life stage or comorbidity with other diagnoses, may have an impact on identifying the most salient and accurate diagnosis. The various chapters in this textbook focus on different types of trauma, crisis, and disaster situations and explore the diagnostic constructs that are most relevant to the situation under examination in the specific chapter. While the current chapter cannot recapitulate the clinical information about trauma that is contained in the *DSM*-5 (APA, 2013), discussions in many of the chapters rely on a basic understanding of two of the trauma-specific diagnostic categories, ASD and PTSD. The criteria for these two diagnostic categories are too numerous to list here, but short descriptions are offered as orienting points; interested readers are encouraged to read and study the *Trauma- and Stressor-Related Disorders* chapter in the *DSM*-5 (APA, 2013).

A significant difference between ASD and PTSD is based on the duration of symptoms. The ASD diagnosis is used when someone has experienced a traumatic event and demonstrates symptoms within the first month following the event; when symptoms persist beyond 1 month, the diagnosis is PTSD. One prominent feature of the PTSD category is that there are separate sets of diagnostic criteria presented for (a) adults, adolescents, and children older than 6 years of age and for (b) children 6 years of age and under. The introduction to the PTSD section offers the following orienting points:

> The essential feature of posttraumatic stress disorder (PTSD) is the development of characteristic symptoms following exposure to one or more traumatic events. . . . The clinical presentation of PTSD varies. In some individuals, fear-based re-experiencing, emotional, and behavioral symptoms may predominate. In others, anhedonic or dys- phoric mood states and negative cognitions may be most distressing. In some other in- dividuals, arousal and reactive-externalizing symptoms are prominent, while in others, dissociative symptoms predominate. Finally, some individuals exhibit combinations of these symptom patterns. (APA, 2013, p. 274)

The previous text points to the importance of clinicians having a firm understanding of differential diagnosis. Differentiating the diagnostic classifications associated with trauma, particularly PTSD, can be difficult, especially for the new or inexperienced clinician. The importance of accurate clinical assessment, discussed in Chapter 26 of this book, cannot be underscored enough.

The history of the psychiatric and psychological diagnosis and treatment of trauma, as well as its codification in the *DSMs*, has been marked by controversy and by a lack of professional agreement (e.g., Bledsoe, 2019; Echterling et al., 2016; Pai et al., 2017). For example, in a review of research literature, Miao et al. (2018, p. 2) state that "the findings of pertinent studies are difficult to generalize because of heterogeneous patient groups, different traumatic events, diagnostic criteria, and study designs." Criticisms of past and current *DSM* codifications have led to increasingly greater discourse surrounding the need for a complex trauma classification (e.g., Briere & Scott, 2006; Courtois, 2004; Herman, 1992/1997; Phillips, 2015). Many have advocated for differentiating between PTSD and complex PTSD (discussions of complex trauma are found in Chapters 1 and 9 of this book), but the architects of the *DSM-5* (APA, 2013) instead elected to implement a separate Trauma- and Stressor-Related Disorders category. While it is essential for mental health professionals to possess requisite diagnostic skills, perhaps of equal concern to most clinicians as the diagnostic categories associated with trauma is the phenomenology of trauma and its clinical manifestation among clients who seek assistance in dealing with the lived aftermath of traumatic events.

Phenomenology of Trauma

People's lived experiences of traumatic events are highly personal and subjective; and at the same time, some of the phenomena associated with trauma are fairly consistent, across cultures and from person to person. Some of the issues related to the core experience of trauma and to trauma as an existential issue of suffering are explored briefly in the following text.

Core Experience of Trauma

In her landmark book, *Trauma and Recovery*, Herman (1992/1997) has identified the core experiences of trauma as terror and disconnection. Stating that "psychological trauma is an affliction of the powerless . . . [in which] the victim is rendered helpless by overwhelming force" (p. 33), Herman has qualified the experience of terror as one of disempowerment, helplessness, and abandonment; she has cast disconnection in similar terms as Courtois (1988, 2004), that is, as shattered trust. When an individual has experienced a traumatic event, the person's worldview and the very foundation of their being can be shaken or crushed, what Stolorow et al. (2002) have framed as "the shattering of an experiential world" (p. 123). Herman has noted that "traumatic events call into question basic human relationships" (p. 51); survivors of trauma may experience disconnection from loved ones or other significant people in their lives, as well as a sense of separation from self.

Hyperarousal is an initial major symptom of trauma, what Herman (1992/1997) has described as a "permanent alert, as if the danger might return at any moment" (p. 35). This startle response is relatively easy for most clinicians to recognize. Herman further has described two additional categorical sets of PTSD symptoms: those that are intrusive and those that are constrictive. Symptoms of intrusion include those readily associated with PTSD, such as "reliving" the trauma through flashbacks and nightmares; symptoms of constriction include some that are less likely to be attributed as quickly to PTSD, such as depression, numbing, and a detached state. One of the most important aspects of Herman's work has been her recognition of what she has termed "the dialectic of trauma" (p. 47). In the absence of appropriate intervention, when a survivor of trauma develops PTSD and the condition goes untreated, the person eventually may begin to vacillate between the previously described symptom sets; the dialectic of trauma is represented by this cycling, back and forth, from intrusive symptoms to constrictive symptoms. It is easy to see, especially if a history of trauma has not been documented adequately, how observing a client who is presenting with either set of symptoms could result in an inaccurate diagnosis. At surface, someone exhibiting intrusive symptoms might appear agitated and anxious, and someone exhibiting constrictive symptoms might appear depressed. Therefore, it is extremely important for clinicians who are working with trauma survivors to ask about trauma history and to recognize this dialectic in order to avoid misdiagnosis.

Stolorow (2007) has stated that one theme of trauma is that it "is built into the basic constitution of human existence" (p. xii). Such a phenomenological perspective of trauma is essential in understanding others' lived experiences of trauma as well as in enabling counselors to help survivors in the recovery and healing process. Herman (1992/1997) has articulated a stage-wise recovery process aimed at addressing the core experiences of trauma. She has detailed the clinical work that needs to take place in each of the following phases: (a) establishing safety, (b) reconstructing the trauma story, and (c) reconnecting with ordinary life. This recovery process corresponds to phenomenological aspects of trauma and assumes the potential for an existential transformation from *victim* to *survivor*. The model illuminates the need for therapists to be intentional in their clinical work with survivors of trauma. In addition, Herman's model astutely aligns with the more recent brain research and PVT, discussed earlier in this chapter; once a survivor's ANS is engaged, and fear either mobilizes or immobilizes the person through their SNS or PNS responses, a counselor needs to reestablish a sense of safety so that the survivor is stabilized enough to work constructively with the traumatic experience.

Suffering as an Existential Component of Trauma

When people are subjected to the most adverse of human situations, they naturally experience psychic pain and suffering. Miller (2004) has posited that most people seek psychotherapy to relieve suffering and are therefore not focused on the clinical aspects of symptomatology, asserting that the science of psychology has long ignored this aspect of the therapeutic encounter. Daneault et al. (2004) have suggested that a major mandate of medicine—and by extension, psychiatry and other psychological practices—is the relief of suffering. Yet very little analysis of the construct of suffering has existed in the professional literature (Makselon, 1998) until fairly recently (e.g., Anderson, 2014; Levers, 2020).

A core consequence of all types of trauma, crisis, and disaster events is human suffering. Mental, emotional, existential, and physical suffering can affect people in a variety of negative ways, including personality changes, health status, and the ability to function on multiple levels. The connection between suffering and illness—*illness* defined from an ethnomedical perspective, relative to cultural construction—is profound and calls for existential and multicultural approaches (Levers, 2006a, 2006b). Suffering also can affect people positively, in the long run; the connection between suffering and transformation has been the subject matter of theological and philosophical discourses for centuries. Although a lacuna exists in much of the contemporary scientific literature regarding a psychology of suffering, the theoretical and existential basis for this discourse exists, for example, among such notable scholars as Bruner (1990), Frankl (1959), Fromm (1947), Bakan (1968), and May (1992). Understanding the nature and the phenomenology of human suffering can assist clinicians in defining the subjective meaning making of trauma survivors, thereby guiding the quality of client-informed interventions. This process is central to the transformation from being a *victim* to being a *survivor* and is a profound step toward recovery.

Trauma as a Systemic Issue

Although the clinical features and phenomenological aspects of trauma involve survivors at the individual level, there are at least three areas of potential systemic impact. First, groups of people may simultaneously experience the same racial trauma, gender-based trauma, natural disaster, accident, or human-made catastrophe; many of them may develop trauma-related symptoms. Second, when groups of people are affected by a traumatic event or a disaster, there is usually a coordinated reaction by an official system of responders; such efforts may have trauma-based implications both for those affected and for those who respond. Third, even when a traumatic event only involves an individual, as explained previously in the discussion regarding the bioecological model, the person is nested within and potentially affected by any or all other systems at the microsystemic, mesosystemic, exosystemic, macrosystemic, and chronosystemic levels. The implications for how a victim or survivor of trauma may be able to navigate these various systems and for how systemic responses to crisis, disaster, and trauma events adequately help or fail to help victims are too numerous for a full discussion in this chapter. However, some of the systemic features of trauma are explored briefly in the text that follows, in terms of their cultural, public health, social justice, and pedagogical dimensions.

Cultural Dimensions of Trauma

Just as cultural assumptions have been made across mental health theories and practices, culture profoundly shapes peoples' experiences of trauma, along with molding the rites and rituals of grief and suffering that enable the expression of trauma (Droždek, 2007b). Locating trauma—and by extension, PTSD—in a global context raises transnational issues. As Breslau (2004) has suggested, "problems [are] generated when the process of defining the disorder is viewed simplistically as a matter of scientific technology rather than as a cultural practice in itself" (p. 121). Expressions of suffering and healing vary across cultures and arise from differing world views; for people outside of Western cultures, as well as for non-Western people who have immigrated to a Western country, an ethnomedical perspective may be useful (*ethnomedicine* is a subspecialty area of medical anthropology, focusing on indigenous paradigms of healing and cultural variations of constructs like illness and disease). Culture has informed the ways in which people make meaning of trauma, the rituals for expressing the impact of trauma, and the manner in which people are able to heal. For example, Castillo (1997) has asserted that "cultural schemas affect the subjective experience and expression of dissociation" (p. 219). Dissociation is but one symptomatic manifestation of trauma that offers a good example of cultural nuance. Dissociation has been pathologized within Western biomedicine. Yet when examining non-Western paradigms of indigenous medicine or traditional healing, dissociation actually may play a proactive role in the transactions between client and healer (e.g., Comaroff, 1978, 1980, 1982; Kleinman, 1986; Levers & Maki, 1995; Moodley, 2005; Torrey, 1986; Turner, 1968) and also can offer adaptive mechanisms (Castillo, 1997) such as with the use of yoga, hypnosis, Tai Chi, mindfulness, and other focus-oriented techniques as part of the recovery process.

Public Health Dimensions of Trauma

Professionals working in the arena of traumatology increasingly have cited the effects of trauma on individuals as a public health issue (e.g., Droždek, 2007a; Musisi, 2004). A growing corpus of literature has highlighted the impact of early childhood adversity on later health across the lifespan (e.g., Felitti et al., 1998; Felitti, 2002; Lanius et al., 2010). Our knowledge about race-related stressors and the impact of trauma on populations of color has advanced, and we have become increasingly aware of the impact of racial trauma (Williams, 2018; Williams & Cooper, 2019; Williams et al., 2018; Williams et al., 2021; Yehuda & Lehrner, 2018). Breslau (2004) has suggested that "epidemiological surveys have been an important vehicle for bringing PTSD into the global health arena" (p. 117).

The rise of all types of technology has increased the capacity for more violence on broader scales; communication technology has increased the potential for members of the public to witness acts of violence, immediately, even when they are not present. The reality of amplified violence increasingly has become a part of the global discourse on trauma (e.g., Krug et al., 2002; Levers, 2012; Levers et al., 2007). Some analysts even have concluded that the issue of trauma has been exploited for political and economic reasons; in her exploration of associated challenges, James (2004) has introduced the notion of a *trauma portfolio*, a kind of hierarchical cataloging of events that have institutional currency. Noor et al. (2012) have examined adversarial groups involved in violent conflicts and have identified the concept of competitive victimhood to describe the dynamic by which one group tries to establish that they have suffered more than the other group, thus leading to greater incidents of public violence. Many of the chapters throughout this book examine these issues more closely. For the purpose of continuing to construct our scaffold for understanding trauma, two salient issues are outlined briefly in the text that follows: the ACE Study and Racial Trauma.

ACE Study

Felitti et al.'s (1998) landmark study illuminated what many clinicians anecdotally began to realize about clients' trauma histories, long before the evidence was aggregated systematically (Levers, 2020). Fortunately, for the field, Felitti et al. (1998) took the time and initiative to investigate what they also had been observing in clinical settings: Many individuals have endured adverse childhood experiences, and these experiences have had real health consequences. Mirroring Bronfenbrenner's (1979, 1981) bioecological model, adverse childhood experiences are risk factors that exist across an individual's multiple environments, and protective factors can mitigate or even extinguish the impact of such adverse experiences.

The Adverse Childhood Experiences (ACE) Study (Felitti et al., 1998) was undertaken from 1995 to 1997 by the Centers for Disease Control and Prevention (CDC) and Kaiser Permanente, the latter being a large managed healthcare consortium. Over 17,000 subjects were involved in the investigation; this constitutes an unusually high number of participants for any research, thus suggesting that the results of the study are quite robust. The number of ACEs experienced by people can have profound influences on future violence, both victimization and perpetration, as well as on health and potential opportunity over the life-span, thereby making adverse childhood experiences an extremely important public health issue. ACEs have been linked to negative outcomes such as risky health behaviors, chronic health conditions, low life potential, and even early death (CDC, 2021). For individuals who have experienced a greater number of ACEs, the risk becomes higher for experiencing these outcomes. Figure 2.3 represents the

Figure 2.3

Adverse Childhood Experiences Pyramid

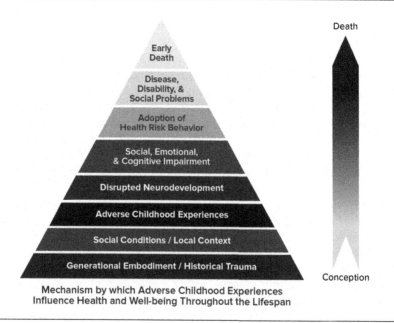

From: Centers for Disease Control and Prevention. (2021, April 6). About the CDC-Kaiser ACE study. *Violence Prevention*. https://www.cdc.gov/violenceprevention/aces/about.html

pyramid of whole-life risks for social impairments and health problems that may result from the core adverse childhood experiences that form the base of the pyramid.

A high ACE score may be an indicator for high risk across a person's life-span. According to "Adverse childhood experiences (ACEs) are stressful or traumatic events, including abuse and neglect. They may also include household dysfunction such as witnessing domestic violence or growing up with family members who have substance use disorders." The base of the pyramid identifies transgenerational or historical trauma, as well as social conditions and local context, thus emphasizing the strong impact that racial trauma and living in conditions circumscribed by poverty or community violence may have on a person. Individuals who have experienced a greater number of ACEs are likely to develop a wider range of health and behavioral health problems. The prevalence of health problems typically is higher for those scoring a greater number of ACEs, and this includes problems associated with risky behaviors such as substance misuse. SAMHSA (2018) and the Village Network (n.d.) identify the following most common ACEs:

- Physical abuse
- Sexual abuse
- Emotional abuse
- Physical neglect
- Emotional neglect
- Intimate partner violence
- Mother treated violently
- Substance misuse within household
- Household mental illness
- Parental separation or divorce
- Incarcerated household member

Clearly, there is a strong association between the health-related effects of ACEs and stress, and this illuminates how stress is implicated in experiences associated with crisis, trauma, and racial trauma.

Racial Trauma

Racial trauma, also referenced as transgenerational trauma and historical trauma, is a source of stress, crisis, and trauma for most, if not all, people of color. Research has established the extent to which race-based stressors can cause serious health and behavioral health issues for people of color (Williams, 2018; Williams & Cooper, 2019; Williams et al., 2018, 2021). Studies have demonstrated that the extreme effects of racial trauma have caused intergenerational transmissions of trauma that ultimately are responsible for epigenetic changes, affecting the function and expression of genes in subsequent generations (Shonkoff et al., 2021; Sotero, 2006; Yehuda & Lehrner, 2018). According to Williams (2018), racism that is deeply embedded within the broader culture continues to affect individuals through structural and institutional mechanisms; research that attends to institutional racism and the health effects of racial hostility has the potential for "enhancing our understanding of the complex association between physical and mental health" (p. 466). Issues associated with racial trauma are detailed more extensively in Chapters 17 and 19 of this book. However, it is essential to point to racial trauma as a major public health concern as well as possessing relevant social justice dimensions.

Social Justice Dimensions of Trauma

Geopolitical atrocities continue to occur internationally, even though the phrase "never again" has been repeated over and over in reference to events such as the enslavement of Africans, the near extinction of indigenous peoples in the Americas, the Jewish Holocaust, apartheid in South Africa, the Bosnian genocide, the Rwandan genocide—and now, *again*, in reference to the

Democratic Republic of Congo, to Sudan, and to the persecution of the Rohingya people in Myanmar. Circumstances like these have exposed people to such a degree of extreme cruelty and unspeakable horror that the ensuing trauma not only affects the individuals directly involved but can live on as transgenerational trauma. Trauma that continues across generations is called "historical trauma," and includes racial trauma, as previously mentioned and also discussed at greater length in other chapters of this book.

Both human-made and natural catastrophes can leave the poorest, the youngest, the oldest, and the weakest in highly vulnerable positions. The world has witnessed the devastation of the most vulnerable in recent climate-related disasters as well as in the ongoing effects of the COVID-19 pandemic. Children (e.g., Lanius et al., 2010; Sanchez et al., 2019) and older adults (e.g., Bonnie & Wallace, 2003; DePrince et al., 2020) have been exploited in many ways that can evoke trauma responses (issues associated with child and adolescent trauma are discussed in Chapters 7 and 8, and with elder trauma in Chapter 12 of this textbook). Immigration processes have become fraught with the potential for trauma, in the United States and in various other parts of the world (e.g., Levers & Hyatt-Burkhart, 2011); these issues are detailed more fully in Chapter 17 of this book.

Trauma-based issues that represent human rights violations need to be examined from a social justice perspective. The effects of a traumatic event can be intensified and worsened when the traumatized person also has cause to feel that they have been betrayed by the very social institutions that should be extending assistance. As an example, this was the palpable pain, witnessed in news feeds across the country and around the world, when victims of Hurricane Katrina were shown, corralled in the most unsanitary conditions and begging for water. Although trauma survivors whose rights have been violated need to be treated individually and to engage in a recovery process, the group aspect of a social justice perspective may require some type of restorative or reparative justice to take place. Restorative justice, which focuses on the needs of the victim rather than legal principles or the punishment of the offender, has been used, as one example, in the *Gacaca* courts in Rwanda, offering a format for reconciliation between victims and perpetrators in a situation where parties need to live together again in the same society (aspects of the Rwandan genocide are discussed in greater detail in Chapter 23 of this book).

Pedagogical Dimensions of Trauma

Opportunities for in-service and professional association trainings concerning all issues related to trauma have swelled during the last several decades. However, preservice clinical instruction, specifically related to the psychosocial impacts of trauma, has been less forthcoming, and the same is true regarding a focus on the clinical supervision of trauma-related cases, although there have been some recent attempts to redress this tremendous training gap. For example, the Council for the Accreditation of Counseling and Related Education Programs (CACREP, 2016) recently instituted the curricular requirement, for both the master's level and doctoral training of professional counselors, that content related to the areas of crises, disasters, and other trauma-causing events be included in the curriculum of accredited programs. Counseling, psychology, and social work programs gradually have been adding courses that deal with trauma and crisis issues, but little is known about pedagogical best practices and trauma (Levers, 2020).

Educators have noted the existence of pedagogical problems and difficulties in teaching matters that are associated with trauma (e.g., Levers, 2020; Simon & Eppert, 1997; Simon et al., 2000; Walcott, 2000). Obviously, care needs to be taken not to overwhelm or traumatize students in the process of helping them to understand the clinical dimensions of trauma. At the same time, educators concerned with trauma issues need to create opportunities for advancing relevant skill sets. Although adding courses that are specific to trauma, especially at the graduate level, is a necessity, embedding trauma-sensitive skills across human services curricula would go a long way in addressing the instructional gap. For example, working with survivors of trauma requires empathic engagement; this skill typically is included in a basic techniques course and so presents an opportunity for illustrating the skill as one related to trauma along with applicability to other mental health issues. In addition to offering an adequate clinical knowledge base within a specialty trauma course, preservice programs could enhance the way they teach basic counseling skills across the curriculum, in order to include issues of trauma. Recent efforts to incorporate trauma-informed educational practices, at P-12 and college levels, appear to be promising (e.g., Carello & Butler, 2015; Quarmby et al., 2021).

Intersection of Constructs Related to Stress, Crisis, Disaster, and Trauma

Issues associated with trauma constitute a major focus of this book. Stress, crisis theory, and crisis intervention are detailed in Chapter 3, and various types of disaster and mass violence situations are examined in Chapters 19 to 25 of this book. Of relevance at this juncture is the nexus of constructs regarding stress, trauma, crisis, and disaster experiences and the importance of differentiating their varying characteristics (Yeager & Roberts, 2015). In some ways, the process of differentiating is paradoxical; the more we look at the differences in these constructs, the more we see the complexity of their intersection, in many human experiences. This is precisely why I have formatted the first four chapters of this book as a scaffold for building upon and understanding these distinct and yet interconnected concepts.

Stress is a common feature of everyday life and has the same psychophysiological effects, whether real or imagined; however, unrelenting stress can be biologically and emotionally harmful. In this instance, a person may need to engage in stress management techniques and prevention activities to alleviate the pressure and tension. A crisis or disaster is usually a time of increased stress or danger. A crisis is an event or situation in which a person perceives a threat to be greater or more intolerable than their ability to cope with or assimilate the circumstances. A disaster is usually a sudden accident or a natural or human-made catastrophe that may or may not be perceived as a crisis or a trauma, depending upon the individual and the context. A traumatic event is typically so overwhelming that the victim experiences a sense of terror or helplessness. Not every stressor constitutes a crisis or a disaster, and not every crisis or disaster is traumatizing. However, a traumatic event typically involves extreme stress and some element of crisis.

It is useful for every mental health professional to be equipped with basic stress management and crisis intervention skills. These skill sets do not rely on long-term counseling as much as assisting clients to regulate their responses to extremely stressful or crisis-oriented situations or disasters; these skills require the counselor to attend to what needs to be done, in the immediate sense. However, survivor responses to traumatic events, especially if the response is enduring enough to qualify as PTSD, usually require longer-term counseling, and this suggests that the mental health professional have clinical preparation in delivering trauma counseling. Determining when a person's sense of intense fear or horror, in response to an overwhelming event, moves from the stress of a crisis to a fully traumatic experience may rely on the clinician's ability to combine two different sets of counseling skills: (a) active and compassionate listening to the client's narrative, and (b) keen assessment and diagnostic skills (Roberts, 2002; SAMHSA, 2014). Developing all of these skill sets requires professional experience but acquiring as much preservice and ongoing in-service training as possible is also an essential factor.

COUNSELING IMPLICATIONS

Several implications arise from the aforementioned overview of a contextual and systemic perspective of trauma and trauma-related issues. Perhaps a pertinent first implication is that the most effective approach to understanding trauma is one that engages multiple disciplines. Scholars and clinicians point to the importance of interdisciplinarity in the study of trauma, from local to transnational trauma events and responses to these events (e.g., Droždek, 2007a; Hamburger et al., 2018). As discipline-based professionals, we can learn from our confederate colleagues of all disciplinary persuasions.

A second implication relates to trauma therapists being adequately grounded in their understandings of both the clinical and contextual factors associated with trauma. This is a double-edged issue of professional responsibility: (a) preservice training programs need to offer adequate instruction concerning the ubiquitous mental health issues of stress, crisis, trauma, and disaster and; (b) clinicians working in the arena of traumatology need to ensure that they have an adequate education, whether preservice or in-service training, to support their work with trauma survivors.

Mental health professionals who work with survivors of trauma can provide more effective and culturally sensitive treatment when they conceptualize client concerns through the bioecological, transactional, neuroscience, and public health models described in this chapter. So a third implication is that these models offer an interdisciplinary format for understanding client risk factors, for engaging and enhancing existing protective factors, and for creating mechanisms that facilitate client recovery. A related fourth implication regards a systemic understanding of the impact of trauma. Because of the very personal nature of how traumatic events are experienced, even those involving mass casualties, along with the overwhelming intensity that is typical of any trauma situation, people who experience a traumatic event are affected profoundly in every area of their lives, including physiologically. To ignore the dynamics between individuals and the relevant systems that play essential roles in everyday living is really to ignore central features of the trauma situation.

When clinicians first recognize trauma and begin to treat the client, this constitutes an ecological transition for the therapist, thus providing a strong reason for seeking clinical supervision, a fifth implication. Working with survivors of trauma entails intellectually demanding and emotionally charged scenarios, ones that require clinicians to maintain professionally appropriate boundaries. In addition to the central importance of boundaries, therapists working with traumatized clients need to be keenly aware of the potential for countertransference. The need for self-reflexive skills, for the ability to formulate intentional treatment strategies, and for unwavering attention to boundary and countertransference issues speaks to the essential importance of clinical supervision when working with trauma (see Chapter 32 of this book for a fuller discussion). Even highly experienced trauma counselors find clinical supervision helpful, and for more seasoned therapists, this can be conducted as peer supervision or even in trauma-informed learning groups that are developed by clinicians to support one another in this intense line of work.

Therapeutic intentionality is an important sixth implication for counseling. For a long time, clinicians working in community settings that are not trauma or survivor specific (different from rape crisis centers and domestic violence shelters, for example, that focus on traumatic events) have tended to provide crisis intervention immediately to distressed or traumatized clients, perhaps without even recognizing the trauma, per se. They then may refer these clients, so that the trauma issues are likely to be identified so much later that there are additional and more complex sets of problems for the clients. This seems to constitute a therapeutic *default* rather than *intentional* therapy. The mental health field has been defaulting on trauma, in this sense, for far too long. In order to avoid systemic failures and to aspire toward best practices, the delivery of mental health services to trauma survivors needs to be trauma informed (trauma-informed care is discussed more fully in Chapters 27 and 28 of this book), to be offered from a pluralistic professional perspective, and to advance strategies of care that are intentional rather than of a default nature.

CONCLUSION

The construct of trauma has sparked controversies for well over a century, and we have arrived at multiple ways of perceiving trauma. This chapter has emphasized that the effects of a traumatic event are perhaps best understood from multidimensional and multidisciplinary perspectives. I have attempted to amplify how a recognition of the physiological effects of trauma on the brain and other organs of the body, along with an awareness of the bioecological and transactional nature of life-span development, can assist therapists in dealing with the aftermath of clients' traumatic experiences. The connection between the personal and the systemic has been highlighted and is germane to the trauma scaffold that we have been constructing, with an aim toward supporting heightened understandings of more complex overlays of traumatic experiences.

A clinician's ability to understand the profound effects of a traumatic event on the psyche of a client goes well beyond codified clinical definitions and includes a phenomenological understanding of clients' lived experiences of trauma. This chapter has noted some of the common criticisms of *DSM* categorizations of trauma-based diagnoses, particularly PTSD, especially as these have established the basis for contemporary arguments that favor the consideration of a complex trauma classification, or a trauma spectrum disorders category. Herman's (1992/1997) helpful separation of PTSD symptoms into intrusive and constrictive sets has been offered, and Herman's notion of a dialectic of trauma has been presented.

In addition to defining trauma from clinical and phenomenological perspectives, insight has been derived from a contextual viewpoint, thereby enabling an examination of the cultural, public health, social justice, and pedagogical dimensions of trauma. This chapter also has reviewed constructs associated with stress, crisis, and disaster, exploring their nexus with relevant trauma issues, to begin to frame a scaffold for understanding the complexity and confluence of these lived experiences. The counseling implications of this chapter's contextual orientation toward trauma have been identified, emphasizing the need for adequate training and clinical supervision. Trauma has been viewed here as a complex human issue that requires informed and intentional individual and systemic responses.

ADDITIONAL RESOURCES

 A robust set of instructor resources designed to supplement this text is located at http://connect.springerpub.com/content/book/978-0-8261-5085-1. Qualifying instructors may request access by emailing textbook@springerpub.com.

PRACTICE-BASED RESOURCES AND REFERENCES

To view a list of resources and all the references, please visit connect.springerpub.com via the following url: http://connect.springerpub.com/content/book/978-0-8261-5085-1/part/part01/chapter/ch02

CHAPTER 3

An Introduction to Stress Management and Crisis Intervention

LISA LÓPEZ LEVERS

CHAPTER OVERVIEW

This chapter focuses on introducing the reader to theories about stress and crisis and on promoting basic stress management and crisis intervention skills. Stress and crisis often intersect with trauma and disaster events and are foundational aspects of the scaffold being created, in the first four chapters of this book, for grasping the profound effects that stress, crisis, disaster, and trauma can have at individual and systemic levels.

LEARNING OBJECTIVES

After reading this chapter, the reader should be able to:

1. Understand the impact of stress;
2. Develop strategies for helping clients to manage stress;
3. Understand the nature of crisis;
4. Define crisis situations;
5. Identify relevant crisis intervention for individuals and communities; and,
6. Develop awareness of how to apply stress management and crisis intervention strategies.

INTRODUCTION

Stress is a regular part of life; people encounter numerous stressors in everyday living. Sometimes stress motivates us to accomplish routine work, but at other times, stress may hinder our ability to be productive. When stress becomes overwhelming for an individual, the person may seek counseling. Similarly, it is not unusual for clients to experience one or more crises, well within the norms of quotidian living. However, when a crisis situation continues to loom, and perhaps becomes intense enough to affect functioning, then the affected person may be prompted to seek counseling. It also is possible for clients to experience crises while they already are in counseling for other reasons. All people experience both minor and major types of stressors and crises across the life-span, so in this sense, stress and crisis are a part of existence; however, when stress or crisis pushes people to the tipping point, then engaging in effective counseling can become imperative. Stress management and crisis intervention are essential skill sets for all mental health and behavioral health professionals and paraprofessionals.

Everyone working in the mental health field can expect to identify, assess, and mediate client stress as well as crisis. Not all stress leads to a crisis or a trauma event. Not every crisis escalates into a traumatizing experience; however, most traumatic events involve some element of crisis and a lot of stress. Not every crisis is a part of a larger disaster, but disaster situations usually include multiple crises and stressors. Stress is an aspect of crisis, trauma, and disaster. For these reasons, it is important for trauma-informed clinicians to be adept at helping their clients to maneuver through and to manage stressors and crises. In other words, professional counselors need to acquire crisis intervention and stress management strategies as a basic component of being a competent clinician; dealing with stress and crisis are foundational components of the scaffold that we are constructing and examining in Chapters 1, 2, 3, and 4 of this textbook.

It is essential that mental health professionals be able to differentiate among the constructs associated with stress, crisis, trauma, and disaster (Yeager & Roberts, 2015). At the same time, it is important to understand the often-complex interrelationships among these dynamics, how they can affect people, and how stress and crisis may be starting points for a longer clinical process. In this chapter, we look at Understanding the Nature of Stress, Understanding the Nature of Crisis, and Counseling Implications, as well as identifying some of the more relevant stress management and crisis intervention strategies, by way of learning how to apply these constructs. After presenting these discussions, we conclude with a brief summary of the chapter. Practice-based resources are available through access to the Springer platform; details for gaining access are noted at the end of the chapter.

UNDERSTANDING THE NATURE OF STRESS

Stress is actually the body's reaction to any situation that feels threatening. This chemical response occurs whether harm or danger is real or imagined, and whether the threat or potential threat exists in the environment or is based on a person's internal perception. As discussed in Chapters 2 and 4 of this textbook, extreme stress engages the fight-or-flight response, as a means of protection. When this happens, the autonomic nervous system (ANS) activates, and the body releases stress hormones, which then produce physiological responses such as increased heart rate, rapid breathing, and tensing of muscles.

In the now classic book, *The Stress of Life*, Selye (1956/1978) was the first to talk extensively about the impact of stress on humans, both biologically and emotionally. As previously mentioned, stress is a hormonally driven, and therefore autonomic, physiological state that occurs in response to situations that demand change. This state is not necessarily always negative; Selye also coined the term "eustress," which implies the kind of "good" stress that can motivate an individual. An example of eustress would be jumping out of bed when the alarm goes off in the morning—we care enough about our work obligations, thus having the right level of eustress, to motivate us to get moving so that we can arrive at work on time. However, when people talk about being "stressed out," the connotation usually relates to a negative state of tension or agitation. Even this kind of pressure is not necessarily a "bad" thing, as under precipitating circumstances stress activates a primitive part of the brain to initiate the fight-or-flight response; stress is like the body's instant messaging system for protecting us from danger. It is when danger has passed and we are unable to "turn off" the stress response that the effects of prolonged stress can begin to take a toll on our bodies, including on important regulating systems like the endocrine and immune systems. Alternatively, sometimes when we are under extreme stress, instead of defaulting to the fight-or-flight response, our bodies instead go into a kind of freeze response, like a deer caught in headlights; this type of inertia may replace the fight-or-flight response or even heighten the original perception of danger.

In a discussion about the symptoms of stress, a *WebMD* article has identified a number of emotional, physical, cognitive, and behavioral symptoms that may be associated with stress overload. (The lists of symptoms can be viewed, categorically, at the *WebMD* site, noted in the reference section [Casarella, 2019].) When we think about stress overload, we need to consider the neurobiological effects of stress, as discussed in Chapters 1 and 2. Prolonged and unattended stress can cause serious physiological problems and may even lead to poor health. As mentioned earlier in the chapter, stress is a part of life, and our bodies equip us with mechanisms for dealing with the ordinary stress of daily living. However, when stress continues unabated or is compounded by additional or more severe stressors, our bodies begin to feel the consequences; our internal alarm system, the fight-or-flight response, remains engaged (Mayo Clinic, 2019). Long-term stress or chronic stress can cause serious health concerns and also may make existing health problems worse. This includes a number of mental health and behavioral health problems, high blood pressure, cardiovascular disease, addiction, and gastrointestinal problems, among others (Casarella, 2019; Harvard Medical School, 2020). The American Psychological Association (2020b) has qualified increasing levels of stress in the United States as being of crisis proportions, and we certainly have seen the entire range of stress responses, from mild to severe, during the COVID-19 pandemic.

In its annual survey on stress in America, the American Psychological Association (APA, 2020b, p. 1) has disclosed that Americans are "profoundly affected by the COVID-19 pandemic, and that the external factors Americans have listed in previous years as significant sources of stress remain present and problematic. These compounding stressors are having real consequences on our minds and bodies." The Centers for Disease Control and Prevention (CDC, 2021) also has emphasized the extent to which the COVID-19 pandemic has had a major impact on our lives. The CDC has identified the following ways in which stress can manifest:

- Feelings of fear, anger, sadness, worry, numbness, or frustration
- Changes in appetite, energy, desires, and interests
- Difficulty concentrating and making decisions
- Difficulty sleeping or nightmares
- Physical reactions, such as headaches, body pains, stomach problems, and skin rashes
- Worsening of chronic health problems
- Worsening of mental health conditions
- Increased use of tobacco, alcohol, and other substances (CDC, 2021, "Coping With Stress," para. 2)

Brief discussions of real and perceived threat, toxic stress, and stress management strategies are in order here.

Real and Perceived Threat

A stress response typically is triggered by something in the environment, for example, unusually heavy traffic on the way to work or a spat with a significant other. In other words, an existing threat in the environment may precipitate an acute stress response. These types of threats usually are resolved in fairly short order, and life goes on. Sometimes people become distressed by what they perceive as a *potential* threat in the environment. The person who encountered heavy traffic on the way to work ends up being a little late, and as the person is moving from the parked vehicle to the office entrance, they become distressed that the tardiness might anger the boss, who could even fire the person. So, the person enters the building in a state of stress and is fearful even to encounter the boss. In reality, the boss also was delayed by the same traffic and arrives a little after the employee, who is already seated at their desk, and can see the boss just arriving. The employee is flooded with a sense of relief. The danger was not real, but the perceived threat still caused a stress reaction, with stress hormones that had been pumping throughout the body, only moments prior, beginning to subside upon the person's sense of relief. The body winds down and returns to homeostasis.

Acute or short-term stress is a part of life that people generally manage on their own. However, when acute stress becomes chronic or longer-term stress, the individual may need to seek mental health or behavioral health assistance. An example of chronic stress might involve that person, mentioned previously, who had a minor spat with a significant other; we can imagine that if the spat becomes ongoing and increasingly more intensive arguing, the relationship might move from one that is vulnerable to one that is compromised. This kind of chronic stress is an indicator that professional help may be needed; unmitigated chronic stress can lead to toxic stress and may result in health problems.

Toxic Stress

Numerous and compounding adverse experiences can lead to excessive activation of the stress response system; this, in turn, can cause wear and tear on the body and on the brain, resulting in toxic stress (Harvard Medical School, 2021). It is important to understand that it is not much an event that is toxic, it is the continual engagement of the sympathetic nervous system and the ongoing biochemical responses that can become toxic to the body and interfere with maintaining good health (Franke, 2014). An essential feature of toxic stress is that the body does not have an opportunity to return to a state of balance or homeostasis; the body is not able to recover fully between onslaughts of neurobiological response to ongoing stress. The COVID-19 pandemic may have provided the "perfect storm" for examples of toxic stress. We know that during the pandemic, instances of substance abuse, intimate partner violence, child abuse, and suicide have increased (Melillo, 2021). We might infer that as people were forced to accommodate to the demands of the pandemic, often under the pressure of multiple stressors and increased isolation, and to adjust to many new norms, high levels of stress became toxic for some.

Stress Management

Whether clients report mild or more intense stress responses, it is important that mental health professionals attend to such complaints and assist clients in learning how to manage stressors in their lives. This may have serious implications for other mental health concerns that a client may present as well as for existing and potential health problems. There is no one-size-fits-all prescription for stress management techniques; it really depends on the particular client, their lifestyle, and their personal preferences. The Mayo Clinic offers some suggestions in one of their publications, and these appear in Box 3.1.

BOX 3.1

Information From the Field: Stress Management Strategies

Stress management strategies include:

- Eating a healthy diet and getting regular exercise and plenty of sleep
- Practicing relaxation techniques such as trying yoga, practicing deep breathing, getting a massage, or learning to meditate
- Taking time for hobbies, such as reading a book or listening to music
- Fostering healthy friendships
- Having a sense of humor
- Volunteering in your community
- Seeking professional counseling when needed

(From Mayo Clinic. (2019, March 19). Stress management. https://www.mayoclinic.org/healthy-lifestyle/stress-management/in-depth/stress/art-20046037)

Helping clients to identify the stressors in their lives and to understand the physiological responses to those stressors can assist in allaying further stress. Working with clients to use the stress management strategies that fit their particular lifestyles can go a long way in cultivating a calmer approach to life and perhaps even a healthier way of living.

UNDERSTANDING THE NATURE OF CRISIS

In the same way that stress is a reality of existence, crisis also is a part of life; we all experience stress and crisis in our lives. However, crisis is an interesting construct, particularly from the perspective of its paradoxical nature, that is, from the viewpoint that it can have positive or negative outcomes. I begin this discussion with popular and clinical connotations and definitions of the word "crisis." In a comment about semantic drift, the Merriam-Webster (2021) describes how the original definition of "crisis" shifted from one based on a pivoting point in an illness, whether getting better or worse, to a more contemporary definition regarding any situation which needs to be addressed. The word "crisis," in its most popular sense, has come to infer some type of instability or even danger. In the American Psychological Association's (2020a), *Dictionary of Psychology*, crisis is defined, in the earlier connotation of the word, as "a turning point for better or worse in the course of an illness," and the later, more clinical connotation as "a situation (e.g., a traumatic change) that produces significant cognitive or emotional stress in those involved in it" ("crisis," para. 1–2). A World Health Organization (WHO, 2012) definition of crisis focuses on its unpredictability and the potential for harm, especially when communities are unprepared. Such popularized and clinical understandings of the word's meaning help to emphasize the potentially paradoxical nature of experiencing crisis and to offer a basis by which a helper potentially can assist a client in addressing, managing, and transforming a crisis into a moment of or an opportunity for growth. In the helping professions, we tend to view a crisis as a troubling but pivotal moment, requiring some type of a change, which often then promotes development and growth, even in the face of adversity, potentially facilitating the person's improved situation. Of course, we need a much broader knowledge base, in order to glean a professional understanding of what constitutes a crisis and what it means to intervene and manage a crisis.

Counselors and other helpers need to possess basic crisis intervention skills, in order to work with clients in crisis, clients experiencing trauma, and survivors of disaster situations. Clearly, helping our clients to manage and contain their crises constitutes a pertinent clinical skill and contributes to building the trauma scaffold that we discussed earlier. Purvis (1994) offers the following useful definition:

> Crisis Management is the careful and tactful management of a situation in which there is trouble or danger that has the possibility of serious and negative consequences. The possible serious and negative consequences might include litigation, injury to individuals and/or property, death of an individual, disruption of the normal routine, and loss of confidence and trust in an individual or an institution. (p. 23)

Purvis further notes that the consequences of a crisis can be real or imagined, and that this depends on the mindset of the person or persons involved, directly and indirectly. It is important for responders to be aware of this and to "respond in a professional, legal, humane, and ethical manner" (Purvis, 1994, p. 23).

James and Gilliland (2017) point to the numerous definitions of crisis, spanning the decades in which we formally have been providing crisis intervention services. A full history of the crisis intervention movement is beyond the scope of this chapter, but crisis intervention strategies primarily emerged in the 1960s and 1970s, most notably within the context of addressing growing drug and alcohol problems, women's concerns during the second wave of the women's movement, and Vietnam veterans returning from combat (James & Gilliland, 2017). Additionally, we see that crisis intervention practices were popularized by the use of Norman Kagan's *Interpersonal Process Recall* (IPR), employed in professional and paraprofessional trainings by crisis hotlines, emerging substance abuse centers, and university programs (Kagan, 1980).

Given the history of training professionals and paraprofessionals in the use of crisis intervention techniques, and how definitions have evolved, in conjunction with the changing needs of society, it is difficult to arrive at a singular and exclusively definitive understanding of crisis. Ultimately, however, James and Gilliland (2017) have offered a succinct and contemporary definition of crisis as the "perception of an event or situation as an intolerable difficulty that exceeds the person's current resources and coping mechanisms" (p. 9). They further have asserted that until a crisis situation is mitigated or resolved, an individual may become increasingly more distraught on multiple levels. These are useful conceptualizations for mental health professionals, especially in their emphasis upon an individual client's own *perceptions* of danger and upon an individual client's *ability to cope* in the moment or in the situation. When a client is in crisis, it is not the time for a clinician to be judgmental about whether the person's experience matches a textbook definition of crisis. If someone tells me that they are in crisis, I am going to take the person at their word, and I am going to assess for that individual's unique capacity to cope, in the here and now. When someone is in crisis mode, we move one step at a time, and at the client's own pace. The Substance Abuse and Mental Health Services Administration (SAMHSA) (2020a, p. 9) sums up crisis work brilliantly: "Perhaps the most potent element of all, in an effective crisis service system, is relationships. To be human. To be compassionate. We know from experience that immediate access to help, hope and healing saves lives." Box 3.2 offers a clinical vignette that illustrates a human crisis and a crisis response.

BOX 3.2

Clinical Vignette: Monique's Crisis

Monique is a 34-year-old, African American mother of two, an 8-year-old daughter and an 11-year-old son. She was diagnosed with breast cancer in late 2019 and began chemotherapy in early 2020. Monique was working as a waitress at the time of her diagnosis, but had to quit her job, both due to the COVID-19 pandemic and to receive treatment. Like so many positions in the food industry, Monique's job did not afford any healthcare benefits, so she had to apply for assistance from a variety of social safety nets, in order to take care of her children as well as her healthcare needs. Not too long after beginning chemotherapy, the public health effects of the COVID-19 pandemic began to take effect. The children had to stay home from school, needing computers for online distance learning, which they were able to obtain from the school. Monique was fearful about leaving her home, due to her compromised immune system. At the beginning of the pandemic, Monique's brother, her only remaining family member, was helping her, especially by bringing groceries to the home for her and the children. But eventually, her brother, a taxi driver, contracted COVID-19, was hospitalized, and died. Monique was frantic. She was facing so much grief as well as an abundance of stressors, many associated with living in poverty, the systemic effects of racism, and dealing with her illness; in addition, she needed to ensure that she could feed her children. When Monique was first prepped for chemotherapy, she was given the name and contact information for a clinical mental health counselor, in case she needed emotional support related to her cancer and chemotherapy. She did not use the information at the time, as she was raised to believe that "needing" counseling is a sign of weakness. But when she found herself in this crisis situation, feeling so desperate, she contacted the counselor, Gwen.

(continued)

Gwen immediately arranged to see Monique via telehealth. They scheduled an appointment for after school time, so that Monique was able to use one of the laptops that the school had given the children for online classes. Although Monique had many pressing psychosocial issues that needed to be addressed, Gwen initially assessed the critical nature of Monique's main crisis concern and ascertained that getting food to the family was a necessary step in beginning to address the crisis. In fact, during that first session, Gwen asked Monique to remain online for several minutes, while she made a call on Monique's behalf. Gwen called a food bank with which she had a good networking relationship. They could deliver a food box that day, if authorized. Gwen came back to Monique, obtained the necessary permission, and placed the request for delivery of free food, beginning that day and then weekly thereafter. Monique was tearful, grateful, and a little shaken that things were moving so quickly. Gwen and Monique discussed the food crisis and how good it was that Monique had reached out to Gwen; Gwen also used the opportunity to help Monique begin to calm down a bit. By addressing the initial crisis of Monique being able to feed her children, the door was opened for further discussion of Monique's other pressing concerns. Gwen and Monique had weekly telehealth sessions through much of the pandemic. As Monique learned to manage her stress level better, and as the crisis situation began to subside, Gwen also was able to assist Monique with relaxation strategies that were helpful in dealing with some of the cancer-related fears and the psychosocial effects of the chemotherapy.

Reflection Questions

1. Why do you think Gwen began, immediately, with the issue of food for the family?
2. How do you think Monique received the suggestion of food before having her other psychological concerns addressed?
3. How do you think assessing and acting on the obvious crisis first might have facilitated a longer-term counseling relationship?
4. How would you have dealt with Monique's initial call?

Crisis Context

Individual crisis situations may be as diverse as the individuals affected by crises; however, it is useful to consider typology. James and Gilliland (2017) have suggested that all individuals may face any number of developmental, personal, or environmental types of crises across the lifespan. While the clinical literature naturally has emphasized the conflictual nature of a crisis, it is important to maintain the strength-based perspective that a crisis also can initiate circumstances for creating meaningful change and building resilience. A helpful operational definition of a crisis is one emphasizing that a crisis also can be a turning point in a person's life, one that promotes personal insight, self-reflection, and change (Levers, 2020). A crisis occurs when someone experiences a personal or environmental stressor or perceives some danger or threat in the environment; how the person responds is critical to whether the individual becomes overwhelmed indefinitely or is able to manage the situation in a self-efficacious way. This leads directly to a discussion about the ways in which mental health professionals can intervene, effectively, in helping clients to resolve their crises successfully.

Crisis Intervention Strategies

Whether real or imagined, a perceived sense of danger can have a profound effect on a person. It is essential that professional counselors be well equipped with crisis intervention skills. A number of crisis intervention models exist and can be used to assist clients in managing and working through their crises. Several stage/step models, the psychological first aid model, and the need for systemic responses are discussed in the text that follows.

Stage/Step Models

One general model for conceptualizing a client's concerns is the *Integrative ACT Intervention Model* (Roberts, 2002), which includes the following three stages: (a) Assessment, (b) Crisis intervention, and (c) Trauma treatment services. Roberts (2005) also has designed a *Seven-Step Crisis Intervention Model*, which is more detailed than his earlier *Integrative ACT Intervention Model* and suggests the following steps:

- Assess lethality,
- Establish rapport,
- Identify problems,
- Deal with feelings,
- Explore alternatives,
- Develop an action plan, and
- Follow up.

As is the case with many stage and step-wise models, these should be considered as points of guidance and adapted to the individual needs presented by specific clients. We never should "push" client responses to fit a predetermined set of stages or steps. Like so many issues that are pertinent to counseling, working with crisis is an iterative and recursive process.

Psychological First Aid

Psychological First Aid (PFA; National Child Traumatic Stress Network & National Center for PTSD, 2006) is an evidence-based modular program, one that has been used widely in responding to crisis, disaster, terrorism, and other emergencies. The National Child Traumatic Stress Network and the National Center for PTSD, a section of the United States Department of Veterans Affairs, jointly developed PFA in 2006. PFA originated as an intervention for disaster response; it has been used extensively by the International Federation of Red Cross and the Red Crescent Societies (Schultz & Forbes, 2014), as well as by the WHO (2013). PFA has been used primarily in disaster response, but because it is a short-term intervention, intended to attenuate distress and facilitate continued care as necessary, it also may be used as a crisis intervention strategy. Due to the reality that crisis and disaster events have become increasingly prevalent, PFA has been developed as a consensus-derived, empirically supported, competency-based training model (McCabe et al., 2014). A wide array of PFA training opportunities has facilitated the use of PFA interventions during the COVID-19 pandemic (Shah et al., 2020).

Crisis Response as a Systemic Issue

While individuals frequently face personal crises, communities and societies face crisis situations as well; therefore, a systemic perspective of crisis intervention strategies also is important. According to SAMHSA (2020b, p. 8), "A comprehensive and integrated crisis network is the first line of defense in preventing tragedies of public and client safety, civil rights, extraordinary and unacceptable loss of lives, and the waste of resources." However, SAMHSA further states that "Effective crisis care that saves lives and dollars requires a systemic approach" (2020b, p. 8). The organization advocates for comprehensive crisis care services that include (a) regional crisis call centers, (b) crisis mobile team response, and (c) crisis receiving and stabilization facilities (SAMHSA, 2020a, 2020b). Such comprehensive crisis services, by definition, address individual crises while also ensuring well-being at community and larger systemic levels.

SAMHSA advises that systemic crisis response efforts should be trauma[...] to SAMHSA's 2020b publication, "trauma-informed care is an essentia[...] treatment" (p. 29). In 2014, SAMHSA established the following set of key gu[...] trauma-informed care:

1. Safety;
2. Trustworthiness and transparency;
3. Peer support and mutual self-help;
4. Collaboration and mutuality;
5. Empowerment, voice, and choice; and,
6. Ensuring cultural, historical and gender considerations inform the care provided (p. 10).

Accordingly, these key principles would inform all treatment and recovery services, including individual crisis intervention and systemic crisis response services. The major directive is to create a service delivery culture that is trauma informed, thus screening for trauma exposure among all clients, including those who are experiencing any type of crisis.

COUNSELING IMPLICATIONS

For many reasons, not the least of which are the COVID-19 pandemic and anthropogenic climate change, it is much more likely now, than ever before, that mental health professionals will be faced with responding to increased levels of stress, more intense crises, and even more frequent disasters; we need to be prepared to provide sufficient services to clients whose lives have been affected. We have seen that stress and crisis not only affect individuals but also communities and societies; stress and crisis have become serious public health issues. Precisely because of the unpredictable nature of most crises and disasters, which can cause enormous suffering and death, the WHO (2012) urges national and local systems to prepare for the unpredictable. Organized response, at this larger systemic level, has become a relatively new role for professional counselors. While such response certainly is within the scope of practice for professional counselors, little instruction concerning stress, crisis, disaster, and trauma is reflected in the mandates of professional accreditation standards. Likewise, the professional code of ethics offers little guidance for ethical conduct or practice issues related to stress, crisis, disaster, and trauma (Tarvydas et al., 2017); Tarvydas et al. (2017) have begun to address these ethical/ professional lacunae by suggesting ethical guidelines for mass trauma and complex humanitarian emergencies, and thus by extension, for addressing stress and crisis (the intersections of professional ethics with crisis, trauma, and disaster are detailed in Chapter 29 of this textbook). Like Rodin's (2014) notion of the dividend that accrues from building resilient communities, we need to move the professional mindset from one that is based solely on preparedness to one that includes adaptation to the increasing stressors and crises associated with contemporary life.

CONCLUSION

This chapter has focused on identifying theories and practices associated with stress and crisis, with a particular emphasis on presenting strategies for stress management and crisis intervention. An additional aim of the chapter has been to illuminate the trauma scaffold being constructed across Chapters 1, 2, 3, and 4 as a means for developing awareness of critical foundational constructs necessary for understanding the more complex issues that are examined in the remaining chapters of this book.

Regardless of which models of stress management and crisis intervention a counselor elects to use, it is important for the counselor to maintain a focus on client needs. It also is imperative

...essional helpers to be familiar with the specific mechanisms and dynamics of the selected ...del and to ensure that the model is compatible with their broader clinical framework and practice. In many ways, effective stress management and crisis intervention skills form a strong foundation in responding effectively to other trauma events and disaster situations.

ADDITIONAL RESOURCES

 A robust set of instructor resources designed to supplement this text is located at http://connect.springerpub.com/content/book/978-0-8261-5085-1. Qualifying instructors may request access by emailing textbook@springerpub.com.

PRACTICE-BASED RESOURCES AND REFERENCES

To view a list of resources and all the references, please visit connect.springerpub.com via the following url: http://connect.springerpub.com/content/book/978-0-8261-5085-1/part/part01/chapter/ch03

CHAPTER 4

Neurobiological Effects of Trauma and Psychopharmacology

JOHN R. TOMKO

CHAPTER OVERVIEW

Posttraumatic stress disorder (PTSD) is a condition that is characterized by profound neurochemical and neuroendocrine changes in the central nervous system (CNS). The physical response to trauma, in those susceptible to its development, can induce physical and behavioral changes. Understanding the impact of these neural changes is the basis for developing a rational medication therapy regimen for a client diagnosed with PTSD. The use of these medications is vital for symptom management so that the benefits of counseling can be realized. This chapter will discuss the neuronal and pathophysiological impact of trauma on the brain while subsequently describing how medications can impact symptom improvement. Medications that are discussed in this chapter include the use of antidepressants, antipsychotics, and other novel agents used in the pharmacotherapy of PTSD. Both U.S. Food and Drug Administration (FDA)-approved medications and "off-label" medications are explored.

LEARNING OBJECTIVES

After reading this chapter, the reader should be able to:

1. Describe the neurochemical changes that develop as a result of trauma;
2. Recognize the core symptoms of PTSD based on the *Diagnostic and Statistical Manual of Mental Disorders*, 5th edition criteria (*DSM-5*);
3. Explain the rationale for the use of specific medications for trauma (both FDA-approved and "off-label");
4. Recognize differences in pharmacotherapeutic treatment modalities based upon the etiology of PTSD; and,
5. Integrate knowledge of the medications into the development of an initial pharmacotherapy regimen for a client case.

INTRODUCTION

The purpose of this chapter is to explore the underlying neurochemistry and pathology of PTSD. Subsequently, medications that are commonly prescribed in the treatment of PTSD are discussed.

Emphasis is placed upon the expected drug mechanism of action in the treatment of this disorder. Through the integration of knowledge of the underlying disorder, coupled with the understanding of drug mechanisms, the reader should achieve a greater appreciation of the pharmacotherapy of PTSD. Armed with this knowledge, mental health professionals can better treat and monitor their clients affected by trauma.

The goals of this chapter are achieved in the discussions found in the following sections: Physical Response to Trauma, the Brain and Physiological Impact of Trauma, The Need for Medications in the Treatment of Posttraumatic Stress Disorder, Commonly Prescribed Medications in Treatment of Posttraumatic Stress Disorder, and Counseling Implications. These discussions are followed by a closing summary and an online list of helpful resources for instructors, students, and clinicians.

PHYSICAL RESPONSE TO TRAUMA

It is generally known that physiological trauma influences a person's health, well-being, and quality of life. Recovery from trauma of this sort may be a long-term, possibly lifelong, and often incomplete process. Psychological trauma, however, may be missed or discounted upon client evaluation, leading to underdiagnosis (Blank, 1994; Grinage, 2003; McPherson, 2003). As in physiological trauma, psychological trauma recovery processes may involve long-term, possibly lifelong, care and management. Trauma of this type affects clients in quality of life, activities of daily living, and can severely influence overall functioning (Grinage, 2003). Exposure to a traumatic event can lead to traumatic stress. The traumatic stress caused by exposure to an actual or perceived risk of death or serious injury, or the threat to physical integrity of oneself or others, can lead to a potentially chronic and debilitating illness referred to asPTSD. PTSD is characterized by a cluster of symptoms that includes persistent intrusive thoughts, phobic avoidance, hyperarousal, and negative changes in cognition and mood. See Table 4.1 for a list of diagnostic criteria. These signs can express in affected clients with such behaviors as impulsivity, aggression, or even depression (American Psychiatric Association, 2013; Davis et al., 2001). Common classifications of such types of psychological or physical trauma which can induce PTSD include abuse (mental, physical, sexual, or verbal); catastrophe (accidents, natural disasters, or terrorism); violent attack (assault, rape, or battery); and combat/warfare exposure. Estimates of the lifetime prevalence of PTSD in the general adult U.S. population are 1% to 12% (Lange et al., 2000; Yehuda, 2004), with an estimated 30% of men and women who have been in war zones having been diagnosed with the disorder (Kessler et al., 1995; Kulka et al., 1990). Early life trauma is recognized as a risk factor for development of psychiatric illnesses later in life, such as major depressive disorder (MDD; Ballenger et al., 2004). It also is known that females develop the condition at between two and four times the rate as males (Grinage, 2003; Yehuda, 2002).

Clients who go on to develop PTSD after exposure to a stressful and traumatic event exhibit the hallmark signs of the disorder, which include reexperiencing of the event, avoidance of reminders of the event, and hyperarousal. Further, these symptoms express in conjunction with negative feelings or beliefs about oneself, distorted cognition, emotional detachment, isolation, or an inability to experience positive emotions. The onset of the disorder is also characterized by three different subtypes of PTSD: acute, chronic, and delayed onset. The acute PTSD subtype has a very rapid onset following the event, with symptoms lasting fewer than 3 months. Chronic PTSD symptoms may last 3 months or longer. Finally, the delayed onset client may begin experiencing symptoms of PTSD 6 months or longer following exposure to a traumatic event (American Psychiatric Association, 2013).

Psychological trauma can lead to significant changes in neurochemical and neurobiological functioning. Early life trauma has been shown to be a significant risk factor for the development of psychiatric illness later in life, including PTSD, other anxiety disorders, and depression. The neurobiological and neurochemical changes that occur as a result of early life stressors may persist or express later in life (Heim & Nemeroff, 1999, 2001). These changes have been well

Table 4.1

Diagnostic Criteria for Posttraumatic Stress Disorder

The person was exposed to: death, threatened death, actual or threatened serious injury, or actual or threatened sexual violence, in the following way(s):

Criterion A required	1. Direct exposure
	2. Witnessing the trauma
	3. Learning that a relative or close friend was exposed to a trauma
	4. Indirect exposure to aversive details of the trauma, usually in the course of professional duties (e.g., first responders, medics)
Criterion B1 required	The traumatic event is persistently re-experienced, in the following way(s):
	1. Intrusive thoughts
	2. Nightmares
	3. Flashbacks
	4. Emotional distress after exposure to traumatic reminders
	5. Physical reactivity after exposure to traumatic reminders
Criterion C1 required	Avoidance of trauma-related stimuli after the trauma, in the following way(s):
	1. Trauma-related thoughts or feelings
	2. Trauma-related reminders
Criterion D2 required	Negative thoughts or feelings that began or worsened after the trauma, in the following way(s):
	1. Inability to recall key features of the trauma
	2. Overly negative thoughts and assumptions about oneself or the world
	3. Exaggerated blame of self or others for causing the trauma
	4. Negative affect
	5. Decreased interest in activities
	6. Feeling isolated
	7. Difficulty experiencing positive affect
Criterion E2 required	Trauma-related arousal and reactivity that began or worsened after the trauma, in the following way(s)
	1. Irritability or aggression
	2. Risky or destructive behavior
	3. Hypervigilance
	4. Heightened startle reaction
	5. Difficulty concentrating
	6. Difficulty sleeping
Criterion F required	Symptoms last for more than 1 month
Criterion G required	Symptoms cause significant distress or functional impairment
Criterion H required	Symptoms are not due to medication, substance use, or other illness

Source: Adapted from Department of Veteran Affairs, Department of Defense. (2017, June). *VA/DoD clinical practice guideline for the management of posttraumatic stress disorder and acute stress disorder)*. https://www.healthquality.va.gov/guidelines/MH/ptsd/VADoDPTSDCPGFinal012418.pdf

documented and have a significant influence upon the development of PTSD (Bremner et al., 1997; Carlson & Earls, 1997; DeBellis, Baum, et al., 1999; DeBellis, Keshaven, et al., 1999).

Although many people have been exposed to trauma in their lives, only a portion go on to develop the signs and symptoms of PTSD. It is estimated that 70% of the world's population has been exposed to trauma, while an estimated 6% of exposed individuals progress onward to develop PTSD (Koenen et al., 2017). Estimates of PTSD development in combat veterans may be as high as 25% (Fulton et al., 2015). The factors for the risk of the development of PTSD are not fully understood. The experiencing of abusive relationships, victimization of physical or mental abuse, surviving violent attacks or overtures, witnessing a violent act or traumatic event, or being interjected into a violent or disturbing situation do not necessarily cause a person to develop PTSD. Clients' risk for development of the disorder and their resilience following exposure to an event are areas that require further study. Studies suggest that previous exposure to trauma and intensity of the response to acute trauma may affect the development of PTSD. Neurochemical changes, particularly lower cortisol levels, may influence information processing of traumatic memories and may be associated with the underlying pathology of PTSD (Yehuda, 2004).

THE BRAIN AND PHYSIOLOGICAL IMPACT OF TRAUMA

Following a traumatic event or witnessing a traumatic event, the CNS begins to develop neurochemical pathways and physiological adaptations to respond to the situation. Areas of the brain which involve memory, such as the amygdala and hippocampus, have increased reactivity to stimuli following acute situations (Yehuda, 2002). People also develop changes in hippocampus function and memory processing, suggesting a possible reason for the symptoms of reexperiencing of a traumatic event. PTSD also has shown increased synaptic activity of norepinephrine in the CNS which is the neurotransmitter released from the locus coeruleus and responsible for the "fight-or-flight" response, as well as increased reactivity of the alpha-2 adrenergic receptors, stimulation of which is responsible for increased heart rate, blood pressure, and anxiety response. Increased norepinephrine, coupled with increased sensitivity of the adrenergic binding sites, promote worsening of the anxiety symptoms common in PTSD (Southwick et al., 1999). Following exposure, persons that have developed PTSD are shown to have significantly higher norepinephrine levels when compared to unaffected controls (Pan et al., 2018).

PTSD, similar to anxiety disorders such as generalized anxiety disorder and panic disorder, are characterized by a CNS imbalance between two distinct neurotransmitters, serotonin and norepinephrine. Serotonin, which is responsible for mood regulation in the brain, is found to be normal to slightly diminished in anxiety disorders. The serotonin center of the brain is located within the upper brainstem in the form of two organelles, the dorsal and rostral raphe nuclei. The raphe nuclei release serotonin for mood regulation as well as other bodily functions such as gastrointestinal regulation, skeletal muscle tone, platelet function, and temperature regulation. Located just near the rostral raphe nuclei is the norepinephrine center of the brain, the locus coeruleus. Norepinephrine release from the locus is greatly increased in trauma and anxiety disorders. Increases in norepinephrine in the brain and periphery are characterized by anxiety, tremors, increased focus, increases in blood pressure, and tachycardia. When an increase in norepinephrine is overlaid with normal to decreased serotonin function, clients present with symptoms attributable to psychic anxiety (Charney et al., 1987). Centrally within the brain and spinal cord, clients present with nervousness, agitation, sleep disturbances, hypervigilance, and heightened memory and thought processing. Peripherally, clients may present with physiological or somatic symptoms of anxiety such as tachycardia; high blood pressure; rapid, shallow breathing; and tremors (see Figure 4.1).

Another type of physiological change that is unique to PTSD, in contrast to the other anxiety disorders, involves CNS and peripheral adaptation of the body's response to corticotropin-releasing hormone (CRH) from the pituitary gland, located in the basal anterior portion of the brain. The pituitary gland works on a feedback mechanism in conjunction with the hypothalamus (located in the midbrain) and the adrenal glands, located on the dorsal area of the kidneys. These organs comprise the hypothalamus–pituitary–adrenal axis (HPA axis). In normal body function, CRH is released by the pituitary gland, located in the basal anterior portion of the brain. The normal progression of function of the HPA axis is as follows: CRH is released from the hypothalamus, which in turn signals the pituitary gland to release adrenocorticotropic

Figure 4.1

Brain Structures That Are Affected by Trauma

Take particular notice of the location of the locus coeruleus, dorsal raphe nucleus, amygdala, hypothalamus, and hippocampus.

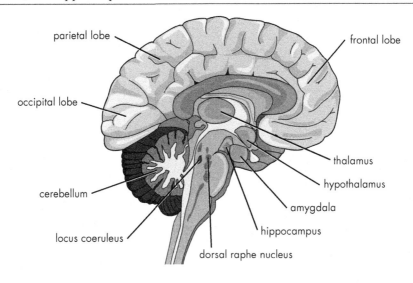

Source: Adapted from Lundbeck Institute. (2000). *The areas of the brain affected in phobia*. CNS Forum. http://www.cnsforum.com/imagebank/item/Neuro_biol_PHB/default.aspx

hormone (ACTH), otherwise called corticotropin. Corticotropin release causes the adrenal glands to release cortisol, a glucocorticoid which has many responsibilities in the body, one of which is mitigation of the stress response. In PTSD, altered response to CRH occurs. Increased levels of CRH are detected in PTSD clients; however, there is diminished response to this CRH release in the pituitary. Therefore, based upon the normal progression of the HPA axis, greatly decreased levels of cortisol are released from the adrenal glands. The net effect is decreased levels of cortisol, which produces a diminished stress response from the body (Yehuda, 2002). Decreased release of cortisol has been evidenced by significantly decreased 24-hour urinary cortisol concentrations in those that have developed PTSD (Pan et al., 2020).

With the presence of a pronounced norepinephrine effect, coupled with a diminished cortisol response, clients who develop PTSD may have an increased and protracted exposure to high levels of norepinephrine. This norepinephrine increase, coupled with an imbalance of normal serotonin concentrations, may cause clients to express signs and symptoms similar to anxiety disorders. In addition to the stress and anxiety response caused as a part of norepinephrine increase, the PTSD client also presents with diminished cortisol production. Because cortisol is attributed to mitigation of the stress response through neuroprotection, the amygdala and hippocampus memory areas of the brain are subject to a sustained exposure to high norepinephrine levels. This sustained exposure to high norepinephrine leads to increased levels of norepinephrine within the cerebrospinal fluid, leading to increased and prolonged excitability and signaling within the CNS. In the absence of the neuroprotective effects of cortisol, sustained norepinephrine exposure within the amygdala and hippocampus may lead to an ingrained response to the offending stimuli. Research has shown that, in addition to amygdala and hippocampal damage, high levels of unchecked norepinephrine may be a possible trigger to emotion expression in the prefrontal cortex area of the brain, the area attributed to executive functioning (Arnsten, 2007). It further has been shown that there are definitive changes in the

Figure 4.2

Relationship of Glial Cells (Astrocytes) to Neuronal Synapse

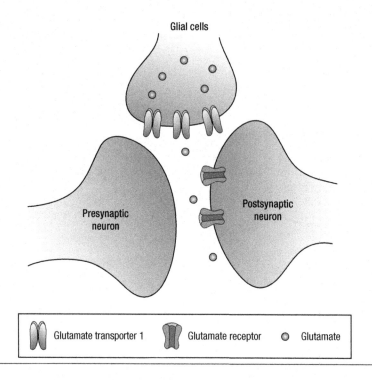

locus coereleus in some diagnosed PTSD clients on autopsy, which possibly may be a reason for prolonged norepinephrine response (Bracha et al., 2005).

Another proposed contributor to the development of PTSD has been the amino acid-based pathology (ABP). Whereas prior theories have emphasized the monoamine theory (e.g., norepinephrine excess), the ABP theory suggests that there is greatly dysregulated glutamatergic activity; thus, excessive release of glutamate from the glial cells results in synaptic damage. As a stimulatory signaling amino acid released from the astrocytes (glial cell), excessive release of glutamate may result in excessive stimulation, loss of neural plasticity, and synaptic damage (Abdallah et al., 2019). See glial cell location in Figure 4.2.

In the treatment of PTSD, psychotherapies (talk therapies) have been considered the mainstay of treatment. Some of the more familiar therapies include several strategies such as cognitive behavioral therapy (CBT) in the form of exposure therapy, stress inoculation, cognitive therapy, and Eye Movement Desensitization and Reprocessing (Seedat et al., 2005), and therapy may include combinations of these CBT methods (Bryant et al., 1999). Supportive counseling also has been employed (Bryant et al., 1998). Clients engage in these therapies to de-escalate, discover root causes of behaviors and reactions, and develop new coping mechanisms to manage the stressors brought about by the trauma response.

As we already know, PTSD is characterized by the four sets of core symptoms exhibited by the disorder; that is, reexperiencing, avoidance, persistent negative alterations in mood and cognition, and hyperarousal. These symptoms persist for greater than 1 month. During psychological treatments, or in the performance of activities of daily living, core symptoms may cause inordinate anxiety, which can pose significant barriers to successful emoting of feelings, beliefs, and reactions. Inability to manage these barriers subsequently may lead to suboptimal outcomes throughout the course of treatment, causing clients to feel overwhelmed and hindering therapeutic alliance formation during these therapeutic encounters. In cases such as these, the addition of medication therapies is warranted. Individuals diagnosed with mild acute PTSD may not need medications to engage in psychotherapy. Clients with the diagnoses of mild chronic PTSD, severe acute PTSD, and severe chronic PTSD would benefit from the dual treatment modalities that combination pharmacotherapy and psychotherapy can provide. Therefore, the choice of whether or not to use medications is based upon severity and duration of symptoms.

The medications used for the treatment of PTSD work on one or all of the core symptoms, allowing the client to engage fully in psychological therapies to gain maximal benefit from treatment. These medications provide the client with resolution of the symptoms during activities of daily living and in psychotherapy sessions, giving clients a better opportunity to experience improved day-to-day functioning while simultaneously allowing them to apply the coping mechanisms garnered during these therapy sessions.

THE NEED FOR MEDICATIONS IN THE TREATMENT OF POSTTRAUMATIC STRESS DISORDER

Medications have become a valuable management tool in the treatment of PTSD. Although talk therapies such as CBT, group therapies, Eye Movement Desensitization and Reprocessing, and others are effective in the treatment of this disorder, medications are a welcome addition to the treatment armamentarium of clinicians. Medications have been shown to be helpful in the management of core symptoms of the disorder, which can aid clients in their engagement in various psychotherapies and assist persons afflicted with the disorder in improving their function in activities of daily living.

Many different agents have been employed in the medical treatment of PTSD, despite the fact that many of these agents do not have approval from the FDA for PTSD treatment. When medications are used that do not have FDA approval for treatment of a specific condition, despite the fact that there is evidence demonstrating effectiveness of the agent, the use of the agent in such circumstances is termed "off-label use" in practice. Most medications that are used to treat PTSD are employed "off-label." Currently, only two medications have FDA approval for the treatment of PTSD. The following sections discuss the various classes of drugs employed in treatment, both FDA-approved medications and off-label medications. The list of commonly prescribed medications, both approved and off-label, are provided in Tables 4.2 to 4.4.

COMMONLY PRESCRIBED MEDICATIONS IN TREATMENT OF POSTTRAUMATIC STRESS DISORDER

Antidepressants: Selective Serotonin Reuptake Inhibitors

Selective serotonin reuptake inhibitor (SSRI) agents are a class of medication that have been studied and used extensively in the treatment of various medical conditions. Each individual agent (with the exception of fluvoxamine) has been approved by the FDA for the treatment of MDD. They also carry FDA approvals for the treatment of various anxiety disorders; however, each individual agent may carry approvals for specific subsets of anxiety disorders.

The mechanism of action of these agents, as described by their drug class, is the prevention of serotonin reuptake into the neural presynaptic vesicles. Simply put, these agents prohibit serotonin from being reabsorbed into the presynaptic nerve terminal, thereby increasing the amount of serotonin available in the nerve synapse. By increasing the available serotonin in the synapse between the neurons, there is an increased amount of serotonin available to stimulate the postsynaptic neuron. Increasing serotonin stimulation at the postsynaptic neuron allows more serotonin-mediated signaling to be carried forth. As previously discussed, serotonin is responsible for mood regulation. Therefore, by increasing serotonin stimulation, clients can see improvement in mood symptoms (Stahl, 2000).

Table 4.2

Antidepressants That Have Been Used in Posttraumatic Stress Disorder

Generic name	Brand name	Usual dosage range (mg/day)
SSRIs		
Sertraline#	Zoloft	25–200
Paroxetine#	Paxil	20–60
	Paxil CR	12.5–62.5
Citalopram	Celexa	20–60
Escitalopram	Lexapro	10–20
Fluoxetine	Prozac	20–80
Fluvoxamine	Luvox*	25–300
SNRIs		
Venlafaxine	Effexor	37.5–225
	Effexor XR	
Duloxetine	Cymbalta	20–120
Mixed mechanism agents		
Mirtazapine	Remeron	15–45
Bupropion	Wellbutrin	75–450
	Wellbutrin SR	
	Wellbutrin XL	
Nefazodone	Serzone*	100–600
Trazodone	Desyrel*	50–600
Tricyclic agents		
Amitriptyline	Elavil*	25–300
Imipramine	Tofranil*	25–300
	Tofranil PM	
Desipramine	Pamelor	25–300
MAOI		
Phenelzine	Nardil	45–90

#FDA approved for PTSD. *Brand name discontinued; generic available.

FDA, U.S. Food and Drug Administration; MAOI, monoamine oxidase inhibitors; PTSD, posttraumatic stress disorder; SNRI, serotonin-norepinephrine reuptake Inhibitor; SSRI, selective serotonin reuptake inhibitors.

This mechanism has been shown to be quite useful in treating MDD, where there is a decrease in serotonin as well as a decrease in norepinephrine. By increasing synaptic serotonin in MDD, the locus coeruleus may respond as well by increasing norepinephrine output. Therefore, serotonin and norepinephrine achieve a balance, which improves mood, energy, and concentration. Trauma and anxiety disorders, however, have a different type of neurochemical imbalance. Anxiety disorders, such as generalized anxiety disorder and panic disorder, as well as PTSD, exhibit an increased amount of norepinephrine in the CNS, contrasted with a relative decrease in serotonin, leading to neurochemical balance. Because CNS serotonin is decreased in anxiety disorders, the attributes of norepinephrine are exhibited that are characteristic of anxiety: psychic anxiety, tremulousness, somatic anxiety, hyperreactivity, increased blood pressure, and increased heart rate. Because the effects of increased norepinephrine express in anxiety disorders due to the inability of serotonin to offset the increase, SSRI agents are helpful in managing all three core symptoms of PTSD through an increase in available serotonin, creating a balance between serotonin and norepinephrine.

Table 4.3

Antipsychotic Agents That Have Been Used in Posttraumatic Stress Disorder

Generic name	Brand name	Usual dosage range (mg/day)
Atypical agents		
Risperidone	Risperdal	2–6
Quetiapine	Seroquel	200–900
	Seroquel XR	
Olanzapine	Zyprexa	5–40
Ziprasidone	Geodon	40–200
Typical agents		
Haloperidol	Haldol*	2–100
Fluphenazine	Prolixin*	2.5–40
Perphenazine	Trilafon*	8–64

*Brand name discontinued; generic available.

Table 4.4

Adjunctive Agents Used in Posttraumatic Stress Disorder*

Generic name	Brand name	Usual dosage range (mg/day)
Clonidine	Catapres	0.1–0.6
Guanfacine	Tenex	1–3
Prazosin	Minipress	1–20

*No agents approved for PTSD.

Upon examination, core symptoms of PTSD can be attributed to increases in CNS norepinephrine as well as decreases in serotonin. Reestablishing this balance can help to improve core symptoms and improve client daily functioning. Clients also are able to participate in their psychological treatments in a more enriching manner and to function at a higher degree in their daily lives.

SSRI agents are considered first-line agents in the pharmacotherapy of PTSD and have been used extensively in client treatment. Of the SSRIs, the only ones that have been approved by the FDA for the treatment of PTSD are sertraline (Zoloft, 2010) and paroxetine (Paxil, 2010). Additionally, they are the only two of any medication class that are FDA approved for the treatment of PTSD. This is not to say that other SSRIs have not been used "off-label" in the treatment of PTSD. As discussed earlier in this chapter, many of these medications have been used off-label in PTSD treatment. This practice is common in medicine, and the use of unapproved agents to treat various conditions sometimes may be considered the standard of practice. An everyday example of this is the use of a daily aspirin tablet for treatment post-heart attack or stroke. Aspirin was never approved by the FDA for this; nonetheless, the agent has been studied and shown to decrease the risk of developing another coronary event by inhibiting platelet aggregation. Likewise, many SSRI agents also have been employed in the treatment of PTSD.

If we stop and take a brief moment to examine the root causes of the psychic and somatic symptoms of PTSD, it can be seen that, based upon the serotonin and norepinephrine imbalance, SSRI agents should be quite effective in restoring balance. Of primary concern, however, is an effect that was discussed; if serotonin is stimulated from the raphe nuclei, a reflexive increase in norepinephrine may occur from the locus coeruleus that may occur more rapidly than the serotonin increase. In order to prevent this, dosing of SSRI agents in PTSD treatment, as well as in other anxiety disorders, usually begins at the low end of the dosing range. Once the client shows a positive improvement from the selected agent, the dose is titrated upward slowly, observing the client for worsening anxiety symptoms. If no worsening occurs, the client continues to be titrated slowly upward to higher drug doses.

It should be kept in mind that SSRI agents do not exhibit an immediate onset of effect. These agents increase synaptic serotonin concentrations slowly, gradually allowing the serotonin concentration to increase in the neural synapses. This concentration increase should occur over 8 to 12 weeks in PTSD, which is slightly longer than in other anxiety disorders or depression; therefore, the resolution of symptoms occurs over time. Clients who are treated with SSRI agents should be educated to have patience for the onset of optimal drug effects. It is also important for them to understand that adherence to psychotherapies and medications will provide them with the best opportunity for positive treatment outcomes.

As SSRI medications begin their action, stimulation caused by increased serotonin may improve mood and offset anxieties with a concurrent increase in headache, nausea, and diarrhea. Some of these side effects may be self-limiting, and as the CNS and gastrointestinal (GI) tract accommodate, the side effects should subside. If they do not subside within a few weeks, clients may need to switch the medication to a different SSRI or other medication treatment. Other side effects that are attributed to the use of SSRI agents include changes in sexual drive or sexual dysfunction as well as weight gain, both of which may be particularly distressing in younger clients.

Although SSRI agents are considered first-line pharmacotherapy, these agents have been shown to be more effective in the treatment of civilian trauma such as domestic violence, rape, and mental abuse as opposed to combat-related trauma. SSRIs may have some value in combat-related trauma, and modest improvement seen in combat-related stress may be caused by lack of chronicity of illness in younger clients, confounded by their use in predominantly male populations (Hertzberg et al., 2000; Zohar et al., 2002). It also has been shown that both paroxetine and sertraline have improved short-term outcomes in PTSD (Beebe et al., 2000; Brady et al., 2000; Davidson, Rothbaum, et al., 2001); however, sertraline also exhibits the added benefit of long-term symptom improvement (Davidson, Pearlstein, et al., 2001). Other types of antidepressants or medications have shown improvement on Clinician Administered PTSD Scale (CAPS) scores than SSRI agents in Veterans Administration-treated clients (Davis et al., 2002).

Other Antidepressants: Adjunct Medications

Although no other antidepressants other than the SSRIs sertraline and paroxetine carry FDA approval for the treatment of PTSD, we know that others are used off-label for treatment. Such is the case for the following classes of antidepressants.

Serotonin–Norepinephrine Reuptake Inhibitors

Perhaps the best studied of these agents in the treatment of PTSD is venlafaxine. Venlafaxine is FDA approved and has been used in the treatment of MDD, generalized anxiety disorder, panic disorder, and social anxiety disorder in order to increase serotonin concentrations at the neural synapse, much in the same way SSRI agents do. The agent is not FDA approved for the treatment of PTSD; however, it has been used for treatment (Hamner & Frueh, 1998; Smajkic et al., 2001). What is interesting about venlafaxine is that it inhibits serotonin at approximately 10 times the rate of inhibiting norepinephrine. Therefore, this medication is usually dosed at the lower dose ranges in anxiety disorders. If doses exceed 225 mg per day, the norepinephrine effects begin to become significant, leading to anxiety and increases in blood pressure. Therefore, venlafaxine is prescribed and FDA approved for anxiety disorders in doses less than 225 mg per day (Preskorn, 1994).

Venlafaxine, although effective, exhibits some side effects that are more severe than those found with SSRIs, namely nausea and headache (Agency for Healthcare Quality and Research, 2007).

Another agent considered an SNRI is duloxetine. Duloxetine is an antidepressant that exhibits both serotonin and norepinephrine reuptake inhibition and is approved for the treatment of MDD, generalized anxiety disorder, diabetic nerve pain, and fibromyalgia (Cymbalta, 2010). Results of trials of duloxetine in PTSD have shown mixed results, and this agent is generally not used in PTSD. One such study indicated that duloxetine may have some benefit in the treatment of PTSD by causing improvements in sleep (Walderhaug et al., 2010). In contrast, another study has shown exacerbations of PTSD core symptoms with the use of the agent (Deneys & Ahearn, 2006). It also should be kept in mind that duloxetine carries a contraindication to use in alcoholism and liver dysfunction. Because substance dependence can co-occur at a high rate in the PTSD client, consideration should be given to the possibility of comorbid alcohol abuse in the PTSD client.

Mirtazapine

Mirtazapine is an agent that has been used adjunctively, or in addition to primary medication treatment, in the treatment of PTSD. Very few clinical studies supporting the use of mirtazapine have been performed; however, its ability to help with sleep induction is the reason it is used as an add-on agent to the primary antidepressant. The drug has a unique mechanism of action, a centrally acting synaptic α2 antagonist. In the neural synapses, α receptors are present that interact with sympathetic neurotransmitters such as norepinephrine. Interacting with α2 receptors on the presynaptic surface of the nerve within the brain (e.g., centrally acting agent) causes negative feedback. This negative feedback leads to a release of serotonin and norepinephrine from the presynaptic vesicles contained in the terminal of the neuron. In summary, the effect makes more serotonin and norepinephrine available to stimulate the postsynaptic neuron receptors, allowing for increased action and transmission from these neurotransmitters (RemeronSolTabs, 2010). Mirtazapine also possesses antihistamine activity, which can cause drowsiness, especially at lower doses (de Boer, 1996). As stated earlier, the drug has been employed in anxiety disorders and depression for sleep in conjunction with the primary antidepressant. Therefore, this agent is used as a part of combination therapy and not as a primary treatment.

Tricyclic Antidepressants

The tricyclic antidepressants (TCA) are some of the oldest marketed antidepressants available. These drugs work by inhibiting reuptake of serotonin and norepinephrine into the neural presynaptic vesicles, thereby increasing the availability of neurotransmitters. This mechanism may sound familiar; the action is similar to the SNRI agents. Unfortunately, these agents also possess action at many other receptor systems in the body, leading to adverse effects. TCA agents interact with the cholinergic system, blocking acetylcholine effects and leading to such side effects as dry mouth, constipation, and urinary retention. They also have an antihistamine effect, leading to drowsiness. TCA agents also can cause cardiac-related adverse effects through blockade of α1 receptors and calcium channel blockade. These interactions can lead to orthostatic hypotension and some cardiac arrhythmias, especially in higher doses. Based on the increased risk of adverse effects with the TCA agents, they are not employed as first-line pharmacotherapy in PTSD today, nor are they approved for use by the FDA.

TCAs that have historically been used in PTSD include desipramine, amitriptyline, and imipramine. These agents were used in the treatment of the disorder prior to the advent of SSRI agents. In the past, amitriptyline was used as a treatment of PTSD much in the same way as SSRI and SNRI agents are employed today. Despite its use, most clients still continued with persistent symptoms of the disorder despite attempts to optimize dose. In one study (Davidson et al., 1990), clients receiving amitriptyline showed greater improvement if they presented with another comorbid disorder versus placebo; however, recovery rates were low in the presence of comorbid disorders such as depression, panic disorder, and alcoholism. Imipramine also has been used historically for management of PTSD symptoms with similar results to amitriptyline (Frank et al., 1988). Bearing this in mind, newer agents such as the SSRI drugs provide much more effective treatment of core symptoms than their older counterparts.

Nefazodone and Trazodone

This agent has been used in the treatment of depression and other anxiety disorders; however, nefazodone is not FDA approved for the treatment of PTSD. Nefazodone is considered a mixed mechanism antidepressant. These agents exhibit a mixed effect upon serotonin; they can work upon serotonin reuptake inhibition like an SSRI, but also block the action of serotonin at certain serotonin receptor subtypes in the post-synapse area (Nefazodone, 2010). This is theorized to improve serotonin transmission through the serotonin receptor subtypes that help to improve mood and anxieties. Nefazodone has been used to improve some PTSD symptoms, subjectively improve sleep quality, and decrease nightmares (Nefazodone, 2010). It also has been shown to cause PTSD symptom improvement in combat-related stress as well as in domestically induced stress (Asnis et al., 2004).

The use of nefazodone has fallen out of favor in recent years, since the inclusion of a "black box" warning from the FDA. It was determined that nefazodone can cause increased risk of irreversible hepatic failure, resulting in death or need for liver transplantation. Clients should be advised to be alert for early signs and symptoms of liver dysfunction (e.g., jaundice, anorexia, gastrointestinal complaints, malaise) and to report them to their doctor immediately if they occur (Frank et al., 1988). Clients who are taking nefazodone should be adherent to physician appointments in order to have their hepatic function monitored by their physician.

Trazodone is another agent with a similar mechanism as nefazodone. Because this agent has a serotonergic effect, it was thought that it would be effective in PTSD. Earlier clinical trials have alluded to this. A preliminary study in PTSD clients showed that trazodone was effective on all three core symptoms of PTSD (Hertzberg et al., 1996). Despite this encouraging data, trazodone is known to cause excessive sedation. Therefore, further trials of the agent were studied as an adjunctive agent, in addition to a primary antidepressant, for improvement of sleep and prevention of nightmares. Insomnia, nightmares, and next-day anger all have been improved. Consequently, trazodone is used in addition to antidepressant agents for improvement in sleep dysregulation due to coexisting depression (Mellman et al., 2003).

Monoamine Oxidase Inhibitors

Antidepressants such as SSRI, SNRI, and TCA agents are known to produce their mechanism of action by prevention of neurotransmitter reuptake into the presynaptic vesicles, leading to increased concentrations of serotonin and norepinephrine available in the neural synapse. In the synapse between neurons, the enzyme monoamine oxidase (MAO) also is present. Its purpose is to degrade excess neurotransmitters such as serotonin and norepinephrine (MAO type A inhibitor [MAOI-A]) and dopamine (MAOI-B). MAOI agents inhibit the enzyme MAO, thus allowing greater concentrations of neurotransmitters to be present in the synapse by preventing their degradation. The agent phenelzine has been used for this purpose in PTSD. This drug has been used in PTSD and, further, has been shown to be effective in the treatment of combat-related stress (Kosten et al., 1991).

Despite their effectiveness, many severe adverse events limit their use in treatment. Clients who are prescribed MAOI agents must be aware of the drug–food interaction with foods containing tyramine. Tyramine restriction is necessary, as tyramine is a precursor of the production of norepinephrine. Ingestion of tyramine-containing foods can lead to increased norepinephrine production. This increase, coupled with the inhibition of the breakdown of norepinephrine caused by MAOI action, may cause a dangerous medical condition known as hypertensive crisis. Hypertensive crisis is the increase in blood pressure to sustained, dangerously high levels. Therefore, clients should be told to avoid such foods as aged cheeses, red wine, legumes, and organ meats. Increased intake of tyrosine should be avoided as well because tyrosine is the precursor to serotonin synthesis.

MAOI drugs are also notorious for numerous drug–drug interactions. Because these drugs inhibit neurotransmitter degradation, the clinician should be careful to avoid MAOI use in clients who are taking other medications which increase neurotransmitter concentrations. Agents used for asthma, attention deficit disorder, Parkinson's disease, certain pain medications (tramadol and meperidine), weight loss medications, dextromethorphan, and even other antidepressants can cause serious, life-threatening interactions. Because of the comorbidity of substance abuse with PTSD, drugs such as amphetamines, cocaine, 3,4-methylenedioxymethamphetamine (MDMA [Ecstasy]), and lysergic acid diethylamide (LSD) can interact with MAOI agents, leading to the same deadly interactions. Because of the potential for these types of drug and food interactions, MAOI agents like phenelzine have been relegated to last-line pharmacotherapy in the treatment of PTSD. Additionally, MAOI agents are not FDA approved for PTSD.

Bupropion

Bupropion has been tried as a possible alternative to SSRI agents as a treatment for PTSD symptoms but has not been approved by the FDA for the treatment of PTSD. The drug works not through serotonin reuptake but upon preventing the reuptake of dopamine and norepinephrine into presynaptic vesicles. Bupropion has been used as a first-line agent in the treatment of depression in clients where sexual dysfunction caused by SSRI agents may be problematic. The use in PTSD, however, has been limited. In one small study (Cañive et al., 1998), the improvement seen in hyperarousal symptoms was significant but was less significant than the change in depressive symptoms in subjects with both PTSD and depression. There was no significant change in reexperiencing, avoidance, or total CAPS scores. Therefore, PTSD symptoms remained essentially unchanged (Cañive et al., 1998).

There has been little research in the form of placebo-controlled studies using bupropion in the treatment of PTSD. Bupropion has been studied in smoking cessation in clients who have been diagnosed with PTSD and was found to be effective for this use; however, no effect was seen upon PTSD symptoms. In this study (Hertzberg et al., 2001), clients were allowed to continue with their previous PTSD treatment, leading to the belief that this agent is an effective smoking deterrent in clients with PTSD. In yet another study (Becker et al., 2007) of 30 clients taking bupropion, and compared to a placebo-controlled group, no between-group differences were found between placebo and bupropion. Despite this, a post hoc analysis of responders showed that clients not previously prescribed an antidepressant were more likely to respond to bupropion (Hertzberg et al., 2001).

Further study of this agent is needed before recommendation of its use can be made in PTSD. The role of bupropion would most likely be as a second-line agent in clients who have experienced severe sexual dysfunction with serotonergic antidepressants.

Antipsychotic Agents: Atypical Antipsychotics

The term "atypical" can be considered almost a misnomer today. This term is used to identify the newer antipsychotic agents, which inhibit serotonin and dopamine activity. The older agents, also known as the "typical" agents, neuroleptics, or phenothiazines, work predominantly on dopamine blockade. Therefore, the newer agents work somewhat differently than the historical agents, hence "atypically." The most studied of these newer agents in the treatment of PTSD are risperidone, olanzapine, and quetiapine. Older "typical" agents such as haloperidol have been used as well.

Both typical and atypical antipsychotics have been used in the treatment of PTSD. Currently, the atypical agents are much more commonly used in pharmacotherapy. Antipsychotic agents have been used as add-on therapy in PTSD clients, especially on reexperiencing symptoms in which there has been inadequate symptom resolution with an antidepressant (Bartzokis et al., 2005; Pivac et al., 2004). Because of dopamine blockade, either of these classes can induce involuntary movement disorders similar to Parkinson's disease. The atypical agents, when used in the recommended dosages, have a much lower propensity to induce these movements. Atypical agents, however, can cause such things as weight gain, increase in serum cholesterol, and increased blood glucose, all of which may lead to worsening hypertension. Clients who are prescribed these medications should be monitored for all of the aforementioned adverse events during therapy.

Recently, information regarding the use of atypical agents in the treatment of combat-related PTSD have questioned their effectiveness. One such study found that the use of risperidone in this subset of traumatized clients, who were also resistant to SSRIs, was no more effective than placebo on the reduction of symptoms as measured by the CAPS scale (Krystal et al., 2011).

Antihypertensive Agents

Certain medications that have been used for the treatment of hypertension (high blood pressure) have been used in the treatment of PTSD for reduction of nightmares. In order to understand how these medications can be helpful in PTSD, we need to understand a bit about how these medications are believed to cause this effect. Prazosin, a postsynaptic $\alpha 1$ antagonist, works by decreasing the stimulation of norepinephrine on the postsynaptic receptors by blocking these receptors. Therefore, norepinephrine action (also called sympathetic outflow) is decreased, leading to increased drowsiness and decreased anxiety. Prazosin has been used in combat-related PTSD in the veteran population (Raskind et al., 2000).

Other agents that have been used for this purpose include clonidine and guanfacine. These agents are centrally acting presynaptic $\alpha 2$ agonists. This means that the drugs attach to the $\alpha 2$ receptors on the nerve terminal. They stimulate these receptors just as norepinephrine would. By stimulating the neuron in this way, the drug provides a negative feedback to the neuron. This essentially tricks the neuron into believing that there is an adequate supply of norepinephrine available in the synapse, causing a decrease in the amount of available norepinephrine in the synapse. The decreased norepinephrine, in turn, decreases the sympathetic outflow, similar to the effect of the aforementioned prazosin (Harmon & Riggs, 1996).

Benzodiazepines

It is interesting to note that benzodiazepine agents have been shown to be of no benefit in PTSD. Benzodiazepines exert their effect by increasing the effect of gamma-aminobutyric acid (GABA). GABA is the predominant inhibitory neurotransmitter within the CNS. Increases in GABA decrease the effect of norepinephrine, leading to anxiety relief (Stahl, 2000). Many of these agents are used as short-term therapy in other anxiety disorders, such as generalized anxiety disorder, in order to cause rapid decrease of the intrusive anxiety symptoms until the predominant drug therapy begins to exert its effect (SSRI agents). Examples of medications in this class include lorazepam, diazepam, alprazolam, and clonazepam. Paradoxically, and perhaps surprisingly, these agents have been shown to produce no positive benefits in PTSD, with no effect on reexperiencing, hypervigilance, or avoidance (Braun et al., 1990). Likewise, early administration following trauma exposure did nothing to prevent development of PTSD (Gelpin et al., 1996). Therefore, because benzodiazepine agents have been shown to be of no benefit in PTSD, their use is discouraged in this population.

Combat-Related Stress; Variations in Recommended Pharmacotherapy

As discussed earlier, Department of Defense and Veterans Administration treatment guidelines for PTSD differ from the pharmacotherapy of domestic-related stress. Table 4.5 provides the

Table 4.5

Level of Evidence for the Use of Medications in Combat-Related Stress

Quality of evidence*	Recommend for	Suggest for	Suggest against	Recommend against	No recommendation for or against
Moderate	Sertraline^		Prazosin (excluding the treatment of PTSD-associated nightmares)		Prazosin for the treatment of PTSD-associated nightmares
	Paroxetine^				
	Fluoxetine				
	Venlafaxine				
Low		Nefazodone±	Quetiapine Olanzapine	Divalproex Tiagabine	Eszopiclone
			Citalopram	Guanfacine	
			Amitriptyline		
Very low		Imipramine Phenelzine±	Lamotrigine Topiramate	Risperidone Benzodiazepines	Bupropion Desipramine
				D-cycloserine	D-serine
				Hydrocortisone	Escitalopram
				Ketamine	Mirtazapine
No data†					Antidepressants
					Doxepin
					Duloxetine‡
					Desvenlafaxine
					Fluvoxamine‡
					Levomilnacipran
					Nortriptyline
					Razodone
					Vilazodone
					Vortioxetine
					Anxiolytic/ Hypnotics
					Buspirone‡
					Cyproheptadine
					Hydroxyzine
					Zaleplon
					Zolpidem

*The Work Group determined there was no high-quality evidence regarding medication monotherapy.
^FDA approved for PTSD.
±Serious potential toxicity, should be managed carefully.
†No data were captured in the evidence review (based on the criteria in Conducting the Systematic Review) and were not considered in development of this table.
‡Studies of these drugs did not meet the inclusion criteria for the systematic evidence review due to poor quality.
Source: Adapted from Department of Veteran Affairs, Department of Defense. (2017, June). *VA/DoD clinical practice guideline for the management of posttraumatic stress disorder and acute stress disorder*). https://www.healthquality.va.gov/guidelines/MH/ptsd/VADoDPTSDCPGFinal012418.pdf

level of evidence for the use of each agent in the treatment of combat-related stress. Notice that sertraline and paroxetine are recommended although the evidence for their use is moderate. Additionally, prazosin is only recommended for the treatment of PTSD-associated nightmares. Antipsychotic agents such as risperidone or quetiapine, other antidepressants, and various other agents are not recommended for combat-related PTSD pharmacotherapy. Thus, the etiology of the development of PTSD should be explored by those caring for these individuals.

Treatment With Medical Marijuana

A number of state governments have legalized the use of cannabis for medicinal use in the forms of edibles, oils, or inhalation. Despite legalization of cannabis in various states, it is still considered illegal by federal law.

Cannabinoids contain two active chemicals in varying concentrations. These are tetrahydrocannabidiol (THC), which is the primary psychoactive chemical, and cannabidiol (CBD), which has no psychoactive properties and may mitigate some adverse effects of THC stimulation. Within the neuronal synapses of various areas of the brain, cannabinoid type 1 (CB-1) receptors exist which are stimulated by a naturally occurring transmitter called anandamide. Cannabinoids work similarly to anandamide but with more potency at the CB-1 receptor. Activating the CB-1 receptors in the amygdala can potentially decrease troublesome memories, fear, and anxiety. Stimulation of CB-1 receptors in the prefrontal cortex can increase serotonin and potentially produce antidepressant properties. Neuronal maturation, improved mood and memory, and a decrease in core PTSD symptoms with a normalization of cortisol may be seen when CB-1 receptors are agonized in the hippocampus. By stimulating the limbic system, there may be a decrease in amygdala and hypothalamus activity. This could assist in regulating the hypothalamic-pituitary axis and cortisol and, therefore, decrease hypervigilance and hyperarousal (Passie et al., 2012).

Despite the theoretical improvements suggested from the use of THC and CBD, analysis of study findings have shown equivocal results. In a recent literature review of medical marijuana use for PTSD treatment (Shishko et al., 2018), the benefits of medical marijuana (MM) were questionable due to severe limitations within the analyzed studies. The majority of evidence was found in anecdotal reports, case studies, or retrospective studies limited by design issues or sample size. One of the larger reviewed studies showed statistically insignificant improvements in PTSD symptoms while the largest reviewed study showed worsening PTSD symptoms following initiation of MM with improvements following discontinuation. The authors concluded that the low level of evidence, coupled with concerns regarding decrease in psychomotor activity and response, short-term memory, motivation, and ability to learn new concepts, results in low level of evidence for recommending MM in PTSD.

Another systematic review of the use of MM in PTSD was undertaken by the Department of Veterans Affairs (Kansagara et al., 2017). Findings were similar insofar as the low level of evidence for benefits of MM in PTSD. The authors also warn that cannabis use is associated with an increased risk of short-term adverse effects; however, data on its effects on long-term physical health vary. MM use is associated with cognitive impairment in active users and potentially serious mental health adverse effects such as psychotic symptoms, though the absolute risk and application specifically to PTSD populations are uncertain. The authors concluded that there is virtually no conclusive information about the benefits of MM in PTSD and limited information on harms, so methodologically strong research in almost any area of inquiry is likely to add to the strength of evidence.

Off-Label Treatment; Ketamine

The ABP theory of PTSD development has led to some clinical trials of the use of intravenous (IV) ketamine infusions for treatment. Ketamine activity occurs at the N-methyl-D-aspartate-type glutamate (NMDA) receptor as an antagonist. The glial cells release NMDA into the synapse; thus, ketamine decreases the effect of NMDA (Rasmussen, 2015). Small clinical trials of ketamine IV have shown rapid reversal of PTSD symptoms in those with chronic PTSD (Feder et al., 2014) as well as in chronic PTSD with comorbid depression (Albott et al., 2018). Despite early positive results with IV ketamine, there are concerns regarding dissociative adverse reactions. The FDA has recently approved an intranasal formulation of esketamine for the treatment of treatment-resistant depression and further larger clinical trials are currently underway for IV ketamine in PTSD with comorbid depression. Therefore, new data will be emerging in regard to the use of these NMDA antagonists in PTSD.

Drug Therapy Duration

Where pharmacological treatment is indicated, clients who are receiving medications for the treatment of PTSD should be continued on medication for varying lengths of time, based on the severity of symptoms and onset of the illness following psychological insult. A client diagnosed with acute onset of the disorder (symptoms present in more than 1 month but less than 3 months) should be continued on drug therapy for 6 to 12 months, at which time a slow downward titration off of the medication should be attempted. In clients who experience chronic trauma symptoms (greater than 3 months), medications should be continued for at least 1 year. If the client experiences adequate response or resolution of symptoms, medications should be continued for 1 to 2 years. At that time, the medication(s) may be slowly decreased in dose until the medication(s) can be safely discontinued. In cases wherein clients are experiencing residual symptoms following optimization of drug therapies, medications may continue for 24 months or longer.

In some clients, medications may be warranted indefinitely based on factors determined by the severity of the condition or social stressors. Such factors as lack of social support, "suicidal ideation," co-occurring mental health diagnosis, propensity for aggression or violence, and poor client function may indicate the need for long-term treatment with pharmacotherapy. Some clients may require medications throughout their lifetime.

Post Medication Recovery

Pharmacotherapy that is used for acute or chronic trauma symptoms is an important treatment for the survivor of trauma by restoring physiological, andneurochemical balance. In cases wherein medications may be decreased slowly or discontinued, it is important for clients to continue with currently prescribed psychotherapeutic modalities. Adherence with these types of treatments can aid clients in coping with symptoms and developing new approaches to management of stress. Insight into the symptoms of their condition is important for clients to develop in order to recognize reemergence of intrusive symptoms, which can cause relapse into the disorder. In such cases of worsening symptoms, clients should be restarted on pharmacotherapy, beginning with the medication or combination of medications that were useful in the prior episode.

Experimental Treatment; Vagal Nerve Stimulation

Newer research has been performed on the use of vagal nerve stimulation (VNS) as a potentially beneficial treatment for PTSD. The vagus nerve, which is the 10th cranial nerve, is implicated in extinguishment of fear response in numerous animal models. The vagus nerve innervates peripheral organ systems and its actions are mixed. Efferent signaling is accounted for by 20% of its transmission whereas 80% of transmission is afferent (Noble, Meruva, et al., 2019). VNS was approved in the United States in 1997 for the treatment of medication-resistant seizure disorders. In seizure disorders, stimulation of both right and left vagus nerves was used; however, stimulation of the right vagus nerve leads to potential slowing of heart rate through extinguishment of peripheral stimulation (Ben-Menachem, 2001). Therefore, VNS in PTSD is focused upon the left vagus nerve, producing extinguishment of peripheral "fight or flight" response. The role of the vagus nerve in this stress/arousal pathway and the specificity of electrical stimulation allow VNS to facilitate memory consolidation and synaptic plasticity (Peña et al., 2013).

The majority of research performed in VNS thus far has been in animal models utilizing rats (Noble, Meruva, et al., 2019). There has been a small pilot study (George et al., 2008) which has shown potential benefit in humans along with some ongoing clinical trials (Clinicaltrials.gov). A review has also suggested that left VNS may be helpful when combined with exposure-based therapies (Noble, Souza, et al., 2019).

COUNSELING IMPLICATIONS

It is important for each and every professional involved in the care of the PTSD client to be cognizant of any changes, both mentally and physically, that occur. Treatment of clients involves many disciplines, and optimal care for those afflicted with the disorder requires an integrated approach to care. Because of regular interactions, counselors are well positioned to observe the client for improvement in core symptoms of the disorder as well as the emergence of side effects. Clients who present with untoward, intolerable side effects such as worsening anxiety, nausea, headache, uncontrolled movements, dizziness, or drowsiness can be referred to their physician for evaluation of the client. Therefore, the accessibility of the counselor, coupled with the therapeutic alliances built with them, provide a perfect "clearing house" for improvements in psychological symptoms, while avoiding side effects or adverse drug reactions that may cause clients to become nonadherent with treatment. This is not to say that counselors are responsible for all clinical aspects of care. Healthcare-aware professionals need to be cognizant of the emergence of psychological symptoms of the disorder and to refer the client to the appropriate member of the care team. Optimal care of the client who presents with physical and mental symptoms cannot be performed in "silos" with little interaction among all professionals involved in treatment. Integrated care between healthcare and mental health professionals provides an all-encompassing, gestalt approach to care so that all aspects of the client's care are well managed.

CONCLUSION

Therapists who care for clients suffering from trauma-related disorders should be keenly aware that this subset of anxiety disorders has both psychological and physiological components, each of which requires optimal treatment. A thorough understanding of the pathology, both physical and mental, provides the groundwork for care and outcomes in the afflicted. Recognition of the client's needs and core symptoms is paramount to provision of favorable therapies, but it is not enough. Understanding how and when to intervene on these needs and symptoms provides clients with meaningful ways of living with and coping with PTSD. Integrating psychotherapy and pharmacotherapy allows the person to alleviate the intrusive core symptoms of the disorder while simultaneously developing coping strategies for improved quality of life. Using both methods, recovery from PTSD can be a distinct reality. Please see Box 4.1 to integrate your knowledge of the medications into the development of an initial pharmacotherapy regimen for a client case.

BOX 4.1

Clinical Vignette

Client Case

A 32-year-old female client presents to the clinic today exhibiting fearfulness and anxiety. She is well known to the clinic staff. About 2 months ago, the client was physically and sexually assaulted in the side parking lot near her local grocery store. The client was treated by the clinic's physician following the assault, and she was referred to a local therapist. She has been attending therapy sessions on a regular basis. Recently, the client complains of difficulty sleeping, with frequent awakenings during the night caused by nightmares. She states that she also drives an extra seven miles to purchase her groceries, stating that she "does not even want to see the place." All laboratory testing and imaging are within normal limits, and her presentation is not consistent with intoxication, infection, or metabolic abnormalities. After assessment, her physician diagnoses her with PTSD.

What would be an appropriate choice for first-line pharmacotherapy?

Answer: An SSRI agent would be initial pharmacotherapy. Because the trauma is associated with an attack in a civilian environment, these agents are considered first-line pharmacotherapy. Of the available agents, both FDA approved and off-label, sertraline has been shown to provide both short-term and long-term benefit. Side note: Because this is a woman of childbearing age, we would want to avoid paroxetine. It is considered a pregnancy category "D" agent, which means that there is higher risk than benefit in using the agent during pregnancy. Paroxetine has been implicated in the development of cardiac abnormalities in fetuses of pregnant women at a higher rate than other antidepressants. If this young woman would happen to become pregnant, we would have to change her therapy. In order to avoid this, sertraline would be chosen, as it is a category "C" agent (physician should weigh risk versus benefit—all other SSRIs are category "C" as well) and may be a safer choice for PTSD management. Therefore, clinical choices must include prevention of any future issues that may occur in an individual client.

If further treatment is necessary, the client may be prescribed an atypical antipsychotic such as risperidone, quetiapine, or olanzapine. Of these, risperidone may cause the least amount of weight gain and be helpful for the re-experiencing symptoms of the disorder.

Lastly, an agent such as the antihypertensive agent prazosin may be helpful at bedtime to decrease sympathetic outflow and help in normalizing frequent nighttime awakenings and nightmares.

ADDITIONAL RESOURCES

A robust set of instructor resources designed to supplement this text is located at http://connect.springerpub.com/content/book/978-0-8261-5085-1. Qualifying instructors may request access by emailing textbook@springerpub.com.

PRACTICE-BASED RESOURCES AND REFERENCES

To view a list of resources and all the references, please visit connect.springerpub.com via the following url: http://connect.springerpub.com/content/book/978-0-8261-5085-1/part/part01/chapter/ch04

CHAPTER 5

Issues of Loss and Grief

JUDITH L. M. MCCOYD AND LISA LÓPEZ LEVERS

Although the world is full of suffering, it is full also of the overcoming of it.
—Helen Keller (1880–1968)

CHAPTER OVERVIEW

This chapter focuses on understanding issues of loss and grief as well as their intersections with trauma experiences. It examines the classical theories associated with loss and grief, describing the transition to a postmodern perspective of how grief is experienced. The chapter describes interventions that can be used with clients experiencing loss and grief, along with the counseling implications. Practice-based resources are available online.

LEARNING OBJECTIVES

After reading this chapter, the reader should be able to:

1. Describe how loss, grief, and trauma are interwoven constructs;
2. Identify a variety of theories associated with grief;
3. Comprehend the implications of complicated bereavement as a traumatic experience;
4. Understand how to help clients make meaning out of loss and grief; and,
5. Identify clinical interventions that are most likely to be effective in the face of loss and grief.

INTRODUCTION

Not all experiences of loss and grief necessarily involve trauma; however, loss, grief, and destabilization are implicit aspects of all types of trauma. This chapter explicates loss and grief contextually and illuminates their centrality to the experience of trauma. We explain the rejection of stage theories of grief and the embrace of postmodern grief concepts that allow culturally sensitive and tailored treatment for those who are bereaved or traumatized. We hope that this chapter enables clinicians to understand the many ways that individuals experience grief,

---

This chapter is a revision of the chapter that appeared in the first edition of this textbook; Dr. Carolyn Ambler Walter, now retired, was one of the authors, and we thank her for her original contribution.

The material in this chapter is drawn from three editions of *Grief and Loss Across the Lifespan: A Biopsychosocial Perspective* (Springer Publishing Company, 2009, 2016, 2021). It has been adapted for use in this volume.

influenced by biological responses to stress, by psychological responses to loss in the face of previous attachments, by social norms and support networks, by cultural attitudes, and by spiritual frameworks. Grief, like trauma, can only be fully understood through a truly bio-psycho-social-spiritual perspective. We expect that the intertwined nature of trauma and loss is clear: losses of people, ideals, and things often are traumatic in the intensity of the loss; trauma always entails a loss of the assumptive world (Beder, 2004) in ways that destabilize just as loss does. We anticipate that clinicians will learn to help mourners make meaning of their losses and validate their experiences of loss. We envision clinicians who are client centered rather than advocates of a particular grief model, and who therefore help mourners process their losses and traumas in a manner tailored to their needs. Clinicians must help mourners explore their (often-changed) assumptions about how the world works, their new identities in the face of the loss, and subsequently help them learn more about themselves and their "fit" in the world. This chapter aims to introduce concepts of loss and grief, describe the phenomenology of loss and grief, and explicate counseling implications. These main sections are followed by a summary of the chapter and an online list of helpful resources for students, clinicians, and instructors.

LOSS, GRIEF, AND TRAUMA

Loss and trauma are intimately interwoven. Loss can occur whenever there is a change in one's world, even with a happy occasion like having a baby (e.g., losses of free time, sleep, intimacy with one's partner). Although losses can span benign through painful events, trauma always carries with it a sense of loss, and usually subsequent grief. When one experiences a traumatic event, such as sexual or physical assault, the losses inevitably include one's sense of safety, self-efficacy, and trust in the world as a good place. Trauma can be interwoven with loss also, as when one loses a loved one in an unexpected or otherwise traumatic manner.

Yet, loss is at the heart of life and growth. This seems a bit paradoxical; however, the reality is that new life, change, and forward movement only come as a result of losing (changing) a prior lifestyle, behavior pattern, or other functioning of the status quo. Trauma and loss both entail a destabilizing set of forces that can leave people in a vulnerable state, questioning their assumptions about the way the world works and their place in it. Reworking one's assumptions about the way the world works and one's identity in that world are a part of negotiating loss. Both trauma and loss open people to the possibility of growth as they process their response to the loss or trauma. Posttraumatic growth (Tedeschi & Calhoun, 2004) is possible after both trauma and traumatic losses. Clinicians who strive to assist clients in their growth must be aware that losses and trauma work involve helping clients to recognize their losses and trauma as valid and grief provoking. Although grief does not follow any set pattern, assisting grievers of loss and trauma involves helping them recognize the value of what they have lost (whether a person, job, or sense of themselves as safe and loved). Once able to recognize the value of what was lost, a critical next step in treatment is telling the story of the trauma or loss until clients develop some sense of meaning and continuity in their life story. Re-building a sense of safety and connection is a third goal that applies to clients who have experienced trauma or loss. In short, there is tremendous overlap in the experience of loss and trauma and the treatment of both.

Three editions of a seminal text on *Grief and Loss Across the Lifespan* (McCoyd et al., 2021) focused on loss as a normative, though destabilizing, experience and process. Loss is customary, though upsetting, and it promotes self-reflection and growth, particularly when the mourner's experience is validated and supported. We view normative losses as those that are relatively common in each age group, although not necessarily experienced by each individual of that age. These types of losses receive little support, precisely for the reason that they are considered "fairly normal." Of course, "normative" becomes an especially interesting concept in the face of trauma.

Whether "normative" in the sociological sense of an event happening (or not) to a large proportion of people, loss and trauma tend to lead individuals to feel that their world is no longer safe, that the person who they have been is changed on some intrinsic level, and that the trust they had in the world to be predictable has disappeared. Work with clients mourning loss and/or trauma is therefore aimed at helping to ameliorate those distressing thoughts and feelings by helping the griever to develop a sense of safety again, assess their identity in light of the loss, and work to help the griever identify what helps them feel the world to be predictable again. Here, we discuss the constructs of loss and grief in light of a normative, growth orientation, while also attending to the implications of complicated bereavement as this may relate to traumatic experiences.

PHENOMENOLOGY OF LOSS AND GRIEF

Loss and trauma are emotionally painful. This is the basic phenomenology of grief. When we lose a person, possession, characteristic, or environment that is important to us, we grieve. When trauma assaults us with feelings of threat, uncertainty, and being overwhelmed, we grieve for our loss of a sense of safety. Nevertheless, losses of various types are a part of human existence and not pathological states. We believe that these loss states can produce growth and insight, with or without professional help, though we also believe that most people process losses more easily when they talk with someone. It is notable that some early work examining the impact of adverse childhood events (ACEs) asserts that having two to three of the ACEs may actually promote better coping as an adult (Seery et al., 2010). Although complicated grief reactions exist (Shear, 2015), we also are aware that people have experienced losses since the beginning of humankind, but that grief therapy has existed for only a little over a century. We write from the perspective of clinicians who fully believe in the power of most human beings to manage their grief responses, while also believing that grief counseling allows clinicians to be present with people as they make this journey in ways that are beneficial and promote the most growth and insight. In this section, we examine the phenomenology of loss and grief through discussions of grief theory and transition to postmodern grief theory.

Classical Grief Theory

Classical grief theory arises from the work of Sigmund Freud, evolving into a task-based set of theories that includes subsequent work by other theorists and researchers (e.g., Lindemann, 1944; Worden, 2018). Also arising from classical origins is the parallel set of stage-oriented grief theories (e.g., Bowlby, 1980/1998; Kübler-Ross, 1969). In the remaining parts of this section, we review the implications of these task-based and stage-oriented theories of grief.

Classical Grief Theory and the Implications of Task-Based Grief Theory

According to Freud (Freud, 1917/1957), "Mourning is regularly the reaction to the loss of a loved person, or to the loss of some abstraction which has taken the place of one, such as one's country, liberty, an ideal, and so on" (p. 243). He proposed that grievers have one task, to decathect (remove emotional energy) from the lost entity. Freud's theory of behavior states that the psyche "cathects" people and loved entities with libidinal energy that must be withdrawn for a mourner to heal after loss. He believed that people experiencing melancholia had not successfully withdrawn the libidinal energy (cathexis) and needed help to do this. Freud was one of the first to address grief, melancholia, and mourning in a scholarly manner. He also contributed the understanding that mourning can occur for things, values, and statuses and does not only occur in response to a death. He also assured that grief and mourning are "not pathological" but goes on to say:

> This demand (to decathect libidinal drive) arouses understandable opposition—it is a matter of general observation that people never willingly abandon a libidinal position, not even, indeed, when a substitution is already beckoning to them. This opposition can be so intense that a turning away from reality takes place. (Freud, 1917/1957, p. 244)

Freud allowed for the possibility of psychotic (turning away from reality) thoughts, feelings, and behaviors as an understandable (and normal) reaction to loss. He asserted (Freud, 1917/1957) that mourning is only completed when the ego becomes free by virtue of decathecting libido from the lost love object and re-cathecting a new love object. He suggested that this generally takes about a year. As a person of Jewish heritage, despite his skepticism of religious belief and practice, he may have internalized the traditional year of mourning that is accepted and ritualized in the Jewish faith.

Freud's was the primary theoretical paradigm for early grief-work efforts. Usually couched in the language of "letting go," counselors have long held to the idea that a mourner must separate from their attachment to the lost entity, and this continues to be a theme running through clinicians' "practice wisdom," despite the development of new theoretical understandings of loss and grief that better explain the process of grief.

Some of the first empirical work to explore the grieving process was done by Lindemann (1944). He studied the responses of people following the Cocoanut Grove nightclub fire in Boston in November 1942 (where many young adults died suddenly), thereby precluding anticipatory grief as a factor that might change mourners' responses. Trauma theory had not yet developed and was not incorporated into his theory about grieving and loss. He theorized that grief normally includes somatic distress, preoccupation with the deceased, guilt, and sometimes hostile reactions. He asserted that eight to ten sessions with a psychiatrist over the course of a month and a half were sufficient to manage grief work (Lindemann, 1944). As an assertion based on research rather than theoretical speculation, this met with widespread acceptance. He believed that tasks of grief must be accomplished, but moved beyond Freud's two tasks of decathexis and recathexis. He postulated the following tasks:

1. Emancipation from bondage to the deceased;
2. Readjustment to the environment in which the deceased is missing; and,
3. Formulation of new relationships.

Although step 1 mirrored decathexis and step 3 mirrored recathexis, Lindemann (1944) contributed the idea that this was not a totally interior, psychological process. He acknowledged through step 2 that bereft individuals live in a social world and that they must adjust to a world that no longer has their loved one living in it. His unfortunate claim of a 4- to 6-week time frame meant that mourners who wanted to be perceived as healthy would avoid grief expression after 4 to 6 weeks. Another unfortunate consequence of Lindemann's study was that grief-work clinicians began to view grief that lasted much longer as pathological in some way. However, Lindemann contributed to our understanding by asserting that distressing symptoms experienced by bereaved people are quite customary, and he expected that the social world has an impact on grief. Simos (1979), a social worker who recognized the limitations of task- and stage-centered grief theories, said, "Anyone who took longer than the prescribed number of weeks to get over a loss was considered maladjusted and treated as emotionally disturbed. Thus, the helping professionals themselves became deterrents to the proper working through of grief" (p. 41).

Most recently, Worden (2018) refined his task-based grief theory and intervention framework. Worden's model includes the following steps:

1. Accept the reality of the loss;
2. Process the pain of the grief;
3. Adjust to a world without the deceased; and,
4. Find a way to remember the deceased while embarking on the rest of one's journey through life.

Worden (2018) originally required experiencing the pain of the grief as the second task, adding the experience of emotional ventilation, something that recently has become known as the grief-work hypothesis. Many embraced Worden's and others' suggestion that emotional ventilation (e.g., crying, mourning, anger) needed to be expressed before one could begin to heal from a significant loss. The implication is that if this type of ventilation did not occur, and if the person were seemingly healthy, the attachment to the lost one must not have been that strong. This has been found to be inaccurate in multiple studies (e.g., Bonanno, 2009; Carr et al., 2006; Konigsberg, 2011; Stroebe & Stroebe, 1991; Wortman & Silver, 2001), which reveal that a significant group of bereaved people actually become worse if emotional ventilation is pushed on them. Worden revised this task to require processing the pain of grief, and to recognize that people do this in a variety of ways. Worden also revised task 4 to allow for recognition that a relationship with the deceased continues in a modified manner—a major step forward in grief work and grief theory.

Freud depathologized grief, and the other task-based theorists helped to explicate what tasks the bereaved needed to accomplish to heal. Yet these tasks could imply an oversimplified "cookie-cutter" type of intervention. Worden (2018) has greatly refined his text to incorporate recognition of mediators of the grief response, criteria for assessing problematic grief, and a model for intervening.

Classical Grief Theory and the Implications of Stage-Oriented Grief Theory

Kübler-Ross (1969) was, like Lindemann (1944), more interested in empirical data than theorizing. She is known as a leader in the field of death and dying, yet her classic stages have been applied to a population that is different from the population she researched. She lived through the societal transition from when people died at home surrounded by family to when people died in hospitals, often with little information about the true status of their prognosis. As part of a seminar on death and dying at Chicago Theological Seminary, she and her students began interviewing dying people about their beliefs and experiences. Her book, *On Death and Dying: What the Dying Have to Teach Doctors, Nurses, Clergy and Their Own Families* (1969), was the source of the now widely reified stages of denial and isolation, anger, bargaining, depression, and acceptance. Her stages of adjustment to a terminal diagnosis are now inaccurately applied to all types of losses, despite their development from an anticipated loss of self after critical illness (M. Stroebe et al., 2017).

The stage of denial is particularly misunderstood. Kübler-Ross (1969) originally conceptualized it as a stage during which the diagnosed would "shop around" to ensure an accurate diagnosis or express hopes that the testing results and terminal diagnosis were incorrect. She viewed this as a "healthy way of dealing with the uncomfortable and painful situation with which these patients have to live for a long time" (p. 39). It is unfortunate that this stage has been misinterpreted widely and misapplied in grief counseling. It often has been viewed as a stage to be "broken through" or confronted, with counselors often applying draconian methods to ensure that denial is not maintained in connection with a death loss. This assertive confrontation of denial has become one of the suspect interventions associated with early grief-work counseling. Yet, in trauma work, denial often is encountered as a tendency to deny the impact of the trauma; individuals are ready to dismiss the impact of trauma without spending much time actually processing the events. One development in trauma work with veterans is to use flooding techniques to have the veteran grapple with the impact of the trauma (Foa & Meadows, 1997). We have come to learn that gently and firmly encouraging re-processing and re-telling of the story is helpful for people experiencing trauma and/or grief.

The fact that denial is viewed as a stage to get through, rather than as the protective adjustment time that Kübler-Ross described, reveals one of the difficulties of stage theories more generally. Individuals, both the bereaved and less reflective clinicians as well, can view these models as a recipe, an intervention plan to be applied with a broad sweep. This assumes a one-size-fits-all quality to mourning. It also implies that knowledge of the stages allows one to move more quickly through them, which is a fallacy with major implications.

Kübler-Ross's (1969) model of moving from this protective denial to a state of anger and irritation (in her study, often directed at caregivers) is usually viewed as a one-way journey. Her original conception involves movement through the stages rather than the back-and-forth or recursive movement seen most commonly among the bereaved. Despite some few who continue to adhere to "stages of grief" that are inaccurate (see M. Stroebe et al., 2017) for the problems of this approach, clinicians must interrogate the model, both because it does not fit empirical data, but also because it implies one-size-fits-all, and anyone with even a bit of cultural humility understands that each person's grief is influenced and made unique by the multiple intersectional identity and contextual factors that affect the griever.

A second classic stage theory grows from the empirical data of Bowlby (1980/1998), who followed children separated from their parents in war-torn countries during World War II. He later studied widows (and a few widowers) and found similar responses. He postulated the following stages:

- **Numbness**: Defined as being shocked and stunned, not as denial; Bowlby identified the protective nature of this stage.
- **Separation Anxiety (yearning/searching)**: Defined as an alternating state of despair and denial, with anger folded in, much like that found in children separated from parents. He believed pathological grief is characterized by being stuck in one of these modes—either yearning, or angry and detached, an assertion supported by Shear's work (2015). Bowlby (1980/1998) noted the following:

    > Thus anger is seen as an intelligible constituent of the urgent though fruitless effort a bereaved person is making to restore the bond that has been severed. So long as anger continues, it seems, loss is not being accepted as permanent and hope is still lingering on. (p. 91)

- **Despair and Disorganization:** As the loss sinks in, there is an attempt to recognize the loss and develop a "new normal." It is a time of lost objects (e.g., keys or other personal items) as well as lost thoughts and lost time.
- **Acquisition of New Roles/Reorganization**: When the bereaved relinquishes attempts at preparing for the deceased's return (e.g., gets rid of clothes) and moves into new aspects of life and relationships with others, the bereaved is viewed as moving through reorganization.

Bowlby's (1980/1998) stages mirror what he recognized in children—they yearn and pine for their parent(s) when separated. He theorized that the attachment style that the child exhibited (secure, anxious, avoidant) would influence the impact of the loss, and that children who were less secure in their attachments would be more likely to exhibit anxious or detached feelings when experiencing a loss. He and others have speculated that these influences carry on into adulthood, with adults playing out their reactions to loss via one of the attachment styles. This is an important conceptualization, with current research actively exploring its basis (Fraley & Shaver, 1999; Kominsky & Jordan, 2016; Zech & Arnold, 2011). Yet, it does not incorporate the reality that bereaved individuals experience a sense of uncertainty about what the future holds, a legitimate uncertainty that is intensified by trauma, as many of the plans for the future change abruptly as a result of loss and separation. This uncertainty itself may provoke anxious behavior (Hirsh et al., 2012) and is an attempt to defend against attachments that may leave the individual open for more emotional distress if circumstances change once again.

Despite the general critique of most stage theory due to its lock-step, one-size-fits-all approach, Maciejewski et al. (2007) found some support for Bowlby's stages, though Roy-Byrne and Shear (2007), "Comment," para. 1) asserted that the authors had "overstated their findings" and that they "drew oversimplified conclusions that reinforce formulaic, unhelpful ways of thinking about bereavement." Concerns remain about stage theories and their susceptibility for being approached as a recipe for grief work. Again, our position is that no model can fit all people's grief experience and their need for tailored support. Newer postmodern theories provide conceptual tools allowing clinicians to better tailor treatments to the unique experiences of individuals experiencing trauma and/or grief.

A recent classic comes from the work of Rando (1993). Rando asserts that individuals move through similar general phases that are fairly universal and chronological. Each phase incorporates "processes" or tasks that she asserts are the outcome of a healthy grieving process. Her model (1993, p. 45) is prescriptive in that it describes a process bereaved people must participate in to proceed toward healing. Using Rando's (1993) terminology for the phases and processes, we offer brief descriptions of each in the following:

- Avoidance Phase:
    1. Recognize the loss. The bereaved must acknowledge and understand the reality of the death.
- Confrontation Phase:
    2. React to the separation. The bereaved must experience the pain of the loss, give it expression, and mourn secondary losses.
    3. Recollect and re-experience the deceased and the relationship. The bereaved is to review and remember the relationship realistically and also review and re-experience the feelings they had as a result of that relationship.
    4. Relinquish the old attachments to the deceased and to the old assumptive world. The bereaved is to let go of previous bonds and beliefs and develop a "new normal" with new relationships and attachments.
- Accommodation Phase:
    5. Readjust to move adaptively into the new world without forgetting the old. The bereaved is to revise their assumptive world, develop a new relationship with the deceased, adopt new ways of being in the world, and form a new identity.
    6. Reinvest. This is a time to invest in new relationships and roles and indicates a resolution to active grieving.

Rando (1993) provides a model with a bit more room for individualized tailoring of the treatment process. It has an inherent assumption that complicated grief is common and requires treatment when grief is deemed to be too extended, too brief (or absent), or when it does not follow the typical trajectory. Despite Rando's obvious compassion and concern for bereaved people, her model is subject to some of the same criticisms as the other models: These models are viewed as normative in a way that means that any deviation from the models is viewed as pathological. In a postmodern world of intersectional identities and multiple cultural contexts, grief theory had to evolve to better capture the multitudinous experiences of human life. Nevertheless, recent work has identified complicated grief as a specific disorder of grief found in about 7% to 10% of grievers, often connected with intense, long-term relationships or with traumatic loss and benefiting from a specialized approach to grief therapy (Iglewicz et al., 2020). Complicated grief is characterized by continuing intense feelings of longing/yearning, rumination on the deceased (or lost entity), sometimes avoidance of discussing the loss, and ongoing inability to begin re-engaging with customary life. We discuss treatment of complicated grief in the Intervention section.

Transition to Postmodern Grief Theory

Some theorists in the Foucauldian tradition critique stage and task theorists for their "disciplining of grief" (Foote & Frank, 1999). They view pathologizing grief as a means to allow therapeutic intervention as a form of diffuse power, which produces conformity to societal norms. This is not overt coercion, but a form of self-care and self-improvement (something Foucault, 1988 calls "technologies of the self") that functions to contain grief within a therapeutic context. Foote and Frank comment:

> Grief, like death itself, is undisciplined, risky, wild. That society seeks to discipline grief, as part of its policing of the border between life and death, is predictable, and it is

equally predictable that modern society would medicalize grief as the means of policing. (Foote & Frank, 1999, p. 170)

Tony Walter (2000), too, has recognized how policing grief can be destructive. He traces the evolution of policing grief from an enforcement of contained, formalized, and time-limited grieving during the Victorian era to a current expectation of more expressive grief with a tendency toward medicalization of the grief process. He asserts that mutual help/self-help support groups have evolved as a form of resistance to policing and medicalization, although they, themselves, are evolving norms that contain an expectation of grieving similar to other group members (T. Walter, 2000). He notes:

> In postmodern times, both old and new maps are challenged by those who claim no maps can be made of a land that is entirely subjective and individual (Stroebe et al., 1992) . . . Yet the evidence presented in this article also suggests that the desire (of both mourners and their comforters) for security, for a map, for fellow travelers, for rules that must be policed, is sufficiently strong that most mourners will never be allowed to be entirely free spirits. (T. Walter, 2000, pp. 111–112)

Postmodern theories of grief grow from a social constructionist understanding of the world (Berger & Luckmann, 1967), which asserts that humans construct their understanding of the world in ways that they then see as self-evident and believe to be true. This "trueness" is part of the construction, because others construct their own truths in different ways. This leads to the postmodern understanding that there are many truths, each created within the context of a person's social and historical milieu, their individual and family experiences, and the person's capacity for reflection and insight. The narrative tradition of therapy (White & Epston, 1990) grew from these social constructionist and postmodern understandings and is predicated on each individual developing their own story with the help of the therapist as someone to help construct, edit, and frame the story. Making meaning of the deceased's life, death, and relationships becomes critical to the bereaved processing their grief (Neimeyer, 2001; Neimeyer & Sands, 2011).

Along with the evolution of this meaning-making approach to grief work, grief theorists and clinicians began to question classic models and templates for grief. The implications of social constructionism and postmodernism include the idea that no individual's grief must follow a certain preset path; decathexis, resolution, "closure," and acceptance are no longer envisioned as unitary end states for all. This allowed Klass et al. (1996) to theorize about what many mourners had been saying all along, that the end of active grieving does not have to entail a separation from the deceased. Indeed, most often, it actually entails continuing bonds that change in quality. Foote and Frank (1999) assert that postmodern meaning-making narrative approaches provide more promise for resistance to disciplining of grief.

Meaning-Making and Grief

Although Frankl (1946/1984) is most associated with *Man's Search for Meaning* and White and Epston (1990) are most associated with the application of meaning-making and storytelling via narrative therapies, Robert Neimeyer is perhaps the best known for applying these concepts to grief theory and intervention. He traces this back to:

> . . . Kant (1787/1965) who emphasized that the mind actively structures experience according to its own principles and procedures. . . . Significant loss—whether of cherished persons, places, projects, or possessions—presents a challenge to one's sense of narrative coherence as well as to the sense of identity for which they were an important source of validation. . . . Bereaved people often seek safe contexts in which they can tell (and retell) their stories of loss, hoping that therapists can bear to hear what others cannot,

validating their pain as real without resorting to simple reassurance. Ultimately, they search for ways of assimilating the multiple meanings of loss into the overarching story of their lives, an effort that professionals can support through careful listening, guided reflection, and a variety of narrative means for fostering fresh perspectives on their losses for themselves and others (Neimeyer, 1998). (as quoted in Neimeyer, 2001, pp. 263–264)

This is quoted at length, because Neimeyer's (2001) explanation fits with our own perspectives—that understanding grief and working with people in grief therapy is a mutual project, not one of diagnosis and therapeutic intervention. Grief counseling is a respectful project and process of hearing and witnessing the stories people tell of their lives and their losses, questioning them in ways that allow them to open other perspectives while also leaving room for them to reject those interpretations. At its best, grief work encourages mourners as they construct and reconstruct stories of meaning that enable them to move into their new lives and their new assumptive worlds in the physical absence of the entity who or which was lost (Box 5.1).

BOX 5.1

Clinical Vignette: Anna's Loss

Anna lost her teenage son in an accident approximately a year before contacting Carol, a professional counselor whose expertise included working with grief. Anna was anxious and tearful when she arrived for her intake session with Carol. Anna opened with a little information about her profound sense of grief after the loss of her child, but much of her initial dialogue focused on her family and friends. It seemed that many of the people in Anna's life believed that she was "stuck" in early "stages" of grief. They pushed her to "get it together" and to "move on" with her life. Anna described receiving both implicit and explicit messages that "it's been a year now" and that "that's long enough." Anna's husband was particularly angry with her for "clinging to the past"—after all, he was "dealing with it," and the boy was his son too. In desperation, Anna decided to seek counseling, particularly as significant people in her life convinced her that she had a "mental problem."

Carol immediately sensed that Anna really had never had an opportunity to tell her story, in her own voice. Carol also came to realize that, even before their son's death, Anna's husband was an emotionally distant person who appeared to ruminate and not express his emotions. Carol helped Anna realize that it was okay to sit with her own feelings and not be influenced by the dictates of others in her life. Throughout a number of sessions, Carol facilitated Anna's growing ability to construct her own narrative about her loss and the significance that this had in her life. Anna finally was able to discuss her true feelings, with a sense of safety, in the counselor's office. She began to make meaning of her son's life and about everything that had happened that led to his death. Carol observed that Anna was becoming less anxious than when she first arrived for counseling, and that she was beginning to self-regulate, allowing for increased relaxation. Eventually, Carol and Anna identified an activity that allowed Anna to engage in prevention efforts related to the type of accident that had taken her son's life. As Anna told Carol, "This doesn't make the pain go away, but it makes it more bearable, and I can feel like I'm doing something proactive and in his memory–I might even be helping to prevent other mothers from going through this agony." They continued to process Anna's feelings about her loss. Anna was beginning to experience a sense of control over her life, decreased anxiety, and her relationships with her family members improved once again.

It is important that clinicians working with people who are grieving recognize that the stories may take multiple forms, and that the task of the therapist is *not* to force an adherence to a "true" or "real" one. Instead, we are there to help the client create their own coherent story while assisting in shining new light on the possibilities of blind spots that may enable a story that fits the client's evolving and dynamic worldview in evermore useful and function-promoting ways. This is a relational project involving a willingness on the part of the clinician to truly engage with the client in an authentic and caring manner, exhibiting genuine curiosity about the way the client is unfolding their story. Successful grief counselors convey realistic hope that this process can enable the client to return to full engagement with their life and loved ones. Clinical work with survivors of trauma benefits from a similar stance.

Dual Process Theory

Dual process theory is another evolution of grief theory built on the ideas of Bowlby (1980/1998) and the stages of disorganization and reorganization. Although Bowlby conceptualized these as discrete stages that one passes through as one heals from a loss, M. Stroebe and Schut (1999, 2010) envisioned an ongoing cyclical process of loss orientation and restoration orientation. This differs from the linear organization stages in that the bereaved person cycles between times of experiencing grief actively and focusing on the loss, and then moving into times of restoration orientation. During the restoration orientation, the bereaved focuses on rebuilding a new life and engaging in new relationships, activities, and other distractions that move the person away from active grieving. It is imperative to understand that these are not viewed in any hierarchy of value for the bereaved; indeed, it is clear that both have value, and that the oscillation between these two orientations provides distraction and restoration time that allows the mourner to move into new roles and activities. Alternately, moving into a loss orientation permits time for processing the loss. Both are necessary. Notably, children and adults seem to oscillate somewhat differently, with children spending more time in restoration orientation (particularly using distraction), whereas adults may linger in loss orientation more frequently. Current research suggests that people with dismissive attachment styles may need more help engaging with the loss orientation, whereas those with an insecure/anxious style may need strong encouragement to engage in the restoration orientation (M. S. Stroebe et al., 2005; Zech & Arnold, 2011), recommendations that have implications for trauma work as well.

Another concept that is implicit within the dual process theory is the revision of the assumptive world. Parkes (1988) was one of the first to write about the assumptive world as a set of assumptions (e.g., my husband will always be there to kiss me good night, buildings will never fall to the ground, pandemics will never affect the United States) that coalesces into a cognitive schema, defining how one views one's world. Parkes defines grief as a psychosocial transition necessitating a readjustment of the assumptive world:

> For a long time it is necessary to take care in everything we think, say, or do; nothing can be taken for granted any more. The familiar world suddenly seems to have become unfamiliar, habits of thought and behavior let us down, and we lose confidence in our own internal world. (Parkes, 1988, p. 57)

Parkes (1988) captures the phenomenology of grief, an issue of "our own internal world," yet the assumptive world entails levels of assumptions from personal to societal, and we argue that these must be understood using an ecological perspective. For instance, on the micro levels, assumptions exist along the lines of "I'll predecease my child"; on the mezzo level, one may hold assumptions like "schools will always be available for education and supervision of children"; but macro level assumptions can be violated too, as when Hurricane Katrina devastated Mississippi and Louisiana, and assumptions that "communities and the country will always take care of people when tragedy hits" were shown to be false. Similarly, when COVID-19 hit the United States, beliefs that the U.S. medical system would be supported by the government to avoid tremendous loss of life was also shown to be false. Whenever assumptions require revision, an individual's world feels uncertain; yet, when these assumptions are dashed at multiple levels, it may be assumed that the challenges to adapting and revising the assumptive world will be greater.

Continuing Bonds and Grief

A pivotal understanding in contemporary grief theory came when Klass et al. (1996) each examined the data from their disparate research populations and realized that all found evidence of the same phenomena—that bereaved people tended to hold on to some type of relationship with the deceased. They challenged the notion that disengaging from the deceased or lost one is the goal of grief and they coined the term "continuing bonds." They observed that bereaved people seem to intuitively maintain connections to the deceased and that they re-worked those connections to allow a sense that the deceased remained a part of their life in varied ways such as through memories, a protective presence that watches over, an entity to pray to, or even just qualities of that person to emulate. They assured bereaved people that they do not need to sever their relationships with the deceased in order to grieve in a healthy manner.

The idea of continuing bonds, therefore, implies that, like meaning making, each individual may have a fairly unique outcome to their grief; yet there is a potential hazard here. Just as bereaved people were "policed" into non-expression of their grief (or more recently into full expression, even when this did not fit their needs), we must remain cognizant that some subgroup of grievers may not feel the need to have continuing bonds, whereas many others can find this comforting. Regardless, the concept of continuing bonds (Klass et al., 1996) was revolutionary and gave the bereaved permission to maintain their sense of relationship with their deceased loved ones.

This not only challenges the concept of "letting go" and "acceptance," but it also challenges notions of closure. "Closure" came into the lexicon during the 1990s and reflects the hope of grievers to be relieved of pain and suffering. Berns' (2011) exposé of closure reveals multiple meanings used for the term, but, more insidious, closure came to justify capitalistic efforts from "burials" in space to "diamonds" made of cremains (Berns, 2011). Berns found that the word "closure" is used for closing a chapter, remembering, forgetting, getting even, knowing, confessing, and forgiving. Closure is therefore a slippery word, not likely symbolizing an ending of grief so much as "justifying" services and products to be sold.

Cultural contexts are important, too. Mexican "Day of the Dead" celebrations and Buddhist worship at shrines of deceased loved ones reflect the practices of only two of many cultures that have allowed maintenance of continued bonds, despite the fact that many Western cultures have not recognized these ties/bonds historically. Individualized assessment of the client, discussion of cultural inputs into the grief process and customs, an intuitive and respectful stance by the therapist, and awareness of the wide range of ways in which people move through and process their grief are all imperative for sensitive, competent grief work with bereaved people. Another imperative is to recognize that although grief is partially a psychological state, it also is defined socially, in both cultural context and normative inputs, and it has physical effects as well. When social expectations are violated, grief and grieving are affected. The concepts of disenfranchised grief and ambiguous grief are fundamentally social, as well, and have been part of the evolving theorizing of grief.

Disenfranchised Grief

Doka (1989, 2002) coined the term "disenfranchised grief" to conceptualize grief that is not recognized, validated, or supported by the social world of the mourner. Essentially, the concept of disenfranchised grief involves grief that does not meet the norms of grief in the griever's culture. Hochschild (1979, 1983) has referred to norms such as these, which guide the individual in what is an "appropriate" feeling in a given situation, as *feeling rules*. Disenfranchised grief comes as a result of breaking the feeling rules, or of living in a time when feeling rules are not established or are discrepant (McCoyd, 2009). This then leaves the griever uncertain as to whether they are "allowed" to feel sad about a loss experience that is not recognized by social peers. Further, it may leave the griever wondering if they are even "allowed" to call the experience a loss (or a trauma). Doka (2002) defines five categories of disenfranchised grief: (a) grief in which the relationship is not recognized, such as gay and lesbian relationships, extramarital relationships, and other relationships that lack social sanction; (b) grief in which the loss is not acknowledged by societal norms as a "legitimate" loss, as when abortion, adoption, pet loss, amputation, and other losses are not viewed as worthy of sympathy; (c) grief in which the griever is excluded, as is often the case for individuals who are children, aged, or developmentally disabled and are (inaccurately) not believed to really experience grief; (d) grief in which the circumstances of death cause stigma or embarrassment, such as when a person dies of AIDS, alcoholism, crime, or in other ways that are viewed as moral failures on the part of the deceased; and (e) grief that is expressed in non-socially sanctioned ways, as when a griever is deemed to be either too expressive, or not expressive enough (Doka, 2002).

The nature of disenfranchised grief means that grieving individuals do not receive the social support and sympathy from others that have been shown to be crucial to being able to process grief and move on from it in healthy ways. The very core of this experience (for most) is to engage the pain of grieving actively. Yet, for many, this pain is exacerbated by social isolation or rejection. Many types of losses fall into some of these categories, particularly losses that are not recognized as worthy of support by others. In these cases, the mere validation that it is accurate to perceive the event as a loss, along with normalizing the grief response, can allow the griever to move through the loss response without the complications that may occur when the griever is bereft not only of the lost entity, but of validation, recognition, and normalization of their grief. Certainly, trauma such as childhood abuse of all forms often entails disenfranchised losses. Indeed, trauma's pain is often disenfranchised by those who suppress their trauma, and validating the grief due to losing one's integrity and sense of safety is often vital to helping the traumatized person to begin to grapple with their trauma and its subsequent grief.

Ambiguous Loss

Ambiguous loss (Boss, 1999) is a form of "frozen grief" which is difficult to process, because the definition of who is lost is so uncertain. In ambiguous loss, the lost entity is

- physically present but psychologically absent–for instance, a loved one with Alzheimer's disease or head trauma/brain injury; or
- physically absent but psychologically present–such as when someone is kidnapped, homeless, or missing in action during a war.

These types of losses are confusing because it is unclear how one is to adjust to them. Without an overt death in the first case, it seems premature and even cruel to grieve in socially sanctioned ways; in the second, to begin to grieve would remove the hope of the return of the lost one to the social milieu. Boss points to the following factors as creating difficulty for those experiencing ambiguous loss:

- Uncertainty means that adjustment cannot occur because it is unclear what one is supposed to adjust to.
- Rituals are not available, and there are few social supports.
- The irrationality of life is on display. It is hard to feel that there is a rational world when nothing seems clear or rational.
- The grief is unending. The uncertainty drags out, and there is little ability for resolution.

These types of losses also confuse formal and informal support people who are just as perplexed about whether to express sympathy or to maintain a stolid sense of normalcy and hope. Disenfranchised and ambiguous losses are heightened in intensity by the lack of social support. This may be why peer support and mutual help groups seem so efficacious with grievers such as these. Theoretically, it is appropriate to create groups for those for whom social nonrecognition of the loss occurs, because the group members are all in similar situations and are aware of a sense of loss. Groups have similar benefits for people who experienced similar traumas. Although having similar types of losses or trauma does not ensure having similar responses, the social contexts can be discussed, and strategies for coping can be addressed.

BIOPSYCHOSOCIAL EFFECTS OF GRIEF

The biopsychosocial approach requires an understanding of the ways that mind and body interact within a social context. The biological impact of psychosocial factors seldom is addressed, explicitly, in much of the therapeutic literature. This said, the link between higher mortality and bereavement has been strong, long-lasting, and significant (Bowling, 1989; Parkes et al., 1969; M. S. Stroebe et al., 1982), including findings that the rates are higher for widowers than widows (Helsing et al., 1982; M. S. Stroebe & Stroebe, 1993). Recent research illustrates that individuals can and do "die of a broken heart" at double the rate of nonbereaved people matched for age and other demographics (Carey et al., 2014; Dande & Pandit, 2013). Understanding the possible mechanisms for the increased mortality and morbidity risk is important.

A full understanding of the interaction of emotions and physical health is beyond the scope of this chapter, but having a basic understanding of how immune systems, neurological systems, and cardiovascular systems may be affected by stress, grief, depression, anxiety, and traumatic events can help clinicians to think about ways of promoting health, despite bereavement, and of recognizing the impact of psychosocial factors on physical health. Koch (2013) provides a useful overview of the ways that mind–body interactions can elicit disease.

The immune system is one of the most potent mediators of the interaction between mental and physical health (Brod et al., 2014; Salovey et al., 2000). A significant body of work (well summarized in Salovey et al., 2000) shows that negative emotions decrease secretory immunoglobulin A (S-IgA), which then causes individuals to be much more susceptible to infection from viruses such as the common cold. Likewise, grief's negative emotions reduce immune system efficiency and inflammation ensues along with decreased activity of T-lymphocytes and natural killer cells (Buckley et al., 2012), reducing ability to fight everything from short-term viral diseases to cancer.

Neurotransmitters and other neurochemical interactions also play a major role in the interaction of mental and physical health. The major mediator of brain chemistry under stress is the hypothalamic–pituitary–adrenal axis (HPA), which, when activated, causes a release of cortisol, the stress hormone. Norepinephrine and adrenocorticotropic hormone (ACTH) are also released when the HPA is activated, with rises in ACTH typically providing a feedback loop with cortisol, which then rises, ideally leading to lowered ACTH production. This feedback loop seems to break down in depressed individuals, with cortisol staying elevated (Buckley et al., 2012). Parentally bereaved children and youth are reported to have disturbed cortisol functioning; their cortisol awakening response becomes blunted, and cortisol levels remain high (Dietz et al., 2013; Kaplow et al., 2013). Cortisol influences sleep-wake cycles and sleep disturbance is highly associated with grief reactions in most age groups. Theoretically, sleep disturbances may contribute to poor health during bereavement (Buckley et al., 2012).

Genes are often viewed as static, but we now understand that genes are "turned on and off," as a result of environmental stresses (Rothstein, 2013). Indeed, the genome can be changed in ways that can be passed down to offspring (epigenetics) (Bienertová-Vašků et al., 2014; Zucchi et al., 2013). These environmental stresses can include the stress of prolonged grief. Associations between complicated grief and genomic findings suggest genes play a part in influencing who experiences complicated (prolonged) grief (O'Connor et al., 2014; Schultze-Florey et al., 2012). Mindfulness work has been shown to reduce the inflammatory responses believed to negatively affect both immune system function and genetic expression (the inflammatory response is regulated by genes) (Creswell et al., 2012). We must continue to learn more about the interactive relationship between genomics and grief.

Gundel et al. (2003) and O'Connor et al. (2007) suggest an intriguing link between the biological effects of grief and the reasons narrative meaning-making is a useful intervention. The researchers used functional magnetic resonance imaging (fMRI) to scan acutely bereaved individuals' brains after interviewing them about their loss. They then said words from the interview to the bereaved and watched the response on the fMRI. They discovered that the posterior cingulate cortex, the cerebellum, and the inferior temporal gyrus are all affected, and each has a role in autobiographical memory and creation of the "storyline" of individual's lives. Van der Kolk et al.'s (1996) understandings about trauma suggest that grief is affected differently when the loss is experienced as traumatic. At this point, the emotional memory of the loss is "stamped in" by the flood of neurotransmitters that occurs at the time of a trauma; further, the amygdala is activated, though often in a less than conscious manner, so that similar events and thoughts may provoke the amygdala to continue to send signals of arousal even when the loss has already occurred (van der Kolk, 1998).

In light of the physiological aspects of bereavement just described, it becomes important for the grief counselor to be aware of how to promote physical health and wellness. Regular exercise, a balanced diet with an increase of B vitamins and antioxidants, increased omega-3 intake, and exposure to light (Zisook & Shuchter, 2001) all need to be encouraged. During the bereavement period, a checkup by a physician is indicated; counselors should encourage conscious provision of self-care and monitoring of risks to one's health.

INTERVENTIONS

As noted in the many task- and stage-related grief theories initially detailed, there is a tendency among grief theorists to identify phases (and associated tasks) through which the mourner must move to heal. Newer theories avoid the prescriptive nature of many of the earlier theories; yet, the onus remains on the bereaved to move through the process. Interestingly, when working with students and others who want to be of use in assisting those who are grieving, their question tends to be "What can I do?" not "What should the bereaved do?" This is actually a much more important question. Lloyd (2002) suggests that the clinician do the following: (a) explore attitudes toward death and dying from psychological, sociological, and philosophical/religious perspectives; (b) explore and analyze the bereaved's constructions of life; and (c) explore the processes of adjustment to the world without the lost entity. Within each area for exploration, attention is paid to how the bereaved redefines roles, rebuilds identities, negotiates transitions, survives trauma, and maintains a hopeful spirit.

Another framework for intervention was developed by McCoyd (1987, October) for use with perinatal loss but has been applied to disenfranchised losses more generally. Called the "Five Vs," this model specifies domains for exploration and intervention; these guide the clinician without resorting to structured, predetermined tasks. The Five Vs are validating, valuing, verifying, ventilation, and being visionary. Validating helps the bereaved to identify any areas where they may not feel that they have social support for grieving and helps them to recognize and validate their right to be a mourner. Valuing and verifying relate to validating by recognizing that the lost entity had value to the mourner and supporting the bereaved in discussing all aspects of the way the lost entity/person had value to them. Verifying is any intervention done to assist the bereaved in gathering concrete mementos or developing rituals that "make real" the loss. These concrete reminders may be used to help enlist the support of social networks. Ventilation has become almost stereotyped in that people are urged to "vent," to "let it all out," or in other ways to be emotionally expressive. Ventilation can be done in various ways and does not always need to incorporate tears. Indeed, if the counselor falls prey to the grief work hypothesis (M. Stroebe & Stroebe, 1991), and insists on tears as a form of ventilation, they risk harming the mourner.

The ventilation domain entails an expectation that the bereaved can talk about the loss with authenticity and consistent affect and content, not necessarily overt tears. Ventilation is often the domain within which meaning making begins to occur as the bereaved is helped to explore the many ways in which the loss has affected the bereaved person's life. This is the time for the grief counselor to remain quietly supportive, avoiding platitudes that could interrupt the mourner's ability to ventilate their thoughts, feelings, and reflections freely. The final domain, being visionary, is often a part of the ending process but is found in small amounts throughout the work. This entails assisting the bereaved person to think through events that are likely to occur in the future and to recognize their potential for intensifying grief feelings. Rando (1993) calls these STUG reactions–sudden temporary upsurges of grief. Often, they come without warning, but in being visionary, the grief counselor can share lessons learned from others about when grief is likely to be heightened. For instance, with perinatal loss, the arrival of the due date for a pregnancy that has been lost is often a time of intensified feelings of grief; the bereaved needs to allow time for reflection and mourning. The Five Vs can provide a model for grief counselors who desire some structure for the work, yet who recognize the importance of allowing the bereaved to follow their own needs and inclinations for grief work.

Rubin's two-track model of bereavement (Rubin et al., 2017) provides yet another approach for assessment and intervention. The focus is two-fold: Track One focuses on the biopsychosocial functioning of the griever and Track Two focuses on the relationship between the griever and the lost entity/person. The premise is that bereavement creates a disruption in the griever's homeostasis and that intervention is geared toward the two tracks using CBT-REBT (cognitive behavioral therapy—rational emotive behavior therapy) techniques to help the griever assess cognitions related to their adaptation to their own functioning post-loss, as well as to the development of the continuing bond to who/what was lost. Focusing on evaluating beliefs and their consequences is different from the more narrative approach embraced in meaning making interventions, but may be preferred by some who want a more structured approach to their grief counseling, particularly in the face of a traumatic component to the loss.

Perhaps the most useful intervention in considering traumatic bereavement is the empirically validated treatment for complicated grief developed by M. K. Shear. Developed to be used in a compassionate, collaborative, and tailored manner, it was previously more structured and now uses lessons learned in the previous iterations to allow broader dissemination of the approach. The seven steps (again, interventions to be used by the therapist rather than stages or tasks of the bereaved) are: (1) understanding and accepting grief, using psychoeducation to help the bereaved understand typical expectations of grief responses and helping them think about what makes their grief complicated; (2) managing painful emotions, which also involves teaching the bereaved to track their grief on a 10-point scale and observe when it is low and when it is high; (3) planning for a meaningful future, which capitalizes on the Dual Process model, by gently urging movement into restoration orientation and goal-setting for the future; (4) strengthening ongoing relationships by helping the bereaved identify at least one confidant in their social group to whom they can talk, (5) telling the story of the death, which is the primary focus of sessions that help reinforce emotional regulation, challenge avoidance, and build meaning making capacity; (6) learning to live with reminders by helping the bereaved identify and emotionally regulate when triggers are present; and (7) establishing an enduring connection with memories of the person who died, by promoting continuing bonds. See the online Resources section for more information to attain detailed training and worksheets.

COUNSELING IMPLICATIONS

The counseling literature suggests that the counselor's own history of grief and loss and their self-reflexive capacity must be understood if they are to assist grievers (e.g., McCoyd et al., 2021; Worden, 2018). Clinicians can experience a parallel process of feeling overwhelmed by client losses and moving into a passive role of hopelessness, thereby making the clinicians less helpful. Clinical supervision is a necessary instrument for dealing with the compassion fatigue that may be associated with counseling complex bereavement. Unidentified countertransference can lead clinicians to do grief work *at* rather than *with* their clients. Attunement to the griever is vital to the work, so self-knowledge must precede work with grievers. Use of the Professional Quality of Life Scale (ProQoL—found in the online Resources section) can help clinicians self-monitor for compassion fatigue and secondary traumatization (issues related to secondary and vicarious trauma are detailed in Chapter 30 of this textbook, and Chapter 31 details counselor self-care).

The efficacy of grief work has been questioned, and the potential for iatrogenic effects raised (e.g., Bonanno & Lilienfeld, 2008; Neimeyer, 2000; W. Stroebe et al., 2005). Nevertheless, Larson and Hoyt (2007) argue that grief therapy is as effective as other forms of psychotherapy. The prudent therapist certainly wants to be aware of theoretical nuances, which may contribute to best practices for particular clients. As the theoretical overview illustrates, there is no one way of doing grief, and, therefore, no one way of doing grief therapy or counseling. We believe counselors must listen deeply and reflectively to the griever discuss their relationship to who/ what was lost, their experience of the loss itself, their concerns about how their life has changed as a result of the loss, and how they anticipate their life evolving as a result of the loss. Helping them consider how to maintain a connection to the entity who/which was lost over time and helping them recognize the reality that this will be a lifelong process of re-evaluating each of those aspects as they age/mature are also critical aspects of the work with grievers.

In 1991, Stroebe and Stroebe asked the question, "Does 'grief work' work?" Their answer at that time was a tepid "maybe." Findings that widowers who avoided emotional expression seemed to have worse outcomes than those who were not actively avoiding their grief showed tepid support for grief work; however, widows did not exhibit this same association. This led the authors to suggest that "the view 'everyone needs to do grief work' is an oversimplification" (M. Stroebe & Stroebe, 1991, p. 481). Indeed, Bonanno et al. (2004), in a prospective study with 276 older couples, found that 46% of the older widows and widowers they interviewed were classified as "resilient," with little depression or active search for meaning-making after their spouse's death, but neither were they considered avoidant. Another 10% were called "depressed improved" and actually improved in mood and coping after the death of the spouse (often those who were caretakers or who had been abused). The people they classified with "common grief" typically experienced depressive symptoms intensifying to about 6 months post loss and then resolving over the course of the following year. This implies that more than half of typically bereaved mourners are capable of adapting to loss, given time and a modicum of supportive social outlets. This reinforces the notion that grief is a normal part of life and something that can promote growth, even in the absence of professional assistance. Yet another 25% or so struggle to manage adaptation after loss, and these individuals, along with those who experience traumatic components to their loss, may benefit from someone with whom to reflect on their loss and its meaning in their lives.

The reflective clinician must weigh skepticism about grief work for all mourners against the paralysis that can result from giving so much weight to these concerns that we neglect to provide support for those who are asking for our assistance. Particularly after traumatic losses, supportive counseling is generally appreciated, and if complicated grief symptoms arise, grief therapy is beneficial. Remaining open and reflective about new understandings in grief theory and trauma theory, while also using the empirical data derived from one's actual interaction with individual clients and how they perceive the work to be useful (or not), are requirements of ethical and sensitive practice in the world of grief support.

CONCLUSION

In this chapter, we have introduced the phenomenology of loss and grief, especially as these constructs apply to losing a loved one, and we have considered the implications for traumatic loss. We have provided an overview of classical grief theory and examined the transition from the classical to more contemporary theories that acknowledge the intersectional nature of grievers' unique experiences. We have emphasized the importance of understanding the biopsychosocial effects of grief, along with explicating recent advances in counseling interventions, especially in situations where bereavement is connected with trauma. We have addressed the implications for counselors working with clients who have experienced the grief and suffering that may result from loss. Grievers deserve our deepest compassion, paired with our most current understanding of how to help them continue to move through their grief and re-engage with their lives.

ADDITIONAL RESOURCES

 A robust set of instructor resources designed to supplement this text is located at http://connect.springerpub.com/content/book/978-0-8261-5085-1. Qualifying instructors may request access by emailing textbook@springerpub.com.

PRACTICE-BASED RESOURCES AND REFERENCES

To view a list of resources and all the references, please visit connect.springerpub.com via the following url: http://connect.springerpub.com/content/book/978-0-8261-5085-1/part/part02/chapter/ch05

CHAPTER 6

Sexual Trauma: An Ecological Approach to Conceptualization and Treatment

LAURA HENSLEY CHOATE

CHAPTER OVERVIEW

Sexual violence is a significant social problem worldwide, occurring at alarmingly high rates and is associated with a host of negative outcomes including posttraumatic stress disorder (PTSD). The purpose of this chapter is to present an ecological model that enhances an understanding of survivor responses to sexual violence and informs treatment for sexual trauma. The chapter will examine the many systems that affect survivors' recovery and will provide an overview of clinical guidelines for treating sexual trauma, including prolonged exposure (PE), trauma-informed CBT (TF-CBT), cognitive processing therapy (CPT), and Eye Movement Desensitization and Reprocessing (EMDR).

LEARNING OBJECTIVES

After reading this chapter, the reader should be able to:

1. Understand posttrauma symptoms that commonly follow an experience of sexual violence, with particular attention to PTSD;
2. Conceptualize a survivor's responses to sexual trauma in terms of an ecological model that includes the multiple systems involved in response to and recovery from sexual violence;
3. Describe evidence-based clinical guidelines for treating sexual trauma, including prolonged exposure (PE), cognitive behavioral therapy (CBT) and cognitive processing therapy (CPT), and Eye Movement Desensitization and Reprocessing (EMDR).

INTRODUCTION

Sexual violence is a significant social problem worldwide, and because of the intimate nature of sexual violence, it is considered one of the most distressing types of trauma an individual can experience (Dworkin et al., 2017). Sexual violence is defined by the Centers for Disease Control and Prevention, the National Center for Injury Prevention and Control, and the Division of Violence Prevention as any sexual act committed against someone without that person's freely given consent, including sexual acts obtained by force, coercion, or perpetrated against an individual unable to give consent due to age, disability, or impairment following voluntary or involuntary substance use. It includes a broad spectrum of nonconsensual sexual activities that are perpetrated upon a victim by partners, spouses, friends, acquaintances, family members, or strangers (Basile et al., 2014; D'Inverno et al., 2019).

It is disconcerting that sexual violence and its resulting trauma occurs at high prevalence rates, particularly for women. According to the National Intimate Partner and Sexual Violence Survey, 44% of all women in the United States will experience some type of contact sexual violence in their lifetimes, with one-third of all women (37%) experiencing unwanted sexual contact, and one in five women (21%) experiencing attempted or completed rape (D'Inverno et al., 2019). Although women are disproportionately affected by all forms of sexual violence, men are also victims of these crimes. Approximately one in 17 men (compared to one in five women) have experienced an attempted or completed rape in their lifetime (Smith et al., 2017), and almost 25% of men report some form of contact sexual violence in their lifetime (D'Inverno et al., 2019).

In addition, women and men of all cultural backgrounds experience sexual violence. When comparing most racial/ethnic groups, there are no statistically significant differences between groups, with the exception of Native American/Alaska Native women, who experience significantly higher rates of sexual assault and violence (34%) than do individuals from all other cultural backgrounds (Tjaden & Thoennes, 2006). To demonstrate the comparison between racial groups, 45% of Native American women experienced contact sexual violence in their lifetime, compared to 38.5% of non-Hispanic White, 35.5% of non-Hispanic Black, 26.9% of Hispanic, and 22.9% of Asian American women (Smith et al., 2017). Further, members of several marginalized groups also experience increased vulnerability to sexual victimization, including individuals with disabilities, sexual and gender minorities, homeless individuals, and individuals engaging in sex work (International Society for Traumatic Stress Studies [ISTSS], 2018). Because of these high prevalence rates that cut across all age groups and populations, counselors need to be knowledgeable about sexual violence and resulting trauma, how it operates in survivors' lives, and how to provide effective treatment.

The purpose of this chapter is to present an ecological model that enhances understanding of survivor responses to sexual violence and informs treatment for sexual trauma. This is accomplished by the discussions offered in the following sections: (a) a brief examination of the symptoms that commonly follow an experience of sexual violence; (b) a conceptualization of an ecological model for use in understanding sexual violence, including descriptions of the systems that affect survivors' recovery; and (c) an overview of clinical guidelines for treating sexual trauma, including prolonged exposure (PE), cognitive behavioral therapy (CBT) and cognitive processing therapy (CPT), and Eye Movement Desensitization and Reprocessing (EMDR). This chapter concludes with counseling implications and an online list of resources for counselors and survivors.

SEXUAL TRAUMA

It is not surprising that trauma resulting from sexual violence is associated with a host of negative mental health problems, including PTSD, anxiety disorders, depression, substance abuse, disordered eating, dissociation, suicidal ideation, and suicide attempts. In fact, in a recent meta-analysis, the experience of sexual assault was associated with an increased risk for and severity of all psychiatric disorders, including a strong increased risk for suicidal ideation and behaviors (Dworkin et al., 2017).

Most individuals develop PTSD-like reactions within days after a sexual assault, and these typically resolve within a month following the event as the individual processes the event; in fact, posttraumatic reactions such as intrusive memories, emotional numbing or withdrawal, or hyper-alertness are considered normal and expected reactions to this type of trauma (American

Psychological Association, 2017). However, if these reactions do not remit but become recurring symptoms, which last over a month, then the symptoms may meet criteria for PTSD. Overall, lifetime prevalence rates indicate that PTSD develops in a significant number of survivors (Scott et al., 2018). Because PTSD is likely to occur in individuals who experience sexual trauma, it is important for counselors to be knowledgeable of PTSD symptoms and how they might manifest in a particular client. The *Diagnostic and Statistical Manual of Mental Disorders* (5th ed.; *DSM-5*; American Psychiatric Association [APA], 2013), groups PTSD symptoms into four clusters: (a) intrusion (e.g., at least one of the following: re-experiencing of the trauma through nightmares, flashbacks, or intense distress at exposure to cues that symbolize or resemble an aspect of the traumatic event); (b) avoidance (e.g., efforts to avoid one or more: thoughts, feelings, physical sensations, people, conversations, activities, places, or physical reminders that arouse recollection of the event); (c) negative alterations in cognitions and mood (e.g., as evidenced by three or more of the following: inability to remember certain aspects of the event, persistent self-blame, negative expectations of one's self, others, or the world; strong and persistent negative emotional reactions, diminished interest or participation in significant activities, feelings of detachment, or inability to experience positive emotions); and (d) alterations in arousal and reactivity at activities associated with the event (e.g., at least three of the following: irritability, aggressiveness, reckless or self-destructive behavior, hypervigiliance, exaggerated startle response, problems with concentration and sleep). To meet *DSM-5* criteria for PTSD, this constellation of symptoms must occur for at least 1 month and cause clinically significant distress or impairment in social, occupational, or other important areas of functioning (APA, 2013). The frequency, severity, and duration of a client's PTSD symptoms may be influenced by many factors, and the primary influences are addressed in the sections that follow.

ECOLOGICAL MODEL FOR CONCEPTUALIZING SEXUAL TRAUMA

Research indicates the importance of understanding a survivor's responses to trauma as a complex interaction between the individual and their environment. An individual's adjustment to trauma can be influenced by multiple systems—including the immediate environment, the broader community, and the larger cultural context in which sexual violence is understood (Campbell et al., 2009). For the purposes of this chapter, I draw on the ecological model of Campbell et al. (2009) for conceptualizing the impact of sexual violence on a survivor's posttrauma functioning. This systems model is based on Bronfenbrenner's (1995) ecological theory of human development and consists of six levels, all of which are described in the paragraphs that follow.

Individual Level

This level refers to the individual survivor's particular sociodemographical characteristics. Although any individual can be a victim of sexual trauma, it is a gendered experience, with women far more likely to be victims, and men far more likely to be perpetrators (e.g., between 91% and 100% of female victims report that the perpetrator was male; Smith et al., 2017). As summarized by ISTSS (2018), some additional individual risk factors include the following:

- Younger individuals are at higher risk for all forms of sexual violence, in general, and for rape in particular. More than 80% of women say they first experienced sexual victimization before the age of 25, 43% before the age of 18, 30% between the ages of 11 and 17, and about 13% when they were 10 or younger. Men report being even younger than women at the time of their first sexual victimization: 51% experienced victimization prior to age 18, 25% between the ages of 11 and 17, and almost 26% were age 10 or under when they were first victimized (D'Inverno et al., 2019).
- Native American/Alaska Native Women are at increased risk of all forms of sexual violence. They are more likely than any other ethnic or racial group to have experienced

a violent sexual assault, such as one involving a weapon or physical injury. In addition, they are more likely than other women to report that the perpetrator was using alcohol at the time of the assault.

■ Individuals with disabilities are raped and sexually assaulted at high rates, One study found that women with disabilities face a five times increased risk of experiencing some form of sexual assault, in the past year, when compared with women who do not have a disability. Men with disabilities are seven times more likely than men without a disability to have experienced completed rape, and five times more likely to have experienced some form of sexual assault during the past year (ISTSS, 2018).

■ Sexual orientation also places one at an increased risk for sexual violence. Bisexual women are at particularly high risk, with 46% of bisexual women experiencing rape in their lifetime (compared to 17% of women who identify as heterosexual and 13% who identify as lesbian; Walters et al., 2013). Gay and bisexual men are also at elevated risk; 47% of bisexual men and 40% of gay men report a history of some form of unwanted or nonconsensual sexual activity.

■ Gender minorities, including transgender and gender nonbinary individuals, experience disproportionately high rates of sexual assault. Around 50% of transgender-identified individuals in the United States say they have experienced unwanted, nonconsensual sexual activity. Male transitioning to female transgender individuals are at higher risk compared to female to male transgender individuals (ISTSS, 2018).

Assault Characteristics Level

This level provides an understanding of the relationship of the survivor to the perpetrator and also refers to the use of alcohol or other drugs during the assault. Sexual trauma is generally classified according to the perpetrator: stranger, date/acquaintance, and marital partner. There is a pervasive stereotype that sexual assault is most likely to be perpetrated by a stranger, although data indicate that sexual assault is most likely to be perpetrated by someone whom the survivor knows, as 80% of rapes are committed by someone known to the victim (U.S. Department of Justice, 2017). Survivors of acquaintance, date, partner, or spousal rapes tend to engage in more self-blame and receive more victim-blame than do those who experience stranger rapes. Sexual violence committed by an intimate partner is particularly traumatic, in that although rape by a stranger may be experienced as a singular event, survivors of intimate partner rape typically endure multiple sexual assaults and must live with the continuous threat of repeated incidents of trauma, including other types of partner violence such as physical and psychological abuse (Temple et al., 2007). In fact, one in four women and one in ten men have experienced contact sexual violence, physical violence, or stalking by an intimate partner and say that they experienced significant short-term or long–term impact (e.g., PTSD, injury) that resulted from these events (Smith et al., 2017).

In addition to the survivor's relationship with the perpetrator, sexual trauma also may be classified as to whether or not alcohol or other drugs were used in the assault. Sexual assault is highly associated with alcohol use, both by the perpetrator and the victim, particularly for college students and in acquaintance rape cases. Frequently, a person is raped while they are unable to give consent for sexual activity because of intoxication; yet, they are hesitant to label the incident as rape, question their role in the assault, and tend to engage in self-blame. In current culture, there remains a prominent myth that if a person is drinking in a social setting and is victimized, then that person is at fault for drinking excessively or by being in that setting in the first place. As a result, women may believe it is their fault if they are sexually assaulted after drinking in social situations (Zaleski et al., 2016). For these reasons, individuals are less likely to report alcohol-related sexual assaults than they are to report stranger rapes, and when they do, they are more likely to be viewed with skepticism and victim-blaming by others.

Chronosystem Level

This level refers to the cumulative effects of multiple developmental transitions in a survivor's life. In the case of sexual trauma, it refers to a survivor's particular history of victimization. There is a considerable line of research indicating that episodes of sexual abuse or assault that occur across two or more developmental periods (e.g., childhood, adolescence, and adulthood) are related to particularly negative outcomes (Charak et al., 2017). Unfortunately, developmental revictimization occurs to a significant number of childhood female sexual abuse survivors; recent studies indicate that 35% of women raped before the age of 18 also experience rape as an adult, compared with 14% of adults with no history of rape (D'Inverno et al., 2019). Survivors of childhood abuse are two to three times more likely to be sexually assaulted in adolescence and adulthood than are individuals from the general population (Tjaden & Thoennes, 2006), and there is some indication that there are even higher revictimization rates among LGBT individuals who experienced childhood sexual abuse (ISTSS, 2018).

Counselors therefore need to assess for and understand a survivor's victimization history, as people who have been victimized previously are more likely to have differing treatment needs than other survivors. Revictimization is associated with increased levels of PTSD symptoms compared to a single incident of trauma (Scott et al., 2018), and those who experience revictimization report greater levels of depression, PTSD, dissociation, anxiety, and substance abuse than do other survivors of sexual trauma (Fortier et al., 2009). Grauerholz (2000) conceptualized the revictimization process as operating within a system composed of the following four levels: (a) a survivor's initial abuse experience and family history (e.g., demographics, severity, duration, relationship to the perpetrator, and negative social reactions to initial disclosure); (b) the exosystem (e.g., lack of resources or safe housing concerns that increase a survivor's vulnerability to future sexual violence); (c) macrosystem factors (e.g., cultural norms and institutions that tend to blame the victim, particularly for causing the revictimization); and (d) microsystem factors (e.g., interpersonal and intrapersonal factors, and the interaction between the perpetrator's behavior and the psychological vulnerability of the survivor).

While recognizing revictimization as a multisystemic problem, recent research in this area has centered on microsystem factors. One reason for developmental revictimization is that childhood sexual abuse significantly interferes with a person's subsequent ability to cope with emotions in an effective manner. Instead, people who were abused are more likely to turn to ways to help avoid or escape painful, persistent emotions. People who are abused as children are more likely to use avoidant coping strategies as an adult, such as engagement in high-risk activities (e.g., binge drinking, risky sexual behavior), which then places a person at higher risk for future victimization (Fortier et al., 2009). A recent study indicates that early experiences of abuse disrupt the development of a child's emotion regulation capacity. With the disruption of emotion-regulatory abilities, as the person enters adolescence and adulthood, they will have trouble with emotional clarity (the ability to be aware of, understand, and accept one's emotions); have poor ability to control impulsive behaviors when distressed; and will have decreased ability to use appropriate strategies to help regulate or modulate emotions effectively (Charak et al., 2017). In addition to emotion regulation deficits, childhood trauma also results in reduced ability to respond effectively to threatening situations. When a person experiences sexual trauma in childhood, these early experiences interfere with the development of their ability to cope with and respond to potentially dangerous situations. These experiences also interfere with their ability to process threatening information, perceive and assess risks accurately, react appropriately to threats, and use effective self-protective responses (Fortier et al., 2009).

Exosystem Level

This level refers to survivors' interactions with formal support services such as medical, legal, law enforcement, or mental health systems. A significant barrier for many survivors is a fear of negative consequences if they reach out for formal support services. These fears are often well-founded; it is common for survivors to report that their contacts with formal systems were quite negative and dehumanizing, and caused them to experience guilt, shame, mistrust, and reluctance to seek further help (ISTSS, 2018). These types of negative interactions can result in what often is termed a "secondary victimization," which is the result of insensitivity, victim blaming, minimization, and negative reactions from medical, legal, law enforcement, and mental health professionals, and which is often experienced as a secondary trauma that does not help but rather exacerbates trauma (Gravelin et al., 2019).

Survivors also report being hesitant to seek access to formal services because of fears that they will be required to make a formal report to legal authorities or to law enforcement. They fear that reporting might bring about reprisal from the perpetrator (or his family and peers), might cause financial and psychological hardship due to court costs and legal involvement, and they might fear negative effects of reporting on the perpetrator's family, friends, and community (the latter point is discussed in greater detail later in this chapter as it relates to cultural values). They also report reluctance to seek services because they have concerns about confidentiality, believe that sexual experiences are private matters, and members of refugee or immigrant groups may have fears of deportation (ISTSS, 2018). Others from marginalized groups may have experienced a long history of not being believed by law enforcement officials, or they may have developed a strong mistrust of agencies, based on both personal experiences and historical knowledge of violations perpetrated by these agencies.

Individuals report that, even when services are available, they have limited awareness of the supports that are available, and they have lack of access to these resources. Formal services tend to be less available and accessible for survivors who are disabled, non-English speaking, or who have low levels of education; such individuals often are unaware of available resources or have limited access to hospitals or rape crisis centers (Bryant-Davis et al., 2009). In addition, many social services are not designed to meet the needs of male survivors or of LGBT individuals. Many survivors from marginalized groups say that a lack of clinicians from their own cultural group is a barrier to help seeking. They believe that clinicians from nonmarginalized groups may lack awareness, knowledge, and skill to understand their native language and to respect their cultural values and practices fully.

Further, individuals might avoid seeking help in order to protect themselves from psychological harm (Patterson et al., 2009; Ullman, 2007). After a sexual trauma, survivors may try to suppress their memories and emotions, deny the impact of the trauma on their current functioning, and fear that if they experience the memories and feelings, they may become overwhelmed. They may delay seeking help from professionals until they can no longer suppress their emotions or when their symptoms become intolerable. As a result, many survivors may delay seeking mental health treatment for years, and even when they do seek treatment, they often present for counseling with a different presenting problem. In addition, survivors may delay seeking mental health treatment because of past negative experiences with the mental health system or with particular mental health professionals, or they might possess beliefs that treatment will cause them to feel worse, that they are unworthy of services, or that mental health treatment will not or cannot help them with their particular experiences (Patterson et al., 2009). Because of these findings, it is therefore important for counselors to be aware that (a) survivors may delay treatment and not seek help until their symptoms are chronic, (b) they may be highly mistrustful of the treatment process, and (c) they may present with a different problem, initially, until they feel comfortable in openly disclosing the sexual violence.

Microsystem Level

This level refers to an individual's social support system. It is a difficult choice for survivors to disclose sexual violence to others, and others' reactions to their disclosure may play an important role in future help-seeking and recovery. When survivors receive negative reactions from informal supports, they report higher levels of PTSD symptoms, poor self-esteem, greater self-blame, and are more likely to engage in maladaptive coping strategies (Ullman & Relyea, 2016). Negative reactions following disclosure can range from overt rejection, blaming the survivor, stigmatizing the survivor (i.e., viewing them as "damaged goods"), or outright disbelief that the incident occurred. Some reactions that seemingly appear to provide support are not effective but actually harmful. For example, it is damaging if a survivor discloses an act of sexual violence to a loved one, and the person acknowledges what happened, but minimizes its impact, tells the survivor to "just stop thinking about it," or even resorts to controlling behaviors to try to protect the survivor (Ullman & Relyea, 2016).

Negative reactions from others, however, can be buffered by the availability of positive social support. Research indicates that social support and positive reactions to disclosure can strongly affect a survivor's reactions to trauma as well as the ability to recover from sexual violence (Ullman & Relyea, 2016). The availability of social support increases the likelihood of early disclosure, which is related to a more positive recovery. In fact, survivors with strong support systems, and those who disclose to family and friends, have more positive physical and mental health following sexual trauma (Ullman, 2007).

Macrosystem Level

This level refers to broader societal factors such as cultural differences in responding to rape and the acceptance of rape myths that exist in a particular culture. It is important to understand a survivor's reactions to sexual violence within a sociocultural context, examining the meaning of sexual assault not only to the individual, but also in terms of how it is perceived within the individual's cultural community. For example, when examining rape within a feminist, gendered context, it is viewed not as a crime about sex but about power that serves to devalue women, limit their freedom, and maintain their inequality (Brownmiller, 1975). Popular culture contributes to and perpetuates this power differential. In current culture, women are hypersexualized and sexually objectified in popular media representations; women are frequently portrayed as sexual objects that exist for the gratification of men's desires. Sexual aggression and violence against women also are normalized in such media as music, music videos, videogames, and pornography (Gravelin et al., 2019).

With sexual objectification occurring so pervasively at the macrolevel, authors recently have used the term "rape culture" to describe certain hypermasculinized settings in which the glorification of coercive sexual behavior becomes part of the group identity. Sexual aggression is an expected and normative behavior within these groups. Such cultural attitudes may be maintained as victims are silenced through stigmatizing, shaming, or not believing women who speak up. When coercive behaviors are normalized, women may begin to question whether they are to blame or whether or not the experience was even a sexual assault (Gravelin et al., 2019). Endorsement of what authors have termed "rape myths" also contribute to the perpetuation of rape culture (see Box 6.1).

BOX 6.1

Rape Myths

Myths about rape may exist within a particular society that influence both survivors' and others' reactions to acts of sexual violence. Women, in particular, are harmed when the following types of commonly accepted rape myths are endorsed:

- Only stranger rape is "real" rape;
- Sexual violence is the norm; it is natural and normal for sexual activity to involve aggressive behavior;

(continued)

- She must have deserved it (rape) because of the way she dressed and where she was when it happened;
- Women are just "asking for it" (rape) if they are out alone, late at night;
- If she is drinking alcohol and is raped, then she should have acted more responsibly with her alcohol consumption;
- She must have wanted it (rape), because she didn't say no or didn't put up a struggle;
- If a woman sexually teases a man, she deserves to be raped;
- Men can't control themselves sexually, once they are aroused; they can't control their urges;
- When she says 'no,' she really means 'yes' and is just playing hard to get (termed "token resistance"; implies the belief that many women say 'no' to sex even though they want to say 'yes' because it is considered 'unladylike' for women to desire sex—so she says 'no' when she really means 'yes');
- A woman who accuses a man of rape is doing it to get back at him for not going out with her" (or she is lying and made the story up for attention or for money);
- It is not really rape if a woman has had many sexual partners; and,
- Men can't be raped.

(Burt, 1980; Gravelin et al., 2019)

It is clear that accepting rape-related myths perpetuated by society can lead to greater levels of negative reactions from others to minimization by the survivor, and to the likelihood of increased victim blaming. All of these can have an impact on an individual's ability to recover from sexual trauma (Campbell et al., 2009).

Recent social justice activism such as the #*MeToo* movement has brought the pervasiveness of rape culture into greater focus, with more survivors speaking out about abuses in the film/television industry, by politicians, on college campuses (and fraternity houses in particular), among professional and elite-level athletes, and the high levels of sexual trauma within the military (Gravelin et al., 2019). It remains to be seen whether this movement will have an impact on decreasing or even eradicating rape culture in the future.

Cultural norms around sexual identity also affect the perpetration of and disclosures about sexual violence against LGBT individuals. For male survivors, cultural beliefs about masculinity (that men cannot be raped) and sexuality ("if a man is raped by another man, he must be gay") may cause blame, stigma, and reluctance to report. As stated previously, men who do not conform to cultural norms of masculinity often are targeted as victims of violence; bisexual men are at especially high risk for sexual violence, as well as transgender individuals who are transitioning from male to female. Further, in cultures where there exists strong homophobia, or even laws against homosexuality, sexual minorities are at particularly high risk for sexual assault. In certain African countries, for example, there still is evidence of what is called "corrective rape" for lesbian women, to "cure" them of their sexuality, as well as experiences of rape/murder for both men and women as a form of "punishment" for their sexual identity (Mwambene & Wheal, 2015).

Finally, a person's experience of sexual violence can be influenced by their racial/ethnic background and cultural values within a particular community. According to Bryant-Davis et al. (2009), the sexual assault of ethnic/racial minority men and women should be understood within the broader context of *societal trauma*, considering that an individual's previous experiences with racism, sexism, classism, heterosexism, cultural violence, or historical violence are cumulative and contribute to the way in which a survivor experiences sexual violence when it occurs. For example, Native American women may have a distrust of government agencies and law enforcement, not only related to their current life experiences but also due to the accumulation of historical abuses and cultural trauma resulting from colonization (ISTSS, 2018). Asian American families may place pressure on survivors to remain silent about their experiences so as not to bring the family shame or dishonor. Finally, Slatton and Richard (2020) write about the societal marginalization of African American women that serves to delegitimize their experience of sexual violence and to increase their reluctance to report when it occurs. Black American women may believe they will be blamed for their own victimization, will not be taken seriously by law enforcement, and that they must uphold the stereotyped role of the Strong Black Woman who should bear her pain without complaint. African American women may also receive pressure from their own communities to refrain from any reporting of intraracial assaults; they are told their primary allegiance should be to protect members of their own race and that a report would be viewed as an attack against the Black community. When receiving this type of pressure, it is understandable that women may be conflicted as to whether to protect African American male perpetrators from incarceration, or to promote their own needs for justice and safety (Slatton & Richard, 2020). The clinical vignette that follows illustrates the importance of viewing sexual assault through a multisystemic lens (Box 6.2).

BOX 6.2

Clinical Vignette: Michelle's Story

Michelle, a 25-year-old African American woman with two children ages 3 and 5, lives with her mother and children. She seeks assistance from Marybeth, a Caucasian counselor (age 45) at the community college she is attending part-time. Michelle has many reservations about being in Marybeth's office and speaks hesitantly, wondering if this White counselor, who is 20 years older than she, actually can be of help to her. While she initially talks about concerns with her young children and time management issues, eventually she reveals that she needs to talk about an incident in which she was raped 1 year ago by a friend of her mother's. At the time of the assault, she was home alone and allowed this friend to come in and wait until her mother returned from work. She never told her mother or anyone in her family of this incident, nor did she discuss it with anyone else until today. She thought she could put the rape out of her mind and told herself to be strong. She questioned whether anyone would even believe her if she told anyone. She is seeking help now, due to recent difficulty going to class, because her professor reminds her of the man who attacked her. She also is experiencing flashbacks, nightmares, and persistent symptoms of anxiety. She keeps asking Marybeth if she is doing the right thing in discussing this private incident.

Marybeth reassures Michelle that she is taking an important step toward recovery by talking about the rape with her. When assessing Michelle's attitudes toward help seeking, she learns about her fears of counseling (i.e., that she will be forced to report the incident to police, that she will have to withdraw from school, that she will be interrogated in court, or that Marybeth will tell her family). She is adamant that she does not want to go to the police, because she has observed male police officers act in a nonresponsive manner with women in her neighborhood who have called them for help with domestic violence. She thinks the police will not believe her, and even if they did, she does not want her mother's friend (who is also African American) to go to jail. She asserts, "There are too many African American men in this city who are already in jail, and I don't want to be responsible for putting another man behind bars." After Marybeth assures Michelle that she will respect her decision not to report and that she will keep her information confidential, she tries to begin to understand

(continued)

Michelle's cultural values and life history that might be contributing to her reactions to the rape. As an African American woman, Michelle says that she learned that it is very important to be strong and independent, to bear any painful burdens in silence. She fears her mother will support her friend and will be angry that she is trying to cause trouble for him, because she believes he is a "good man." When asked about social support, Michelle states that she is close to her sister and a few women at her church, but she does not want to tell anyone about this, because she fears it is pointless; they either will blame her or just tell her to "be strong and this will pass."

TRAUMA-INFORMED TREATMENTS FOR SEXUAL VIOLENCE

Counselors generally provide assistance to survivors coping with sexual assault in two ways: either through referring to or providing crisis intervention in the immediate aftermath of the event, or through providing treatment, at a later time, when the survivor can no longer tolerate the symptoms that have emerged following the sexual trauma. As highlighted in the previous sections, it is important for counselors to be prepared with the knowledge and skill to provide contextually-sensitive trauma-focused treatment.

The treatment approaches outlined in the following text are based on clinical practice guidelines for PTSD and are recommended as efficacious by major mental health organizations (American Psychiatric Association PTSD Guideline Watch, 2009; American Psychological Association Clinical Practice Guideline for the Treatment of PTSD, 2017; ISTSS Practice Guideline for PTSD, 2019; Veterans Affairs/Department of Defense Practice Guideline for the Management of PTSD and Acute Stress Disorder, 2017). The evidence-based, recommended treatment approaches are designed to reduce PTSD symptoms that occur following sexual trauma, and they include the following: (a) psychoeducation about trauma and commonly experienced PTSD symptoms, (b) PE to facilitate the client's ability to process memories related to the event, (c) cognitive therapy and CBT with a trauma focus (i.e., trauma-focused CBT for children and adolescents, CPT, and [EMDR), both to process memories associated with the event as well as to help restructure the client's maladaptive beliefs about the impact of the event.

Psychoeducation

When counselors work with sexual trauma survivors, they first should work to develop a trusting therapeutic alliance, as survivors may have great reluctance to discuss their memories of the trauma and may have had negative experiences with other service clinicians. Counselors should demonstrate empathy and positive regard for clients as they carefully assess client concerns through the multisystemic lens described in this chapter. This type of assessment is imperative in developing a treatment approach that is tailored to the client's specific needs. As part of building rapport, survivors of sexual trauma benefit from receiving information regarding commonly experienced reactions to sexual assault (e.g., guilt, anger, shame, powerlessness, helplessness, fear) and the symptoms of PTSD, as described previously. Many survivors express that they feel relief when they realize that they are not "crazy," but rather are experiencing a normal and expected reaction to a highly traumatic event, and that PTSD symptoms persist, because the natural process of recovery has been interrupted. They feel a sense of hope that effective treatments exist that can help to resolve their distress. The counselor also should be prepared to provide information and resources about medical and legal decisions and assist the survivor in gaining access to local sexual trauma services, as appropriate (American Psychiatric Association, 2009; American Psychological Association, 2017).

Exposure-Based Therapy

PE is another research-based approach that is strongly recommended in clinical practice guidelines. The goal of PE is to assist a survivor in working through painful memories, situations, thoughts, and emotions associated with the traumatic event and which currently evoke anxiety and fear (Foa et al., 2007). The client is asked to create a verbal and written narrative that provides a detailed recounting of the traumatic event. This PE to the memory is done with the goal of habituation (and resulting decrease in anxiety and fear). As noted previously, many survivors of sexual trauma engage in avoidant coping strategies in order to avoid this intense anxiety and fear (Fortier et al., 2009), and it is understandable that they will be resistant to this strategy when it is presented to them in counseling. To encourage clients to undertake this difficult work, counselors should express empathy and acknowledge a survivor's fear, spend time educating the client about the rationale for this treatment strategy, and convey positive expectations for recovery. Counselors can explain the rationale for PE to clients in the following way:

1. Memories, people, places, and activities associated with the trauma are now stored as a fear network in your brain. Any time you encounter anything associated with the trauma, your fear network is activated, causing symptoms like nightmares, flashbacks, and intrusive thoughts. These are uncomfortable and make you highly anxious, so you do what you can to avoid the memories or anything else that might remind you of the trauma.
2. Each time you avoid them, however, you do not finish the process of digesting painful experiences, and so they keep returning in the form of intrusive symptoms.
3. You can begin to process the experience by gradually allowing yourself to access the memories, thoughts, and feelings in your imagination, holding them there without pushing them away.
4. You also will practice facing those activities, places, and situations that currently evoke fear.
5. Eventually, you will be able to think about the trauma and resume your normal activities without experiencing intense fear.

After providing a rationale, the counselor can then teach a breathing technique to help the client manage her anxiety as she begins formal processing of the trauma. When the client is ready to begin the process, the counselor can use *imaginal exposure* to assist the client in repeatedly recounting memories associated with the trauma, until the memories no longer cause intense anxiety and fear (Foa et al., 2007). Clients are asked to close their eyes, to imagine the traumatic event in vivid detail, and to describe it as if it were happening in the present. This narrative is recited repeatedly, in sessions, and is recorded for listening, outside of sessions. Writing about the event in a journal also may be helpful for continued practice. This is an extremely difficult phase of treatment for clients as they face the thoughts, feelings, and images associated with the event, which they have been attempting to avoid, out of fear. Counselors should acknowledge this difficulty and encourage clients in their willingness to process the event, gradually, in order to cope with their fears.

PE also involves *in vivo exposure*, a process through which clients are asked to focus on activities and situations associated with the event that they currently avoid because it evokes intense fear and disrupts daily functioning. The client hierarchically lists all avoided situations and activities, ranking them from least to most distressing. It should be noted that the counselor should review this list to ensure that these situations or activities are actually safe and that it includes only those things that are interfering with the client's ability to engage in their daily routines. Starting with the activity or situation that is least distressing, the client remains in this particular environment for a minimum of 30 minutes. This time is recommended because it is long enough for the client to experience fear, to evaluate the actual level of danger present in the situation, and to allow the fear and anxiety to decrease. Anxiety management techniques can be used during this time. Over the course of counseling, the client can progress through the hierarchy until they are able to resume daily routines and functioning (Foa et al., 2007).

Trauma-Focused Cognitive and Cognitive-Behavioral Approaches

According to practice guidelines, cognitive and CBT-based approaches are effective in reducing symptoms associated with sexual trauma. In these approaches, clients learn to identify the automatic thoughts or beliefs that they experience during negative emotional states related to the sexual trauma. The counselor's ability to understand the client's broader context can assist the client in fully identifying and exploring thoughts as well as the meaning that the client places on the impact of the traumatic event. As clients identify these thoughts and beliefs, they also learn about typical cognitive distortions related to sexual trauma, learn to evaluate distortions, challenge them, and eventually replace them with more rational or beneficial thoughts.

Trauma-Focused Cognitive Behavioral Therapy

TF-CBT is a structured model of trauma-based treatment for children, adolescents, and their caregivers. The goal of this approach is to help the client process traumatic memories, to overcome problematic thoughts and behaviors, and to develop effective coping and interpersonal skills. The approach also includes a parenting component that focuses on stress management, positive parenting, behavior management, and effective communication (Cohen et al., 2016). The key components of TF-CBT can be summarized according to the acronym PRACTICE:

P: Psychoeducation (about trauma, PTSD); parenting skills (positive parenting, communication)
R: Relaxation techniques (e.g., practicing focused breathing, progressive muscle relaxation)
A: Affective expression and regulation (identifying and expressing emotions appropriately)
C: Cognitive coping and processing (identifying and correcting unhelpful thoughts, understanding how thoughts, feelings, and behaviors are connected)
T: Trauma narrative and processing (creating a verbal, written, and other creative recounting of traumatic events)
I: In vivo exposure (gradual exposure to trauma reminders in a child's environment so that the child can learn to control emotional reactions, as fear is reduced)
C: Conjoint parent/child sessions (working with a family to teach effective communication, and to provide the child with an opportunity to share the trauma narrative with caregivers)
E: Enhancing personal safety and future growth (education and training on personal safety, healthy relationships and sexuality, and encouraging the use of new skills in future situations) (Child Welfare Information Gateway, 2018; Cohen et al., 2016).

Cognitive Processing Therapy

One form of CBT that originally was designed specifically for rape-related trauma in adults is CPT (Resick et al., 2017). CPT recently has been expanded and shows strong success in treating PTSD in multiple populations, including military veterans and for military sexual trauma (VAA/DOD, 2017). In CPT, PTSD is conceptualized as a disorder of halted or interrupted recovery. While painful memories are typically processed and resolve naturally, over time, for some individuals, recovery becomes stuck due to repeated avoidance of the feared memories, thoughts, feelings, and places associated with the event. Recovery also can become stuck when the impact of the trauma results in the development of unhelpful beliefs about the self, others, and the world. Therefore, the goal of CPT is to help the client break the pattern of avoidance, through repeated exposure to the traumatic memory, so that the memory can be processed adequately. A second goal is to challenge and restructure unhelpful beliefs that have developed related to the trauma.

In therapy, the client is asked to write an impact statement—a statement regarding why she thinks the event happened, and the impact that it has had on her beliefs about self, others, and the world. The client and counselor then explore the client's interpretation of the event, along with the implications of the trauma, as these relate to the client's belief system. Through the counselor's line of questioning, the client can start to consider alternative viewpoints and multiple ways in which to view the trauma. The therapist can use questions such as:

- What is the evidence for and against this idea?
- Is your belief a habit or based on facts? Is the source of information reliable?
- Are you using words or phrases that are extreme or exaggerated (i.e., always, forever, never, need, should, must, can't, and every time)?
- Are you taking the situation out of context and only focusing on one aspect of the event?
- Are your judgments about yourself or the event based on feelings rather than facts?

In identifying and examining the client belief system, the counselor first helps the client analyze her beliefs regarding self-blame. Resick et al. (2017) encourage counselors to help their clients to distinguish between responsibility and blame in a situation. On the one hand, *responsibility* is related to the actions an individual took in a situation that contributed to a certain outcome. In contrast, *blame* involves a combination of both responsibility and intentionality. The following questions might be posed to the client: What did you do in the situation, and did you intend to cause or contribute to the resulting outcome? Did you intend for harm to come to you or to others?

As described throughout this chapter, self-blame is perpetuated by cultural beliefs and by negative reactions from others in the survivor's life who engage in victim blame. Individuals who incorporate self-blame into their overall view of themselves tend to be the most stuck in recovery. It therefore is important for counselors to help their clients distinguish between avoiding attributions of self-blame assigned to their *character* (e.g., "I am a bad person and deserved to be raped") versus accepting responsibility for some aspect of their *behavior* (e.g., "I made a decision that day that I might not make now"). Guilt often is related to self-blame, in that the survivor may perceive that they are to blame for putting themselves in the situation or for not doing enough to fight back or to prevent the crime. The counselor can assist the client in examining self-blaming and guilt-related beliefs and can help the client begin to replace these thoughts with more logical and growth-enhancing self-statements (e.g., "I did not do everything right in this situation, but the perpetrator is fully responsible for this crime. I will now do everything I can to reclaim the power taken away from me by this crime").

In addition to attributions about self-blame, survivors learn skills to identify and challenge "stuck points" in five specific areas: safety, trust, power/control, esteem, and intimacy. The CPT stuck points are described briefly in the following text.

Safety: The first stuck point to explore relates to prior and current beliefs about safety. The client is asked to examine her prior beliefs about safety (e.g., Did you believe others were basically safe and that you had what it takes to protect yourself in the world? Or did you grow up believing that others are dangerous and that you were unable to protect yourself?). The nature of these prior beliefs will be altered because of the trauma. Through a gentle questioning process, the counselor can help the client develop a more balanced view that incorporates the traumatic event but that does not lead to avoidance or undue fear. An example of a new and balanced view might be: "I can't control my safety at all times, but I can take steps to protect myself from harm. There may be some people I encounter, who intend to harm others, but it is unrealistic to expect that everyone I meet is going to harm me."

Trust: Disruptions in trust of self and others is a common stuck point for survivors. For some individuals who had a prior trusting outlook (e.g., "I have good judgment," and "Others are trustworthy"), this belief will become disrupted, while for those who held previous negative beliefs about trust in self or others ("I can't trust myself to make good decisions," and "Others can't ever be trusted"), their worldview might be reinforced to an extreme degree that contributes to fear and isolation. The client will need to develop a more balanced belief that accepts and incorporates the traumatic event. For example, a new belief might be: "I can learn from my experiences and I can trust myself to make the best decisions I can in the future. There may be some people I cannot trust to talk to about what happened to me, but they can be trusted to support me in other areas."

Power and Control: During an act of sexual violence, an individual is stripped of their power, and often survivors continue to feel powerless and out of control long after the trauma has ended.

In examining her prior beliefs, the counselor can help determine if she viewed herself as always in control of her life (e.g., I can control what happens to me and I can always protect myself") or if she viewed herself as powerless to effect change (e.g., "I am powerless in most situations"). The goal in therapy is to help the client create a more balanced view of power and control, one in which she recognizes that she will not have total control over every situation, but in which she recognizes that she is not helpless. For example, "I do not have total control over my reactions, other people, or everything that might happen in my life, but I definitely have some control over my reactions to events and the power to influence the outcome of many situations." Counselors also can assist the client in focusing on restoring their sense of personal power, particularly regarding decisions made in the present. As a part of regaining power and control, counselors should encourage clients to take an active role in the counseling process, providing them with as many choices as possible and allowing for flexibility in the timing and pacing of sessions.

Self-Esteem: In their CPT treatment manual, Resick et al. (2017) recommend helping clients to focus on the effect that the sexual trauma has had on their self-image and self-esteem. Clients can uncover negative beliefs, such as "I am unlovable" or "I am damaged goods," which have surfaced or have been reinforced by the trauma. Through CPT, clients can learn to separate the events and their reactions from their views of themselves as individuals (e.g., "Being a survivor of sexual trauma is a part of who I am, but it does not define me. I have strengths and a sense of self that this trauma did not disrupt"). As a part of this process, the survivor gradually can learn to view the sexual violence as a traumatic yet growth-enhancing event. It is helpful for clients to know that growth often occurs after a traumatic event, including greater self-awareness, strength, maturity, a more flexible worldview, increased empathy, greater sensitivity to the suffering of others, and changes in relationships, spirituality, life philosophy, or overall values.

Intimacy: Because sexual violence often is committed by someone the survivor knows and trusts, a client's capacity for intimacy may be disrupted. If a survivor questions their judgment in selecting safe relationships, engages in self-blame, and receives victim-blaming reactions, they can develop particular problems in intimacy with both existing and new relationships. To change these stuck points, clients can explore beliefs that they have developed, related to relationships and about the world in general (e.g., "People can't be trusted and I should not allow them to be too close"). They can then modify any beliefs that are impediments to their recovery, evaluate current relationships and their interactions with others who can provide support, and fully explore the need for positive connections with others as part of the recovery process. For example, one area that is common for survivors is the need to process any disappointment they feel in others who reacted in an unsupportive manner following disclosure of the trauma. They can then decide if they want to communicate their feelings openly to the people involved (Box 6.3). They can be encouraged that, by communicating directly about their feelings, the overall level of safety and trust in the relationship might be clarified, and overall communication actually might be enhanced. A helpful and more balanced view of intimacy, then, may be: "I can still be close to people, and I have the right to choose whether or not I want to be intimate with others. I don't have to be close to everyone, but I don't have to push everyone away either."

BOX 6.3

Clinical Vignette: Michelle's Treatment and Recovery

Recall the case of Michelle from earlier in the chapter. Once in treatment, the counselor, Marybeth, first reassures Michelle that her symptoms are normal reactions to a traumatic event such as rape. She educates her about symptoms of PTSD and describes the elements of recommended treatment approaches. With Michelle's permission, they gradually create a trauma narrative and impact statement. Marybeth asks Michelle to describe the rape in detail and to re-experience her emotions around the event. Over time, Michelle learns to use relaxation techniques, while sitting

(continued)

at her desk before class, and then once the professor enters the room. She uncovers self-blaming thoughts that are keeping her stuck: "I deserved this," "I can trust no one," "I am disgusting because this happened to me." She then learns to let go of some of her blame, guilt, and mistrust of others. While she decides not to tell anyone in her family about the rape at this time, she discusses the benefits and consequences of doing so in the future. With Marybeth's encouragement, Michelle is able to disclose the rape to one friend and is relieved when she fully supports her. Gradually, she experiences some symptom relief and is able to function better at home and school.

Eye Movement Desensitization and Reprocessing

Although initially developed 30 years ago (Shapiro, 2001), EMDR has emerged as an effective and widely accepted treatment for PTSD. It is a treatment that integrates elements of the exposure-based and cognitive therapies described previously and focuses on changing the way that traumatic memories are stored in the brain. When under extreme stress, our natural fight, flight, or freeze instincts are activated. When PTSD symptoms develop, it is assumed that the memory (including images, cognitions, affects, and bodily sensations) has been stored in the brain exactly as it was at the time of the event. When the memory or anything associated with the memory is triggered, the original fight/flight or freeze response is reactivated and is experienced by the individual as if the event is happening again in the present moment. Because this is so unpleasant, the individual does what is possible to keep this from happening and tries to avoid memories and associations with the trauma.

EMDR uses bilateral brain stimulation through eye movements, taps, or tones to help the individual to process these distressing memories directly. While undergoing bilateral brain stimulation, the person is asked to recall the image, associated cognitions, affects, and physical sensations. The treatment assumes that as both the left and right hemispheres are activated in processing the memory, the brain becomes better able to integrate the memory with less emotion and more logical reasoning. With integration, the individual finally can experience the memory as not actually happening in the present, but rather, experience it as an occurrence in the past that is now over. The memory remains, but the fight/flight or freeze response (along with distressing symptoms) is no longer reactivated (EMDR International Association, 2020). The sessions are structured according to the following phases (summarized from American Psychological Association, 2017):

- **History**: The counselor conducts a history of the trauma, develops a treatment plan, and ensures the client has adequate resources for affect management and containment both within and outside of sessions.
- **Assessment**: The client is asked to view a list of common negative core beliefs about self, others, and the world. The client is asked to rate the validity of their belief on a scale from one to seven ("How true does this feel to you with one being completely false and seven being completely true?") and is also asked to rate the memory on a scale that measures the level of distress she experiences related to that memory.
- **Desensitization**: The client focuses on a segment of the memory while exposed to eye movements (or tones or tapping) that bilaterally stimulate both hemispheres of the brain. The client's memory exposure is interrupted after a few moments, and she is then asked about what new thoughts or feelings emerged for her. Ideally there is a new understanding about the experience and its impact. The process continues until the particular memory is experienced as no longer distressing.
- **Installation**: The client is asked to compare the prior negative cognition with a new, more positive and integrated belief about self, others, and the world.
- **Body Scan**: The client is asked to scan the body and to note if any remaining somatic distress is present.

■ **Closure**: The counselor ends the session and assesses for safety and containment until the next session.

■ **Re-evaluation**: At the start of the next session, the counselor assesses for any new memories or thoughts that have emerged since the last session, and these are used as targets for the current session.

EMDR continues to gain popularity among clinicians around the world, but it is clear that it is a complex and highly structured treatment that involves considerable training and skill to be utilized ethically and effectively. Counselors should not practice EMDR without appropriate training and supervised experience (see Eye Movement Desensitization and Reprocessing International Association for training and certification requirements).

COUNSELING IMPLICATIONS

Counselors who work with survivors of sexual trauma can provide more sensitive and effective treatment when they conceptualize client concerns through the ecological model presented in this chapter. It should be clear that counseling treatment that is focused solely on an individual's posttraumatic symptoms is inadequate, as the counselor ultimately fails to address the client's unique responses as affected by the multiple systems that operate in their life. The more the counselor can understand the client's background, cultural values, previous victimization history, relationship to the perpetrator, current level of support, and experiences with victim blame from other service clinicians, the more effective the counselor will be in tailoring treatment to the client's specific needs. While providing this multisystemic understanding of a client's responses to sexual trauma, counselors also should be knowledgeable of clinical practice guidelines for sexual trauma. Because these treatments require clients to address the memories and situations that produce intense fear and anxiety, so they can be fully processed, counselors should balance treatment techniques with adequate support and validation, so that the client remains in control of the direction of their treatment. As the counselor demonstrates empathy and an understanding of the client in context, the client can remain empowered as they undertake the difficult but growth-enhancing process toward recovery.

CONCLUSION

In summary, because of the pervasiveness of sexual violence and resulting trauma, it is important for counselors to be able to provide treatment for sexual trauma in a contextually sensitive manner, while also remaining knowledgeable of evidence-based approaches to treatment. Future research should prioritize a multisystemic approach to the conceptualization of sexual violence. Research also is needed to refine current treatment components and how these may be best tailored for individual clients, based on their sociocultural context.

ADDITIONAL RESOURCES

 SPRINGER PUBLISHING **CONNECT™**　A robust set of instructor resources designed to supplement this text is located at http://connect.springerpub.com/content/book/978-0-8261-5085-1. Qualifying instructors may request access by emailing textbook@springerpub.com.

PRACTICE-BASED RESOURCES AND REFERENCES

To view a list of resources and all the references, please visit connect.springerpub.com via the following url: http://connect.springerpub.com/content/book/978-0-8261-5085-1/part/part02/chapter/ch06

CHAPTER 7

Trauma Experienced in Early Childhood

ANDREA DOYLE AND LISA LÓPEZ LEVERS

CHAPTER OVERVIEW

The purpose of this chapter is to outline some of the consequences of trauma that occur during early childhood. The chapter discusses particular trauma-relevant issues in early childhood, identifies therapeutic responses, and examines the counseling implications. These major sections are followed by a summary of the chapter and an online list of relevant resources.

LEARNING OBJECTIVES

After reading this chapter, the reader should be able to:

1. Become cognizant of the developmental issues in early childhood that interface with and complicate diagnosis;
2. Become aware of the main treatment approaches to trauma in early childhood, how they differ, and how they intersect; and,
3. Develop insight regarding the counseling implications of treating the effects of trauma experienced in early childhood.

INTRODUCTION

Advances in developmental science have marked an increased recognition of the formative nature of early childhood for growth and development across the life-span. Early childhood encompasses the first 8 years of life—including infancy, toddlerhood, preschool, and the early elementary school years. During these years, children develop critical cognitive, social-emotional, and physical competencies that will enable them to negotiate early developmental challenges successfully and to support their future well-being (Durwin & Reese-Weber, 2021; National Research Council, 2000). These early years also are marked by increased vulnerability to traumatic events, such as child abuse and neglect or witnessing intimate partner violence (IPV) or domestic violence (DV). According to Harvard University's Center on the Developing Child (2021), "Toxic Stress," p. 1), "healthy development can be derailed by excessive or

This chapter is a revision of the chapter that appeared in the first edition of this textbook. Dr. Staci Perlman, who passed away in 2015, was one of the authors; we honor and thank her for her original contribution here, as well as for all of her work in advocating for children and youth.

prolonged activation of stress response systems in the body and brain [and] such toxic stress can have damaging effects on learning, behavior, and health across the lifespan."

After a significant decline in number and rate of abused children from 2006 to 2007, as cited in the first publication of this chapter in 2012, the rate and number of abused and neglected children continued to decrease until 2012, when both began to rise again. In 2017, there were approximately 674,000 abused and neglected children in the United States, at a rate of nine per thousand (U.S. Department of Health and Human Services, Children's Bureau, National Child Abuse and Neglect Data System [NCANDS], 2019). As in previous years, rates of abuse and neglect have been greatest among infants and young children (Administration for Children and Families, 2020). Similarly, nearly 60% of children who have witnessed DV are younger than the age of 6 (Fantuzzo & Fusco, 2007; Fusco & Fantuzzo, 2009). Given the critical nature of early childhood for children's development, experiences of trauma in these early years can have a particularly adverse influence on development. From birth to age 5, children are exposed disproportionately to traumatic events relative to older children, but until the last decade, they have been underrepresented in the trauma research literature. Children of color and those living in poverty particularly are affected by the social and behavioral determinants of toxic stress and trauma (Lieberman et al., 2011; Morsy & Rothstein, 2019).

Early childhood can be a toxic or even dangerous time for young children (Center on the Developing Child, 2021), and risk factors associated with poverty and ethnicity may increase the threat of toxic stress and trauma (Kim & Drake, 2018). Some children have experienced untold suffering due to the long-term consequences of child abuse and neglect (Child Welfare Information Gateway, 2019). The purpose of this chapter is to provide an overview of the influence of trauma on early childhood development and to illuminate ways to begin mitigating the effects. This is accomplished through discussions in the following sections: development in early childhood, the influence of trauma on early development, and practice implications for working with young children who have experienced trauma. These sections are followed by concluding remarks and an online list of practice-based resources.

EARLY CHILDHOOD DEVELOPMENT

Early childhood is a critical time for brain development (Centers for Disease Control and Prevention [CDC], 2021; Shonkoff & Phillips, 2000). Between birth and age 2, the brain more than triples in size, reaching 75% of its adult size by age 2 (Davies, 2004; National Research Council, 2000). Neural development begins soon after conception and continues at a rapid rate through early childhood (Durwin & Reese-Weber, 2021; Nelson & Bosquet, 2000). The early stages of neural development consist largely of primitive cells migrating to and forming specific parts of the brain. Once this migration of cells has been completed, the processes of synaptogenesis and myelination begin (Durwin & Reese-Weber, 2021; Nelson & Bosquet, 2000). Synaptogenesis is the process by which connections are made between brain cells, and myelination functions to increase the speed with which cells communicate with one another. The rate of development for synaptic connections is highest in the first few years of life. It is largely contingent on the quantity and quality of stimulation to which children are exposed—or neural plasticity. Positive early experiences have been associated with increased synaptic connections, whereas negative, adverse, or traumatic early experiences have been associated with decreased synaptic connections—or pruning (Durwin & Reese-Weber, 2021; Perry et al., 1995; Siegel, 1999). A primary source of information about the world, and thus a primary source of neural development, comes from infants' and young children's interactions with their caregivers (Siegel, 1999). For this reason, the development of the relationship between infants and their caregivers is a primary early developmental task.

Attachment as a Developmental Competency in Early Childhood

A fundamental task of early childhood is the development of a secure attachment relationship(s) with a parent or guardian. Bowlby (1982), who originated attachment theory, defined "attachment" as "any form of behavior that results in a person attaining or maintaining proximity to some other clearly identified individual who is conceived as better able to cope with the world" (p. 26). Attachment relationships are transactional, in that they result from the mutual interactions between the infant and their caregiver, and they serve to provide the infant with a "sense of security," "affective" regulation, "expression of feelings and communication," and a secure base from which to explore the world (Cicchetti & Valentino, 2006; Davies, 2004; Sroufe et al., 1999; Tronick, 2017).

Starting at birth, infants begin a process of moving through phases of attachment. The first phase of attachment, "orientation and signals with only limited discrimination of figure," occurs in the first 8 weeks of life (Ainsworth, 1964; Bowlby, 1982, p. 266). During this phase, the infant is relatively indiscriminant in terms of the target of their attachment behaviors. The second phase occurs between the eighth and 12th week of life and involves "orientation and signals towards one (or more) discriminated figure(s)" (Bowlby, 1982, p. 266). In other words, the infant is beginning to show preference for one or more specific caregivers. The third phase of attachment is characterized by "maintenance of proximity to a discriminated figure by means of locomotion as well as signals" (p. 267). This phase lasts from about 12 weeks to 18 months. During the third phase, typically, developing infants gain mobility skills through crawling or walking. In doing so, they gain the capacity to retain close physical proximity to their caregiver. The fourth phase of attachment begins at about 18 months and lasts indefinitely. This phase is characterized by "formation of goal-corrected partnership" (p. 267).

As the infant progresses through each of these attachment phases, they engage in attachment behaviors. These behaviors are elicited with the purpose of drawing a caregiver into closer proximity, and as the child moves through the phases of attachment, the behaviors become increasingly discriminating in favor of the primary caregiver (Ainsworth, 1964). Even very young infants show evidence of these behaviors. For instance, as noted by Lieberman and Knorr (2007), a baby may cry, smile, track, cling, or follow a caregiver in an attempt to bring the caregiver closer.

The nature of the caregiver's response to the infant's attachment behaviors has a direct relationship with the resulting pattern of attachment. Consistent and sensitive caregiver responses to infant attachment behaviors are positively associated with the creation of a secure attachment (Rothbaum et al., 2000; True et al., 2001). In accordance with attachment theory, the development of a secure attachment relationship is critical to children's early development. It is from the safety and security of the secure attachment relationship that an infant gains the confidence to explore the world around them. Research has indicated that the lack of secure attachment may result in a child exhibiting social competency deficits (Durwin & Reese-Weber, 2021).

When parents/caregivers respond inconsistently, unpredictably, or adversely, infants are at risk for developing one of three forms of insecure attachment relationships: avoidant, ambivalent/ resistant, and disorganized/disoriented (Schuder & Lyons-Ruth, 2007). Infants whose primary caregivers either reject or discourage their children's attachment behaviors typically exhibit "avoidant" attachment styles. Infants demonstrating an avoidant attachment style often seem indifferent to the presence or absence of their caregiver (Ringel, 2011). Although these children are capable of exploring the world around them, research demonstrates that these children are thought to camouflage their emotional need for their caregivers through a seeming indifference to whether or not the caregiver is present. In fact, research examining the cortisol (stress hormone) levels of children with avoidant attachment styles has found that children with this attachment style have higher cortisol levels than children with secure attachment styles (Mueller & Tronick, 2019).

Children evidencing an anxious-avoidant attachment style are less likely to feel confident exploring the world around them, and they are more likely to evidence stronger attachment behaviors toward their caregivers. Unlike children with ambivalent attachments, these children are hypersensitive to maintaining proximity to their caregiver. Caregivers of children with anxious-avoidant attachment behaviors have been found to be inconsistent in their responses to their children. At times, they are highly attentive; at other times, they are largely emotionally absent.

The final attachment style is referred to as "disorganized" attachment. This attachment style is characterized by unstable, unpredictable patterns of attachment behaviors (Wenar & Kerig, 2000). This style of attachment frequently is observed in children who have experienced abuse or neglect and is the result of children seeking protection from a caregiver in times of stress, even if/when the caregiver is abusive.

Other Developmental Competencies in Early Childhood

In addition to the formation of a secure attachment relationship, the infancy, toddlerhood, preschool, and early elementary school years are marked by the acquisition of several other stage-salient developmental competencies (Durwin & Reese-Weber, 2021). These are outlined below.

Infancy:

- **Beginning gross motor regulation:** Gross motor development follows cephalocaudal (head to toe) and proximodistal (inside to out) trends. This means that infants will learn to lift their heads before they learn to sit up or crawl.
- **Self-regulation:** At birth, infants are completely dependent on their parents or caregivers to meet their needs. Parents/caregivers regulate the infant's sleep and eating cycles. Through interactions with parents/caregivers, infants eventually begin to regulate these cycles for themselves. According to Piaget (1952), the infant learns that they can have control over and interact with their environment.
- **Secure attachment formation:** The formation of a secure attachment is tied into the infant's development of trust versus mistrust, that is, the degree to which the infant experiences the world as a good and positive place (Erikson, 1968).

Toddlerhood:

- **Language:** During the toddler years, young children learn to speak, and they experience a rapid growth in vocabulary.
- **Gross motor development:** By the end of the first year/beginning of the second year of life, children start to walk. Their increasing mobility offers children the opportunity to explore the world around them. Children with a secure attachment relationship can use their parent/guardian as a secure base. That is, the child feels safe to explore the uncertainty of the world around them and becomes secure in the knowledge that their parent/caregiver is there, if needed. Children without a secure attachment relationship may be more reticent or fearful of exploring their environments.
- **Autonomy:** According to Erikson (1968), the "conflict" of the toddler years is autonomy versus shame/doubt. The language and gross motor development of the toddler years lends itself to an increasing sense of independence. During this developmental stage, young children are eager, almost adamant, about trying to perform tasks on their own. When supported by their parents/caregivers, toddlers begin to develop a positive sense of self. Children whose parents/caregivers either overregulate or underregulate these opportunities may experience feelings of shame or doubt regarding their ability to accomplish new tasks.
- **Continued self-regulation:** The newly acquired autonomy of the toddler years also offers increased possibilities of frustration (for instance, being unable to reach something or do something that they want to do). Toddlers in this stage do not yet have the cognitive or language capacities to manage these frustrations, which can result in "temper tantrums," particularly early in the toddler years. Toddlers evidence gains in self-regulation toward the end of the toddler years as they simultaneously gain increased language and cognitive capacities.

▨ **Egocentrism:** According to Piaget (1952), toddlers and preschoolers have an egocentric view of the world. This means that the child believes that others around them experience the world the same way they do.

Preschool Years:

▨ **Cause–effect thinking:** Preschool children's increasing cognitive capacities provide them with the ability to begin thinking about events in cause–effect terms (Piaget, 1952). Early in the development of this competency, children may confuse the sequencing of events or not account for the influence of other events (Davies, 2004). This confusion, coupled with a tendency toward egocentric thinking, may leave preschool age children prone to believing that they "caused" traumatic events.

▨ **Initiative:** The developmental crisis of the preschool years is initiative versus guilt (Erikson, 1968). During this stage, children are eager to try to do new things.

TRAUMA AND EARLY CHILDHOOD

Given the importance of the formation of a secure attachment relationship in early childhood, disturbances to the parent/caregiver–child relationship in these early years are particularly traumatic for young children. Young children depend on their parents/caregivers for protection from external stressors and for helping them to understand how to respond to stressful/traumatic events (Lieberman & Van Horn, 2008; Sparrow, 2007; Winston & Chicot, 2016). When parents cannot provide this protection, or the parents themselves are the source of the stress, young children's development and well-being becomes increasingly vulnerable to poor outcomes (Child Welfare Information Gateway, 2019; Dorsey et al., 2017).

Child Maltreatment

In 2017, as in prior years, younger children were mistreated at higher rates than older children; the rate for children ages 0 to 3 was three times that of the rate for those aged 16 to 17 (U.S. Department of Health and Human Services, Children's Bureau, National Child Abuse and Neglect Data System [NCANDS], 2019). Child maltreatment includes experiences of physical abuse, neglect, sexual abuse, and emotional abuse. These experiences represent a proximal disruption to the caregiver–child relationship and thus have the potential to exert a strong influence on children's development (Cicchetti, 2004). In cases of child maltreatment, the child's caregiver often is both the threat/source of traumatic experiences as well as a source of comfort. As a result, the child is likely to experience an approach–avoidance relationship with the parent or a disorganized attachment (Milot et al., 2010; Schuder & Lyons-Ruth, 2007). Very young children who experience child maltreatment are at increased risk for evidencing poor developmental outcomes, including increased behavioral problems as well as poor educational well-being (Cook et al., 2005; De Bellis, 2001; Fantuzzo et al., 2011; Hildyard & Wolfe, 2002; Milot et al., 2010; Perlman & Fantuzzo, 2010).

Domestic Violence and Intimate Partner Violence

An estimated 10% of U.S. children are exposed annually to DV, with approximately 25% experiencing at least one event during childhood (Carlson, 2000; Huecker et al., 2021). Young children are more likely than older children to be exposed to DV (Crusto et al., 2010; Fantuzzo & Fusco, 2007). In a Canadian study, up to 34% of legitimate investigations of child maltreatment were characterized as child exposure to IPV (Trocmé, 2010). Research has demonstrated that young children who have witnessed DV show elevated trauma symptoms (Bogat et al., 2006; Graham-Bermann et al., 2008; Levendosky et al., 2002; Scheeringa & Zeanah, 1995; Tsavoussis et al., 2014). Studies by Scheeringa and Zeanah (1995) and Bogat et al. (2006) examined trauma symptomology in infants and young children who had witnessed DV. Scheeringa and Zeanah (1995) found that children show increased arousal and new fears after witnessing DV. The researchers suggested that this may be due, in part, to concerns that (subsequent to witnessing DV) the child perceives that their caregiver is less capable of acting as a "protective shield" (Scheeringa & Zeanah, 1995). Additionally, Bogat et al. found that just less than half of all infants who witnessed DV exhibited at least one trauma symptom (numbing, increased arousal, or fear/aggression), and that the number of symptoms that infants experienced after DV was directly related to the number of symptoms exhibited by their mother. Levendosky et al. (2002) examined trauma symptoms among preschoolers who had witnessed DV. Preschool children who witnessed DV showed high levels of re-experiencing and hyperarousal. Notably, children who lived in households in which DV was occurring, but who did *not* witness the DV event, still demonstrated increased levels of trauma symptoms.

Environmental Trauma

Following the September 11, 2001 terrorist attacks, recent natural disasters (e.g., Hurricane Katrina), school shootings like the Sandy Hook Elementary School massacre, and the COVID-19 pandemic, increased attention has been paid to how these events affect very young children. Chemtob et al. (2010) conducted a study assessing the impact of September 11 on preschool children. This study examined maternal PTSD following September 11 and related it to child behaviors. Findings indicated that children of mothers with co-occurring depression and PTSD were more likely than their peers to evidence increased behavioral problems. Similarly, Celebi Oncu et al. (2010) conducted a study examining trauma symptoms following the 1999 Turkish earthquake. Children who had experienced the natural disaster engaged in more negative storytelling than children who did not experience the natural disaster, even 2 years after the disaster event.

In the aftermath of the Sandy Hook Elementary School shootings, more and more schools have established trauma-informed care at the organizational level (Berger, 2019; Overstreet & Chafouleas, 2016). However, significant challenges remain, including the generation of funding quickly enough to conduct research on how best to intervene as well as the implementation of evidence-based practices that individually focused health insurances will support (Grolnick et al., 2018; Sandy Hook Advisory Commission, 2015; Thomas et al., 2019), when research findings point to multi-tiered approaches to intervention (Berger, 2019). Because of the worldwide devastation of the COVID-19 pandemic, the lives of most individuals have been affected, and children have been particularly vulnerable. Studies already have indicated the need to focus on C-19-related losses and the well-being of children (e.g., Gassman-Pines et al., 2020; Patrick et al., 2020), and this concern, unfortunately, is likely to continue well into the future.

Young children may experience another type of environmental trauma, in the form of bullying. While not necessarily traumatizing, a pattern of bullying may become traumatic for a young child. Cyberbullying, a variation of bullying more typically associated with preteens and teens, has become more prevalent among younger children. The Anti-Defamation League (ADL, 2021) has identified the warning signs that a child or teen may be experiencing cyberbullying, including but not limited to moodiness after online or phone activity, withdrawing or not engaging, refusing to go to school, atypical academic failures, and depression.

EFFECTS OF TRAUMA IN EARLY CHILDHOOD

The effects of traumatic experiences in early childhood vary and are based on several factors, including the individual child's stage of development and the nature of the traumatic event.

Given that very young infants cannot yet express their emotions verbally, the effects of trauma experienced in infancy usually are manifested through changes in the infant's behaviors. Infants experiencing trauma may evidence higher levels of agitation, fussiness, and dysregulation of normal routines, including sleeping and eating (Lieberman & Knorr, 2007). Toddlers and preschoolers experiencing trauma may have the capacity to convey their experiences verbally, as well as to use their increased mobility to engage in flight-or-fight responses to traumatic events. However, because egocentric thinking also marks these years, children experiencing trauma in these developmental stages are more likely than older children to attribute the cause of the traumatic event to themselves. For instance, a preschooler, who is physically abused by their parent, is likely to believe that they did something to cause the physical abuse. Traumatic events in early childhood might constitute a pattern of adverse childhood experiences that, as noted in the discussion about the ACE Study in Chapter 2, "Theoretical Contexts of Trauma Counseling," may have deleterious implications across the life-span. Additionally, there may be transgenerational significance, as recent research has indicated that the adverse childhood experiences of parents may result in developmental delays among young children (Folger et al., 2018), which, in turn, may have further developmental consequences.

Posttraumatic Stress Disorder in Early Childhood

Posttraumatic stress disorder (PTSD) in children above the age of 6 is diagnosed using the same *DSM-5* criteria that are used to diagnose PTSD in adults (National Center for PTSD, U.S. Department of Veterans Affairs, 2021). However, PTSD symptoms manifest differently in very young children than they do in older children or adults, and symptoms may persist for longer times (Coates & Gaensbauer, 2009; Scheeringa & Zeanah, 1995; Scheeringa et al., 2005; Vasileva et al., 2018). In fact, different from previous versions of the *Diagnostic and Statistical Manuals*, the *DSM-5* (American Psychiatric Association, 2013) introduced a new developmental subtype of PTSD for children ages 6 years and younger: Posttraumatic Stress Disorder in Preschool Children (Scheeringa, 2019).

For very young children, intrusive symptoms of trauma often are manifest as repetitive play (Coates & Gaensbauer, 2009). According to Coates and Gaensbauer (2009), young children who have experienced trauma may engage in play that is devoid of "fun or creative spontaneity" (p. 613). These play experiences may resemble the traumatic event in either content or expression of the emotions/affect from the traumatic experience (Coates & Gaensbauer, 2009; Markese, 2007). Avoidance symptoms manifest in terms of the child's developmental capacity (Scheeringa, 2019). If the child is mobile, they physically may avoid reminders of the traumatic event. On the other hand, if the child is not yet mobile, they actively may seek to avoid eye contact or, in the case of abuse or neglect, noticeably may be distraught by the presence of the abusive caregiver (Coates & Gaensbauer, 2009; Markese, 2007). Markese (2007) also points out that young children may avoid "symbolic play," that is, substituting one object for another or pretending as a means of avoiding the traumatic experience. Finally, symptoms of increased arousal can manifest in very young children as increased irritability, aggression, and temper tantrums, and in some cases also may resemble symptoms of attention deficit hyperactivity disorder (ADHD; Markese, 2007). Thus, care should be taken in the diagnosis of young children evidencing signs of ADHD.

One other significant difference in the diagnosis of PTSD in very young children, compared to older children or adults, is that very young children need to evidence only *one* symptom in select diagnostic criteria to PTSD (Scheeringa, 2019). In general, the *DSM-5* changes include diagnostic thresholds for PTSD that have been lowered for children (and adolescents). Additionally, for children aged 6 or less, separate, more developmentally sensitive criteria have been added. These new criteria include caregiver-child–related losses such as foster care placement (Scheeringa et al., 2011) as an important precipitant of trauma and behavioral PTSD symptoms. According to the *DSM-5*, PTSD symptoms can develop any time after age 1 (Substance Abuse and Mental Health Services Administration, 2016).

Increased attention has been focused on preverbal experiences of traumatic events. Initially, it was believed that because infants and toddlers could not verbally express their experiences of trauma, these experiences did not have a long-term impact on their development. We now understand this differently. Infants begin storing memories as young as 2 months of age (Durwin & Reese-Weber, 2021; Markese, 2007). These memories are stored as "somatosensory experiences" in the brain (van der Kolk, 1994, 2014). In other words, traumatic experiences in infancy and toddlerhood are stored in the brain as sensory experiences, even if the child cannot yet verbalize these experiences (Green et al., 2010; Markese, 2007). The influence of these experiences on infant and toddler development is seen by the presence of the PTSD symptoms noted previously, as well as an increased likelihood of evidencing disorganized attachment relationships with caregivers (Markese, 2007). The short clinical vignette, presented in Box 7.1, illustrates the early childhood experience of one child.

BOX 7.1

Clinical Vignette: Mark

Mark is a 4-year-old foster child who experienced early childhood maltreatment. He has been in three different placements. He recently was removed from a family that he loved, but the family members could not handle the intensity of Mark's emotional and behavioral outbursts. At the preschool that he attended, it was routine for teachers to place him in "time-out," because they considered Mark's behaviors to be too challenging for their classrooms. Mark's temper tantrums continued to escalate.

Reflection Questions:

- How do you begin to conceptualize Mark's situation?
- What theories of childhood development might be useful to consider in this case?
- Was the school-based method of discipline helpful or harmful to Mark?

THERAPEUTIC INTERVENTIONS

Given the primacy of the parent–child relationship in early childhood, therapeutic interventions for young children who have experienced trauma should focus on the parent–child relationship (Lieberman & Van Horn, 2009; Osofsky & Lieberman, 2011). Recent research has supported evidence-based, neuroscience-informed approaches to a variety of counseling interventions, including behavior modification, play therapy, cognitive behavioral therapy (CBT) and Eye Movement Desensitization and Reprocessing (EMDR)(Beckley-Forest, 2021; Dorsey et al., 2017; Field & Ghoston, 2020). Several strategies, which can be used by mental health professionals working with young children, are identified and discussed in the text that follows.

Child–Parent Psychotherapy

One evidence-based intervention approach is child–parent psychotherapy (CPP; Lieberman & Van Horn, 2009; Lieberman et al., 2019). Lieberman and Van Horn suggest that "CPP has the goal of making the trauma *knowable* and *sayable* as a shared child–parent experience in which the parent becomes capable of acknowledging the reality of the events and the legitimacy of the child's resulting terror, anger, and broken trust" (p. 714). According to this approach, CPP has four primary goals:

(1) Create a common language to describe what happened; (2) regulate the overwhelming affects associated with the experience; (3) enhance the parents' capacity to respond . . . to the child's basic needs . . . and (4) restore [the child's] trust in the parent's ability to protect [him or her] from external and internal danger. (Lieberman & Van Horn, 2009, p. 710)

Initial CPP therapy sessions are attended by the parent/caregiver and are focused on developing an understanding of the nature and magnitude of the traumatic experience. Following these initial sessions, both the child and the parent attend therapy sessions. In the case of preverbal infants or toddlers, much of the therapeutic effort is focused on helping the parent or caregiver to identify how their own childhood experiences are influencing their parenting. The use of CPP with older, verbal children focuses more on helping the child create a narrative about the traumatic experience. This is accomplished through the use of play, by assisting the parent/caregiver in reclaiming their protective role with the child, and by rebuilding a trusting, positive relationship between the child and caregiver. To date, CPP has been found to be an effective intervention for young children who have experienced one or more traumatic events (Ippen et al., 2011; Lieberman et al., 2005, 2006) and has shown effectiveness across various ethnicities and socioeconomic backgrounds (Lieberman et al., 2006).

Parent–Child Interaction Therapy

Another evidence-based approach for working with young children who have experienced trauma is parent–child interaction therapy (PCIT; Eyberg, 1988; Vanderzee et al., 2019). Similar to CPP, PCIT focuses on the parent–child interaction. PCIT was developed for use with young children (ages 4 to 7) who have been identified as having behavioral problems, and it consists of a two-phase intervention (child-directed interaction [CDI] followed by parent-directed interaction [PDI]) that is implemented across 14 to 20 weeks (Timmer et al., 2010). During the CDI phase, the therapist focuses on enhancing the parent–child relationship by encouraging and supporting parents in recognizing their children's positive behaviors. During the PDI phase, the parent is taught specific parenting techniques for behavioral management to reduce the rates of child behavior problems. PCIT has been found to be effective for working with children who have been victims of or are at risk of experiencing child maltreatment, as well as children who have witnessed DV (Herschell & McNeil, 2005; Timmer et al., 2010).

Trauma-Focused Cognitive Behavioral Therapy

Trauma-focused cognitive behavioral therapy (TF-CBT) is another evidence-based approach for working with parents and children who have experienced traumatic events (Cohen & Mannarino, 1993; Vanderzee et al., 2019). This intervention initially was developed to treat young children who had experienced sexual abuse but has since been adapted for use with children who have experienced other forms of trauma (Cohen et al., 2006). TF-CBT combines CBT with trauma-informed practice throughout a series of individual and combined sessions with the parent and child. TF-CBT uses a nine-component model (PRACTICE): (P)sychoeducation, (P)arenting skills, (R)elaxation skills, (A)ffective modulation skills, (C)ognitive coping skills, (T)rauma narrative and processing, (I)n vivo mastery of trauma reminders, (C)onjoint child–parent sessions, and (E)nhancing safety and future development (Cohen et al., 2010). The intervention lasts for approximately 12 weeks (Scheeringa et al., 2007). This intervention has been effective for use with preschool-age children across an array of traumatic experiences, including child sexual abuse, motor vehicle accidents, and natural/environmental disasters (Cohen et al., 2006, 2010; Scheeringa et al., 2007; Silverman et al., 2008; Vanderzee et al., 2019). A free training on TF-CBT is available to clinicians on the SAMHSA website (https://tfcbt2.musc.edu).

Play Therapy

Given that trauma that is experienced in infancy and toddlerhood is stored as sensory experiences in the brain, symbolic play can offer children a chance to process and heal following trauma (Green et al., 2010; Malchiodi, 2020; A. Stewart et al., 2020). Young children can, in effect, reenact the traumatic experience through symbolic play. During these play experiences, children have control over how directly they interact with the traumatic experience and, with the guidance of a therapist, can begin to create a narrative surrounding the experience. The therapist's warm, empathic response to the child's play can begin to rebuild the child's sense of trust and attachment toward an adult caregiver. Sandtray therapy is one variation of play therapy that has been used successfully with children who have experienced trauma (e.g., Homeyer & Sweeney, 2017).

Promising Practices

In addition to interventions that have a strong empirical base such as CPP and play therapy, several new strategies have emerged for working with young children who have experienced trauma. These interventions, discussed briefly in the text that follows, include *Ways of Seeing*, mindfulness-based parenting programs, and bibliotherapy.

Ways of Seeing

A promising new strategy that addresses the importance of the parent–child relationship is *Ways of Seeing* (Tortora, 2010, 2019). This intervention is a "multisensory psychotherapeutic treatment approach" that incorporates "dance/movement principles" (p. 37). This method capitalizes on very young children's sensory processing of their experiences. In *Ways of Seeing*, the therapist observes interactions between the parent/caregiver and child in the following areas: (a) quality of eye gaze, (b) facial expression, (c) use of space, (d) quality and frequency of touch and/or physical contact, (e) body shapes, (f) tempo of nonverbal movement style, (g) vocal patterns, and (h) nonverbal behavior and regulation (Tortora, 2010). In this intervention model, the therapist meets weekly with the parent and child. These weekly sessions are videotaped and then viewed by the therapist and parent to examine nonverbal interactions between the parent and child. The nonverbal interactions form the basis of the intervention, with a focus on helping parents/caregivers to understand how their own childhood experiences influence their parenting and on improving the nonverbal interactions between the child and parent/caregiver. This approach most recently has been studied in young children with cancer (Tortora, 2019). Additionally, expressive therapies such as dance, as well as play, have a healing effect on the neurobiology of the traumatized child (Malchiodi, 2015).

Mindfulness-Based Parenting Programs

Mindfulness-based parenting programs (MBPPs) are being used to address parent–child interactions (Burns, 2018; Cohen & Semple, 2010). These programs build on relationally oriented mindfulness programs to focus specifically on parent–child relationships by increasing self-awareness, intentionality, and resilience while also attending to cultural diversity (Beckley-Forest, 2021; Field & Ghoston, 2020). Recent research has suggested that positive psychology interventions, which are aimed at enhancing happiness, hope, and resilience among youth, may influence positive mental health experiences (Lenz, 2021). Yoga and other MBPPS are being used in clinical trials with traumatized children, with good outcomes (Ortiz & Sibinga, 2017).

Bibliotherapy

A final intervention for young children who have experienced trauma, which warrants discussion, is bibliotherapy (De Vries et al., 2017; Duncan, 2010). This approach involves the use of children's literature as a way of helping young children process events. Children's literature can provide a means for helping children learn adaptive messages about coping with traumatic experiences (Duncan, 2010). Although this method has been found to reduce child behavioral problems, it should be used in conjunction with other forms of therapy (Jack & Ronan, 2008) and be culturally affirming (Field & Ghoston, 2020; P. E. Stewart & Ames, 2014).

COUNSELING IMPLICATIONS

While once an area of debate, over the last two decades, there has been a growing body of research that diminishes any doubt that children younger than 6 and as young as age 1 can develop posttraumatic stress symptoms (PTSS). There is also evidence that multi-tiered, systemic approaches are best for trauma-informed care; however, policy has not necessarily paralleled the evidence, and implementation of systemic approaches sometimes has been sidelined in favor of individual approaches, which is driven by the health insurance industry. Yet, in spite of policy issues and a lack of access to needed services, children continue to experience trauma, and children continue to face environmental risks that impede their developmental trajectories.

Identifying childhood risk factors is crucial in understanding the context for and the effects of child maltreatment and childhood trauma. However, it is important to identify existing childhood protective factors, as well as to advocate for strategies that can enhance existing protective factors and even construct new ones. Figure 7.1 illustrates a possible interaction between risk factors and protective factors.

Figure 7.1

Possible Interaction Between Risk Factors and Protective Factors

Source: Child Welfare Information Gateway. (2019). *Fact sheet: Long-term consequences of child abuse and neglect.* Retrieved from https://www.childwelfare.gov/pubPDFs/long_term_consequences.pdf

CONCLUSION

Early childhood experiences, both positive and negative, lay the groundwork for future growth and development. Of utmost importance during these years is the formation and maintenance of a positive attachment relationship with one or more caregivers. Traumatic events such as child maltreatment and DV can undermine the protective nature of these early relationships. Given the primacy of a positive attachment relationship for young children's growth and development, this relationship is the focal point of many interventions targeting young children who have experienced trauma. These interventions emphasize healing the parent–child relationship and aim to build resilience, as well as giving the child the opportunity to develop a narrative for the traumatic event (especially in the case of children who have experienced preverbal trauma).

ADDITIONAL RESOURCES

 | A robust set of instructor resources designed to supplement this text is located at http://connect.springerpub.com/content/book/978-0-8261-5085-1. Qualifying instructors may request access by emailing textbook@springerpub.com.

PRACTICE-BASED RESOURCES AND REFERENCES

To view a list of resources and all the references, please visit connect.springerpub.com via the following url: http://connect.springerpub.com/content/book/978-0-8261-5085-1/part/part02/chapter/ch07

CHAPTER 8

Trauma Experienced in Adolescence

ANDREA DOYLE AND STACI PERLMAN

CHAPTER OVERVIEW

The purpose of this chapter is to outline particular consequences of trauma when it occurs during adolescence, as well as what one might expect subsequent to earlier childhood traumatic events that occurred. This aim is accomplished in the following sections: (a) Trauma-Relevant Issues in Adolescence and (b) Counseling Implications. These major sections are followed by a summary of the chapter and an online list of relevant resources.

LEARNING OBJECTIVES

After reading this chapter, the reader should be able to:

1. Be cognizant of the developmental issues in adolescence that interface and complicate diagnosis; and
2. Be aware of the main treatment approaches to trauma in adolescents as well as how they differ and how they intersect.

INTRODUCTION

The national average of child abuse and neglect victims in 2019 was 8.9 victims per 1,000 children (U.S. Department of Health and Human Services, Administration for Children and Families, Administration on Children, Youth, and Families, Children's Bureau, 2021).

Both children and adolescents are subject to extremely high rates of abuse and neglect, victimization, and intentional and unintentional injury (Centers for Disease Control and Prevention, 2016; Finkelhor et al., 2009; McCaig & Ly, 2002; McDonald et al., 2006). Over 67% of children report at least one traumatic event by the age of 16 (Substance Abuse and Mental Health Services Association [SAMHSA], 2020). By the age of 11, 11% of youth have experienced a traumatic event; by the age of 18, 43% of youth have experienced such an event (Eckes & Radunovich, 2007). This increased exposure to and experience of trauma during adolescence is partly tied to behaviors characteristic of this particular developmental stage.

This chapter is a revision of the chapter that appeared in the first edition of this textbook; Dr. Staci Perlman, who passed away in 2015, was one of the authors; we honor and thank her for her original contribution here, as well as for all her work in advocating for children and youth.

TRAUMA-RELEVANT ISSUES IN ADOLESCENCE

Stemming from the Latin *adolescere* "to grow up," adolescence is the phase between childhood and adulthood, generally considered to be the ages between 13 and 19. Characterized by a rush of hormones and a budding sexuality that leads to fundamental physical changes, it is also a time of experimentation and risk taking. Because of this risk taking, adolescents have a high probability of experiencing traumatic events (Ben-Zur & Zeidner, 2009; Tull et al., 2016). They also are at risk of trauma that is related to bullying at school, cyberbullying, violence in the home as well as the community, drug experimentation, and other dangerous situations (Gaete et al., 2017; Shaw, 2000). In the course of defining who they are, many teens take risks and defy their parents in an effort to differentiate boundaries between parents and self (Gilmore & Meersand, 2015; Hales & Yudofsky, 2003). Typical traumatic experiences specific to this stage include date rape (Rickert & Wiemann, 1998), gang shootings (depending on community context) (Kelly et al., 2012), and teen suicide. This section presents discussions about the issues that are relevant to the discourse on trauma experienced in adolescence: Stages of Development, Effects of Trauma, Typical Responses to Trauma, Gender Differences, Age- and Stage-Appropriate Considerations, Multiple Diagnostic Categories, and Family Issues.

Stages of Development

Adolescence is a period of rapid cognitive development, characterized by the capacity for abstract thinking (Piaget, 1952). The development of the prefrontal cortex, associated with executive functioning, allows for more coordination and management of thinking and behavior (Choudhury et al., 2006), which is necessary for the development of autonomy and engaging in relationships (Cook et al., 2005). Experiences during this developmental period play a major role in identity formation (Erikson, 1968), moral development (Gilligan, 1993; Kohlberg, 1958), and personality, thus shaping adulthood (Smith & Handler, 2007).

The developmental tasks of adolescence are as follows:

- Accepting the physical changes and sexual impulses brought on by puberty
- Attaining independence from parents (economically, emotionally)
- Developing mature relationships with peers and adults outside the family
- Developing the capacity for intimacy with a romantic partner
- Establishing a set of moral values and ethical behavior
- Consolidating a coherent social role (including gender, vocation, and ethnic identity)
- Pursuing a vocation or career (Becker et al., 2003; Gilmore & Meersand, 2015; Havighurst, 1949)

Although these stages are considered universal across cultures, for adolescents of color, ethnic identity has unique stages (Phinney, 1989). Ethnic and racial identity-achieved adolescents demonstrate more solid ego identity, psychological adjustment, and better health outcomes (Phinney, 1989; Phinney & Ong, 2007; Rivas-Drake et al., 2014). This period of development involves a search for an integrated and stable ego identity. This process proceeds as teens make sense of their current self-perceptions with their "self perceptions from earlier periods and with their cultural and biological heritage" (Brodzinsky, 1987, p. 37).

Effects of Trauma

Following a particular type of trauma, namely disaster, children assume greater responsibilities and face several morally challenging situations that may lead to premature moral development (Goenjian et al., 1999; Nucci & Turiel, 2009). By the same token, posttraumatic stress disorder (PTSD) symptoms and negative self-schemas may lead to lacunae in moral functioning (Chaplo et al., 2019; Goenjian et al., 1999). Trauma that is associated with disaster may beget further trauma. For example, we know that in Haiti, post-earthquake, there was a growing prevalence of sexual assaults, with accounts of girls as young as 12 years old being treated for sexually transmitted infections resulting from rapes (Bayard, 2010).

Within Erikson's theory of development, adolescence falls in the stage of identity versus identity diffusion. At the extreme, dissociative identity disorder can result from early trauma (Sanders & Giolas, 1991; Trond, 2005). A more frequent reaction of traumatized adolescents is premature closure of identity formation (Figley, 1985) or entrance into adulthood. Posttraumatic "acting out" can include absences from school, early sexual debut, and delinquency (Filipas & Ullman, 2006; Finkelhor, 1990; Margolin & Vickerman, 2011; Newman, 1976; Steiner et al., 1997). Substance use is often a way of self-medicating in an effort to offset depressed mood, but what starts out as experimentation and a way of coping, in the short term, can lead to problems in brain development and later addiction if used regularly (Gaete et al., 2017; Mayhew et al., 2000).

Adolescent survivors from the Jewish Holocaust of World War II, for example, experienced persistent identity diffusion, interpersonal distress, and difficulties with school and work (W. Koenig, 1964; L. Koenig et al., 2004). Unlike younger children, who are likely to misinterpret the trauma as something that resulted as a consequence of their own behavior, adolescents possess the developmental capacity for abstract and contextual understanding of the sequential nature of events over time and how their choices might fit into the chain of events leading up to a trauma (Figley, 1985). Finkelhor (1995) distinguishes between *localized* versus developmental effects of trauma. The symptoms associated with PTSD are considered localized and will dissipate over time or with treatment. Developmental effects are more generalized and pervasive and challenge the attainment of age-appropriate tasks such as emotional regulation and development of positive self-esteem (Finkelhor, 1995). Similarly, traumatic events must be distinguished between a single event versus a chronic process (Margolin & Vickerman, 2011; Shaw, 2000), the latter of which can have more generalized effects.

Adolescents may withdraw and become less communicative subsequent to a trauma, whereas toddlers are likely to cry, and grade school children may experience disturbances in sleep or somatic complaints (Zubenko & Capozzoli, 2002). As children become teenagers, their symptoms resemble those of adults (Wolfe & Mash, 2006). There is some evidence that a person's cognitive style may affect symptomatology. Moran and Eckenrode (1992) found that those with a higher internal locus of control were less depressed than those with a more external locus of control. Traditionally, the prevailing thinking in psychology has been that males externalize, whereas females tend to internalize negative life experiences (Leadbeater et al., 1999), and this thinking has been subject to some debate as gender roles have changed with time (Ara, 2016). However, this notion of internalizing or externalizing is worthy of comment, as it has implications for prognosis and treatment. Internalizing is an intrapsychic reaction to trauma that manifests itself as depression, anxiety, or low self-esteem (Feuer et al., 2001). Externalizing or "acting out" usually manifests in aggressive ways such as seen in conduct disorders. Disorders of internalization and externalization represent a breakdown of the developmental path as a response to crisis.

Typical Responses to Trauma

Research in the area of trauma demonstrates the primacy of human attachments in assessment, treatment, and adolescent development (Brown, 2008). Trauma undermines trust and human connections. When trust is damaged by adults failing to protect from or actually perpetrating trauma, basic worldviews and foundational aspects of relationships change (H. A. Barnes et al., 2019; Nader, 2007). The inability to trust caretakers, God, or the universe makes it challenging to feel safe again following trauma (H. A. Barnes et al., 2019; Nader, 2007).

Fear and anxiety, reexperiencing of the trauma, increased arousal, avoidance, anger and irritability, guilt, shame, grief, depression, negative self-image and worldview, disinterest in sex, and abuse of substances are all common reactions to trauma (Foa et al., 2011). Essentially, trauma is an assault to the brain (Steven Berkowitz, 2010 August 6, personal communication) that alters the way the brain performs, impairing cognitive, psychological, and neurological functioning. The potential for injury to the brain needs to be considered carefully within the context of the increased brain development during adolescence (Hales & Yudofsky, 2003). There is evidence that the stress associated with traumatic events can change major structural components of the central nervous system and the neuroendocrine system, leaving a lasting effect (Herringa, 2017; Shaw, 2000; Spear, 2000).

Gender Differences

Females are more at risk for victimization, especially sexual, in interpersonal relationships than males are, whereas males are at greater risk for physical abuse and assault (Capaldi et al., 2012; Feuer et al., 2001; Kessler et al., 1995; Yehuda, 2004). Young women and men tend to experience and process the distress associated with traumatic events differently (Briere & Scott, 2006). The counselor should be sensitive to ways in which traumatized adolescents display or suppress their emotional reactions based on gender expectations. Males are more likely to be exposed to traumatic stressors, but females are more likely to experience PTSD (Inslicht et al., 2013; Olff, 2017; Stuber et al., 2006). Gustafsson et al. (2009) found no difference in occurrence of trauma by gender, but found differences by age, with older adolescents reporting more trauma events, a finding noted also by Nucci and Turiel (2009). Margolin and Gordis (2004) found that females and Caucasians were less likely to be victims or perpetrators, that middle adolescents were more likely to be perpetrators only, and that adolescents with substance-using peers were more likely to be victims and/or perpetrators of violence. In their juvenile detainee sample, Abram et al. (2004) found slightly higher rates of traumatic incidents in males.

Horowitz et al. (1995) proposed the concept of "compounded community trauma" in their study of urban female adolescents, finding that they experienced a mean of 28 violent events. Of these young women, 90% experienced hyperarousal, 89% had symptoms of reexperiencing, 80% used avoidance as a coping mechanism, and 67% met criteria for PTSD. An increased number of types of violent events was positively correlated with meeting PTSD criteria and with greater symptom severity. The young women endured prolonged and repeated exposure to multiple types of community as well as domestic violent events over time, via multiple modalities of contact. The take-home message here is that the effects of trauma are cumulative. Regardless of gender, there is evidence that neighborhood violence is shaping teens' brains (Saxbe, 2018).

Age- and Stage-Appropriate Considerations

Evidence from studies of combat trauma, disasters, and rape results points to differential effects on adolescents. Adolescents who fought in Vietnam, for example, were more likely to develop PTSD than older soldiers; van der Kolk (1985) speculated that this differential effect was caused by the intensity of their attachment to their peer soldiers and the consequent magnitude of the loss that the young soldiers experienced when their friends were killed. When one considers that most young people are entering the military in their late teens and early 20s, and that PTSD as well as depression are serious problems for soldiers who return home from the war, it is important to keep in mind that the soldier is a developing adolescent. An average of 10% of returning soldiers from Iraq and Afghanistan suffer from PTSD and/or depression, with many displaying violent behavior as well (Thomas et al., 2010). Hardoff and Halevy (2006) note that the capacity for abstract thinking and planning for the future, typical of late adolescence, runs counter to the military demand for obedience, leaving family, and threats of physical injury and emotional stress.

Upon discharge from the military, the chronologically mature young adult faces the questions of the late teens, with normal adolescent growth having been forestalled by war (Hardoff & Halevy, 2006). The authors urge those who care for soldiers in their late teens and early 20s to consider the time of military service as an additional developmental stage of late adolescence. Additionally, adolescent children of deployed older soldiers also are affected by the trauma of war. In a study of stress levels among adolescents with family members serving in Iraq at the beginning of Operation Iraqi Freedom in March 2003 and at the end of the campaign in May of the same year, V. A. Barnes et al. (2007) found that at both time points, adolescents of military parents experienced PTSD symptoms; this finding was especially true if a parent had been deployed (issues related to veterans and trauma are detailed further in Chapter 25).

Davidson et al. (1996) found the greatest likelihood of later suicide attempts in those who were assaulted prior to age 16. Similarly, Breslau et al. (1997) found that women who experienced trauma of any kind prior to age 15 were more vulnerable to developing PTSD than were those whose trauma occurred at a later age. Two years after the Buffalo Creek disaster, adolescents were found to have higher levels of distress than younger children (Green et al., 1991). A major factor contributing to this tragedy was a loss of community as well as a belief in duplicity on the part of the mining company whose carelessness led to the disaster. These may have been particularly traumatic stresses for the adolescents, for whom normal development would dictate orienting socially outside the family and a realization that adults in authority are fallible.

Adolescents may be less vulnerable than children or adults to certain kinds of trauma. Studies of Holocaust survivors of World War II indicate that the most devastating effects were on those who were infants during this massive trauma (Kestenbaum & Brenner, 1996); adolescents who survived did relatively well, faring better than adult survivors. The separation from parents was most detrimental for the youngest children; the thinking here is that older children and adolescents had at least a period of earlier healthy development to sustain them. Resourcefulness, group cohesion, a sense of invulnerability, rebelliousness, and a willingness to take risks were protective factors and enhanced the likelihood of adolescents surviving. Similar findings emerged from Weine et al.'s (1995, 1998) studies of Bosnian survivors of ethnic cleansing, which indicated that adolescents were less traumatized than were adults. In their sample, however, younger survivors tended to experience less torture and other extreme conditions than did adults. The authors suggest that the relatively low rate of PTSD, compared to adults and also in comparison to Cambodian adolescent survivors of the "killing fields," may be related to normal prior development, the time-limited nature of the trauma, adversity, lack of sexual or physical abuse, reuniting with family, or simply insufficient time for the development of delayed-onset PTSD. More optimistically, they suggest that these results may be owing to adolescent resilience.

Terr et al. (1997) studied the reactions of children and adolescents who had witnessed the 1986 Challenger space explosion on television while at school, which was particularly relevant to school children, because a teacher was among the crew members who all perished. In contrast to children who exhibited symptoms, teenagers had changes in their thinking. During the 14 months after the explosion, adolescents developed negative attitudes toward God, institutions, and the future.

Multiple Diagnostic Categories

PTSD frequently co-occurs with other diagnostic categories (Giaconia et al., 1995; Kessler et al., 1995). Traumatic experiences can lead to disruptive behavior disorders, other internalizing disorders, personality disorders, and physical illnesses (Ohan et al., 2002). Adolescents who have experienced trauma as children are more likely to develop anxiety-related disorders and fears and are more likely to show a pattern of risky sexual behaviors (Norwood et al., 2000). Different types of exposure to traumatic events lend themselves to different subsequent diagnoses. Children's exposure to violence often goes unnoticed or unreported; therefore, symptoms often are diagnosed as maladjustment (Margolin & Gordis, 2004; Margolin & Vickerman, 2011). In an epidemiological study of juvenile delinquents in detention, Abram et al. (2004) found that 11% of adolescents in jail met criteria for PTSD, and that 93% had experienced at least one trauma in their lifetime; the mean was 15 traumatic events. A history of family violence is the most significant difference between groups of delinquents and nondelinquent youth (Office of Juvenile Justice and Delinquency Prevention, 2013).

In a review of the relationships among eating disorders (EDs), trauma, and comorbid psychiatric disorders, with a particular focus on PTSD, Brewerton (2007) concluded the following: childhood sexual abuse (CSA) is a nonspecific risk factor for EDs; other forms of abuse and neglect, besides CSA, have been linked to EDs; trauma is more common in bulimia, compared to other EDs; multiple traumatic events and/or specific types of trauma are associated with EDs; ED severity is not necessarily associated with trauma, but trauma is associated with greater comorbidity (including and often mediated by PTSD) in research participants with ED; subthreshold PTSD also may be a risk factor for bulimia; and recovery from the ED and comorbid disorders is contingent upon the trauma and PTSD symptoms being addressed.

A range of posttraumatic responses does not necessarily meet full criteria for PTSD. Evidence from community samples suggests that partial syndromes are much more common than PTSD in the general population and also following a specific traumatic event such as a natural disaster. These subclinical conditions also can coincide with significant impairment. Adolescent posttraumatic symptoms can include avoidance, reexperiencing, and arousal that parallel those in adults who meet PTSD criteria (American Psychiatric Association, 2013). Trauma-specific fears, depression and anxiety, and hostility are also common. Even though full PTSD criteria may not be met, a young person can experience significant distress that may interfere with daily functioning. Other disorders may follow trauma, even if posttraumatic symptoms are not immediately present.

The ultimate outcome of experiencing trauma during adolescence may include increased sensitivity to loss and an increased vulnerability to anxiety and depression. More serious reactions include dissociation, ranging from chronic psychic numbing to dissociative identity disorders and interpersonal difficulty. Trauma-related psychopathology that is comorbid with depression, conduct disorder, or substance misuse markedly complicates treatment of the adolescent. Therefore, it is important to assess for a history of trauma and how the adolescent coped at the time of the event.

PTSD itself is difficult to detect without systematic screening (Abram et al., 2004; Havens et al., 2012). PTSD and child abuse often go unrecognized in adolescents (Cohen, 1998; Havens et al., 2012). Symptoms of PTSD overlap with other disorders such that it may be missed. For example, ADHD may be the diagnosis ascribed to the interpersonal problems, hyperactivity, and distractibility that accompany PTSD; this type of presentation necessitates looking beyond the presenting symptoms to assess for early trauma (Wolfe & Mash, 2006). Greenwald (2002) has asserted that trauma mediates the development of conduct problems in adolescence; the trauma can account for the lack of empathy and for the impulsivity, anger, and acting out. Community violence is a significant risk factor for conduct problems in early adolescence (age 10–14), according to Pearce et al. (2003). Protective factors that offset conduct problems include a strong religious faith and parental involvement. The involvement of a caring adult is a factor that mitigates most effects of community violence (Lynn-Whaley & Sugarmann, 2017) as well as witnessing intimate partner violence (Alaggia & Donohue, 2018).

As a final note on trauma in adolescents and differential diagnosis, let us consider the issue of substance use as possibly an antidote for trauma symptoms or symptoms of substance use looking like trauma symptoms. Equally, contributory factors to borderline personality disorder can include trauma as part of an early invalidating environment. Indeed, there was a push at one point for borderline personality disorder to be renamed complex trauma disorder, but the bid was lost in the latest edition of the *DSM,* and notwithstanding the fact that adolescence, by virtue of the developmental stage in and of itself, leads to risky experimental behavior. Untangling the host of symptoms to form a diagnosis depends on gathering a careful history of symptoms, with attention to frequency, intensity, duration, time of onset, and contextual factors such as the bioecological environment.

Family Issues

The impact of a traumatic event may depend on the extent to which it disrupts family functioning. Gustafsson et al. (2009) found that interpersonal violence was more strongly associated with symptoms than with non-interpersonal violence. The major categories of violence are child maltreatment, aggression between parents, and community violence, which often co-occur (Margolin & Gordis, 2004; Margolin & Vickerman, 2011). Each year, more than 10 million children witness physical aggression between their parents (Margolin & Gordis, 2004; Margolin & Vickerman, 2011). Exposure to violence very often occurs in familial settings. Possible consequences include break-up or relocation of family, family conflict, poverty, parental unemployment, parental substance misuse, and psychopathology. Thus, life stresses and trauma can become cyclical. Common short-term effects of exposure to violence are behavioral disorders such as aggression and delinquency, emotional and mood disorders, posttraumatic stress, health-related problems, somatic symptoms, and academic and cognitive problems (Margolin & Gordis, 2004; Margolin & Vickerman, 2011).

COUNSELING IMPLICATIONS

Adolescence is an opportunity to rework earlier traumas (Blos, 1962). The importance of this favorable period for therapeutic action cannot be underestimated, as earlier interventions bode well for better adaptation in later developmental stages. This section offers discussions on stage-appropriate interventions and present-day promising practices.

Trauma-Informed Treatment Strategies or Clinical Models Specific to the Trauma

Cognitive behavioral therapy is particularly effective in treating symptomatic adolescents exposed to trauma (Villalba & Lewis, 2007). Eye Movement Desensitization and Reprocessing (EMDR) also can work with some traumatized individuals (Roth & Fonagy, 2005).

Trauma can affect several developmental domains such as attachment systems, biology, affect regulation, dissociation, behavioral control, cognition, and self-concept. Bath (2008) examined trauma interventions for complex trauma and specified three pillars upon which interventions should be based. This three-pronged interactive approach involves steps that caregivers can take to strengthen the three pillars: safety, connections, and managing emotional impulses. The outcome of complex trauma is often PTSD; however, because the PTSD criteria are meant for adults, many adolescents go undiagnosed and untreated. Unfortunately, according to Bath and others (Gamache Martin et al., 2016), adolescents often come to view adults as threats instead of supports. But all home, school, and community caretakers who interact with traumatized children potentially contribute to their maturation and healing.

Bath argues that in order for healing to occur, safety, affect regulation, and coping and self-management skills must be established. The first pillar, safety, represents a core developmental need (Bowlby, 1988; Erikson, 1950; Maslow, 1943). Therefore, when working with adolescents who have experienced trauma, it is essential to create a sense of safety (transparency, availability, consistency). The second pillar demands the development of comfortable connections between the adolescent and their caretakers. The author further argues that third-pillar interventions should teach adolescents the ability to manage emotions or self-regulate. Similarly, Dombo and Sabatino (2019) have taken this notion of pillars and written a manual for creating trauma-informed schools.

Margolin and Gordis (2004) propose community interventions such as mentoring programs and structured school-based activities. Particularly for trauma symptoms stemming from community-based violence, community interventions without involving all of the community systems, such as police and schools, are less likely to succeed (Horowitz et al., 1995). Given the developmental shift to looking more toward peers than family, group interventions often are employed (Aronson & Kahn, 2004; van der Kolk, 1987). After the 1988 Armenian earthquake, trauma/grief-focused brief psychotherapy was employed in schools in order to mitigate PTSD symptoms and prevent aggravation of comorbid depression among young adolescents (Goenjian et al., 1997). The results support the broad use of such school-based interventions after major disasters and demonstrate the cross-cultural applicability of Western psychotherapeutic approaches.

Promising Practices

The *Community Service Foundation & Buxmont Academy* (CSF Buxmont) operates a Pennsylvania-based alternative school that uses restorative practices. A student confronts traumatic life challenges with the help of group problem-solving with supportive peers (Lange, 2008). The use of peer groups at this developmental stage is a recurring thread among best practices for traumatized youth.

The *Sanctuary Model of Trauma-Informed Organizational Change* (Bloom, 1997) builds respectful culture in community mental health organizations and schools so that troubled youth and their caregivers are not subject to victimization. The therapeutic community focuses on the needs of traumatized youth through a psychoeducational model called SELF, which addresses the challenges of **S**afety, **E**motional management, **L**oss, and **F**uture.

The *UCLA Trauma Psychiatry Program* has developed a school-based intervention program for children and adolescents who have been exposed to trauma, and who are chronically distressed with resultant problems in school or with peer and family functioning (see Saltzman et al., 2001). The program includes a systematic approach to screening for trauma, a manual-based 16- to 20-week trauma/grief-focused group psychotherapy protocol, along with individual and family therapy and measurement scales to determine any reduction in symptomatology as well as any increase in adaptive functioning.

Miller Children's Abuse and Violence Intervention Center (MCAVIC) in Long Beach, California, created the *Integrative Treatment of Complex Trauma for Adolescents* (ITCT-A), which focuses on the treatment of multiple traumatized youth. This program is a comprehensive manual-based multimodal treatment (Briere & Lanktree, 2008), which is freely available to the public.

It is worth noting that dialectical behavioral therapy (DBT) is being widely used in various residential programs for youth who cannot remain in the home of the family of origin. Although not always articulated, many of these youths are in residential care because of a history of trauma. DBT has been conceptualized as a trauma-based model for those with borderline personality disorder (BPD; Swenson, 2000). Originally developed for women diagnosed with BPD who exhibited suicidal and parasuicidal behaviors and very often had histories of trauma, DBT has since been used in state-run adolescent residential programs such as Echo Glen in Washington State (see Trupin et al., 2002) and the McLean Adolescent Unit, affiliated with Harvard. Additionally, a community-based DBT program for adolescent females shows promise (Geddes et al., 2013). Two randomized controlled trials have demonstrated robust success with suicidal adolescents in reducing suicidal symptoms and hospitalization for self-injury (McCauley et al., 2018). The symptoms of BPD are similar to those of a risk-taking adolescent who is just learning how to modulate emotions, such that the skills offered by this approach resonate with the tasks of this developmental phase. DBT treatment consists of individual behavioral treatment, skills coaching, and a psychoeducational group, in which cognitive and behavioral skills, including mindfulness, can be learned and practiced. Critical to DBT with adolescents, and what distinguishes it from DBT with adults, is involvement of the parents, who learn the same skills that the adolescent learns so that they can coach the youth through any emergent distress.

By the same token, a mentalization approach to adolescents with borderline symptoms has gained some traction as an evidence-based approach (Abate et al., 2017; Taubner & Curth, 2013); there is now a treatment protocol, Mentalization-Based Treatment for Adolescents or MBT-A, available with a move toward therapist certification in this treatment modality (see Anna Freud Centre).

Trauma-focused CBT for children is a well-established best practice promoted by SAMHSA, with training material freely available on their website. There is now growing evidence for its use with teens in particular (Cohen et al., 2016).

What all of the sampling of available approaches, discussed previously, have in common are their multipronged, relational approaches with a strong peer group work component. This use of the mutual aid of peers is consistent with the importance of peers as well as self-determination at this stage of life. The use of cognitive behavioral procedures for identifying triggers and emotional responses is also a core component of these programs and consistent with traditional approaches to treating trauma in adults. Cognitive approaches promote exposure to and tolerance of the emotions that persons suffering from trauma often attempt to avoid (Lang & Sharma-Patel, 2011). Whatever the approach, there is some evidence that telling one's story and being able to do so in a coherent narrative is a good prognostic sign (Briere & Scott, 2006; Pennebaker, 1993). The cognitive skills and motivation necessary for constructing a coherent narrative related to one's life story normally develop during adolescence (Habermas & Bluck, 2000). Efforts in treatment are geared toward being able to face and articulate the trauma in a way that the adolescent can convey their experience without reliving it in the moment.

Clinical Tensions

Adolescence by its very nature is a time of conflict and contradiction (Box 8.1). Developmentally, at a time when there is a natural move away from parents, there is still a need to feel connected. Particularly with regard to a traumatic event or series of traumatic events, the need for a caring adult with whom to process is paramount. Adversity is the opportunity for growth and trauma can either hinder or enhance growth and development depending on supports available.

BOX 8.1

Normal Adolescent Contradictions

The contradictions of normal adolescence are described by Raphael-Leff (2011) as follows:

- Ideas of "invincibility" coupled with panic attacks and lack of confidence
- Social withdrawal yet deep concern regarding relationships
- Silence, need for privacy, sensitivity to external intrusions
- Talkativeness, loud music, barriers to block out internal intrusions
- Confusion, impulsiveness, sadness, resentment
- Self-preoccupation, exquisite sensitivity yet lower attunement to the emotions of others

The previous conflicts coincide with hope for the future and a sense of loss of childhood. Development does not occur in a straight line, but rather often involves the return of earlier childhood behavioral patterns, marshalled by the youth to manage the loss of childhood as well as the awakening of a sexual self. Family power dynamics shift as adolescents strive for independence. Ironically, as physical and psychological changes associated with puberty threaten confidence in competing with peers, or succeeding academically, the early adolescent seeks the reassurance of parents. Careful attention of caregivers to boundaries—flexible enough to adjust with the age of the youth—is important. The tendency to want to control the youth or abandon control completely is ever present. Either approach, too much control or too little, increases the likelihood of the adolescent's "withdrawal or defiant rebellion in his/her search for adequate limit-setting coupled with warmth and support" (Raphael-Leff, 2011).

As previously discussed, it is important for teens to be able to talk to a caring adult, and to be able to respond in a validating way. Table 8.1 from the National Child and Traumatic Stress Network gives some very useful and nuanced responses to teens' experience of the disaster/trauma.

Table 8.1

Parent Tips for Helping Adolescents After Disasters

Reactions	Responses	Examples of Things to Do and Say
Detachment, shame, and guilt	• Provide a safe time to discuss with your teen the events and their feelings. • Emphasize that these feelings are common, and correct excessive self-blame with realistic explanations of what actually could have been done.	• "Many teens—and adults—feel like you do, angry and blaming themselves that they could have done more. You're not at fault. Remember even the firefighters said there was nothing more we could have done."
Self-consciousness: About their fears, sense of vulnerability, fear of being labeled abnormal	• Help teens understand that these feelings are common. • Encourage relationships with family and peers for needed support during the recovery period.	• "I was feeling the same thing. Scared and helpless. Most people feel like this when a disaster happens, even if they look calm on the outside." • "My cell phone is working again; why don't you see if you can get a hold of Pete to see how he is doing." • "And thanks for playing the game with your little sister. She's much better now."
Acting out behavior: Using alcohol or drugs, sexually acting out, accident-prone behavior	• Help teens understand that acting out behavior is a dangerous way to express strong feelings (like anger) over what happened. • Limit access to alcohol and drugs. • Talk about the danger of high-risk sexual activity. • On a time-limited basis, keep a closer watch on where they are going and what they are planning to do.	• "Many teens–and some adults—feel out of control and angry after a disaster like this. They think drinking or taking drugs will help somehow. It's very normal to feel that way–but it's not a good idea to act on it." • "It's important during these times that I know where you are and how to contact you." Assure them that this extra checking-in is temporary, just until things have stabilized.
Fear of recurrence and reactions to reminders	• Help to identify different reminders (people, places, sounds, smells, feelings, time of day) and to clarify the difference between the event and the reminders that occur after it. • Explain to teens that media coverage of the disaster can trigger fears of it happening again.	• "When you're reminded, you might try saying to yourself, 'I am upset now because I am being reminded, but it is different now because there is no hurricane and I am safe.'" • Suggest, "Watching the news report could make it worse, because they are playing the same images over and over. How about turning it off now?"
Abrupt shifts in interpersonal relationships: Teens may pull away from parents, family, and even from peers; they may respond strongly to parent's reactions in the crisis.	• Explain that the strain on relationship is expected. Emphasize that everyone needs family and friends for support during the recovery period. • Encourage tolerance for different family members' courses of recovery. • Accept responsibility for your own feelings.	• Spend more time talking as a family about how everyone is doing. Say, "You know, the fact that we're crabby with each other is completely normal, given what we've been through. I think we're handling things amazingly. It's a good thing we have each other." • You might say, "I appreciate your being calm when your brother was screaming last night. I know he woke you up, too." • "I want to apologize for being irritable with you yesterday. I am going to work harder to stay calm myself."

(continued)

Table 8.1

Parent Tips for Helping Adolescents After Disasters (*continued*)

Reactions	Responses	Examples of Things to Do and Say
Radical changes in attitude	• Explain that changes in people's attitudes after a disaster are common, but often return back over time.	• "We are all under great stress. When people's lives are disrupted this way, we all feel more scared, angry—even full of revenge. It might not seem like it, but we all will feel better when we get back to a more structured routine."
Premature entrance into adulthood (wanting to leave school, get married)	• Encourage postponing major life decisions. Find other ways to make the teens feel more in control.	• "I know you're thinking about quitting school and getting a job to help out. But it's important not to make big decisions right now. A crisis time is not a great time to make major changes."
Concern for other survivors and families	• Encourage constructive activities on behalf of others, but do not let them burden themselves with undue responsibility.	• Help teens to identify projects that are age-appropriate and meaningful (clearing rubble from school grounds, collecting money or supplies for those in need).

Source: Reproduced with permission from the *Psychological First Aid Field Operations Guide* (PFA), 2nd Edition (2006).

Examining the response to the various reactions to disaster, or trauma, listed in Table 8.1 essentially instructs us that the response is one of validation of the youth's experiences, which can mitigate any emotional dysregulation, and also serves to contextualize the reaction leading to cognitive understanding.

CONCLUSION

Adolescence is not only a time when there is increased risk for trauma because of the risk-taking typical of this developmental stage, but it also offers an opportunity to rework earlier traumas, a "second chance" (Blos, 1967; Eissler, 1958; Raphael-Leff, 2011). Intervention approaches typically include cognitive behavioral techniques to assist the young person in identifying triggers to deal with symptoms associated with PTSD; group interventions also are key during this developmental phase, when peers become much more important. Being able to tell one's story in a linear coherent narrative, without the intrusion of posttraumatic stress symptoms, assists in the identity formation so crucial to this developmental stage of life.

ADDITIONAL RESOURCES

SPRINGER PUBLISHING
C**O**NNECT™

A robust set of instructor resources designed to supplement this text is located at http://connect.springerpub.com/content/book/978-0-8261-5085-1. Qualifying instructors may request access by emailing textbook@springerpub.com.

PRACTICE-BASED RESOURCES AND REFERENCES

To view a list of resources and all the references, please visit connect.springerpub.com via the following url: http://connect.springerpub.com/content/book/978-0-8261-5085-1/part/part02/chapter/ch08

CHAPTER 9

Treating Adults With Complex Trauma or a Complexity of Traumas

CAROL M. SMITH

CHAPTER OVERVIEW

This chapter reviews current knowledge in the helping professions regarding adults with complex trauma. *Complex trauma* is defined and deconstructed, locating the individual within relevant social systems. The chapter clarifies otherwise inexplicable characteristics of adults carrying significant trauma histories. The neurobiology of trauma informs treatment planning. Phases of treatment are reinforced, as well as current best practices and limits of what psychotherapy or mental health counseling can achieve. The chapter briefly compares Eastern and Western approaches to emotional discomfort and offers relevant guidance. The chapter closes with counseling implications of current treatment models and evidence-based best practices, which are discussed in more detail in later chapters.

LEARNING OBJECTIVES

After reading this chapter, the reader should be able to:

1. Distinguish multiple meanings about what is meant by the phrase *complex trauma*;
2. Recognize typical clinical characteristics of adults with significant trauma;
3. Describe the treatment implications of the *neurobiology* of complex trauma;
4. Review current best practice approaches in treating complex trauma; and,
5. Recognize the limits of treatment for complex trauma.

INTRODUCTION

This chapter focuses on the therapeutic encounter with adult survivors of developmental (complex) trauma and those who present with a *complexity of traumas*. Working with adults who have significant trauma histories is uniquely challenging. Challenges include characteristics that some label as mistrust (or naivete), resistance (or anxious attachment), acting out (or self-harm), emotional blunting/flat affect (or emotional outbursts/histrionics), lack of engagement (or manipulation), or shame (or shamelessness). These behavioral *labels* are not ends in themselves; rather, they point to a person living with a history of significant trauma.

This chapter addresses the clinical *footnotes* of working with adults who have survived some of the worst experiences conceivable, some of which are nearly incomprehensible in intensity and scope. Unpacking a trauma history includes consideration of the neural substrates of trauma; how trauma *inhabits* a body, emotions, and thought patterns; and how survivors learn to survive in ways that were uniquely ingenious at the time of the trauma(s) but that now create more problems than they solve. A comparison of *Western* and *Eastern* approaches to emotional pain facilitates making sense of a traumatic history and provides a foundation for posttraumatic growth and development. This chapter emphasizes the importance of following a phasic approach to treatment and why. While planning what treatment can accomplish for adults living with significant trauma histories, it is also incumbent on the therapist to explain the limits of therapy. The chapter introduces current best practices and addresses the implications for counselors providing counseling to adults with significant trauma.

COMPLEX TRAUMA AND CLINICAL TENSIONS

Mental health professionals use the phrase "complex trauma" in at least two ways. "Complex trauma" can refer either to "developmental trauma," which typically occurs in childhood as an enduring characteristic of household or generational patterns (Courtois, 2004; Ford & Smith, 2008; van der Kolk, 2005; van Dijke et al., 2015), or to a "complexity of traumas," which refers to any combination of sequential or contemporaneous traumatic events (traumas within traumas), or simultaneous preexisting mental health disorders or addiction(s) and either sequential or contemporaneous traumatic events, or all of the above (Briere & Scott, 2015; Lawson, 2017). For example, refugee immigrants, who have typically lost their homes, livelihoods, and many family members, experience long stays in displacement camps, significant cultural intolerance, stigma, and physical or sexual assault in host countries, and find it nearly impossible to find meaningful work by which they can rebuild their lives (Panter-Brick et al., 2018; Riber, 2017; Ter Heide et al., 2016). (Further details regarding immigration-related trauma appear in Chapter 17, "Racial, Ethnic, and Immigration Intolerance: A Framework for Understanding Violence and Trauma.")

Knowing that the phrase "complex trauma" refers either to developmental trauma or to a complexity of traumas (or both) helps the therapist to recognize multiple types and instances of traumatic stress, or traumas within traumas, that manifest in a bewildering array of characteristics in clients, and which can significantly complicate treatment. A clinical example of someone experiencing complex trauma appears in Box 9.1.

BOX 9.1

Clinical Vignette: Christa

Christa (*composite example*) provides an example of a complexity of traumas: Christa left home and eighth grade at age 14 to escape the neglect of her addicted mother and the sexual predation of her third stepfather, only to fall in with sex traffickers who provided food and a place to stay in exchange for trafficking her. They plied her with heroin to blunt the pains of being trafficked. At 18 she managed to escape and hitchhiked across the country. Still addicted, she pitched a tent on railway land and found a job waiting tables. When COVID-19 shut the restaurants to which she could walk or take the bus, she tried to find space in a women's shelter and get help obtaining a car so she could find additional work. While unable to find permanent shelter or a car, she attended shelter workshops whenever possible and sought medication-assisted treatment to overcome her addiction. Christa became pregnant while working on her GED and obtaining skills training through a local Job Corps. Christa

(continued)

delivered a baby girl, Destiny, in the emergency department and was discharged later that day with a bag of diapers, a stroller, and formula vouchers. Job Corps secured an efficiency apartment for them when Destiny was 2 months old. As Destiny's needs have increased in the ensuing months, Christa cannot afford childcare and finds it hard to concentrate or sustain her energy for her GED and work training. She is unable to make ends meet. She is not sleeping and is considering returning to sex work because the sisterhood of workers will watch Destiny when she is working. While she knows her situation is not ideal, Christa does not consider herself to be victimized or out of the ordinary, because almost everyone she knows shares a similar history.

Despite the potential complexity of a given trauma history, whether an adult seeks mental healthcare for a traumatic childhood, or a series of traumatic experiences, both the presentation and treatment planning are similar (Briere & Scott, 2015; Lawson, 2017; McCormack & Thomson, 2017). Although the traumas are complex and seemingly overwhelming, it may be reassuring to know that treatment approaches remain clear and consistent for all adults with significant trauma histories.

CLIENT CHARACTERISTICS

The *Diagnostic and Statistical Manual of Mental Disorders* (5th ed.; *DSM-5*; American Psychiatric Association [APA], 2013) moved the diagnosis of Posttraumatic Stress Disorder (PTSD) from the section on Anxiety Disorders (*DSM-IV-TR*, APA, 2000) to a newly created section on Trauma and Stressor-Related Disorders, in recognition that traumatic stress is a distinct category (APA, 2013; McFarlane, 2014; Miller et al., 2014). The new *DSM* section includes Reactive Attachment Disorder (RAD), Disinhibited Social Engagement Disorder (DSED), Posttraumatic Stress Disorder (PTSD), and Adjustment Disorders. The section follows Anxiety Disorders and Obsessive-Compulsive and Related Disorders, and precedes *DSM* sections on Dissociative Disorders and Somatic Symptom and Related Disorders. The section's location in the *DSM-5* is pertinent to a broad understanding of trauma and underscores the etiological relevance of these clinical presentations, which can co-occur. The authors of the *DSM-5* not only recognize traumatic stress as its own distinct category, worthy of study and expertise, but also acknowledge that its etiology relates to the sections which precede and follow it in the manual. Trauma's neighboring sections in the *DSM* are near it because they relate to trauma, both conceptually and clinically. Interestingly, the potential entry of developmental trauma disorder (DTD) was proposed but not included in the *DSM-5* (Bremness & Polzin, 2014). Future editions of the *DSM* almost certainly will include more trauma-related diagnoses and recognition that both trauma, and reactions to trauma, occur on a continuum or *spectrum* (Carmassi et al., 2020; Monson et al., 2017; O'Donnell et al., 2011).

Any of the following may apply to adults with traumatic histories who are seeking mental healthcare:

- They may reveal that they have a difficult time with relationships (*see* V- and Z-codes in *DSM-5*);
- They do not remember much of their childhoods (dissociative amnesia);
- They may be self-medicating with marijuana, alcohol, or multiple substances (substance use disorders [SUD]); and,
- They may qualify for an anxiety disorder or major depressive disorder (MDD), dissociative identity disorder (DID), panic disorder, somatic disorders, sleep–wake disorders, sexual dysfunctions, conduct disorders, personality disorders, or paraphilic disorders.

In short—excluding schizophrenia and neurocognitive and neurodevelopmental disorders—adults with a complexity of traumas may spend years collecting diagnoses spanning the *DSM-5* and still not have an accurate clinical explanation for what is wrong. While this can feel completely overwhelming to an inexperienced clinician, it is reassuring to understand that "what is wrong" is actually *trauma.* If mental health professionals can recognize and treat trauma, the majority of diagnoses in the *DSM* can be eliminated (Breuer & Freud, 1893; Kira et al., 2013; McCormack & Thomson, 2017; Zanville & Cattaneo, 2009).

Trust and Boundaries

Adults with substantial histories of trauma have great difficulty trusting others or forming healthy attachments—for good reason—given their histories (Garcia, 2017; Larsen et al., 2011; Miranda et al., 2020; Unthank, 2019). Therefore, these clients initially may frustrate clinicians with an aloof, guarded, and blunted presentation. They do not seem to engage in the counseling process, offer little information or detail when asked open questions, appear to withhold candid answers, or deflect inquiries that even modestly approach trauma or victimization. On the other hand, they may present as angry, irritable, defensive, suspicious about the clinician's motives or line of inquiry, or doubt the clinician's credentials or competence to work compatibly with them. Alternatively, they can be charming, manipulative, disingenuous, and bafflingly opaque in their initial sessions, giving the impression that nothing is wrong and there is no reason for therapy to take place. Because interpersonal trauma unavoidably ruptures the fundamental trust on which human relationships are built, adults with substantial trauma histories have compelling reasons *not* to trust relationships with others (Garcia, 2017; Larsen et al., 2011).

A lack of confidence in others creates an unsolvable dilemma in a world that essentially requires human beings to form trusting relationships in order to live healthy lives (Garcia, 2017; Larsen et al., 2011; Unthank, 2019). Therefore, a fundamental goal of therapy is to establish a trusting relationship. A trusting relationship grows through the intentional use of unconditional positive regard (Rogers, 1957), patience, appreciating that *trust issues* are evidence of the quality of previous relationships rather than current therapeutic rapport, and tolerating repeated *tests* of the therapeutic relationship while maintaining consistent interpersonal boundaries of the professional—rather than personal—relationship. It is essential to remember that a therapeutic encounter represents a professional relationship, despite the intensely intimate content and topics addressed in therapy.

Adults with complex histories of trauma may use *self-blame* and a deep sense of *shame* to keep others at a distance (Unthank, 2019). They may have very little regard for their own personal boundaries, considering themselves unworthy of respect or genuine caring (Blanco et al., 2016; Horowitz & Stermac, 2018; Unthank, 2019). Client mistrust regarding the therapeutic relationship and related disturbances in the client's interpersonal boundaries with others are characteristics of trauma rather than interpersonal deficits. Further, they do not reflect the quality of the therapist. Clinicians are wise to remind themselves, frequently, that trauma disrupts many assumptions about how the world works. Therefore, trauma manifests in characteristics that otherwise would sabotage the clinical encounter. In the end, competent clinicians will be patient, soft-spoken, and tolerant. As trust in the therapeutic relationship builds, therapeutic progress accelerates.

Dysregulation

Adults with a complexity of traumas present with an array of other emotional characteristics. For example, they may struggle with regulation, pivoting between a dull, flat affect and emotional lability, sometimes within the same session (Frei et al., 2020; Horowitz & Stermac, 2018; Poole et al., 2017; Siegel, 2009). Clients may seek relief in self-injury (Frei et al., 2020; Horowitz & Stermac, 2018), risky behavior (Felitti et al., 1998; Modrowski & Kerig, 2019), or substance use as a way of self-medicating (Ghorbani et al., 2019). Clients describe an overwhelming spectrum of somatic complaints (headaches, gastrointestinal complaints, muscle aches, stiffness, unexplained pain), and benefit from therapists who recognize how uncomfortable it can be for individuals who have been physically violated, targeted, or seriously injured simply to inhabit a human body (McGuire, 2018), which feels chronically unsafe (Herman, 1992; van der Kolk, 2014).

Triggers

Traumatic experiences may not be accessible as thoughts or part of a personal narrative. Rather, the experiences are stored as fragments of senses throughout the body, and restored by relevant body positions, pains, smells, sights, or sounds (Ogden & Fisher, 2015; Stein & Kendall, 2004; van der Kolk, 2005, 2014). Memories or disjointed sensations of "something wrong" can be triggered by subtle or obvious cues. They can be caused by anniversaries or relevant circumstances: such as having one's child reach the survivor's age of abuse; the physical gestures used by authoritative figures; or cues like smells, textures, or patterns in carpet, fabric, music, or artwork. Interestingly, *trigger warnings* on college campuses and in media are not only unhelpful, paradoxically, they reinforce survivors' views of their trauma as "central to their identity" (Jones et al., 2020, p. 905).

Dissociation

Finally, adults with complex histories of traumas may be unaware of one of their most effective defense mechanisms–*dissociation*. Dissociation refers to an automatic and spontaneous division of pieces of thought processes from personal awareness. In other words, dissociation serves to create conceptual and categorical distance between a person and the unbearable things that person has experienced. Dissociation allows a person to sustain two or more incompatible actualities without recognizing the incompatibility (APA, 2013).

Dissociation allows a child to love an abusive figure, a teen to feel safe in a dangerous family, and an adult to remain devoted to a violent partner. Dissociation occurs when individuals must choose between the two major needs of *safety* and *belonging*, outlined by Maslow's hierarchy of needs (Maslow, 1943) as *mutually exclusive categories*. They can either be safe without belonging, or they can belong without safety, but not both simultaneously. The ingenious psychological and self-preserving answer to this existential conundrum is *dissociation*. Dissociative symptoms include dynamics like a fragmented sense of one's personality, *derealization* (distancing from the actuality of an experience; this is not really happening) ,and *depersonalization* (detaching from one's sense of living in the experience; this is not really happening *to me*) (APA, 2013). In extreme cases, people with extensive histories of trauma may qualify for DID (APA, 2013), which is characterized by more than one distinct personality and sense of history existing in the same person. DID is an elegant solution to an unsolvable problem for a youngster growing up in a dangerous and violating environment. When something unbearable and unconscionable occurs to a person (typically a developing child), the mind distances itself from the experience, to the extent that "it not only did not really happen; and did not happen to me; it actually happened to someone else altogether."

Some learn to dissociate as a tool for survival (Alayarian, 2019; Kumar et al., 2019; Lawson & Akay-Sullivan, 2020; McGuire, 2018) and grow up without knowing that they dissociate. Difficulties ensue when individuals engage in dissociation whenever circumstances feel overwhelming, with an accompanying degradation to the mean, meaning that it takes less stress to produce a dissociative response. This is especially problematic when individuals have difficulty piecing together a coherent personal historical narrative for almost any span of their life stories (Alayarian, 2019). The challenge in treatment is to distinguish between healthy and self-defeating forms of dissociation, and to help clients know that, as adults, they have more coping strategies at their disposal than they did as children. They can use healthier and more life-affirming methods, such as dosing and distancing, to process distressing events in manageable ways.

NEUROBIOLOGY OF COMPLEX TRAUMA

To explain the neurobiology of complex trauma, it is helpful to revisit an historic evolutionary model, an oversimplification now replaced by clearer scientific understanding of physical development. The triune brain model (MacLean, 1990) nevertheless serves as a metaphorical organization of brain *functioning* rather than *development*. The triune brain model describes three systems: the *brainstem* (which controls fine motor movements, smooth muscle function, regulation of heart rate and breathing, and the ability to maintain consciousness); the *limbic system* (which is the emotion and memory center of the brain), and the *cerebral cortex* (which controls executive functions like the ability to sustain attention, make choices between right and wrong, put things in sequence, find the right word, and make sense of experiences).

Bessel van der Kolk (2014) maintains that the structures deepest within the brain and closest to the midline (a.k.a. the *corpus callosum*) are those which are most relevant to the individual's sense of self, while the structures toward the surfaces of the brain have to do with social relationships and interactions with the world. Given the limbic system's location in the center of the brain, the limbic system is where the *sense of self* resides. The limbic system houses basic emotions, memories, alertness to danger, and self-in-environment. The function of two key structures–the *amygdala* and the *hippocampus*–are essential to a contemporary understanding of the neurobiology of trauma. The neuroscience of trauma is explored in more detail in Chapter 2, "Theoretical Contexts of Trauma Counseling."

Amygdala and Hippocampus

The amygdalae are two almond-shaped structures, one on either side of the midline (*corpus callosum*) of the brain. The hippocampi are two seahorse-shaped structures, one on either side of the corpus callosum. The amygdala uses the neurotransmitter norepinephrine to determine *how* perceived external stimuli are encoded and consolidated as memories through the amygdala-hippocampal connection. The effect of this relationship is an upside-down U-shaped curve (a.k.a. the Yerkes-Dodson curve). Too little norepinephrine means that memories are not likely to be consolidated and stored. A medium ("just right") amount of norepinephrine enhances alertness, focus, and memories. Too much norepinephrine "hijacks" memory consolidation and facilitates amnesia and dissociation, which is the typical signature of a life of complex trauma.

Executive Functions: Flipping Our Lids

When an individual is frightened or sufficiently stressed, the upper cortical layer in the brain (where all of the executive functions and self-regulation skills reside) goes offline, and the limbic system takes over, doing whatever it can to fight, flee, freeze, or faint, in order to avoid a stressor. This is called *flipping one's lid* because it is like unwrapping the cortex from the midbrain (Box 9.2).

BOX 9.2

Brain Function Illustration

An illustration of the brain's trauma process is to make a fist with one's fingers curled over the thumb, and then to flip the fingers up straight and open. In the model, the wrist represents the brainstem. The thumb represents the limbic system, and wrapped fingers represent the cortex. When trauma, stress, or both occur, "flip the lid," by uncurling the fingers from over the thumb. In this model, the cortex (represented by the fingers) "goes off-line," leaving the limbic system (emotions; represented by the thumb) and brainstem (represented by the wrist) to manage the situation with more basic responses and instincts.

When a person is exposed to multiple, uncontrollable sources of stress, particularly traumatic stress, the amygdala becomes primed or sensitized to excrete norepinephrine, and in greater amounts. This priming increases not only the volume of neurotransmitters (primarily norepinephrine) employed by the amygdala, but also the physical size of the amygdala (Kuo et al., 2012). Increased norepinephrine in the brain, over time, impairs the functioning of the prefrontal cortex. Higher levels of stress lead to higher amounts of norepinephrine circulating in the brain and body. Over time, progressively less stress is required to reach a high level of norepinephrine in the brain. This process is also known as *kindling*.

Neural Pathways

Neural pathways are the paths through which nerve signals travel, using neurons in the brain or body. Simple neural pathways control things like a knee-jerk response in the leg. More complex neural pathways control things like habits, or well-learned coordinated skills (such as typing, musical passages on an instrument, dance, or athletic moves). Neural pathways are also significantly involved in cognitive activities such as memories, mind-sets, worldviews, and schemas.

Each time the brain is stimulated by information, the brain creates new neural pathways. Specifically, neural stimulation encourages new dendritic growth (branching of the nerve cells) in the brain. As these fibers lengthen, they increase the physical surface available both for receiving information and for passing it along to the next nerve. Increased dendrites (short, branched extensions of the nerve cells) are central to thought, memory, and information processing in the brain. The more dendrites the brain has at its disposal, the more quickly and smoothly it can process information, make connections, see patterns, form meanings, predict implications, and so on. Just as physical bridges and roadways provide faster travel for cars, neural pathways provide faster and smoother transfers for communication within the cortex, or between the cortex and connected structures, such as the limbic system. Neural pathways increase processing power in the brain by dedicating familiar information to familiar pathways, which frees the cortex to attend to new information. The more a given pathway is stimulated, the stronger it becomes. For example, if a person accentuates negative schemas or mind-sets, the brain programs cognitive neural pathways toward negativity. Likewise, traumatic stress tends to emphasize negative, vulnerable, and hypervigilant mind-sets. In order to counteract these negative neural pathways, people with complex trauma benefit from purposefully working on and exposing themselves to new, positive, and trustworthy information and experiences. Essentially, if a person emphasizes positive materials and mind-set, the brain accommodates by creating and reinforcing positive neural pathways. Simple repetition of behaviors, motions, or thoughts strengthen and deepen neural pathways.

Broca's Area

One of the key areas in the prefrontal cortex that shuts down during traumatic stress is *Broca's area,* or the area in the cortex responsible for producing speech. This is one reason why van der Kolk (2001, 2005, 2014) describes traumatized people as those who are *frozen in speechless terror*. This means that people who have experienced traumatic stress have an exceptionally difficult time talking about what exactly happened. This is not because it is too challenging, emotionally, to talk about it (although this is partly true), but because Broca's area has become inactivated during the traumatic stress, and therefore cannot assist in the typically easy process of putting experiences into words. The physiological underpinnings of words and descriptive language are simply not available. It also means that many cognitively based talk therapies, while necessary, are insufficient to resolve a traumatic experience.

Inability to talk about a trauma does not mean, however, that the individual is unaffected by—or is not thinking about—the trauma. Exactly the opposite occurs. *Because* the person cannot put it into words, *because* Broca's area was offline, and *because* the person cannot talk it out, the person tends to become developmentally stuck and unable to move forward. The person becomes stuck in a frustrating process of trying to make sense of the events, trying to put them into words (generally without success), and trying to organize thoughts about what happened, why, and what the events *mean*. This expressive work is no small task.

Some adults with complex trauma not only have difficulty generating speech about their traumatic stress, they also have difficulty recognizing and processing language, especially feelings-based language, about traumatic stress. A study of veterans (Freeman et al., 2009) showed that those with PTSD displayed significant inability to comprehend or discriminate between components of affective (emotions-based) speech. The degree of difficulty recognizing and understanding emotional language for the veterans with PTSD was similar to those who have ischemic brain injury (stroke). Please see Box 9.3 for a recap of the neurological implications of trauma.

BOX 9.3

Neural Recap

Quick recap: Traumatic stress decreases neural connections, and ultimately cellular volume, in the hippocampus (it gets smaller and less efficient). Traumatic stress increases the size of the amygdalae on both sides of the brain, making them more sensitive and alert to any signs of threat in the environment. Traumatic stress causes breakdown in the connectivity of the two hemispheres of the brain via the corpus callosum, diminishing the ability of the two brain halves to communicate and integrate with each other. Traumatic stress decreases whole brain volume (Perry, 2009; van der Kolk, 2014), especially in the cortex, where the majority of thinking and sense making occurs. Not only does traumatic stress kindle the fight–flight–freeze–faint response, but it also deregulates it so that the response is both less predictable and less manageable when it occurs. Traumatic stress also dysregulates neurotransmitters and hormones in the brain (and the body) so that they are out of balance with one another, leading to mood swings, impulse control problems, difficulty regulating affect, and self-awareness. This lack of balance also characterizes classic depression and anxiety disorders, as well as anger control problems.

TRAUMA AND THE DEVELOPING BRAIN

Brain development occurs from the bottom up, both physically and in terms of functionality (Perry, 2009). It is sequential, in a predetermined order, and higher levels of development depend on lower levels having developed appropriately first. Brain development starts before birth and a series of critical windows of development must happen in a sequential order for a brain to be fully developed and healthy. Critical windows are periods of potential in brain development that are critical to functionality. Therefore, the same trauma will affect a younger child more profoundly than an older child because of the sequential nature of brain development. Trauma early in life makes a person more vulnerable to future trauma. Brain development concludes around ages 28 to 30, and then slowly declines over the rest of one's lifetime.

Timing is everything regarding trauma and development. The earlier a trauma occurs, the more profoundly it affects brain development (Garner, 2013; Perry, 2009; Whittle et al., 2013). The longer a trauma lasts, the worse it is. The more it is directed personally at a child, the more pervasive its consequences (Perry, 2009; Shonkoff & Garner, 2012). A salutary feature of brain development is "malleability," meaning that a very young brain (neonatal until about age 4) is more malleable, meaning that it changes and develops easily with learning and experience. However, very young brains are also more vulnerable (McCrory et al., 2010). A young brain (ages 5 to 25) is less vulnerable than a *very* young brain, but also less malleable. An old brain (after about age 65) is less malleable and more vulnerable to physical insults such as head injury or stroke. Trauma early in life is so profound, because a young child is creating templates for expectations about the world, other people, and the child's place in the world. Children learn at very early ages (less than 24 months) whether the world is safe, whether others are trustworthy and predictable, and whether the environment is safe and caring (Perry, 2009). Children also learn whether they are essentially okay and acceptable, whether they belong to the family group, and whether they have personal agency.

EAST–WEST UNDERSTANDINGS OF SUFFERING AND PAIN

Lifetime prevalence for anxiety disorders in the United States is 31.2% (National Comorbidity Survey, 2007) compared to 5% in China (Shen et al., 2006). Likewise, lifetime prevalence for depression in the United States is 21.4% (National Comorbidity Survey, 2007) compared to 2.5% in Japan (Kawakami et al., 2005). While people who live in eastern countries may be less happy overall, they experience fewer mental health disorders (DeVaus et al., 2018). Because individuals from different cultures think in different ways about their emotions, and their responses also differ (DeVaus et al., 2018), it is instructive to contrast East and West systems of thought (Nisbett et al., 2001).

People from Western cultures tend to favor analytical thinking, breaking things down into a binomial either/or taxonomy of exclusive categories, for example: sadness/happiness; myself/others; good/evil; cause/effect; wellness/illness (Nisbett et al., 2001). People from Eastern cultures employ holistic thinking (both/and), and, rather than separating opposites, see them as coexisting simultaneously; for example, yin/yang symbolism, and events within context, and the interdependence of individuals within the collective (DeVaus et al., 2018; Spokas, 2019).

Eastern conceptions of emotions can be instructive for people in the West, particularly those coming to terms with a history of complex trauma. First, in Eastern conceptualizations, emotions co-occur (Goetz & Peng, 2019; Nisbett et al., 2001; Spokas, 2019); happiness can be found even in sad events—such as funerals, relationships that end, leaving home—and sadness can accompany positive experiences—such as weddings, childbirth, promotions, and birthdays. Second, emotions about the same event evolve over time (Nisbett et al., 2001; Spokas, 2019); for example, realizing that a divorce, while painful at the time, was also a relief and a release from painful interactions. This is important because it conveys the impermanence of feelings and events. Negative events, even trauma, become less threatening, because they are temporary (DeVaus et al., 2018). Finally, emotions are embedded in context (Goetz & Peng, 2019; Nisbett et al., 2001), meaning that negative experiences can be reframed. It is possible to do something about one's current emotional state by taking care of oneself currently, rather than ruminating on what happened previously. One way to manage negative feelings is to pay less attention to them, while attending to the needs of the situation (Adler, 1927) and one's effect on other people. The focus of one's attention affects one's beliefs about the world and causality (Goetz & Peng, 2019; Nisbett et al., 2001). Westerners turn inward and tend to conceptualize negative affect states as "What is wrong with me?" asking "How can I feel better?" By contrast, Easterners consider the self-in-context and ask, "What is wrong with the situation?" and "What can be done about it?"

Therefore, mental health professionals can provide clear cognitive tools to assist adults with histories of complex trauma, by emphasizing the duality and impermanence of emotions. While emotions provide the fuel for action (Adler, 1927), the specific *choice* of action can be made by the executive functions of the individual. Emotions co-occur (more than one emotion can happen simultaneously), they are embedded in a context (time, place, role), and they change over time (as new meanings and perspectives are considered). Emotions do not necessarily control the individual dealing with a complexity of traumas. Rather, the individual is empowered to consider the meaning and purpose of emotions, and then decides mindfully what to do with this information. Further, it may be a relief to expand one's conceptualization of a traumatic event by considering the individual in the *context* of other people, circumstances, roles, and the needs of a given situation. An individual may, by shifting perspectives, and by considering context and the passage of time, rally current, more developed ways of coping, and situate a personal event in the larger narrative of one's loved ones, community, culture, overall life history, goals for the future, and desires for positive change. Larger perspective and contextualization can foster significant change and posttraumatic growth.

PHASES AND ESSENTIAL ELEMENTS OF TREATMENT

Herman's (1992) phasic approach to treatment provides a structural framework for planning treatment. Three phases–establishing safety, working through, and consolidating gains–provide a roadmap for best practices. Some clients do not proceed through all three phases, and competent therapists do well to recognize that each client is unique with unique needs. It is not best practice to plunge into a debriefing of "what happened" unless the client is confident of the safety of the therapeutic relationship and context and wishes to tell the story. Some clients are satisfied with establishing safety and have no desire to rehash or unpack negative experiences—and being forced to do so, by well-intentioned therapists, actually can cause additional harm. Although it used to be axiomatic that, in order to heal, the traumatic history needs to be spoken and examined in detail, that is no longer the case (Webber & Mascari, 2017). In fact, some clients do not want or need to tell their story at all, ever. Mental health therapists can be content not to know what happened, because they do not need to know in order to help clients significantly and in lasting ways.

Essential elements of treating individuals with a complexity of traumas include matching the intervention to the functionality of the client (Perry, 2006, 2009); valuing the client while validating the client's feelings, thoughts, and experiences (Rogers, 1957); providing clear structure for both individual sessions and the overall span of treatment; dosing difficult emotions and affect (should the client choose to work through a given trauma); co-creating anchors for emotional grounding and tolerance; containment of content; installation of hope (Yalom & Leszcz, 2005); experiential fostering of creativity and spontaneity; and finally, reconceptualizing *trauma* as a *superpower*. While some of these essential elements are self-evident and are covered in detail elsewhere in this textbook, others deserve more discussion here.

Matching Intervention to Functionality

Perry (2006, 2009), in introducing the Neurosequential Model of Therapeutics (NMT), clarified that it is fruitless to provide therapy that does not match the developmental need of a given child. Perry discovered that some children, due to the traumatic nature of their upbringing, missed critical windows of development and therefore benefit more readily from remediation at specific areas of neurological development. For example, a child who has a poorly organized brainstem struggles with emotional self-regulation, focus, and impulsivity, and therefore would benefit from repetitive physical activities to balance emotional and physiological regulation (Perry, 2009). Examples of such activities include patterned breathing, a game of repeating verbal call and response, gently rolling a ball back and forth, learning to take turns, and simple yoga poses and stretches. These needs may persist into adulthood for people with a complexity of traumas, and therefore such lower level, somatic and physiological interventions are very helpful in learning to inhabit a human body safely, in the here and now.

Structuring, Dosing, Anchors, and Containment

Structuring, dosing, anchors, and containment refer to the calming and encouraging provision of bringing order to the chaos of feelings, flashbacks, and somatic experiences of humans with complex trauma histories. "Structuring" simply refers to the intentional and repeated use of words like "first," "before," "after," "later," "then," and "finally" to provide order and continuity in the process of any given therapeutic encounter as well as the overarching plan of treatment, in general, from beginning to end. This is good practice, because it provides a road map and a sense of progression for the client. "Dosing" is a specific type of structuring, which guides the client in managing negative affect and difficult memories. The client is empowered to determine how much will be managed in a given session or even in a given intervention, with the options of slowing down, backing off, hitting the proverbial brakes, and recognizing that enough has been accomplished for a given intervention, day, or season of working through a memory or history. Dosing in mental health treatment parallels medication prescriptions–take two a day in the morning, guidance for exercise–do three sets of 20 once a day, or building muscle–hold for 60 seconds.

Anchors

Anchors refer to identified examples of somatosensory phenomena in the immediate environment to assist with coming back to the here and now. A counselor can ask the client to identify two objects in the room (e.g., flower vase, yellow figurine) to serve as visual anchors, two sounds in the environment (ventilation inside, birdsong outside) to serve as auditory anchors, and, if it feels right, two textures or feelings (soft blanket, sitting down) to reconnect to current circumstances when working with emotionally challenging material. The counselor can use the identified anchors to help the client return to the here and now, should the client seem to be dissociating or getting lost in a given memory. The counselor can ask the client, who seems to be dissociating, to name the two visual anchors and focus on them, to name the two auditory anchors and experience them, to activate the two feelings by touching the textures or shifting postures–this brings the client out of the troubling memory and back to the here and now in the therapeutic encounter.

Containment

Containment refers to providing a physiological or metaphorical way to hold, or keep safe, the traumatic material discussed in therapy. For example, some clients choose to build a physical box themselves, or decorate a premade box and use it to *contain* writings, symbolic objects, poetry, photographs, and the *essence* of a trauma history. At the end of the session, everything goes back into the box, and the box either can stay in the therapy room for safekeeping, or the client can take the box, with the understanding that any intrusive thoughts or feelings that happen between sessions are moved into the box to be dealt with later at the next session. Langberg (1999) provided therapy in a converted turn-of-the-century house still containing an ornate cast-iron pot-bellied stove. A client spontaneously asked to leave her trauma in the stove for safekeeping until the next week, thus creating a containment mechanism that was also extended to other clients. The strategic employment of structuring, dosing, anchors, and containment provides clients with control, empowerment, tangible handles, and indicators of progress through the duration of the therapeutic relationship.

Tolerance of Emotions and Installation of Hope

Frei et al. (2020) found that those who were preoccupied with their feelings or mood were significantly more likely to engage in self-harm. These clients can benefit immensely from learning to tolerate negative affect, to regard negative feeling states as temporary and flowing, and to make sense of such feelings in life-affirming ways. The therapist, by creating a safe space for experiencing, staying with, and tolerating emotions as they arise in therapy, teaches clients that emotions are not, after all, frightening or overwhelming, and *can* be tolerated by allowing them to happen; to begin, wax, wane, and conclude, like waves on the surface of the water. Like being in waves of the ocean, clients may first feel tossed around and as if they are drowning. However, with guidance and support, clients learn not only to navigate, but also to discover that the seas become gentler, and the waves of emotions are less intense, less unfamiliar, and easier to endure; eventually, clients even learn to honor and value the full spectrum of emotions.

Yalom and Leszcz (2005) wrote about the *installation of hope* as an essential element of group counseling. This holds true for individual counseling as well, especially for adults with a complexity of traumas who may have lost sight of what hope feels like. Therapists gently and persistently express trust and hope in the client with phrases like, *it is okay that this feels overwhelming now; stay with it, stay with me; you are finding your way through this feeling; I trust that you can do this; as long as there is breath there is hope; we fall down seven and get up eight; I am eager to see what life is like for you on the other side of this; I know you can do this;* and so on. The adult client may have very little self-confidence, and may be plagued with self-doubts, and double guessing every thought. The therapeutic alliance is strengthened as the mental health professional consistently repeats phrases of trust, confidence, and hope, metaphorically leaning toward a future of health and life-affirming wholeness that the client may not yet be able to consider. The installation of hope is a key element of restoring the ability to live life as it comes, without being stuck in a dark and painful past.

Experiential Creativity and Spontaneity

Suffering has long been recognized as a source of creativity. Many of the greatest works of art and musical compositions were born of suffering, persecution, longing, or loss. Nevertheless, people with complex histories of trauma may have lost all sense of creativity, experiencing joy, or savoring any moment. Instead, they survive in a grey haze of "just hold it together" or "feeling dead inside" and existing, rather than living. Talk therapy alone is insufficient for helping many clients overcome trauma and re-engage with the full experience of living a human life. Instead, trauma-competent counselors purposely engage as many sense modalities (sight, hearing, taste, smell, touch, and posture) as possible to help the client re-experience what it feels like to *live* rather than *exist*. Each activity in the therapeutic encounter is strengthened as it capitalizes on *current experiences* which counteract and balance the old darkness and sadness of traumatic memories. Experiences that involve successive accomplishments (e.g., gentle exposure to unsettling material, paired with progressive relaxation and increased tolerance); multiple senses combined with creativity such as artwork, music, movement, and making something that expresses healing; and intentional uses of creating new, positive, and symbolically meaningful memories will—due to their salience and immediacy—accelerate healing and solidify gains achieved in the therapeutic encounter.

Trauma as a Superpower

Almost all superheroes have a traumatic backstory involving loss, bereavement, vulnerability, betrayal, exclusion, or rejection. Adler (1927) declared that a central component of a person's development is the overcoming of a felt sense of defectiveness or inadequacy. Nietzshe and Large (1888/1998) claimed that that which does not kill us makes us stronger. Inspirational speakers, people held in high honor, nearly every Olympic athlete, and many unsung heroes carry astonishingly difficult histories, most of which will never be known by the general public. The suffering and emotional complexity of these difficult histories become transformed as a motivational force for overcoming, for striving for strength and competence. Adults with complex trauma histories can be assured that they have joined the ranks of superheroes, by virtue of having survived their ordeal, and by doing the deeply personal and difficult work of therapy. This is not an observation that a counselor shares flippantly in early sessions, but rather, it is revealed gently, toward the end of therapy, while gains are being solidified and the client is moving toward the closing of the therapeutic encounter. Trauma is actually a secret superpower.

It once subjugated, but now enervates and motivates with surprisingly enduring drive and intensity. One's history does not need to be shared with everyone (or even anyone), but as the trauma is transformed and transcended, it can be kept to oneself with a smile.

LIMITATIONS OF TREATMENT

Adults with complex trauma histories need to know that mental health therapy alone will not solve everything. Even the best mental health treatment has limitations. For example, psychotherapy and/or counseling alone, for many people, works best when combined with tailored psychopharmacology (Brown et al., 2021; Fortney et al., 2018; Johnson & Possemato, 2019). Even when the best physical healthcare is combined with the best mental healthcare, other facets of human experience such as physical fitness, nutrition, spirituality, creativity, economics and finances, politics, social supports, and community environment are beyond the scope of mental health intervention. In order to experience true holistic vitality, it is incumbent on the individual to address each and every sphere of life, and this effort represents lifelong work for all people, regardless of immediate circumstances.

Furthermore, trauma treatment cannot change the fact that the trauma occurred. Something awful happened, and nothing can turn back the clock and make it as if it never happened. It did. Coming to terms with the reality of the trauma is a major element of processing a traumatic history, but nothing can alter the fact of its existence in a person's life history. Therapeutic treatment can address the existential ruptures—such as betrayal; breaches of trust; usurpation of naïve beliefs about safety, belonging, and the reliability of others; the despair of helplessness and horror; loss of agency; and the realization that truly awful things happen in the best of all possible worlds— but treatment cannot undo the fact that these ruptures occurred. They, too, like the trauma itself, actually happened and have an inevitable effect on an individual's worldview and approach to life. Clients and therapists alike confront the limitations of the human condition, and the ability to change or adapt to the world. Some limitations are painful and impervious to change. It is then up to the individual to adjust and accommodate because no other options exist. Sometimes trauma therapy means coming face to face with unbearable pain and somehow learning to live with it. Sometimes bearing witness in silence is the only appropriate response.

Finally, there are individual limitations that must be faced as well. Sometimes a therapist is confronted with a client's history and clinical presentation that is essentially and personally overwhelming. Even seasoned therapists need the self-awareness to know when to ask for supervision, consultation, and even referral to a more experienced clinician. More frequently, clients are not ready to make the changes required by therapy. They may not be ready to step into the unknown. They may not feel safe enough, or they may not have enough self-confidence, or they may feel like they do not have enough therapeutic resources at their immediate disposal to work through the more challenging and painful aspects of trauma work. Sometimes they simply are not ready, and there is no reprehensibility in this. A wise therapist knows when to recognize that a client needs more time before moving forward and can propose either a break or an end to therapy, at least for the time. In the end, an experienced clinician knows when it is time to let go and release the client to live their life without further therapy. It is commendable to know "when the work is enough, and it is time to move on."

CURRENT MODELS OF TREATMENT

While the American Counseling Association does not yet offer practice guidelines on trauma, the Clinical Practice Guideline from the American Psychological Association (2017) strongly recommends cognitive behavioral therapy (CBT), including trauma-focused cognitive behavioral therapy (TF-CBT), cognitive processing therapy (CPT), and prolonged exposure therapy (PE). It suggests the use of brief eclectic psychotherapy (BEP), Eye Movement Desensitization and

Reprocessing (EMDR), and narrative exposure therapy (NET). The guidelines suggest that pharmacology, including fluoxetine, paroxetine, sertraline, and venlafaxine, is helpful but notes "there is insufficient evidence from the systematic review on direct comparisons between psychotherapy and medications for PTSD" (American Psychological Association, 2017, p. ES-7). The guideline is based on empirical studies, especially double-blind, placebo-control studies in the research literature (Guideline Development Panel for the Treatment of PTSD in Adults, American Psychological Association, 2019).

Practice guides are limited by their inclusion criteria, which exclude approaches that do not lend themselves to double-blind, placebo-controlled studies. Therapeutic approaches to traumatic stress do not always lend themselves to quantitative reductions, and therefore, by definition, cannot be included in research that depends on a reductionistic, quantitative approach. Like many things in life, trauma and its recovery are ideographic, nonbinary, holistic, and qualitative, defying categories, taxonomies, and quantitative principles of accounting. Nevertheless, the most promising and effective approaches to therapy for trauma in adults include elements of many sensory modalities, and select interventions based on the neurocognitive needs of the client. In other words, the best approaches provide for basic physiological and emotional regulation and grounding first, and then move through therapy that focuses on emotions and emotion tolerance, followed by cognitive approaches, and finishes with meaning-making and other existential considerations.

Therapeutic models proliferate today, but the most prominent include the NMT (Perry, 2006), sensorimotor psychotherapy (Ogden & Minton, 2000), emotion-focused coping (Folkman & Lazarus, 1985; Guerreiro et al., 2013), EMDR (Shapiro, 1993), TF-CBT (Cohen et al., 2000), Brainspotting (Corrigan & Grand, 2013), and somatic experiencing and integration (Levine, 1997, 2010). While emotion-focused coping is viewed as a promising outpatient treatment for trauma, it should be used with caution, as a recent study found that it predicted inpatient self-harm in response to psychiatric hospitalization (Frei et al., 2020). The most experienced therapists use a multimodal approach, tailoring planning to the needs of the individual, and, like sensorimotor psychotherapy (Ogden & Fisher, 2015), include elements that access multiple senses (e.g., sight, hearing, smell, taste, touch, body posture, and bodily awareness). They also integrate music (Bensimon, 2021), movement, nature, animal therapy, creativity, spirituality, symbolism and symbolic objects, therapeutic ritual, and meaning-making in treatment planning.

COUNSELING IMPLICATIONS

Counseling implications for treating adults with complex trauma or a complexity of traumas include the need for creativity, patience, and analytic synthesis by the clinician. *Analytic synthesis* refers to the ability to analyze the needs of the client, and synthesize what the clinician knows about trauma, the neurobiology of trauma, and available best practices in trauma treatment to create tailored and bespoke treatment plans for the benefit of *this* particular client at *this* particular point in the client's journey of healing.

The information in this chapter implies that mental health clinicians continually renew familiarity with emerging best practices in the field and understand that an integrative approach is most effective. Mental health professionals recognize their own cultural limitations and approach therapy with cultural humility and an appreciation of both Western and Eastern approaches to mental pain and suffering. An understanding of the neural substrates of trauma is essential so that the clinician accurately can match a planned intervention with the demonstrated needs of the client (e.g., basic neurophysiological regulation, emotional grounding, cognitive processing, and existential meaning-making). Adults with complex trauma histories, or who have endured a complexity of trauma, represent both the most challenging and the most rewarding work in the mental health field. When trust and a therapeutic bond can be established, and when the client has developed the courage to step into change, the shared labor of healing is manifestly rewarding and meaningful for both the client and the clinician.

CONCLUSION

This chapter addressed the therapeutic encounter with adult survivors of developmental (complex) trauma and those who present with a *complexity of traumas*. The challenges of working with adults with significant trauma histories include seemingly internally inconsistent characteristics such as too little or too much trust, difficulties in forming attachments, acting out or self-defeating behaviors, emotional flatness or lability, disengagement, manipulation, shame, and shamelessness. These characteristics indicate that the person is living with a history of significant trauma.

This chapter addressed the clinical *footnotes* of working with adults who have survived traumatic experiences, to inform a clinician's tailoring and choice of interventions. The neural substrates of trauma explain how trauma *inhabits* a body, emotions, and thought patterns, and how survivors learn to survive in ways that were uniquely ingenious at the time the trauma(s) occurred but ultimately create more problems than they solve. A comparison of *Western* and *Eastern* approaches to emotional pain facilitates making sense of a traumatic history and provides a foundation for posttraumatic growth and development. This chapter emphasized the importance of following a phasic approach to treatment and explained the importance of its sequence. While planning what treatment can accomplish for adults living with significant trauma histories, it is also incumbent on the therapist to recognize the limits of therapy, and explain these, when appropriate, to clients. The chapter described current best practices and addressed the implications for counselors providing counseling to adults with significant trauma.

Wise therapists carry a wealth of knowledge about trauma and renew their familiarity with best practices on a regular basis. Essentially, the best therapy occurs in a solid and trustworthy therapeutic encounter, when interventions are intentionally tailored to the specific needs of the client and involve as many sensory modalities and positive, creative experiences as possible. The therapist is wise to express unshakeable faith in the process and growth of the client, and to provide structure in an otherwise chaotic sense of personal history. Therapy with adults who have a complexity of traumas is both uniquely complex and challenging, and deeply rewarding work for both the therapist and client. By working through the disruption of life caused by a complicated history of trauma, clients' futures change permanently for the better, for them, and for all the lives they subsequently touch. It is an honor to work with these brave clients, and to be entrusted with their courage.

ADDITIONAL RESOURCES

 A robust set of instructor resources designed to supplement this text is located at http://connect.springerpub.com/content/book/978-0-8261-5085-1. Qualifying instructors may request access by emailing textbook@springerpub.com.

PRACTICE-BASED RESOURCES AND REFERENCES

To view a list of resources and all the references, please visit connect.springerpub.com via the following url: http://connect.springerpub.com/content/book/978-0-8261-5085-1/part/part02/chapter/ch09

CHAPTER 10

Intimate Partner Violence

CAROLE JUSTICE, FRANK M. OCHBERG, LISA LÓPEZ LEVERS, AND NANCY N. FAIR

CHAPTER OVERVIEW

This chapter focuses on issues associated with intimate partner violence (IPV). It examines the impact on survivors of IPV as well as on families, communities, and societies. The chapter presents theories for contextualizing and understanding IPV as well as offering strategies for counseling survivors of IPV.

LEARNING OBJECTIVES

After reading this chapter, the reader should be able to:

1. Define important terms that are associated with IPV;
2. Develop an awareness of the prevailing theories related to IPV;
3. Identify trauma issues concerning the experience of IPV;
4. Recognize the prevalence of IPV across all sectors of society;
5. Develop insight regarding the implications of IPV for survivors; and,
6. Summarize effective counseling approaches for working with IPV.

INTRODUCTION

In order to understand some of the powerful dynamics associated with the lived experiences of intimate partner violence (IPV), we begin by offering an illustrative case. By way of introducing the topic, we present the real-life case of Kristin in Box 10.1.

BOX 10.1

From the Field: The Strange Case of Kristin

In August of 1973, a Swedish bank teller in Stockholm was taken hostage and held in a bank vault for several days by two armed assailants, one named Olsson and the other named Olofsson. By the end of her captivity, the young bank teller, Kristin, had become enamored with

(continued)

Olsson, to the point where she broke off her engagement to her fiancé and spoke vigorously in defense of her captor to the Swedish prime minister.

Shortly after the incident in Sweden, one of the authors of this chapter (F. M. O.), who was the psychiatrist on the National Task Force on Terrorism and Disorder, became intrigued by the case, which was one of a rash of hostage events that occurred in the 1970s. Law enforcement officials and behavioral scientists were just beginning to collaborate intensely on cases like Kristin's, which involved an unexpected bond forming between captive and captor. Kidnap and hostage experts already had been aware of such cases, and psychoanalyst Anna Freud had described similar situations in Nazi concentration camps as "identification with the aggressor."

Interviews in the Stockholm case and many others afterward, however, did not support the idea that captives were identifying with an aggressor; rather, the hostages described being stunned, shocked, and certain they would die. A human being in such a situation then becomes like an infant—dependent on captors for food, water, and other basic necessities.

In each one of these cases, small acts of kindness by the captors gradually began to evoke feelings much deeper than relief. As one Dutch ex-hostage stated about the men who chose not to kill him, "We knew they were killers, but they gave us blankets, cigarettes." What the hostages seemed to experience was more like an infant's primitive feelings of security, calm, and, in a way, gratitude when basic needs are met. These are the feelings that eventually develop and differentiate into varieties of affection and love (Ochberg, 1988). The attachment goes both ways, with the captor often developing reciprocal feelings toward the hostage. When this occurs, both captive and captor usually have developed a distrust of outsiders, including the rescuers, who then become the common enemy.

The dynamics of hostage situations that involve the formation of a bond between captor and captive were identified as a pattern (Ochberg, 1975, personal communication) that later came to be known as the Stockholm syndrome. Although the syndrome was identified for the purpose of assisting negotiators in developing effective strategies for facilitating hostage release in rare situations like Kristin's, it also is especially useful for helping clinicians to understand the bonds of attachment that often exist in abusive intimate partner relationships (Martinez, 2001; Ochberg, 1998). As Graham et al. (1994) summarized, the four conditions of the syndrome are (a) the victim's perception of threat to survival; (b) the victim's perception of some kindness, no matter how small, from the abuser; (c) the victim's isolation from others who might offer an alternative perspective to the abuser's; and, (d) the victim's perception that there is no escape.

In addition to applying the lessons learned from hostage situations to the trauma of IPV, this chapter examines various effects, social costs, contextual theories, and implications for counseling regarding survivors of IPV. This is achieved in the following sections: defining relevant terms, offering background statistics, discussing the trauma associated with IPV, outlining the theoretical contexts for understanding IPV, identifying the counseling implications, and summarizing the salient points. This chapter concludes with a listing of helpful resources for instructors, clinicians, students, and clients.

DEFINITIONS

IPV, as a topic, has been studied in multiple academic disciplines and has been described using a variety of terms. To enhance the reader's understanding of IPV in this chapter, some of the terms and constructs are defined in the following subsections: Victims and Abusers, Intimate Partners, and Intimate Partner Violence.

Victims and Abusers

Violence is an unfortunate fact of our human existence. The cruelty of war, sexual assault, revenge and honor-motivated killings, bullying, and hate crimes assault our senses on a daily basis. Efforts to identify root causes have produced volumes of theoretical and research data that have added to the public understanding of the social, biological, and emotional origins of violence; unfortunately, these efforts have not reduced the prevalence of victimization. IPV, a relatively new term, is an area that has been the subject of copious research under a variety of labels, including *domestic abuse*, *wife beating*, and *domestic violence*.

While IPV research includes studies of female violence against male partners (e.g., Straus et al., 1980) as well as same-sex and transgender IPV (e.g., Rollè et al., 2018; Yerke & DeFeo, 2016), most partner–abuse victims have been, and continue to be, overwhelmingly female. The historic roots of spousal abuse run deep and reflect the male dominance that is prevalent in many societies. Women have been bought, sold, and traded as chattel for centuries; they have been denied education and land ownership, and they are not yet considered fully independent human beings in many cultures. Politically, even in the industrialized West, women's rights have been granted nominally but continue to be undermined or ignored by certain male groups, and often in their own homes by their partners (Ochberg, 1978/2008, 1988, 1998). Estimates from the National Crime Victimization Survey (NCVS) have indicated that, in 1998, about one million violent crimes qualifying as IPV were committed against individuals. Of that one million, 876,340 or about 85% were against women. More recent statistics from the NCVS have indicated that "For the 10-year aggregate period 2003 to 2012, domestic violence accounted for 21% of all violent victimizations" (Truman & Morgan, 2014, p. 1). Tjaden and Thoennes (2000) have studied the prevalence and consequences of male-to-female and female-to-male IPV, finding that women experienced higher rates of violence by marital/opposite sex partners than did men. Women have reported more frequent, longer lasting violence, as well as more threats and fear of bodily harm. Women victims of IPV have been significantly more likely than men to report that they had been injured, have received medical care and mental health counseling, have lost time from work, and have sought legal intervention.

Studies have expanded the definition of interpersonal violence beyond that of physical assaults to include psychological violence, defined as "put-downs, name calling, and controlling behavior" (Thompson et al., 2006, p. 4). These expansive definitions, over time, have raised awareness resulting in recognition that IPV is not just a justice system issue, but also a serious public health issue (Karakurt et al., 2016). This recognition has provided the opportunity for obtaining increased surveillance and prevalence data and encourages a broad-brushstroke, multisystemic approach to understanding and addressing interpersonal violence in society. Based on the criminal justice statistics that continue to indicate that women are victimized more often by intimate partners, references to abusers in this chapter use the pronoun "he," whereas victims are referred to as "she." However, the authors fully acknowledge the presence of victims and perpetrators of all genders, including within the context of same-sex couples, a subject that is explored in detail in later sections of this chapter.

Intimate Partners

The federal definition of intimate partners has changed over the last couple of decades. Previously, intimate partners were defined by the U.S. Department of Justice (Rennison & Welchans, 2000, p. 1) as "current or former spouses, boyfriends, or girlfriends," and the term assumed that the partnerships may be either heterosexual or homosexual. However, the current federal definition of intimate partners has been broadened, legislatively, and an IPV victim now is viewed as:

a spouse or former spouse, a person who shares a child in common with the abuser, a person who cohabits or has cohabited as a spouse with the abuser, or a person who is or has been in a social relationship of a romantic or intimate nature with the abuser, as determined by the length of the relationship, the type of relationship, and the frequency of interaction between the persons involved in the relationship, and any other person similarly situated to a spouse who is protected by the domestic or family violence laws of the state or tribal jurisdiction in which the injury occurred or where the victim resides. (U.S. Code of Federal Regulations, Section 2266(7), n.d.)

This definition is mirrored in other federal laws related to IPV including Title 25 of the Code of Federal Regulations Section 11.454 as well as in the reauthorized *Violence Against Women's Act of 2013* (Public Law 113-4). While named the *Violence Against Women's Act* (VAWA), it is gender-neutral in providing these protections, based upon the acts and the relationships of the parties, not the sex or sexual orientation of the victim or perpetrator.

Intimate Partner Violence

In 1994, Congress passed the VAWA as part of the Violent Crime Control and Law Enforcement Act of 1994. The Act was brought forth in recognition of the severity of the crimes associated with domestic violence, sexual assault, and stalking and marked the first comprehensive federal legislative package designed to end violence against women. This was done in recognition that the states were failing in their duty to offer this protection. The protections provided through this Act subsequently were expanded and improved in the *Violence Against Women Act of 2000* (H.R.1248—106th Congress, VAWA, 2000), the *Violence Against Women and Department of Justice Reauthorization Act of 2005* (USDOJ, 2005), the *Violence Against Women Reauthorization Act of 2013* (S.47—[113th], VAWA, 2013), and the *Violence Against Women Reauthorization Act of 2021* (H.R.1620—117th Congress, VAWA, 2021). This legislation also has provided for federal grants to assist in developing protections and services that uphold the civil rights of women experiencing gender-based crimes and for the collection of extensive data concerning these crimes (Women's Legal Defense and Education Fund, n.d.).

The passage of VAWA took interpersonal violence out from the shadows, bringing it into the light of day. While originally focused on the narrower definition of spouse abuse and domestic violence, with each iteration of VAWA came greater exposition of the comprehensive nature of these crimes and of the other social justice issues that required attention, within the context of civil rights, implicit bias, and systemic racism. VAWA is a federal act, which, in many ways, has an impact on a minority of U.S. citizens for whom federal law has jurisdictional preference. State, local, and tribal laws rely on different definitions of interpersonal violence passed by their respective legislative body; local practices in enforcement differ as much as the locations in which they exist. However, VAWA, with its "guidance" of how to define and address gender-based, relational violence, is coupled with its substantial funding streams to those in compliance with its recommendations, as well as with requirements such as providing for Full Faith and credit to domestic violence protection (18 USC 2265) across state lines. This funding "carrot" has made a major impact in changing laws, practices, hearts, and minds.

BACKGROUND STATISTICS

The numbers of individuals affected by IPV, including victims, family members, and society as a whole, are staggering. IPV may result in any number of criminal charges ranging from trespass, to disturbing the peace, to sexual assault, to homicide—and every type of crime in between. Criminal justice statistics are perhaps the least reliable, however, in judging the scale and scope of IPV. How crimes are reported by law enforcement and subsequently charged by prosecutors is a very subjective process, one that is rife with the potential for bias, problems surrounding the differences in definitions, and idiosyncrasies. This partly is due to the new electronic data gathering systems such as the Uniform Crime Reporting program, which only allows for a limited number of crimes to be reported upon an arrest. VAWA grantees, required to fill out copious statistical reports in return for the receipt of grant funds, find it difficult to report accurate data, as they are required to report local data into a "one size fits all" type of reporting form. Additionally, for the various reasons to be discussed later in this chapter, victims also underreport IPV. Therefore, statistics purporting to capture this information should be viewed as indicative but not entirely correct in providing the breadth and depth of the issue. The following statistics, therefore, are only suggestive of the scope of IPV, both in the United States and abroad.

The Centers for Disease Control and Prevention's (CDC) National Intimate Partner and Sexual Violence Survey (NISVS; CDC, 2015) indicates that about one in four women and nearly one in ten men have experienced contact sexual violence, physical violence, and/or stalking by an intimate partner during their lifetime and have reported some form of IPV-related impact. Over 43 million women and 38 million men have experienced psychological aggression by an intimate partner in their lifetime. When IPV occurs in adolescence, it is called teen dating violence (TDV), and it affects millions of U.S. teens each year. About 11 million women and five million men who reported experiencing contact sexual violence, physical violence, or stalking by an intimate partner in their lifetime said that they first experienced these forms of violence before age 18 (CDC, 2015).

IPV is a significant public health issue, with both individual and societal costs (Breiding et al., 2014; Karakurt et al., 2016). About 35% of female IPV survivors and more than 11% of male IPV survivors have experienced some form of physical injury related to IPV. IPV is a pattern; many victims experience repeat acts of violence not captured in the number of 10 million adults abused annually (National Congress of American Indians [NCAI], 2013). Data from U.S. crime reports have indicated that one in five homicide victims are killed by an intimate partner. From 2016 to 2018, the number of IPV victimizations in the United States increased 42%, and in 2018, partner violence accounted for 20% of all reported violent crime (Morgan & Oudekerk, 2019). Of U.S. women homicide victims, over 50% were killed by a current or former male intimate partner (Niolon et al., 2017). An abuser's access to a firearm increases the risk of femicide by at least 400% (J. D. Campbell et al., 2003). The Federal Bureau of Investigation reports that 6,410 women were murdered by an intimate partner using a gun between 2001 and 2012 (cited in Gerney & Parsons, 2014).

Reports of increasing international rates of IPV during the COVID-19 pandemic have been alarming (Boserup et al., 2020; Rodriguez, 2021; Roesch et al., 2020). The home page of the National Coalition Against Domestic Violence (NCADV, 2021) has a rolling count calendar of data collected from its coalition members across the United States. On December 27, 2020, they reported the following: there were 621 gun-related domestic violence deaths in 2020; 10 million people a year were physically abused by an intimate partner; 20,000 calls a day were placed to domestic violence hotlines; and, 20% of women in the United States reported being raped. (NCADV, 2021). These advocacy-based data sources contain grassroots data that often are missing from more institutional statistical sources.

Racial and Sexual Minorities

As profound as the previously noted statistics may be, research statistics regarding IPV among racial groups and sexual minorities in the United States are even more compelling (Petrosky et al., 2017). Black et al. (2011) provided the following 2010 rates of reported contact sexual violence, physical violence, and/or stalking for women in their lifetimes by race/ethnicity:

- 53.8% multiracial non-Hispanic women—38.95% multiracial non-Hispanic men;
- 46.0% American Indian/Alaskan Native women—45.3% of American Indian/Alaskan Native men;
- 45.1% of non-Hispanic Black women—40.1% of non-Hispanic Black men;
- 34.6% non-Hispanic White women—27.4% of non-Hispanic White men;
- 34.4% of Hispanic women—30% of Hispanic men; and,
- 19.6% of Asian or Pacific Islander women—13.7% of Asian or Pacific Islander men.

As startling as these 2010 data are, they still appear to be the tip of the iceberg on this issue among the "statistically insignificant" populations reported out as "other" or not reported out at all. Rosay (2016) delineated the findings of a National Institute of Justice study on violence against American Indian/Alaskan Native women and men; the results showed that 83.3% of American Indian/Alaskan women and 81.6% of American Indian/Alaska Native men have experienced violence in their lifetime. Among the women, 56.1% experienced sexual violence, 55.5% experienced physical violence by an intimate partner, and 46.8% experienced stalking. Among the men, 27.5% experienced sexual violence, 43.2% experienced physical violence by an intimate partner, and 18.6% experienced stalking (Rosay, 2016). According to the Bureau of Justice Statistics (n.d.) and the U.S. Department of Justice (2005), the violent victimizations experienced by American Indians are committed by persons not of the same race and at a substantially higher rate of interracial violence than experienced by White or Black victims. The Asian Pacific Institute on Gender-Based Violence (2020) has been collecting statistics on physical abuse and sexual assault since 2001. In its *Facts & Stats Report*, Yoshihama et al. (2020) reported that, based upon studies that used some type of probability samples, 16% to 55% of Asian women report experiencing intimate physical and/or sexual violence during their lifetime.

The CDC (2015) reported that 43.8% of lesbians and 61.1% of bisexual women experienced IPV or sexual assault, physical violence, or stalking, while 26% of gay men and 37.3% of bisexual men reported such violence. The 2015 U.S. Transgender Survey (James et al., 2016) found that 54% of transgender and nonbinary respondents experienced IPV in their lifetimes. Balsam et al. (2005) compared lesbian, gay, and bisexual (LGB) adults to their heterosexual siblings' experiences, with multiple types of violence across the life-span, and found that sexual orientation was a significant predictor of most of the victimization variables, including partner psychological abuse and physical victimization in adulthood.

Adolescent IPV is being measured through use of the CDC's (2019) *Youth Risk Behavior Surveillance System* (YRBSS). This survey monitors six categories of health-related behaviors that contribute to the leading causes of death and disability among youth and adults. YBRSS is a school-based survey conducted in a majority of states/jurisdictions by the CDC through local education and health agencies. In 2019, 12.2% of youth reported that they experienced physical dating violence, and 3.0% that they experienced sexual dating violence. However, when reviewing the microdata, 22.3% of LGB and 18.7% "not sure" gender respondents reported physical dating violence, and 5.8% of LGB and 9.4% of "not sure" gender respondents reported experiencing sexual dating violence. The sexual identity categories of choice were heterosexual, lesbian, gay or bisexual, and not sure (CDC, 2019). LGBTQ+ youth of color are also at greater risk for physical and sexual dating violence, when compared to non-LGBTQ+ White youth. In a Women of Color Network factsheet (2018a), citing the work of Breiding et al. (2014), these issues were illuminated in the following way: "Domestic Violence (DV) occurs among all race/ethnicities and socio-economic classes. DV is a pattern of many behaviors directed at achieving and maintaining power and control over an intimate partner, such as physical violence, psychological aggression, stalking, and coercion" (p. 1). For victims of color, as well as for other marginalized populations, distrust of law enforcement (fear of subjecting themselves and loved ones to a criminal and civil justice system they see as sexist, and/or racially and culturally biased) and obtaining safety (physical, economic, emotional, and legal) become even more challenging (Breiding et al., 2014; Yoshihama et al., 2020).

Intimate Partner Violence and Women With Disabilities

Women with developmental disabilities have among the highest rates of physical, sexual, and emotional violence perpetrated by intimate partners and family members. Women with disabilities have a 40% greater risk of violence than women without disabilities and are at particular risk for severe violence. Studies estimate that 80% of women with disabilities have been sexually assaulted, and that they are three times more likely to have been assaulted than women without disabilities. A nationally representative sample has shown that both men and women living with disabilities in the United States "were at increased risk for recent sexual violence, compared to those without a disability" (Basile et al., 2016, p. 928). Additionally, victims with disabilities have increased challenges in acquiring access to services including limited resources, lack of transportation (especially in rural communities), and lack of knowledge or ability to obtain resources. Victims with disabilities are more vulnerable to threats by their abusers, if they report the abuse (Brownridge, 2006).

Findings From a Multicountry Study

As a part of the World Health Organization's (WHO) project on women and domestic violence, Garcia-Moreno et al. (2006) interviewed 24,097 women about IPV at 15 sites in 11 countries, including Bangladesh, Brazil, Ethiopia, Japan, Namibia, Peru, Samoa, Serbia, Montenegro, Thailand, and the United Republic of Tanzania. The findings indicated a lifetime prevalence of physical and/or sexual partner violence from between 15% and 71%, with two sites having a prevalence of less than 25%, seven between 25% and 50%, and six between 50% and 75%. In all but one of the sites, women were at much greater risk of violence by a partner than from violence by other people. The findings confirmed that physical and sexual violence against women is a worldwide problem, with the variations in prevalence indicating that risk factors vary by culture and that these factors can be addressed.

THE TRAUMA OF INTIMATE PARTNER VIOLENCE

A poster produced by the San Francisco District Attorney's Family Violence Project and appearing in the medical journal *The Lancet* (J. C. Campbell, 2002) displays an x-ray of a fractured skull, along with the statement "A bad relationship can hurt more than your feelings." The message is shockingly direct in its ability to draw our attention to the often-tragic results of IPV. The broken bones leave no room for ambiguity in the mind of the reader as to the real and permanent damage that can be caused by IPV. Not visible in the poster, and less easily conveyed to an observer, are other serious long-term consequences of IPV. These include physical health effects not visible on x-rays, mental health problems such as chronic posttraumatic stress disorder (PTSD), and the subsequent social issues that inevitably occur in cultures where violence and trauma are common events.

The Traumatic Consequences of Intimate Partner Violence on Individuals

The traumatic consequences of IPV are numerous and far reaching. Some of the physical and psychological effects are detailed in the following subsections of this chapter.

Physical Effects

IPV has been recognized as a significant public health issue that has many individual and societal costs (M. A. Dutton et al., 2015). The physical effects of IPV often are first discovered in medical settings, such as emergency departments, physicians' offices, or clinics. This may occur when victims are seeking care for conditions related to injuries or as part of a routine checkup. According to J. C. Campbell (2002), battered women are more likely to have been injured in the head, face, neck, thorax, and abdomen than women hurt in nonbattering incidents. The short-term physical effects of violence can encompass minor injuries or serious conditions. They can include bruises, cuts, broken bones, or injuries to organs and other parts of the body and can be difficult or impossible to see without scans, x-rays, or other medical tests (U.S. Department of Health and Human Services [USDHHS], 2019). J. C. Campbell and Messing (2017) also describes the long-term consequences of battering, such as fear and stress that can result in chronic conditions like headaches, neck pain, and back problems. However, these conditions also can be related to traumatic brain injuries (TBIs; including concussion) and to damage caused by strangulation, two conditions that historically have not been given the attention they need, considering their seriousness as well as their frequency in IPV. This lack of attention is due to unawareness by victims of the seriousness of these injuries, unfamiliarity by physicians and mental health professionals about these conditions as IPV related, and by systemic bias that often dismisses complaints by women as emotional instead of physical conditions. Recent studies show that 34% of abused pregnant women report being "choked," while 47% of women victims of IPV report being "choked." When IPV women were asked, in both a shelter and hospital study, what made them believe they were in danger or not, the majority of women perceiving a great amount of danger mentioned "choking" as a tactic used against them that made them believe their partner might kill them (J. C. Campbell & Messing, 2017; Stuart & Campbell, 1989). In fact, we now know that victims of prior non-fatal strangulations are 800% more likely, later, to become a homicide victim at the hands of the same batterer.

It is important to note that strangulation actually is not choking, the word most commonly used to describe the act by a victim, or suffocation in the true sense of the word. Strangulation is the external compression of the neck that either directly can block the airway, thus preventing breathing, or can impede the flow of blood to and from the brain by closing off arteries and jugular veins. When a victim is strangled, research findings indicate that loss of consciousness can occur within 5 to 10 seconds and brain death within 4 to 5 minutes. The seriousness of internal injuries may take a few hours to be discerned, and death can occur even days later. The absence of visible injury can result in the minimization of the assault, even by the victim, who actually may not remember much of the event, due to the nature of the assault (McClane et al., 2001). Signs and symptoms of strangulation include voice changes in 50% of victims, swallowing and breathing changes, mental status changes, involuntary urination or defecation, visible injuries to neck, petechiae (tiny purple, red, or brown spots on the skin), ligature marks, lung changes, or brain damage. The largest nonfatal strangulation case study conducted to date (the San Diego Study) found that most cases lacked physical evidence or visible injury of strangulation; while major signs and symptoms of strangulation corroborated the assaults, little visible injury was detected, and no symptoms were documented or reported in 67% of cases (McClane et al., 2001).

The scope of the problem of TBI in the context of IPV is enormous. Upwards of 90% of all individuals with a history of interpersonal violence have concomitant signs and symptoms of TBI (Lifshitz et al., 2019). In addition to strangulation-related brain injuries, a serious risk of physical abuse is concussion and other TBIs from being hit on the head or falling and hitting the head. TBI can cause any of the following: headache or a feeling of pressure, loss of consciousness, confusion, dizziness, nausea and vomiting, slurred speech, memory loss, trouble concentrating, and sleep loss. Some symptoms of TBI may take a few days to show up, while others may last a year or longer, depending upon the severity or cause; some injuries may be permanent, especially when there are multiple battering events over time. TBI can cause depression and anxiety and interfere with the ability to plan and carry out tasks. This, in turn, can make it more difficult for women who are in an abusive relationship to leave (USDHHS, 2019). The connections among these common conditions and their antecedent causes often are unclear to healthcare clinicians, as well as to victims themselves, resulting in neglect for those clients who repeatedly seek medical care for vague and persistent symptoms while the traumatic origins of the problem remain unaddressed. Overlooked, strangulation and TBI effects can be mistaken as emotional or psychological issues related to the assaults, and the survivors may be referred to mental health professionals for treatment, while the physical needs of the victims go unmet.

Large-scale research conducted by Felitti et al. (1998) establishes the connection between adverse childhood experiences (ACE study) and problems in adulthood, ranging from chronic physical health issues to long-term psychiatric disorders. It also is well established that children exposed to domestic violence are at increased risk for physical abuse and other forms of child maltreatment (Appel & Holden, 1998; Edleson, 1999; Jouriles et al., 2008; Osofsky, 2003). It is perhaps less understood, however, that children who experience a head injury before young adulthood report greater interpersonal violence in young adulthood than participants who had never had a head injury, thus supporting findings that link a history of head injury to later interpersonal violence (Stoddard & Zimmerman, 2011). This information stresses the importance of a holistic approach to assessing for unseen injuries that affect the physical and psychological well-being of victims of IPV.

The CDC (2020) reports that negative health outcomes associated with IPV include a range of conditions, many of which are chronic, affecting the circulatory, digestive, reproductive, musculoskeletal, and nervous systems. J. C. Campbell (2002) notes that gynecological problems related to forced sex by intimate partners are "the most consistent, longest lasting, and largest physical health difference between battered and non-battered women" (p. 1332). Women's vulnerabilities that result from domestic violence create risk for contracting HIV, additional violence, and not obtaining and adhering to treatment (Bent-Goodley, 2017). Women in abusive relationships may be forced to engage in sexual acts both with a partner and with others (Lichtenstein, 2006). J. C. Campbell's findings among heterosexual women are extended by Heintz and Melendez (2006), who report an increased risk of HIV/STDs among lesbian, gay, bisexual, and transgendered (LGBT) individuals as a result of forced sex by intimate partners. Members of sexual minorities also report a higher incidence of battering as a direct consequence of asking their partners to practice safe sex.

The identification and treatment of IPV-related injury and illness often is hindered by the reluctance of victims to report their partners' violence to medical personnel. They fear that police and legal intervention may follow, further jeopardizing their physical safety and financial security, as their family or community support system may take the side of the abuser. They also fear not being believed, especially when they may have difficulty explaining the attack, due to distortion of memory related to the trauma or to related physical injuries. Lack of a prompt and appropriate law enforcement response in many communities of color and in rural areas is another common reason for nonreporting. In addition, shame and social stigma, which may be attached to being battered by a partner or spouse, prevent many victims from seeking medical help for all but the most severe injuries, which then, often, are attributed to falls or other accidents.

Cultural and religious beliefs also factor into nonreporting of IPV, especially in minority and marginalized populations. If the victim is a member of a minority population, personal experiences of racism and prejudices may contribute to a reluctance to seek help for physical problems associated with IPV. The Women of Color Network Report (2018b) provides an in-depth analysis of the factors that contribute to the underreporting of IPV among minority groups. Historically, the relationship between intimate partners has been considered private, particularly in cultures that tacitly or overtly condone men's domination of women. In many heterosexual marriages, women are subject to the control of their husbands, a situation that often is supported through selective interpretation of religious teachings. These beliefs may present barriers for those needing or seeking mental health treatment.

Many women who have experienced violence cope with this trauma by using drugs, drinking alcohol, smoking, or overeating. Research shows that about 90% of women with substance abuse problems have experienced physical or sexual violence (USDHHS, 2019). This leads to credibility issues with law enforcement officials, who may be biased against the victim due to intoxication, thus placing the victim at further risk if police do not remove the abuser or take the victim to safe shelter. People who perpetrate IPV intentionally may use mental health and substance use issues to undermine and control their partners, deliberately keeping them from achieving their treatment and recovery goals. For example, it is not uncommon for abusive partners to introduce a partner to opioids or other illicit substances. The abuser then may control the drug supply and threaten the victim with withdrawal, loss of custody of children, incarceration, or physical violence when the victim tries to reduce use, access treatment, call police, or resist demands to engage in illegal activities, including participating in human trafficking. These forms of abuse— referred to as mental health and substance use coercion—jeopardize the well-being of survivors and their children. They can compromise the effectiveness of mental health and substance abuse treatment, underscoring the need for physicians and behavioral health agencies to implement policies and practices for addressing IPV (National Center on Domestic Violence, Trauma & Mental Health, 2019).

Psychological Effects

A meta-analysis (Golding, 1999) and a systematic review (Lagdon et al., 2014) of studies of the psychological effects of IPV have revealed that depression and PTSD, which have a high degree of comorbidity, are the most prevalent mental health problems associated with intimate partner trauma; the occurrence of PTSD in battered women is statistically much higher than in non-abused women. Diez et al. (2009) observed psychological health indicators such as antidepressant intake, sleep disorders, lack of concentration, loss of energy, and difficulties making decisions to be higher in abused women. Coker et al. (2002) confirmed that behaviors that may have an adverse effect on mental well-being, such as alcohol consumption and drug use, tend to be more prevalent in female victims of IPV. We know that the brain injuries and related chronic physical conditions also contribute to the prevalence of these mental health symptoms in this population.

PTSD has been defined as applying equally to military trauma, criminal violence, and natural disaster. Ochberg (1988), however, has proposed that victims of deliberate cruelty such as IPV are likely to suffer from symptoms that represent "victimization" rather than "traumatization"—a distinction that recognizes the *perpetrator's behavior* rather than the victim's reaction as the source of deleterious effects associated with IPV. Victims frequently suffer from a wide range of abuse, over a period of time, and have no way of knowing when or if they will be safe. Law enforcement personnel have been reluctant to intervene in domestic violence situations because attempts to separate the abuser from the victim may result in the formation of a united front against the police—a phenomenon that leads us back to the Stockholm syndrome principle of alliance between abuser and victim that was introduced at the beginning of this chapter. Misunderstanding of the complex dynamics involved in IPV relationships has led to general skepticism about the abused person's status as a victim or as a sufferer of traumatic stress, although social science research has begun to change these misperceptions. These misperceptions may be further traumatizing to the survivors of IPV events.

The Consequences of Intimate Partner Violence on Society

The consequences of IPV on individual victims, as we have detailed earlier, can be measured in the lives of those who suffer its effects. In the previous section of this chapter, we examined some of the physical and psychological effects of IPV on individual victims. This section explores some of the consequences of IPV on society, including its likely contribution to the intergenerational transmission of violence, termed the *cycle of violence* by Widom (1989) in her critical examination of the literature linking IPV, child abuse, and other social stressors. In discussing the intergenerational nature of violence, it is important to recognize that most individuals who have been abused as children do not go on to become abusers as adults (Lisak et al., 1996; Rakovec-Felser, 2014). However, it is equally important to know that studies have clearly identified childhood abuse as a crucial risk factor for later violence (Lisak & Miller, 2003; Maxfield et al., 2000; Weeks & Widom, 1998; Widom, 2000). These seemingly contradictory statistics are more easily understood if we are able to picture victims of abuse as a relatively large group of individuals, while recognizing that victimizers represent only a small number of those who have been abused and may not belong to the victimized group at all, but generally victimize more than one person. Among victimizers, however, as stated earlier, studies have shown that a large percentage of this group *has* been victimized, thus implicating childhood victimization as a risk factor for becoming a violent adult. The following subsections describe the less quantifiable but pervasive social costs of IPV.

The Cycle of Violence in Relationships

People in abusive relationships often describe a pattern of behavior, which has been characterized as the cycle of violence; this pattern may serve as a mechanism for locking someone into an abusive relationship. The perpetrator uses abusive behavior to exert power and control over another person—or persons, in the case of a family setting. The abuser "needs" a victim to control, and without intervention, may become a serial abuser. The cycle of violence dynamics can be expressed as three phases: the tension-building phase, the acute or crisis phase of abuse, and the "honeymoon" phase, in which a sense of relief or calm is restored (Walker, 1980). During the tension phase, the abuser may become tense or irritable, prompting the victim to "walk on eggshells." In the abuse phase, the perpetrator acts violently (physically, sexually, and/or emotionally) toward the victim. The relief or honeymoon phase is characterized by abuser behaviors that include apologies, remorse, and promises to change. It is during this latter phase that the blame shifts away from the abuser (e.g., it was the alcohol, drugs, or a hard day at the office), or the abuser finds something that the woman did or did not do as the excuse for his abusive behavior, rather than accepting responsibility for his actions. This gaslighting type of behavior is designed to erode the woman's self-esteem, discredit her within the family, and manipulate her to try harder to mend the broken relationship/family unit. Walker points out that the perpetrators of the cycle of violence are found in all socioeconomic classes and professions. Some professions, in which abusers have heightened responsibility for their performance but lack ultimate control over the desired outcomes (e.g., lawyers, doctors, law enforcement officers, professional athletes), may lend to greater vulnerability, in terms of the power-and-control coping style afforded by the cycle of violence. Similarly, their victims often (but not necessarily) are those engaged in helping professions (e.g., counselors, nurses, physicians, teachers, social workers) who believe that their efforts can help change the relational dynamic (Walker, 1980).

Social Costs and Multiple Losses

The social costs of IPV can be expressed in several ways. Societal resources are required to evaluate and treat the victims of violence; these resources include victim service organizations, child welfare agencies, mental health services, and medical facilities. The willingness of taxpayers and governments to fund resources is not commensurate with the need. While funding from the *Violence Against Women Act* has assisted in developing necessary services over the years, the majority of these funds are provided through competitive grant solicitations that are time limited. This leaves the costs of services to local communities competing for other necessary resources. States also receive federal funds for victim services and provide small grants for victim-witness support services within their district attorney offices; they may offer small competitive grants to local governments, tribes, and other nonprofit groups. It is important for everyone involved in this work to become knowledgeable of existing resources that can aid in services to clients and that can point toward other avenues of assistance that may be available. The most stable source of funds for victim services in each state flows through a victim compensation account, generally administered by state and federal attorney general offices. The most frequently allowed costs include payment for medical expenses incurred due to the abuse, mental health counseling services for the victim (and secondary victims of the crime, like children and non-offending family members), reimbursement for lost employment revenue, and childcare or transportation related to seeking care and investigative/court appearances. Funeral expenses also may be compensated, up to a certain amount, in the case of homicide victims.

One of the most damaging effects of IPV is its impact on succeeding generations of human relationships and its profound reduction of quality of life. Lisak and Beszterczey (2007) reviewed the life histories of 43 death row inmates, finding that more than 80% of the men had witnessed IPV in their childhood homes and 100% had experienced some form of neglect, along with other forms of abuse. The researchers also found that subjects who had been abused were likely to have come from families with multigenerational histories of abuse. Although the study sample represented the extreme end of the continuum of long-term effects of familial violence, the consequences for the lives of the participants gives us a glimpse of the pervasive effects of IPV.

An insightful overview of children exposed to violence is provided in the *Report of the Attorney General's National Task Force on Children Exposed to Violence* (Listenbee et al., 2012); the report indicates that exposure to violence is a national crisis that affects almost two in every three children, nationwide. The report provides comprehensive data on the extent of violence in the daily lives of children, indicating that approximately one in 15 youths, or 6.6%, had been exposed to some form of physical assault between their parents in the past year. If exposure to other forms of family violence in the household is included, then one in nine youths (11.1%) were exposed to physical or psychological violence in the family during the previous year. Lifetime percentages were higher, reflecting the longer period of possible exposure. The lifetime percentage was 17.8% for exposure to physical IPV alone. If, in addition to IPV exposure, parental assault of a sibling and violence between other teens and adults in the household are included, then lifetime exposure to physical or psychological violence within the family rises to 25.6% (Finkelhor et al., 2015). A focus solely on IPV misses a substantial amount of the violence to which children are exposed within the "safety" of their home. Given the effects of IPV on victims, the reported figures still may minimize the actual amount and severity of violence. Exposure to IPV is distressing to children and is associated with a host of mental health symptoms, both in childhood and later in life. The losses suffered by victims of IPV include and exceed those of individuals who have been traumatized by non-IPV events (Koss et al., 1994). Loss of health, financial security, home, children, pregnancies, and even life itself are tragic legacies of victims of IPV.

Less easily observable losses can include a decreased ability to assess one's situation, as caused by shock, grief, and despair. Koss et al. (1994) point out that as victims deploy more *internal* coping strategies (e.g., denial, dissociation, numbing), there is often a decrease in *external* activity that would be more likely to change the IPV situation. This often is expressed in terms of victims needing to use their energy to stay alive and cope with the dangerous situation; this is energy that, if redirected, could be used to seek assistance, or escape the situation. Symonds (1978) speculated on a "state of terror" experienced by a victim, which can contribute to a sense of loss of control or agency within one's life, seriously impairing the victim's ability to appraise her own situation. We once again are reminded of Ochberg's (1988) list of complex symptoms, which may be seen in survivors of intentional cruelty. The presence of any or all of these difficulties, identified in Box 10.2, implies a loss to the individual as well as a loss to society.

BOX 10.2

Clinical Information: Ochberg's (1988) List of Complex Symptoms

1. **Shame:** Implies an impairment of a person's ability to relate to self and others accurately, thereby depriving society of the full benefit of that individual's selfhood and gifts.
2. **Self-blame:** Implies that the victim carries a sense of being somehow responsible for her own victimization, thereby diverting attention from the perpetrator's culpability.
3. **Subjugation:** Implies that the victim's sense of powerlessness may prevent her from effectively protecting herself and her children, thus perpetuating the cycle of violence.
4. **Morbid hatred:** Implies that the victim's life energy may be diverted from self-actualization to obsession with rage/revenge, increasing the possibility of mental illness, addiction, and legal problems.

(continued)

5. **Paradoxical gratitude:** Implies that the victim may employ a survival strategy that keeps her in an abusive relationship.
6. **Defilement:** Implies that the sense of being "damaged" by the abuse will be likely to affect the victim's sense of self and may contribute to problems with eating disorders, body image, and identity.
7. **Sexual inhibition:** Implies that the victim may be less able to engage in healthy intimate relationships and may live out a pattern of choosing battering partners due to a confused notion of intimacy and the nature of sexual relationships.
8. **Resignation:** Implies loss of the victim's ability to persevere, resulting in lifelong struggles with depression, learned helplessness, and unfulfilled potential.
9. **Second injury or second wound:** Implies the likelihood that the victim will experience retraumatization at the hands of those agencies and individuals charged with helping victims, thus creating multiple layers of wounding and dysfunction. Implicit biases (gender, sexual, racial, and cultural) in the American justice, health, and social care systems clearly have an impact.
10. **Socioeconomic status downward drift:** Implies that the victim's situation may result in a decreased ability to work and to care for herself and her children, resulting in dependence on welfare, foster care, or disability funds for survival. Between 21% and 60% of victims of domestic violence lose their jobs due to reasons stemming from the abuse (NCADV, 2015).

So far in this chapter, we have examined some of the characteristics of IPV and its prevalence, as well as having identified individual and social costs related to IPV. In the following section, we review relevant literature for the purpose of identifying theoretical contexts for understanding IPV.

THEORETICAL CONTEXTS FOR UNDERSTANDING INTIMATE PARTNER VIOLENCE

According to Koss et al. (1994), early literature on the subject of IPV tended to speculate on possible psychopathological characteristics of the victims rather than social contributions to the problem or perpetrator characteristics. Women's verbal and emotional aggression against their partners was viewed as a precipitant to male violence, whereas other studies (e.g., Straus, 1993) sought to evaluate IPV from a gender-neutral standpoint, asserting that males were victims of IPV as often as females. However, our understandings about the dynamics of IPV have increased over the ensuing years. The literature on this topic has evolved, and a number of theories have emerged that have elucidated societal assessments of IPV over the decades. The following subsections briefly identify and describe some of the most commonly held theories about IPV, as well as specific risk factors for IPV. These subsections include perspectives from feminist theory; family systems theory; the biomedical model; and more contemporary and comprehensive paradigms, such as an ecological development model, attachment theory, and Polyvagal Theory (PVT). Disciplines represented in these perspectives range from psychology and counseling to nursing, medicine, and criminal justice.

Feminist Theory

Feminist theories of IPV originated with the upsurge in attention brought to the victimization of women in the 1970s, defining IPV as primarily a social problem to be corrected by empowering women and reeducating men. Feminist theories identify gender-based power differentials as central to the issue of IPV, citing the domestic relationship's structure as a parallel process mirroring the patriarchal pattern of society's organizational structures (Healey et al., 1998; Shore, 2019).

Strengths and Criticisms of Feminist Theory

We need only to look at the history of batterer intervention programs in the United States to recognize the impact of feminist theory on the subject of IPV. Healey et al. (1998) note that treatment programs for batterers were established as a result of feminist activism and focused on changing sex role attitudes, which claim that women's behavior provokes men's violence. Some theorists have claimed that feminist theory relies too heavily on a social model of IPV, to the exclusion of other factors, such as childhood abuse and personality disorders (D. G. Dutton & Painter, 1993a; Namy et al., 2017). According to critics, feminist theory fails to predict which men will become violent, assuming that all men are exposed to similar patriarchal values.

Family Systems Theory

Family systems theory advances the idea that each individual should be viewed not in isolation, but rather in terms of the interactions, transitions, and relationships within the family. In its most fundamental application, family systems theory offers a framework for observing and understanding patterns of relationships as well as the transmission of behavioral patterns over multiple generations, which is particularly important when attempting to understand IPV. It also emphasizes that families are a subsystem within larger systems, such as the community, which interact with and influence one another, as well as contributing to the maintenance of particular patterns of behavior (Hyde-Nolan & Juliao, 2012). Family systems theory further supports an understanding of individual behavior and its reciprocal effect upon the family unit, rather than focusing on the individual pathology of any singular family member.

Strengths and Criticisms of the Family Systems Theory

The family systems theory provides a treatment framework for IPV couples who may want to remain together and for those who wish to address the intergenerational cycle of violence within the family. Some cite the model's emphasis on relationship strengths, rather than pathology, as a useful approach, particularly in light of statistics indicating that more than half of IPV couples remain together (Murray, 2006; Sirles et al., 1993). Counseling models using this approach also have been rated as highly effective within some cultural settings, for example, those living in extended-family groups, in cultural enclaves (including American Indian/Alaskan Native communities), and for families experiencing intergenerational trauma, especially as related to substance use disorder (see Substance Abuse and Mental Health Services Administration [SAMHSA], 2020). In a robust systematic review and meta-analysis, Karakurt et al. (2016, p. 567) have stated that "Preliminary data suggest that couple's therapy is a viable treatment in select situations."

Predictably, most criticisms of the model's use with IPV couples cite concern for victim safety. Given the inequities of power intrinsic to IPV, critics speculate that speaking honestly in the presence of the batterer is inherently dangerous, particularly if the couple continues to live together. Other critics note the potential for victim blaming, while the victimizer is not held responsible for the violence (Healey et al., 1998; Murray, 2006). Professional expertise should be used in assessing when to introduce or whether to select this approach, in view of cultural and safety considerations.

The Biomedical Model

The biomedical model is a framework in which victims' psychological symptoms are catalogued and the individual is then assigned a diagnosis. The connections between symptoms displayed and antecedent trauma are deemed secondary, if not irrelevant, to client treatment. Treatment is predicated upon the assumption that many psychological disorders arise from faulty brain chemistry that requires psychiatric medication for correction, with or without adjunctive psychotherapy. However, as a result of the identification of trauma-based disorders, particularly PTSD, research into the origins of trauma as well as its connection to common mental health diagnoses have made a purely biomedical model less relevant in working with IPV (Herman, 1992; van der Kolk et al., 1996). Problems such as anxiety, dissociation, depression, and personality disorders all have been the subjects of extensive study, linking them to traumatic antecedent events in the lives of the victim, perpetrator, or both (van der Kolk et al., 1996).

Strengths and Criticisms of the Biomedical Model

The primary utility of the biomedical model is its acceptance as the prevailing paradigm by which diagnosable mental difficulties are understood. Some perceive this as a way toward destigmatization of mental illness, through promotion of the diagnosis as just another form of medical illness, on par with heart disease and diabetes and substance abuse disorder. The downside of this view is that medicalization of the symptoms suffered by trauma survivors requires the sufferer to accept her symptoms as a mental illness rather than to understand them as the natural outcomes of traumatic experience. This may result in the secondary wounding and decreased credibility of the victim described earlier in this chapter (Ochberg, 1998). It also can discount or overlook actual medical conditions resulting from TBI in or strangulation of IPV victims, when the underlying cause (traumatic abuse) is not considered as the presenting condition, and only psychological approaches are being considered. The original biomedical perspective, within the contemporary landscape, more often is combined with an integrated approach to care that is trauma-informed as well as infused with knowledge derived from brain research. The latter is comprised of modern medical technologies including SPECT (single photon computed tomography) scans and functional MRI (magnetic resonance imagery) scans, which also serve to improve diagnosis and pharmaceutical approaches. Precisely because IPV-related causes of physical injuries often are not reported when a victim seeks medical treatment, it becomes essential that the biomedical model include an integrative, trauma-informed approach.

Ecological Development, Attachment, and Polyvagal Theory

In attempting to understand the complexity of IPV, the reader may wish to consider comprehensive models of human development and behavior that take into account the biological, developmental, and psychosocial factors that contribute to the genesis of IPV. Bronfenbrenner's (1979) ecological development model and Bowlby's (1969) attachment model offer broader developmental and relational models for conceptualizing IPV; Porges' (2007, 2011) PVT is especially helpful in understanding the neurobiological effects of trauma on the IPV survivor.

Bronfenbrenner's (1979) ecological development model, when applied to a framework for understanding IPV, implies an acknowledgment of the biological characteristics with which humans are endowed, along with developmentally mediated psychological factors, as seen within a multifaceted social context. Bronfenbrenner's reference to *micro-, meso-, exo-, macro-,* and *chronosystem* structures in an individual's ecology acknowledges the impact of multiple layers of the relational environment upon an individual's experience at any given moment. The ecological model, along with attachment theory (Bowlby, 1969), which focuses predominantly on the impact of children's early relationships with caregivers, and the more recent understanding of the neurobiology of trauma, together provide a more balanced view of the factors associated with IPV.

Attachment theory is a framework upon which extensive enhancements have been constructed by social scientists from a variety of disciplines. Bowlby (1969) based his theory on his observations and his belief that human infants have a biologically driven developmental need to be cared for by a person who is older and wiser (usually the mother) for purposes of safety and survival as well as regulation of affect. The quality of this initial attachment bond acts as a template for future adult attachments. If early attachment is disrupted by separation, illness, or trauma, the child's ability to soothe herself in the presence of stress may be underdeveloped; this is a deficit that has particular relevance to IPV, because attachment-seeking behavior continues throughout the life-span (Bowlby, 1984).

Based on Bowlby's (1984) work, Fonagy (1999) proposed that adult relationship violence is an exaggerated response of the attachment system. As stated previously, seeking solace through close relationships is a normal human behavior and one that may erupt into intimate partner discord if early dysfunctional attachment patterns are experienced as being present in the adult romantic relationship. Bronfenbrenner (1979) emphasized the importance of *experience* as key, because it is the experience of the individual in a particular context that takes precedence over any objective observations that may be made regarding the situation. An emotional experience template, forged in a childhood of abuse and domestic violence, has been implicated in the prevalence of IPV in adulthood (Fonagy, 1999).

Studies on the neurobiology of attachment (e.g., Schore, 1999; Siegel, 1999) have provided support for attachment theory by demonstrating the link between biological and psychological models of development, thereby deconstructing artificial barriers that historically have existed between the two. Of particular relevance is the recent neurobiological research (e.g., Porges, 2007, 2011), which has elucidated the engagement of the autonomic nervous system (ANS) during a traumatic event, as well as the effects of trauma on the vagus nerve and its interactions with the brain and other major organs of the body. Although these issues have been detailed throughout this textbook, particularly in Chapters 2 and 4, it is essential to note here that these same physiological processes are engaged before, during, and after IPV events.

In a situation that usually is unsafe, the IPV victim may be in a constant state of hypervigilance, with the ANS continually scanning the environment in an effort to detect any existing threats. Being in a constant state of alertness—ready for mobilization, ready for fight or flight—has numerous physiological and psychological consequences. Conversely, in a situation that usually is unsafe, the IPV victim may be too fearful to mobilize, and therefore becomes unable to respond in any meaningful way, thus becoming too immobilized to protect herself. A full discussion of PVT and its implications for IPV is beyond the scope of this chapter. However, the professional literature (e.g., Dana, 2018; Porges & Dana, 2018) describes clinical applications of PVT, and, as one research example, PVT has been used as the theoretical framework for investigating intimate partner stalking/pursuit and attachment style (Creamer & Hand, 2021). The advances in this area of study, particularly relative to brain science, have provided new dimensions in our understanding of traumas, such as IPV, as the result of a complex interplay of biological, psychological, social, and cultural risk factors for both victim and perpetrator.

Risk Factors—The Victim

As we demonstrated earlier in this chapter, the Stockholm syndrome pattern of attachment between captive and captor is echoed in many IPV situations, where the cycle of tension, abuse, and relief reoccurs in the life of the victim, with the relief phase offering intermittent moments of hope and optimism that may keep the victim in the relationship (Ochberg, 1998). D. G. Dutton and Painter (1993b), in fact, cite the intermittency of abuse as a factor in the level of stress experienced by women who chose to leave their batterers, with extremes of negative and positive batterer behavior associated with the most post-separation distress. In other words, women whose abusers were extremely violent, but who *also displayed the most kindness and remorse* during the relief phase of the IPV cycle, had the most difficulty separating from their batterers.

Bornstein (2006) cites economic and emotional dependency as risk factors in the etiology of IPV relationships for both women and men. For women in particular, the cultural traditions of economic dependency and social disempowerment contribute to the possibility of victimization by a male partner, as does her partner's excessive emotional dependency. Economic dependency may escalate to economic abuse, which refers to when an abuser takes control of or limits access to shared or individual assets, or when the abuser limits the current or future earning potential of the victim as a strategy for power and control. In economic abuse, the abuser separates the victim from her own resources, rights, and choices, isolating the victim financially and creating a forced dependence for the victim and other family members (NCADV, 2015). Cunradi et al. (2000) found that couples living in impoverished neighborhoods are at increased risk for IPV. Wallace (2007) reminds us that most women in IPV relationships are looking for signs that the perpetrator is not all bad. The woman has invested a lot in the relationship and hopes for a future for herself and for any children she might have with the perpetrator. Wallace (2007, p. 33) also lists the following beliefs and behaviors that may result from the conditions imposed by the Stockholm syndrome-type pattern of perceived threats and social isolation imposed by batterers:

- She develops an overwhelming need to pacify the batterer, in order to survive;
- She adopts the batterer's perspective of the world;
- She feels intense feelings of gratitude toward the batterer; and,
- She rejects offers of help or rescue, which she may believe could aggravate the batterer.

Kearney (2001) supports the argument for a multifactorial model of IPV, in that it includes influences from social and cultural institutions (e.g., religions, traditional expectations of women) as well as factors that possibly could be connected to attachment patterns or childhood experiences of witnessing domestic violence (e.g., caretaker role, use of denial). The women in Kearney's study also reported that changes in their relationships (for the worse) had occurred over time, with most of the women endorsing a definition of love that included a need to endure. We can conclude that women's interpersonal relational style (Gilligan, 1982), combined with attachment experiences and viewed within an IPV context, may make them vulnerable to a pattern of coping strategies that often is misunderstood by those outside the relationship who may focus on the perceived shortcomings of the victim rather than the actions of the perpetrator.

Risk Factors — The Perpetrator

Fonagy (1999) suggests that many men who commit violent acts against women lack the ability to mentalize, that is, to imagine their attachment figure's thoughts. This is a state that Fonagy attributes to a childhood rendered so physically or emotionally unsafe that the child copes by refusing to imagine the state of mind of a parent who wishes to harm him. This pattern, persisting into adulthood, may form the basis for IPV relationships between batterers and their partners (who in some cases also may be attachment disordered). Similarly, Meloy (2002) believes that men who fail to develop secure attachments in childhood are at greatest risk for IPV, basing this hypothesis on a growing body of research that empirically supports the connection between insecure attachments and adult (often intergenerational) relationship violence.

A study by Mauricio et al. (2007) found that both antisocial and borderline personality disorders were related to attachment styles that served as mechanisms for both physical and psychological violence in a sample of male batterers referred for treatment. The authors state that their findings suggest that intervention programs may need to address batterers' personality disorders more directly to improve outcomes. Heyman and Slep (2002) found that the frequency of family of origin violence predicted adulthood child and partner abuse in a retrospective study of more than 6,000 participants in a national family violence survey. Israel and Stover (2009) studied distress levels in children exposed to violent father figures and reported significantly more symptoms in these children, leading us to speculate about the interconnectedness of these studies' findings as well as the implications for society.

As the majority of IPV continues to be perpetrated by males against females, it is germane to include information on the topic of the culture of male privilege and entitlement found in our society. This underlying construct is found across cultural and racial groups and forms an important basis upon which interpersonal violence against women is perpetrated. Examples of male privilege and entitlement include the following: He is trusted and seen as more credible than women; he experiences fewer barriers and more access to money, jobs, status, and so forth; he gets to do what he wants, when he wants; he has an expectation that women should be accommodating; he feels entitled to make big decisions alone, expecting women to "make it happen"; his (men's) way is the right way and more valuable than a woman's; he views male roles as superior and female roles as inferior; he faces no consequences for bad behaviors; he feels entitled to monopolize conversations and discussions; and he feels entitled to interrupt and/or ignore women (Hill, 2020). Male privilege and entitlement are found in minority cultural communities as well as in dominant cultures where, in some settings, they have replaced more egalitarian traditions. Teaching of misogynic beliefs and exposure to this behavior in the family and in a culture further leads to the lack of agency and dehumanization of women, thus serving to sanction IPV.

Operating From an Ecological, Attachment, and Neurobiological Paradigm With Intimate Partner Violence

Specific features of the ecological model, attachment theory, and recent neurobiological research offer a broad context for understanding IPV. For this reason, a succinct discussion of the strengths and criticisms of this paradigmatic approach is far more complex than merely presenting these details of the models; such a critique requires greater comprehensive theoretical explication, and therefore is beyond the scope of this chapter. However, there are several reasons why this paradigm merits further investigation by therapists working with IPV and trauma:

1. The ecological model provides a multilevel social systems framework that accommodates strengths from feminist and family systems theories;
2. Attachment theory includes elements from the biomedical model and family systems theory;
3. PVT facilitates an understanding of recent neurobiological research, the effects of trauma on the brain, and the application of brain science in working with IPV; and
4. The ecological model, attachment theory, and PVT combined offer social and individual developmental as well as neurobiological dimensions to the study of IPV and trauma.

COUNSELING IMPLICATIONS

Given the prevalence of IPV in our culture, professional counselors are likely to encounter victims and perpetrators among their clientele over the course of their careers, whether the IPV is disclosed or goes undisclosed. To work effectively with these clients, the counselor can benefit from increasing their knowledge base about IPV. The following subsections refer to aspects of IPV with which professional counselors may want to become familiar.

Treatment for Victims

Given that there are many forms, facets, and stages within the IPV cycle, generalizations about victim interventions should be avoided. Those who are still in physical danger need to acquire physical safety, financial assistance, and legal protection. Providers of these services include victim advocates, domestic violence shelters, attorneys and legal aid programs, and others with relevant experience and resources. It is only after basic needs are met and safety is achieved that the victim may be able to address the effects of trauma more fully, as well as to address any self-defeating patterns of her own in therapy with a trauma-competent counselor (Ochberg, 1998).

Counselors should be aware that shelters are often the safest refuges for victims, because the family of origin may represent another source of betrayal and abuse for the battered individual. Shelters offer protection from the abuser and have the added benefit of esteem-building groups for residents. Careful discussion about what constitutes supportive behavior can help counselors and their clients to identify an appropriate crisis plan along with trustworthy contacts (DiBlasi & Smith, 2020; Ochberg, 1998). Some shelter programs provide transitional housing, along with life skills and counseling services, and many offer after-shelter support groups that can assist survivors of IPV as they rebuild their lives. Shelters are much less available in rural and tribal communities, thus making safe shelter and transportation to a safe shelter challenging. However, other ways of meeting these emergency needs may be available through community resources.

Once the client's safety is established and the therapy process begins, it is important for counselors to use an empowerment approach, in which the client is given as many choices as possible in determining the course of her own life. Counselors also need to be prepared to encounter the depression as well as the often contradictory or paradoxical behavior patterns of abused women. These behavior patterns may confuse the therapist, especially as these clients often are labeled "borderline," due to the frequent limit-testing and emotional demands (Walker, 1991). Maintaining a professional relationship without implying friendship beyond appropriate boundaries is the most helpful response (Ochberg, 1998). A successful competent intervention usually incorporates an awareness of one's own biases and prejudices, cultural humility, and recognition of professional power (the power differential between the counselor and the client), in order to avoid imposing one's own values on others. Counselors need to remember to offer respect, not rescue, and suggestions, not orders, thus minimizing trigger effects in the victim, building trust, and supporting cultural healing traditions and spiritual practices that may aid in recovery.

Treatment for Batterers

The challenge of IPV is that while violence is the common denominator in the definition, the causes and conditions of individual abusers are as varied as the types of violence that they perpetrate. No "one size fits all." However, as the majority of perpetrators may end up in treatment through court referrals, it is important to review the research on the models used and recidivism rates found within the justice system involved. The Duluth model (Pence & Paymar, 1993) uses group-facilitated exercises to change abusive and threatening behavior in males who engage in IPV. The Duluth model views the principal cause of domestic violence as being determined by a social, cultural, and personal ideology that imposes power and control through violence. The model focuses on changing offenders' dominant and controlling behaviors.

An evaluation by the National Institute of Justice (NIJ, 2019) indicated that the efficacy of batterer intervention programs showed mixed results. An NIJ meta-analysis (2013b) assessed the Duluth model as effective for reducing recidivism, as this applies to violent offenses; the same study determined the model to be promising in terms of the reduction of victimization. The results found fewer partner reports for violence in the intervention group relative to comparison groups. Because the Duluth model is psychoeducational in nature, it should be used as an *adjunct* to other forms of therapy that may be necessary. A similar analysis by the NIJ (2013a) rated cognitive behavioral therapy (CBT) as *not effective* as a batterers' intervention model, citing analyses of four randomized trials, which found no statistically significant effect of CBT on the likelihood that CBT participants would not commit violence against their partners. This affirmed three quasi-experimental studies (Babcock et al., 2004), using partner reports of violence for analysis and finding no statistically significant effect on victimization rates of partners of domestic violence offenders who participated in CBT.

One efficacious method for working with batterers blends attachment theory and cognitive approaches, taking into account the early childhood risk factors mentioned earlier in this chapter (Bowen, n.d.). Lawson et al. (2006) have reported significant changes in abuser attachment styles as well as decreased violent behavior in men who participated in a 17-week course of integrated cognitive behavioral/psychodynamic group treatment. Renn (2009) has advocated for couple therapy in certain batterer cases, following a careful risk assessment. Renn has asserted the following:

> Couple violence . . . is a complex phenomenon and has both relational and individual origins. Understanding the traumas and adult attachment styles that people bring to their intimate relationships in the context of their early attachment histories may help us to assess whether or not, and under what specific circumstances, couple violence is more likely to occur. (p. 2)

Regardless of the model applied in the treatment of batterers, true personal change that generalizes into societal change only can be accomplished by holding batterers and social institutions accountable for the damage that they inflict or fail to prevent. It is equally important to address underlying substance abuse and mental health conditions that contribute to the violence as well as to focus on the wellness of the person and his ability to engage in healthy relationships. The cost to society is too great for these issues to be ignored.

Multicultural Considerations

In order for counselors to address IPV effectively, it is necessary first to address our own biases and myths about IPV along with those of the dominant culture in which we live or practice. This includes considerations of implicit bias concerning racial, ethnic, religious, cultural, socio-economic backgrounds, gender identity, gender roles, disability issues, and beliefs regarding the types of intimate partner relationships that make up society. When clinicians are working with IPV victims from different cultural backgrounds, they need to assist clients in understanding the meaning of victimization within that cultural group; counselors then need to explore how treatment issues can be effective and appropriate. Cultural and spiritual practices should be encouraged, if desired by the client, as an adjunct to other Western models of treatment. Of course, everyone is an individual, and even among cultural groups, diversity exists concerning beliefs and norms, overlaid by specific family and community conditions. In general, the overarching hope expressed by survivors of IPV is that they want the violence to stop, they want to feel safe, and they want to heal.

Prevention

The focus of this chapter has been on defining and identifying IPV, along with exploring how its sequelae may present major public health and social problems for the entire culture, as well as for individuals and their families. Primary and secondary prevention programs have been made available through the CDC (Niolon et al., 2017), SAMHSA (2020), the U.S. Department of Justice (2014), and the National Institute of Justice (2007). The burden of effecting such preventative changes, however, cannot and should not be borne by victim service and public health agencies alone. True cultural change requires public acknowledgment of the problem by political forces, as well as action by governmental agencies responsible for defining needs; allocating funds; and upholding the rights of women, children, and other marginalized populations. Personal and professional activity that holds public officials accountable for initiating and supporting measures to protect vulnerable members of the population may be one of the most important ways in which counselors can advocate for their clients, as well as for their work, and for society as a whole.

The Importance of Education and Self-Reflection

In closing this chapter, the authors wish to acknowledge the critical need for undergraduate and graduate education that addresses IPV trauma and its effects on individuals and society. Few professional counseling or other preservice training programs offer courses that teach students how to identify and work with trauma, and those that do so usually offer them as elective courses (Kitzrow, 2002). Based on the statistics presented in this chapter, the likelihood of a counselor encountering clients affected by IPV is high. Therefore, the following suggestions are offered for counselors to:

1. Seek out and use continuing education to learn how to deal effectively and compassionately with IPV and trauma in general. Such advanced training should include the use of self-reflection as a professional development strategy, enabling the counselor to identify their own biases, feelings, and values;
2. Engage in clinical supervision, preferably with a clinically advanced professional who understands and works with IPV or other types of trauma;
3. Find like-minded colleagues with whom the challenges and rewards of working with IPV clients may be shared; and,
4. Finally, and perhaps most importantly, develop a system of self-care that acknowledges the secondary stress and vicarious trauma that may arise from working with trauma survivors, and that addresses any personal IPV trauma.

Counseling victims of IPV is difficult but rewarding work, requiring not only an understanding of the complex dynamics of the individuals involved, but also awareness of the multiple factors that enter into the creation of an IPV social environment. As Gold (2000) so aptly states, referring to childhood abuse survivors, "Their best hope, and consequently that of the rest of us, is to recognize that although they have been abandoned and feel alienated and alone, their destiny, and that of society as a whole, are in actuality inextricably intertwined" (p. 244).

CONCLUSION

In this chapter, we have presented the concept of IPV as trauma experienced mainly by females at the hands of males, but one that exists as a form of power differential that can include same-sex couples as well. We introduced this chapter with the case of Kristin, the Swedish bank teller, whose paradoxical bonding with her kidnapper became known as the Stockholm syndrome—a pattern of primitive attachment that is echoed in the lives of many victims of IPV. Although viewed by the world as strange initially, Kristin's survival strategy has been rendered more understandable through research that identifies the connections between PTSD and victimization of all types.

The effects of trauma are reflected in the physical, psychological, emotional, and social aspects of the victim's life and often are entwined, intricately, in the individual's earliest development due to the intergenerational transmission of violence. The losses associated with IPV are many—for the victim and for society. Perhaps among the most profound are the loss of a sense of interpersonal safety and facing the betrayal that abuse by an intimate partner brings to the relationship. The interdependent nature of human existence dictates that individual trauma truly does not happen in isolation; rather, it affects the entire culture through subsequent generations of traumatized children, who may grow up to be traumatized adults who, in their turn, create traumatized societies.

The risk factors associated with IPV may originate from within social, biological, or developmental contexts, or, most likely, a combination of all three. Just as individual trauma exists within a larger cultural context, the environment of IPV is created within that same complex contextual framework. IPV is a part of our cultural tapestry; no single thread representing IPV can be followed from beginning to end, nor can it be removed from the larger picture, into which it has been interwoven, without changing the prevailing pattern, all of which imply serious challenges for counselors involved in the change process inherent in working with IPV.

ADDITIONAL RESOURCES

 A robust set of instructor resources designed to supplement this text is located at http://connect.springerpub.com/content/book/978-0-8261-5085-1. Qualifying instructors may request access by emailing textbook@springerpub.com.

PRACTICE-BASED RESOURCES AND REFERENCES

To view a list of resources and all the references, please visit connect.springerpub.com via the following url: http://connect.springerpub.com/content/book/978-0-8261-5085-1/part/part02/chapter/ch10

Trauma Survivorship and Disability

ELIAS MPOFU, BRADLEY MCDANIELS, AND JUSTIN WATTS

CHAPTER OVERVIEW

This chapter focuses on the central role of disability in how people experience, deal with, and overcome traumatic experiences. Stress can emerge from a variety of health conditions (e.g., congenital disability, adventitious disability, chronic illness) and can be exacerbated significantly when one experiences trauma. Disability and trauma are not mutually exclusive experiences; in fact, they are not infrequently seen in tandem. Although trauma is frequently associated with large-scale natural events (e.g., hurricane, tornado, war), people with disabilities (PWD) experience various degrees of trauma due to pervasive societal discrimination, which can result in a number of psychopathologies necessitating affective type treatments. Despite trauma survivorship being common in nearly all societies around the globe, the evidence base has been thin, but the number of available interventions with promising options has been evolving quickly. The recovery from the effects of both disability and trauma is a process that requires an understanding of the diversity of factors that contribute to the trauma as well as the customization of treatments to individuals' life situations.

LEARNING OBJECTIVES

After reading this chapter, the reader should be able to:

1. Define trauma and trauma survivorship;
2. Characterize the relationship between disability experience and trauma;
3. Outline the common sources and types of trauma experience with disability;
4. Discuss the relative significance of personal and environmental factors in trauma survivorship; and
5. Evaluate the evidence base on emerging counseling interventions for trauma survivors.

INTRODUCTION

An analysis of global disability concerns suggests that the impact of trauma, crisis, and disaster on persons with disabilities has emerged as an important trend in the international disability-related literature (Levers, 2011). Yet, theory and research-based literature regarding disability and trauma remains limited, despite the fact that these issues are often profoundly distressing.

While people with disabilities (PWD) are at higher risk for traumatic experiences, limitations in health and rehabilitation services often hinder their access to support interventions they require to participate fully in society (Raoul et al., 2007). Disability trauma from work injury is prevalent in the United States, with nearly one in ten sustaining a serious injury-related disability (Haegerich et al., 2014). And, although most injuries can be treated and managed, survivors experience trauma from the larger challenges presented by adapting to the acquired disability (Zaloshnja et al., 2008). For people with developmental disabilities, trauma-informed care is a best practice due to their high trauma vulnerability in everyday settings (Rich et al., 2020). Trauma survivorship is associated with chronic distress long after traumatic events have ceased, affecting multiple life domains and areas of functioning (Shenk et al., 2012). In the next section, relevant trauma issues, as well as disability-related terms and concepts, will be defined and context for understanding the intersection between trauma survivorship and disability will be provided.

DEFINING RELEVANT TRAUMA ISSUES

The trauma experience typically follows "an event, series of events, or set of circumstances that is physically or emotionally harmful or life threatening and that has lasting effects on the individual's functioning and mental, physical, social, emotional, or spiritual well-being" (Substance Abuse and Mental Health Services Administration [SAMHSA], 2014; p. 7, see also American Psychiatric Association [APA], 2013). Moreover, trauma is not always the result of a singular event; it can occur and be intensified by recurring or new traumatic experiences. Recent updates to the *ICD-11* have also included a diagnosis of complex posttraumatic stress disorder (CPTSD; Barbano et al., 2019; World Health Organization [WHO], 2018), which typically occurs after prolonged (or chronic) exposure to distressing events (e.g., prolonged torture, child-maltreatment or child adversity, extreme domestic violence).

Posttraumatic Stress Disorder

Posttraumatic stress disorder (PTSD) is a clinical diagnosis that develops in some people in response to a traumatic experience and includes at least one of the following: (a) reliving the trauma (e.g., flashbacks, nightmares); (b) avoidance (e.g., avoiding persons, places, or things that might serve as reminders of the trauma); (c) hyperarousal; and (d) negative affect (Steenkamp et al., 2017). Most adults will survive at least one traumatic event in their lives (Bonanno & Mancini, 2012), but not all will experience PTSD.

Historically, trauma has been associated with the experience and survivorship of wars (Mullins, 1999). Necessarily, physical trauma and collateral disability were the archetypical forms of trauma. As a result of the necessity to provide quality medical interventions for these wounded military personnel, military, and large municipal hospitals contributed to the development of comprehensive trauma systems (Blaisdell, 1992). A trauma system is an organized multidisciplinary consortium providing and managing treatment beneficial to injured persons via the provision of timely and coordinated care (Mullins, 1999). Prior to the 1960s, trauma survivorship efforts of governmental agencies in the United States were focused mostly on reducing the country's overarching burden of injury. The 1966 National Research Council (NRC), in conjunction with the National Academy of Sciences, issued a report entitled *Accidental Death and Disability: The Neglected Disease of Modern Society*. This report was the beginning of a nationwide effort to combat trauma and was a landmark publication highlighting the priority focus on surviving physical trauma. The overarching goal of this report was to translate the lessons learned from the wartime experiences with trauma into society at large. This report sought to stimulate innovative interventions for physical trauma and to improve treatment, especially in emergency departments. With the publication of this report, trauma became a political concern.

Trauma Survivorship

Trauma survivorship is described as being a "physical, emotional, and spiritual makeover" for a transformational and triumphant personal identity in the face of life-threatening adversity (Carr, 2008). The concept of trauma survivorship gained prominence from cancer survivorship research (National Cancer Institute, the American Cancer Society, LIVESTRONG: the Lance Armstrong Foundation, and the Centers for Disease Control and Prevention, NCI, ACS, LIVESTRONG, CDC, 2010), examining how people with a cancer diagnosis, erstwhile considered a death sentence, could recover their lives with lifestyle changes and triumphantly thrive with cancer instead of withdrawing into themselves, which would hasten their mortality (Bell & Ristovski-Slijepcevic, 2013). A robust corpus of literature exists documenting the phenomenon of psychological growth following suffering and trauma (Lerner & Blow, 2011; Tedeschi & Calhoun, 1995). Tedeschi and Calhoun (1996) framed this paradoxical process of positive psychological change following intense and highly stressful events as *posttraumatic growth* (PTG; 1996). PTG is not a mere return to pretrauma baseline of functioning; it is an enhancement of one's previous self that does not result from the trauma per-se but from the resultant struggle to survive (Joseph & Linley, 2008; Tedeschi & Calhoun, 2004). A traumatic event(s) may be the catalyst to short-term or long-term disability, depending on survivorship competencies and resources. Resilience is one such resource. Broadly, resilience is defined as "the ability to adapt successfully to adversity, stressful life events, significant threat, or trauma" (Feder et al., 2019, p. 443).

Disability

The International Classification of Functioning, Disability, and Health (ICF) defines "disability" as "the outcome or result of a complex relationship between an individual's health condition on the and personal factors, and of the factors that represent the circumstances in which the individual lives" (WHO, 2001. p. 17). Disability, including both temporary and permanent impairments, can be the result of a traumatic experience; however, not all trauma results in disability. Much research addressing the effect of trauma on individuals does so from a somewhat myopic point of view, as it largely disregards the experiences of habitually disregarded segments of society (Suarez, 2013). Indeed, the construct of disability, as collateral to or from the experience of an event (or series of events) that would comprise trauma, is substantially influenced by aspects of culture, including discriminatory practices that deny PWD access to resources typically available to others in the community (Mpofu et al., 2012). PWD historically have been excluded from educational programs involving violence prevention, healthy relationships, and sexuality (McDaniels & Fleming, 2016). As a result of inadequate sexuality education and ignorance about safe-sex practices, PWD are at an increased risk of HIV and unwanted pregnancies (Doyle et al., 2020).

Discrimination on the Basis of Disability

Disability-related discrimination relates to "any distinction, exclusion, or restriction of a person, based on disability, which has the purpose or effect of impairing or nullifying the recognition, enjoyment, or exercise of all human rights and fundamental freedoms in the political, economic, social, cultural, civil, or any other field" (Convention on the Rights of Persons With Disabilities, 2006, Article 2, Definitions). This concept includes direct and indirect discrimination, underscoring that disability rights are human rights.

Discrimination as Context

PWD face particular discrimination and neglect related to basic rights such as the right to food, shelter, or even to life. The scale of exclusion due to disabilities is often dramatic; for example, globally, poor children with disabilities are less likely to receive early education, and many adults with disabilities have limited opportunities for competitive employment (WHO, 2001). In addition to the violation of human rights experienced by PWD because of practical impediments, foremost among them being negative attitudes, PWD may be denied their legal rights (e.g., employment, inclusive education; Konrad et al., 2013). Research has demonstrated that discrimination plays a role in exacerbating psychological distress in addition to increasing symptoms of PTSD, suggesting that social context is an important factor to consider when examining the well-being of socially marginalized groups (Matheson et al., 2019).

Most of the bias faced by PWD is premised on the three pillars of attitudinal, environmental, and institutional disability discrimination (Handicap International [HI] and CBM, 2006). These practices may lead to greater distress for PWD (both in severity of distress and duration) than the physical trauma of loss of a limb, sight, hearing, or any other physical trauma. Discrimination and exclusion of PWD is both a potential cause and effect of trauma. Following is a brief discussion of the different types of discrimination faced by PWD.

Attitudinal Discrimination

Stereotypes and stigma regarding disability exist across all cultures and permeate all social classes, even in the contemporary landscape that emphasizes disability as a human rights issue. Before discussing stigma and stereotype, we must define attitude. A classic definition of attitude is an evaluative psychological tendency that is either positively or negatively valenced (Eagly & Chaiken, 1993). Stigma, on the other hand, is inherently negative and is recognized by disapproval, shame, or disgrace, resulting in disadvantage and devaluation (Martin, 2010). This disapproval is based on any characteristic that is judged to be different from the norm (Bellanca & Pote, 2013), and stigma is manifested by stereotypes (Ohan et al., 2015), which are beliefs or cognitive schemas that characterize people into groups based on arbitrary characteristics of differentiation and results in discrimination (e.g., disability, race, ethnicity).

Among the various forms of discrimination, attitudinal discrimination toward PWD often creates the most difficult obstacles. Despite concerted efforts made through education and social inclusion policies, negative attitudes and perceptions persist (Barr & Bracchitta, 2015). Such stigma often arises from scapegoating or "othering" people who appear to be different in some way (these and related constructs are discussed more fully in Chapter 16). Among the number of deleterious outcomes, violence may be the result of objectification of PWD. Whereas numerous environmental circumstances (e.g., socioeconomic status, race, ethnicity) may render any PWD more vulnerable to violence, gender (e.g., female) is among the most salient characteristics associated with heightened vulnerability to interpersonal violence.

Environmental Discrimination

Despite decades of effort and the passage of scores of legislative acts to make communities accessible to all, PWD continue to be confronted with environmental barriers (Agaronnik et al., 2019). Attitudinal, environmental, and social factors continue to impede community participation (e.g., leisure, employment) and further marginalize PWDs (Anaby et al., 2013). Two forms of environmental discrimination that preclude accessibility of PWD exist: architectural (e.g., buildings, transportation, infrastructure) and social (e.g., presentation of information that is available to all). For example, transportation is critical for allowing PWD to fully participate in their communities, and when transportation is unavailable or inaccessible, access to community services is hindered (Hammel et al., 2015; McDaniels et al., 2018). It is not unusual for essential facilities, like those offering health and medical services, to lack accessibility for persons with mobility challenges, which can obviate receiving needed care and create unnecessary anxiety. Social inaccessibility, on the other hand, occurs when information is presented in formats that are not disability friendly (e.g., written only, computer-based).

Institutional Discrimination

Institutional discrimination is the societal mistreatment of a person or group of people based on stereotypical beliefs. This type of discrimination can be either intentional or unintentional. Examples include not hiring a PWD for a job or not allowing PWDs to participate in sexuality education.

Trauma Linked to Disability Discrimination

Over one's lifetime, PWDs are confronted with a variety of stressful events (e.g., perceptions of incompetence, social rejection) which may have significant deleterious effects (Hipes et al., 2016). The accumulation of these stressful experiences can become untenable and lead to additional psychological and emotional sequelae. In particular, discrimination and feelings of devaluation are among the most important "disability-relevant social stressors" (Brown, 2017, p. 99). These stressors are more typically observed in marginalized populations and higher levels of discrimination are associated with more severe depressive symptoms (R. L. Brown, 2014) and potentially PTSD (J. G. Allen, 2005).

Children with disabilities may be particularly susceptible to trauma, which includes physical abuse, sexual abuse, antipathy (i.e., rejection), psychological abuse (i.e., cruelty), emotional neglect, and physical neglect (Watts, O'Sullivan, & Shenk,, 2018). Trauma in childhood is especially problematic because it can influence the course of psychological, social, and physiological development with effects often extending into adulthood. The experience of chronic stress in childhood has also been linked to increased risk for chronic illness and disability later in life along with the early adoption of maladaptive coping behaviors (e.g., substance abuse; Felitti et al., 1998).

CONTEMPORARY VIEWS OF TRAUMA SURVIVORSHIP AND DISABILITY

Contemporary understanding of trauma survivorship is more holistic and considers physical, psychological, and social aspects and how they interact to affect quality of life. Although not an inclusive list, trauma survivors may experience PTSD, generalized anxiety disorder, major depressive disorder (MDD) (Anwar et al., 2011; Warren et al., 2014), acute stress disorder (ASD), and dissociative disorders (Gold, 2008). Thus, consideration of the psychological, social, and postmodern effects of trauma survivorship is important.

Psychological Perspectives

PWDs have been marginalized for decades, which has led to cumulative historical trauma. Cumulative trauma results from natural or man-made disasters and involves injury to a group's identity (Saul, 2013). "The collective trauma works its way slowly and even insidiously into the awareness of those who suffer from it" resulting in loneliness and loss of self (Erikson, 1976, p. 154). Trauma as a psychological phenomenon is recognized in the works of Carlson (1997), among others, who regarded an event as traumatic if (a) an individual's perception of the event results in negative consequences (i.e., physical pain, injury, or death); (b) they perceive the sudden onset of the event as an immediate threat; and (c) the individual perceives the event as out of their control. Practically speaking, trauma survivorship consists of two factors, if one experienced the event (whatever it might be) as subjectively shocking (Solomon & Canino, 1990), and the event produced "symptoms of . . . stress," including intrusion, numbing, and arousal (Norris, 1992, p. 490). In other words, survivorship of the traumatic event(s) presents a challenge to the individual's adaptive system, the mechanism for supporting psychosocial equilibrium within one's environment (Silove, 1999). Historically, the phenomenon of trauma has been associated more with disability experience and much less with adaptive competencies.

Sociological Approaches

Sociological perspectives, such as the work of Silove (1999), provide a systematic model to operationalize survivor adaptive systems. Silove considered five adaptive systems—safety, attachment, justice, existential meaning, and identity/role—which provide a homeostasis between an individual and their environment. In reference to the safety system, experiencing a threat to one's health or life may initiate a psychobiological mechanism to ensure and preserve safety (e.g., fight or flight). In addition, connectedness or a sense of belonging is paramount to psychological well-being (Williams & Galliher, 2006), and the disruption of social ties results in a disturbance to one's interpersonal relationships leading to a host of detrimental mental health issues. For instance, in war trauma, specific tactics may be used to impact a person's sense of community negatively so that they feel alone and useless. Social connectedness not only moderates the effects of stress on mental health outcomes but also mitigates the impact of discrimination (Lee & Ahn, 2011). According to Nussbaum (2000), affiliation is one of the two essential capabilities that can "organize and suffuse all others" (p. 82). Social resources are critical to buffering stress and coping with problems and are associated with positive mental health outcomes (Umberson & Montez, 2010). Prior roles such as father, provider, and so forth, are diminished or eliminated. This disruption may result in actual (e.g., the death of a family member) or symbolic (e.g., self-worth) losses to which an individual must adapt.

Postmodern Approaches

Postmodern approaches (e.g., Stolorow, 2009) consider the experience of trauma a natural part of the human condition. According to Stolorow, "human beings would be much more capable of living in their existential vulnerability, anxiety, and grief, rather than having to revert to the defensive, destructive evasions" (p. 208). Postmodern perspectives on trauma consider trauma survivorship to be largely the result of environmental and societal domains (Anwar et al., 2011). When trauma survivorship is viewed in this manner, the potential of subsequent disability is based on the framework that (a) persons are not equally susceptible to or affected by traumatic experiences, (b) persons may or may not receive clinical care, and (c) clinical intervention posttrauma does not guarantee recovery in and of itself. Survivorship is compromised with continual distress and inadequate support within the recovery environment. Thus, providing psychosocial support to trauma survivors is critical for mitigating subsequent disability.

Human Rights Perspective

Trauma can be the result of natural or man-made circumstances. Of those that are man-made, physical, emotional, and psychological abuse are violations of one's human rights. International, civil, and human rights movements have cast trauma survivorship as a global issue, perhaps more than any other historical movement (Gruskin, 2004). For instance, protection from the experience of man-made traumatic events and the rehabilitation of survivors aligns with the United Nations' (1966) International Covenant on Civil and Political Rights (ICCPR). The ICCPR obligates governmental entities to respect the dignity and security of all persons via protection of physical integrity, procedural fairness in laws, freedom of speech and religion, and the right to political participation. This covenant is exemplified by related resolutions of the United Nations' organization such as the resolution in 1973 on Libya to protect citizens from predatory regimes threatening to murder citizens who hold contrary political ideology. As time passes, so-called second-generation human rights refer to survivors' entitlements to have access to basic necessities, whereas third-generation human rights entail respect of cultural values such as maintaining heritage, a sense of community, and the right to self-determination. These rights are These rights to human dignity are essential, should be guaranteed to every person, and must remain a top priority (United Nations, 1948). Thus, human rights norms and standards have provided a broad-based view to understanding trauma survivorship. Combining health and human rights in a public health framework provides a benchmark for the assessment of progress and the success or failure of trauma protection and safety policy implementation (Gruskin & Loft, 2002).

SURVIVORSHIP AND VICARIOUS TRAUMATIZATION

The psychological effects of traumatic events are not limited to the one who experienced the event; anyone who has a relationship with the survivor is also susceptible, including those who provide services to the individual (e.g., first responders, counselors). Figley (1995, p. 573) posited that stress/trauma is a "normal and natural byproduct" of being in relationship with traumatized people. Vicarious traumatization (VT) consists of a variety of psychological effects (e.g., nightmares, intrusive thoughts) experienced by repeated exposure to other people's trauma, which can lead to long-term consequences to both involved (Pearlman & Saakvitne, 2013). VT is constructed over time and insidiously invades one's everyday life. Secondary traumatic stress, another closely related phenomenon, is defined as a PTSD-like syndrome (Melvin, 2015). Family members are also at risk of developing symptoms of PTSD through the vicarious experiencing of the event of their loved one. Historically, a diagnosis of PTSD was given only to the one who was actually exposed to the event; however, with the revisions of the *DSM-V* (APA, 2013), the diagnostic criteria allow for "learning that the traumatic event(s) occurred to a close family member or close friend" (APA, 2013, p. 271). The inference is clear—traumatic events and PTSD can affect anyone who interacts with the traumatized individual.

Congenital Disability

The process of childbirth has been described as an existential event that affects the entire family constellation (Nilsson et al., 2010). When childbirth is traumatic (e.g., the discovery of a congenital disability), families commonly experience both psychological and emotional trauma (Obeidat et al., 2009) with some describing their experience with the pediatric ICU as "being in hell" (Widding & Farooqi, 2016, p. 160). Most parents are ill-equipped to assume the myriad responsibilities associated with ensuring the child's medical needs are met, and they frequently fail to attend to their personal needs (Bishop et al., 2019). Parents may dwell on the traumatic experience (e.g., guilt, blame, anxiety, depression) and blame themselves for their child's condition. Once receiving the unwelcomed news of a diagnosis, parents may react with ambivalence, denial, anger, guilt, and sorrow (Barnhill & Barnhill, 2010).

Acquired Disability

Despite the reactionary similarities between adjusting to a family member with a congenital disability and one who acquires a disability, one stark contrast is, with an acquired disability, families mourn the "loss" of the family member while simultaneously being introduced to the "new" person within the family unit. Acquired disability typically arises from traumatic events such as accidental injuries as in motor vehicle accidents (MVA), falls, and war injuries; therefore, families not only have to deal with the immediate effects of trauma but also with the resultant, long-term consequences of disability. Like families who have a child born with congenital disabilities, those who are confronted by an acquired disability are thrust into uncharted territory replete with dramatic family role changes, financial uncertainty, unpredictability, stress, and anxiety that they were unable to prepare for (Degeneffe, 2015). The family becomes the primary source of affective and caregiving support (e.g., advocacy, service coordination, daily living needs) (Degeneffe & Burcham, 2008). The case of Sue, in Box 11.1, is illustrative.

BOX 11.1

Clinical Vignette: The Case of Sue

You are working as a vocational rehabilitation counselor at the U.S. Department of Veterans Affairs. You received a supported employment referral for Sue, a 56-year-old female Caucasian veteran. With supported employment, participants have work reentry support of job coaches both onsite and also from a facilitator (or case manager) of a vocational rehabilitation agency. Sue has a diagnosis of paranoid schizophrenia and military sexual trauma.

During your initial consultation meeting, Sue described her interests and preferences for work. She also talked about her prior job as a secretary. Sue explained that she needed to quit her last job because she was having problems getting along with her male coworkers. Sue discussed how she has felt uncomfortable around men since she was sexually assaulted when she served in the military 15 years ago. Currently, she feels worried about her male neighbors because she believes that they are attracted to her and may try to pursue her. Consequently, Sue has not been sleeping well.

You accept Sue into your supported employment program, but you plan to recommend that she seek counseling for her current stress and anxiety.

Reflection Questions

1. How do you use the supported employment counseling to address Sue's current stress and anxiety?
2. What other counseling intervention options would be appropriate for Sue and why?
3. What is the evidence for the interventions you recommend?

RESEARCH ON TRAUMA SURVIVORSHIP AND DISABILITY

Traumatic events are complex and challenging to study (Norris, 1992). Prior trauma studies have relied on small, homogeneous samples, often focusing on only one particular event (e.g., traumatic brain injuries [TBI], stroke) at a time. Such a narrow method of evaluation has limited knowledge gains in the frequency and severity of traumatic events that occur in society. Even when considering the limitations of previous research, a theoretical/empirical understanding of the construct of trauma is important for several reasons. As noted previously, clinically, exposure to trauma is linked to dissociative disorders, depression, anxiety, substance abuse, personality disorders, and psychosis (Anwar et al., 2011; Gold, 2008; Warren et al., 2014). Exposure to trauma has been linked to various health-risk behaviors such as childhood physical and verbal abuse (Williamson et al., 2002); spousal, sexual, physical, and emotional abuse (Dube et al., 2003); and smoking, alcohol abuse, and high-risk sexual behavior. The case of James, in Box 11.2, is illustrative.

BOX 11.2

Clinical Vignette: The Case of James

James is a 35-year-old African American man who returned home from combat in Afghanistan 6 months ago. He is seeking counseling services from the local Veterans Administration because of PTSD. While in Afghanistan, James obtained an injury caused by an explosion and had to have a right below-the-knee amputation. He recovered at the local veterans' hospital and now

(continued)

uses a prosthetic leg for mobility. During the clinical interview, James mentioned that upon returning home, he and his wife of 5 years are arguing a lot. He finds himself constantly losing his temper with her. James drinks about four to six alcoholic beverages per day to cope with stress. He states that drinking helps him to cope with the images of combat scenarios that haunt his dreams and the amputation he endured.

Reflection Questions

1. What other background information may be needed before developing a treatment intervention to help James?
2. Considering courtesy trauma, what issues may James's wife be experiencing?
3. Choose one counseling intervention that has been proven efficacious in helping persons with war-related PTSD. What are the benefits, risks, and considerations associated with using the intervention?

When examining the relationship between trauma exposure and physiological/psychological maladjustment, there is, at times, a direct causal relationship; however, the overall relationship is much more complex (Morrison et al., 2003). For instance, in the case of multiple traumatic experiences, exposure to trauma may make one more susceptible to future trauma (Gold, 2008).

Trauma Centrality, Identity, and Self-Efficacy

Research emphasizes trauma centrality, when the memory of a traumatic occurrence can become a central part of a survivor's identity (Rubin et al., 2008). Survivor identity is negatively correlated to PTSD symptoms in soldiers exposed to combat stress, even when controlling for depression and dissociation (A. D. Brown et al., 2010). The implications of this study suggest that trauma centrality may contribute to the development and continuation of PTSD.

Additionally, a meta-analysis (Luszczynska et al., 2009) provides evidence in support of an association between self-efficacy and PTSD symptoms on health-related outcomes such as distress, anxiety, and depression among survivors. Effect sizes were medium to large, in terms of cross-sectional studies of self-efficacy on general distress, severity, and frequency of PTSD ($r = -.36$ to $-.77$).

Premorbid Personality Characteristics and Posttraumatic Stress Disorder

The biopsychosocial impacts of PTSD are well-documented; what is less clear are the premorbid factors that increase the likelihood of clinically relevant PTSD. Studies have investigated the development of PTSD following the events of 9/11 (DiGrande et al., 2008) and in military personnel who were deployed to missions in Iraq and Afghanistan (Jacobsen et al., 2015) and reported that only 12.6% and 6% reported symptoms consistent with PTSD, respectively. Among the proposed explanations for these curious findings are the differences in premorbid vulnerabilities (e.g., genes, epigenetics, personality characteristics; [M. T. Allen et al., 2019]). Personality characteristics that are positively correlated with PTSD include: (a) trait anxiety (Phipps et al., 2009), (b) behavioral inhibition (Tyrka et al., 2008), (c) emotional dysregulation (Weiss et al., 2019), and (d) type D personality (i.e., negative affect, social inhibition; M. T. Allen et al., 2018). Other contextual factors that are positively associated with an increased propensity to develop PTSD include prior trauma, prior psychological adjustment issues, family history of psychopathology, perceived life threat during the trauma, posttrauma social support, peritraumatic emotional responses, and peritraumatic dissociation (Ozer et al., 2003). Ozer et al. (2003, p. 31) suggest that "the specific processes by which these factors may serve to influence the development of PTSD remain largely unexamined" and "further specification of the intervening as well as directly explanatory variable would point to areas of opportunity for intervention and possible attenuation or prevention of the development of PTSD."

In terms of future research, it is necessary not only to continue to investigate the association between traumatic experiences and physical/psychological impairment (Gold, 2008), but more importantly, to identify protective factors and evaluate promising strategies for enhancing them. Specifically, researchers should investigate the factors (e.g., resiliency, social support) that lead persons exposed to trauma to experience or not experience the adverse ramifications. Further exploration is needed, because researchers found that participants receiving treatment for PTSD who completed trauma-related questionnaires reported more feelings of sadness compared to participants completing nontrauma-related questionnaires (Ferrier-Auerbach et al., 2009). Lastly, current research specifically relating to PTSD resulting from the experience of child-maltreatment is quite limited (Ehring et al., 2014). In a review of over 40 randomized controlled studies examining the impact of effective counseling approaches for PTSD, only 10% examined the effectiveness of these approaches for individuals with child-maltreatment histories (Cloitre, 2009), emphasizing that current approaches may not effectively address issues that child-maltreatment survivors might experience (i.e., interpersonal disturbance and emotion dysregulation).

CURRENT PRACTICES IN TREATING TRAUMA IN SURVIVORS WITH DISABILITY

As the field of disability studies has progressed from the medical model of disability to the more comprehensive ICF model, the field of trauma studies has recently begun to broaden the focus of PTSD interventions from the singularly shortsighted fixation on individual characteristics to appreciating the links between individual experiences and their macrosystem (Bonnan-White et al., 2018). This purposive shift toward a holistic approach to trauma survivors, and those who have comorbid disabilities, allows for complementary interventions that include the contributions of oppression and marginalization. When one is from more than one marginalized group (e.g., trauma survivor, one with a disability), the experiences of trauma qualitatively differ from what one from a dominant group experience (Bryant-Davis, 2019).

Trauma-informed care (TIC) is widely accepted as the necessary framework when working with individuals who have experienced trauma. TIC is a holistic approach that incorporates the effects of trauma on psychosocial functioning (SAMHSA, 2014). TIC is not a form of trauma-focused therapy; rather, it is a general orientation for service delivery that views the individual's issues through the lens of their traumatic experience (S. M. Brown et al., 2012) to foster the development of adaptive coping in the context of oppression. Clinicians who provide trauma-counseling interventions to individuals with disabilities face challenging dilemmas not only about how to provide evidence-based treatment to more than one condition, but which one should be the focus. Most PTSD or trauma counseling theories and techniques are applicable to treating trauma in PWD. However, intervention strategies, resources, or facilities may need to be modified to meet the unique needs of people with specific disabilities.

Trauma-Focused Therapies

Over the past two decades, PTSD and its associated trauma-focused treatments have received a great deal of attention. Despite the interest in efficacious interventions, no treatment has proven to be superior. Several meta-analyses have reported that there is no difference in efficacy between various types of trauma-focused treatments (Australian Centre for Posttraumatic Mental Health [ACPMH], 2007; Bisson & Andrew, 2009; Seidler & Wagner, 2006). However, one factor is clearly associated with therapy completion and positive outcomes—the therapeutic alliance, which may be critical when working with individuals with trauma histories who may have trust issues (Watts, O'Sullivan, & Chatters, 2018). Along with improved diagnostic criteria and several notable trauma-inducing events (e.g., Iraq/Afghanistan conflicts, 9/11), a number of promising therapies to treat PTSD have evolved.

Currently, trauma-focused approaches (e.g., trauma-focused cognitive behavior therapy [TF-CBT]) are promoted as first-line treatment for PTSD (American Psychiatric Association, 2004; ACPMH, 2007), and the Department of Veterans Affairs and the Department of Defense (2017) have issued clinical practice guidelines recommending several specific TF-CBT interventions: cognitive processing therapy (CPT; Resick et al., 2016), prolonged exposure (PE; Foa et al., 2007), and Eye Movement Desensitization and Reprocessing (EMDR) first-line therapy (Shapiro, 2017). Collectively, the symptoms of PTSD are amenable to interventions, but roughly one-third of people have symptoms that are somewhat unresponsive to traditional trauma-focused options (Watkins et al., 2018). Although not specifically trauma-focused (debate continues regarding the necessity of "trauma-focused" labels), a variety of PTSD treatments have been studied and can be successfully "delivered in a trauma-focused framework" (Schnurr, 2017, p. 57).

Alternative and Complementary Interventions

Complementary and alternative medicine (CAM) are practices that augment traditional medical care but are unlikely to become first-line treatment options (Wynn, 2015). A variety of current nontrauma-focused treatments hold promise, such as affective and interpersonal regulation, yogic breathing, mindfulness training, acupuncture, and behavioral activation (Jakupcak et al., 2006). Further research is warranted to continue to investigate the efficacy of these new interventions for trauma.

Treatment Outcomes With Co-Occurring Conditions

Although trauma alone can result in significant psychosocial challenges, comorbidities frequently accompany a PTSD diagnosis (Kang et al., 2019). More than one-half of all people diagnosed with PTSD have co-occurring anxiety, mood, or substance use disorders (SUD; Pietrzak et al., 2011), which may contribute to increased disability and poor health outcomes (Schlenger et al., 2015). Challenges related to treating individuals with PTSD and SUD, for example, include more severe symptomatology and treatment dropout (Norman et al., 2012). Positive comprehensive trauma treatment delivery outcomes with people with co-occurring trauma and disability have been reported. For instance, a collaborative care (CC) pilot intervention, which reduced symptoms of PTSD and alcohol abuse among inpatients with physical injuries (Zatzick et al., 2004), was shown to be effective compared to the control (nontreatment condition) group. CC is a disease management strategy that integrates evidence-based mental health interventions into medical care. Collaborative interventions have the potential to improve rehabilitation from trauma and disability.

Impact of Disability Service Delivery Services

Physical, psychological, and vocational functioning often become personal barriers facing working-age adults with disabilities who seek employment opportunities. With respect to employment opportunities for PWDs resulting from trauma, psychosocial factors play a significant role even though the exact impact of such factors on employment status is difficult to determine (Smeets et al., 2007).

Although PTSD or trauma survivorship counseling interventions are appropriate for treating trauma in PWDs, there is limited understanding of the unique treatment needs for individuals with disabilities. Researchers should continue to investigate service delivery models for individuals with co-occurring physical disabilities (e.g., spinal cord injury, traumatic brain injury) and trauma (Zatzick et al., 2001). Moreover, clinicians should aim to develop evidence-based interventions that could assist individuals who experience trauma from the diagnosis of a chronic illness or disability (e.g., HIV, multiple sclerosis, Parkinson's disease). To elaborate, these interventions are important for persons with co-occurring trauma and disability in order to improve rehabilitation outcomes, specifically in the area of socioeconomic participation.

COUNSELING IMPLICATIONS

Addressing issues related to disability and trauma requires a bipartite approach (Cowles et al., 2020), one that addresses both the physical trauma of having acquired a disability and the psychological trauma of having experienced discrimination, marginalization, and exclusion. The use of this approach means both mainstreaming of disability into all strategic plans as well as supporting specific disability initiatives for the empowerment of PWDs.

The type of service provision model that is used typically influences the approach that is applicable in providing disability support services. The outdated charity model, which sees PWD as victims of their impairments and consequently in need of special services and care in special institutions, has seen the creation of special institutions that remove PWD from communities. This approach discriminates against PWD and does not address trauma that is caused by discrimination. The medical model tends to consider PWD as clients who need fixing to make them "normal," and places PWD into the passive mode; all the while, rehabilitation "experts" make all the decisions for them, thereby, again, not addressing the disability trauma caused by discrimination. The social model, the multidimensional model, and the political perspective model tend to address issues of disability mainstreaming, inclusion, participation of PWD, and involvement of disabled people's organizations in empowerment programs. In this regard, the emphasis is not only on medical rehabilitation, but rather, it is on the support services that are required by PWD to participate fully in family and community activities and to access equitable services. The greatest implication for counseling relates to the aforementioned types of systemic service-provision features that may have profound effects upon PWD who have experienced trauma.

CONCLUSION

Disability and trauma are both complex, multifaceted constructs, and causation directionality is likely bidirectional. Conceptualization of trauma has evolved over time to emphasize contextual factors that influence competencies and strength that contribute to the outcomes of traumatic experiences. Human rights approaches provide a transcultural understanding of trauma experiences that are important for policy on protections from trauma and necessary resources for survivors. The research evidence suggests that disability (e.g., PTSD) from trauma experience and survivorship is influenced by a variety of factors (e.g., social support, premorbid functioning). Evidence is accumulating on the efficacy and effectiveness of trauma-focused therapies, along with a host of promising options for treating trauma survivors with disability. Recovery from both trauma and disability are not events; they are journeys that often last for a lifetime. Survivorship is an inclusive concept for understanding the lived experience of trauma and also the recovery process.

ADDITIONAL RESOURCES

 A robust set of instructor resources designed to supplement this text is located at http://connect.springerpub.com/content/book/978-0-8261-5085-1. Qualifying instructors may request access by emailing textbook@springerpub.com.

PRACTICE-BASED RESOURCES AND REFERENCES

To view a list of resources and all the references, please visit connect.springerpub.com via the following url: http://connect.springerpub.com/content/book/978-0-8261-5085-1/part/part02/chapter/ch11

CHAPTER 12

Older Adults' Health Resourcing

ELIAS MPOFU

CHAPTER OVERVIEW

This chapter focuses on aging as a natural process that affects every one of us. It provides an interdisciplinary overview on how older adults' health needs and the relationships for them change with the aging process, conspiring their biopsychosocial vulnerabilities and assets during the later life years. Most importantly, it discusses the developmental aspects of aging, the meaning of age, issues affecting older adult people, and the significance of relationship support to successful aging. In doing so, the chapter surveys the demographics of aging and the evidence from aging-related research important to the health resourcing of older adults. Finally, the chapter considers a case illustration on the implications of aging to healthcare resourcing from family, cultural, and social policy perspectives.

LEARNING OBJECTIVES

After reading this chapter, the reader should be able to:

1. Define key terms that are relevant to aging, along the life course and in the context of health and function;
2. Outline the significance of relationship transitions associated with the aging processes and outcomes;
3. Examine how health and function in old age relates to practices for successful aging;
4. Evaluate the role of demography of aging and interdisciplinary perspectives, in order to understand vulnerabilities from the aging process and practices to mitigate those vulnerabilities; and,
5. Explain the role of family and support systems as well as living arrangements for successful aging in older adult populations.

INTRODUCTION

The global older adults population aged 60 years and above is projected to increase by 12.5% to approximately 2 billion in 2050, representing one in five people, world-wide (United Nations' World Population Ageing [UNWPA], 2012, United Nations Population Fund [UNPF], 2019; World Health Organization and the National Institute on Aging [WHO & NIA], 2019). The population of older adults aged 65 and older in the United States will double between 2011 and 2050, and that of the "oldest old," aged 85 and older, will increase tenfold in the same period (Administration on Aging, 2010; WHO & NIA, 2019). Yet, "many older people today experience much poorer health trajectories" from preventable conditions and which could at least be "delayed by engaging in healthy behaviors across the life course" (WHO, 2017, p. 6). The WHO advocates for "age-friendly help to foster Healthy Ageing in two ways: by supporting the building and maintenance of intrinsic capacity across the life course, and by enabling greater functional ability so that people with varying levels of capacity can do the things they value" (p. 6). With aging, people's health becomes more complex, requiring integrated healthcare relationships beyond those designed for acute conditions.

While many older adults will experience health, vitality, and longevity unknown to previous generations (Butler, 2009), they also will age with or into disability, immune compromise, chronic inflammation conditions, and frailty (Beard et al., 2016; Franceschi et al., 2018). For these reasons, the longevity gained by many older adults also places them at elevated risk for trauma from conditions associated with the aging processes and the health relationship qualities that they may lack in mitigating those aging processes (O'Neill, 2017). Quite regrettable is the fact that older adults are at elevated risk for abuse and neglect by carers, who may be family and/or other clinicians (Falk, 2012; Yon et al., 2017). Moreover, in the presence of diminishing physical and financial resources, the quality of health relationships of older adults is critical for their successful aging. Successful aging refers to achieving a desired health-related quality of life, even with functioning limitations, by maintaining one's self-efficacy (Cosco et al., 2014).

This chapter discusses relationship health qualities among older adults, which is important for their wellness in the face of decreasing health and function. First, it describes the major aging process conditions for which older adults would require health support for successful aging. Second, the chapter addresses the health relationship vulnerabilities of older adults, including from risks for abuse and maltreatment, and considering diversity among older adults as important for understanding their care needs with aging process conditions. Third, this chapter proposes health relationship resourcing approaches at the personal, family, community, and policy care levels for successful aging.

AGING PROCESS HEALTH CHANGES

Older adults experience significant assaults on their physical, mental, and social health from the aging process. These assaults on health may occur in parallel, with devastating impacts on well-being. They also may occur variably among older adults in terms of timing, intensity, or severity. To add to the complexity of managing aging-related processes, their occurrence in any one older adult is not entirely predictable, and when they do occur, the outcomes may vary, depending on type, timing, and presence of preexisting conditions. The aging process health of older adulthood requires multilayered interventions to mitigate personal-lifestyle, sociobehavioral, medical, and environmental health issues, often a combination of interventions. Among the best documented of health traumas of old age include immune suppression immunosenescence and inflammaging, cancer, neurodegenerative conditions, physical frailty, and sarcopenia.

Immunosenescence and Inflammaging

Older adults have diversity in terms of their immune functioning, which is important for their relationship health, as far as they might require the support of family and other caregivers. Immune function declines with aging, a process called immunosenescence. This process varies widely among older adults, and some have earlier and pervasive onset of immunosenescence, while others have later age onset of immunosenescence. Moreover, of those presenting with immunosenescence, some may be with low to mild forms or more severe forms. The rate of decline in immune bodily capabilities would vary among older adults, and may change within older adults influenced by their evolving biological functioning (such as the body's ability to engage in cell repair), as well as lifestyle and life situation demands (Franceschi et al., 2018). The concept of life situation is a person-centric and context-sensitive way to address real world, everyday activities in which individuals engage and that they perceive to be normal or routine practices in the home or community (Jurczyk et al., 2015).

Indicators of immunosenescence include higher vulnerability to infections and to inflammaging, which is an inflammation syndrome. The immunosenescence is associated with the lower immune white blood B cells and T cells for recognizing and fighting invader micro-organisms like viruses and bacteria that may enter the body in various ways. With the aging process, the production of white blood cells, which detect a pathogen in the body systems, declines, and the body is less capable to detect and neutralize the invading microorganism, which could be COVID-19, for example. Elevated immunosenesence is associated with chronic inflammation syndrome (inflammaging) or persistent low-grade inflammation, degrading the immune response from the body systems to infections (Baylis et al., 2013). While "a moderate inflammation is beneficial and fundamental to activate a [healthy] response to a stress," chronic and elevated inflammation is detrimental (Castellani et al., 2016; Franceschi et al., 2018, p. 5). Older people are susceptible to infectious disease and may have one or more chronic or infectious diseases, making them especially vulnerable to additional infectious diseases (WHO & NIA, 2019) (also as demonstrated by the morbidity and mortality from the global COVID-19 pandemic).

With the aging process, risk for chronic inflammation syndrome is exacerbated by lifestyle issues such as weight gain and mental distress as well as poor access to timely healthcare (Bosma-den Boer et al., 2012). Chronic inflammation is associated with aging autoimmune diseases, such as rheumatoid arthritis, ankylosing spondylitis, osteoarthritis, systemic lupus erythematosus, psoriasis, inflammatory bowel diseases, multiple sclerosis, and others (Franceschi et al., 2018). Chronic inflammation is also associated with cardiovascular, respiratory, and renal dysregulation. The health support needs for older adults would vary by their location on the immunosenescence spectrum (low, high); inflammaging status (episodic, chronic); lifestyle factors; and access to timely healthcare services. Yet, there is a tendency by the general population to treat older adults as necessarily immune compromised, while also not recognizing the diversity in their immune function that explains differences in their health outcomes.

Cancer

While cancer occurrence is a life-long potential, in older adults the risk is elevated (Parry et al., 2011). With the aging process, the chances increase significantly that transforming mutations might occur; this is likely due to the damage that results from allowing cells to progress into malignancy and to metastasize (DeNardo et al., 2010). This effect probably transpires in the presence of an elevated level of inflammaging, from a compromised immune response attempting to manage cancerous cells (Grivennikov et al., 2010). The presence of immune inflammatory cells is associated with tumor growth and cancer cell proliferation, as well as invasiveness. As previously noted, inflammaging is a risk factor for a variety of health conditions of old age; the higher prevalence of inflammaging with aging would explain the association between cancer and old age. Because the inflammaging response is universal in humans, theoretically, it would portend cancer type occurrence at some point in advanced age for some older adults. Of course, learning of a cancer diagnosis is distressful for most individuals and may be traumatizing to many.

A significant proportion (66%) of older adults are cancer survivors, so they can expect to be alive in 5 years (Aziz, 2007). Cancer survivorship refers to lived health quality with a history of cancer diagnosis navigating the complexities of treatment phase care, optimizing the physiological, psychosocial, and functional health outcomes (Feuerstein, 2007; Mohile et al., 2016). Older adult cancer survivors may experience organ senescence or the failure of compensatory mechanisms, with the passage of time, from acute organ toxicities such as radiation pneumonitis, chronic congestive heart failure, inflammaging-related neurodegenerative conditions, and malignancies. Older age care survivors require extensive health support relationships to sustain a meaningful life (Rowland et al., 2006).

Neurodegenerative Conditions

Alzheimer's disease (AD) and Parkinson's disease (PD) are two neurodegenerative conditions associated with the aging process (Boyko et al., 2017; Nelson et al., 2012). Their onset may be incipient and may include later-stage clinical manifestations, with signs of dementia, including memory impairment, time–space disorientation, and difficulties in performing erstwhile basic and/or instrumental activities of daily living. About 25% to 30% of older adults, over 85 years of age, will have dementia (WHO & NIA, 2019). One in eight Americans has Alzheimer's disease, and close to half of all people older than 85 years, the fastest growing segment of the U.S. population, has Alzheimer's disease (Alzheimer's Association, 2011). At mild-to-advanced stages, AD and PD would be traumatizing to the older adults and carers, requiring relationship resourcing and resilience. Certain bacterial infections are hypothesized to activate the pathways involved in neurodegeneration and AD, in the presence of cerebral inflammatory responses (Houeland et al., 2010). PD appears to be associated with accelerated aging, affecting specific neurons in the brain, and to be on a continuum between physiological aging and neurodegenerative age-related motor disorders (Franceschi et al., 2018). PD also appears to be associated with neuroinflammation and perhaps even result from environmental stressors (Codolo et al., 2013). Health relationship demands with AD and PD are extensive and unremitting; they are further compounded by the loss of personal agency, over time, among the afflicted as well as by resource depletion risk of the carers (Kalaria et al., 2008; Kim et al., 2007; Riggs, 2001).

Physical Frailty and Sarcopenia

Frailty is characterized by a loss of physical functions of agility, energy depletion, poor hand grip, and also a poor response to, and recovery from, environmental stress (Aguayo et al., 2017). Older adults with frailty have a high risk for falls, which could be fatal. However, frailty is peculiar as it displays a wide spectrum of phenotypes, depending on the criteria that are considered for its definition, as well as the age range of the subjects studied. Frailty in earlier-age older adults can be treated with physical exercise and nutrition supplements (Michel et al., 2015). Frailty from low-grade inflammaging may be a case of accelerated aging and may be reversible with appropriate treatments (Fried & Ferrucci, 2016). Among the "oldest old," frailty may be accompanied with sarcopenia, which is the progressive decline of skeletal muscle mass, strength, and function associated with chronic inflammation and other conditions (Budui et al., 2015). Immunosenescence and systemic inflammaging from the aging process increase the risk for sarcopenia (Baylis et al., 2013), the onset of which requires intensive health supports in managing it (Greenlund & Nair, 2003).

HEALTH RELATIONSHIP VULNERABILITIES OF OLDER ADULTS

An underlying health relationship vulnerability of older adults is from ageism, the ascription of social stigma by young and middle-aged people against older adults, placing them at risk for human rights abuses (Voss et al., 2018). Ageism also has the effect of treating older adults as somewhat diseased, burdensome, and revulsive. This serves to disempower older adults, denying the older adults the credit for their time-tested wisdom in managing their life situations (Nahmiash, 2004). Uncertainty in personal relationships increases with age, amplifying the subjective demands and prominence that older adults place on initiating and maintaining close relationships, as well as exposing older adults to risk for abuse and exploitation.

Older Adult Abuse

Older adult abuse refers to "acts carried out with the intention to cause physical pain or injury; psychological or verbal abuse, . . . emotional pain or injury and sexual abuse financial exploitation, involving the misappropriation of an older person's money or property; and neglect, or the failure of a designated caregiver to meet the needs of a dependent older person" (Lachs & Pillemer, 2015, p. 1974). Globally, an estimated 15.7% of older adults (or 141 million) have experienced abuse (Yon et al., 2017). Within this population of older adults with an abuse history, 6.8% have experienced psychological abuse, 4.2% financial abuse, 2.6% physical abuse, and 0.9% sexual abuse. About 9% of older adults aged 57 to 85 years reported that they have experienced verbal abuse and 3.5% reported financial abuse in the past year (Laumann et al., 2008). These prevalent types of older adult abuse tend to co-occur (Labrum, 2017; U.S. Government Accountability Office [GAO], 2011) and are especially pervasive among older adults with disability (Fang & Yan, 2018). Most older adults age with or into disability, predisposing them to multiple forms of abuse, depending on their life situations.

Older adult abuse is likely to occur among persons with chronic illness or disability, which impairs the person's independence and judgment and, in turn, makes it easier for the care provider who intends to cause harm or injury to the older adult (Nerenberg, 2008). While the specific content of the actions of older adult abuse may vary by cultural setting, abusive actions are perpetrated knowingly or intentionally by a caregiver or other person in a position of trust or guardianship over a vulnerable senior-age person (Enguidanos et al., 2014). Abuse can take place in residential care facilities and may include restraint, nutritional deficiency, and overmedication (Glendenning, 1999). In the United States, older adults are protected by federal/state/district statutes, but abuse actions may need to be linked to another crime, such as assault, theft, or fraud. This is a complex issue, and legal differences occur across locations (U.S. GAO, 2011). At the same time, older adult abuse is often under the public awareness radar (Gorbien & Eisenstein, 2005), making it less likely that older adults will get the social justice that they deserve in order to live safely and in fulfilling ways (Fulmer, 2003). For instance, they are likely to be left behind in catastrophic event evacuations, even while having physical mobility and transportation limitations (Cloyd & Dyer, 2010; Dostal, 2015). Older adult abuse in residential care facilities is seriously underreported (Gibbs & Mosqueda, 2004; Phillips et al., 2013).

Some older adults may present with self-neglect, defined by poor self-management; this then impairs the elder's own health and safety, and has a negative impact on the person's ability to take care of their own hygiene, nutritional needs, shelter, and/or medical care (National Center on Elder Abuse [NCEA], n.d.). Self-neglect is not a form of older adult abuse. However, what may seem like a case of self-neglect could be the result of ongoing abuse by carers or other persons involved with the older adult's life situation. Examples include cases in which carers are negligent of hygiene, nutritional, and medical care needs of the older adults they have committed to assist (Glendenning, 1999) or acts of financial fraud on an older adult, risking their well-being (Smith, 2000). A vulnerable older adult may respond with self-neglect, believing that they are unable to extract themselves from an abusive relationship with a carer or other person (Enguidanos et al., 2014; Naik et al., 2008). For example, an older adult might endure maltreatment, fearing to be socially rejected or ostracized (Enguidanos et al., 2014). Self-neglect also might result from the challenges of self-management, in terms of aging process conditions (as with cognitive impairment and depression) that take away erstwhile abilities in the absence of alternative mitigation plans (Burnett et al., 2014; Pavlou & Lachs, 2006).

Social Vulnerabilities

Global trends suggest that the older age population will soon outgrow the number of people available to provide the supports needed (WHO & NIA, 2019), and increasingly, older adults will need cost-effective technology supports to manage their health needs (Hall et al., 2012).

Social vulnerabilities of older adults include a foreboding sense of uncertainty about personal relationships that once were taken for granted. On the one hand, older adults may experience social vulnerability from the loss of family or due to a partner or carer relocating to another place or passing away. On the other hand, they may experience social strain from conflictual social interactions with family or with the partner or carer with whom they live, thus harming their psychological well-being (Ten-Bruggencate et al., 2018; Tough et al., 2017). The latter issue may be even more pervasive among older adults who are cognizant of their diminishing social network resources (Wheaton, 1985). The fact that older adults seek to regulate their relationships by investing in closer rather than more distal relationships makes them particularly vulnerable to risks for unwanted social isolation, which would harm their physical and mental health (Tomini et al., 2016). In addition, the rise of "elder orphans," those older adults who live in the community without family, carers, or surrogates, is receiving greater attention from mental health professionals, due to the higher potential for elder orphans to experience a sense of isolation, depression, and anxiety (e.g., Roofeh et al., 2020).

A majority of older adults is aging with or into disabilities (sees previous section), for which they would need supports. Activities of daily living (ADLs) include both basic (bADL) and instrumental (IADL) functions. bADLs involve primarily personal care actions such as bathing, dressing, feeding, toileting, continence, and transfers, while iADLs involve participation in life situations like shopping, recreation and leisure, traveling, managing finances, and use of communication tools (WHO, 2001). With the aging process, declines in physical and cognitive function are associated with declines in the performance of ADLs, often requiring the help of carers and/or other clinicians.

Decision-Making in Older Adults

Aging-related declines begin to affect the efficiency by which older adults make deliberative or sequential staged decisions over extended time or activity frames. Rather, older adults would elect a shorter decision period and settle for a decision that carries emotional appeal. This would add to their vulnerability in high stakes healthcare decisions that require complex consideration of many options.

Most decisions that people make are tagged with some degree of affect and are comprised of positive and negative markers, colored by level of experience, real or imaginary (Slovic et al., 2007). Affect acts as a prism for action or effort investment choices, predisposing some pieces of information over other competing data points. It also serves to conserve decision-making energy by simplifying harder choices for intuitively appealing ones, substituting for what sometimes may be more relevant information (Kahneman, 2011). By definition, a decision results in a commitment to a categorical course of action, and the decisions people take or forgo have consequences for their health outcomes. People are known to adopt or forgo products and behaviors by their incentive values (Charness & Gneezy, 2009). However, decision science theory postulates that risk for personal loss would influence a decision more than opportunity for an equivalent gain or preserving current resources. Consequential real-world decisions about community living options are value based, as when "a subjective measure like utility is used to assign the relative desirability of each choice" (Gold & Shadlen, 2007, p. 560).

AGING PROCESS HEALTH RESOURCING

The aging process conditions, which older adults negotiate for successful aging, require comprehensive responses to mitigate the effects, including personal resourcing for self-managing their own health, social support by family, clinician support, and living arrangements. These resources optimize when working interactively, and their particular qualities would differ across individuals. Personal factors or "the particular background of an individual's life and living, including features of the individual that are not part of a health condition or health states," can affect functioning "positively or negatively" (Grotkamp et al., 2012; p. 48). These include individual differences such as gender, age, ethnicity, learning orientation, educational level, social background, past and current experience, overall behavior pattern, and so forth.

While older adults may perceive successful aging differently, they would seek to "select" and "optimize" present and prospective relationship capabilities for living well with an aging process condition (WHO & NIA, 2019). The hierarchical compensatory model (Barnett & Cantu, 2019; Pinquart & Sörensen, 2002) proposes that older adults would invest in health resources that they perceived to be accessible and efficient in meeting their needs, rather than in those requiring high effort demands to access or utilize. In making their choices about which health relationships to implement, older adults would consider their specific life situations. There is evidence to suggest that cues and prompts in the environment (as in life situations) make it likely that decisions regarding behavior will be made and implemented (Milkman et al., 2011). Box 12.1, which appears at the end of this section, illuminates these dynamics.

Technologies may help older adults aging with disability to participate and live independently in their communities. Use of computer and internet technologies by older adults (65+ years of age) is on the increase from 12% in 2002, to 67% in 2016 (Anderson & Perrin, 2017), a 42% increase in a decade and a half. By 2017, about 75% of U.S. households had a desktop or laptop, while 77% of adults in the United States had a handheld device such as a smartphone, and 51% had a computer tablet (U.S. Bureau of the Census, 2017). Within the senior population of adults, 82% of the younger older adults (<69 years) utilized internet-based resources, compared to 90% of the general adult population who regularly utilize online resources (Anderson & Perrin, 2017). Use of smart technology by older adults is employed more extensively by relatively young older adults (<65 years) who are more educated, have higher annual incomes, are healthier and more active, and are recognized members of their communities rather than a part of underrepresented segments of older adults (Anderson & Perrin, 2017; Berner et al., 2012; Cresci et al., 2010). This becomes particularly important with use adoption of smart technologies, in which there is a huge digital disparity divide that hinders older people with lower technology-use literacy from any cause, including intersectionalities in social disadvantage from lower socioeconomic status, disability, race, gender, disability, and rurality.

Personal Resourcing

With the aging process, gaps increasingly occur between what a person decides and what they actually do and can do (Glass et al., 1999). This has significant implications for self-management by older adults aging with or into disability. Older adults tend to invest in personal resourcing for health relationships that they perceive to be accessible to them, appropriate, and lower in intensity of resource-support demands, including decisional influences (Bruine de Bruin et al., 2012; Finucane et al., 2002).

Self-management is at the core of independent community living and participation, benefiting older adults in terms of autonomy, self-determination, and prioritization of personal values for preferred lifestyle (Mpofu, 2014; Ruchinskas, 2010). While older adults have aging-related declines in the efficiency of their decision-making, preferring to make deliberative or sequential-staged decisions over extended time or activity frames (Bruine de Bruin et al., 2012), they also show remarkable efficiency in motivated selectivity in decision-making, drawing upon their greater experience in managing their life situations (Peters et al., 2007). For this reason, older adults managing aging-related health trauma would make effective life situation decisions that are based on past experiences in providing appropriate guidance (Mata & Nunes, 2010) and about issues with which they had a higher affect investment (Slovic et al., 2007). There is evidence to suggest that affect may be resilient to the aging process, and affect-laden decisions would be a serviceable vehicle for life-situation decisions in older age (Peters et al., 2007).

Social Resourcing

In their social resourcing for health, older adults would prioritize spouses and children as their inner circle of social support, while other relatives and friends are in the middle circle (Huxhold et al., 2014). Other social partners would be in the outermost circle. Predictably, people in the inner circle, advantaged by the proximity in relationships, may have a stronger influence on life satisfaction than people in the outer circles (Antonucci, 1994). Family members are physically and psychologically closer to individuals than other people (e.g., friends, acquaintances) and typically provide relatively more social support than would other social relationships (O'Connor, 1995; Yeung & Fung, 2007). Thus, family and partners would be an important social referent group for older adults in their health management decisions.

People are more likely to adopt healthcare decisions that they perceive to be in line with how social referent group others (like family, partners, or significant others) would behave in a similar choice situation, perceiving them to be a source of accurate information about the appropriate behavior for the context (Holroyd-Leduc et al., 2016; Popejoy, 2005). This social influence occurs mostly through implicit communication by others in the person's social network regarding the desirability of health actions of the individual (Melnick & Li, 2018). The latter behavioral choice may be explained by the prosocial motives that people hold about their health decisions (Betsch et al., 2015), the implementation of which would serve to enhance their self-image with social referent group others, like family (Vietri et al., 2012). Moreover, older adults' decisional values may change over time, based on experience and interpretation of present and emerging social sources of information, thus altering the implicit decision rules about a desired health goal state (Gold & Shadlen, 2007; Pinquart & Sörensen, 2002).

Clinician Resourcing

Older adults would rely on their clinician relationship for guidance on their health decision choices. The effect would occur through in-built situational supports for a behavior, saving the person the additional effort to decide and act on a behavior (Chapman et al., 2016; Rodrigues et al., 2015). For instance, the decision to opt out of a health support is more likely than the choice to opt in, so that clients with the choice to opt out for a flu-shot appointment were more likely to keep the appointment, compared to those with the option to schedule an appointment if they wished (Chapman et al., 2016). Even a question about when to carry out a health action (e.g., cancer screening: Rodrigues et al., 2015; taking a flu-shot: Milkman et al., 2011) increased the probability of a pro-health decision implementation as much as making the decision to adopt a pro-health decision as the default decision (Patel et al., 2014). This effect most likely occurs through solution need priming, as with older adults who, upon being asked to consider use adoption of a clinician, supported aging process support for their everyday living. However, once a decision magnitude value is reached, the tendency to adopt a present choice decision as the default becomes subjectively compelling, so that additional valuable information may pass for noise and not be considered.

Recommendation of a particular decision by healthcare clinicians also enhanced its chances of a pro-health decision implementation (Brewer et al., 2017), probably due to the recommendation assuming a default decision status. Finally, a decision-maker's sense of self-control is enhanced through self-binding to a course of action with the use of a commitment device (Mochon et al., 2017; Schwartz et al., 2014). However, older adults would vary in their adherence to health maintenance, as prescribed by clinicians, based on their individual preferences (Jansen et al., 2016).

Use of Smart Technologies

The use of sensor-monitoring devices that measure and support daily functioning by older adults living independently is on the increase, enabling their aging in place, in the comfort of their homes, and with a sense of community safety. Those older adults with assisted living also increasingly use smart technologies to (self) monitor their daily living and community participation access (Bruce, 2012). These digital devices serve to support older adults' ADLs: bADLs, and iADLs. As mentioned earlier in this chapter, bADLs primarily involve personal care actions such as bathing, dressing, feeding, toileting, continence, and transfers, while iADLs involve participation in life situations like shopping, recreation and leisure, traveling, managing finances, and use of communication tools. With the aging process, declines in physical and cognitive function are associated with declines in the performance of ADLs, and the use of sensor surveillance technologies for tracking the older adult's functional status may be needed for successful aging in place or for quality-assisted living (Cornelis et al., 2017). Sensors can be wearable, allowing for ongoing monitoring of the older adult's physiological and accelometric activity statuses, while nonwearable (environment attached) devices utilize interconnected devices with or without internet connectivity to support participation in life situations. Smart homes are those residences equipped with interconnected devices to allow information exchanges between or among end users, who may be older adults who live in a home, and others elsewhere who may be clinicians.

Box 12.1 illuminates many of the older adult-related resources that have been discussed throughout this chapter.

Mr. Kempton was a lifelong smoker and occasional drinker, and this, in some respects, can affect overall health and susceptibility to certain health conditions. Being from the Baby

BOX 12.1

Health Relationships Resourcing Following Stroke in Older Age

Mr. Roger Kempton is a 67-year-old man who is a retired Transportation Security Administration officer. He is living with aging process-related stroke conditions characterized by a right middle cerebral artery territory cerebral infarct with residual left hemiparesis, left sensory loss, visual field deficits, dysphagia, and receptive aphasia. Mr. Kempton also experiences right shoulder pain. He has a history of smoking and occasional alcohol drinking.

From the stroke experience, Mr. Kempton has moderate loss of muscle power functions of right upper and lower limbs. He also has difficulties following simple two-step directives, and impaired spoken language comprehension. Mr. Kempton needs assistance with mobility and activities of daily living, including with walking, self–care, and acquisition of goods and services. He has stopped attending local senior person group activities.

Mr. Kempton lives alone in a split-level house in a rural area. The side access of the house has four stairs with a steep unpaved pathway. The house has two stairs at the front access and two stairs between the living area and kitchen, without any rails. In addition, the shower recess and toilet have no rails. The fact that he is living alone without family is a major barrier to his well-being.

Personal resourcing. Mr. Kempton is eligible for aged care community services. An older adult age helper from a local community agency is providing personal activities like showering, house cleaning, and meal preparation. Mr. Kempton asked for his daughter, in an enduring guardianship process, to assist him; this was due to his impaired communication functions, and would save him undue burden self-managing his life situation following his stroke experience. He also expressed a preference to move in with his daughter, who has a disability-friendly single story house.

Social resourcing. Following his stroke experience, Mr. Kempton is provided with community transport to visit a local day center and for shopping, thus increasing social participation. He required a disability taxi or disability community transport.

(continued)

Clinician resourcing To resource Mr. Kempton for self-managing his physical functioning, he is taking physical therapy from his clinicians for muscle strengthening and balance and mobility training with an aid.

Assistive technology. The community agency also provided for an electronic home safety sensor for quick-help calls. Moreover, home modifications for his independent living included a ramp for wheelchair access and a walking frame to facilitate community access.

Boomer generation (1946–1964), his birth cohort has experienced chronic conditions exacerbated by the environmental exposures of their time, such as unregulated pollution, use of materials with asbestos, and the lead paint that was in many old houses, thus predisposing them to lung disease with susceptibility from smoking. Smoking was trendy among the Baby Boomers, and unregulated for most of the period that Mr. Kempton was an adult, as the long-term dangers were not well recognized.

Successful aging is likely among those aging with the health support resources for it. Being a retired transportation officer, Mr. Kempton would have had decent financial resources, inclusive of retirement savings and health insurance coverage. However, his rural residence may have constrained access to critical care services that simply were not available in rural locations.

CONCLUSION

The older adult population will endure one or more of the aging process-related health conditions for which they need a broad spectrum of relationships and resources to manage. At the same time, older adults are at an elevated risk for abuse and exploration in their relationships with family and other caregivers, for which they would need resourcing to mitigate potential or experienced risk. Older adult abuse is often an invisible phenomenon. Those most at risk of abuse are the "oldest old" (aged over 85 years). They may be socially isolated, living with several aging process conditions and with diminishing physical, social, and financial resources. Caregivers of older adults need to anticipate the typical aging process conditions that older adults would live with to best cultivate and support health support relationships with the older adults. Health relationship partnerships with older adults are critical to preventing, stopping, and ameliorating risk for abuse on them, for which they would be faced with diminishing resources to counteract in the face of also managing aging process conditions.

The older adult population is diverse, not only regarding their demographics, but also related to the aging processes with which they live and for which they would seek supportive relationships. This chapter addressed the major aging processing for which older adults would require supportive health relationships across a broad range of interactions, from their own self-management to the support of family and significant others, along with that of clinicians. Caregivers of older adults such as their physicians, case managers, nurses, and social workers seek to assist older adults in achieving a health-related quality of life. These supports are optimized with relationship building and maintenance in which the older adults themselves are active participants. Treating older adults as mere passengers in their own life journeys would be tantamount to maltreatment and abuse.

By focusing specifically on the decisional needs of older adults in the health relationship resourcing that they would need, the risk of patronizing older adults and providing them with suboptimal or unwanted health support is minimized. While relationship resourcing of older adults may not be the panacea for age-related structural disadvantage inequity in health services, approaches that are based on an understanding of the major aging process health conditions would contribute to implementing interventions for their overall health and well-being. Use of smart technologies increasingly will play a major role in the health relationship self-management of older adults. Such technologies will make a difference to the extent that they provide options to address present and emerging health needs from the aging process.

ADDITIONAL RESOURCES

 A robust set of instructor resources designed to supplement this text is located at http://connect.springerpub.com/content/book/978-0-8261-5085-1. Qualifying instructors may request access by emailing textbook@springerpub.com.

PRACTICE-BASED RESOURCES AND REFERENCES

To view a list of resources and all the references, please visit connect.springerpub.com via the following url: http://connect.springerpub.com/content/book/978-0-8261-5085-1/part/part02/chapter/ch12

CHAPTER 13

Addictions and Psychological Trauma: Implications for Counseling Strategies

RACHEL WURZMAN

CHAPTER OVERVIEW

This chapter focuses on conceptualizing addiction in relationship to the experience of trauma. It briefly covers some of the major theoretical orientations used to understand how addiction develops in individuals with diagnosable substance use disorders and co-occurring trauma. The chapter highlights the importance of social neuroscience and identifies stigma-related obstacles to recovery. The chapter concludes with discussions of treatment approaches and strategies as well as the counseling implications of co-occurring substance use and trauma disorders.

LEARNING OBJECTIVES

After reading this chapter, the reader should be able to:

1. Define addiction;
2. Conceptualize addiction in relation to trauma;
3. Develop an understanding of the relevant neuroscience related to co-occurring substance abuse and trauma;
4. Appreciate the role of social health in biopsychosocial treatments; and
5. Identify pertinent treatment approaches and counseling strategies.

   "Not why the addiction, but why the pain." – Gabor Mate

INTRODUCTION

Many have noted that addiction and trauma go hand in hand. Trauma counselors are likely to encounter clients frequently whose use of substances or compulsive behaviors is problematic. Understanding what addiction is and appreciating the heterogenicity of addictive disorder presentations, particularly with coincident trauma, is necessary for sound decision-making about when clients require additional services or a higher level of care. It ultimately is necessary to treat addiction and trauma in an integrated fashion, as failure to address one often sabotages attempts to treat the other.

This chapter is a revision of the chapter that appeared in the first edition of this textbook, written by Patricia A. Burke and Bruce Carruth, and we thank them for their original contribution here.

Some studies report that up to 95% of clients with a substance use disorder (SUD) also report a history of trauma in one form or another, and posttraumatic stress disorder (PTSD) is one of the co-occurring disorders with the highest prevalence in clients undergoing substance use treatment (Brown et al., 1999). While estimates vary, most studies of co-occurring disorders report that at least 50% of people seeking treatment for an SUD meet the criteria for PTSD. Co-occurring PTSD and SUDs have problematic prognoses, as they tend to relapse more quickly and experience stronger cravings for drugs, alcohol, addictive foods, and compulsive behaviors compared to those without PTSD (Coffey et al., 2002).

This chapter introduces distinct yet complementary ways of conceptualizing addiction and its relationship to the experience of trauma. It offers an overview of principles and approaches to treating co-occurring trauma and addictive disorders, as well as important considerations regarding social supports and recovery groups as adjuncts to treatment. This is accomplished in the following major sections of the chapter: Defining Addiction: Substance Use and Related "Addictive" Disorders; Ways of Conceptualizing Addiction in Relation to Trauma; Social Neuroscience: The Missing Link Between Trauma and Addiction; Presentations of Trauma and Addiction; Sequential, Parallel, and Integrated Treatment of Addiction and Psychological Trauma; Treatment Approaches and Counseling Strategies; Counseling Implications; and the Conclusion.

DEFINING ADDICTION: SUBSTANCE USE AND RELATED "ADDICTIVE" DISORDERS

The American Society of Addiction Medicine (2021) defines "addiction" as both a medical disease and as involving environmental interactions. Importantly, addiction as a construct is not the same thing as becoming physically dependent upon a substance and experiencing physical withdrawal symptoms. For some substances, such as alcohol, opioids, and sugar (among others), prolonged use requires more of the substance to produce the same effect ("tolerance"), and abrupt cessation of the substance will result in physical symptoms ("withdrawal"), which can be life-threatening for substances like alcohol and opioids. (Sugar withdrawal entails a much-attenuated version of these withdrawal syndromes without any risk of mortality, but sugar affects many of the same neurotransmitter systems in the same brain regions, which is why it has long been known to help ease withdrawal from drugs and alcohol.) Yet while physical withdrawal and dependence is one factor that is considered in diagnosing an SUD, it is not a sufficient cause, or even the primary biological mechanism driving compulsive substance use. Other more important changes occur in the brain. Such changes may lead to loss of control over use, a change in the capacity to feel pleasure and motivation with respect to anything other than the drug, and changes in inhibitory control and decision-making circuits that cause a person to be unable to stop seeking and using the substance despite profoundly negative consequences. These brain changes also readily occur in response to repeated exposure to drugs that do not have a physical withdrawal profile, such as cocaine. Not everyone who uses highly addictive drugs, such as crack cocaine or even heroin, becomes addicted—in fact, it is a minority who do. Substantial scientific research is devoted to understanding the complex interplay among biological, psychological, and social factors that render some individuals more vulnerable than others to becoming more readily or quickly addicted, relative to length or intensity of drug exposure.

In addition to SUDs, the *Diagnostic and Statistical Manual of Mental Disorders* (5th ed.; *DSM-5*; American Psychiatric Association, 2013) introduces the diagnostic category of "Substance-Related and Addictive Disorders" to refer to so-called "process addictions," or compulsive behaviors that exhibit the same features of SUDs. These include factors such as loss of control over the behavior (i.e., doing more than intended or for longer than intended), continuing to engage in the behavior despite severe negative consequences and/or a desire to stop, needing more over time to get the same effect (tolerance), and even withdrawal symptoms. At the time of this writing, only gambling disorder has been officially specified in this category, but several other behaviors were considered, including shopping, internet gaming, pornography viewing, nonsuicidal self-mutilation ("cutting"), and food addiction (Potenza, 2014). The committees considered that there was insufficient evidence at the time to include these as diagnostic entities, but they identified the need for further research, and additions to the category of substance-related and addictive disorders have been anticipated over time. In a later section of this chapter, frameworks for conceptualizing addiction in relation to trauma are offered in order to guide the trauma counselor in addressing these other compulsive behaviors when they function analogously to substance use in clients' lives.

A more colloquial way of conceptualizing addiction is also relevant to consider. As Dr. Gabor Maté observed in a recorded interview with this author, we live in a culture that breeds compulsive behavior as a means to soothe the prickly emotional edges of rugged individualism and shame-based self-reliance (SeekHealing, 2020). Popular cultural conceptions of addictions may encompass things like "bingeing Netflix" or obsessively consuming social media feeds focusing on niche interests, adult coloring books, and excessive indulgence in hobbies such as knitting or baking. This broad definition of addiction contains two elements related to compulsion: (a) a pattern of obsessive thinking about engaging in a behavior that elicits a feeling of being high or intoxicated or that reduces anxiety or hyperarousal and (b) feeling compelled to persist in that behavior despite negative consequences. Human beings have a tendency to turn compulsively to activities and behaviors that help us to self-soothe or emotionally self-regulate when we feel pain that overwhelms our resources for coping.

While these more normalized impulsive and/or compulsive behaviors often do not rise to the level of "real" addiction phenomena, they are useful to consider for a few reasons. First, they reveal something essential about the human condition to which the clinician, family member, and individual with an SUD can relate alike: we all impulsively make decisions that do not serve us when we feel painfully uncomfortable or disconnected from others or our lives. We begin to see that the concept of harm reduction is relevant to all drug use *and* compulsive behavioral engagement, with human beings attempting to balance the harms of continuing to experience painful emotions with the harms caused by the means for relief. This understanding can help normalize addiction, in ways that reduce both stigma and self-stigma, which are significant obstacles to recovery. Second, these manifestations reveal addictive behaviors as existing on a spectrum of normal to pathological, depending primarily on the degree to which a behavior impairs one's functioning in life. Yet it follows from this that such impairment may be more related to the social consequences of the behavioral dependence (often related to its stigma or legality) than the actual pattern of its use; we might consider caffeine versus morphine as an example. A compulsive behavior that is less mind-altering—say, compulsive book-coloring, television-binging, or shopping—can nevertheless lead to loss of employment and relationships. If we consider that there is a spectrum of compulsive reward-seeking behaviors that humans use to escape feelings of dis-ease or pain, then we can shift our focus to intervening with the factors that contribute to such dis-ease, which may be biological, psychological, and/or *relational* in nature.

Considering how biological, psychological, and relational social factors interact in complex ways to generate the powerful human motivational drive for relief, we finally arrive at the other universal human experience: trauma. Whether "big T" or "little t" trauma, all humans experience stressors which outstrip our capacity for coping at one time or another. Elsewhere in this volume is extensive discussion about what influences resilience to and recovery from the enduring effects of such experiences. In this chapter, we consider some of the underlying reasons for why addictive disorders are so astoundingly prevalent in individuals with traumatic histories, which involves both social and neurobiological consequences of trauma-begotten shame and isolation. Approaching both the conception and treatment of trauma and addiction through this lens adds nuance to considerations of best practices for intervening and treating both categories of disorders, and especially their co-occurrence. Ultimately, this perspective elevates the importance not only of biological and psychological treatment, but also social-relational interventions, which, until recently, have received little attention, despite the nominally biopsychosocial model used widely in assessment and treatment.

WAYS OF CONCEPTUALIZING ADDICTION IN RELATION TO TRAUMA

The Disease Model

There are several ways to conceptualize addiction, and it benefits the trauma counselor to be aware of these. The most dominant is the disease model, which considers that SUDs and so-called "process addictions" or behavioral addictions are the product of abnormalities in brain circuitries responsible for reward, motivation, memory, and related functions. While it is recognized that abnormalities in these brain regions and circuits lead to characteristic biological, psychological, social, and spiritual manifestations, the disease model asserts that the primary mechanism of addiction is neurological.

Over the past few decades, a wealth of research has supported this view, which considers that while the initial consumption of the substance or performance of the behavior may have been voluntary, over time the exposure to the neuropharmacological consequences of these substances and behaviors changes the brain such that it becomes nearly impossible to stop using them. According to Volkow et al. (2016), three major neurobiological processes are implicated. First, reward circuits in the brain become desensitized, which interrupts the capacity to feel pleasure and dampens the motivation for participating in everyday activities. Second, there is an increase in stress reactivity and its coupling to conditioned responses, which increases the incidence of cravings for drugs and behaviors and elicits negative emotions when these cravings are not sated. Third, there is a weakened influence of the brain regions responsible for decision making, inhibitory control, and self-regulation—referred to collectively as executive function—which leads to repeated relapse to use of the substance or behavior (Volkow et al., 2016).

The disease model does not suppose that addiction, as a chronic, recurring illness, is simply biological in nature and expression. Proponents of the disease model such as Alan Leshner, former director of the National Institute of Drug Abuse, consider that in addition to biology, behavior and social context matter (Leshner, 1997). They consider that a complex interplay between environmental and biological (especially genetic) factors determines who may become addicted to a substance and who may not. Understanding these factors is important, because even with powerful drugs such as opioids, which create physical dependence and withdrawal in everyone, it is actually a minority of people who are exposed to such drugs and become addicted.

Trauma-Centric Explanations

Developmental trauma is one of the greatest risk factors for addiction, with extraordinarily high percentages of childhood trauma of various types found in studies of individuals experiencing addiction. The famous Adverse Childhood Experiences Study (ACES; Felitti et al., 1998) found that for every additional adverse childhood experience (ACE), the risk of early life substance abuse rose exponentially with each additional ACE experienced; if an individual had five or more ACEs, they had seven to ten times greater risk for substance abuse.

There are two complementary explanations for this relationship between trauma and addiction. The first is that trauma, by definition, generates stress that overwhelms an individual's capacity to cope. People who use drugs often self-medicate in order to cope with the psychic and somatic consequences of trauma such as emotional dysregulation (both numbness and overwhelming pain), flashbacks, and shame. Developmental trauma is particularly associated with addiction, because it interferes with the development of brain systems responsible for stress responses, memory, motivation, impulse control, and behavioral "autopilot." This results in an inability to control the impulse to use a substance under stressful circumstances—and unfortunately, such brains are predisposed to perceive everyday occurrences as more stressful (Maté, 2010, p. 203) (Box 13.1).

BOX 13.1

A Note About Food Addiction

Of the potential "substance-related and addictive disorders," food addiction merits special attention for two reasons. First, the accumulating evidence makes it likely to become one of the next "behavioral addictions" to join gambling disorder as an explicit diagnosis. Second, the putative category of food addiction is highly relevant to trauma counseling because eating disorders, and especially binge-eating, are so prevalent in individuals with developmental and especially sexual trauma (Madowitz et al., 2015). Particularly for individuals who experienced childhood sexual abuse or rape, morbid obesity affords a feeling of safety and "sexual invisibility" by eliminating sexual attraction as a potential threat source. For many traumatized individuals, highly rewarding food use and binge-eating also provide a means to "ground" into one's body, in much the same way as has been proposed for "cutting" behaviors (van der Kolk, 2014). Alternatively, some behaviors may enable dissociation from the body, as with food restriction or the innate chemical consequences of purging. In this way, food and compulsive food behaviors are used as "drugs" to self-soothe and/or escape from an uncomfortably dysphoric experience, which traumatized individuals may perpetually feel, particularly when under stress.

Evidence for considering food addiction within the neurobiological umbrella of other addictions is steadily accumulating. Sugar and highly concentrated saturated fat have been shown to activate the endogenous opioid system in the same way as alcohol and painkillers (Colantuoni et al., 2002). Excessive exercise and induced vomiting also cause a rush of endogenous opioid release, which may lead, over time, to both tolerance to and withdrawal from purging behaviors in bulimia nervosa, leading some to suggest that such "behavioral addictions" are simply endogenous opioid addictions (Milkman & Sunderwirth, 2009). Similarly, the release of stress hormones, adrenaline, and norepinephrine with fasting may render anorexia an endogenous stimulant addiction in some individuals, with accompanying cravings for food restriction, and withdrawal symptoms when eating regularly.

It remains controversial whether certain ingredients such as sugars, high concentrations of saturated fat, and flour may have intrinsically addictive properties and whether food addiction is a construct that warrants consideration alongside (or apart from) eating disorders. However, its proponents note that similar neurobiological features have been reported for gambling, substance use (including tobacco), and binge-eating disorder (Potenza, 2014). There are some who think that food addiction is simply an extreme form or advanced state of progression of the named eating disorders. Others have hypothesized that multiple cases of each recognized eating disorder may meet a common set of criteria but actually exist on one of two different spectrums, an obsessive-compulsive/anxiety spectrum or an addiction spectrum (with the latter more frequently encompassing bulimia nervosa and binge-eating disorder than anorexia nervosa and orthorexia, but not necessarily to their exclusion). The difference between locating an eating disorder construct on one or the other spectrum may have to do with the way that some brains and bodies of individuals with eating disorders react abnormally to specific food ingredients, much like the phenomenon that occurs when people meeting diagnostic criteria for alcohol use disorder take the first drink.

While there are more women diagnosed with eating disorders than men, evidence suggests that the actual prevalence of lifetime eating disorders of women to men may be as high as 3 to 1 (Ziółkowska & Mroczkowska, 2020). Eating disorders in men are underdiagnosed, due to stigma and a lack of recognition, and may be diagnosed more frequently in nonheterosexual men due to stereotypes. Eating disorders may present differently with men, associated with a preoccupation with muscularity instead of thinness, and while many men with bulimia nervosa also purge through vomiting, purging behavior as a compulsive exercise may go unrecognized by clinicians. Eating disorders and food addiction should be screened for,

(continued)

particularly in men with histories of childhood trauma and substance abuse disorders. In one study, men with opioid use disorders (OUDs) have been found to be three times as likely to have food addiction or a binge-type eating disorder compared to control men (Canan et al., 2017). This connection to OUDs is unsurprising, when one considers that Naloxone, the opioid blocker that reverses overdose, was shown to reduce consumption of sweet high-fat foods in both obese and lean female binge eaters (Drewnowski et al., 1995). The National Comorbidity Survey-Replication found that a lifetime diagnosis of SUDs is associated with as much as a threefold risk of anorexia nervosa, an eightfold risk of bulimia nervosa, and a fivefold risk of binge-eating disorder, although these factors varied somewhat by the substance of abuse (Hudson et al., 2007).

Just as trauma is associated with an elevated risk for SUDs, the same is true for eating disorders and food addiction. For both men and women, sexual and physical abuse are associated with significantly higher rates of eating disorders, with emotional abuse more tied to eating disorders in women and physical neglect more tied to eating disorders in men. It also is common for individuals with traumatic histories to become cross-addicted in recovery and to substitute food for drug and alcohol use, and vice versa (Afifi et al., 2017). This is important for the trauma counselor to be aware of, particularly if a newly alcohol- or drug-abstinent client starts gaining weight rapidly. Later in the chapter, resources for individuals manifesting behaviors with food that resemble alcohol use disorders are suggested. As with all addictions, it is necessary to integrate trauma treatment with addiction treatment to avoid treatment sabotage by forcing abstinence without adequate trauma support, thereby leaving individuals without their only defensive coping mechanism for the effects of trauma.

SOCIAL NEUROSCIENCE: THE MISSING LINK BETWEEN TRAUMA AND ADDICTION

Systems and Spectrums

Addiction is not a monolithic entity. While the diagnostic criteria for SUDs may be met, the subjective phenomena and use patterns may vary widely among individuals. Some people have patterns of prolonged binges punctuating long stretches of abstinence; some people become obsessively preoccupied with using a substance after the very first exposure, while others find their experience of a particular substance changed after a particular life event, triggering an escalation in use and eventual loss of control. Phenomenological examinations of addiction patterns reveal different subjective experiences of the same diagnosed entity. For example, many people who are self-medicating with alcohol may begin drinking addictively after exposure to a traumatic event to cope with posttraumatic symptoms, and may become physically dependent—clearly qualifying for an SUD. Yet a subset of these people may not be a true instance of the "alcoholism" phenomenon as it was described by the first 100 "recovered alcoholics" of Alcoholics Anonymous (1939) in their eponymous book. That book's understanding reflected the then-prevailing medical perspective that alcoholism involved a physical "allergy" to alcohol. This "allergy" manifests as uncontrolled drinking after a single drink. The other qualifier was an experience of "mental blank spots" occurring at varying frequencies that prevented the individual, in the moment, from having any mental defense against that first drink (such as sufficient recall of a painful memory of previous experience). However, some individuals who have experienced severe trauma may drink to oblivion, not because of a physically mediated inability to stop drinking induced by the first drink, but because they are always intentionally seeking oblivion. (Of course, these conditions are not mutually exclusive, and individuals may be aware of only one while both may be operative.)

Typically, in individuals who qualify for an alcohol use disorder (AUD) diagnosis, the prolonged effect of alcohol on the brain alters brain circuits permanently, and the inability to drink moderately becomes permanently hard-wired, like the development of a severe allergy to a previously safe substance. However, a subset of people exists who may present with an identical pattern of drinking and consequences as others with an AUD. Some of these people find that, once they adequately have treated their trauma, they are again able to drink moderately. Many such people experience a deterioration of overall mental health, after resuming substance use, or else they may manifest cross-addictions, such as with food. This is *not* the norm, and it counters the prevailing wisdom of "once an alcoholic, always an alcoholic." Because it is exceedingly rare that such experiments have positive outcomes for clients (and many are lethally disastrous), it is not considered ethical to allow for the possibility that a person might drink again safely one day. However, the existence of such people who, after trauma treatment, no longer feel compulsively driven to drink excessively bespeaks the actual heterogenicity of the phenomena which may all check the same set of diagnostic boxes. They demonstrate that, from a phenomenological standpoint, not everyone who drinks according to the same pattern has the same physical reaction to alcohol.

The concept that the same constellation of symptoms can arise from different combinations of physical manifestations is known as the *spectrum model*. *Spectrum disorders* are those disorders associated with a common larger set of symptoms that may present in different combinations and to different degrees in different individuals. SUDs not only occur on a spectrum from mild to severe (from a diagnostic standpoint, depending on how many of the listed symptoms are present), but they also occur on a spectrum of different patterns, such as an intermittent binge pattern, compared to a daily use pattern with physical dependence. The diagnostic concept of *spectrum* also connotes addictive phenomena that exist on a spectrum from normal (i.e., drinking more than intended occasionally) to pathological (i.e., drinking to blackout every time despite consistent intentions to have only one drink). Often, the boundary between normal and pathological is arbitrary, or determined by the consequences or degree of functional impairment. The spectrum model of neuropsychiatric disorders also is used to account for diagnoses that tend to co-occur, such as attention deficit disorder and depression, or Tourette syndrome, obsessive-compulsive disorder, and anxiety. The reason why these symptoms and diagnoses manifest in clusters is because each symptom or disorder may involve brain circuits that are critically implicated in other symptoms or disorders as well. If a particular brain circuit functions abnormally in a given way, either or both disorders may result, depending on the combination of other brain abnormalities that also are present (Wurzman, in press).

When we look at the brain as a set of circuits that sometimes share brain regions, like transfer stations of different colored subway lines, we begin to see that the brain is not a collection of brain regions but of functional brain systems that share brain regions. A systems understanding of the brain and a spectrum understanding of diagnoses are implicitly tied to one another, because spectrums of symptoms can be explained by systems that share "hubs" for brain activity involved in several functions. If something affects a hub, it will have downstream effects on multiple systems in characteristic ways. If something affects a set of hubs, it starts to limit the range of brain states that the set of symptoms can create. As a result, some brain states may start appearing more often than others, and these may be clustered according to which brain hubs have been affected. This tendency for the brain to occupy certain states more than others is what manifests as chronic inattention, depression, or anxiety—among many other possibilities.

Why is a systems understanding of the brain and the spectrum disorder model relevant to understanding trauma and addiction as co-occurring disorders? There are a few reasons. First, it follows from these understandings that something like trauma, which presents a functional insult to certain brain systems, can, over time, cause a spectrum of other symptoms to emerge by changing the function of key "hubs" for brain activity responsible for operations such as behavioral inhibition or emotional reactivity. In other words, the experience of trauma *or* experiences that may commonly follow trauma, such as perceived social isolation, may alter the activity of brain systems that *also* play a role in addiction. (By this logic, one might argue that trauma itself could be thought of as a spectrum disorder.) Second, it gives us a neurobiological understanding of the biopsychosocial model that clinicians commonly use for assessment and/or treatment. The biopsychosocial model considers that addiction results from a complex interplay among biological, psychological, and social factors. A systems understanding of the brain can help to explain how social factors could set the conditions for neurobiological abnormalities to emerge, or how cognitive behavioral therapy can lead to neurochemical shifts toward health, as a result of practicing less distorted thought patterns. Third, and perhaps most important, it suggests that biological, psychological, *or* social factors left *unaddressed* during treatment can act like dead weight to the system's *status quo*, preventing the individual's brain from shifting patterns among sets of brain-state patterns frequently experienced to patterned sets of brain-states that are more conducive to recovery and behavioral change (Wurzman, in press).

Social Neuroscience Implications for the Biopsychosocial Model in Addiction

As mentioned, the biopsychosocial model considers that addiction presentation is influenced by a complex interplay among biological, psychological, and social factors. Herein may lie a key clue as to why addiction has been so challenging to treat. Treatment systems often give lip service adherence to the biopsychosocial model for addiction, but in action, they often fail to appreciate some of the most critical implications of the model. Most important is the concept that if biological, psychological, and social factors have a complex interaction, then an intervention or stressor that influences any one of these factors will therefore have detectable effects in the other two domains. Each has the power to influence the presentation of any given SUD, but none can be considered in isolation of the others. For example, prolonged exposure to certain drugs such as opioids, alcohol, or methamphetamine changes the neurobiological substrate on which these drugs act. The neural microcircuitry that underlies the drug's effects as well as the neural circuits involved in volition, cognitive control, and impulse inhibition all become modified by exposure to the substance over time, such that it is no longer possible for an individual consciously to override an urge or impulse to use, despite a strong desire to do so. However, to reduce this to a mere biological phenomenon misses the essential point that factors other than drugs (or even comorbid diagnoses) can induce plasticity and "tune" the settings of these circuits (Wurzman, in press).

One such variable capable of "tuning" the brain's reward circuitry is social connection. Recent neuroscientific advances have demonstrated that social reward systems overlap with reward and motivational circuits associated with addictive drug effects. Social exclusion activates networks involved in pain perception, including the anterior insula activity, which also is seen to correlate with subjective cravings for addictive drugs in humans (Garavan, 2010). This is just one example of how functional neuroanatomy supports the biopsychosocial model, with relational social variables influencing the sensitivity of neural circuits that underlie addictive behaviors. It also highlights another consideration for proponents of the biopsychosocial model: the need to consider social factors as relational, instead of merely "social determinants of health" (e.g., housing near drug trafficking, active addiction in family members, socioeconomic stress) (Hunter-Reel et al., 2009). The biopsychosocial model most often makes reference to these nonrelational social factors as targets for intervention in treatment. While that is certainly a wise course of action, emerging neuroscience linking human disconnection and social deprivation with increased addictive and compulsive behaviors, coupled with evidence that social reward and addictive reward circuits overlap, suggests that relational dimensions of social factors, such as meaningful interpersonal connections, may be an even more important target for intervention (Heilig et al., 2016).

Currently, we have excellent interventions for biological factors in addiction: we have opioid agonist therapies for treating OUDs; we have medications for treating comorbid psychiatric and medical diagnoses; and we can intervene to improve functions like sleep and nutrition. There is a strong evidence base for practice in the psychological domain as well, including the following interventions (detailed in Chapter 27, "Trauma, Crisis, and Disaster Interventions:

Integrative Approaches to Therapy" and Chapter 28, "Selected Strategies and Techniques for Counseling Survivors of Trauma"): cognitive and dialectical behavioral therapies to address cognitive distortions and emotional dysregulation; motivational interviewing to help clients move through the stages of change; relapse prevention training to teach clients constructive ways to cope with triggers and cravings; narrative therapy for social empowerment; Eye Movement Desensitization and Reprocessing (EMDR) therapy; and somatic therapies for treating trauma. Compared with these mental health treatments, existing social interventions are of a categorically different order. Presently, they tend to be limited to arranging for access to safe, sober housing; vocational rehabilitation; and perhaps a suggestion to find a volunteer position "to do service." Unlike mental health therapies, these do not aim to modify an individual's internal experience directly. The closer equivalent to mental health treatments would be interventions that support an individual to experience being vulnerable yet safe in relationship with others. Professionals are increasingly recognizing the need to support clients with social skills training and, even more importantly, safe contexts in which to practice experiencing healthy relationships and being a part of a community—and new programs are emerging to meet this need. Without the means to meet the relational needs of clients entering recovery, neurobiological and psychological interventions frequently are stymied by difficulties in shifting brain-state patterns, due to the gravity of neurochemical consequences of social disconnection. Social health interventions, if they lead to experiences of authentic human connection, have the potential to affect, directly, brain circuitry that is hijacked by addictive drug use, and therefore can act in synergy with the bio- and psychological interventions seeking to install new neural and behavioral patterns (Wurzman, in press). While these interventions are new and still experimental, as the field of social health is emerging, successful pilot programs and a strong theoretical rationale bodes well for their ultimate validation. One such program, SeekHealing, is featured in Box 13.2.

BOX 13.2

From the Field: SeekHealing: A Community-Sourced Social Health Intervention for Trauma and Addiction

Jennifer Nicolaisen, Co-Founder and Executive Director, SeekHealing, Asheville, NC

SeekHealing began when the founder's close friend survived an opioid overdose and partnered with the founder to begin a holistic healing journey. As part of this process, the two discovered the role of meaningful social connection and community belonging as critical elements in addiction recovery. Jennifer teamed up with a social cognitive neuroscientist and neuroethicist, Dr. Wurzman, and together they began to view the low recovery rates and the opioid overdose epidemic—indeed, all of the so-called "deaths of despair"—as symptoms of a broader epidemic of loneliness. The co-founders created SeekHealing to provide intentional experiences of human connection and to help individuals in communities acquire skills to socialize in healthy ways. The model is designed to serve alongside medical mental health treatment services.

Launched in 2017 in Asheville, NC, the Pilot program initially focused on serving individuals facing an addiction crisis or at risk for overdose. However, it soon became apparent that other participants who did not have a lived experience of bonding to a substance but rather experienced acutely painful disconnection associated with past trauma, recovery from other mental health conditions, or chronic health conditions were also benefiting from SeekHealing's programming. This created a spreading awareness of the need to address *social health* as a construct distinct from social determinants of health or mental health in all of these groups.

As a social health provider, SeekHealing curates and delivers the relational tools, experiential offerings, and community-driven resources that support a stable social climate and

(continued)

reduce the isolating tendencies that drive negative mental health well-being, such as substance abuse and depression. In creating (and iterating) a program where connection has been authentic, deep, and safe, SeekHealing discovered several key elements that are essential as core values for social health interventions. These include mutuality, nonhierarchy, nonjudgment, curiosity, and restraint from "fixing" or giving advice (or obtaining prior consent if advice is offered).

SeekHealing provides participants with a laboratory for focusing on their social health, while complementing the outcome-oriented elements of their other recovery systems. Centered around Community Calendar (CC), the project has regularly scheduled support meetings (in-person and online) where people can practice prosocial skills and healthy communication techniques, called Connection Practice. Other offerings include Art Therapy, Sound Meditation, Yoga, and Food From The Heart. All events are open to the public at no cost, based on a harm-reduction model, and guided by SeekHealing facilitators and volunteers. Facilitators are community members who receive 50+ hours of training and mentorship based on trauma-informed practices, transpersonal psychology, peer support, nonviolent communication, and attachment theory, developed with Dr. Gabor Mate as advisor. Participants—many of whom do not have lived experience with addiction—are led through relational exercises working to eliminate the stigma of trauma and addiction issues created by the division of staff and participants in a clinical setting. Connection Missions consist of technology-assisted, in-person outreach to activate social opportunities between volunteers and people who are isolated, struggling with active substance use cycles, or need emotional health support. These social opportunities include meal deliveries, check-in phone calls and texts, personal naloxone deliveries, herbal first aid, and pairing individuals to practice connection skills with each other. Connection Missions operate with mutuality: yesterday's "volunteer" might become the one receiving help on a less-resourced day, and vice-versa.

Additional support services are provided to individuals at risk of drug overdoses or other acute deaths of despair through the Extra Care Program, which in addition to the offerings of the CC also provides a stipend for access to holistic healing services provided by "connection agents" in the community. Their offerings include yoga, chi gong, acupuncture, ortho-bionomy, reiki, traditional psychotherapy and EMDR, spiritual counseling, nutritional and herbal support, and more, all provided with a commitment to compassionate curiosity and nonjudgment. These participants also receive more proactive outreach and meet regularly with a program coordinator, to structure and guide their engagement and to be matched with higher levels of community support when necessary. Services within the program are never contingent on abstinence. Because the program is not limited to people in recovery from an SUD and the concept of harm reduction is normalized, SeekHealing serves as a bridge to help those in early recovery reintegrate into the broader community without the experience of stigma.

SeekHealing believes that there is no mental health without social health. More information can be found at https://seekhealing.org/

The COVID-19 pandemic in 2020 and 2021 made for an unfortunate "natural" experiment of what happens when we increase social disconnection and relational deprivation. Many people's patterns of alcohol and drug use escalated sharply during the period of enforced physical distancing, leading to a loss of control and, in many cases, the first episode of substance use or disorder and treatment. Opioid overdoses, already epidemic, skyrocketed even higher. People who initially engaged in "stress baking" were qualifying for binge eating disorders by the end of the year. On the other hand, where it was available, providing for the relational needs of individuals amplified healing and recovery from the effects of social isolation exacerbated by COVID-19. While social health interventions are not a panacea, nor do they replace the need for biological and psychological interventions, they increasingly are being recognized as an essential complement to empower existing treatments to have lasting success in individuals.

Trauma, Shame, and Social Disconnection

Trauma, whether experienced during development or adulthood, is a powerful factor leading to social disconnection. Traumatic experiences often profoundly impair one's embodiment, in the sense that one may lose the ability to connect with one's inner experience, which is essential for being able to connect meaningfully with other individuals. Without the capacity to access a shared experience, relationships may become superficial and unsatisfying at best, and fearfully threatening at worst. Big attachment traumas such as abuse from a caregiver or sudden abandonment by a trusted partner, but also small attachment traumas such as ordinary day-to-day emotional wounds, can make connection feel scary and threatening. The common thread between traumas of widely varying magnitudes is the shame and feeling of "not enough" that emerges. Shame is a powerful emotion that promotes isolation and disconnection. This emotion is particularly deadly for clients who are seeking recovery from an SUD, because the trauma and its resulting shame often prevent individuals from accessing tools that could lead to connection with others. In 12-step programs, this manifests as the dreaded "10,000 pound phone phenomenon" where sponsees find it nearly impossible to take their sponsor's suggestions to reach out to either newcomers or experienced members of the program. This makes it impossible to "work the solution" that these programs offer, and the ultimate result is often a return to substance use.

The need to treat the trauma, in order to enable someone to tolerate abstinence (or the actions required to maintain that state), is discussed later in this chapter. It is important to note here, however, that the biggest consequences of trauma manifest relationally. Our trauma histories emerge in social contexts and deeply shape our social experience. The ways in which we have framed the disease model of addiction, historically, have been relatively inattentive to relational social factors. It is therefore unsurprising that, until recently, there has been a corresponding underemphasis on the role of trauma as a casual mechanism of addiction, relative to biological factors such as genetics and the lasting physical effects of drug use on the brain. Given the incredibly high rates of PTSD and SUD co-occurrence, and the nearly ubiquitous experience of some form of trauma in people diagnosed with SUDs, we need more research to understand better how social health has an impact on both pathology and recovery in addiction and trauma. Such research may clarify and confirm the consequence of neglecting social health in addiction and trauma treatment, respectively. It also may provide novel insights into barriers to recovery in present systems. If brain dynamics influencing behavior exist on biopsychosocial spectrums, social health interventions may just unlock the key to a truly integrative treatment of co-occurring disorders.

PRESENTATIONS OF TRAUMA AND ADDICTION

The relationship among the psychological/emotional aftereffects of trauma, including depression, anxiety, panic, PTSD, eating disorders, and addiction, is complex. Like all co-occurring conditions, trauma-related disorders and addictions can present themselves in several ways. For example, the development of an addiction can be an adaptive strategy for managing the emotional and psychological responses to trauma, and addiction to substances can make people more vulnerable to trauma, including rape and other kinds of violence that can cause trauma complications like PTSD.

Although the research literature indicates a strong association between trauma complications and SUDs, clinicians should not make assumptions about causal relationships. Najavits et al. (2020) suggest that co-occurring conditions like PTSD and SUDs can precede each other, follow each other, contribute to the development or course of each other, or arise independently of one another. Regardless of how trauma-related conditions and addiction present themselves and in what order, both disorders must be addressed simultaneously in treatment (Najavits et al., 2020). Furthermore, treatment is less effective in split systems, where clients may be rejected from mental health facilities until abstinent, or conversely, rejected from substance use facilities until stabilized (Najavits, 2006).

SEQUENTIAL, PARALLEL, AND INTEGRATED TREATMENT OF ADDICTION AND PSYCHOLOGICAL TRAUMA

Treatment for co-occurring trauma-related disorders and addiction can occur along three treatment trajectories: sequential, parallel, and integrated therapy. Burke and Carruth (2012, p. 214) described these trajectories, briefly, as follows:

- **Sequential treatment:** One disorder is defined as "primary" and is treated first, followed by treatment of the "secondary" disorder.
- **Parallel treatment:** Disorders are treated concurrently but in separate treatment systems or by separate clinicians, generally without much coordination between the two treatments.
- **Integrated therapy treatment:** Both disorders are treated concurrently by the same clinician or treatment system, with recognition of how each disorder impacts the recovery from the other and with a high degree of coordination within the treatment system.

Most clinicians would agree that the third option is the most efficacious; unfortunately, however, this often is not what happens in practice. First, the treatment system for substance use often does not interact with mental health treatment systems that typically address trauma-related disorders (and vice versa). Such lack of communication is not conducive for sequential treatment. Clinicians in addiction treatment settings focus on getting people sober first, assuming that the trauma symptoms may subside or can be dealt with later by a mental health clinician. Clinicians in mental health treatment settings focus on managing trauma-related symptoms first, assuming that the alcohol and drug use or other addictive behaviors may subside or can be treated later by substance abuse professionals or self-help recovery groups. When trauma is a significant factor in maintaining substance use, and integrated treatment is not available, clients often must have their trauma addressed prior to attempting complete abstinence—at least to the extent of being able to self-soothe and cultivate a sense of safety. Without some means to cope with intense and/or frightening feelings, many people are not able to tolerate abstinence long enough for substance abuse treatment to be effective. Clearly, this is an arena in which the mental health and the substance abuse sectors need to coordinate services in ways that best benefit clients.

TREATMENT APPROACHES AND COUNSELING STRATEGIES

There is no single treatment approach or strategy to address such a broad-based and complex issue as psychological trauma and co-occurring SUDs. Najavits et al. (2020, p. 545) argue in favor of a public health approach to treating PTSD/SUD comorbidity, in which the therapeutic options "meet a reasonable standard of evidence and also meet the standard of being feasible in real-world settings (a public health paradigm)." Counselors have to consider the unique needs of the client, the context in which services are provided, and counselors' own levels of training and skill in treating these co-occurring conditions. In this section, I examine some overarching approaches and specific strategies for integrated treatment of SUDs and trauma.

Treating the Symptom Versus Treating the Problem

A basic dilemma in both addiction and trauma treatment concerns symptom management versus treating the underlying dynamic. The primary symptoms of SUDs are obsession, compulsion, and harm caused by drug use. The primary symptoms of trauma are interpersonal withdrawal, hypersensitivity, and intrusion. Treatment systems addressing trauma-related disorders and addiction generally favor short-term, symptom-management approaches. This approach deems treatment successful if symptoms subside. In effect, no symptom, no problem!

SUD treatment programs tend to put their personnel and financial resources into helping people get "clean and sober," rather than focusing on the more costly strategy of helping people change a way of life. Most clinical resources go into the first 30 to 90 days of substance abuse recovery. The result is that many people are left without long-term assistance at a critical time in their recovery when they are most likely to have a resurgence of trauma-related symptoms and, thus, are prone to relapse back into alcohol/drug use or addictive behaviors. These people then end up becoming the "walking wounded"; perhaps they are not using drugs, but they may continue to live a limited life. Likewise, in trauma treatment, the bulk of clinical resources go into reducing symptoms of hyperarousal, interpersonal withdrawal, and intrusion (often through psychopharmacology). But this simply creates short-term relief for many clients who continue to experience the underlying symptoms of trauma: disturbed interpersonal relationships, low self-esteem, a lack of hope and optimism, diminished self-efficacy, and difficulty experiencing the joys of life. As discussed previously in this chapter, and again in the text that follows, social health interventions that focus on relational health and the experience of deep interpersonal and community connection can amplify the effects of both trauma and substance use treatment. This can happen by restoring a sense of meaning in life and by providing access to a nonprofessional support system, which many individuals have lost due to their substance use.

It should be noted that clients with both disorders can become willing coconspirators in ending treatment too quickly. For instance, when clients are no longer experiencing intrusive nightmares or have not had a drink in 30 days, they may be only too willing to declare themselves "better" and no longer in need of treatment. Few people voluntarily wish to explore their painful inner functioning and past to understand how these wounds manifest in their current lives and interfere with self-esteem, relationships, and a sense of belonging.

For some adult traumas, particularly "single-event" traumas such as a rape, an armed robbery, a near-death health crisis, or the death of a spouse, it may be appropriate to address only the trauma symptoms and not "delve deeper" unless the client signals that such exploration might be useful. They might signal the need to delve deeper, for instance, by suggesting that the single event activates other traumas in their history or by reports of long-disavowed affective states that emerge when ego defenses are down, such as upon awakening in the morning. When higher-functioning people go through a traumatic time, the risk of significant wounding at the level of self-functioning is lower than with a person who does not have very good coping skills. However, even for higher-functioning people, it might be wise to see if symptoms of a self-wound appear before probing. In a similar vein, some people can, with positive support from others (and sometimes strong sanctions against continuing the behavior), cease a destructive compulsive pattern such as alcohol or drug use, compulsive sexual behavior, shoplifting, or gambling and not need additional treatment. However, anecdotal evidence suggests that these clients are the exception, not the norm.

Many clients with SUDs can look—and are—remarkably improved after 30, 60, or 90 days of abstinence. However, a part of what is clinically relevant in this circumstance is that the psychological defense that individuals have employed—and continue to employ—to look "good enough" to self and others may be hiding enormous underlying pain. In some cases, the rebound from the physical effects of the substance or behavior causes a temporarily inflated sense of well-being known as the "pink cloud" phase of recovery. Stressful life events often trigger a precipitous "fall off of the pink cloud," and what appeared as a high level of functioning can deteriorate extremely rapidly into a return to substance use.

Not every client with co-occurring trauma-related and addiction disorders needs long-term treatment. Some clients can benefit from relatively short-term intensive treatment, followed by supportive counseling or self-help programs. However, it is critically important to be cognizant of the fact that many, and perhaps a majority, of this particular category of clients need more.

Finally, these additional services have to be matched to the specific needs of the clients. No one treatment protocol effectively can address the wide range of treatment and recovery needs of people with such diverse presentations of trauma and addiction disorders.

Staging Treatment

It is helpful to think of both trauma and addiction treatment as occurring in stages. The symptoms presented in early treatment are not necessarily the symptoms that become evident later on. Likewise, treatment needs vary depending on the phase of treatment. Finally, the role of the clinician may differ significantly depending on where the client is in their recovery. This subsection focuses on early treatment, because this is the point at which the interaction of trauma symptoms and addiction symptoms are most likely to be prominent. Once a client has stabilized in recovery, it is often more common for the client to be able to separate symptoms of one disorder from the other. Likewise, in more extended recovery, symptoms like low self-esteem, relational difficulties, lowered self-efficacy, repression of specific emotions, and overreactivity to environmental stressors often blend; it becomes more difficult, in these later stages, to describe a symptom as specific to trauma or to addictive illness.

In general, early treatment is focused on goals such as symptom management, reducing triggers and cues, stabilizing the psychosocial environment, learning about trauma and about addictive illness, developing a better understanding of recovery, and developing hope that life can be better. As clients master these tasks, other dynamics in a second stage of treatment may begin to be more prominent. The latter are marked by some of the following: being able or unable to manage success; continuing or not continuing relational patterns that are self-destructive or unfulfilling; and confronting problems that arose during the process of addiction, or have evolved as a result of trauma, such as bad decisions about jobs or careers, patterns of family relations that are limiting or retraumatizing, or decisions about the future of marriage or other important relationships. These are most often problems that predated treatment entry, but it is only after a period of stabilization that they emerge to the forefront. These dilemmas for the client require different treatment strategies and change the therapeutic stance of the clinician. In earlier treatment, the clinician might have been more directive, more focused on therapeutic boundaries, and more structured in the therapeutic endeavor, thus allowing the client to develop a dependent therapeutic relationship.

As treatment progresses, the clinician might elect to focus more on the client's affect, encouraging insight and supporting the client in making their own decisions; at this point, the therapist begins to appear less confrontational. In an even later stage of treatment, the clinician might take on more of an advisor role, walking alongside clients as they make their own decisions. A final stage of treatment involves the client's separation from the clinician, allowing the client to "let go" of a resource that has been a significant part of their lifeline for the duration of therapy. Being able to achieve their own separation healthily, in and of itself, can be a major therapeutic step for people who have experienced significant abandonment or attachment trauma.

Counseling Strategies in the Early Stages of Treatment

There are several specific counseling strategies that are useful in the early stages of treatment of trauma after-effects, SUDs, and process addictions. Perhaps the most important strategy is to create a safe working relationship, balancing the client's need for control and therapeutic relationship boundaries. While clients need clear boundaries to establish safety in the therapeutic relationship, when working with people with trauma-related disorders and addiction, the clinician also must recognize that the client needs to feel a sense of control in the relationship—a sense of control that was shattered during the trauma experience. Trauma has an impact on how people perceive the world, that is, their thoughts, judgments, intuitions, and their relationship to their emotions and physical experience. People sometimes shrink their world of experience in an effort to make it controllable, while simultaneously and paradoxically feeling out of control.

Addiction also can have an impact on how people perceive the world: their thoughts, judgments, intuition, and their relationship to their emotions and physical experience. Obsessive thinking and compulsive behaviors associated with addiction are actually coping strategies (or responses to trauma) and are employed by traumatized people to gain a sense of control; however, this paradoxically may increase their experience of being out of control. The person who suffers from trauma complications and addiction is dancing this dance of control in a vicious circle. The goal of the clinician is to dance with the client in a mutual process of following and leading, in order to enhance the client's sense of empowerment in the context of a safe relationship. Unfortunately, the rhythm of the dance is rendered "less than smooth" by some of the differences between "standard" trauma and SUD treatment. For example, in traditional SUD treatment programs, it is often a goal to get clients to "admit" that they are alcoholics or addicts and to confront those who do not. For trauma survivors, the shame that is associated with feelings about the loss of control that is engendered by this "admission" may activate the shame of the trauma experience and become overwhelming, or the push to make an admission may feel like another violation of personal boundaries. In the Seeking Safety model of treating the co-occurring conditions of trauma after-effects and addiction, Najavits (2006, p. 245) states that "the heavily confrontational style of some SUD group therapies [should be] avoided to maintain the safety of a trauma-focused treatment. Accountability, but not harsh confrontation, is emphasized."

It is more useful in the context of SUD and trauma-focused treatment not to focus on confronting clients about making an identity declaration of addiction, but rather to use collaborative counseling strategies that facilitate agreement about which addictive behaviors the client is willing to change and how those changes can occur. One such collaborative method is motivational interviewing, which is a value-centered approach to helping people change health risk behaviors (Miller & Rollnick, 2013). Although the ultimate goal of addiction treatment is abstinence from substance use, harmful compulsive behaviors, and process addictions, this collaborative approach to counseling recognizes that stabilization and harm reduction are important intermediate goals. Such an approach enhances a mutually agreed upon agenda of behavior change between client and clinician. The client can regain a sense of control over their life and can manifest a sense of empowerment by retaining a measure of control over the treatment agenda.

Other counseling strategies, which are essential to the successful treatment of SUD and trauma, involve employing supportive psychotherapy to explore the relationship between trauma aftereffects like PTSD and SUDs, along with psychoeducational methods to address the roles that substance use and compulsive behaviors have in reducing the heightened anxiety, hyperarousal, and flashbacks that frequently occur when people stop using substances and/or engaging in compulsive behaviors. The key here is to educate people about the effects of trauma and how substance use and addictive behaviors are understandable responses to the trauma aftereffects. An implicit subtlety here is for clinicians to emphasize that harmful behaviors such as cutting, drinking to pass out, and compulsive overeating are not to be dismissed or excused but are to be understood in the context of the client's traumatic experience. Supportive psychotherapy and psychoeducation can help clients to understand that they have choices about the strategies they employ to cope with trauma. These approaches also reinforce that although substance use may provide temporary relief from some of the intensity of the trauma effects, in the long run, it leaves them feeling more out of control than in control.

Processing of trauma memories needs to be delayed until a client's SUD and compulsive behaviors are stabilized and they have established sufficient coping strategies to manage intense affect. Much of the clinical literature indicates that clients run the risk of increased substance use, or relapse back into substance use, after a period of abstinence, if specific trauma memories are processed prematurely in treatment. According to Najavits (2006, p. 244), "Opening up the 'Pandora's box' of trauma memories may destabilize clients when they are most in need of stabilization." Najavits further points out that clients "may not feel ready for trauma processing early in SUD recovery; others may want to talk about the past but may underestimate the intense emotions and new disturbing memories" (Najavits, 2006, p. 244).

Traumatic experiences can overwhelm people's sense of control, connection, and meaning; they then tend to engage in a defensive strategy of disconnection that serves to protect them, superficially, from further threat, whether actual or perceived (Herman, 1992). People with SUDs and process addictions also tend to become isolated and disconnected from meaningful relationships with family, friends, coworkers, and others. For a person suffering from addiction, the drug or the compulsive behavior becomes like a capricious lover, and the relationship to that love object takes precedence over all other relationships. Therefore, an essential counseling strategy—especially in the early stages of treatment and recovery, when clients give up or dramatically change their relationship to the drug or compulsive behavior and are feeling isolated, alone, anxious, and depressed—is to work collaboratively with clients to replace this unhealthy relationship with healthy social supports. Such supports historically have included recovery support groups like-Alcoholics Anonymous (AA), Narcotics Anonymous (NA), Overeaters Anonymous (OA), Women for Recovery, Self-Management And Recovery Training (SMART), and so forth, although newer models continue to emerge.

Engagement in social support networks helps clients to reestablish meaningful connection to others and to decrease isolation. A renewed sense of connection can help reduce the hyperarousal that people with trauma complications suffer, although this is true only if they feel safe. However, participation in these groups often presents difficult challenges to individuals with trauma histories, such as an expectation of making outreach phone calls. All 12-step groups are autonomous, and some meetings contain individuals with more hostile views of psychiatry, which can leave clients fearful to disclose or discuss the way that their experiences with trauma have affected their substance use. It is also important to understand that while fellowship and close, supportive relationships occur in 12-step groups, they are not the primary focus, nor are they guaranteed, simply by attending meetings. The fellowships, where members come to encounter one another and support each other in the program, are distinct from the actual *program* of recovery, which is the 12 steps. While a general improvement in relationships is a promise of working the 12 steps, not all groups provide similar degrees of social support to members, nor are recovery rates necessarily linked to such social support.

Newer, innovative organizations, such as SeekHealing, focus more explicitly on social support and relational health and have been designed to meet the human need for authentic, meaningful social connection. They tend to be more "pan-recovery" oriented, in that participants may be healing from addiction, trauma, other mental health conditions resulting from or exacerbated by social disconnection, or simply loneliness. Because not everyone in the groups has a diagnosis, and participation is drawn from a wide variety of individuals in the broader community, "little r" recovery groups such as SeekHealing provide a means for individuals to reconnect with the broader community, outside of the often-siloed communities of people with lived addiction experience. As evidence grows for the effectiveness for these interventions, meetings focused on social health may become a very valuable complement to participation in psychotherapy and other "capital R" recovery groups.

Recovery Support Groups as an Adjunct to Counseling

As noted earlier, recovery support groups can be an important adjunct to individual counseling for people with co-occurring conditions of SUDs and trauma-related conditions. Most recovery support groups are patterned after AA, which is based on the 12 steps of recovery. The 12 steps are principles for living that accomplish the following: emphasizing powerlessness over the substance or addictive behavior; making amends with people harmed as a result of destructive, addictive behavior; and developing a spiritual connection to self, others, and something greater than the self. Types of 12-step support groups that might be useful for people with co-occurring addiction and trauma-related conditions include AA, NA, Drug Addicts Anonymous (a newer fellowship in which qualification for membership overlaps with NA, but the Big Book and AA literature is used to guide the action of working the steps), Cocaine Anonymous (CA), Heroin Anonymous, (HA), OA, Gamblers Anonymous (GA), and Emotions Anonymous (EA), among others.

Another 12-step group, Adult Children of Alcoholics and Dysfunctional Families (ACA, or ACoA), is explicitly aimed at recovering from the effects of developmental trauma and adverse childhood experiences, which often occur (but not exclusively) in family systems with alcoholism or addiction. This program has a slightly different approach to the 12 steps, in that it focuses on re-parenting one's inner child as a part of the spiritual path to recovery and encourages a "blameless inventory" of not only oneself, but the whole family. However, clinicians are cautioned that abstinence from compulsive use of substances, food, or behaviors is required before ACA steps can be worked effectively. Some seasoned members of these fellowships recommend that individuals struggling with addictions first achieve stable sobriety before delving into this "deeper layer of the onion" of the work, as ACA meetings also may be triggering. Other recovery support groups that are not based on the 12-step model include Women for Sobriety, which incorporates a spiritual component, and SMART and Secular Organizations for Sobriety (SOS), which do not include spiritual components. Refuge Recovery and its offshoot, Recovery Dharma, which maintain a spiritual emphasis rooted in Buddhist principles of non-attachment, are increasingly popular alternatives to 12-step groups.

In addition to social support, recovery support groups and fellowships also provide cognitive reframing functions that are consistent with cognitive behavioral therapy (CBT), which have demonstrated efficacy in treating SUDs and PTSD. For example, AA slogans, which often are hung on banners in meeting locations, such as "one day at a time," provide people with a kind of reminder to return to the present moment when their minds project into the future or get obsessively stuck in ruminating about the past.

The spiritual focus of many recovery support groups can be helpful to clients who have suffered the devastating effects of trauma by helping people reconnect to meaning in their lives. In addition, numerous studies have shown that alcohol or other drug abuse is associated with a lack of meaning in life, and those without an active religious or spiritual life are more likely to fill this void with alcohol or drugs (Laudet et al., 2006). Although the spiritual aspects of recovery support groups are not for everyone, it is important to explore this potential resource with clients in counseling.

Facilitating active involvement in recovery support groups is an important aspect of the counseling process with people who suffer from addictions and trauma complications. This counseling strategy involves exploring clients' understanding of recovery support groups, dispelling myths and misunderstandings, educating clients about the benefits and potential risks of participation, helping clients resolve ambivalence about attendance, helping clients decide on and locate appropriate meetings, and monitoring clients' reactions to meetings.

Many clients feel ambivalent and anxious about attending recovery support groups. Many feel ashamed about being identified as an "alcoholic" or "addict," and others simply are uncomfortable in groups. Such clients may respond more favorably to meetings like those of SeekHealing that feature a participatory destigmatization model, in which all compulsive means of dissociating from difficult emotional experiences—up to and including binge-streaming television shows—are considered as harm reduction, and accordingly normalized. SeekHealing thereby deliberately obscures the distinction between an "addict" and "non-addict" in favor of experiencing a sense of authentic connection over universal human experiences. Still, in all recovery support groups, clients with histories of trauma may feel overstimulated by the environment and experience a reactivation of trauma memories. It is important to work collaboratively with clients in resolving their initial ambivalence about attendance at meetings and to develop a desensitization plan.

Peer support specialists, or "recovery coaches," also can support clients by helping them to navigate between treatment systems and community support, including recovery meetings. They can assist in lowering the barriers, which some clients experience, to attending meetings, particularly if they also have subjective experience with trauma recovery in addition to addiction. Finding the right support group for each client is an important part of this collaborative counseling strategy. For example, women who have been sexually traumatized by men often find the predominantly male atmosphere of AA, NA, CA, and other recovery support groups to be anxiety provoking. Women's groups of AA and/or Women for Sobriety meetings might be more acceptable for these clients. It is important for clinicians to respect clients' trauma experiences and to encourage them to investigate acceptable meetings. Miller and Rollnick (2013) suggest that any plan, developed in collaboration with clients to help them change health-risk behaviors, needs to be accessible, acceptable, and appropriate for each individual.

It is possible for some individuals to find that the support group environment is inadvertently retraumatizing. Retraumatization can occur in various ways in self-help support groups. For instance, hearing other participants openly describe trauma events in their lives can open memories and disavowed affects for some individuals, particularly those new to the program. Individuals with weak interpersonal boundaries may misinterpret the interest and attention given to them by others and then feel rejected and abandoned. Some individuals can become prematurely involved in sexual relationships with other support group members and unconsciously "reenact" their trauma experiences.

The role of the "sponsor" in 12-step self-help environments can be particularly therapeutic, but it also can be fraught. A sponsor is another member of the group with more experience in recovery, who acts as a mentor and coach for newly recovering individuals—ideally to guide them through the 12 steps. However, the intimacy of these relationships varies widely; sometimes sponsorship becomes a close and nurturing relationship beyond mere guidance with step work. It is not uncommon to hear an individual say, for example, "My sponsor in AA was like the father I never had." Having someone in the role of a safe and nurturing parent figure, as a client moves through the recovery process, cannot be underestimated. However, styles of sponsorship vary widely, and, in some instances with sponsors who have not yet addressed their own relational issues, these relationships may become highly codependent, controlling, or even abusive.

Healthy sponsors help sponsees to work the steps and to get connected to a "higher power," but do not recast themselves as anyone's higher power, instead modeling and encouraging sponsees toward spiritual action to help them cope with life's turbulent moments. However, as with parenting, people often sponsor the way they were sponsored, and varying means of influence may be normalized in such relationships. This is not necessarily unhealthy, but it is very important that clinicians monitor the client's participation in self-help environments, supporting the person's involvement, helping the individual to integrate their learning in different recovery environments, and being observant for signs of potential retraumatization. Being able to handle the potential retraumatization in a positive and productive way can be particularly therapeutic for individuals in early recovery, especially for those who have a limited repertoire of coping skills. Relationships in 12-step programs can be catalysts for growth, even when challenging.

Self-help programs offer the potential for powerful therapeutic growth through the process of identification, sharing, and belonging. This is particularly true for clients who have experienced abandonment trauma, thereby interfering with their ability to bond with others. Self-help programs can aid clients to experience intimate sharing in a safe environment and especially to have a sense of belonging; such programs can offer significant therapeutic gains that may not be available in individual counseling settings. Clients in self-help programs can proceed at their own pace, have the opportunity for meaningful feedback from others, and can learn to modulate their own sharing and involvement.

Spirituality in Trauma and Addiction Treatment

An additional counseling strategy, which can be employed at all stages of the treatment process, is to work collaboratively with clients to enhance hope and resilience through the exploration of their own understanding of spirituality. Unlike religion, spirituality does not refer to any particular dogma or set of beliefs. Rather, spirituality is primarily concerned with the personal search for meaning and a felt sense of connection with some ultimate or transcendent reality. A popular quote in 12-step recovery rooms is, "Religion is for people who are afraid of hell—spirituality is for people who have already been there." Spirituality can enhance a person's vitality and sense of interconnectedness with all existence (Grim & Grim, 2019), thus combating the pervasive sense of disconnection that both traumatized and addicted people chronically experience (Herman, 1992). Research has demonstrated that alcohol/drug use also is associated with a lack of meaning in life. Active spiritual involvement can reduce the risk of substance abuse, contribute to the formation of a resilient worldview, strengthen long-term recovery, increase coping skills and resilience to stress, enhance hope, and act as a protective factor in preventing alcohol and drug abuse (Burke, 2006).

Exploration of spirituality in counseling needs to be inclusive; it needs to honor the client's own experience and to assist the client in understanding the broader meaning of personal trauma. For example, instead of getting caught in discussions about religious beliefs, which often can become impersonal debates, it is important to ask clients about their spiritual practices, such as walking in nature, praying, or meditating, which might be considered helpful during times of high anxiety or when there is a temptation to drink, use drugs, or engage in addictive behaviors. It also is important to explore spiritual experiences, values and ethical principles, relationships to spiritual teachers, connection to sacred space, and how spiritual communities (whether a meditation group, church, AA group, and so on) have been or could be a resource to help people stay sober and reconnect with social supports (Burke, 2006). The exploration of spiritual community, in an inclusive and collaborative way, can support clients with SUD and trauma complications; it holds the potential for helping to find hope, rebounding from adversity, connecting with a greater meaning and purpose, and reconnecting with social supports that had been lost after the original trauma.

COUNSELING IMPLICATIONS

Due to the complexity of working with clients with co-occurring issues of psychological trauma and SUDs, along with the demands of high-stress treatment environments, clinicians are at risk. They are at risk for developing secondary trauma (signs of PTSD related to exposure to clients' trauma material), vicarious traumatization also known as compassion fatigue (a negative shift in worldview and self-identity), burnout (the general psychological stress of working with difficult clients), and intense countertransference reactions (these relevant clinical issues are discussed in Chapter 30, "Vicarious Traumatization"). To prevent and/or reduce these risks, it is essential for clinicians to develop comprehensive personal and professional self-care plans that include a relapse prevention plan for those who are themselves in recovery from SUDs or process addictions (the importance of self-care is detailed in Chapter 31).

Although personal responsibility is important, the clinical and research literature suggests that a team approach, whereby members of the treatment team or supervision group share in the responsibility of caring for complex and challenging clients, can prevent or mitigate the impact of secondary trauma as well as intense countertransference reactions by clinicians (Burke et al., 2006). The literature also suggests that treatment agencies can support clinicians in their efforts by adopting a trauma-informed approach that normalizes secondary trauma reactions and vicarious traumatization, validates and encourages clinician self-care, and creates an atmosphere of empowerment and respect for both the client and the counselor (Substance Abuse and Mental Health Services Administration [SAMHSA], 2014a, 2014b).

CONCLUSION

A complex relationship exists between psychological trauma and addictive disorders. Although not every clinician who works with people with these co-occurring conditions needs to be an expert in the treatment of both, it is essential to be able to recognize the expression of both in clients and to be trauma and addiction informed. This means being able to recognize that trauma-related conditions such as PTSD, clinical depression, and anxiety as well as symptoms like hyperarousal, interpersonal withdrawal, and intrusive re-experiencing of trauma memories arise in the treatment of SUD and process addictions, especially once clients are no longer using such substances. These trauma-related symptoms need to be addressed in the early stages of recovery from addiction. In addition, the long-term social, psychological, and neurobiological impacts of trauma also must be addressed in order for people to move beyond these difficult experiences and live fully satisfying and meaningful lives. A spiritually sensitive focus in counseling can aid in this meaning-making function, enhance resilience, and provide hope and reconnection to community. Social health interventions that provide meaningful interpersonal connection amplify the effects of biopsychological treatments. Hope and connection are what make life meaningful and are essential ingredients in recovery from both trauma and addictions.

ADDITIONAL RESOURCES

 A robust set of instructor resources designed to supplement this text is located at http://connect.springerpub.com/content/book/978-0-8261-5085-1. Qualifying instructors may request access by emailing textbook@springerpub.com.

PRACTICE-BASED RESOURCES AND REFERENCES

To view a list of resources and all the references, please visit connect.springerpub.com via the following url: http://connect.springerpub.com/content/book/978-0-8261-5085-1/part/part02/chapter/ch13

CHAPTER 14

Criminal Victimization

LAURENCE MILLER

CHAPTER OVERVIEW

This chapter focuses on the effects of criminal victimization and ways that counselors can respond effectively. This chapter discusses specific counseling responses, including symptom management, short-term mental health stabilization, and longer-term counseling and psychotherapeutic strategies. The counseling implications for working with crime victims are elaborated.

LEARNING OBJECTIVES

After reading this chapter, the reader should be able to:

1. Define various types of criminal assault;
2. Understand the psychology of victims of crime;
3. Use specific responses for responding to victims of crime; and,
4. Develop strategies for immediate response, short-term intervention, and longer-term counseling for victims of crime.

INTRODUCTION

Although almost any kind of violence can happen to anyone, certain types of criminal victimization appear to be relatively common in the clinical practice of trauma counselors. These are discussed briefly in the following sections: Criminal Assault; Sexual Assault; Theft and Robbery; Crime in the Community; and Real Crime, Fear of Crime, and the "Mean World Syndrome."

Criminal Assault

Each year, more than 25 million Americans are victimized by some form of crime. Rapes, robberies, and assaults account for 2.2 million injuries and more than 700,000 hospital stays annually. Although the most violent crimes are committed by family members or close associates of the victim (Bidinotto, 1996; Herman, 2002; Kirwin, 1997; Miller, 2008a, in press-a), what most people fear most is an attack by a malevolent stranger.

Several diagnosable psychiatric syndromes may be seen following criminal assault (Miller, 2019). Depression, anxiety, posttraumatic stress disorder (PTSD), and substance abuse are common psychological disorders found in victims of robbery, rape, and burglary, and a high proportion of panic attacks trace their onset to some traumatically stressful experience. About half of crime-induced PTSD cases persist after 3 months, and clinical experience suggests that such traumatic effects may last for years or longer in some victims. Men appear to be subject to economic assaults, such as muggings and robberies, in similar situations as women, but are far less likely to be subject to sexual assault. However, it may be more difficult for a man to report any kind of assault for fear of shame, ridicule, or disbelief (Breslau et al., 1991, 1998; Davis & Breslau, 1994; Falsetti & Resnick, 1995; Frank & Stewart, 1984; Hough, 1985; Kilpatrick & Acierno, 2003; Norris, 1992; Resnick et al., 1997; Resnick et al., 1993; Rothbaum et al., 1992; Saunders et al., 1989; Uhde et al., 1985).

One of the realities of doing crime victim work is the realization that perpetrators and victims do not come in neat, separate, and diametrically opposed packages. Whereas some victims are targeted through no fault of their own, others may lead questionable or marginal lifestyles that all too often put them in the wrong place at the wrong time. Women who work in the adult entertainment industry may be targeted for sexual assault by males who feel "entitled" to have sex with women in these trades. People looking to buy or sell drugs may be assaulted and robbed. Members of a rival gang may be attacked for straying into alien territory or in retaliation for real or imagined aggression of their own. In such cases, counselors may have to negotiate the delicate task of suspending moral judgment in order to form a successful treatment relationship, while at the same time forthrightly addressing the risky behavior, in order to prevent (as much as possible) a repeat of the victimization (Miller, 2008a, in press-a).

Sexual Assault

Sexual assault affects one-fourth of women and up to 7% of men, and is associated with significantly increased risk of anxiety, depression, substance abuse, and PTSD (Elliott et al., 2004; Resick, 1993). As with all traumas, individual differences account for the severity of PTSD symptoms after sexual assault (Bowman, 1997, 1999). In particular, the PTSD symptoms of women who perceive negative events as uncontrollable tend to be more severe than those in women who believe that they have some ability to predict and control what happens to them (Kushner et al., 1993).

In addition to the general effects of crime victim trauma, some authorities have characterized the relationship between sexual violence and health as the *radiating impact of violent victimization* (Macy, 2007; Riger et al., 2002). In this conceptualization, violence influences women's physical and mental health, as well as radiating out to affect careers, friendships, families, and whole communities. Despite this impact, a surprisingly small number of sexual assault victims seek mental health services for problems related to their assault (George et al., 1992; Golding et al., 1989; Ullman, 2007).

Theft and Robbery

Although typically not lethal, to steal something from another person constitutes a fundamental violation of that person's dignity and bespeaks a callous disregard for their rights as a human being. This is why most of us react with that burning sting of outrage upon being tricked or strong armed out of what we believe is rightfully ours.

Theft refers to the illicit appropriation of resources that rightfully belong to someone else—in other words, someone taking what is not theirs. Although technically frowned upon in all cultures and considered a crime in societies with formal legal systems, it is nevertheless a cultural universal, occurring frequently in all human groups, as well as in many other animal species (Kanazawa, 2008). More than 90% of theft and robbery crimes are committed by men, especially those who are poor, less intelligent, and have less education (Herrnstein & Murray, 1994; Kanazawa, 2004, 2008; Kanazawa & Still, 2000; Miller, 2012; Wilson & Herrnstein, 1985).

Burglaries involve breaking into a structure to steal something, usually without physical confrontation, although some burglaries can turn violent if the thief is surprised by the occupants. Some criminals also combine burglary with rape. Burglaries make up 11% of all thefts, and burglars are typically young males of low educational and socioeconomic status, with histories of substance abuse and other criminal behavior. The skill level of burglars can range from rank amateurs, such as bored teens breaking into a private residence, to professionals who hit wealthy homes or businesses that contain valuable items or large amounts of cash. Most private dwellings are burglarized during the day when occupants are likely to be out, whereas businesses typically are struck at night. Some burglars report experiencing a thrill or rush at breaking into a dwelling and stealing items. This thrill may take on a frankly sexual nature in the case of *fetish burglaries* in which intimate items are stolen, or in more violent cases, where rape accompanies the burglary. Some burglars may urinate, defecate, or masturbate in the burgled dwelling or otherwise vandalize the premises. Where the criminals force their way into the dwelling by overpowering the occupants, this is referred to as a *home invasion* (Bureau of Justice Statistics, 2003, 2006; Conklin, 1992; Miller, 2012; Palermo & Kocsis, 2005; Pitts, 2001).

Crime in the Community

The *Diagnostic and Statistical Manual of Mental Disorders* (5th ed.; [*DSM-5*; American Psychiatric Association, 2013) recognizes that posttraumatic stress reactions can occur in persons who observe terrible events happening to others, even if they are not directly affected, including witnessing crimes of violence or threats of violence against others. Indeed, certain segments of the population may be exposed to traumatically stressful events on a fairly regular basis, for example, residents of crime-ridden and socioeconomically depressed inner-city neighborhoods. Precipitating events include sudden injuries, serious accidents, physical assaults, and rape, as well as having one's life threatened, receiving news of the death or injury of a close friend or relative, narrowly escaping injury in an assault or accident, or having one's home destroyed in a fire. Many of these individuals experience anxiety, depression, cognitive impairment, medical symptoms, and PTSD that persist for a year or longer. Furthermore, this appears to produce a vicious cycle—the so-called "cycle of violence"—with victims of aggression showing more aggression toward others (Breslau & Davis, 1992; Breslau et al., 1991, 1998; Garbarino, 1997; Scarpa, 2001; Scarpa & Haden, 2006; Scarpa et al., 2002).

Real Crime, Fear of Crime, and the "Mean World Syndrome"

Inasmuch as most members of the general public have little direct experience with crime, our beliefs about crime and the criminal justice system are largely based on what we see on TV and read in the newspapers or online, where sensational and violent crimes are often overrepresented, leading to a type of media-induced trauma known as *mean world syndrome* (Budiansky et al., 1996). This may have the paradoxical effect of oversensitizing people to nonexistent or insignificant threats, while at the same time numbing the public's understanding of the true impact of crime victimization when it does occur (Miller, 1995, 2008a; Miller & Dion, 2000; Miller et al., 1999).

THE PSYCHOLOGY OF CRIME VICTIMIZATION

Russell and Beigel (1990) conceive of crime victimization as comprising several layers in relation to a person's core self: *property crime*, like burglary and vandalism, generally hurts victims at the outermost self-layer, that is, their belongings, although the theft or destruction of certain meaning-laden family heirlooms can have a much greater emotional impact. *Armed robbery*, which involves personal contact with the criminal and threat to the physical self of the victim, invades a deeper psychological layer, while *assault and battery* penetrates still deeper, injuring the victim both physically and psychologically. *Rape* goes to the very core of the self, perverts the sense of safety and intimacy that sexual contact is supposed to have, and affects the victim's basic beliefs, values, emotions, and sense of security in the world.

Society's response to crime also plays a role in how supported or abandoned victims feel (Russell & Beigel, 1990). For example, society often regards victimization as contagious. In modern American culture, with its emphasis on fierce competition for limitless success and the perfect life, victims are often equated with losers. Most of us want to believe that crime victimization is something that happens to somebody else. The victim must have done something to bring it on themselves; otherwise, "I'm just as vulnerable too, and who wants to believe that?" We thus may be reluctant to empathize or associate with crime victims for fear that their bad luck will "rub off." All of these beliefs and reactions further contribute to the feelings of blame and shame that many crime victims experience (Miller, 1996a, 1998a, 1998b, 2001b, 2007b).

CRIME VICTIMIZATION: THERAPEUTIC AND COUNSELING GUIDELINES

Proper psychological intervention with crime victims ideally takes place at three levels and at three points in time: (a) at or close to the crime scene itself, involving crisis intervention and short-term psychological stabilization; (b) intermediate-level stress management and symptom-reduction strategies to allow the crime victim to achieve a sense of normalcy and control; and (c) more extensive counseling and therapy to help the victim work through the traumatic event and regain a sense of existential groundedness (Miller, 1998a, 1998b, 2008a, 2012, 2020).

On-Scene Crisis Intervention: Guidelines for First Responders

Ideally, effective mental health intervention for crime victims begins the moment the first responders arrive. For most crimes, this consists of police and paramedics, sometimes accompanied by a special mental health trauma clinician. In other cases, the first mental health contact occurs in the emergency department if the victim is taken to a hospital. Whoever the first responders are, they need to be aware that they are in a unique position to help the crime victim deal with the impact of their ordeal and to help restore a sense of safety and control to an otherwise frightening and overwhelming situation (Herman, 2002; Miller, 2000, 2008a, 2010).

First responders may face a confusing scenario when arriving at a crime scene. Traumatized victims may be in a state of shock and disorientation during the initial stage of the crisis reaction, feeling helpless, vulnerable, and frightened. Other victims may manifest fight–flight–or–freeze panic, and some actually may try to flee the crime scene. Some victims may be confrontational or combative with arriving police or paramedics, adding to the confusion as to who is the victim and who is the offender; this is most likely to occur in cases of barroom brawls, domestic disturbances, or neighbor disputes. In some instances, virtual physical and emotional paralysis may occur, rendering the victim unable to make rational decisions, speak coherently, or even move purposefully, much less seek medical attention or report the incident to the police. Balancing concern for victim welfare and the need to obtain detailed information thus becomes a delicate dance and requires some degree of interpersonal skill on the part of the interviewer (Box 14.1).

BOX 14.1

Tips From the Field

The following offers some practical recommendations for first responders who have to deal with crime victims on scene (Clark, 1988; Frederick, 1986; Miller, 1998a, 1998b, 2006a, 2010; Silbert, 1976).

(continued)

Introduce Yourself

As soon as you arrive, identify yourself by name and full title to the victim and bystanders. Even with a uniform or ID tag, you may need to repeat the introduction several times; victims who are still in shock may respond to you as if you are the criminal, especially if you arrived quickly on the scene, unintentionally heightening their shock and disorientation. Children traumatized by adults may respond with fear to any new adult in their environment.

Apply Medical First Aid

It is typically the job of paramedics to render emergency medical care. But even as a mental health counselor, if you are one of the first responders on the scene, you may be the only one available to apply basic first aid until further medical help arrives. For whoever carries out this task, calmly explain to the crime victim what you are doing, especially when you are touching the victim or doing an otherwise intimate procedure, such as applying a breathing mask or removing clothing. If possible, encourage the victim to help you treat her, if she is capable and wants to, by having her hold a bandage or letting her undo her own clothing in order to afford some sense of control.

Respect the Victim's Wishes

When feasible, allow a requested family member or friend to remain with the victim during medical treatment or questioning by the police. If the present officer makes the victim uncomfortable, try to have a less threatening backup officer fill in for the questioning (e.g., a female officer for a rape victim; an ethnically or culturally familiar officer for a minority victim).

Validate the Victim's Reactions

Always try to normalize and validate the traumatic ordeal the victim has just been through and, as realistically as possible, reinforce their resilience and coping efforts thus far. In general, build on the victim's own resources to increase their feelings of self-efficacy and control, for example: "I can see this must have been a terrible experience for you; most people would be feeling pretty much like you are under these circumstances, but I'm glad to see you're handling it as well as you are."

Investigate Sensibly and Sensitively

Police typically prefer to interview crime victims as soon as possible to obtain fresh information that can be used to apprehend and prosecute the offender. Mental health clinicians who are on scene can assist and advise law enforcement personnel in these actions. This includes avoiding even unintentional accusatory or incriminatory statements, such as "What were you doing in that building so late at night?" A sympathetic, supportive, and nonjudgmental approach to law enforcement interviewing can do much to restore the crime victim's trust and confidence and thereby facilitate all aspects of the criminal investigation (Miller, 2006a, 2008a, 2010, 2012).

Present a Plan

Related to the issue of restoring control is having some kind of clear plan to provide further structure and order to an otherwise overwhelming situation. Such a plan needs to be backed up with concrete suggestions for action: "We're going to move to a safe area and have the medics take care of these cuts; then I'm going to ask you a couple of questions, if that's all right. After I'm done, I'm going to explain what happens next in the police process and legal area, and then I'll give you a card with some phone numbers of victim assistance agencies you can contact. I'm also going to give you my card, and you can contact me at any time for any reason. Do you understand? Do you have any questions?"

(continued)

Employ Humor Judiciously

A tasteful witticism may add some perspective to the crisis situation and ease an otherwise tense situation, but traumatized people tend to become very literal and concrete under stress, and well-meaning humor may be mistaken for mocking or lack of serious concern. As with all such recommendations, use your professional judgment.

Utilize Interpersonal Calming and Coping Techniques

Never overlook the interpersonal power of a reassuring presence, both verbally and physically. Project a model of composure for the victim to emulate. Eye contact should be neither a detached glance nor a fixed glare, but more of a concerned, connected gaze. Stand close enough to the victim to provide proximal contact comfort, but do not crowd or intimidate by invading the victim's personal space. Use physical touch carefully. Sometimes, a brief pat on the shoulder or comforting grasp of the hand can be very reassuring, but it may frighten a victim who just has been physically assaulted. Take your cue from the victim.

SYMPTOM MANAGEMENT AND SHORT-TERM MENTAL HEALTH STABILIZATION

Clinicians often wonder, "When does crisis intervention end and 'real' psychotherapy begin?" However, the border between short- and long-term therapies is a fluid one, as is the line between so-called *superficial* and *deep* therapies. Much depends on the client. For example, helping a crime victim gain control of their bodily reactions—panic attacks, churning gut, and so forth—in the days and weeks following a physical beating, armed robbery, hostage scenario, or sexual assault may be an essential first step toward tackling the issues of safety and predictability that are raised in more extensive traditional trauma therapy. For other victims, even a cursory attempt to deal with symptoms must await the achievement of some degree of therapeutic confidence and stability. For many clients, this is a reciprocal cycle, with small increments in confidence permitting small steps toward symptom control, which in turn produce greater confidence and further attempts at mastery, and so on. In still other cases, clients may come to understand that although symptoms may be managed and controlled, they may never completely disappear but can be relegated to the background of consciousness, like "mental shrapnel" that only aches on occasion (Everstine & Everstine, 1993; Matsakis, 1994; Miller, 1994b, 1998b, 2012).

Modulating Arousal

The following sections present a flexible menu of cognitive behavioral symptom-control techniques that I have culled from diverse areas of practice and have used with diverse clinical populations, including crime victims, accident victims, law enforcement critical incident stress, military psychology, sports psychology, and others (Miller, 1989a, 1989b, 1994a, 2006a, 2006b, 2008a, 2008b, 2008c, 2012, 2013, 2020).

Progressive Muscle Relaxation

For more than half a century, the technique of *progressive muscle relaxation* (Jacobson, 1938) has been the standard recipe of stress management and is by now so well-known that it only needs to be summarized here. The basic rationale is that much of what we experience as uncomfortably heightened arousal arises out of feedback from tensed muscles and other bodily signals of arousal. Essentially, then, the progressive relaxation exercise focuses on one muscle group or body area at a time and guides the subject through an alternate tense-and-relax sequence until all major muscle groups are in a state of relative physiological quiescence. This is typically combined with slow, steady, and diaphragmatic breathing (deep stomach breathing as opposed to shallow chest breathing) and one or more mental cuing or imagery techniques (see on the following texts) to further induce a state of psychophysiological calm.

The technique is first practiced in a peaceful, stress-free environment, such as in the therapist's office or in stress management class, guided by the clinician's or instructor's soothing words or by the use of a commercially prepared or custom-made relaxation tape, CD, computer, or cell phone app. Later, with continued practice in a variety of settings and conditions, traumatized crime victims should be able to self-induce the relaxed state on their own, in their natural environment, without external prompting, and without having to go through the whole tense-and-relax sequence each time. As an example, they can use it while sitting in traffic or at their desk at work.

Cued Relaxation

Once the progressive relaxation procedure has been practiced and mastered, many individuals are able to employ a kind of instant relaxation or *cued relaxation* technique. By voluntarily reducing muscular tension, taking a calming breath, and using a cue word, the subject learns to lower their physiological arousal immediately and thereby induce a more calm and focused mental state. The *cue word* or phrase may range from the spiritual ("God is with me," "Om") to the mundane ("Chill"; "Okay, I'm good") and is basically any word or phrase that the subject has learned to associate with the full relaxation response and that they can now say to themselves to signal their body to relax.

Similarly, a *cue image* is any mental scene the subject can invoke that has a calming effect, especially by virtue of having been paired with the initial relaxation response practice. Have your client pick the modality or technique that works best for them: the key is to invoke some cue that enables the client to quickly and voluntarily lower their arousal level to a degree that is appropriate for the situation they are in (Hays & Brown, 2004; Miller, 1994a, 2006b, 2008a, 2008b).

Centering

This is a technique derived from Eastern meditation (Asken, 1993) that involves combining diaphragmatic breathing with a *centering cue image*. The instruction to the client is as follows: "Begin by taking a slow, deep diaphragmatic breath. As you breathe out, slowly let your eyes close (or remain open if this is more comfortable for you) and focus your awareness on some internal or external point, such as your lower abdomen or an imaginary spot on the wall. Repeat this process until you feel yourself becoming calmer." As with all of these techniques, increased practice yields greater proficiency.

Mindfulness

For some people, "trying to relax" is a contradiction in terms; the more they try to force themselves to relax, the more tense they get. That is because, by definition, relaxation is something one has to learn to *let* happen, not something one can *make* happen, and some individuals are just too challenged by the process to allow this to take place comfortably. This may be especially common following a traumatic crime victimization, where "relaxation" may connote letting one's guard down and becoming more vulnerable. In *mindfulness* training (Kabat-Zinn, 1994, 2003; Marra, 2005), the individual makes no conscious effort to relax, but simply allows themselves to take in the sensations and images in the surrounding environment without trying to control them. Eventually, by taking the demand element out of the process, relaxation often will occur as a beneficial side effect. This technique may be especially useful with crime victims who already have enough to feel ashamed about without having to face the prospect of "failing" a relaxation assignment. Mindfulness training allows productive engagement with a therapeutic exercise that has as little demand as possible, thus allowing whatever small progress that occurs to be counted as a step in the right direction.

COUNSELING AND PSYCHOTHERAPY OF CRIME VICTIMS

Effective as they are, therapeutic symptom-reduction strategies have their limitations in dealing with the full cognitive and emotional range of posttraumatic stress reactions and bringing about a reintegrative healing of the personality after crime victimization. For many victims, some form of constructive confrontation with the traumatic experience and its meaning has to take place in order to achieve a workable degree of mastery and resolution (Miller, 1998b, 2008b). It is important to bear in mind that symptom-oriented therapies and reintegrative therapies are not mutually exclusive; in fact, they reinforce each other, that is, sometimes, sufficient therapeutic trust, ego bolstering, and self-mastery through self-control must take place to lay the groundwork for more detailed direct exploration of the traumatic event itself (Brom et al., 1989; Everstine & Everstine, 1993; McCann & Pearlman, 1990).

Counseling and Therapeutic Strategies

As used here, a therapeutic *strategy* refers to an overall approach or game plan for addressing a problem or therapeutic issue, whereas a therapeutic *technique* is the actual nuts-and-bolts practical application of that strategy. For example, one strategy may be to help a victim feel more comfortable interacting with coworkers from the same ethnic group as their attacker by increased positive interaction with these peers. Specific techniques would include relaxation training, rehearsal and role-playing exercises, and gradually increasing time spent in interaction with these coworkers. In general, the effectiveness of any therapeutic strategy is determined by the timeliness, tone, style, and intent of the intervention. Effective psychological interventions with crime victims include the components discussed briefly in the succeeding subsections (Blau, 1994; Fullerton et al., 1992; Miller, 1994b, 1998a, 1998b, 2006a, 2008a, 2020; Wester & Lyubelsky, 2005).

Create a Sanctuary

One essential component of the therapeutic environment should be to provide a feeling of safety. The crime victim should be assured that what they say will be used only for the purposes of their healing and strengthening. Indeed, once the initial wariness passes, many victims report that they find the counselor's office a refuge—perhaps the only refuge—from the legal and family stresses that swirl around them in the wake of the crime, the only place where they can be "real." Of course, the limits of confidentiality must be carefully explained to the client, as she probably will be involved in legal proceedings, and the counselor's records may be subpoenaed or the counselor may be called to testify in court (Miller, 1996b, 2001a, 2007a, 2009).

Focus on Critical Areas of Concern

As with the general emphasis on quick mobilization of therapeutic gains and the client's sense of self-control, crime victim psychotherapy initially should be goal directed. It should remain focused on resolving specific adaptation and recovery issues related to the crisis at hand, which is a corollary of the next principle.

Specify Desired Outcomes

In the beginning, the clinician needs to help the crime victim to operationalize these therapeutic objectives, in line with the emphasis on achieving practical goals. For example, the client might state, "I'd like to feel more at ease with my work and my family." The therapist can help him to objectify this general desire to more specific and achievable goals, such as, "I want to reduce the number of intrusive thoughts about the attack to a level where I can ride to work without panicking at each red light," or "I'd like to be able to step back for a few seconds to regain my composure before I blow up at my wife and kids again over nothing."

Of course, few distraught clients will come to the first session with a preset list of concrete goals; indeed, traumatized victims often are confused initially about what they hope to accomplish in therapy (e.g., "I just want the pain to go away," "I want to be able to sleep," "I want to think clearly again."). In the early phases, then, it is primarily the counselor's task to help the victim sort out, focus, and operationalize their goals so that there can be a way of assessing if the therapy process is accomplishing them. Once again, without being overly rigid, specifying a doable goal and then setting to work on it can serve to focus and empower the out-of-control client.

Develop a General Plan

From the first session, after one or more workable goals have been elaborated, it is useful to develop an initial game plan that can be modified as counseling progresses. All the details need not be worked out at this point, and most likely, the plan will be revised as new information comes in. But the counselor needs to start somewhere, so developing a general road map allows the clinician to identify implementation and self-management strategies.

Identify Practical Initial Implementations

Clinicians should hit the ground running by beginning interventions as soon as possible. There is almost always some practical information, advice, or recommendation to provide, even in the first session. This induces confidence quickly, motivates further progress, and allows the counselor to get valuable feedback from initial treatment efforts thus far that can guide further interventions. Of course, counselors do not want to appear to be "pushing" these on the client; rather, interventions can be presented as a brief menu of options, allowing the client to make the choice when and if they are ready.

Review Assets and Encourage Self-Efficacy

Consistent with the overarching aim of posttraumatic psychotherapy as a strengthening, not weakening, process, it is as important to know what personal strengths and resources the client has as it is to understand their vulnerabilities. Counselors always strive to capitalize on strengths to overcome or work around weaknesses.

Counseling and Therapeutic Techniques

Adapted and expanded from psychological work with public safety personnel, the following therapeutic intervention techniques also have been found effective in working with traumatized crime victims (Blau, 1994; Miller, 1998b, 2000, 2006a, 2008a, 2008b, 2012, 2020; Miller & Dion, 2000; Silva, 1991). As always, clinicians should adapt and improvise these guidelines to the specific needs of their individual clients.

Attentive Listening

Attentive or active listening is a basic counseling skill. It includes good eye contact, appropriate body language, genuine interest, and interpersonal engagement, without inappropriate comment or unnecessary interruption.

Empathic Presence

Empathic presence is a therapeutic attitude that conveys availability, concern, and awareness of the disruptive emotions being experienced by the traumatized, distressed crime victim. Several victims have commented that they were put off by their counselor's detached, clinically aloof demeanor and did not feel as if the clinician really was prepared to engage them. Some of this may have to do with countertransference, vicarious traumatization, and emotional contagion issues on the part of the counselor (McCann & Pearlman, 1990; Pearlman & Mac Ian, 1995). Alternatively, some victims may be unusually demanding of the counselor's time and devotion, necessitating the setting of realistic limits, while still retaining empathic engagement.

Reassurance

In acute stress situations, this should take the form of realistically reassuring the crime victim that routine matters will be taken care of, that deferred responsibilities will be handled by others, and that the victim has the support of their family, the mental health clinician, and the criminal justice system. It is also helpful to let the victim know, in a non-alarming manner, what they are likely to experience in the days, weeks, and months ahead. How much information is to be imparted, at what pace, and at what stages in the treatment process should be carefully calibrated to the client's recovering ego strength in order to avoid retraumatization. The key is to balance realism with reassurance.

Supportive Counseling

This includes active listening, restatement of content, clarification of feelings, and validation. It also may include such concrete services as community referral and networking with liaison agencies, if necessary.

Interpretive Counseling

This type of intervention should be used when the crime victim's emotional reaction is significantly greater or reaches into wider areas of the subject's life than the circumstances of the critical incident seem to warrant. In appropriate cases, this therapeutic technique can stimulate the victim to explore underlying emotional, personality, or psychodynamic issues that may be intensifying a naturally stressful traumatic event (Horowitz, 1986). In a few cases, this may lead to continuing, ongoing psychotherapy for broader life issues. The counselor should be careful, however, not to reflexively attribute any atypical reaction of the crime to their criminal victimization as stemming from "unresolved" childhood issues. These may well be important, but the counselor needs to be sure to understand what is happening in the here-and-now before delving into past psychodynamics.

Humor

Humor has its place in many forms of psychotherapy (Fry & Salameh, 1987) and may be especially useful in working with some traumatized crime victims (Fullerton et al., 1992; Henry, 2004; Miller, 1994b, 1998a, 1998b, 2006a, 2008a; Silva, 1991). In general, if the therapist and client can enjoy a laugh together, this may lead to the sharing of more intimate feelings. Humor serves to bring a sense of balance, perspective, and clarity to a world that seems to have been warped and polluted by malevolence and horror. "Show me a man who knows what's funny," Mark Twain said, "and I'll show you a man who knows what's not."

However, it is usually wise to maintain proper boundaries regarding destructive types of self-mockery or inappropriate projective hostility on the client's part. This may occur in the form of sleazy, cynical, or mean-spirited sniping, character assassination, or self-deprecation. Also, recalling the caveat for first responders mentioned previously, counselors should remember that many traumatized individuals tend to be quite concrete and suspicious at the outset of therapy, and certain well-intentioned kidding and cajoling may be perceived as insulting to the crime victim or dismissive of the seriousness of their plight; therefore, clinicians should always try to know the client and take their cues from them.

Utilizing Cognitive Defenses

In psychology, "defense mechanisms" are the mental stratagems the mind uses to protect itself from unpleasant thoughts, feelings, impulses, and memories. Although the normal use of such defenses enables the average person to avoid conflict and ambiguity and maintain some consistency to their personality and belief system, most mental health clinicians would agree that an overuse of defenses to wall off too much unpleasant thought and feeling can lead to a rigid and dysfunctional approach to coping with life. Accordingly, much of the work in traditional psychotherapy involves carefully helping clients to relinquish their pathological defenses so that they can learn to deal with internal conflicts more constructively. However, in the face of acutely traumatizing experiences, the last thing the affected person needs is to have their defenses stripped away.

For an acute psychological trauma, the proper use of psychological defenses can serve as an important "psychological splint" that enables the person to function in the immediate posttraumatic aftermath and eventually be able to productively resolve and integrate the traumatic experience when the luxury of therapeutic time can be afforded (Janik, 1991). In many cases, the clinician discovers that traumatized crime victims need little help in applying defense mechanisms on their own (Durham et al., 1985; Henry, 2004; Taylor et al., 1983). Examples of common defenses—all of which can have both constructive and maladaptive effects, depending on how they are used—include the following.

Denial: "I'm just going to put it out of my mind, focus on other things, and avoid situations or people who remind me of it."

Rationalization: "I had no choice; things happen for a reason; it could have been worse; other people have it worse; most people would react the same way I am."

Displacement/projection: "It was my boss's fault for sending me down to the basement so late at night; the police took forever to respond to the 911 call; the district attorney is going soft on this case because of politics."

Refocusing on positive attributes: "This was an isolated event—I'm usually a cautious, capable person. I'm a smart, strong person; I can get through this."

Refocusing on positive behaviors: "Okay, I'm going to follow safety procedures more carefully and talk to management about getting better security around here. I'm going to advocate for more safety training so nothing like this happens to anyone here again."

Where necessary, at least in the short term, counselors should know when to actively support and bolster psychological defenses that temporarily enable the traumatized crime victim to continue functioning (Janik, 1991). Only when defenses are used inappropriately and for too long, when they begin to hold the crime victim back from facing their fears and reentering the world, should we gently confront the now-maladaptive aspects in an atmosphere of safety and support (Miller, 1998b, 2008a).

Existential Issues, Therapeutic Integration, and Closure

In virtually every case of significant trauma, the victim struggles with shattered assumptions and fantasies about fairness, justice, security, and the meaning of life. Accordingly, it is a legitimate and, in some cases, essential part of the task of psychotherapy to help them come to terms with these existential issues. Some clients obsess over what they did or should have done to avoid or escape more serious harm or to help other people, and with these individuals, the therapeutic task becomes one of reorienting these clients to a more realistic state of self-acceptance. Many clients need to pass the anniversary date of the traumatic event, especially when their trauma was severe, before they can begin to bring the trauma response to closure. The process of simultaneously externalizing and integrating the crime trauma allows the last stages of recovery to take place. As the client approaches closure, the therapist can help them form a newly realistic and adaptive self-image, which becomes the foundation for a healthy future (Calhoun & Tedeschi, 1999; Everstine & Everstine, 1993; Rudofossi, 2007; Tedeschi & Calhoun, 2004; Tedeschi & Kilmer, 2005).

Indeed, the diversity of human personality and the variation in severity and circumstances of the traumatic event virtually guarantee that different victims will have different reactions and that the therapeutic outcomes will vary as well. Thus, posttraumatic integration can be approached from one or more of three main perspectives (Everly, 1994, 1995).

Trauma Integrated Into the Client's Existing Worldview

The message here is that these things happen—people do hurt other people and undeserved injuries do befall innocent victims—but that the affected person is not helpless or hopeless, because there are certain precautions one can take to minimize the risk of this happening in the future. Such a message allows the person to feel reasonably safe again.

Trauma Understood as a Parallel Aspect of the Existing Worldview

The trauma is seen as an "exception to the rule." According to this interpretation, society sets up laws and structures to keep most of us safe most of the time, so this tragedy, while certainly awful, is really an isolated incident that, most likely, never will happen to the same person again. Of course, this must be realistically based; as noted earlier, in some communities, risk of repeated exposure to crime is a grim reality.

Trauma Illustrates the Need to Create a New and Modified Worldview

The trauma can be used to demonstrate the invalidity of the client's existing perspective and the need to construct an alternative one in which the trauma more readily fits. For example, the assault shows the victim that the world is not entirely filled with good people, that justice does not always work out, and that sometimes the innocent suffer and the guilty go free. But the counselor can assist the client in fashioning a new way of looking at things that encourages both realism and cautious optimism; the client can learn to be clear headed, even skeptical, about human nature and motives but without allowing themselves to turn into a soul-shriveled cynic.

I have found that the subject's personality has a strong effect on which integrative strategy is most effective. For example, predominantly externalizing clients seem to adhere to the once-in-a-lifetime "lightning does not strike twice" type of explanation, putting their trust in fate or God or sheer statistical improbability. The "what can I personally do to keep this from happening again" type of reframe appeals more to clients who already possessed a degree of self-efficacy before the trauma and are therefore willing and able to try to solve problems by their own efforts once the therapist shows them the way. Still others may blend various perspectives together.

Finally, counselors must be mindful of victims who suffer from *enhanced integration* of the traumatic theme into their self-concept and life narrative (Berntsen & Rubin, 2007). For these individuals, the crime victimization becomes the exclusive focal point of their entire existence, and their lives become a ceaseless search for validation of their martyrdom. For such clients, the therapeutic emphasis must be on emotionally decoupling from the traumatic victimization and finding non–crime-related activities that encourage these individuals to resume a "civilian" life. In such circumstances, these clients may subtly or overtly shift gears to another alleged source of their woundedness and betrayal, such as family traumas, illness, or disability. Alternatively, they may quit treatment with one counselor and start over with another, more sympathetic counselor until that relationship sours as well, and so on.

Existential treatment strategies that focus on a quest for meaning may productively channel the worldview conflicts generated by the trauma event, such as helping the client to formulate an acceptable "survivor mission" (Shalev et al., 1993). Indeed, in the best cases, the rift and subsequent reintegration of the personality leads to an expanded self-concept and even a new level of psychological and spiritual growth (Bonanno, 2005; Calhoun & Tedeschi, 1999; Tedeschi & Calhoun, 1995, 2004; Tedeschi & Kilmer, 2005). Some trauma survivors are thus able to make positive personal or career changes out of a renewed sense of purpose and value in their lives. Of course, not all crime victims are able to achieve this successful reintegration of the ordeal, and many may struggle with at least some vestige of emotional damage for a long time, perhaps for life (Everstine & Everstine, 1993; Matsakis, 1994; McCann & Pearlman, 1990). Therefore, the main caution about these transformational therapeutic conceptualizations is that they be presented as an opportunity, not an obligation.

The extraction of meaning from adversity is something that ultimately must come from the crime victim themselves and not be foisted on them by the therapist. Such forced existential conversions usually are motivated by a need to reinforce the therapist's own meaning system, or they may be part of what I call a therapeutic "Clarence-the-angel fantasy" (Miller, 1998b), wherein the enlightened counselor swoops down and, by virtue of the clinician's brilliantly insightful ministrations, rescues the client from their darkest hour and gives them a proverbial new lease on life.

Realistically, we can hardly expect all or even most of our traumatized clients miraculously to transcend their tragedy and thereby acquire a fresh, revitalized outlook on life—how many *counselors* would respond this well? But human beings do crave meaning (Yalom, 1980), and if a philosophical or religious orientation can nourish the client in their journey back to the land of the living, then our therapeutic role must sometimes stretch to include some measure of guidance in affairs of the spirit.

COUNSELING IMPLICATIONS

Psychotherapy with traumatized crime victims must span the range from concrete, supportive, and directive approaches to the most abstract, and even—in the broadest sense—spiritual modalities. Short-term crisis intervention can help restore a feeling of stability and control early in the trauma evolution process and possibly prevent the development of more disabling posttraumatic manifestations down the road.

Psychophysiological and cognitive-behavioral symptom-reduction strategies can help break the vicious cycle of escalating distress leading to greater helplessness, more severe distress, and so on. Psychologically integrative therapy and counseling approaches can help crime victims put their experiences into a narrative context to regain a sense of order and meaning in the world. Counselors who work with crime victims should master the fundamental skills of trauma therapy but be knowledgeable and flexible enough to allow each client's individual personality and recovery trajectory to guide intervention efforts.

CONCLUSION

Psychotherapeutic work with crime victim survivors often forces the clinician to confront the effects of human callousness and cruelty in all of its flesh-and-blood starkness. Working with these clients requires skill, dedication, patience, perseverance, flexibility, tolerance of partial solutions, and, sometimes, a strong stomach. But in many cases, the clinician will have the satisfaction of knowing that they have made a substantial impact, not just on the crime victim themselves, but on the larger radiating orbit of family, coworkers, and community.

ADDITIONAL RESOURCES

 A robust set of instructor resources designed to supplement this text is located at http://connect.springerpub.com/content/book/978-0-8261-5085-1. Qualifying instructors may request access by emailing textbook@springerpub.com.

PRACTICE-BASED RESOURCES AND REFERENCES

To view a list of resources and all the references, please visit connect.springerpub.com via the following url: http://connect.springerpub.com/content/book/978-0-8261-5085-1/part/part02/chapter/ch14

CHAPTER 15

Traumatic Aftermath of Homicide and Suicide

JAYNA BONFINI

CHAPTER OVERVIEW

This chapter focuses on the loss, grief, and trauma that survivors may experience in the aftermath of a homicide or suicide. The chapter examines the various effects of homicide and suicide and discusses treatment strategies for working with survivors.

LEARNING OBJECTIVES

After reading this chapter, the reader should be able to:

1. Understand the impact of homicides and suicides on survivors;
2. Develop empathy concerning multiple losses;
3. Discern the potential effect of COVID-19 pandemic isolation on homicide and suicide rates;
4. Identify the diagnostic considerations associated with the loss of a loved one through homicide or suicide; and,
5. Understand the treatment strategies that are most relevant to survivors of homicide and suicide.

INTRODUCTION

There is no way that anyone can prepare for the loss of a loved one through homicide or suicide. These events leave tremendous pain and suffering in their wake. The suddenness, the violence, and the preventability of such deaths complicate and compound the grieving process for survivors. Mental health professionals are positioned uniquely to assist clients in dealing with these traumatic losses, to process their grief, and to minimize the secondary victimization that many survivors experience after a homicide or suicide. This chapter reviews the literature describing the impact of homicide and suicide on those left behind. Treatment issues and strategies for working with survivors are also discussed.

TRAUMA OF HOMICIDE

Each year, over 19,000 people die due to homicide in the United States (Centers for Disease Control and Prevention [CDC], 2017). The Center for Victim Research estimates that approximately 64,000 to 213,000 experience homicide co-victimization each year, which translates to a range of 20 to 70 people per 100,000 annually who are surviving the loss of a murdered loved one (Bastomski & Duane, 2019, pp. 3–4). While few studies measuring the national prevalence of homicide co-victimization exist, we know that every homicide leaves behind family members and loved ones—survivors and co-victims—whose lives are forever changed (Bastomski & Duane, 2019; Spungen, 1998). Losing a loved one to homicide may result in psychological trauma that shatters a person's sense of security and well-being.

Family Survivors

Family members may make sense of their loved one's murder in their own way. Some may try to get back to "normal"; others might not, as they realize the need for a new normal. There may be traumatic reminders throughout the grieving process, and dealing with the criminal justice system often may cause survivors to relive the horror (Spungen, 1998). Some traumatic reminders include news accounts of the murder or similar events; seeing or identifying the murderer; holidays, birthdays, or anniversaries of the loved one's death; and the occurrence of life events that the deceased will never experience (e.g., driving a car, walking their daughter down the aisle, celebrating a child's first steps). Other reactions and contextual factors that affect family members include inexplicability, social stigma, and involvement with the criminal justice system.

Inexplicability

The horror and disbelief of hearing of a loved one's murder is beyond comprehension. It is an ugly situation to process, and individuals often demand to know every piece of information around the death, in order to try to make sense of the situation. Survivors often experience dissociation, or a disruption in how their minds handle information. They may feel disconnected from thoughts, feelings, memories, and surroundings. Survivors often ask the same five questions: (1) What happened? (2) Why did this happen? (3) Why did I act as I did then? (4) Why did I act as I have since then? And (5) What if this happens again? (Figley, 1985, p. 404).

Social Stigma

The way the person died often determines the aftermath of the murder. For example, if a victim engaged in high-risk behavior before the murder (e.g., addiction, gang membership), survivors may feel isolated from others and disenfranchised from their ability to grieve the loss, because others believe that the victim put themselves at risk. In fact, the victim and the victim's family may be blamed irrationally for the murder, as "if only they did X, their loved one would still be alive." This reinforces the assumption of their own personal invulnerability and that people get what they deserve. However, as we know, this is a façade and tragedy can befall any family.

Involvement With the Criminal Justice System

Pleas, motions, hearings, trials, sentencings, appeals, and other aspects of involvement with the criminal justice system can be overwhelming to survivors of homicide. Each step of the legal process can bring strong emotions to surface and cause emotional distress. For example, in cases where there is sufficient evidence for a jury to find the defendant guilty, family members may feel that the sentence was not long enough. Plea bargaining, which dominates the criminal process in the United States, can bring a great deal of frustration to homicide survivors (Reed & Caraballo, 2021). Finally, in cases where the killer is unknown or where there is insufficient evidence for a guilty verdict, the survivor may feel even more helpless or angry.

Multiple Losses

Victims of violent crime frequently experience more than one traumatic event in their lifetimes (Saunders, 2003). Furthermore, criminal victimization is correlated with demographic factors such as racial/ethnic status and socioeconomic status, which represent risk factors for psychiatric disorders (Kilpatrick & Acierno, 2003). Therefore, it sometimes is difficult to attribute psychiatric symptoms to a particular traumatic event. More studies are needed that control for risk factors such as demographic variables and prior trauma history, in order to better understand the effects of traumatic events like homicide victimization. Box 15.1 illustrates one person's experience with multiple losses.

BOX 15.1

Case Illustration: Susan

Susan is a 58-year-old woman, married for 35 years to Rick, 59. They have two grown children: Jeremy, 28, and Natalie, 24. Susan works as a reading specialist at a local elementary school, and her husband owns a landscaping business. The family is close-knit, and during the busy summer months of Rick's business, the whole family worked together on landscaping projects and routine maintenance.

Late one evening, police officers rang the family's doorbell and informed Susan and Rick that Jeremy had been murdered. Susan does not recall what happened in the next moment, and the hours and days after receiving the news are missing from her memory. She went with Rick to choose a casket and plan a funeral, but she reports that she cannot tell you who attended the funeral, what was said, or even what she wore. She asked, "What are you supposed to wear to your child's funeral anyway?"

Susan began to be aware of feelings and sensations as the initial shock began to subside. Her appetite was nonexistent, and she was unable to sleep for more than an hour or two at most. Susan had recurrent nightmares of Jeremy asking for help or calling out to her asking why he died. Susan would wake up shaking and wracked with a sense of guilt that she had been unable to help and protect her son. She took a leave of absence from work until the end of the academic year.

Rick, concerned for Susan's health, was able to convince her to leave the home and visit a doctor. Susan's doctor prescribed medication to help with sleep and depressive symptoms. Susan began to regain her strength and emotional stability, as she was able to rest and recover from her profound loss.

When an arrest was made, a month later, Susan and Rick were told that the case against the alleged perpetrator was strong and that a trial date would be in 6 months. Susan and Rick were informed by the district attorney that the trial would start on a particular date. However, when they arrived, they learned that, at the last minute, the trial had been postponed. This was very frustrating to both Susan and Rick, who were hoping for a sense of closure, as well as justice for Jeremy.

When the trial finally commenced, Susan found it difficult to observe images from the crime scene and had to leave the courtroom temporarily. She found it difficult to breathe and had thoughts of Jeremy's suffering in his final moments. A guilty verdict was ultimately returned, and Susan, Rick, and Natalie prepared victim impact statements to express their pain and injuries as a result of Jeremy's murder. The killer was sentenced to prison, for 20 years, for murder in the second degree.

Once the legal case was closed, Susan thought her life would return to "normal," or as close to normal as she could imagine, but without Jeremy. Unfortunately, the trial brought up some

(continued)

of the feelings, nightmares, and anxiety that she experienced during the time after Jeremy's funeral. Her flashbacks worsened, and her sleep suffered; she also became reclusive, spending days in Jeremy's childhood bedroom surrounded by his photos, old sports trophies, and other items that reminded her of him. Rick, again concerned, called their family doctor who referred Susan to a trauma counselor.

The trauma counselor, Tamara, diagnosed Susan with posttraumatic stress disorder (PTSD). During the initial assessment, Tamara discovered that Susan blamed herself for Jeremy's death, because she had encouraged him to move into his own apartment the year prior. Susan wanted him to be more independent and to live as a young adult and not a "perpetual teenager" in her home. Tamara was able to reframe this distortion for Susan and began a course of Eye Movement Desensitization and Reprocessing (EMDR) to help Susan cope with the traumatic images. Tamara also referred Susan to a psychiatrist to obtain medication to help relieve the symptoms of hypervigilance and avoidance that she was experiencing.

Susan's symptoms subsided over time, and after more than a year, Susan felt that she was ready to take what she had learned about this process and help others in similar situations. Susan worked with another homicide survivor to start a local support group aimed at helping other families and friends to navigate the thoughts, feelings, and sensations that surround such a seismic loss.

TRAUMA OF SUICIDE

Suicide long has been considered a global public health problem, with about 800,000 people taking their lives each year (World Health Organization [WHO], 2019). It is a complex and multidimensional phenomenon. Individuals who attempt suicide frequently describe feelings of hopelessness, despair, and social isolation as triggers for acting on suicidal impulses (Feigelman & Feigelman, 2008). According to WHO data, each suicide is accompanied by more than 20 suicide attempts (WHO, 2019). In 2019, the most recent year that full data are accessible from the CDC, the number of deaths totaled 47,511 in the United States. It is in the top 10 causes of death across all age groups and the second-leading cause of death in persons under the age of 34 (CDC, 2017).

The literature describes suicide as affecting between five nuclear family members and 80 relatives, friends, and acquaintances (Andriessen et al., 2017; Berman, 2011). A meta-analysis by Andriessen et al. (2017) found that 4.3% of people have experienced a suicide in the previous year, with 21.8% being exposed to suicide during their lifetimes. This makes suicide a highly pervasive phenomenon, with the group of suicide survivors being one of the largest at-risk communities for mental health disorders. Suicide survivors show increased risk of complicated grief, depressive and anxiety disorders, substance-abuse disorders, and suicidal behavior (Jordan & McIntosh, 2011).

Grieving suicide survivors are a particular group of individuals. Grief is the natural reaction to the loss of someone significant, as the survivor processes emotional, psychological, physical, and behavioral responses to the death (Jordan & McIntosh, 2011). However, people grieving suicide loss also present an important component of shock and possible trauma, as well as feelings of abandonment, rejection, unacceptance, and shame related to the circumstances of death (Jordan & McIntosh, 2011).

Family Survivors

When a loved one is murdered, there is often a desire for an explanation; the question "Why?" emerges. Why did this happen? However, when a loved one dies by suicide, the "Why?"

Table 15.1

Relationship Loss Issues for Survivors of Suicide

Loss of a Child	Loss of a Parent	Loss of a Sibling	Loss of a Spouse/Partner
• Rejection • Guilt • Shame • Blame • Stigma • Fear of exposure as failure • Anger	• Abandonment • Legacy of suicide • Children acting out in grief • Secondary loss of surviving parent • Guilt • Responsibility • Blame • Parentification	• Loss of victim as well as parent(s) • Added family responsibility • Anger • Blame parent for failure • Overresponsibility • Parentification	• Abandonment • Rejection • Blame • Survivor guilt • Anger • Stigma • Others blame spouse • Expectations of others

question is coupled with the question of responsibility. In homicide, the horrific intent of the murderer might explain what happened; this intent, coupled with actions, certainly points to responsibility, especially in the court of law. However, the responsibility question is not always so clear with respect to suicide. Jordan (2020) explains that most survivors begin by blaming themselves for the death. "Many survivors repeatedly review a litany of their own 'sins of omission and commission' in trying to assign responsibility for the death" (Jordan, 2020).

Those who are left behind in the wake of a suicide are left trying to understand how to deal with an inexplicable act. They are left to mourn a parent, child, or sibling who was a part of their life since the moment they were born, or to mourn a spouse whose love and life they shared, or to grieve their very best friend and companion. In his 2020 article summarizing his 40 years of experience working with suicide survivors, John Jordan outlined the mourning process after a suicide and how it differs from more normative causes of death. First, there is a greater need to seek an explanation for the death and to make sense of the death (Jordan, 2020). Second, survivors experience greater levels of guilt and felt responsibility for the death, or, at a minimum, for a failure to somehow foresee and prevent the suicide (Jordan, 2020). Third, there is a greater level of stigmatization and shame about this mode of death, and a greater need to conceal the fact that the death was a suicide (Jordan, 2020). Fourth, survivors receive more avoidance by, and isolation from, social support from their regular social networks (Jordan, 2020). And, fifth, exposure to the loss of a loved one to suicide increases the chances of suicidal thinking and behavior in the person exposed (Jordan, 2020).

The type of relationship that was lost influences the reactions of the survivor. Because the needs, responsibilities, hopes, and expectations associated with each type of relationship vary, the personal meanings and social implications of each type of death also differ. Table 15.1 demonstrates relationship loss issues that may arise when a loved one dies by suicide, as highlighted in Flatt's (2007) Suicide Survivors' Support Group Guide.

Loss of a Child

Katrina Fuller lost her son, Landon, 11, to suicide in late April 2020, after the schools were closed across the country and stay-at-home orders imposed to minimize the spread of COVID-19. The closures were hard on many people; for some, it was completely destabilizing. Landon took the shutdowns especially hard (MacGillis, 2021). He was an outgoing kid who loved school, enjoyed attending church, and liked riding bikes with his friends in the neighborhood. He was lonely and had written in his journal that the lockdowns were driving him crazy and that all he wanted was to go to school and play outside with his friends (MacGillis, 2021). It was too much for him to bear. As Katrina and her family tried to recover from this loss, several months later, a letter arrived at the grieving family's home. It was a form letter from the state Public Education

Department indicating that Landon had been truant from his online classes in Fall 2020 (MacGillis, 2021). Her sadness turned to anger at the insensitive oversight.

Katrina started hearing from other families from around the country, including a mother of a 6-year-old. "These are kids without mental health issues, with good families, kids that are loved," Katrina said. "I've heard it all," Fuller said with respect to explanations. "I've blamed myself" (MacGillis, 2021).

Parents who lose a child experience unique circumstances that can intensify and prolong the mourning process. They struggle to make sense as to why their 11-, 15-, 19-, or 25-year-old child did not ask them for help. Sometimes there are warning signs of the person's intentions. However, clues may be so disguised that even a trained professional may not recognize them. Occasionally there are no discernible signs, and the child's suicide becomes a catastrophic decision that may never be understood. While mental illness often plays a role in suicide, not everyone who dies by suicide is mentally ill (Stone et al., 2018). For every family that has experienced years of treatments, hospitalizations, and medications with their child, others experience none at all.

Loss of a Parent

In the wake of a parent suicide, many children and young teens are devastated and "experience profound grief, guilt, and anxiety that may persist for months and even years" (Jamison, 1999, p. 302). Losing a parent to suicide at an early age is often a catalyst for the child's own psychiatric disorders and even suicide; however, it is the simultaneous developmental, environmental, and genetic factors, which come together, that increase the risk for also dying by suicide (Wilcox et al., 2010). Children can be surprisingly resilient, and research demonstrates that a supportive environment and attention to any emergent mental health symptoms may offset even such a major stressor as a parent's suicide (Cohen et al., 2006; Jamison, 1999; Janet Kuramoto et al., 2009; Wilcox et al., 2010). Like other trauma survivors, there may be a critical window for intervention in the aftermath of a parent's suicide, during which clinicians carefully can monitor and refer children for psychiatric evaluation and, if needed, residential care (Wilcox et al., 2010).

Siblings

People who lose a sibling to suicide often experience anger, complicated grief reactions, depression, posttraumatic stress disorder, and even thoughts of taking their own lives (Bolton et al., 2017). Until recently, these survivors were overlooked in medical research, However, according to several studies of survivors, those who lose a sibling to suicide, especially one of the same sex or close in age, have more serious mood disorders and thoughts of suicide themselves than survivors who lose a sibling for any other reason (Bolton et al., 2017; Royden, 2019). It might be difficult, as well, for siblings to find support within their families, as they are struggling with the loss, and in some families, siblings feel that they should not show their pain for the sake of their parents (Royden, 2019).

Spouse

Companionship in many marriages consists of sharing daily routines, responsibilities, and bed and often the sharing of intimate lives. In all cases, the death of a spouse to suicide necessitates that the survivor find substitute companions or tolerate a lonelier life. In addition to dealing with the traumatic loss, the surviving spouse is left with unfamiliar tasks to be accomplished. For example, the loss of a spouse may mean the loss of the family's chief income producer, which then imposes on the survivor a need to manage the household finances and to compensate for the spouse's absence. This is especially difficult if the couple has young children to support.

Writing in *Night Falls Fast: Understanding Suicide*, Jamison (1999) recounts a woman's experience after the death of her husband: "The guilt and 'if onlys' escalated and seemed to be endless, especially for me. My husband's parents, who were very close to us before the suicide, blamed me for my husband's depression and refused to enter our home" (p. 302). In this way, the couple's children lost both their father and their paternal grandparents to suicide.

Survivors experience greater levels of guilt and felt responsibility for the death (or at a minimum, for a failure, somehow, to foresee and to prevent the suicide). There is a greater level of stigmatization and shame about this mode of death, and a greater need to conceal the fact that the death was a suicide. In her aforementioned book, Jamison (1999) recounts a story of the denial of suicide. One of her colleagues, an eminent scientist, suffered from bipolar disorder and killed himself. His wife refused to belief that he had died by suicide and forbade it from being mentioned at his funeral or memorial service. She unknowingly "made it very hard for his fellow professors, graduate students, and laboratory staff to deal with his death and move on with their lives. Even a year later, his students and colleagues found it difficult to discuss the suicide" (Jamison, p. 299).

There is an expression in the support community that goes along the lines of "No one brings you a casserole when your family member dies by suicide" (or when your loved one is an addict or has another stigmatized mental health diagnosis). Survivors experience more avoidance by, and isolation from, their supports and from their regular social networks. Additionally, as in other sudden, unexpected, and often violent deaths such as homicide, suicide also seems to produce higher levels of PTSD-type symptoms such as avoidance and hyperarousal (Bonanno et al., 2007). This often is accompanied by a significant disruption of the survivors' assumptive world (e.g., beliefs such as "my life is predictable" and "I can keep my loved ones safe from harm" (Parkes, 2001, 2013).

CURRENT RESEARCH: COVID-19'S IMPACT

At the time of this writing, we do not yet know the full impact of COVID-19 in terms of homicide and suicide survivors as a full report of the 2020 data is not yet available. However, COVID-19 brought together extreme cases of social isolation and/or unrest and economic unease against a background of fragile and undersupported public health systems. With such risk factors, it is unsurprising that the homicide and suicide rates increased during 2020—as well as the ranks of survivors left behind. Indeed, this pandemic fundamentally has disrupted the ways in which survivors process death and grieving. In-person funerals have been replaced by scaled-down or virtual events. Relatives and friends expressing condolences often have provided them via a smartphone screen instead of in person.

In a recent report by the National Commission on COVID-19 and criminal justice, homicide rates in a sample of 34 cities were 30% higher in 2020 than in 2019, a jump that claimed an additional 1,268 lives in those cities alone. Rosenfeld et al. (2021) said that urgent action is needed to address the increase, including subduing the pandemic, improving police legitimacy, and expanding proven antiviolence programs in cities hardest hit by crime.

While homicide rates in 2020 were higher than 2019 levels during every month of the year, the rise was steepest in June, coinciding with mass protests after the May 25 killing of George Floyd by a Minneapolis police officer. The three largest cities in the sample, New York, Los Angeles, and Chicago, accounted for 40% of the 1,268 additional murder victims in 2020 (Rosenfeld et al., 2021). Rosenfeld et al. (2021) reported that "While there is variation among the cities, what is most notable is that homicide rose substantially in the vast majority of them" (p. 18). Overall, a rise in murders of this magnitude suggests that the increase in the national homicide rate is likely to exceed the previous largest single-year increase of 13% in 1968 (Rosenfeld et al., 2021). That determination, however, cannot be verified until official crime statistics are released by the federal government in late 2021. It should be noted that homicide has dropped significantly in the United States since the early 1990s, although brief spikes occurred in 2005, 2006, 2015, and 2016. Even with the 2020 increases, the homicide rate for the cities in the Rosenfeld et al. study was just over half of what it was for those same cities 25 years ago (11.4 deaths per 100,000 residents in those cities versus 19.4 per 100,000 in 1995) (Rosenfeld et al., 2021).

Suicide and COVID-19

The compulsory lockdowns for people during the spring of 2020 confined nearly half of the world's population to their households. This lockdown, to stop the spread of COVID-19, led to a decrease in contacts and deprived individuals from their support and care structures as people received help only for basic daily needs. During this time, Pinto et al. (2020) explained, "Emotional and affective support was scarce, with a marked increase in feelings of loneliness and isolation" (p. 2). Even prior to COVID-19, the suicide rates had been climbing, in addition to rising rates of anxiety, depression, and substance abuse. During the week of June 24, 2020, CDC data showed that younger adults, racial/ethnic minorities, essential workers, and unpaid adult caregivers reported having experienced disproportionately worse mental health outcomes, increased substance use, and elevated suicidal ideation (Czeisler et al., 2020). Alarmingly, nearly a quarter of young adults experienced suicidal thoughts (Czeisler et al., 2020).

The full data set for 2020 is not yet completed; sadly, it seems that 2020 will be another year of suicide increases (Czeisler et al., 2020). If these trends continue, or if it will be a 1 or 2 year increase due to the pandemic, only time will tell. We know that some of the strategies that successfully have prevented homicides and suicide in the past are not available until the vaccines become more widespread, and society resumes a semblance of normalcy. However, in the meantime, mental health, medical care, and services for justice-involved individuals require a great deal of face-to-face contact, typically among service providers and the people who are most likely both to commit these offenses and to be the victims of them. Not everyone has the capability to engage in telehealth and videoconferencing, and this makes it difficult for those who cannot meet in person.

DIAGNOSTIC CONSIDERATIONS

Intense grief is typical, after we lose someone close, and remains intense until we adapt to the loss. For an estimated 10% to 15% of bereaved people in the general population, adaptation is problematic (Bryant, 2013). The rates for bereaved people experiencing difficulty in adapting are higher when the death is sudden, unexpected, or violent, such as in homicide and suicide (Bastomski & Duane, 2019). Evidence indicates that many survivors are diagnosed with posttraumatic stress disorder (PTSD), depression, suicidal ideation, and/or complicated grief as a result of their experiences.

Posttraumatic Stress Disorder

As individuals, we often have the deepest connections with those that we love—these relationships help make us who we are. They contribute to our sense of identity and have the power to transform us, for good or bad. Because of this, the death of a loved one can create numerous psychological issues, including the development of PTSD, particularly if the loss is tragic and unexpected. By definition, PTSD can occur when someone has experienced, witnessed, or been confronted with a terrible event. News of an unexpected death already brings up especially strong emotions, because it catches us off guard. A tragic death magnifies these feelings. In fact, a 2014 study by Keyes et al. (2014) noted that, "unexpected death was associated consistently with elevated odds of new onsets of PTSD, panic disorder, and depressive episodes at all stages of the life course." The symptoms of PTSD (American Psychiatric Association, 2013; Mitchell & Terhorst, 2017) include:

- Being frequently angry, tense, or jumpy;
- Physical symptoms like heart palpitations, sweating, or hyperventilating;
- Flashbacks of the trauma or dwelling on what the person might have gone through in their final moments;

- Persistent avoidance of things or events that remind us of the person or place where the tragedy occurred;
- Avoiding the emotions surrounding the death or event;
- Problems sleeping or nightmares;
- Changing personal routine to avoid reminders of the event;
- Distorted feelings of guilt and blaming; and,
- Negative thoughts.

Most of the time, people slowly begin to recover from the initial shock and grief of a death. For those with PTSD, however, the symptoms dramatically affect their day-to-day lives, and they experience the symptoms for at least a month, perhaps longer. While some survivors may eventually recover on their own, it is best to seek counseling and other assistance to overcome PTSD symptoms.

Major Depressive Disorder

The death of a loved one can lead to major depressive disorder (MDD; Bastomski & Duane, 2019; Bellini et al., 2018), which can be diagnosed in the fallout of a traumatic death. People with MDD experience symptoms like persistent sadness, loss of interest in activities, and sleep and appetite disturbance (American Psychiatric Association, 2013). Additionally, suicide survivors may be at an increased risk for suicide themselves, particularly if they have lost a romantic partner or child to suicide, as discussed previously. This risk is even higher if the suicide survivor has a mental health diagnosis such as PTSD or MDD (Bellini et al., 2018).

Prolonged/Complicated Grief

There is no predictable trajectory to the traumatic grief related to homicide and suicide. Acute grief symptoms—such as feelings of shock, sadness, and yearning—usually lessen in intensity over time, enabling the bereaved to reengage with life. However, approximately 10% of bereaved people find that grief persists with substantial distress and impairment for years after a loss—a condition called complicated grief (Columbia Center for Complicated Grief, 2018). Complicated grief is diagnosed when grief and related symptoms remain severe beyond the first year, interfering substantially with healthy functioning and impeding the survivor's ability to integrate the loss and move forward (Columbia Center for Complicated Grief, 2018). Risk factors for complicated grief are elevated after a traumatic loss, such as to suicide or homicide. Indeed, homicide survivors experience complicated grief at a rate two to three times higher than the general population (Columbia Center for Complicated Grief, 2018).

RELEVANT MULTICULTURAL ISSUES

It is well-established that grief due to homicide or suicide is difficult regardless of race, age, gender, or socioeconomic status. However, certain populations are more vulnerable and may be at heightened risk. Throughout the United States, homicide and its survivors are geographically concentrated in large cities (e.g., New York, Los Angeles, Chicago) with larger Black and Latinx populations and part of a broader pattern of structural inequalities (Rosenfeld et al., 2021). Black and Latinx people face an elevated risk of homicide and homicide co-victimization compared to their White counterparts (CDC, 2017). Additionally, Native Americans also face higher rates of homicide compared to Whites. Based on a lack of research that examines the rate of homicide survivorship or co-victimization among Native Americans, it is not possible to present an accurate estimate of the risk that Native Americans face (Bastomski & Duane, 2019, p. 5). We can only make an inference, based on the prevalence rates and existing literature, that the risk is elevated.

Race and ethnicity are correlated with high risk of homicide survivorship. In particular, Black adults, adolescents, and children, as well as Latinx adolescents and children, are substantially overrepresented as homicide survivors (Bastomski & Duane, 2019; Turner et al., 2018). Alarmingly, evidence suggests that homicide survivors/co-victims are concentrated among adolescents. Bastomski and Duane (2019) explain, "people are most likely to identify as a survivor during this time . . . the difference in reporting could reflect variation in how younger people perceive loss" (p. 5).

Conversely, the prevalence rate for suicide is higher among White Americans, well above those for Asian Americans, Black Americans, and Hispanics (Frakt, 2020). Case and Deaton (2017) found that both White non-Hispanic men and White women are facing a mortality crisis with what they refer to as "deaths of despair" (e.g., deaths by suicide, alcohol, and drugs; p. 11). White deaths of despair have increased in all regions of the country at every level of urbanization (Case & Deaton, 2017, p. 12). The epidemic has spread from the Southwest, where it was centered in 2000, first to Appalachia and then to Florida and the west coast by the mid-2000s; it is now, unfortunately, nationwide (Case & Deaton, 2017, p. 12). Additionally, the CDC found higher suicide rates in rural America than in medium/small and large metropolitan counties. Most gun deaths in America are suicides, not murders; White men are more likely to own a gun (CDC, 2017; Frakt, 2020).

Protective factors such as the Christian or Catholic faith for Black Americans and the Latinx populations, respectively, and kinship responsibilities held by Asian Americans may keep their suicide prevalence and survivorship rate lower than Whites (Frakt, 2020). This is despite lower unemployment and other markers of success (Frakt, 2020).

TRAUMA-INFORMED TREATMENT STRATEGIES

Survivors of suicide and homicide face unique challenges that can impede the normal grieving process. As mentioned in an earlier section, this puts survivors at an increased risk for developing complicated grief, MDD, PTSD, and suicidal ideation. If left untreated, these conditions can lead to prolonged suffering, impaired functioning, negative health outcomes, and even fatalities. There are several effective treatment therapies for addressing significant mental health disorders after the sudden or traumatic death of a loved one, including cognitive behavioral therapy (CBT), EMDR, and somatic experiencing. Sometimes medications are used in conjunction with these modalities.

Cognitive Behavioral Therapy

A tragedy and the resulting trauma may alter survivors' thinking as they try to process what happened. For example, they might feel overwhelming guilt, as if they were somehow responsible for the event. Or they may feel detached from the world or from those they love. These negative thoughts can cause avoidance of the things normally enjoyed, or they can cause survivors to worry obsessively that they may lose someone else in a similar manner. Initially developed by Aaron Beck in 1964, CBT focuses on the relationship among thoughts, feelings, and behaviors, and notes how changes in one domain may improve functioning in the others (Beck, 1976). Altering a person's unhelpful or faulty thinking may lead to healthier coping and improved emotional regulation.

Counselors using CBT encourage clients to evaluate their thinking patterns and assumptions in order to identify unhelpful patterns in thoughts, such as overgeneralizing bad outcomes and applying this type of overgeneralization to all situations. By using CBT, clients learn to overcome the kind of negative thinking that diminishes anything positive or even neutral, and that positions clients to expect catastrophic outcomes. Counselors aim for their clients to achieve a more balanced and effective pattern of thought. The intention is to help clients to reconceptualize their understandings of traumatic experiences, as well as their understanding of themselves and their ability to cope (Monson & Shnaider, 2014). Additionally, clients are exposed to the trauma narrative, whereby they are reminded of the emotions associated with the traumatic loss. This helps clients to reduce avoidance and maladaptive associations with the trauma in a controlled and measured way, working collaboratively with the counselor at the client's own pace (Monson & Shnaider, 2014).

Eye Movement Desensitization and Reprocessing

EMDR helps people to process trauma on an emotional level. With PTSD, traumatic thoughts and memories work against the brain's healing process. Flashbacks, nightmares, and disturbing emotions cycle through the brain, keeping the ordeal in the forefront of the person's mind. EMDR therapy can break that cycle by using bilateral (both sides of the body) stimuli to tap into the biological mechanisms that the brain uses during rapid eye movement (REM) sleep (Shapiro & Maxfield, 2002). The theory is that using REM, while recalling the disturbing thoughts or memories of the trauma, helps the brain to process it naturally, allowing the mind to heal. A therapist might use such bilateral stimulation as hand-tapping, eye movements (e.g., following a pattern of lights, following fingers moving back and forth), vibrations, and musical tones.

More than 30 positive controlled outcome studies have been done on EMDR therapy. Some of the studies show that 84% to 90% of single-trauma victims no longer have posttraumatic stress disorder after only three 90-minute sessions. Another study, funded by the HMO Kaiser Permanente, found that 100% of the single-trauma victims and 77% of multiple-trauma victims no longer were diagnosed with PTSD after only six 50-minute sessions (EMDRIA, 2021). Given the large research base demonstrating EMDR's effectiveness for the treatment for trauma, it is well-regarded by organizations such as the American Psychiatric Association and the World Health Organization (EMDRIA, 2021).

Somatic Experiencing®

The Somatic Experiencing method is a body-oriented approach to recovery from trauma and other stress disorders. Created by Levine (1997), Somatic Experiencing releases traumatic shock to transform emotional trauma. It differs from cognitive therapies in that its major interventional strategy involves bottom-up processing by directing the client's attention to internal sensations, both visceral and muscular-skeletal, rather than to primarily cognitive or emotional experiences (Payne et al., 2015). Somatic Experiencing specifically avoids direct and intense evocation of traumatic memories and instead approaches the charged memories indirectly and gradually.

Family Therapy

In addition to individual therapy, family therapy may be helpful for those attempting to reconstruct their worldview after a homicide or suicide. The goal of family therapy, in the aftermath of homicide and suicide, is to assist the loved ones in the completion of unfinished business between themselves and those whom they lost. It also is helpful to recognize the remaining roles and relationships in the family that have been left behind.

Counselors who work with families are aware of the diversity of family dynamics that must be addressed and accommodated in treatment. This applies to reactions to tragedy as well. Vesper and Cohen (1999) describe five types of family reactions in the face of traumatic loss, including in the case of criminal victimization and its aftermath. The "contemptuous family" copes with adversity by getting upset, berating and blaming each other, and/or denying the existence of problems. Counselors may have to start with getting family members to communicate over small matters before addressing big issues like their common loss. The "brittle family" members are reluctant to depend on one another for support; they prefer to rely on outsiders for care and concern. The counselor may take advantage of this and serve as a bridge to connect family members. The "hierarchical family" functions with a sense of internal unity and purpose.

However, it has little flexibility, and specific family members—usually the older persons or eldest child—make the decisions. While this structure can inject an element of order and stability to chaos, the risk is that the cohesion may crumble if the hierarchy breaks down. The counselor should encourage flexibility in decision-making. The "enduring family" relies on religious faith to deal with tragedy. They expect that God deems the consequences that are appropriate, and that challenges sometimes will occur that are part of a greater plan. As long as this remains a healthy and inclusive way of coping, counselors should reinforce meaning-making. Last, and healthiest, is the "functional family," which supports and bolsters more devastated family members while working to care for one another. For these families, the counselor's task is to encourage members to keep providing positive support (Vesper & Cohen, 1999).

Group Therapy

In her seminal work, *Trauma and Recovery*, Herman (1997) writes that while a survivors' group is a good idea, it requires careful planning by the group leader, as groups that start out with an overabundance of hope may dissolve, thereby causing additional pain. Potential group members must be screened to ensure that the modality is appropriate for all participants. Herman notes that the "destructive potential of groups is equal to their therapeutic promise" (p. 217). However, when groups are successful, survivors of homicide and suicide are given the opportunity to share feelings with others, to promote self-esteem, as they alternatively receive and provide help to others, and to find personal meaning in the traumatic events that led them there. Herman (1997) explains:

> Commonality with other people carries with it all the meanings of the word common. It means belonging to a society, having a public role, being part of that which is universal. It means having a feeling of familiarity, of being known, of communion. It means taking part in the customary, the commonplace, the ordinary, and the everyday. It also carries with it a feeling of smallness, or insignificance, a sense that one's own troubles are 'as a drop of rain in the sea.' The survivor who has achieved commonality with others can rest from her labors. Her recovery is accomplished; all that remains before her is her life. (pp. 235–236)

Peer Support Groups

Peer support groups have been founded by survivors who already have worked through many of the issues in the aftermath of homicide, and who wish to help others who are similarly situated. Support groups are a safe place for survivors to share experiences and feelings. Many survivors who recently have lost a loved one learn that others have had the same reactions to a horrific experience, and it provides them with hope that they, too, will be able to cope. A list of resources for peer support groups is located in the online version of this chapter. Box 15.2 describes a clinical pitfall that could jeopardize an attempt at counseling a client who needs services.

BOX 15.2

Clinical Pitfall

Commonly, some counselors aim to "fix" the presenting problem, as soon as possible, by using interventions that are dictated by their clinical approaches. For example, Larry, a counselor using CBT, asked his client James, a grieving widower, to "change his negative thinking" about his wife's death by suicide. While CBT can be helpful in treating survivors following

(continued)

a traumatic loss, Larry first must strive to create a secure attachment with James, in order to understand, fully, the long-term impact that such a loss may have on James, who had hoped to grow old with his wife. Having a theoretical underpinning is necessary in treatment. However, counselors must be patient and fully present with a client, going at the client's pace. It is difficult to work with people who are in extreme pain, and counselors must remember that the survivor does not have a choice. Survivors cannot undo what has happened to their loved ones. Counselors working with this population must tolerate the persistence of the pain of this experience and be willing to sit with clients as they work through this intense pain.

COUNSELING IMPLICATIONS

We should note that clinicians often lack experience and training in working with survivors of suicide and homicide. Indeed, many clinicians may find it overwhelming and exhausting to work with clients who are grieving. Those who work with homicide and suicide survivors must develop an ability to listen empathically to the repeated and often vivid descriptions of violent images, poignant memories, and even fantasies for revenge. Validating a client's suffering makes the counselor vulnerable to vicarious traumatization (vicarious traumatization is detailed in Chapter 30, "Vicarious Traumatization," but it is important to discuss it briefly, here, as it relates to working with homicide and suicide survivors). It is believed that counselors working with trauma survivors experience vicarious trauma because of the work that they do with individuals who are in a great deal of pain due to abnormal events. Vicarious traumatization refers to negative changes in the clinician's view of self, others, and the world, resulting from repeated empathic engagement with clients' trauma-related thoughts, memories, and emotions (Pearlman & Saakvitne, 1995).

Vicarious trauma is the emotional residue of exposure that counselors have from working with traumatized people; as counselors hear clients' trauma stories, the counselors become witnesses to the pain, fear, and terror that trauma survivors have endured (Pearlman & Saakvitne, 1995). This is not simply burnout; vicarious trauma is a state of stress, tension, and preoccupation concerning the trauma experiences described by clients. Symptoms might include an avoidance of talking or thinking about what the trauma survivor has been talking about, being numb to the client's pain, or being in a persistent state of arousal. Counselors should be aware of the signs and symptoms of vicarious trauma along with the potential emotional effects of working with trauma survivors. Counselors must be careful not to assume feelings and experiences that belong to clients. Obtaining appropriate clinical supervision and attending to self-care needs are incredibly important for counselors working with this population.

Counselor as Homicide Survivor

Losing a client to homicide is distinct from other forms of termination or bereavement, in that it is violent, transgressive, and intentional (Milman et al., 2018). Resilience is an essential component for counselors whose clients are murdered. Counselors who have a strong support network, who maintain a sense of hope and optimism, and who remember to practice self-care are more likely and better able to overcome adverse events. Bolstering resilience can allow mental health professionals to become better able to cope with such a loss and to experience posttraumatic growth following the death of a person in treatment.

Counselor as Suicide Survivor

The potential for losing a client to suicide is always a risk for mental health professionals. Whenever it happens, everyone associated with the client is affected by the tragedy. Box 15.3 presents a clinical illustration of when a counselor is the survivor of a client's suicide.

BOX 15.3

Clinical Illustration: Surviving Candice's Suicide

Candice was a 38-year old homemaker and mother of two. She was from a small town in Eastern Ohio and moved to Pittsburgh 12 years ago, when she married her husband. She initially was referred to counseling for depression, following an acrimonious divorce after her husband's affair. Candice and her ex-husband only communicated through the "Family Wizard" platform, which was monitored by the court and their attorneys; they had a strict schedule, with respect to joint custody of the two sons, ages 11 and 9. Candice believed that the male judge had sided with her ex-husband in awarding joint custody. She had wanted sole custody of their children. Instead, she had her children half of the time and her ex and his new girlfriend had them the other half. Her ex-husband objected to her receiving spousal support; however, she had not worked since they married 12 years ago, per her ex-husband's desire to have a stay-at-home spouse. To resume her teaching career, Candice needed to retake qualifying examinations and other continuing education. The judge awarded 3 years of spousal support, estimating that this would be how long it would take Candice to get her career on track and support herself.

After a few months of outpatient therapy and a referral to a psychiatrist for an antidepressant, Candice's mood began to improve. She began to practice self-care, started a workout routine with other women, and embarked on a path to be recertified as a teacher. Candice talked with her counselor about taking a trip to visit family in Ohio and reconnect with old friends. However, on the day prior to her leaving, her ex-husband called their oldest son and announced that he was now engaged and that the boys would be big brothers to an eventual half-sibling. The boys would celebrate the happy news with their father and new stepmother-to-be that weekend. Candice met her ex at the designated drop-off point, as planned, that next morning. Directly after hugging her boys goodbye, Candice got in her car, drove to a bridge, and jumped off. Her counselor initially learned of her death on Facebook.

One of the tragedies of Candice's suicide is that she had been improving and charting a new path of independence, and then a setback—news of her ex-husband moving on and building a new family—leveled her. Counselors must address the aftermath of client suicide. The loss is significant, both personally and professionally. Hendin et al. (2000) surveyed 26 therapists who lost a client to suicide. They found that emotional reactions of guilt were common, as were shock, grief, fear of blame, self-doubt, shame, anger, and a sense of betrayal. Twenty-one of the 26 therapists identified at least one major change that they could have made, thinking that if only they did X or said Y, the suicide could have been prevented (Hendin et al., 2000). Some of the therapists were reluctant to accept subsequent suicidal clients into their practices as a result of the client suicide. Finally, although colleagues were supportive, institutional responses, case reviews, and debriefs were rarely helpful, as these either attributed blame or offered false reassurance that the suicide was inevitable (Hendin et al., 2000).

There is a paucity of information regarding self-care after the loss of a client to suicide. However, it is of the utmost importance, because a client's suicide can generate counselor feelings of low self-esteem, professional incompetence, and thoughts about the counselor's own mortality.

Many competent clinicians—about a quarter of all counselors (Meyers, 2015)—lose a client to suicide. We are humans first, before we are professionals, and we need to take the time to discuss our feelings and review the case with a trusted colleague, preferably one who has been in the same position. Counselors who experience a client's suicide are also at risk for mental health problems, like anyone else surviving a traumatic loss. Unfortunately, the pressures of work and lack of time often have an impact on counselors' ability to take appropriate measures for their own self-care after client suicide (Scupham & Goss, 2020). However, it is paramount for counselors to be given space to grieve, to have open communication in the workplace, and to receive peer support and supervision. For counselors in private practice, client suicide raises the need for external support to be accessible as well.

CONCLUSION

This chapter addressed the many factors surrounding the violent and sudden nature of homicide and suicide, as well as how such an event may affect a survivor's ability to cope in the aftermath. Survivors of homicide and suicide need competent counselors to help them with processing their traumatic experiences. Counselors working with this population must be prepared to listen to graphic detail and difficult emotions from grief-stricken clients, while engaging their own support systems to prevent vicarious traumatization.

ADDITIONAL RESOURCES

 SPRINGER PUBLISHING **CONNECT™** | A robust set of instructor resources designed to supplement this text is located at http://connect.springerpub.com/content/book/978-0-8261-5085-1. Qualifying instructors may request access by emailing textbook@springerpub.com.

PRACTICE-BASED RESOURCES AND REFERENCES

To view a list of resources and all the references, please visit connect.springerpub.com via the following url: http://connect.springerpub.com/content/book/978-0-8261-5085-1/part/part02/chapter/ch15

CHAPTER 16

The Moral Psychology of Evil: A Roadmap

TOM R. HANAUER

CHAPTER OVERVIEW

This chapter examines the construct of evil from the perspective of moral psychology. The chapter first discusses contemporary theories of evil and common misconceptions about evil. The chapter then draws on examples from social psychology in order to examine the psychological and situational causes of evil actions. The relation between trauma and evil is then explored with an emphasis on Primo Levi's account of Auschwitz and the concept of the "gray zone." Finally, the chapter discusses the nature and possibility of healing and reconciliation ("moral repair") after evil has been done.

LEARNING OBJECTIVES

After reading this chapter, the reader should be able to:

1. Understand issues related to evil from an interdisciplinary moral psychological perspective;
2. Develop awareness of contemporary theories of evil and common misconceptions about evil;
3. Distinguish between a "situationist" and "dispositionalist" explanation of evil, based on examples from social psychology;
4. Become familiar with the concept of the "gray zone" and the traumatic effects it has on its inhabitants;
5. Identify problematic areas and possibilities concerning healing and reconciliation that are associated with evil.

INTRODUCTION

Lynching was a common event in the American South during the late 19th and into the early decades of the 20th centuries. James Allen and Jon Lewis recount one ghastly case that took place in Morven, Georgia, on the 19th of May 1918:

> The brutalities meted out in these years often exceeded the most vivid of imaginations. After learning of the lynching of her husband, Mary Turner—in her eighth month of pregnancy—vowed to find those responsible, swear out warrants against them, and

have them punished in the courts. For making such a threat, a mob of several hundred men and women determined to "teach her a lesson." After tying her ankles together, they hung her from a tree, head downward. Dousing her clothes with gasoline, they burned them from her body. While she was still alive, someone used a knife ordinarily reserved for splitting hogs to cut open the woman's abdomen. The infant fell from her womb to the ground and cried briefly, whereupon a member of this Valdosta, Georgia, mob crushed the baby's head beneath his heel. Hundreds of bullets were then fired into Mary Turner's body, completing the work of the mob. The *Associated Press*, in its notice of the affair, observed that Mary Turner had made "*unwise remarks*" about the execution of her husband, "*and the people, in their indignant mood, took exceptions to her remarks, as well as her attitude.*" (Allen & Lewis, 1999, p. 14)

Mary Turner's story provides a paradigmatic portrait of evil. The lynchers were not merely doing something "bad." To call their actions bad—even *very, very* bad—would be an egregious understatement. "Evil," however, seems like the appropriate predicate: it is a word that we reserve today for the most heinous actions, the vilest of deeds. Evil sits atop the highest rung in the hierarchy of moral wrongs. We respond to evil with revulsion, but also with incredulity. These sorts of wrongs often strike us as incomprehensible. They seem to transcend the very boundaries of sensibility. Thus, the common refrain about evil is: "How could somebody do something *like that*?" This chapter outlines some approaches to answering this question from the perspective of moral psychology. Moral psychology is an interdisciplinary enterprise. It combines the resources of psychology and philosophy in a mutually reinforcing attempt to illuminate concepts and answer questions about human behavior in morally significant contexts (Doris, 2006/2020). But moral psychology is not merely oriented toward explanatory ends. It seeks to address the ethical matters themselves that are at stake in our discussion. For instance, a moral-psychological account of evil should help us determine how (and whether) we can avoid evil and what we should do about its presence in the world. This too is an aim of this chapter.

The remainder of the chapter is split into the following sections. In the second section, I clarify the object of our investigation—the nature of evil—by outlining a contemporary theory of evil offered by the philosopher Claudia Card (2002, 2010). I also address some "myths" or misconceptions that are commonly held about evil. In the third section, I canvass some of the major axes of the debate in moral psychology between so-called "situationist" and "dispositionalist" explanations of evil by drawing on the empirical work in social psychology of Stanley Milgram, Phillip Zimbardo, and others. In the fourth section, I turn to examining a particular kind of evil—what Levi (1986/1989/2017) calls the *gray zone*—that poses serious questions about healing and reconciliation in the face of evil and its harms. I conclude with a summary of the chapter content, followed by a list of practice-based resources available online.

THEORIZING AND DEMYTHOLOGIZING EVIL

The term "evil" carries a lot of baggage, and different people place different meanings on the word itself. The construct of "evil" insinuates different nuances across various disciplines and professions. In this section, I present a philosophical theory of evil and debunk some common myths about it.

Card's Theory

Evil—like the term "good"—is an irreducibly normative concept. It is not employed simply to describe a phenomenon, for example, an action, motive, or person. To call some phenomenon, X, "evil" is to *evaluate* X, or to *prescribe* a certain action or emotional response to X, or *recommend* a mode of comportment toward X. In Western history, the concept of evil has had a relatively broad usage; the domain of "evil" was roughly coextensive with that of the "bad." It designated anything that could be counted as one of the "minuses" of life: everything from disease, earthquakes, and even ugliness, to malevolence, violence, and blasphemy. This is the notion that is operative in theological discussions about the "problem of evil." Roughly, the problem deals with explaining how the existence of evil could be compatible with the existence of an omnipotent, omniscient, and omnibenevolent God (For some representative works, see Augustine's [1960] *Confessions*; Hick's [1966/2010] *Evil and the God of Love*; Mackie's [1955] "Evil and Omnipotence"; and Adams' [1999], *Horrendous Evils and the Goodness of God*). However, over the last two centuries, the concept of evil has narrowed in its scope to refer more exclusively to moral wrongdoings, or rather, to a certain subset of moral wrongdoings.

Intuitively, there is a difference between doing something wrong, say, stealing a chocolate bar from the grocery store, and doing something evil, such as setting the neighbor's dog on fire out of mere boredom. This raises the following questions: What is the difference between lesser wrongs and evil wrongs? What is the evil-making feature of moral wrongdoing? An applicable theory of evil is offered here, partially as an answer to these questions. There are, of course, various theories of evil that purport to answer these questions (for a useful examination of theories of evil, see Calder's [2013/2018] article, "The Concept of Evil" in the *Stanford Encyclopedia of Philosophy*). For the purpose of this chapter, and in light of a major topic of this textbook, trauma, I examine Card's (2010) influential account of evil in her book, *Confronting Evils*. I provide the essential details of her theory and offer some elaborations along the way.

Card's (2002) theory is known as "the atrocity paradigm." The theory is specifically tailored to account for the sense in which actions, institutions, and practices can be evil, but it is not intended as a theory of evil personhood. Card specifically seeks to avoid attributing evil to persons. Accordingly, for Card, individuals can *do* evil without *being* evil. I return to this important point later. The theory is called the "atrocity paradigm" because it takes atrocities to be paradigms or models of evil. Some examples of atrocities offered by Card include the 1937 Rape of Nanjing, the Tuskegee Experiment, the World War II (WWII) Japanese military's Unit 731, and the Cambodian Genocide. Card's idea is that we can generate an illuminating, helpful, and socially useful concept of evil by focusing on uncontroversial cases of evil and seeing which features constitute their "evilness." *This, however, does not mean that all evils are atrocities.* The sadistic cyberbullying of an innocent person is plausibly evil, but it is not necessarily an atrocity. The theory is also not meant to capture all possible notions and applications of the term "evil." In fact, it is unclear whether this is entirely possible or even desirable. Rather, it is meant to isolate and construct a concept of evil that is ethically significant and useful for secular, public, and moral discourse. The theory also does not imply that evils are especially rare or "extraordinary." Indeed, Card (2010, p. 17) thinks that evils are unfortunately all too common.

So, what is the theory? Card says that her theory combines the following two historically contrasting approaches to theorizing about evil:

1. **Stoicism**: evilness consists in the intention and/or motive behind the deed.
2. **Epicureanism**: evil consists in the experience of the harm that results from the deed.

The Stoic component is about agency—it is internal to the action and its doer. The Epicurean component is about the action's results or consequences. In Card's theory, an evil action is a (a) *reasonably foreseeable* (b) *intolerable harm* that is (c) *produced by inexcusable wrongdoing*. The first and third are the Stoic components, while the second is the Epicurean one. But, for an action to be evil, Card says, it needs to be comprised of all three components.

Reasonable Foreseeability. Reasonable foreseeability applies to the predictability of the results of the action (or policy). For a person's actions to count as evil, it must be the case that the agent who performs it foresees, or could have been expected to foresee, its consequences, if they had exercised due care (Card, 2010, p. 28). So, for instance, people who transported slaves across the Transatlantic Passage often did foresee that much of their "cargo"—upwards of 50%—would die as a result of the voyage (Rediker, 2007). But, even if they did not die, it would have been easily foreseeable, given the conditions in which the enslaved persons were held. Evil actions are ones that cause a reasonably foreseeable intolerable harm to others for morally inexcusable reasons.

Intolerable Harm. Intolerable harm, Card (2010, p. 8) says, consists in depriving "victims of basics ordinarily needed to make a life (or death) decent." The notion of intolerability is a normative one; it signifies what people *should not* have to tolerate, not what they *can* (or cannot) tolerate. Card's claim is that people should not have to tolerate anything that robs them of a minimally decent life.

Is intolerable harm a subjective matter? Not entirely, Card (2010) claims; although there is some variation, of course. Life might be intolerable for a person with diabetes if she is deprived of her insulin shots, but not for a nondiabetic individual. Card (2010, p. 104) says that "*Intolerable harm consists in gravely diminishing or destroying capacities central to the meaning or value of an organism's life.*" For human beings, some examples could include:

> access to non-toxic air, water, food, sleep, freedom from severe and prolonged pain or humiliation and from debilitating fear, having affective ties with others, having the ability to make choices and act on them, and having a sense of one's worth. (2010, p. 105)

These basic things are essential for a decent life, that is, a life that meets minimal standards of quality or that is simply not a bad one. Evils, then, cause intolerable harms of the sorts mentioned previously. Atrocities are paradigmatic examples of such harms. As a function of fair critique, I would add that "intolerable harm" is perhaps the weakest component of Card's theory, as it seems to be open to counterexamples. For instance, if John concocts a sadistic plan to murder Oscar, but he fails to accomplish it due to sheer incompetence or bad luck, does this mean that his actions were not evil? They did not produce intolerable harm, but they nevertheless do seem to be evil. This may be addressed by adding a counterfactual clause, according to which the action *would have* caused intolerable harm, if performed successfully.

Inexcusable Wrongdoing. Evils lack two kinds of excuses: (a) metaphysical and (b) moral. Metaphysical excuses focus on the aspects and conditions of the agent. *Nonculpable ignorance* is an example of a standard metaphysical excuse. John left a knife on the kitchen counter; Sally accidentally slips and cuts her finger on the knife. Is John responsible? "No," we would say, *if* he could not have reasonably known or foreseen such an occurrence. Sometimes, however, we can reasonably expect an agent to know better and, hence, to have acted otherwise than they did. Perhaps John did not intend to park a car illegally, but he is still getting a fine. Ignorance is not always a good excuse. Metaphysical excuses also can be offered when the person lacks certain agential capacities altogether, rather than merely lacking the relevant information. Sally's newborn vomited on a friend—is the baby's behavior excusable? She cannot control herself nor could she possibly know that such behavior is inappropriate. She cannot yet appreciate and follow nuanced social norms. The question of whether she "ought to have done otherwise" does not make much sense in such a case. To hold her responsible would simply be bizarre. Compulsion is yet another common metaphysical excuse. The kleptomaniac cannot control themselves; they steal things compulsively. It is an illness or mental condition that overrides or disrupts the capacity to exercise autonomous agency. These sorts of excuses are meant to reduce or completely revoke someone's culpability by reducing or denying their responsibility.

Moral excuses are meant to reduce someone's culpability, but without denying their responsibility or agency. In these cases, the person takes responsibility for the wrongdoing—and recognizes it as wrong—but claims to have had a good or "morally appropriate" or "morally defensible" reason for doing it (Card, 2010, p. 17). Morally defensible reasons are ones that count, morally, in favor of an action. For instance, Joan's water breaks; she is going into labor. Alex, her spouse, dangerously speeds down with her to the hospital. He knows that he is endangering others; he knows that it is morally wrong, but he says, "I had a good reason, I needed to get my wife to the hospital as soon as possible." That is a moral excuse. Card adds, importantly, that for something to count as a moral excuse, it is not enough for the agent to *think* that it is a good (moral) reason, but it actually must *be* a good (excusing) moral reason. The fact that someone thinks she is acting rightly does not mean that she really is acting rightly or that she is absolved from responsibility for the actions she has performed.

Evil actions, according to Card (2010, p. 20), lack both moral and metaphysical excuses. She writes, "When a deed is inexcusable, morally and metaphysically, the doer's culpability is unmitigated." This means that evildoers are blameworthy. Although, we should note, they are not necessarily always blameworthy to the *same degree*. We should also note that not all inexcusable wrongs are evil; however, according to Card, all evils are inexcusable wrongs. This means that the wrongdoer ought to have acted differently and that there is nothing that could get them "off the hook" for the actions they have done. (For a fascinating and influential discussion of evil and responsibility, the interested reader can see Watson [1987]. Watson argues that [some] cases of evil seem to suggest that the evildoer is so insensitive to proper moral reasons that they may cease to be proper objects of blame altogether. Watson uses the example of Robert Harris, an especially callous murderer, to discuss the relationship between evil, responsibility, and childhood abuse.)

Demythologizing Evil

Card's (2002, 2010) theory, then, is that evil actions are reasonably foreseeable, inexcusable wrongs that produce intolerable harm. This yields a number of important and preliminary results (the list here is highly indebted to Eric Schwitzgebel's lectures for a class on evil at the University of California—Riverside):

1. Evildoers need not *intend to harm* others. An organization like NAMBLA (North American Man/Boy Love Association) might see itself as promoting good, ethical, and healthy romantic love between children and older men, but it is undeniably harmful in its aims. In other words, evildoers need not be malicious, or intend to harm someone for the sake of harming them.
2. Evildoers need not be *selfish*. It is possible for someone to participate in evils for the sake of one's family or one's country. "Crime families," for instance, often act for the sake of their organization rather than purely in their own self-interest. Likewise, many Nazis apparently saw themselves as protecting the German people and their nation against its foreign and domestic "enemies."
3. Evildoers need not be deeply *wicked* or *cruel*. In other words, they need not be acting for the sake of "evil itself." As Satan, in Milton's *Paradise Lost*, says, "evil be thou my good" (Milton, 2005, p. 108). Some evildoers are just callous. For instance, imagine that Joseph runs over Julie with his car, paralyzing her for life, simply in order to get home faster. Julie did not do anything to deserve this, she just happened to be in Joseph's way. He did not even want to make her suffer; rather, he just did not care about her at all. This is still a reasonably foreseeable and inexcusable wrong that causes intolerable harm: evil.
4. Evildoers can commit evil acts on the basis of *moral principles*. For instance, some Confederate soldiers during the Civil War may have sincerely believed that they were fighting for "states' rights," but that does not serve as a good moral excuse for promoting the institution of slavery. In other cases, someone might have a good moral aim, but choose an inexcusably immoral *means* to achieve that aim. For example, it is surely morally good to help one's child do well in school, but not by threatening physical violence to a teacher if she does not give the child an A.

The previous results can be marshalled to address some common myths about evil. First, recall the claim from the introduction that evil is "incomprehensible." This myth often is grounded in the supernatural aura of evil, or in really "extraordinary" cases of serial killers, for example. It seems impossible to imagine ourselves in the shoes of such people. We cannot—and often enough do not *want to*—imagine ourselves lynching, raping, murdering, or engaging in the cruelties and horrors that we identify as evil. But Card's (2002, 2010) theory suggests that some cases of evil are perfectly intelligible; evil is unfortunately human—all too human. People can commit evil or participate in evils out of laziness, apathy, self-interest, blind conformism, approval-seeking, or even sheer thoughtlessness. These are not incomprehensible motives or unintelligible psychological states. Arendt (1964) famously was struck by the figure of Adolph Eichmann—the high-ranking SS officer who organized transports to death camps during WWII and who was captured in Argentina and brought to trial in Israel in 1960—and his superficiality, his lack of imagination, his thoughtlessness and emptiness. Eichmann was not a monster, Arendt famously said, he was merely a boring, paper-pushing, bourgeois bureaucrat. Eichmann, in Arendt's famous phrase, is the face of the "banality of evil." The horrifying thing about Eichmann is not his extraordinariness, but rather his ordinariness. We all know an Eichmann. More frighteningly still, we might even be one ourselves.

The second myth is that people can be neatly categorized into "good" and "evil" groupings. This Manichean myth is perhaps a result of our tendency toward "us" and "them" thinking, that is, creating in-group and out-group divisions. We (in-group), of course, are "the good ones" and they are the "evil ones." The feeling of moral superiority that this affords reassures us of the rightness of our ways and solidifies our bond with the members of our group. For instance, in 2015, ISIS filmed the gruesome execution of a captured Jordanian pilot. He was set aflame in a cage. Some in the United States have taken this barbaric act as a confirmation of the complete "backwardness" of the Middle East, and, by contrast, the moral superiority of the United States and the West. It is easy to forget, however, that until the middle of the last century, lynching was not only commonplace in the United States, but so were the burning of the bodies of lynching victims and their commemoration in postcards and other memorabilia, including collecting pieces of clothes, teeth, and bones from the charred bodies of the victims (Allen & Lewis, 1999). But, against the Manichean myth, Card's (2002, 2010) theory suggests that "perpetrator" and "victim" are not absolutes. They are idealized constructs that map imperfectly onto the real world. People are often both perpetrators and victims of evil. This is a possibility that is hard to digest; we do not want to think that anyone who can be a victim of evil also can be a perpetrator of evil. Yet if we are serious about stopping evil—rather than just protecting our egos—then this is a possibility that we should accept.

The dichotomous thinking surrounding good and evil closely relates to the assumed "extraordinariness" and rarity of evil. Card (2002, 2010) thinks that evil is not necessarily rare. This may be especially true in relation to practices that are widespread in one's community. It is hard to recognize some practice as evil if *everyone* is doing it. The neighbors are "good, respectable people" after all, so whatever they are doing cannot be evil, and would it not be terribly arrogant to assume that *I* know better than all the members of my community? The need to maintain communal ties creates a powerful tendency toward a general policy of unquestioning conformism (see Schwitzgebel's [2019] "Aiming for Moral Mediocrity" for a helpful discussion of this topic). Also, perpetrators tend to misperceive the harms that they inflict. They may diminish the gravity of the harms. For example, they may claim that it was not "*that* bad," or they may ignore victims altogether. Baumeister (1997a, 1997b), in discussions about threatened egotism and self-defeating responses, has suggested that victims, conversely, may tend to exaggerate the terribleness of the harm or the maliciousness of the perpetrator's motives. This is not to imply in any way that a victim has not been harmed, but rather, it speaks to the workings of cognitive schema and the way in which human beings, perhaps as a part of human nature, sometimes may magnify perceived danger as being "larger than life." For the purpose of the discussion at hand, this means that, if we want to identify someone as "evil," then we are more likely to exaggerate their intentional or motivational features and the degree of harm that they cause, but it also means that we are less likely to examine critically the harms that we ourselves have a part in creating. So, for instance, it is fair to assume that most meat-eaters in modern, affluent, industrialized countries are aware of the horrors suffered by animals in factory farms, yet it is not uncommon for them to doubt whether the animals feel much pain or whether their pain bears any substantive moral weight. More commonly still, meat-eaters probably rarely think much at all about the morality of modern meat production and consumption, nor do they consciously consider the typically horrific process that gave "birth" to the hamburger they are biting into. (For more on animal ethics, see Donaldson and Kymlicka [2011] and Will Kymlicka, *Zoopolis*, Singer [1975/2009], *Animal Liberation*, Norcross [2004], "Puppies, Pigs, and People," and Diamond [1978], "Eating Animals and Eating People."). Is this a reasonable mode of thought, or is it one that reflects precisely the claim that evildoers dismiss the harms inflicted on their victims or, indeed, the reality of victimhood itself?

EXPLAINING EVIL

In this section, I explicate a social psychological context for understanding and explaining evil. In the first subsection, I discuss the basic distinctions between two explanatory paradigms in psychology: situationism and dispositionalism. The second subsection offers a discussion of relevant social psychology experiments. The third subsection seeks to draw some conclusions from these experiments about which paradigm—situationism or dispositionalism—offers a better framework for explaining evil, especially in relation to ordinary agents.

Social Psychology and Character: Dispositions and Situations

Evil, as we have said, is not incomprehensible, nor is it necessarily extraordinary; but it is nevertheless a complex phenomenon that cries out for explanation. It is especially important to understand the factors that push people to commit evil actions if we are committed to preventing evil. In moral psychology, there are two major explanatory paradigms for people's behavior: dispositionalism and situationism. Dispositionalism is the commonsense view that human behavior is (often) the product of *character traits*, or the tendencies that constitute our "character" or personality.

Character traits are dispositions to feel, think, and act in certain ways. If I have some character trait, C, then I may be disposed, or I may have the tendency, to consistently act in certain ways and feel or think certain things. For instance, if I am compassionate, then I may be disposed to feel compassion and act compassionately toward others. The explanations that we offer for human behavior—in ourselves and in others—often rely on the attribution of such character traits. For example, Juan lied to me again, because he is *disloyal* or *insincere* or *selfish* or *forgetful*; or Maria helps me with my homework, because she is *kind* and *empathic* and *generous*. Character traits are assumed to have the following features:

1. **Character traits are stable:** If someone has a character trait, C, then it is very hard to lose or drastically alter that character trait;
2. **Character traits have a wide cross-situational consistency:** If someone has a character trait, C, then it determines and explains the person's behavior across a wide variety of situations, for example, if a person is compassionate, then that person predictably and consistently feels compassion upon seeing people in need of serious help—whether on the TV or in the street—and regardless of (many) situational factors;
3. **Character traits persist over time:** If someone has a character trait, C, then the person continues to have C throughout time, without major and sudden modification or alterations, for example, if a person is compassionate on Tuesday, then we can reliably expect that she will be compassionate next Tuesday as well.

Situationism challenges dispositionalism. According to situationism, character traits do not have the immense influence on our behavior as is assumed with dispositionalism. According to situationism, *minor and insubstantial situational factors have a much greater weight in determining and (hence) explaining human behavior than character traits do*. The insubstantiality of the factors is an important point. John Doris, a proponent of situationism, notes that there is nothing very controversial about the claim that *substantial* situational factors have an immense influence on action—I cannot, for instance, act courageously and save a drowning child unless there is a child who is drowning and in need of saving. So, the situationist point is a subtle one: "the problem is not that substantial situational factors have substantial effects on what people do, but that seemingly insubstantial situational factors have substantial effects on what people do" (Doris, 2002, p. 28). If the situationist is correct, then character traits—if they exist at all—do not really have the important role that we think they do in governing and explaining human behavior. Minor situational factors should not be able to offset robust, stable, cross-situational, and persistent characterological dispositions. We should note that situationism does not deny that *people can be or are (sometimes) compassionate, altruistic, cruel,* and so on. Situationism simply claims that people's prosocial (altruism) or antisocial (malice) behavior often is determined by situational factors rather than character traits (Doris, 2002, p. 35). Altruism is real, it is just not rooted in these global, stable, persistent character traits that typically are assumed to explain and determine people's actions.

The support for the situationist thesis comes from decades of empirical work in social psychology. There is a large number of experiments that demonstrate the power of minor situational factors in the determination of human action. Doris (2002, p. 35) writes that, "Situationism is motivated by a pattern of results, not by the results of any particular study." These studies, taken together, strongly suggest that character-based moral psychology is fallacious on the situationist view. The same person can be courageous in one situation but cowardly in another, or compassionate in one case, but cruel in another, and so forth. The upshot of situationism is clear: the determining force is situational, not characterological. If this is true, it has enormous implications for how we should explain evil actions. To demonstrate this, we will examine a few of the most notable (and controversial) experiments in social psychology.

Social Psychology Experiments

Some of the most (in)famous experiments in social psychology have offered glimpses into the human psyche that assist in understanding the nature of evil. I offer several of the most prominent examples in this subsection.

Omission Experiments

First, Isen and Levin (1972) conducted a famous experiment that involved unwitting subjects finding a dime in a phone booth—which served as a mood-booster of sorts in the 1970s. The subjects, after finding the coin, witnessed a confederate dropping a pile of papers on the ground, seemingly by accident. Isen and Levin wanted to see if finding a coin would have an effect on people's willingness and motivation to help. The results were that 87% of those who found the dime decided to help. The mood boost from finding a dime seemed to have played an enormous role in determining their behavior; only 4% of those who did not find the dime decided to help. The dispositionalist assumes that one's character predicts whether someone will stop to help a stranger. But what seemed to make the difference was the situation—the coin—and *not* the person's character, unless we are ready to assume that the people who happened to find the coin also, by chance, happened to be more compassionate persons than those who did not find one.

Another famous experiment, by Latane and Rodin (1969), tested the effects of group size on bystanders' willingness to help. The subjects (university students) were told that they were participating in a market research study. They were given a questionnaire by a "representative," who then went behind a curtain that divided the room. The subjects then were interrupted by a loud crash and cries of pain coming from behind the curtain, implying that a serious accident has taken place. Doris (2002, p. 32) reports that "Seventy percent of bystanders offered help when they waited alone, compared with seven percent in the company of an unresponsive confederate." This is astounding. If people had robust character traits—like compassion—then minor situational factors, like having another person in the room with them, certainly should not make them *less* likely to offer help to someone in need. This important psychological phenomenon often is called "diffusion of responsibility" or the "bystander effect": A bystander feels less responsible for doing something, in an emergency, as the number of other bystanders increases. The feeling of responsibility is weakened, as it is "diffused" throughout the group. (For the interested reader, Miller's [2017] book, *The Character Gap*, provides many more examples of these kinds of experiments along with a discussion of situationism and its philosophical merits and implications.)

Milgram Experiments

The previously described experiments were about *omissions* of compassion. The participants failed to offer assistance, but they did not actively hurt anyone. They did not purposefully cause the confederate to drop their papers, for instance. This might suggest that there is room for dispositionalism about certain character traits, for example, compassionate people may be unwilling to severely harm other human beings as a result of minor situational factors, even if they are not so willing to provide active assistance in other situations. But, unfortunately, some experiments—specifically, the Milgram and the Stanford Prison experiments—suggest that even this is false. This research is much more disturbing.

Stanley Milgram, a psychologist at Yale, was interested in the Holocaust: Why did ordinary Germans agree to murder millions of innocent people? They could not *all* have been monsters. They could not *all* have been sadists. So, what is the explanation? Milgram's experiments were designed to test obedience to authority—will people agree to *murder* if commanded to do so by an authority figure? The answer, for many, was yes: they are willing to murder on command. In the standard condition of the experiment, 65% of the participants agreed to deliver lethal, 450-volt shocks to a protesting "learner" situated in another room. Most participants protested, but nevertheless continued on at the insistence of the experimenter. Dispositionalism, and commonsense, would have assumed that *no one* would comply with such orders, unless they are disposed toward sadism or extreme submissiveness, and so forth. Doris writes the following:

> Milgram's experiments show how apparently noncoercive situational factors may induce destructive behavior despite the apparent presence of contrary evaluative and dispositional structures. Furthermore, personality research has failed to find a convincing explanation of the Milgram results that references individual differences. Accordingly, Milgram gives us reason to doubt the robustness of dispositions implicated in compassion-relevant moral behavior; his experiments are powerful evidence for situationism. (2002, p. 39)

The obedient participants were not horrible or monstrous people. Their verbal and bodily responses demonstrated their conflicted internal states. But the situation outweighed whatever character traits they supposedly had. Compliance varied enormously once Milgram introduced slight variations to the experimental scenario. For example, if the teacher had to hold the learner's hand down on a shock plate, obedience dropped dramatically. Participants also were much less likely to comply if the instructions were given by phone or delivered via tape recorder. But, then, there is also almost *100%* compliance whenever the participant could only hear frantic pounding on the wall, but not the learner's actual, agonized voice behind it. In general, the factors that seemed to matter most for rates of obedience were *proximity* to the experimenter and *distance* from the learner. Milgram's conclusion was that most of us would obey a malevolent authority figure in *some* situations, even if we are not directly *forced* to do anything by that authority figure.

One important situational phenomenon that the experiment demonstrates has come to be known as the "foot-in-the-door." The "teachers" are asked to start with a relatively mild electric shock, 15-volts, but they then are instructed to increase the voltage in incremental steps until they suddenly have reached a lethal or obviously harmful level. Once someone has agreed to take the initial step, the failure to take another step poses a challenge to the *justification* of the initial one—if administering a 100-volt shock is wrong, then was it not wrong to have administered a 75-volt one? . . . 45-volt? . . . 15-volt? This "stepwise" progression of the experiment may have had an even greater influence than the authority itself.

Therefore, Doris (2002) claims, the empirical studies in social psychology tell a pretty consistent story: trivial situational factors have large effects on behavior. This challenges the commonsense dispositionalist view that character determines and explains people's behavior. This is also, of course, very disturbing. Doris explains, "What the experiments . . . highlight . . . is the power of the situation; the majority of subjects [in Milgram's experiments] were willing to torture another individual to what seemed the door of death without any more direct pressure than the polite insistence of the experimenter" (Doris, 2002, p. 42).

The Stanford Prison Experiment

Zimbardo (2007), a social psychologist at Stanford University, conducted another infamous experiment in the early 1970s that aimed to investigate group dynamics in prisons. He constructed a makeshift prison in the basement of Stanford's psychology department, where he closely could observe and monitor the interactions of the experiment's participants. The participants—24 in all—were predominantly White, middle-class, university students, who had no known psychological disorders or abnormalities. They were divided up randomly into two equally numbered groups of guards and prisoners; there were nine prisoners (three on reserve) and nine guards (another three on reserve).

The prisoners initially were arrested at an unannounced time on a Sunday morning by actual Palo Alto police officers and taken into custody before being moved, blindfolded and handcuffed, into the experimental Stanford jail. Each prisoner was assigned a number, and the numbers were essentially their new "names." They were *required* to address each other by their numbers only (Zimbardo, 2007). The guards and the "warden" (a research assistant) had a detailed list of 17 rules that the prisoners were required to memorize and follow. The rules restricted everything from food access and bathroom use to speech and body movement. For instance, rule 14 states that "All prisoners in each cell will stand whenever the warden, the prison superintendent, or any other visitors arrive on the premises. Prisoners will wait on orders to be seated or to resume activities" (Zimbardo, 2007, p. 44). Notably, the prisoners also were subject to punishment for any rule violation, and some guards showed rather sadistic creativity with the punishments that they imposed and in their general rule-enforcement tactics as they slipped further into their roles—for example, throwing them in the "Hole," demanding the prisoners "sing" their numbers during roll call, or forcing them to do pushups for purposes of humiliation (Zimbardo, 2007, p. 49). Although the guards were forbidden from engaging in physical torture, abuse, or harm, they were allowed to create the psychological conditions that Zimbardo (2007, p. 55) associated with prisons: fear, anxiety, boredom, constant surveillance, powerlessness, deindividuation, and so forth.

The experiment infamously ended very prematurely, after 6 days, following an escalation in guard brutality and prisoners' responses. Prisoners started revolting before the third day was over; and one prisoner—8612—seemed to experience a mental breakdown and was "released" early. Prisoners were sprayed with a fire extinguisher, forced to defecate and urinate in buckets, and had their mattresses and even clothes taken away. The experience of losing their freedom and autonomy so suddenly and dramatically, being reduced to mere numbers, and being subjected to psychological abuse and humiliation caused visible distress, depression, and anxiety in the prisoners. The guards also used various mechanisms to disrupt solidarity among the prisoners, for example, when prisoner 416 went on a hunger strike, the others were deprived of blankets and were instructed to insult "416" (Zimbardo, 2007).

In a few days, as Zimbardo says, "the boundaries between reality and simulation have seemed to erode completely" (Zimbardo, 2007, p. 142). The guards acted as if they really were guards, and the prisoners answered exclusively to their numbers rather than their names. Zimbardo's (2007, p. 142) explanation is that, "Role playing has become role internalization: the actors have assumed the characters and identities of their fictional roles." Inhabiting the role of a "guard" allowed the individuals themselves to distance themselves from their actions: "it is not *me*, it is just the part I am *playing*." In addition, this also may represent a need to fulfill the type of aggressive and hypermasculine demands or descriptions that usually are associated with being a "correctional officer." This might further disincline the guards from recognizing or caring about the suffering of the inmates, as "that's what women do, and you're not supposed to be soft with criminals anyway." It is no wonder, indeed, that homophobic slurs and sexual humiliation made an appearance in the guard's control tactics (Zimbardo, 2007, pp. 119–120). To be sure, not all of the guards were sadistic, but none of the guards made any substantive effort to intervene with or to stop the sadistic ones. Finally, the experiment's creation of two (artificially) antagonistic groups probably further cemented the pressures that the participants may have felt to identify with and endorse the behavior of their own group members over those of the other. The Stanford Prison Experiment thus seems to confirm the situationist claim—the situational factors seemed to overpower whatever dispositional inclinations even the participants themselves assumed they had. As one of the guards reported, "I was actually beginning to feel like a guard and had really thought I was incapable of this kind of behavior. I was surprised—no, I was dismayed—to find out that I could really be a—uh—that I could act in a manner so absolutely unaccustomed to anything I would really dream of doing" (Zimbardo, 2007, p. 158).

Evil Situations and Ordinary Agents

The commonsense assumption, as we have noted, is that evil actions are explainable in terms of evil dispositions—or that evil actions are done by evil *people*. The Southerners who lynched Mary Turner, for instance, did something evil because they were evil. But the work of Zimbardo, Milgram, and other social psychologists suggests that evil-*doing* is not necessarily indicative of evil-*being*. It is entirely possible for normal, ordinary, and otherwise decent people to do evil things *if* certain situational factors are met. Although situationism emphasizes the effects of relatively minor situational factors on behavior, it is important to note (again) that more familiar and wider-scoped situational factors are of course important too. Culture, social norms, law, and language, for instance, play especially important situational roles in the production of evil. Tirrell (2012), in her "Genocidal Language Games," provides an illuminating analysis of the role that terms like "inyenzi" ("cockroach") played in the 1994 Rwandan genocide. "Inyenzi" was used as a descriptor for Tutsis; connecting them to cockroaches was not merely dehumanizing, it also licensed and motivated a certain type of response. One does not respect or reason with cockroaches, one exterminates them as the disgusting, disease-ridden, pestilential horde that they are. (Note, though, that the influence of culture and language, or indeed any situational factors, does not necessarily imply that perpetrators are not responsible for their actions.) But none of this demonstrates definitively that personality is not real or that behavioral dispositions have no predictive or explanatory power.

Staub (1989) has argued that people with certain personality types are more likely to become perpetrators, for example, those who have an "authoritarian personality." The distinguishing mark of the authoritarian personality is the "tendency to order the world and relate to people according to their position and power in hierarchies"; admiration and obedience is rendered to the superior, contempt and abuse is heaped on the inferior (Staub, 1989, p. 75). Yet even here we should remember that situational factors (such as parenting styles) have a substantial contribution. Parents who are overly punitive, who do not show affection, who emphasize "traditional" values, and who will not acknowledge "bad" emotions, like anger, sexual desire, and so on, are more likely to produce "submissiveness to authority and a tendency to devalue the powerless," that is, an authoritarian personality, in their offspring (Staub, 1989, p. 73). And "[w]hen obedience is the highest value," Staub (1989, p. 74) writes, "self-guidance becomes impossible." Therefore, both dispositional and situational factors are worth taking into consideration. For our purposes, in any case, it is sufficient to note that the practical importance of situationism is embedded in its plausible suggestion that we often are lacking in self-knowledge about the underlying drivers and determinants of our actions. Although it is fair to assume that 100% of Milgram's participants would not have believed they were capable of consensually killing a person on command, 65% of them, in fact, did consent to do so. No one would like to imagine herself capable of such acts, but if one is an ordinary person—like Milgram's participants—then one does not *know* with certainty that they are immune to the situational pressures of authority. For the situationist, the most effective strategy for avoiding evil, therefore, is avoiding situations that promote evil while creating more situations that increase altruism or promote helping behavior instead. People do worse, the situationist suggests, when they just trust that their "character" will overcome the relevant situational forces. Zimbardo's own suggestion is to create more opportunities for people to see and think of themselves as potential "heroes," or as agents who can intervene in difficult moral situations despite the counterpressures they might face. In his inversion of Arendt's famous phrase, Zimbardo (2007, p. 21) thinks that we ought to cultivate the "banality of heroism."

But are we conceding too much to the situationists when we heed their evil-avoidance advice? For instance, one might ask, what about the capacity for rational reflection and empathy? Those seems like good guides for the avoidance of evil; so, we should just cultivate empathy and promote reflexivity. Perhaps, but the importance and effectiveness of both rational reflection and empathy are surprisingly controversial subjects. Haidt (2012) has done numerous experiments demonstrating the inefficacy of moral reasoning (detailed in his book, *The Righteous Mind*). Reasoning, he claims, is used to *rationalize* an intuitive, emotional judgment that an agent has already made. In Hume's (1739/1986) famous phrase, "reason is and ought to be only the slave of the passions." Reason, on this view, cannot by itself provide moral guidance. It can only determine the best means to whatever happens to be our moral or immoral ends. Likewise, in the case of empathy, research has uncovered some uncomfortable problems. As Prinz (2011) notes, "empathy . . . is easily manipulated. Evidence from jury studies suggest that jurors hand down harsher sentences when the victims are visibly emotional and lighter sentences when defendants display regret" (p. 227). More perniciously, individuals tend to empathize more with those who look like them than those who are perceived as different or alien. In a study, Xu et al. (2009) discovered that White people feel more empathy for other White people than they do for ethnically Chinese people, and the same holds the other way around. (For more on the problems with empathy, see Jesse Prinz, "Against Empathy.")

TRAUMA AND EVIL: LEVI'S GRAY ZONE

In this section, I offer a discussion of Primo Levi's concept of the "gray zone," which challenges our assumptions about evil, but, more importantly, offers some important psychological insights from the victims' perspective into the kinds of trauma and harm that evil engenders. I end with a discussion about the possibility and nature of healing and reconciliation after evil has left its mark on victims.

There is another common myth about evil that we have not had an opportunity to introduce: It is typical to assume that our moral status—as good or evil—is under our direct, personal, and complete control. Perhaps, we think, there is not much that we can do about our circumstances. We do not choose our bodies, or genes, or the environment into which we are born, but we *do* choose the basic moral orientation of our "souls." It is always possible, we think, to avoid wrongdoing, it is always possible to retain one's fundamental goodness; good and evil are not subject to *luck*. This is a myth that is closely linked with the desire to maintain the view that we are decent or good people, and to bifurcate others into the "innocent" and the "guilty," the "victim" and the "perpetrator." There is an especially strong pull to assume that one cannot simultaneously be a victim and a perpetrator. The blurring of these categories makes us especially uncomfortable. There is a simple reason for this, I suggest: Victims deserve sympathy, perpetrators deserve blame. Therefore, someone who seems to fit both categories at once "confuses our need to judge," as the Jewish-Italian author and Holocaust survivor, Levi (1986/1989/2017, p. 42), says. The dualistic Manichean narrative, which our moral concepts and judgments are tailored to fit, is incapable of recognizing, appreciating, and hence coping with moral ambiguity. The world unfortunately tends to be morally messier than our (implicit) Manicheanism demands. Levi's concept of the "gray zone," as we will see, is especially disruptive to this Manichean bifurcation between good and evil. The purpose of this section of the chapter, however, is not to dwell on the superficiality of Manicheanism. The purpose, rather, is to confront the uniquely traumatic experience of *being involuntarily placed within a deeply morally compromised position* where the line between "victim" and "perpetrator" begins to intersect and blur.

Levi's (1986/1989/2017, p. 42) final book, *The Drowned and the Saved*, is a meditation on his experiences at Auschwitz. Levi refers to Auschwitz as a "gray zone," but he does not provide a strict definition of the term. Instead, he writes, the gray zone is a place where "two camps of masters and servants both diverge and converge," thereby confusing our need for moral clarity and judgment. Card (2002), commenting on Levi, provides some helpful clarification. Gray zones, she says, have three dominant features:

1. **Victimhood**: The involuntary inhabitants of the gray zone are themselves victims;
2. **Complicity**: The inhabitants are implicated through their choices in perpetrating some of the same or similar evils on others who are already victims like themselves; and,
3. **Stress**: The inhabitants act under extraordinary and prolonged stress (Card, 2002, p. 224). I suggest adding a fourth condition, too:
4. **Systematicity**: The gray zone has been designed to promote and exploit the previously mentioned conditions among an interrelated group and for an indefinite time.

The prisoners of gray zones, as Card explains, are given positions of power over their fellow inmates (Card, 2002, p. 212). Levi describes a number of important examples of these (*Kapos* and the *Sonderkommando*) that we will examine in the text that follows. As Card notes, the inhabitants of gray zones have often already been deprived of all their worldly possessions *and* their loved ones before or shortly after their arrival (Card, 2002, p. 224). They may have already endured months or years of cruelty, humiliation, exploitation, degradation, poverty, hunger, and squalor. The inhabitants of gray zones therefore operate in an environment where their attachments to the world and to other people are being or have been forcibly and systematically eroded. And the only vestiges that are left of their humanity—their life and body—are themselves now under a constant and looming threat of being lost too (Card, 2002, p. 224). In this regard, it is important to note that the choices agents make within gray zones are often morally problematic, but *not* necessarily evil. Gray zones are gray precisely because of the moral ambiguity of their inhabitants, although those who *culpably create* gray zones are not themselves morally ambiguous; their actions are unquestionably evil. Gray zones often tempt victims to imagine that complicity with evil actually can be better on the whole, that is, bring about more good overall: "I cannot be of any use to anyone, if I am dead." But, according to Card (2002, p. 223), some things may yet be worse than not "being useful." It might, she suggests, be worse to become a tool for evil itself. Card's assumption is that *evil is the worst thing one can be or do*. This is a good reason for identifying gray zones as one of the deepest possible kinds of evils—indeed, *diabolical* evils— since gray zones threaten to destroy not just lives and bodies, but the goodness of the victims themselves. That is Satanic in the classical sense of the term: Satan as a literal corrupter of souls.

The Trauma of Gray Zones

The traumatic nature of gray zones emerges most clearly once we examine the particular effects it has on its inhabitants. Levi's (1986/1989/2017) account of Auschwitz will serve as our guide. Auschwitz is a paradigmatic but extreme case of a gray zone. The characteristic effects of the gray zone in Auschwitz, then, are meant to apply more widely to other cases, though not necessarily to the same degree or in the same way. Gray zones have four characteristic effects: (1) alienation; (2) loss of moral innocence; (3) disintegration of selfhood; and (4) survivor's shame. I discuss and explain each characteristic in what follows.

(1) **Alienation:** Gray zones alienate their inhabitants from one another. The complicity of inhabitants threatens to *disable the possibility of solidarity* with other victims.

According to Levi, human beings have a powerful need for an "us versus them" narrative. This need is linked closely to the "Manichean myth" mentioned earlier. It is a need that leads us to reduce many social phenomena to conflicts between in-groups ("friend") and out-groups ("enemy"). Levi claims that this is partly why spectator sports—football, basketball, and so on—are so popular. They satisfy the craving for a clean narrative that ordinary life simply cannot provide due to its moral ambiguity and complexity. The gray zone of Auschwitz of course did not satisfy the Manichean craving—Auschwitz was already incomprehensible enough, a world without "why," as Levi (1958/1996) puts it elsewhere—but it went much further. According to Levi, Auschwitz outright crushed this craving at its roots:

> The world into which one was precipitated was terrible, yes, but also indecipherable: it did not conform to any model; the enemy was all around but also inside. . . . One entered hoping at least for the solidarity of one's companions in misfortune, but the hoped for allies, except in special cases, were not there; there were instead a thousand sealed off monads, and between them a desperate covert and continuous struggle. (1986, p. 38)

The gray zone reduces the possibility of solidarity by alienating the victims from one another. The inmates knew they were being flung into a hell, but even in hell we have an implicit and minimal expectation to be able to suffer *with* and *alongside* others. Gray zones are designed to minimize this possibility of solidarity-in-suffering by pinning inmates against themselves and giving them positions of authority over one another. The impossibility of bonding with other inmates ensured: (a) that rebellion will be less likely, and (b) that collaboration with the Nazis will be more likely. In this sense, the gray zone exhibits some distant echoes of Marx's (2007/1844) notion of alienated labor under capitalism, where Marx claims that workers are alienated not just from their own "species essence" and the products of their labor, but also from *one another*. Workers come to see other members of their class as competitors in the job market, for instance. If the worker does not agree to take the starvation wages offered by the owner of capital, he knows that someone else, who is even more desperate than he, will accept these wages; or some workers are offered higher-salaried positions that involve overseeing lower-tiered workers and keeping them in line (the so-called "professional managerial class"). This diminishes the possibility of solidarity between workers, thus forestalling unionization, organization, strikes, and so on, all to the benefit of the owners, of course. The "alienated labor" of the gray zone, though, is far more sinister than the Marxist version, as will soon become clear. Here is where we encounter the second important effect of the gray zone:

(2) **Loss of Moral Innocence**: Gray zones force their inhabitants into situations and conditions that compromise their moral integrity; our innocence is lost when the harms and wrongs that are unjustly inflicted on others are the result of choices we have made, that is, when our decisions are responsible for their suffering, even if no better course of action was available to us at the time of making these decisions. (Card, 2002, p. 222)

The surest way to drive an alienating wedge between fellow victims and sufferers is to make them resent and distrust each other. Or, more preferably, to turn them into antagonistic enemies. Levi explains, first, that not everyone in Auschwitz inhabited the gray zone to an *equal degree*; and some, in his judgment, are more blameworthy than others. For instance, Levi (1986/1989/2017) distinguishes between lower-level functionaries and *Kapos*. The lower-level functionaries included interpreters, lice checkers, cleaners of various sorts, and so forth (Levi, 1986/1989/2017, p. 44). These inmates perhaps received a slightly better ration of food or something equivalent for their complicity, but their complicity certainly did not spare them from the same kind of suffering experienced by the general or nonprivileged camp population. More importantly, this kind of complicity did not necessarily pin the victims *against* one another as enemies.

Judgment becomes much murkier, Levi says, when we examine the *Kapos* or those inmates who were given positions of authority over other inmates in exchange for certain privileges. The *Kapos* were the "managers" of labor units, barracks, and other daily tasks in camp life that were carried out by inmates. Their role was primarily to maintain maximum efficiency, productivity, and order among the inmates. The *Kapo* system shifted the burdens of policing and organizing onto the prisoners themselves—the prisoners were to order, police, and punish each other. The *Kapos*, as Levi (1986/1989/2017), p. 46) reports, were allowed to brutalize inmates in whatever manner they like, even if doing so resulted in an inmate's death. The *Kapo* system really did, therefore, make the inmates enemies of one another.

But the most horrifying case of collaboration that Levi (1986/1989/2017) describes is surely that of the "Special Squad," the *Sonderkommando* (*SK*). The *SK* was tasked with such things as,

[maintaining] order among new arrivals . . . who were to be sent to the gas chambers, to extract corpses from the chambers, to pull gold teeth from jaws, to cut women's hair, to sort and classify clothes, shoes, and the contents of the luggage, to transport the bodies to the crematoria and oversee the operation of the ovens, to extract and eliminate the ashes. (Levi, 1986/1989/2017, p. 50)

The members of the *SK* were kept apart from the general camp population, and they too were killed routinely. There was a total of 12 squads in Auschwitz's history; and, as a rule, the first assignment of each new squad was to burn the bodies of the preceding one (Levi, 1986/1989/2017, p. 50).

Levi (1986/1989/2017, p. 53) says that the creation of the *SK* was National Socialism's (i.e., the Nazis) most diabolical act. The diabolical depth of the creation of this unit consists in the attempt to offload the genocidal work—and especially the *guilt* for the genocide as such—onto the Jews themselves. In 1943, the camp was 90% to 95% Jewish, and its aim had become to fulfill the "Final Solution," or the total extermination of the Jewish people. Levi (1986/1989/2017, p. 53) sums up the second effect aptly when he writes that the *SK* "represented an attempt to shift onto others—specifically, the victims—the burden of guilt, so that they were deprived of even the solace of innocence." It is essential, however, to note that, for Levi, the *system*, not the inmates, is primarily responsible: the *fascist, totalitarian state*. The conditions under which they acted do not eliminate culpability, Levi (1986/1989/2017, p. 44) says, "but," he continues, "I know of no human tribunal to which one could delegate the judgment." It is clear, in the case of the *Sonderkommando*, that they were acting under the most extreme duress and coercion imaginable. Nevertheless, from the victims' *own* view, it is doubtful whether this exoneration matters much. There is nothing that can erase the fact of their participation in these horrors. There is nothing that can erase fully the destructive effect it has had on their self-conception. (For more on this kind of phenomenon, where an agent is not "guilty," but nevertheless feels something like as if she were so, see Williams [1981] discussion of "agent regret" in his *Moral Luck*.) This is where the third effect becomes most significant:

(3) **Disintegration of Selfhood:** Gray zones aim to annihilate the inhabitants' self-conception through a betrayal of their deepest commitments and the values that they identify with or that make them *who* they are.

The complicity in the atrocities at Auschwitz could not have happened if the victims did not have their humanity, character, self-respect—or what Levi calls their "soul"—reduced to nothingness. Most victims, upon arrival, had already spent years or months in an enclosed ghetto, as mentioned. They already were deprived of their rights, property, livelihood, and so on, by the Nazi regime. The Nazis euphemistically would tell them, their soon-to-be victims, that they were to be "resettled in the east" when shipping them off in crammed cattle cars to be gassed in a death camp or worked to death in a labor camp. Upon arrival, all of their leftover property was confiscated; all their body hair was shaved; they were given ragged prisoners' uniforms; their identities were reduced literally to numbers that were tattooed onto the skin of their arms. They were separated from their families, in most cases, forever. But, even here, one might think that one's character and "soul" can remain intact. A person's body can be destroyed, tortured, and humiliated, but the most important and central thing about a person, that which makes someone *who* they are, the values and commitments that one endorses and that constitute one's identity, one's moral decency and humanity—*that*, we think, cannot be "taken" from us by anyone other than ourselves.

The gray zone's aim is to eliminate this essential core of personhood. For Levi (1986/1989/ 2017), this core seems to be *moral* in its fundamental character. The same seems true for Card (2002, p. 217), who claims that becoming evil might be the gravest danger faced by people who endure prolonged conditions of oppression and domination. As we saw, she thinks that becoming evil might be worse than death itself. The death of the body is preferable to the death of the soul. And Levi (1986/1989/2017), as we will see in the text that follows, seems to echo this point too.

The disintegration of selfhood in the gray zones begins with the previously mentioned events, but it continues. Prolonged and excessive hunger, fatigue, fear, and brutality reduce the inmates to a semi-animalistic condition. These are the conditions in which people will compromise their dignity, their values, their commitments—their selfhood—for morsels of food. These are the conditions that ensure prisoners will turn on one another and, in doing so, hasten the annihilation of their own selfhood. Wiesel (1960), another Auschwitz survivor, relates an utterly horrific story of this sort in *Night*. He recounts how a son literally strangled his father to death over a stale piece of bread at the time of the winter death march that Auschwitz inmates were forced to endure in 1945 during the war's final days. As Levi (1986/1989/2017, p. 52) says, for the Nazis, "it must be shown that the Jews, the subrace, the submen, bow to any and all humiliation, even to destroying themselves." But that is not all. Self-destruction can transcend even the disintegration of one's selfhood, the total unraveling of one's self-understanding, self-conception, or the betrayal of one's deepest values, commitments, and so on. The ultimate level of self-destruction consists in *remaking the self in the image of its oppressor*. This is perhaps clearest in the case of the *SK*. The *SK* was designed to destroy the self by making the victims resemble their Nazi oppressors (Levi, 1986/1989/2017, p. 54).

The diabolical essence of the gray zone is encapsulated in turning the victims into the mirrors of their oppressors. In the case of Auschwitz, this meant destroying the victims' souls by making them resemble the already disintegrated souls of the Nazis themselves. This theme in Levi's work is helpful for thinking about how identities are formed under oppression more generally. As many feminists, anti-colonial, and anti-racist writers have emphasized, oppressed subjectivity typically involves the internalization of the oppressor's perspective. See, for example, Bartky's (1990, 2002) analysis of women's subjectivity-formation under patriarchy. Patriarchal cultures formulate norms for how women "ought" to be—that is, how they ought to look, think, behave, and so on—and these norms are enshrined in "disciplinary" practices that women are expected to follow (think of dieting, makeup routines, and so on). But, as Bartky (2002, p. 25) writes, "The norms of feminine body discipline are not imposed upon fully formed subjects; they are importantly implicated in the very construction of our subjectivities." Women come to internalize these norms and practices; they are incorporated into their sense of self, their identity, and they thereby come to structure their conception of their own self-worth and value—they become, for instance, "essential to her sense of herself as a sexually desiring and desirable subject" (Bartky, 2002, p. 25). Yet, in patriarchal cultures, these norms and practices essentially are tied to the satisfaction, interests, and standards of *men*. Thus, as Bartky explains, women are internalizing the perspective of men; it is not just that they come to see and understand themselves through the eyes of their oppressors; rather, they come to *identify* with their oppressors' perspective as if it were their own. The result is a kind of "psychic fragmentation" where one part of the self is used constantly to monitor, criticize, police, judge, and discipline the other. Fanon (1952/1986) offers a similar theory in relation to colonized subjectivity in his *Black Skin, White Masks*. Colonized peoples come to form their identities *derivatively* from their oppressors. The colonized persons internalize the racist standards of their colonizers, such that, "The colonized is elevated above his jungle status in proportion to his adoption of the mother country's cultural status" (Fanon, 1952/1986, p. 18). So, in French colonies, like Fanon's birthplace of Martinique, the person who masters the French language is considered to be more "civilized" than his "pidgin-speaking" brethren, that is, "he becomes whiter as he renounces his blackness, his jungle" (Fanon, 1952/1986, p. 18).

The deformation of the soul—this transformation of the oppressed into a copy of the oppressors—reveals yet another one of Levi's central themes: the moral fragility of human beings. There are very few people, Levi claims, who would have had the "moral armature" needed to resist under the conditions of the Nazi gray zone (Levi, 1986/1989/2017, p. 68). Collaboration exercises a powerful appeal. Collaborators had numerous motivations to comply. Sheer terror, fear, and prudence were, of course, typical motivators. But Levi also notes the allure of the semblance or feeling of having *any* power at all in an otherwise completely powerless and despondent situation (Levi, 1986/1989/2017, p. 43). Consider Chaim Rumkowski, for example. As Levi reports, he was the head of the Jewish Council of the Lodz Ghetto in Poland (roughly equivalent to a mayor) and a major collaborator. He tried to make his ghetto as productive as possible to the Nazis. Jewish productivity, he must have believed, would save the Jews of the ghetto from the extermination promised by the "Final Solution." In the process, however, he notoriously exploited the situation to acquire—and then abuse—the limited amount of power and authority that he actually had. He subsequently (and cynically) became known as "King Chaim" and the Lodz ghetto was eventually liquidated with almost all of its inhabitants shipped off to be gassed as Auschwitz (Rumkowski himself arriving and eventually dying there too, but by private car rather than in a crammed train). Levi (1986/1989/2017, p. 67) takes Rumkowski to be an instructive case for the morally corrupting influence that political power exerts on individuals: "At the foot of every absolute throne, men such as Rumkowski crowd in order to grab their small portion of power." Resisting the lure of power—even under the worst circumstances—is something that requires a strong moral backbone.

Similarly, Levi (1986/1989/2017, p. 56) thinks we should recognize moral fragility in the fact that "compassion and brutality" can be present in the same person at the same time. Levi recounts a story about an *SS* commander, Eric Mushfeldt, who seemed to feel a second of compassion for a girl who survived the gas chamber. Is this proof that, at bottom, commander Mushfeldt was a good person after all? In some sense, Mushfeldt's story can be said to demonstrate *im*moral fragility. His compassion demonstrates the fragility of his brutality, which, unfortunately, was not fragile enough. Mushfeldt had an underling finish the job the gas chamber failed to do and execute the girl with a shot of his rifle. Finally, Levi (1986/1989/2017) turns the question on his readers:

> National Socialism exercises a frightful power of corruption, against which it is difficult to guard oneself. It degrades its victims and makes them similar to itself, because it needs both great and small complicities. To resist requires a truly solid moral armature. . . . How would each of us behave if driven by necessity and at the same time lured by seduction? . . . Like Rumkowski, we too are so dazzled by power and prestige as to forget our essential fragility. Willingly or not we come to terms with power, forgetting that we are all in the ghetto, that the ghetto is walled in, that outside the ghetto reign the lords of death, and that close by the train is waiting. (pp. 68–69)

This brings us to the final characteristic effect of gray zones:

(4) **Survivor's Shame:** The threat of disintegration of selfhood, loss of moral innocence, complicity in crimes, and the unwillingness to extend compassion or foster solidarity is conducive to producing a distinctive sense of shame in gray zone survivors (Card, 2002, p. 213).

There is a common distinction drawn between shame and guilt. People feel guilty when they have *done* something wrong, but they feel shame about who or what they *are*. The target of shame is not an action, but the self as a whole. It is true, of course, that one can be ashamed because of something one has done, but the target of the shame is not the action per se, but one's identity. I might, for instance, feel guilty about failing to call out a coworker's racist remarks, but ashamed for being a coward or failing to live up to my values. (But see Williams' [1993] *Shame and Necessity* for an account that complicates the relationship between shame and guilt.)

Gray zone survivors are apt to feel both shame and guilt as a result of the traumas from the disintegration of selfhood, loss of moral innocence, and alienation they experience in the gray zone. Guilt for specific acts or omissions is likely to be persistent; but, as Levi (1986/1989/2017, p. 81) writes, there is also a deep and significant sense of shame in the feeling that one was not as *worthy* of surviving as one's fellows, that one is alive at the expense of someone who was a better, wiser, more virtuous human being than oneself. Indeed, the title of Levi's (1986/1989/2017) book, *The Drowned and the Saved*, maps precisely onto this persistent sense of survivors' shame that the "saved" are the unworthy. As Levi (1986/1989/2017, p. 82) claims, the "saved" were not typically those who were morally best—the kind, the compassionate, the selfless—but, rather, those who were the most egoistic and violent, those who were willing to collaborate with the enemy or trample on their fellows, those who traded their souls for a (meager) chance at prolonging their existence: "The worst survived, that is, the fittest; the best all died." [Levi's claim here sits in some tension with his remark that no court is in a position to judge survivors. Yet this also seems perfectly in line with the ambiguous nature of the gray zone. It draws our emotions in multiple and often conflicting directions; it muddies our judgment (Levi, 1986/1989/2017, p. 42). Levi's claim also perhaps overplays people's agency in gray zones. The immense role luck played in survival seems undeniable. But whichever way we interpret the claim, Levi's thought provides a strong phenomenological example of the kind of shame that survivors of atrocities are apt to experience.]

After Evil?

How is the power of finding meaning could change the whole trauma experience.

Evil involves intolerable harms; it can completely destroy or engulf the good in people's lives, and it can annihilate our solidarity and relationships with others precisely where they may be needed most, as, for instance, in gray zones. This raises a final question: How is it possible to cope with traumatic experiences of this sort? Some thinkers, like the psychologist Viktor Frankl, himself an Auschwitz survivor, have emphasized the need for meaning as the driving motor of human life. As Frankl (1959/1985) explains in *Man's Search for Meaning*, "being human always points, and is directed, to something, or someone, other than oneself—be it a meaning to fulfill or another human being to encounter" (p. 133). And he continues,

> We must never forget that we may also find meaning in life even when confronted with a hopeless situation, when facing a fate that cannot be changed. For what then matters is to bear witness to the uniquely human potential at its best, which is to transform a personal tragedy into a triumph, to turn one's predicament into a human achievement. When we are no longer able to change a situation—just think of an incurable disease such as inoperable cancer—we are challenged to change ourselves. (Frankl, 1959/1985, p. 135)

Frankl's approach is focused on the self as an existential subject, as a being who is, in Sartre's (1957) phrase, "condemned to be free," that is, a being who must take responsibility for their life and give it meaning through action (p. 23). But Frankl's approach deemphasizes the *moral* dimension of evil. Unlike cancer, evil involves moral wrongdoing. It therefore gives rise not just to the question of how *I*, as a victim, can proceed with my life, but also: What do perpetrators *owe* their victims? Is it possible to remedy or *mend* the deep forms of damage that they have done? Is *reconciliation* between evildoers and victims even possible? We close, then, with some discussion of these questions through the topic of moral repair. (For a substantive critique of Frankl's approach, please see Lawrence Langer's [1980] essay, "The Dilemma of Choice in the Death Camps.")

The philosopher Margaret Urban Walker understands moral repair as aiming at rebuilding or stabilizing moral relationships between wrongdoers and those they have wronged. As Urban Walker (2006) explains, there are three basic conditions for "making amends" or repairing relationships when wrongdoing has occurred. The wrongdoer must (1) *take responsibility* for their actions and their consequences; (2) *acknowledge* that those actions were wrong and their consequences harmful; and (3) engage in *reparative actions* (apology, for instance) that expresses the wrongdoer's will to "set right something for which amends are *owed*" (Urban Walker, 2006, p. 191). Yet, as Urban Walker (2006, p. 191) notes, it often seems like "the magnitude of injury and the disposition to take responsibility are inversely related." If Walker is right, this means that evildoers may be the least likely to take responsibility and engage in moral repair. Urban Walker (2006, p. 195) explains that "reparative gestures, including admissions, apologies, and amends, but also excuses . . . are favored where they are most likely to 'work.'" According to Walker, this regards cases in which the wrongdoer thinks they could regain social standing, mend the broken relationship, or (eventually) diminish their sense of guilt and the resentment that is directed toward them by the victim and others. So, although moral repair is *most* needed after evil, evil makes it perhaps the *least* likely to be available. Evil, in other words, poses the most significant roadblocks for the possibility of successful moral repair. Taking responsibility for evil means acknowledging and affirming shared norms that define what one has done as *inexcusably terrible*—and this introduces the possibility of a deep sense of guilt along with the acknowledgment of the aptness of resentment from the wronged party or the community. It also opens the door to costly demands for rectification by the victim(s). Taking responsibility for evil further requires evildoers to relinquish control over their narrative and to accept the authoritative role of victims (or relevant communities) in framing the events, as well as the victims' right to express their own accounts of the wrongs they have suffered and the emotions these events have wrought.

Nevertheless, moral repair after evil is not impossible. Successful moral repair requires establishing a mutual sense of *confidence* that the wrongdoer and the victim have a shared set of moral standards and values, *trust* that these standards and values will be upheld or acknowledged if they are violated, and *hope* that this trust is not misplaced and that "unacceptable treatment will not prevail" (Urban Walker, 2006, p. 210). Urban Walker (2006, p. 199) claims that successful moral repair depends ultimately on "what deep reservoirs of trust and still flowing springs of hope can be tapped." But then, what should be done in cases where evildoers fail to share the same values or norms as the victims or refuse to recognize the victim's right to hold the perpetrator(s) accountable? The victims in such cases may be completely invisible *as victims* to the perpetrators. And, what if the "reservoirs of trust and hopefulness" that are necessary for stabilizing relationships may be completely annihilated by the wrongs of the evildoers? Victims may reasonably have reservations about rebuilding confidence. This could potentially mean that evildoers would have to commit to a seemingly impossible task or a deeply morally demanding one of endless repair (Urban Walker, 2006).

In these cases, it is important to note that *communities* also may bear responsibility for moral repair rather than just perpetrators. Moral repair at the communal level has its own distinctive vicissitudes too, however. Kizuk (2020) provides an instructive example of this in her discussion of "settler shame" in the Canadian context. Kizuk has called attention to the ways in which the Canadian Truth and Reconciliation Commission, which ostensibly seeks moral repair for indigenous groups in Canada, is directed toward reaffirming the identity of settler Canadians themselves, rather than promoting justice for indigenous groups. The shame that the settler Canadians feel is directed toward their recognition that they cannot uphold their identities as "the peaceful, benevolent Canadian," but the shame itself (and its "performance") becomes a means through which their original, positive, self-identity can be restored. This is not to say that the Truth and Reconciliation Commission is wholly bad for the indigenous participants. But as Kizuk (2020, p. 7) writes, "The problem of settler shame is that it tends toward repairing the damaged self by using the indigenous other as a mute foil to enact peace upon."

Kizuk highlights some valuable lessons for communal moral repair more generally. Communities and agents who engage in reparative gestures should remain cognizant of the *power dynamics* that are already present between the parties; it is easy for those in power to frame narratives in accordance with their material, social, and psychological interests, even under the genuine guise of "justice." And, as Kizuk (2020, p. 12) writes, "The material demands of transformative justice require a new affective attunement for settlers that is neither fleeting nor self-focused and that does not use Indigenous peoples' pain as a canvas on which to explore our own reflexivity."

Ultimately, the "reservoirs" of confidence, trust, and hope may never be fully restored. But morality demands that we at least do what we can for the victims; that we provide them with the proper platform to express their emotions, frame their narratives, and voice their social, political, and material demands; that we take those emotions, narratives, and demands with seriousness, compassion, respect, and love. Moral repair after evil may be an endless and difficult, perhaps in some cases even impossible, task, but it is one that morality nevertheless demands we undertake.

CONCLUSION

In this chapter, we examined evil through the lens of moral psychology. Following Card's (2010) lead, we saw that those who *do* evil need not themselves *be* evil, and that evil can be an entirely ordinary or "banal" phenomenon. The susceptibility of ordinary agents to engage in evil was borne out by our examination of its causal determinants, specifically situational factors and personality. "Situationists" like Doris (2002) play down significantly the role of character in explaining evil behavior. Numerous experiments in social psychology, when considered together, demonstrate that even small situational factors have enormous behavioral effects, and thus, that our commonsense reliance on explaining people's behavior via their personality (what Ross and Nisbett (1991) call the "fundamental attribution error") may perhaps be more misleading than true. But we also noted that the approach of moral psychology is not merely concerned with *explaining* evil, it is also concerned with how we *should* respond to it, for instance, how we can avoid doing evil ourselves and what should be done after someone has been traumatized by evil. In relation to this, we discussed the trauma involved in what Primo Levi has called the "gray zone," where victims are made complicit by their perpetrators in their own victimization as well as the victimization of others.

Repairing relationships and restoring people's sense of trust, confidence, and hope in others and the world is, of course, a very difficult task after evil has been done. However, although it presents many obstacles and challenges, moral repair is not impossible. Because perpetrators often are unwilling to engage in moral repair, though, the responsibility often falls on communities to take up the work of moral repair in the face of evil. One hopes that, armed with a theory of evil, a proper understanding of one's susceptibility (as an ordinary person) to doing evil, as well as an awareness of the effects that evil and gray zones can have on their victims, people—whether as part of a community or as individuals—will more readily recognize and act in ways that both reduce the prevalence of evil and remedy its life-destroying effects. In a century in which impending climate catastrophe unimaginably threatens to exacerbate every single form of oppression that already exists, an informed commitment to combatting evil could go a long way indeed.

ADDITIONAL RESOURCES

A robust set of instructor resources designed to supplement this text is located at http://connect.springerpub.com/content/book/978-0-8261-5085-1. Qualifying instructors may request access by emailing textbook@springerpub.com.

PRACTICE-BASED RESOURCES AND REFERENCES

To view a list of resources and all the references, please visit connect.springerpub.com via the following url:: http://connect.springerpub.com/content/book/978-0-8261-5085-1/part/part03/chapter/ch16

CHAPTER 17

Racial, Ethnic, and Immigration Intolerance: A Framework for Understanding Violence and Trauma

WAGANESH A. ZELEKE AND LISA LÓPEZ LEVERS

CHAPTER OVERVIEW

This chapter focuses on the intolerance experienced by marginalized groups of people, based on race, ethnicity, and immigration status. It reviews current knowledge about violence-based trauma among minority groups and offers discussions that highlight historical patterns of and risk factors for PTSD. The chapter briefly summarizes interventions and treatments that relate to race-based, ethnicity-based, historical, and intergenerational trauma.

LEARNING OBJECTIVES

After reading this chapter, the reader should be able to:

1. Define ethnic, racial, and immigration intolerance and trauma as well as transgenerational trauma;
2. Develop greater awareness about the experience of violence-based and historical trauma among minority groups;
3. Recognize various factors that contribute to an increased risk for PTSD among individuals from minority racial backgrounds and among immigrants;
4. Discuss community protective factors related to treating trauma among populations affected by race-, ethnicity-, and immigration-related intolerance; and,
5. Identify appropriate interventions and treatments that are relevant to race-, ethnicity-, and immigration-based violence and trauma.

INTRODUCTION

Issues related to ethnicity and race have served as a prelude to social interactions throughout history and across national boundaries; they have become increasingly more volatile in the United States. Ethnicity and race have played a significant role in shaping immigration policy, politics, and reactions throughout U.S. history. Immigration has re-emerged as an important issue in ideological perception and public policy in the United States, as well as in many other Western nations. Political views pertaining to immigration among Americans especially are divided, with both support for and hate against the "other." For some, race and immigration evoke cultural and economic anxieties as well as raising concerns about the use of public resources. In contrast, for others, race and immigration represent a myriad of benefits to and new opportunities for the country.

Responses to contemporary notions about race, ethnicity, and immigration phenomena range from nativist and xenophobic reactions of alarm and fear to an appreciation of multicultural diversity and even the sense of an inevitable triumph of Democracy. In recent times, racism, xenophobia, and immigration restriction practices have created controversies over the lines historically drawn between races, between aliens and citizens, between "haves" and "have-nots," and between "us" and "them"; explosive tensions have been shared, and individuals and their families have been harmed, along with local communities and society in general. Intolerance of human beings, based on race, ethnicity, immigration status, and the intersectionality of any of these, either together or along with existing social inequities, is an area of high public salience, with significant implications for policy, social outcomes, and well-being.

Intolerance refers to a lack of acceptance of or hostility toward others, based explicitly on their minority status. Racial, ethnic, and immigration intolerance in America broadly is perceived to be on the rise in recent years, and research has documented an increase in manifestations of intolerant attitudes, both in national policy and more widely in the behaviors of individuals (e.g., Quillian et al., 2017; Shonkoff et al., 2021; D. R. Williams, 2018). Intolerance that is based on race, ethnicity, and immigration has a stressful impact on immigrants and racial- or ethnic-minority groups, causing emotional pain, suffering, and even trauma (Gorski & Goodman, 2015; Levers, 2020; Levers & Hyatt-Burkhart, 2012; Wilkerson, 2020; M. T. Williams et al., 2021).

In this chapter, we aim to broaden the usual conceptualization of violence and trauma as a theoretical framework by elaborating on the nature, causes, symptoms, and effects of racial, ethnic, and immigration-status intolerance. We specifically amplify this framework by offering discussions in the following sections: (a) Posttraumatic Stress Disorder in the Context of Race, Ethnicity, and Immigration Status; (b) Colonial Oppression; (c) Systemic Oppression and Immigration Intolerance; (d) Race-Based Hate Crimes; (e) Transgenerational Trauma; (f) Trauma-Informed Interventions; and (g) Counseling Implications. Within these discussions, we propose a movement away from simplistic conceptualizations to richer engagement with a *humanizing* rather than *objectifying* context, one that supports racial, ethnic, and immigrant minority groups who far too often must deal with hate-based and historical trauma.

POSTTRAUMATIC STRESS DISORDER IN THE CONTEXT OF RACE, ETHNICITY, AND IMMIGRATION STATUS

Posttraumatic stress disorder (PTSD) is a serious condition that can develop after a person has witnessed or has experienced a traumatic event. The current diagnostic criteria for PTSD that appear in the Diagnostic and Statistical Manual of Mental Disorders (5th ed.; *DSM-5*; American Psychiatric Association [APA], 2013) include cognitive, behavioral, and affective presentations of the disorder. Under "Criterion A," the *DSM-5* contains an important prerequisite for the identification and diagnosis of PTSD: a history of trauma exposure. Certain experiences that are not covered under the "Criterion A" umbrella still can cause a traumatic reaction. This has led to arguments for legitimizing exposure to oppressive and racist acts as traumatic events worthy of consideration in the diagnosis of PTSD. Scholars in the field state that exposure to race-, ethnicity-, or immigration-based hate acts can cause or trigger traumatic reactions (e.g., O'Neill et al., 2018; Shonkoff et al., 2021; D. R. Williams, 2018; M. T. Williams et al., 2018, 2021). The Anti-Defamation League (ADL, 2019) has constructed a *Pyramid of Hate* to illuminate the cascading societal attitudes that can lead to unthinkable acts of violence; a pertinent description and downloadable PDF of the pyramid are available on the ADL website (see References).

Race-, ethnicity-, and immigration-based trauma can be defined as a traumatic response to race-, ethnicity-, or immigration-related experiences that are collectively characterized as racism and xenophobia. Tenets of racism are based upon belief systems, held by individuals, that are deterministic in nature and premise the superiority of one group over another. However, as reported by the BBC (2020), a recent push to add "systemic oppression" to the formal definition of racism has been successful. Xenophobia commonly refers to a fear of strangers or those from other countries, and by extension, to an extreme dislike or even hatred of anything foreign. Both racism and xenophobia have led to overt or covert actions such as prejudice, discrimination, or violence against a perceived subordinate racial or immigrant group based on attitudes of superiority held by the dominant group. These covert or overt actions, carried out by individuals or societies, have the potential to cause racial- or immigration-based trauma.

Research shows that over time, the trauma begotten of race- or immigration-based intolerance can result in significant psychological and physiological damage in people of color and immigrants (Shonkoff et al., 2021; D. R. Williams, 2018). Race- or immigration-based traumatic stress is a shared experience among people of color and among immigrants. This cumulative and overwhelming emotional and psychological response to race- and hate-based trauma often is referred to as historical trauma. Historical trauma is an example of transgenerational trauma and consists of at least three factors: (1) the traumatic events result in collective suffering, (2) the event is widespread, and (3) the intent of those inflicting the trauma is malicious (O'Neill et al., 2018). Historical trauma grows out of the intolerance for and eventual devaluation and persecution of marginalized groups of people by some members of the dominant group; historical trauma clearly is a product of "othering."

The intolerance under scrutiny here has manifested, in far too many arenas, as White supremacist and White nationalist ideologies of exclusion and hatred. These ideologies embrace the perceived privilege of those who possess self-perceptions of "having power" over those viewed as "not worthy" of privilege or personal agency. According to Zalaquett and Haynes-Thoby (2020, p. 229), "These unearned privileges usually are not available to people of color. White privilege is mostly invisible to those who have it and, therefore, is very difficult to acknowledge." Sue et al. (2019) have referred to this phenomenon of invisibility as the *invisible veil*, thereby implying that racism has become so institutionalized that the very people who perpetrate its intolerance also are incapable of perceiving it, ostensibly without a mechanism for assisting them with some degree of self-awareness about the matter. Such "invisible" attitudes of intolerance cause great harm. For example, a former U.S. senator asserted the following, in an April 26, 2021 CNN broadcast (Lock, 2021, "Transcript of Santorum's remarks on Native Americans," para. 1–5):

> If you think about this country, I don't know of any other country in the world that was settled predominantly by people who were coming . . . here, mostly from Europe, and they set up a country. . . . We came here and created a blank slate. We birthed a nation from nothing. I mean, there was nothing here. I mean, yes, we have Native Americans but candidly there isn't much Native American culture in American culture. It was born of the people who came here . . .

The "blank slate" narrative just presented is astonishing. It ignores the genocide of many of the indigenous peoples who inhabited the Americas, long before the arrival of European colonizers. It also ignores the forced abduction of many African peoples from their homelands, kidnapped to the "New World" and enslaved, in order to construct the very foundation for establishing the "dream" world reality of the colonizers. The factual history of the "founding of America" is far removed from any notion of "creating" a "blank slate"; indeed, statements of privilege, such as the one made by the senator, betray any sense of the sanctity of life, cause damage to others, and sustain the lived experiences of historical trauma.

The conceptualization of race-, ethnic-, and immigration-based violence and its effects can be viewed from varied theoretical approaches across different fields of studies. The following section illuminates the experiences of Black, Indigenous, and people of color (BIPOC), as well as immigrants, who have been exposed to traumatic events from an anticolonial lens. This anticolonial approach offers a way for understanding how colonial oppression and systemic racism can cause additional life stressors to those who have been oppressed and even harm their mental and physical health; this approach offers a critical discourse regarding individuals exposed to oppression as well as a discussion of how exposure to oppression affects their families and entire generations.

COLONIAL OPPRESSION

The word "colonize" derives from the Latin "colonus," which means to inhabit, settle, farm, and cultivate. According to the Oxford English Dictionary (2021, "colonization," p. 1), "colonization" describes "The action or process of settling among and establishing control over the indigenous people of an area . . . [and] The action of appropriating a place or domain for one's own use." This definition indicates the taking over of land and resources, with or without violence and displacement. Most of us are familiar with the type of external colonization that we learned about in history courses, when people from one land move into and colonize another land, as was the case with European colonizers "conquering" the Americas or parts of the African, Asian, and Australian continents. However, scholars (e.g., Blauner, 1972, 2001) have posited an important distinction between external and internal colonization. Internal colonization occurs when a dominant culture undermines and exterminates another culture within the same area. Internal colonization is less obvious; it often is subconscious and more insidious.

In this section, we focus on the history and nature of internal colonization and the act of oppression in the United States. Even though the phenomenon of internal colonialism in the United States differs somewhat from other parts of the world, we hope that the focus on the United States can serve as an example for examining internal colonialism as a form of oppression that may exist in any given country. The theory of internal colonization explains the ways in which inequality and dominion are sustained within a society, even though a foreign power may not be in control. Internal colonization is a condition of oppression, and the term is used by social science scholars to conceptualize the historical and cultural conditions and experiences that result directly from the actions of imperial governments (Blauner, 2018).

Blauner (1972, 2001, 2018) provides a model to conceptualize colonialism and the oppressive nature of colonial acts. His model addresses four basic components of the colonization complex: (a) forced, involuntary entry into a land and among its people; (b) destruction of indigenous culture, values, social orientation, and way of life; (c) imposition of legal order on the indigenous culture, by the invading culture, with an aim to dominate; and (d) justification of these actions through the use of prejudice, racist beliefs, and stereotypes (cited in Canadian Association for Refugee and Forced Migration Studies [CARFMS], 2021, "colonization complex," p. 1). As defined by this complex, representatives of the dominant power regulate the lives of the subordinate group. This, in turn, establishes a principle of social domination and racism, by which a group is viewed as inferior or different; the alleged biological characteristics of the subordinate group members are exploited and controlled by the dominant group, and the dominant group oppresses the subordinate group socially and physically. Other scholars (e.g., George, 2012; Schaefer, 2015) have described colonial oppression as a way to maintain control over a group's political, social, economic, and cultural capital and mores.

The history of the United States is written and taught from the perspective of the dominant culture. Even though the United State is among the most diverse democracies in the world, much of its history reveals an internal colonialism that has had traumatic consequences for minority groups and has affected subsequent generations. This history includes brutality against Native Americans and disregarding treaties with Native American Nations, internment of Japanese-American citizens during World War II, constitutionally encoded enslavement of Africans, as well as the racial profiling of Latinos, African Americans, and immigrants in general. Table 17.1 summarizes the types of colonial oppressions, aimed at various groups in the United States, which have led to their experiences of historical trauma.

Racism in the United States is systemic and has very deep roots. We must excavate to the deepest levels to eradicate this toxic malevolence. We also must call out everyday acts of racism—what

Table 17.1

Oppressive Acts and Traumatic Experience of Minority Groups

Oppressive Act	Group	Traumatic Experience as a Result of the Oppressive Act
Removal Act	Native American Nations	– Forced relocation (died of hunger, disease)
The Dawes Act		– Trail of Tears march (exhaustion)
		– Forced placement in boarding schools
		– Loss of tribal lands and erosion of tribal traditions
Constitutional encoding of enslavement	Africans	– Segregation
Chattel Slavery	African Americans	– Denied basic human rights
Slavery Abolished		– Enslavement
Ku Klux Klan		– Tortured
Lynching		– Prohibited from education
"Great migration"		– Restricted movement and behavior
Urbanizing Blacks		– Rape
		– Brutal punishment
Internment during World War II	Asian Americans	– Denied citizenship and naturalization
Chinese Exclusion Act		– Prevented from marrying Caucasians
		– Prevented from owning land
Racial profiling	Latinos/Hispanics	– Racism
	African Americans	– Racist biases
	Immigrants	– Exposure to racist abuse in the media
		– Discrimination
Crimmigration	Immigrants	– Harsh criminal sanctions
Between 2005 and 2015, anti-immigrant legislative acts increased by 500%, from 38 to 222		– Criminalizing certain migrant groups
		– Violence
		– Sanctions and injuries

Hannah Arendt (1963) has identified as the "banality of evil." Gorski and Goodman (2015) have suggested that the area of multicultural counseling needs to be decolonized. Goodman (2015, p. 55) further states that the "creation of trauma-informed practices is a critical step forward . . . because this framework acknowledges that trauma can have complex and long-lasting impacts on clients and must be addressed throughout all human services in order for our work to be effective." Following Gorski and Goodman, perhaps the entire arena of trauma counseling needs to be decolonized. While it is beyond the scope of this chapter to present the histories of all groups of oppressed people, in the following subsections, we discuss the colonial oppression of a few of the more highly targeted groups in the United States. We have selected groups that represent both indigenous people and immigrants, including those who already were here and were invaded, those who arrived willingly, those who fled dangerous conditions in their homelands, and those who were forcibly enslaved. We have elected to frame the discussion in terms of colonization, in order to reflect the multilayered dimensions and strata of historical trauma.

Colonial Oppression and Native Americans

As a result of oppressive systems and policies designed by individuals from dominant European cultures, Native Americans have been subjected to internal colonialism. The act of internal colonization traumatized indigenous populations and caused the loss of many lives, loss of families, loss of land, and loss of culture for the last 500 years (Whitbeck et al., 2004). In 1830, President Andrew Jackson signed the Indian Removal Act, which authorized the federal government to relocate Native Americans, forcibly, to the southeast to create room for White settlements. This displacement caused the deaths of many Native Americans due to hunger, disease, and exhaustion on a forced march west of the Mississippi River. Additionally, in 1887, President Grover Cleveland passed the General Allotment Act, also known as the Dawes Act, which forcibly converted communally held tribal lands into small, individually owned lots and allowed the government to seize two-thirds of reservation lands and redistribute them to White Americans. These experiences caused the forced erosion of tribal traditions, the displacement of thousands of families, and the loss of 90 million acres of valuable land. The loss of tribal lands continued between 1945 and 1968, with federal laws terminating more than 100 tribal nations' recognition, thus placing them under state jurisdiction.

Indigenous peoples were forced onto "reservations," tracts of land that were not their tribal homes, but rather, spaces determined by the government. In some instances, tribal groups who were historical enemies were placed on the same reservation by legislators (Wyoming State Historical Society, 2018). The government removed indigenous children from their families and forced the children to attend government boarding schools, circa 1879, such as the Carlisle Indian Industrial School. Severing children from their families and indigenous cultures was another act of oppression that traumatized generations of Native Americans. Many of the children, dispossessed of their families and sent to these schools, experienced severe abuse and neglect, including regular physical and sexual assaults. Many of the schools were operated by religious organizations, and the abuse was at the hands of duly officiated members of religious groups. Contemporary Tribal Elders continue to share horrific memories about the school-based violence of their early childhood experiences (Pember, 2019).

Colonial Oppression and Asian Americans

People emigrating from Asia have had varied experiences upon arriving in the United States. Immigrants, along with U.S. citizens whose heritages have derived from China, Japan, India, other parts of Asia, and the Pacific Islands (both of Asian and indigenous heritage)—all people of color—are likely to have experienced discrimination in the United States. As a continuation of our discussion about colonial experiences, Asian Americans long have been considered as a "threat" to the nation, as the "other"; historically, they were looked down upon, considered to be of lower status, and they have been discriminated against, exploited, violently attacked, and murdered.

In the 19th century, Asian Americans were referred to as the "yellow peril" and viewed as "unclean," which fueled the passage of the Chinese Exclusion Act, the first law that restricted immigration based on race. Although Chinese laborers largely were responsible for building the transcontinental railroad east, from California, the "Chinese Must Go" movement in 1880s was vehement and caused the decline of Chinese immigrants from 39,500 in 1882 to only 10 in 1887 (Asia Society, 2021). In 1924, all Asian immigrants, including Chinese, Japanese, Koreans, and Indians, with the exception of Filipino "nationals," were fully excluded by law, denied citizenship and naturalization, and prevented from marrying Caucasians or owning land. Because of the U.S. colonization of the Philippines, many Filipinos emigrated to the United States to work. They were denigrated and reviled for supposedly being "unclean" and "uncivilized," which was a standard trope for the "swarthy other" viewed through the lens of bigotry. In 1942, President Franklin Roosevelt's Executive Order 9066 to isolate and incarcerate individuals, under suspicion as "enemy aliens," served as the impetus for the internment of over 120,000 Japanese Americans during WWII. These instances constituted additional examples of the vile historical oppression against Asian Americans in the United States. Even though this Executive

Order, along with earlier discriminatory laws, affected German and Italian Americans as well, the vast majority of those incarcerated in the early 1940s were of Japanese descent and lived in five west coast states. Many of them were second- and third-generation Americans—they were born in the United States, and they were citizens. Silence and attempts to assimilate into mainstream society were common coping reactions following the internment. The descendants of those who were interned have tried to cope with the trauma by seeking redress and by reviving connections with their Japanese heritage and culture (Nagata et al., 2019).

U.S. immigration laws remained discriminatory toward Asians until 1965, when, in response to the larger civil rights movement, nonrestrictive annual quotas of 20,000 immigrants per country were established. Fewer people have emigrated from other parts of Asia but nonetheless have experienced discrimination. Asian Americans from smaller countries like Viet Nam, Laos, Thailand, and Nepal have immigrated to the United States in immigration waves over the last several decades, often as refugees fleeing dangerous situations in their countries of origins. Asian Americans, like most marginalized groups, have been found to be at risk for mental health disparities. For example, PTSD, depression, anxiety, panic disorder, and other mental health disorders have been common in Cambodian and Vietnamese American refugees (Constante, 2020). Of course, immigration law in the United States has become a contentious issue, and vile, vicious, and pernicious perpetrations of racism against Asian Americans have reemerged as an artifact of misperceptions about and reactions to the COVID-19 pandemic.

Colonial Oppression and Africans/African Americans: Enslavement

During much of the 17th and 18th centuries, prominent U.S. citizens in all of the 13 colonies—both in the North and the South—incorporated slavery into accepted law (Congress.Gov., n.d.). Slavery was more than a labor system; it was an uneven, exploitative, and immoral covenant that, when threatened or endangered, gave White colonists an exaggerated sense of their own status of superiority, perpetuating their shared racial bond and identity. The practice of slavery continued on a large scale, even after it was declared illegal, which in and of itself was a complex issue, in terms of an historical date. The preliminary Emancipation Proclamation was signed in 1862, the Emancipation Proclamation was signed in 1863, and the 13th Amendment to the U.S. Constitution was passed in 1865; however, the pathway to freedom was paved with obstacles. During this time, captive Africans faced the challenge of surviving in a society that had avowed each of them as private property. They had no legal right to make decisions about their own lives and could be bought, sold, tortured, rewarded, educated, or killed at the slaveholder's will. Even after emancipation, freedom for African Americans has remained elusive; through Jim Crow laws, through the civil rights movement, through voter suppression, and through the contemporary Black Lives Matter movement, equity and justice, assumptive attributes of American Democracy encoded in law and in the Constitution, are not necessarily the quotidian reality of many Black lives in the United States.

The long legal—and ultimately de facto—existence of slavery helped to create the American caste system that endures today. Wilkerson (2020) brilliantly identified and examined eight pillars that undergird caste systems across civilizations, emphasizing how Nazi Germany assessed American racial systems as a means toward Jewish subjugation. The course of enslavement, its brutality and savagery, its contemporary retrograde to Jim Crow, has carried a high cost for African Americans, not the least of which is transgenerational or historical trauma. African Americans experience much higher rates of poverty, unemployment, educational disparity, and negative health outcomes compared to the majority group in the United States. The biopsychosocial disparities and possible epigenetic changes associated with historical trauma have further complicated well-being and life-span issues for African Americans (Daskalakis et al., 2018). The legacy of enslavement has shaped the entire contemporary situation of African Americans.

Oppressive ideas about African Americans and about Blackness, forged first through European and then "New World American" colonial violence, ultimately spread, influencing culture and even science for centuries. It also shaped the premise for an utter devaluation, by

Whites and the systems they have controlled, of African American life in the United States. Scholars in the fields of sociology, anthropology, and psychology have argued that colonialism is at the root of the current trend of police violence against African Americans and their communities (Bryant-Davis et al., 2017). Present day policing practices that include brutality have manifested in the killings of George Floyd, Breonna Taylor, and so many others. These atrocities continue to mirror the colonialism that has shaped the history of African Americans since their earliest arrival, as enslaved Africans, in the 16th century (while captive Africans were brought to the Jamestown Colony in 1619, their initial arrival in North America was in the 1500s) (Guasco, 2017).

SYSTEMIC OPPRESSION AND IMMIGRATION INTOLERANCE

Many factors may influence the decision for a person to choose to emigrate from one location to another. Individuals, as well as entire families, may experience immigration-related trauma before, during, and after the immigration process (Levers & Hyatt-Burkhart, 2012). Immigration also can cause transgenerational trauma, as a person's or their family's reason to immigrate can affect their perceptions about the process. If a family is forced out of their homeland due to safety concerns, perhaps arising from persecution by their own people or even from a dominant culture, it can create stress and maybe trauma symptoms. Individuals may pass along traumatic symptomatology that affects their children's ability to trust other people or to create effective personal and interpersonal boundaries. Several issues may contribute to this type of transgenerational trauma.

First, in addition to the psychological effects of immigration, there are also environmental impacts on immigration. There often may be hundreds or thousands of people trying to reach resource officers to emigrate from their country-of-origin; however, long lines and the unavailability of people to help may hamper a sense of well-being during the immigration process. This could lead to extensive trauma for children or unaccompanied young adults who are trying to immigrate without a guardian present. This type of trauma can cause mental health strains for these young individuals as they continue to develop and grow.

Second, culture plays an important role in the immigration process. During their journey to the United States, immigrants are at further risk of experiencing extortion, sexual assault, violence, robberies, kidnapping, exposure to extreme temperature resulting in hypothermia or hyperthermia, and even death. Trauma, in this capacity, could affect how individuals experience their direct environment, thus causing them to feel uneasy about what is happening around them. Again, this may add to the potential struggle with ongoing mental health concerns related to the immigration process.

Finally, immigrants face perhaps even greater psychological stressors after reaching their new destination. They often encounter additional and potentially traumatizing impediments that may threaten their well-being; these include racism, ethnocentrism, nativism, isolation, and fear of deportation. As they live in the United States, immigrants (e.g., African immigrants, Latinx immigrants, Asian immigrants, and other immigrants of color) often experience the negative effects of systemic oppression. They often are perceived as "outsiders" or "others" for many reasons, including differences in race, ethnicity, and immigration status. Othering is the process by which individuals who are perceived as "'different' in a given society are rejected and oppressed" (Chavez-Dueñas et al., 2019, p. 50).

Nativism, racism, and ethnocentrism contribute to trauma among immigrants, their families, and their communities. Nativist ideologies maintain cultural stereotypes about immigrant people, involving a number of unfounded negative perceptions that immigrants refuse to assimilate and refuse to learn the language of the new country, that they cause fiscal problems, and that generally they are not "legitimate" and are living in the country without proper authorization (Chavez-Dueñas et al., 2019). A resurgence of nativism in the United States has increased the likelihood of violence against immigrants, causing greater fear and trauma in immigrant communities.

Racial- and Ethnic-Based Trauma Among Immigrants

The levels of ethnic, racial, and immigration intolerance in America and other Western countries are perceived widely as being on the rise. Numerous reports from human rights advocacy groups have documented this rise and have expressed concern. According to the Council of Europe (2012), racism and intolerance have been on the rise in Europe, resulting in tensions that have led to racist violence. Reports by the Southern Poverty Law Center (2017, 2020, 2021) reflect parallel levels of hatred, rooted in racism and intolerance, in the United States.

The intolerance of migrants commonly is referenced as nativism. Nativism reflects the intersection of racism and nationalism, initiating an intense opposition to and intolerance of migrants, whom the nativists deem as foreign and therefore inferior (Vallejo, 2013). Nativist attitudes toward ethnic minorities arise, in part, from the belief that foreigners are a threat to the national culture. Intolerance toward immigrants centers on several interrelated themes. Race- and immigration-based stress involves any threatening or dangerous event, real or perceived, that leads to experiences of discrimination based on race or immigration status. According to Comas-Díaz et al. (2019), these include threats of harm, actual injury, any humiliating or shaming acts, and witnessing harm to other people of color or immigrants due to real or perceived racism or immigration intolerance. Immigrants may be exposed to traumatic events prior to their immigration as well as during their journey (Levers & Hyatt-Burkhart, 2012). They also may experience high levels of stress related to racism, ethnocentrism, and nativism once they arrive in the United States. This, in turn, may result in or exacerbate already-existing ethno-racial trauma among immigrants, which then can affect their mental health, well-being, and everyday functioning (Aranda & Vaquera, 2015). Chavez-Dueñas et al. (2019) have defined ethno-racial trauma as "the individual and or collective psychological distress and fear of danger that results from experiencing and witnessing discrimination, threats of harm, violence, and intimidation directed at ethno-racial minority groups or immigrants" (p. 49).

The links among racism, xenophobia, and trauma are evident in many social science studies (e.g., Comas-Díaz & Jacobsen, 2001; D. R. Williams, 2018; M. T. Williams et al., 2021). Research from a variety of academic fields provides various perspectives for conceptualizing and understanding the intersectionality of race, ethnicity, and immigration intolerance that comprises the trauma resulting from racism. Race- or immigration-based trauma does not occur in a vacuum and thereby is worsened by the cumulative impact of multiple traumas, such as community violence, victimization, and combat. From an ecological perspective, the race- and immigration-based violence that leads to trauma exists at interpersonal, environmental, institutional, and cultural levels; it affects the physical, emotional, psychological, and social health of individuals and communities.

RACE-BASED HATE CRIMES

Hate crimes are criminal acts that have been motivated, in whole or in significant part, "by bias against race, color, religion, national origin, sexual orientation, gender, gender identity, or disability" (U.S. Department of Justice, n.d., "Terminology," p. 1). The Hate Crimes Statistics Act, which was signed into law by President George H. W. Bush in April 1990, created a voluntary program for police agencies to submit data to the FBI, through the attorney general; in the most recent report (at the time of writing), for 2020, there were 15,136 law enforcement agencies that had provided data (Federal Bureau of Investigations [FBI], 2021). To offer a general picture, hate crimes reported to police in America's 10 largest cities rose 12.5% in 2017 (Levin & Reitzel, 2018). In contrast to the increase in hate crime in the 10 largest cities, the nation experienced a slight drop in crime during the first part of that same year, with the decrease in property crime being greater than in violent crime (Levin & Reitzel, 2018). Levin and Reitzel reported that, at the time, "The most common type of hate crime bias categories in the nation's ten largest cities in 2017 were anti-Black, anti-Semitic, anti-gay and anti-Latino, but there was wide variation across different cities for this and other factors" (p. 8). However, anti-Asian hate crimes surged to 149%

in 2020, while overall hate crimes in the United States dropped by 7% in 2020 (Center for the Study of Hate & Extremism, 2020).

Race- and immigration-based hate crimes have been described as private or public behaviors that are intended to emphasize and devalue the status of minorities or a member of a minority group (Abu-Rasm & Suarez, 2009). Race-based hate crimes have been the most common types of hate crime, and they increased significantly between 2016 and 2019. According to the U.S. Department of Justice (2019a), 2018 hate crime statistics released by the FBI indicated that there were 7,036 single-bias incidents involving 8,646 victims and 84 multiple-bias hate crime incidents involving 173 victims. More than half of the incidents (59.6%) were race-, ethnic-, and ancestry-bias hate crimes. Figures reported to the FBI varied only slightly in 2019, with the following incidents of hate crime: 7,103 single-bias incidents involved 8,552 victims, and 211 multiple-bias hate crime incidents involved 260 victims (U.S. Department of Justice, 2019b).

Context of Race and Immigration-Based Trauma

Hate crimes may manifest as various forms of race-based harassment or discrimination. Hate crimes can look very different, depending on a number of factors; they may include various forms of murder, rape, assault, intimidation, or destruction of property (Abu-Rasm & Suarez, 2009). Hate crimes are used to intimidate individuals, manipulating or forcing them into submission. These events typically are traumatic to the individual who is experiencing them, but the events also can be traumatizing to the entire community or culture of the targeted individual; ultimately, hate crimes harm and degrade the whole society in which they occur. Such dynamics can perpetuate the symptomatology for transgenerational trauma. Victims of transgenerational trauma may experience an increase in fear, hopelessness, defensiveness, and vigilance; they may feel like the dominant culture is unwelcoming of their identity, which paradoxically may cause them to separate from their minority group status. This may be an effort, conscious or unconscious, to protect against potential further aggression; individuals may receive or communicate what Cherepanov (2020) has referred to as "survival messages." However, such trauma-based separation may disrupt important familial and cultural attachments; in the process of self-protective separation, individuals may lose important support systems, which in turn can inhibit continued recovery (Abu-Rasm & Suarez, 2009; Cherepanov, 2020).

Effects of Race and Immigration-Based Trauma

The legacy of race- and immigration-based displacement, oppression, and unresolved grief across generations has affected not only individuals, but also has caused families and communities to endure higher levels of financial insecurity and poorer overall physical and mental health (Comas-Díaz et al., 2019; Duran, 2006; Geter et al., 2018; Rensink, 2011; D. R. Williams, 2018; M. T. Williams et al., 2021). For example, according to a U.S. Department of Health and Human Services report (2021), the 2019 data showed that 20.3% of the American Indian/Alaska Native population lived at the poverty level, as compared to 9% of non-Hispanic Whites. As a result, members of this population have been at greater risk of experiencing psychological distress and are more likely to have poorer physical and mental health. Their suicide rates have been the highest of any racial/ethnic group in the United States and have been increasing since 2003 (Leavitt et al., 2018). Suicide has been the eighth-leading cause of death for American Indians and Alaska Natives, across all ages; suicide has been the second-leading cause of death for American Indian and Alaska Native youth from 10 to 24 years of age (National Indian Council on Aging, 2019).

Research has shown that trauma reactions from racism or ethno-violence can be as psychologically debilitating as trauma reactions from natural disasters and other events usually associated with trauma (D. R. Williams, 2018). The effects of violence, racism, and ethnic oppression heighten the risk of experiencing psychological harm. Race- and immigration-based trauma carries psychophysiological effects such as hypervigilance, flashbacks, nightmares, avoidance, suspiciousness, and somatic expressions like headaches and heart palpitations, among others that are similar to PTSD symptoms (Comas-Díaz et al., 2019). Although racial trauma exhibits these similarities, it differs from PTSD. For example, according to Comas-Diaz et al. (2019, p. 2), "racial trauma involves ongoing injuries due to the exposure (direct and or vicarious) and re-exposure to race-based stressors." All of these psychological and physical effects of racial trauma also may cause hidden wounds among those who have been oppressed (Comas-Diaz et al., 2019; Geter et al., 2018; Rensink, 2011; D. R. Williams, 2018; M. T. Williams et al., 2021). One of the prominent effects of racial trauma is its transmission to the next and subsequent generations, even possibly effecting epigenetic changes (Daskalakis et al., 2018; Yehuda & Lehrner, 2018). The next section discusses how the impact of racial trauma passes from generation to generation.

TRANSGENERATIONAL TRAUMA

While theories about and understandings of intergenerational and transgenerational trauma are relatively new to the field of psychology, they have been receiving a lot of attention in recent years (Atkinson et al., 2014; Braga et al., 2012; DeAngelis, 2019; Yehuda & Lehrner, 2018). Simply stated, the construct of transgenerational trauma has offered a perspective about how parental exposure to extremely adverse events can have an impact not only on the parents' children but also on subsequent familial generations. Initially this idea was investigated after World War II, in response to the experiences of Holocaust survivors' children. In the mid-1960s, psychologists began to notice a significant number of children of Holocaust survivors, who were presenting with affective and emotional symptoms, transmitted from the previous generation, and who were seeking mental health treatment (Rakoff et al., 1966). Some of the symptoms included a mistrust of the dominant culture, an incapacity for expressing feelings, a continuous fear of danger, separation anxiety, unclear boundaries, and overprotection among family members (Braga et al., 2012, "Background," p. 4). Since that time, a number of field studies have provided evidence supporting the idea of intergenerational or transgenerational trauma and illuminating how parental trauma exposure can affect offspring (van Steenwyk et al., 2018). Researchers continue to investigate the experience of trauma passed from one generation to the next through the possible expression of epigenetic mechanisms (Daskalakis et al., 2018; Yehuda & Lehrner, 2018).

Transgenerational trauma can be caused by a multitude of different traumatic experiences; just a few types of examples include the effects of extreme poverty, a sudden or violent death of a family member, a crime against a family member, a parent or other family member dispatched to go to war, and the assault or torture of a family member. The impact of historical trauma typically is more complex than individual trauma. Historical trauma can affect a family's health and wellness negatively. It can result in a greater loss of identity, purpose, and meaning; this, in turn, can have an impact upon multiple generations, perhaps even "normalizing" the sequelae of the trauma. The National Child Traumatic Stress Network (2017) has reported that some of the common traumatic stress reactions related to race and immigration include "increased vigilance and suspicion, increased sensitivity to threat, sense of a foreshortened future, and more maladaptive responses to stress such as aggression or substance use" (p. 3).

Understanding the legacy of trauma, as it passes generationally, is key to understanding how families operate for generations to come (DeAngelis, 2019; van Steenwyk et al., 2018). Transgenerational trauma can affect how parents choose to raise their families. A family that has experienced transgenerational trauma may raise its children to be more cautious and distrusting of the dominant culture, as familial members were taught in that same manner. Or perhaps something happened within their lives which caused them to raise their family using a more conservative or cautious style. Massive transgenerational trauma, as with a genocide for example, can affect individuals, their families, communities, and entire societies profoundly and in multidimensional ways (Danieli, 1998; DeAngelis; 2019; Mukamana et al., 2019). Understanding transgenerational trauma can help mental health professionals in identifying patterns among affected people and families.

Another implication of transgenerational trauma includes better understandings of and working relationships both with the individuals and within the public health sector. If large populations of individuals who are experiencing transgenerational trauma are more ready to seek public health services, it allows more data to be collected about their lives. This could identify a plethora of variables that potentially can be linked together to create a fuller scaffold for working with these individuals. Sotero (2006) has suggested that gaining this invaluable information can lead to developing better training protocols, which in turn can enhance how individuals affected by historical trauma might adapt and readapt to the communities in which they live in. In addition, a broader public health perspective provides a context for understanding transgenerational trauma, thus allowing for better treatment interventions that can empower individuals to address their needs culturally, throughout the community, and to build resilience (Ortega-Williams et al., 2021).

Healing in the Context of Racial Trauma

Healing from racial trauma can be a challenging process (Anderson & Stevenson, 2019). The wounds caused by racial trauma occur within a sociohistorical and political context; they are complex, they typically recur, and they may traverse generations. Counseling with racial and ethnic groups of people who experience systemic racism, violence, and other forms of bias, particularly as a result of historical trauma, requires a framework for trauma recovery that concurrently addresses both the harm that has been inflicted and the strength and resiliency needed to overcome such discrimination (Ortega-Williams et al., 2021). Scholars and clinicians have developed a variety of approaches to assess, intervene with, and help recover from race-based trauma and historical trauma. However, the practice of cultural sensitivity, cultural competence, and cultural humility approaches to trauma comprises skill sets that still are under development. Moreover, the current definitions of "trauma," "traumatic stress," and "trauma treatment" are embedded in Euro-centric perspectives of counseling (Goodman, 2015; Gorski & Goodman, 2015; Hernández-Wolfe, 2015; Hook et al., 2017). Consequently, many trauma and PTSD treatments tend to lack cultural relevance for most people with racial and ethnic minority backgrounds (Hinton & Good, 2015).

Schnyder et al. (2016) found that PTSD treatment-seeking survivors did not necessarily share their therapists' cultural perspectives. The researchers concluded that clinicians working with PTSD clients needed to increase their cultural sensitivity and competence. Both researchers and clinicians need to contextualize their work with BIPOC who present with racial trauma symptoms, by using culturally responsive and racially informed interventions. Emergent work on race- and trauma-informed therapeutic approaches must draw upon individual and cultural resilience; enhancing and building resilience is key to advancing personal and collective transformation, healing, well-being, and recovery.

Multicultural Pluralism, Cultural Humility, Social Justice, and the Effects of Trauma

Multicultural pluralism has referenced situations in which a minority group, living within a larger majority group, is able to maintain its cultural identities and values (Hook et al., 2017). This type of coexistence has proven ideal, as it accepts and accounts for the qualities and values of both majority and minority groups. Coexistence has been positive for immigrants who are seeking a new way of life. This type of situation also has helped individuals who have experienced transgenerational or historical trauma to feel more welcomed and comfortable within the dominant society. It has been important for nondominant cultures to feel this acceptance and support from the dominant society. This can be fostered through social advocacy and social justice actions aimed at sensitizing and educating members of the dominant society. Those who have experienced transgenerational trauma can feel supported within their own culture but also sense acceptance by the dominant culture in order to prevent or reduce prolonged trauma symptomatology.

Cultural humility has been described as the ability to maintain an open perspective to the aspects of cultural identity that are important to the individuals of another culture (Hook et al., 2017; Waters & Asbill, 2013). The notion of cultural humility has encouraged us all to develop the highest levels of cultural competency; the pathway to achieving this includes a lifelong commitment to being able to self-evaluate and critique self and others as well as an understanding of the imbalance in power among various groups within the population (Hook et al., 2017; Waters & Asbill, 2013). Minorities have not had a seat at the table in most aspects of life, as compared with the dominant culture. Therapists should advocate for these groups in order to promote equality and equity. Finally, cultural humility has been instrumental in developing partnerships with people and groups to promote advocacy and support throughout the community (Hook et al., 2017; Waters & Asbill, 2013).

Social justice has been defined as a societal state in which members have the same rights, opportunities, obligations, and social benefits (Turner & Pope, 2009). Social justice has played an important role in making sure that individuals feel supported and accepted. Clinicians may need to advocate for their clients' rights in order to aspire toward and produce positive social change. Those who have experienced transgenerational trauma need therapists who can advance their rights and advocate for social justice within the larger dominant culture.

All three of these systemic dynamics—multicultural pluralism, cultural humility, and social justice—constitute important skill sets for therapists to possess. These characteristics can aid therapists in being able to conduct their jobs ethically and to the fullest ability, helping to change the future, especially for clients who have "inherited" historical trauma. Additionally, these skills also are useful in understanding all clients and how best to serve them.

TRAUMA-INFORMED INTERVENTIONS

Healing race- and immigration-based trauma requires a focus on what Chavez-Dueñas et al. (2019, p. 55) refer to as "both the symptoms of the trauma (internal) and the interlocking systems of oppression (external) that cause and maintain psychological distress." Intervention for and treatment of race- and immigration-based trauma begin with understanding the symptoms of intergenerational and transgenerational trauma. At both personal and community levels, the symptoms of historical loss and trauma can manifest as societal-environmental, psychological, and physiological concerns. For example, intimate partner violence, physical violence, and sexual assault are three-and-a-half times higher than the national average in Native American communities (Sue et al., 2019), and Native American children are one of the most overrepresented groups in child protective services (National Conference of State Legislatures, 2021). Certain psychological issues can indicate the need to screen for a trauma history, across ethnic or racial groups. These may include high levels of alcohol consumption among any ethnic group, co-occurring disorders, substance abuse and mental health disorders, low or vacant self-esteem, loss of cultural identity, lack of positive role models, history of abuse and neglect, self-medication to numb emotional pain, feelings of hopelessness, and loss of familial and cultural connections (DeGruy, 2005; Sue et al., 2019). Members of minority groups, particularly BIPOC, are overrepresented in some types of healthcare problems, such as heart disease, tuberculosis, sexually transmitted diseases, and injuries. Metabolic diseases like diabetes are more prevalent among BIPOC than other racial groups in the United States. Life expectancy at birth for the Native American population, as one example, is 5.5 years less than that of all U.S. populations combined (Indian Health Service, 2019). In the remaining parts of this section, we discuss related assessment and treatment issues.

Clinical Assessment: *Diagnostic and Statistical Manual of Mental Disorders, Fifth Edition*, Framework

Traumatic stress caused by racism, xenophobia, and racial trauma can be difficult to recognize due to many factors such as lack of clinician awareness, discomfort surrounding conversations about race in a clinical setting, and a lack of validated measures for its assessment. It is crucial for counselors to uncover racial trauma using culturally informed case conceptualization and exploration of client experiences of racism as a basis for the diagnosis of PTSD, when warranted. Even though connections between racism and trauma are accepted and understood widely in the psychological literature, the lack of practical guidelines and assessment tools may hinder counselors in fully diagnosing and exploring the traumatic experiences of clients based on racial or immigration intolerance. One helpful assessment protocol is described in the text that follows.

Synthesizing the existing literature, existing measures for assessment of racial trauma, and accepted clinical practice, M. T. Williams et al. (2018) developed the *UConn Racial/Ethnic Stress and Trauma Survey* (UnRESTS). The UnRESTS is a semistructured clinician-administered interview protocol, designed specifically for use with clients who are members of stigmatized racial and ethnic groups. The UnRESTS protocol incorporates information and includes items that inquire about the racial and ethnic groups with which clients identify. The racial and ethnic identity sections of the protocol emphasize the client's socialization to race as well as how the person feels about and toward the racial/ethnic group. This information can inform the clinician about the context of the clients' distress. The assessment protocol allows counselors to explore clients' experiences related to explicit racism, both direct and vicarious, along with more subtle forms of racism, including microaggressions. The UnRESTS concludes with a checklist aimed at discovering if symptoms are present and whether they comport with *DSM-5* criteria for PTSD.

Clinical Treatment

In the mental health fields, numerous scientist-clinicians have developed approaches for treating and intervening with racial and intergenerational trauma (Chavez-Dueñas et al., 2019; Comas-Díaz, 2016; M. T. Williams et al., 2018). Common approaches in helping clients to recover from racial trauma range from psychotherapy, group counseling, and community methods to ethnopolitical interventions. One such community-based model, *Trauma-Informed Community Development* (TICD), is detailed in Chapter 19, "Historical Trauma and Trauma-Affected Communities," of this textbook; a second community-based intervention, HEART, is presented below.

Community-Based Intervention Framework: *Healing Ethno And Racial Trauma*

Chavez-Dueñas et al. (2019) have proposed a framework intended "to stimulate healing from ethno-racial trauma" (p. 49). They have titled this community-based intervention as the *Healing Ethno And Racial Trauma* model, or HEART. Comprised of four phases, the framework is grounded in the principles of liberation psychology and trauma-informed care. The phases are goal driven to ensure that counselors have culturally sensitive guidelines for "helping individuals, families, and communities to achieve growth, wellness, and healing" (p. 49). Although the framework originated with an aim toward helping Latinx immigrants to become aware of and to cope with the systemic oppression that causes ethno-racial trauma, we believe that this model can be of utility in working with various types of race- and immigration-based trauma. The four phases that comprise the HEART framework can be applied within the context of what Chavez-Dueñas et al. have identified as a sanctuary space, that is, a space in which individuals with racial/ethnic minority status are permitted to:

> (a) authentically express themselves, be affirmed, and acknowledged; (b) reprocess and mourn the losses associated with ethno-racial trauma; (c) integrate experiences of ethno-racial trauma and connect to cultural elements and practices that heal; and (d) create strategies for protecting, liberating, resisting, and organizing for social action. (p. 56)

The authors describe the intention behind each phase and offer suggestions for clinicians and clinician organizations to help clients navigate the four phases, described briefly in the text that follows.

Phase 1: Establishing Sanctuary Spaces for Individuals Experiencing Ethno-Racial Trauma
Clinicians can create a sense of physical and emotional safety through respect, validation, and affirmation with a focus on "assisting individuals, families, and communities [to] gain immediate

relief from the effects of psychological distress caused by ethno-racial trauma" (Chavez-Dueñas et al., 2019, p. 57).

Phase 2: Acknowledge, Reprocess, and Cope With Symptoms of Ethno-Racial Trauma

In Phase 2, Chavez-Dueñas et al. (2019) have encouraged counselors to shift their perspectives of trauma from a purely diagnostic and symptom-based perspective to one that contextualizes the lived experiences of marginalized clients. In this regard, the objectives of Phase 2 are to assist clients to "(a) acknowledge the impact of ethno-racial trauma, (b) process the experience in a sanctuary space, (c) develop culturally responsive ways of coping, and (d) contextualize their distress by challenging assumptions about the source(s) of their difficulties" (Chavez-Dueñas et al., 2019, p. 57).

Phase 3: Strengthen and Connect Individuals, Families, and Communities to Survival Strategies and Cultural Traditions That Heal

In this phase, Chavez-Dueñas et al. (2019) have promoted that counselors encourage connections as a means for building resilience and nurturing healing. This phase has focused on helping clients "to strengthen their connection with their culture, or build a connection if one does not exist" (Chavez-Dueñas et al., 2019, p. 57).

Phase 4: Liberation and Resistance

This phase has advanced a social justice orientation for immigrants. The activity of this phase has encouraged taking collective social action, based upon the premise that "healing takes place when people (a) gain awareness of the systemic roots of the challenges, and (b) learn strategies to act in ways that resist oppression and lead to social change" (Chavez-Dueñas et al., 2019, p. 59). Healing, in the form of liberation and resistance, becomes possible precisely because the process incorporates social justice action.

COUNSELING IMPLICATIONS

When working as a counselor, one of the most important aspects of treatment is the ability to understand a client's trauma (George, 2012). Many individuals who have immigrated to a new country have a higher rate of trauma symptomatology, both physically and psychologically, and counselors need to understand this (de Arellano et al., 2018; Levers & Hyatt-Burkhart, 2012; Mpofu et al., 2021). Likewise, it is essential that clinicians understand and explore the lived experiences of daily microaggressions and historical trauma while working with clients who have experienced racial and ethnic trauma (Torres & Taknint, 2015). When counseling any clients who have experienced transgenerational trauma, it is imperative to assess for PTSD. In this context, PTSD may arise from hearing or witnessing a traumatic event(s) but it also can be learned from social roles and networks as well as from the acculturation stressors that are passed down from family members (George, 2012). Transgenerational trauma can be complicated, and it may present dense clinical dynamics, requiring extreme fortitude on the parts of both counselor and client in working through these issues in treatment. George has suggested that the best way to provide support for refugees is in a group setting. Group-based interventions, whether conducted with refugees or other members of minority or immigrant groups, must include a high level of cultural competency and operate from a strengths-based perspective. Cultural competency is necessary for understanding clients' values, beliefs, and ethnicity, along with their social and cultural needs. Counselors need to understand the dynamics among individuals, their families, and their cultures. These factors play an important role in how a client interacts within the family, society, their own culture, and the dominant culture.

Transgenerational trauma can affect how a therapist and client may interact during their working relationship. Working with a family as a whole unit can allow for the family system to develop a level of trust and understanding without perpetuating ideas of separation. George

(2012) advocates for using a strengths-based approach to empower clients to draw on their resilience. This resilience is anchored in the very act of their immigration to a new land and in their ability to figure out how to operate within a new society. Maximizing internal strengths can enable clients to continue to face upcoming difficulties with greater positivity and generativity, thus improving the client's overall sense of well-being.

Weine et al. (2008) have suggested the *Coffee and Family Education and Support* (CAFES) intervention, which empowers individuals to work with their family members to foster support and champion wellness. The model encourages families to discuss issues that would help to decrease the effects of transgenerational trauma. Therapists can facilitate such conversations, thereby enabling family members to create a safe and trusting working environment for all who are involved. Additionally, George (2012) has stated that art therapy may be a useful tool for working with children who are at risk of experiencing transgenerational trauma. This strategy can encourage children to draw their environment and explore the different contexts of their lives. Art therapy also can allow therapists to address children's patterns of resilience through their various life experiences.

CONCLUSION

This chapter has presented a framework for understanding the violence and trauma that result from racial, ethnic, and immigration intolerance. In constructing this framework, we have offered discussions about context-based PTSD, various facets of oppression and transgenerational or historical trauma, trauma-informed interventions, and the counseling implications for working with clients who are affected by race-, ethnicity-, and immigration-based trauma. When counseling individuals and their families who have these experiences, it is important to understand their stories—their lived experiences—prior to creating treatment plans. A systems- or family-based approach seems to be one effective form of treatment, as it allows individuals to feel safe and to trust the therapeutic relationship. Additionally, a strengths-based approach reminds individuals of the profound resilience that they have manifest throughout their journeys. These approaches open communication among family members and reinforce their support systems. A strengths-based approach also improves the overall well-being of the individual's mental health. Trauma-informed treatment approaches include being sensitive to the individual and to the person's trauma narrative. Understanding and working with clients on various aspects of their lives can improve how they are interacting with their families and with other systems. Ultimately, it is important to be culturally competent in providing counseling, to be culturally sensitive to the trauma stories that are entrusted to us, and to demonstrate cultural humility in offering safe sanctuaries for people to heal from their trauma.

ADDITIONAL RESOURCES

A robust set of instructor resources designed to supplement this text is located at http://connect.springerpub.com/content/book/978-0-8261-5085-1. Qualifying instructors may request access by emailing textbook@springerpub.com.

PRACTICE-BASED RESOURCES AND REFERENCES

To view a list of resources and all the references, please visit connect.springerpub.com via the following url: http://connect.springerpub.com/content/book/978-0-8261-5085-1/part/part03/chapter/ch17

Understanding and Responding to Affectional and Transgender Prejudice and Victimization

CORY VIEHL, MISTY M. GINICOLA, AMY ELLIS, AND
R. JOSEPH CHARETTE II

CHAPTER OVERVIEW

In addition to traumas that heterosexual and cisgender people experience, queer and transgender people face a heterosexist and cissexist culture, in which marginalization and trauma against them is normalized or minimized. In this chapter, the experience of hate crimes and violence, relational and interpersonal trauma, religious based-trauma, and sociocultural and political-based trauma are covered in relation to how it impacts Lesbian, Gay, Bisexual, Trans, and Queer (LGBTQ) people. Clinical and counseling implications are discussed. The increase in mental health challenges is explained via the minority stress model. Implications for diagnosis and trauma-informed practices for queer and transgender people are discussed. Additionally, the role of the mental health professional as a social justice advocate is explored, including how social justice frameworks can be incorporated in the counseling environment.

LEARNING OBJECTIVES

After reading this chapter, the reader should be able to:

1. Define key terminology including sex, gender, gender expression, and gender identity, as well as affectional orientation identities;
2. Describe unique stressors and experiences of trauma specific to queer and transgender communities and people;
3. Describe the psychological, social, and emotional effects of trauma on queer and transgender communities and people;
4. Identify implications and unique clinical considerations within counseling and counselor education, including diagnosis and evidence-based interventions, using a clinical vignette; and,
5. Identify actions and steps, working from a social justice and advocacy lens, specific to queer and transgender communities and people.

Although in general the authors use the term "queer and trans people" to describe this populations, the authors may use different acronyms for this population throughout the chapter as it relates to the research reviewed, i.e., the populations discussed in the literature cited may not include all queer and trans people, but rather only certain identities from the population, e.g., LGBT, LGB, and so on.

INTRODUCTION

Queer and transgender people face a world in which they receive the message about who they are, at the core of their being, and that who they are is wrong, immoral, devalued, and even despised. Despite progress in human rights legislation and increasing societal acceptance, queer and transgender people continue to face marginalization, prejudice, discrimination, harassment, bullying, and violence (Federal Bureau of Investigation [FBI], 2019; Kosciw et al., 2018). The purpose of this chapter is to explore the important aspects of trauma for mental health professionals to consider for this population. Relevant definitions are offered, along with examining the context in which queer and transgender people experience these various forms of trauma: a world with heterosexism and cissexism. The most common types of trauma, including hate crimes, relational trauma, religious-based trauma, and sociocultural and political-based trauma, are discussed. Implications for counseling and for social justice advocacy are explored, along with narratives, a case study, and reflection questions. The resources and references (online only) also serve as sources for further learning on this topic.

RELEVANT DEFINITIONS

A key concept to understand, in considering trauma for queer and trans populations, is the difference between sex and gender identity. **Sex** refers to the classification made by a medical or birthing professional at birth; babies, after a cursory external examination, are designated male, female, or intersex (a difference of sex development where a child has ambiguous genitalia or a combination of a penis, scrotum, and labia/vagina; Ginicola et al., 2017). While this cursory examination considers external genitals, it typically does not consider (unless the child is identified as intersex) an examination of their internal genitalia, chromosomes, or the child's internal sense of their gender, that is, their self-awareness of and personal sense of gender (Ginicola et al., 2017). Gender is "the feelings, attitudes, and behavior associated with a person's sex," experienced and expressed through a cultural lens (Ginicola et al., 2017, p. 362). As children grow up in a culture, the norms and expectations for gendered differences are learned through exposure to the culture; children quickly learn what colors, dress, behavior, and personality characteristics are associated with a specific gender within their culture (Martin & Ruble, 2010). Within this context, children develop their own gender identity, which includes their deeply internal feelings and sense of self that surround being male, female, neither, other-gendered, or a combination of genders; gender identity also similarly involves their own internal sense of masculinity, femininity, and/or other-gendered self (Ginicola et al., 2017). Research indicates that evidence of gender identity can be seen as early as 18 months in all children and is typically stable and consistent by the time the child reaches 3 to 4 years of age (Martin & Ruble, 2010). People may express their gender externally through their demeanor, body language, activities, behavior, clothing, and hairstyle, among others—a concept termed "gender expression." A person may identify with a binary conception of gender—male versus female, or may identify as trans/transgender (T), which is a person whose gender identity does not align with the sex they were designated at birth (Ginicola et al., 2017). People may identify as a trans man, trans woman, or with a nonbinary identity, which can be agender (no gender within their identity), other-gendered (another gender beyond the binary of male or female), gender-expansive, or a combination of genders (Ginicola et al., 2017).

While understanding of one's own gender develops first, understanding of a person's affectional identity is usually experienced in childhood or adolescence (Ginicola et al., 2017). Whereas gender is an understanding of who one is, affectional identity is an understanding of who one loves (Ginicola et al., 2017). Affectional identity is the "direction in which one is predisposed to bond emotionally, physically, sexually, psychologically, and spiritually with others" (Ginicola et al., 2017, p. 359). Once called sexual orientation, counseling and psychology organizations have moved to replace this term, as it emphasizes sexual behavior over other bonding, which is not an accurate depiction (Harper et al., 2013). The term "sexual orientation" also excludes persons who identify as asexual (A), which are persons who feel little to no sexual attraction toward other persons but may feel and express romantic love (Ginicola et al., 2017). Within these identities, people may identify as lesbian (L; female-identified person who bonds with other female persons), gay male (G; male-identified person who bonds with other male persons), bisexual (B) and pansexual (P; which are both referring to a person who bonds with people from similar and other genders), queer (Q; an umbrella term for all affectional identities, and an individual identity that is not reflected, experienced, and/or expressed in conventional heterosexual or gay terms), or asexual, among other identities (Ginicola et al., 2017). Within the research, these communities are often collectively referred to as Affectional and Gender Minorities (AGM).

CONTEXT

Heterosexism is the assumption that all individuals do or should identify as heterosexual and perpetuates heterosexuality as the normative experience (Harper et al., 2013). Cissexism is the assumption that all individuals have a gender identity that is aligned with the sex and gender assigned to the individual at birth (Ginicola et al., 2017; Harper et al., 2013). Along with racism, sexism, and nativism, heterosexism has been intentionally woven into the legal and social structure of our society (Koski et al., 2019). Cissexism is embedded in the academy and social research (Lombardi, 2018). The presence of any "ism" fosters the conditions for marginalization and assigning lowered worth and value to those within those populations (Davis et al., 2020). Queer and transgender people exist within this context that devalues their identities, which has an impact on all people's internal and external sense of the acceptability of queerness and nonheterosexual or cisgender identities.

The existence of queer and transgender people challenges the cisnormative and heteronormative social norms, which can lead to the direct and indirect experience of homophobia and transphobia. This challenge can manifest as an "aversion, fear, hatred, or intolerance" toward queer and trans people (Harper et al., 2013, p. 41). It is this challenge to the heterosexual and cisgender expectation of identity that causes queer and trans people to experience discrimination, oppression, and violence. An individual's identity as queer or trans in itself is not a risk factor. Rather, experiencing heterosexism and cissexism in response to one's identity, is a risk factor for traumatization and continued experiences of re-traumatization. Queer and trans people live in a constant battle to liberate themselves from heterosexist and cissexist sociocultural constraints. The lived experience of queer and trans people is one of *experiencing* and *surviving* multiple and repeated forms of trauma (Harper et al., 2013).

MOST COMMON TYPES OF TRAUMA

The term "trauma" is one that can refer to both an event and consequences from experiencing that event. Therefore, when someone says that a person has been through a trauma, it is unclear whether they mean that they have lived through a catastrophic incident, are exhibiting the signs of traumatization, or both. Potentially traumatic events (PTE) are those events that are regarded as threatening to one's life or physical safety, or witnessing that threat occur against someone else, or sexual violence. However, not all traumatic events result in symptomatology such as posttraumatic stress, dissociation, depression and anxiety, substance use, eating disorders, and so on. Thus, one can experience trauma without being traumatized. However, one cannot be described as traumatized without first having experienced a trauma (American Psychiatric Association [APA], 2013).

This warrants further discussion as to the definition of trauma events. The field often distinguishes between big "T" traumas and little "t" traumas. Big "T" traumas, as previously referenced, follow closely in line with the *Diagnostic and Statistical Manual of Mental Disorders* (5th ed.; *DSM-5*; APA, 2013) diagnosis of Posttraumatic Stress Disorder (PTSD). Criterion A in the *DSM-5* defines and requires an event to precipitate the symptoms associated with posttraumatic stress. Some examples that would meet this definition of a trauma event, and are relevant in the AGM community, include sexual assault, intimate partner violence (IPV), physical violence, hate violence, urban violence, and threatened death or violence. The effects of such trauma events may lead to Criterions B to E: symptoms of avoidance, hyperarousal, intrusion, and negative thoughts and mood (APA, 2013).

Little "t" trauma events and experiences often co-occur with big "T" trauma events. Where the *DSM-5* would define a trauma event as life-threatening, little "t" trauma events are regarded as ego-threatening. Some specific examples include inadequate access to behavioral and medical healthcare, stigmatization and discrimination, internalized homoprejudice, biprejudice, and transprejudice, as well as homelessness and unemployment. These examples are unified by one commonality: they occur and are present at the hands of collective others. That is, being denied access to housing, employment, and healthcare is systemic and organizational, as well as personal (e.g., being denied employment after interviewing and presenting one's gender expression as noncisgender). Stigmatization and discrimination are macro-level events as well (e.g., laws and regulations that exist that are not directly targeting one specific individual), but often manifest in personalized interactions (e.g., inappropriate or hateful remarks, being denied an opportunity or service). None of the aforementioned examples threaten the physical integrity or mortality of an individual, yet they may, and often do, result in minority stress and trauma responses (e.g., Meyer, 2003; Stenersen et al., 2019).

Hate Crimes Against This Population

Definition and Prevalence

The FBI defines a "hate crime" as a "criminal offense against a person or property motivated in whole or in part by an offender's bias against a race, religion, disability, sexual orientation, ethnicity, gender, or gender identity" (FBI, 2019, Hate Crimes section). According to the FBI (2019) *Hate Crime Statistics*, a report that includes data submitted by over 16,000 law enforcement agencies and provides information pertaining to the offenses and victims, people with AGM identities are at an increased risk of being victims of hate crimes. Roughly 17.4% of all hate crimes reported were motivated by the offender's affectional (15.8%) and gender identity (1.6%) biases. Similarly, Herek (2009) found that in a study of 662 LGB-identified individuals, 20% of participants reported having experienced a crime related to their affectional identities. In a special report by Human Rights Campaign (HRC; Marzullo & Libman, 2009), affectional identity was the third highest motivator reported in all hate crimes. It is important to note that these rates are also very likely to be underestimates; Marzullo and Libman (2009) further noted that hate crimes against LGBTQ individuals are underreported for various reasons including the fact that victims may not wish to "out" themselves when reporting. Additionally, AGM identity-biased hate crimes may be underreported by officers and agencies due to lack of experience and education on these topics as well as the officer's own biases. Officers' strong religious fundamentalism, overall negative attitudes toward LGBTQ persons, victim blaming, a general lack of criminal justice training, and lack of applied experiences with discussing affectional identities are all predictors of an AGM hate crime being mishandled (Marzullo & Libman, 2009).

Experiencing Hate Crimes

Given the information on increased rates of hate crimes that are experienced by individuals based on their AGM identities, it is important to discuss the adverse consequences associated with experiencing such crimes. Hate crimes carry additional negative consequences, because they target a person's identity, and this is particularly salient when those identities are consistently subjected to *stigma-related stress* (i.e., expectations of rejection, fear of victimization; Meyer, 2003; Pachankis, 2007) as is the case with respect to AGM identities. Individuals with AGM identities live in a state of fear of being a victim of a hate crime and are forced to make decisions whether to conceal their identities in order to protect themselves (Herek, 2009).

Additionally, research has demonstrated a link between hate crimes and significant psychological distress and suicide among AGM individuals (e.g., Duncan & Hatzenbuehler, 2014; Herek, 2009). Heidt et al. (2005) reported higher incidents of reported depressive symptoms, PTSD, and overall psychological distress in a study of AGM individuals who experienced crimes related to their sexual identity. Herek (2009) expanded on this phenomenon and discussed the constructs of *felt stigma* and *enacted stigma* in relation to *criminal victimization* in a sample of 662 participants and concluded that the "psychological toll" that hate crimes take on the well-being of AGM individuals should be closely considered by mental health professionals and researchers moving forward (p. 9).

It is also important to note the intersection of minority stress (discussed further in the *Clinical and Counseling Implications* section, in the text that follows) experienced by AGM individuals and the resulting expectations of rejection and internalized homoprejudice (Meyer, 2013). The long-term effects of lived experiences of minority stress, coupled with the devastating psychological distress experienced as a result of hate crimes based on sexual and gender identities, can have detrimental effects on individuals who hold these identities and results in increased prevalence of suicidal ideation and attempts. In a study of sexual minority youths, Duncan and Hatzenbuehler (2014) demonstrated a significant correlation between living in neighborhoods with higher LGBTQ assault crimes and reported suicidal ideation and attempts. Specifically, AGM individuals from these neighborhoods were significantly more likely to report both suicidal ideation and attempts (Duncan & Hatzenbuehler, 2014).

Multiple Losses — Relational and Interpersonal Trauma

Relational or interpersonal trauma (IPT), often referred to as complex trauma or complex relational trauma, is the prolonged and repeated experience of stress that is characterized by feeling trapped, rejection, betrayal, violation of boundaries, confusion, and feelings of helplessness within a significant relationship (Schore, 2013). Relational trauma can look like bullying, harassment, abuse (physical, emotional, or psychological), threats of violence, perpetration of violence, rejection, and destruction of healthy attachment in significant relationships (Herman, 1992, 2015). Beginning in childhood, the prevalence of IPT has been shown to be higher for queer and trans identified individuals in comparison to heterosexual children (Balsam et al., 2005; Roberts et al., 2010). IPT has been conceptualized in the literature as primarily occurring among children who experience long-term abuse or maltreatment during their developmental years (Herman, 2015; Schore, 2013). This characterization fails to acknowledge that experiencing and surviving in relational trauma can happen across the life-span. The nature of experiencing relational trauma is that it is prolonged, repeated, and ambient (Schore, 2013).

Queer and transgender people are also at an increased risk of experiencing relational trauma within the workplace in the form of prejudice and discrimination (Chung et al., 2009). Affectional identity has also been correlated with higher rates of burnout (Rabelo & Cortina, 2014; Viehl & Dispenza, 2015), as well as lower job satisfaction as a result of workplace heterosexism (Lyons et al., 2005; Velez et al., 2013; Waldo, 1999). Rabelo and Cortina (2014) noted that these negative workplace experiences included harassment, discrimination, and "sex stereotypes" by heterosexual colleagues.

The long-term effects of experiencing relational trauma during developmental years have been studied (Schore, 2013). What remains unexamined is the experience of individuals who encounter relational trauma across the life-span, and withstand the long-term effects, while continuing to be exposed to relational trauma from multiple sources. Queer and trans people are affected by relational trauma, beginning in childhood, and continue to experience and re-experience this trauma through adolescence and adulthood. The ways in which queer and trans people experience prejudice, discrimination, oppression, and violence have been examined in the literature; however, characterizing these experiences as forms of relational trauma has not yet been examined.

Research also has indicated that queer people are more likely to be at higher risk for child sexual abuse (CSA); Xu and Zheng (2017) found that 24% of gay men and 21% of bisexual men reported CSA, while 37% of lesbian women and 36% of bisexual women report CSA. This is compared to 8% of heterosexual men and 18% of heterosexual women (Pereda et al., 2009). Lesbian, gay, and bisexual individuals experience IPV, all forms of sexual violence, and stalking at rates equal to or higher than that of heterosexual individuals (Walters et al., 2013). These types of violence disproportionately affect bisexual women with approximately 46% experiencing rape in their lifetime (Walters et al., 2013). Compared to 21% of heterosexual men who report experiencing sexual violence, approximately 40% of gay men and 47% of bisexual men experience some form of sexual violence in their lifetime (Walters et al., 2013). When interpreting this data, it is crucial to remember that these numbers may not reflect the full scope of victimization of queer people, as many instances go unreported for fear of further violence, being outed, or not being believed. Additionally, demographic data about sexual and affectional identity is not always collected in local, state, and national surveys measuring victimization and violence.

Religious-Based Trauma

An area in which queer and trans people may also readily experience trauma is through their religious communities, particularly those linked to their families of origin. Often used as a rationale for the harassment and violence toward queer and trans people, religion has been weaponized in the current culture as *religious freedom* legislation, giving permission to discriminate openly and legally against queer and trans people (American Civil Liberties Union, 2020). The experience of religious-based trauma often is described as the experience of spiritual abuse (Oakley & Kinmond, 2013). Spiritual abuse is a deeply emotional attack, "coercion and control of one individual by another in a spiritual context" (Oakley & Kinmond, 2013, p. 21).

The perpetrators of spiritual abuse may not only be religious leaders, but also family members who ascribe to a disaffirming religion that holds a dogmatic belief system that rejects gender and affectional variance as abnormal and sinful (Oakley, 2009). Perpetrators of spiritual abuse may not only be unaware of the traumatic impact of their behavior on their victim, they also may feel and express that they are acting in accordance with a moral imperative and that their cruelty is, in fact, kindness (Blue, 1993). Because disaffirming religions are accepted in the mainstream, these religious messages, paired with the disaffirming cultural context, can be isolating and confusing for the victim—as they receive multiple messages regarding the devaluing of their identities in multiple contexts, which may compound their experience of trauma and internalization of the abuse (Oakley & Kinmond, 2013).

For a person growing up in such a religious context, their understanding of who they are as a queer or trans person, as well as the meanings associated with their AGM identities, can be experienced as problematic, abnormal, and also as a threat—to their soul, their families, and their communities (Wolkomir, 2006). In a study by Ginicola and Smith (2016), one participant reflected the following:

> I grew up in Southern Mississippi, in a place where Baptist is the only religion. My parents were, and still are, ultra conservative Evangelical Christians. We were in a church every time the doors opened. . . . I heard a sermon . . . concerning homosexuality. 'If a man lie with a man as he lieth with a woman' . . . In that moment, I had two revelations: one, I am a homosexual, and two, I am going to burn in hell for all eternity.

Often these experiences may render a victim feeling powerless and disconnected from reality; their experience of themselves does not match what is being told to them as absolute truth (Oakley & Kinmond, 2013). If an individual reaches out to a disaffirming family member or a religious leader, disclosing their experience and their identity, the individual may not only discredit their experience, but attempt to convince them that their sense of reality is distorted, leaving the victim confused and disconnected from their realities and perceptions (Oakley & Kinmond, 2013).

Leaving the abuser or abusing institution becomes incredibly difficult; in many cases, the primary source of support and community is also the primary source of victimization and abuse (Kinmond & Oakley, 2015). Breaking away from the abuse may occur gradually or very abruptly (Winell, 2006). However, even with breaking away, the psychological, physical, spiritual, and emotional damage continues to be carried with the survivor (Winell, 2006). In addition to many survivors reporting loss of their spirituality, they also report posttraumatic symptoms, which would meet *DSM-5* Criteria (Criteria B, C, D, & E; APA, 2013; Wehr, 2000; Winell, 2006).

Sociocultural- and Political-Based Trauma

Legal victories such as the end of "Don't Ask, Don't Tell" and the passage of federal marriage equality would give the impression that queer and trans people are free of sociocultural- and political-based trauma. The passage of sweeping legislation supports the idea that queer and trans people are now equal, in their protection and freedom under the law, to heterosexual people. Despite advances in the movement for equality, these two landmark victories do not represent the end of the fight for queer and trans liberation (Ball, 2019).

Relying on these victorious policies to signal equality for queer and trans people fails to recognize a foundational component of equality, which is equity. Sociocultural factors such as political policies, political attitudes, and religious discourse continue to influence attitudes (Israel et al., 2011) toward queer and trans people. This broadens the gap between groups within queer and trans communities who remain systemically oppressed. Many queer and trans people continue to work without legal protections for their jobs, as this legislation is left to be determined at the state and local levels. Queer and trans people face discrimination from faith-based organizations that hold disaffirming belief systems. Legislation specifically protecting trans people from discrimination and violence is almost nonexistent. Whether by failing to provide necessary protection or allowing legislation to pass that negatively impacts queer and trans people, political systems commit institutional betrayal and violation of queer and trans people's human rights (Smith & Freyd, 2013). As these political disparities become more apparent, opportunities to enact change that supports queer and trans people also will become more apparent and important. This public debate has the potential to support queer and trans people and re-traumatize them as the validity of their existence is debated in public (Levitt et al., 2009).

Queer and trans people also experience relational trauma at the sociopolitical level within personal relationships and from political entities. Queer and trans people may experience betrayal and damage to personal relationships from the potential harm of political policies being downplayed by family, friends, and communities (Drabble et al., 2018). Queer and trans people also experience a systematic lack of policies that protect their rights, relative to majority groups and communities (Flores et al., 2015). This experience has become more salient as potentially harmful policies targeted at limiting the rights of all marginalized individuals and communities emerged under the Trump administration (Drabble et al., 2018; Koski et al., 2019). In addition to targeted policies, the Trump administration did not take a proactive stance to defend queer and trans people when hate crimes were committed against queer and trans people in his name (Koski et al., 2019). However, on his second day in office, President Biden issued an "Executive Order on Preventing and Combating Discrimination on the Basis of Gender Identity or Sexual Orientation," which serves to roll back the persistent attacks of the previous administration on queer and trans people (American Civil Liberties Union, 2021).

At the sociopolitical level, "marginalized communities may feel that the political norms, institutions, and conventions on which they are dependent for protections have betrayed them"

(Drabble et al., 2018, p. 497). Experiencing repeated and prolonged betrayal can cause queer and trans individuals to feel powerless (Flores et al., 2015). Even in experiencing powerlessness and betrayal, queer and trans people have demonstrated resilience and resistance to fight back against harmful policies that attempt to limit or completely take away their rights; however, the battle against these policies is traumatic (Levitt et al., 2009). This can occur in personal relationships with family or friends or through action taken at a broader level to affect change. Existing in a time when the legitimacy of one's existence is repeatedly a topic of public debate (Levitt et al., 2009) is a form of relational trauma, and the fight against these policies can be further traumatizing. At the sociopolitical level, such policies can cause psychological turmoil among queer and trans people, as they fear that legal progress cannot be made without direct involvement from queer and trans people who are marginalized and devalued by the same society they wish to change (Levitt et al., 2009). Engaging in a constant battle against legal and political entities for the right to exist can result in continued experiences of relational trauma and withdrawing from fighting can result in continued oppression and discrimination (Levitt et al., 2009).

CLINICAL AND COUNSELING IMPLICATIONS

Increased Mental Health Challenges

An array of existential assaults on queer and trans people was presented in the previous text. Navigation of these multiple complex layers of traumas, conflicts, and stressors has been found to correlate with negative outcomes for persons with marginalized identities; one of the major impacts of experiencing high minority stress is a higher prevalence of mental health concerns. Minority stress posits that the prejudice and stigma experienced by AGM individuals creates unique and chronic stressors; therefore, these stressors are correlated with adverse physical and mental health concerns (Meyer & Frost, 2013 as cited in Meyer, 2015; Parent et al., 2019). In addition to the overall adverse mental health concerns, experiences of minority stress among AGM individuals have been correlated with internalized negative self-esteem (Herek et al., 2009), experiences of interpersonal trauma (IPT; Stenersen et al., 2019), and internalized homophobia and transphobia (King et al., 2008; Meyer, 2015).

Research with LGBTQ adolescents demonstrates increased risks and rates of substance use (Kann et al., 2016; Marshal et al., 2008), as well as suicidal thoughts and behaviors (Marshal et al., 2011; S. T. Russell & Joyner, 2001). LGBTQ adults and aging adults also have reported significant mental health disparities when compared to heterosexual and cisgender individuals including increased depression, substance use, and suicidal attempts (Cochran et al., 2003; King et al., 2008; Meyer, 2003). Much of the literature on the discrepancy in mental health concerns, when compared to heterosexual and cisgender individuals, centers on the prevalence of stigmatization, prejudice, and discrimination as contributors to the negative lived experiences of LGBTQ individuals and the subsequent development of these negative health outcomes (Herek, 2009; Meyer, 2003; Pachankis, 2007). The clinical vignette that is presented in Box 18.1 illustrates some of the mental health issues discussed in this section.

BOX 18.1

Clinical Vignette: The Case of Jessica

Jessica, a 34-year-old Latinx female, presented to counseling with mild levels of anxiety and depression. She is an artist and an art educator. She reported that she was struggling with how to have a relationship with her family, who were devout Catholics. She reported growing up in

(continued)

that religious context had been very difficult. She was unaware of her queerness until she was older because there were so many negative messages about sexuality, about being a woman, and about being different—outside of the highly controlled identities within her church. She went to a religious primary and secondary school and was sent to college at a religious-based university. There she began to question her beliefs and her identity. Now as an adult, she has rejected the beliefs of her parents, but struggles with "finding her voice" and not "becoming invisible" when she is around them for visits. She also discloses that she was sexually abused as a child from someone within the church community.

Within sessions, she presents as intelligent, insightful, and motivated to heal from these experiences. She reports that she avoids religion and religious discussions whenever possible, becomes anxious and dreads the visits with her family, and when they inevitably want to pray with her or have an impromptu "Bible Study," she withdraws, cries, and feels like she will "crawl out of her skin." After these experiences, she reports that she feels "fuzzy" and disconnected from everyone; in response, she says she usually goes to sleep and may feel better the next day. She reports having distressing memories and dreams of being in church and being highly controlled. She also reports feeling similarly when hearing news reports about legislation, hate crimes against LGBTQ people, attacks against women, suppression of feminists, and the political divide, which is often fueled by religious differences.

Case Questions

1. What are your own feelings, biases, thoughts, and assumptions when hearing Jessica's story?
2. Identify the complex layers of trauma for Jessica's past and current situation. What types of trauma has Jessica directly or indirectly experienced?
3. How might you approach creating a safe, trauma-informed, and affirming space for Jessica?

Increased mental health concerns among AGM individuals are associated with stigma-related stress, including expectations of rejection and fear of victimization (Meyer, 2003; Pachankis & Branstrom, 2018). These stressors have been shown to emerge early in development and correspond with subsequent social isolation and psychological distress (Hatzenbuehler, 2009; Hatzenbuehler et al., 2008). As a result of these stressors, many AGM individuals feel forced to conceal their identities in social and workplace environments, which consistently has been shown to have detrimental effects on the identity development and well-being of AGM persons (A. Bryan & Mayock, 2017; Chung et al., 2009; Meyer, 2003; Pachankis, 2007). As such, AGM individuals and communities are at a greater risk of experiencing mental health disparities due to their lived experiences. Therefore, it is incumbent on clinicians to consider the experiences of their AGM-identified clients when considering clinical practices such as diagnosis, which may further perpetuate experiences of minority stress.

Diagnostic Issues

Although there are *DSM-5* limitations in diagnosing "little t" trauma, the *International Classification of Diseases* (*ICD-11*; World Health Organization, 2018) offers a "sibling" diagnosis to PTSD, that of Complex PTSD (C-PTSD). Complex trauma events are defined as prolonged and repeated, as well as interpersonal in nature. As noted earlier regarding interpersonal traumas, complex trauma previously was regarded as exclusively occurring in childhood and/or perpetrated by one's caregiver(s). However, it is now recognized as being able to occur exclusively in adulthood, and also in noncaregiver relationships (e.g., IPV). The original concept of complex trauma described situations in which the victim was held emotionally or physically captive (Herman, 2001). The authors argue that the common experiences of AGM-identifying individuals feeling constrained in their identity, expression, and behaviors is also a form of complex trauma. In addition to the classic PTSD symptoms of intrusion, arousal, and avoidance, C-PTSD has three additional symptoms: **a**ffect regulation difficulties, **i**dentity issues in regard to having a poor sense of self, and **r**elational impairment. These symptoms, which can be remembered as **AIR**, reflect the interpersonal and relational nature of complex traumatization. Given that the AGM community is disproportionately exposed to physical and sexual violence in adulthood, childhood sexual and physical abuse, IPV, and hate crimes, it is often the case that they likely meet criteria for complex trauma as well as trauma events as typically defined in the *DSM-5*.

Beyond traumatic symptomatology, research finds that AGM individuals have higher rates of other mental health problems (e.g., depression, anxiety, substance abuse or misuse) as compared to cisgender and heterosexual individuals (Dhejne et al., 2016; Semlyen et al., 2016). In fact, of those diagnosed with PTSD, 80% have a comorbid diagnosis (Kessler et al., 1995).

Often, depression and anxiety are comorbid with PTSD. Depression and anxiety may precede and increase risk for developing PTSD, may share an overlap in symptoms, or may be secondary or symptomatic responses to traumatization (Ginzburg et al., 2010). In this case, resolving the trauma also would mitigate the comorbid symptoms. However, in individuals with prolonged and repeated abuse or traumatization, the depression and anxiety, although secondary, can be debilitating and may be the primary presenting concern. Understanding and conceptualizing this would be important in determining the best course of treatment, often focusing on safety and stabilization of the depression and anxiety first, and then focusing on resolving the trauma.

Additional diagnoses may be forms of coping with societal stigmatization, hate and prejudice, and other traumas. For example, alcohol and substance abuse may be used as a form of numbing or coping with fear-based and/or depressive and anxious emotions (Parent et al., 2019; Reisner et al., 2015; Weber, 2008). Substances also may be used to aid in sexual intimacy to "dissociate" from intrusive reminders of past sexual violations (Pantalone et al., 2017).

Diagnosis of personality disorders may be more prevalent as well. Indeed, discerning among PTSD, C-PTSD, and borderline personality disorder (BPD) can be challenging. Symptoms of affective instability, poor self-concept, and interpersonal difficulties are hallmark symptoms of BPD. They are also the core features (AIR) of C-PTSD. Cloitre et al. (2014) created profile analyses to compare and contrast the three conditions. In the C-PTSD group, they were significantly more likely to endorse nightmares and avoidance of thoughts, as compared to BPD. Further, for those with BPD and compared against C-PTSD, they endorsed more frantic efforts in relationships, unstable relationships, an unstable sense of self, impulsiveness, self-harm, mood changes, temper, and paranoia/dissociation.

Another discerning factor would be chronology. By definition, C-PTSD arises as a result of trauma events; therefore, gathering a timeline of trauma events and their correspondence with various symptoms would be necessary. Less helpful in diagnosis, but also an indicator, is that a hallmark feature of personality disorders is chronicity; if after treatment the symptoms of disturbances in affect, identity, and relationships remit, then it would be accurate to say that the diagnosis was C-PTSD.

Trauma-Informed and Trauma-Focused Interventions for Queer and Trans People

Trauma-Informed Affirmative Care as an Approach and Style

Research remains somewhat mixed on the treatment-seeking behaviors within this population. For example, research supports the notion that affectional minorities are more likely to seek out services from a mental health clinician (Cochran et al., 2003). More specifically, Cochran et al. (2003) found that more than half of gay and bisexual men and more than 60% of lesbian and bisexual women visited a mental health clinician, saw a medical doctor for an emotional concern, attended a self-help group, or took psychotropic medication in the previous 12 months. As a comparison, only 25% of heterosexual men and almost 36% of heterosexual women reported engaging in those services (Cochran et al., 2003). This also has been replicated more recently: nonheterosexual individuals were two to four times more likely to see a mental health clinician as compared to heterosexual individuals (Platt et al., 2018). However, the methodology of these studies is often problematic in that it defines "treatment utilization" as attending one or more visits. That is, someone who engages for 30 visits to a therapist or counselor would be coded as just as engaged as someone who visits a clinician one time and then "drops out" of treatment. Thus, a more accurate term might be initiation of services. Additionally, the extant literature does not focus or address trans and gender expansive individuals. It is more than likely that these results generalize to gender minorities, given that this community faces additional biases from clinicians and staff within a counseling and medical context (Stotzer et al., 2013). Micro- and macro-aggressions such as using incorrect pronouns, inadequate or lacking knowledge of differences between biology and identity, and discomfort in talking about sexual health and well-being may all lead to disengagement, or dropping out, of therapeutic care.

In fact, while AGM individuals may initiate treatment at higher rates than their heterosexual counterparts, they also report greater dissatisfaction in their clinicians, usually due to lack of clinicians' cultural competence in working within this community (Hudson-Sharp & Metcalf, 2016). Compounding this is a lack of clinicians who are trained in trauma-informed therapy (see Cook et al., 2017) and subsequently lack the necessary competencies to deliver trauma-informed and trauma-focused interventions.

Affirmative care and trauma-informed care share many overlapping similarities, to the point where one could argue that affirmative care *is* trauma-informed care. In fact, affirmative trauma-informed care can contribute to posttraumatic growth, a sense of growth that comes from challenging one's beliefs and facing a psychological struggle (Calhoun & Tedeschi, 2006). Both styles are approaches of interacting with clients from a strengths-based perspective, with a focus on client empowerment and resilience. The two models emphasize the responsibility of the clinician to acknowledge, confront, and continuously revise one's biases and assumptions. In affirmative care, therapist biases might include what it means to be AGM and who is really a part of the community; in trauma-informed care, therapist biases may be present in regard to believing that only certain genders can be traumatized or assuming disorders of personality when presented with relational disruptions. Treatment goals are established collaboratively, with an intention to reduce hierarchical and authoritarian experiences in the context of the therapeutic relationship. Further, affirmative trauma-informed care requires the tailoring of evidence-based interventions based on clients' intersecting identities and experiences, and a focus on developing and enhancing skills to navigate various domains within society. For an overview of trauma-based competencies, see Cook et al. (2014).

Given the prolonged and repeated nature of trauma facing queer and trans people, and the presence of additional traumatic experiences that may not be considered at a diagnostic threshold, Herman's (1992) three-phase model also should be considered. The model emphasizes the need to build a trauma-informed, secure and trusting, affirmative relationship prior to any trauma-focused work. In the first phase, building rapport within a strong therapeutic foundation is emphasized. This stage also emphasizes the need to build up coping skills, which can be used in lieu of maladaptive skills. To prevent regression in treatment when beginning the challenging work of trauma processing, clients need emotion regulation and distress tolerance skills. Then, in phase 2, they are able to begin the emotionally difficult task of processing and resolving their trauma by employing their new skillset. In the third phase, the focus is on reintegration, in which the individual learns how to live their best life in social, occupational, relational, and intrapersonal domains. The benefit of such a model is that it does not immediately focus on trauma, which can be destabilizing. Rather, it focuses on skill development and the here-and-now, which can consist of issues such as unemployment, homelessness, and familial and/or spiritual rejection, among others. By focusing on present-day issues to create a safer system, as well as teaching affect regulation and distress tolerance skills, this leaves space for eventual trauma processing through formal evidence-based trauma exposures or nonmanualized narrative forms.

Evidence-Based Trauma Interventions

Trauma-focused care refers to the evidence-based interventions specifically targeting PTSD symptoms. The APA (2017) developed PTSD Treatment Guidelines based on a systematic review of empirical studies evaluating psychotherapy outcomes. Cognitive-behavioral therapy, prolonged exposure (PE), and cognitive processing therapy (CPT) emerged as robust interventions with large effect sizes in reducing trauma symptoms. It should be noted, however, that the experimental studies selected for inclusion did not include AGM populations and likely require tailoring (Livingston et al., 2019). Both PE and CPT involve some form of exposure-based exercise. In PE, the goal is to practice both imaginal and in vivo exposures; in CPT, the goal is to challenge cognitive distortions that emerge after writing a detailed narrative of the traumatic event. In sum, these treatments are effective for a Criterion A event and Criterions B to E symptoms. An additional consideration is that these are treatments for *post*traumatic stress. These would not be effective when considering that many AGM individuals may be presenting to treatment with current traumatization (e.g., IPV, risk for assault and hate crimes, trafficking, or exploitation).

Evidence-based treatments for trauma, as is, may not be appropriately tailored to the AGM community. As an example, consider CPT that focuses on breaking and replacing "stuck points," or maladaptive thoughts. A common stuck point includes, "I cannot keep myself safe," with the intended goal of having the individual reframe this to, "I may not be able to keep myself safe in all situations." Taken at face value, this may be insensitive to the real threat of outside violence. Therefore, a key recommendation is to apply a stigma-informed approach (G. M. Russell & Hawkey, 2017), in which the clinician acknowledges the proclivity to blame oneself and disproportionately accept responsibility and move to one of externalizing and understanding occurrences in the context of a larger macrosystem.

SOCIAL JUSTICE AND ADVOCACY ACTIONS

Though a common theme throughout the research literature has indicated that queer and trans individuals experience higher rates or are at an increased risk of mental health concerns when compared to heterosexual and cisgender-identified individuals, it is important to consider that these studies often are framed as correlational, with outcomes based on identities of the individuals rather than examining the systems and social/cultural milieu which oppresses and marginalizes these identities (A. Bryan & Mayock, 2017). In addition to considering appropriate and ethical clinical responses with this population, counselors and related mental health professionals also need to understand and act within their role as a social justice advocate to address the oppressive systems that cause and perpetuate this trauma (American Counseling Association, 2014; Ratts et al., 2010, 2015).

At the individual level, mental health professionals should investigate their lived privilege and biases when working with this population (Ratts et al., 2015). Likewise, mental health professionals need to do their own work in investigating their internalized and oppressive beliefs regarding gender and affectional variance (Singh, 2016). In what ways might a hidden bias or privileged viewpoint injure the client? For example, a counselor may behave in a microaggressive manner to a client, which could lead to cessation of counseling, increase mistrust of counselors, and increase their experience of trauma. A counselor may evidence discomfort in their body language surrounding the experiences a queer client is discussing, may use outdated or problematic terminology (e.g., use the term "homosexual" which is an outdated and stigmatized term that is no longer used), or express heteronormative assumptions about a client. It is incumbent on mental health professionals and educators to incorporate supervision and training that is aimed at addressing these oppressive systems, rather than minimizing or dismissing one's lived experiences as an LGBTQ individual (S. Bryan, 2018).

Using a liberation framework, therapists should provide psychoeducation and a trauma-informed space to allow clients to empower themselves (Ratts et al., 2010). When the client faces barriers within the systems they are navigating, counselors should collaborate with and work on behalf of the client to assist in planning and implementing a plan of action to counter barriers and find resources (Ratts et al., 2010). For example, counselors could take a feminist approach and encourage a liberation dialogue by discussing the role of the oppressive culture; dialoguing with clients on what has been taken away from them through the process of growing up in a heterosexist and cissexist culture can be liberating and healing (Richmond et al., 2017; Singh, 2016). Counselors could provide psychoeducation that queer and trans persons were important figures in indigenous cultures, seen as inherently valuable and spiritual; exploring how society and colonization have changed positive perceptions to ones that are oppressive for LGBTQ people and other marginalized people may be helpful for clients (Singh, 2016). Additionally, counselors also should explore the ways that clients resist these oppressive and traumatic experiences; their resilience and survival are strength-based themes, which can be helpful to explore in an effort to assist clients to self-empower (Singh, 2016).

At the community level, mental health professionals should serve as a support for the queer and trans communities in fighting systemic barriers that they face (Ratts et al., 2010). Counselors should stay connected to advocacy organizations like the Human Rights Campaign and the Society for Sexual, Affectional, Intersex, and Gender Expansive Identities to remain knowledgeable about issues facing these populations, develop alliances with community members and stakeholders, and educate other important stakeholders in community centers and schools. For example, a therapist could advocate to have a speaker from this population come to a clinical mental health agency to offer professional development, review their site's trauma-informed practices, and assess the LGBTQ-affirming practices of the agency. Ensuring that there is an affirming counseling space, appropriate language on forms, and quality, well-trained staff is important in creating a context in which healing can occur for these populations.

Finally, at a social and political level, mental health professionals can find ways for members of the community to have their voices heard about the issues that impact these populations, as well as combat practices that perpetuate cissexism and heterosexism and lead to further experiences of trauma (Ratts et al., 2010). Some of these issues include advocating for better law enforcement training around issues of diversity, including sexual and gender identity, to increase awareness and responsiveness to hate crimes (Human Rights Campaign, 2018). Additionally, mental health professionals can advocate for increased research and advocacy for trans populations, as these communities are experiencing more frequent and more violent attacks than LGB communities (Clements-Nolle et al., 2006). Finally, counselors can advocate for state and national protection for all queer and trans people from discrimination in any context (Burgess et al., 2007).

CONCLUSION

Despite improving acceptance in the culture, queer and trans people continue to face adversity, marginalization, and trauma that impact them at a holistic level: mind, body, and spirit. Who they are, at a core level, can be denigrated; they may experience stressors and trauma at an interpersonal level, within their peer groups, families, communities, faith systems, and work. They also may face continued political and social marginalization, invalidating their humanity and access to human rights. As helping professionals, we are challenged to investigate our own internalized oppressive beliefs and experiences surrounding gender and queerness; provide a safe, trauma-informed, and affirming space for all clients; and promote healing, liberation, and self-empowerment with LGBTQ clients through the use of affirmative and trauma-informed practices.

ADDITIONAL RESOURCES

A robust set of instructor resources designed to supplement this text is located at http://connect.springerpub.com/content/book/978-0-8261-5085-1. Qualifying instructors may request access by emailing textbook@springerpub.com.

PRACTICE-BASED RESOURCES AND REFERENCES

To view a list of resources and all the references, please visit connect.springerpub.com via the following url: http://connect.springerpub.com/content/book/978-0-8261-5085-1/part/part03/chapter/ch18

CHAPTER 19

Historical Trauma and Trauma-Affected Communities

MATTHEW J. WALSH, REVEREND PAUL T. ABERNATHY, AND LISA LÓPEZ LEVERS

CHAPTER OVERVIEW

This chapter focuses on the importance of understanding historical trauma and how its legacy influences communities that have been affected by trauma. One major purpose of this chapter is to explore the lived experiences of individuals and communities exposed to trauma, in ways that can lead to trauma-informed interventions, especially among those affected by historical trauma. One such research-based strategy is highlighted and discussed in detail.

LEARNING OBJECTIVES

After reading this chapter, the reader should be able to:

1. Understand the impact of trauma on communities;
2. Develop insight about the effects of historical trauma;
3. Re-imagine community development from a trauma-informed framework to produce a bio-behavioral change at the micro-community level;
4. Describe a new framework through which to understand trauma as a communally experienced, multigenerational, and layered phenomenon;
5. Understand how to design a salient community-engaged/community-embedded research strategy from a bio-ecological perspective; and,
6. Identify elements of a context-sensitive model for sustainable integrated healthcare in low-resource communities.

INTRODUCTION

Trauma affects individuals living in communities around the world. While urban areas have higher densities of populations, more people living in poverty, and more communities with higher crime rates, people living in suburban and rural areas also experience trauma. The reality, however, is that historically marginalized groups of people and lower-resourced communities have experienced historical trauma as well as more frequent incidences of traumatic events. The purpose of this chapter is to explore the lived experience of trauma from an individual and community or collective perspective. To frame our discussion, we explore the following topics: First, we describe the phenomena of historical trauma, the developmental impact it can leave on subsequent generations, and the intersection with low resource communities; second, we explore developmental aspects of trauma, including complex trauma and Adverse Childhood Experiences (ACEs); third, we expand on the idea of community trauma, highlighting ecological influences, and presenting the idea of trauma-affected communities; and, finally, we offer a salient example of a research-based, trauma-informed response to community trauma from the *Neighborhood Resilience Project*. This is followed by a brief conclusion and an online list of practice-based resources.

THE LIVED EXPERIENCE OF TRAUMA

The lived experience of trauma can be elusive and profound, not just for the individual who has experienced the event or events, but also for the community. The lived experience of trauma can affect the individual and the community in a variety of ways that are not always completely understood to the individual and the community. Trauma can have an impact on the body; the environment; identity formation; interpretations of the past, present, and future; and our relationships with others. Herman (1992/1997) states that traumatic events "violate the victim's faith in a natural or divine order and cast the victim into a state of existential crisis" (p. 51). Such existential crisis reverberates in the words of one community resident who participated in an inquiry about community-based violence (Walsh, 2015):

> My mom went to Jail. . . . My grandmother would beat me because I reminded her of my mom . . . because she did not want me, I felt like I was not worthy. . . . I was the lost girl, the girl that wasn't worthy.

Trauma can alter the very existence and meaning that an individual gives to their life (Frankl, 2006; Janoff-Bulman, 1992). These existential influences can hinder an individual's ability to trust, hope, and care for themselves or for others, resulting in a "disconnect" between an individual's perceived sense of self, as well as relationships with others (Herman, 1992/1997). Trauma can attack the core of an individual's normal living and coping mechanisms and cause the individual to retreat into the self or to become isolated from others. For many residents from Walsh's (2015) community-based study, trauma informs their understanding of the world and how they interact with their environment, as well as how the environment affects them developmentally. Identity formation and the ability to reach or recognize an individual's potential are based in large part on the meaning-making relationship with the community and the environment. If an individual feels that they have no potential or feel trapped in a prescribed socioeconomic status (SES) or role, their sense of self can become stagnant or distressed. Likewise, if they view the community as distressed, that person may view the self as distressed and stagnant. Within the broader discussion of lived trauma in this section, we examine the relevance of historical trauma, the developmental effects of trauma, the role of attachment and the environment, the importance of the ACE study, and community trauma in the following subsections.

Historical Trauma

Historical trauma theory provides a context for understanding community trauma and illuminates potential barriers to treatment. As introduced in Chapter 1, "An Introduction to Counseling Survivors of Trauma: Beginning to Understand the Historical and Psychosocial Implications of Trauma, Stress, Crisis, and Disaster," historical trauma theory tries to understand *how* and *why* certain populations have a greater likelihood of disease and other disparities. It also is important to understand the confluence of historical trauma, racism, poverty, and other forms of oppression. According to David and Derthick:

Despite its pervasiveness and harmful impacts, however, it seems as though many of us still do not have a clear understanding of oppression, its many manifestations, and its consequences. Many of us may have heard of racism, sexism, and even heterosexism or homophobia . . . but do not see the need to address them—believing that such "isms" are not legitimate concerns and are just products of some people's ideological movement toward "political correctness"—thereby failing to understand that "isms" are oppressive and are therefore harmful. Even among those of us who are familiar with specific "isms" and agree that they are social ills that need to be addressed, many seem to not see that the core commonality between these various forms of "isms" is that they are problematic precisely because they are oppressive. (David & Derthick, 2017, p. 2)

Sotero (2006) has described historical trauma theory as a relatively new concept in public health that aims to assess the higher prevalence of disease among populations exposed to long-term traumatic experiences (e.g., racism, slavery, genocide) across generations. J. C. Alexander (2004) examined the construct of cultural trauma as a constructivist concept. He asserted that events are not inherently traumatic; rather, it is the beliefs of individuals and societal groups that make them such (J. C. Alexander, 2004). Although some events are considered to be nefarious, universally, in short, Alexander posits that it is not so much the events, per se, but their meanings, which disturb and shock the social consciousness.

The process of cultural trauma, according to Eyerman (2002), has evolved from the reconstruction and reconceptualization of collective memory and identity. Estrada (2009) has pointed out that it is precisely the intergenerational stress, in response to atrocious and traumatic social and historical events, that is at the core of historical trauma theory. This applies to many groups of indigenous and oppressed peoples around the world, for instance, colonized Africans across the continent of Africa, African Americans and other previously enslaved peoples of the African diaspora, Native American and First Nations people of North America, colonized indigenous peoples throughout South America, Aboriginal people of Australia and New Zealand, and various populations throughout Asia, among others (Walk Free Foundation, 2018). Wilkerson (2020) eloquently identifies the existence of racism in the United States as a caste system, outlining the eight pillars of caste systems that can be found universally. The concept of historical trauma, or collective trauma, implies that the experience involves generational transmission across a group of people who have established a cohesive identity or a sense of group affinity (de Mendelssohn, 2008; Evans-Campbell, 2008).

As research into generational trauma is still a relatively recent phenomenon, there remains work to be done in refining definitions, explaining modes of transmission, and delineating the impacts of intergenerational trauma. Such detailed exploration is not the focus of this chapter; however, an overview of the salient research to date is in order. At its core, intergenerational or cultural trauma is suggested to be a result of a population's identification with the emotional distress and suffering of previous generations (M. Y. H. Brave Heart, 2003, 2007; M. Y. H. Brave Heart et al., 2005). There appear to be common characteristics of the type of events that lead to cultural trauma. Most notably, an "outside" group, whose intent is to subjugate or to cause harm, generally perpetrates the incidents. Although natural disasters have been found to contribute to collective trauma, it is generally the course of human events that seems to breed the greatest devastation. Additionally, events that are experienced by a large number of members of a specific group, for whom the event created significant distress and bereavement, tend to create trauma that is transmitted to future generations (M. Y. H. Brave Heart, 2003, 2007; Brave Heart & DeBruyn, 1998; M. Y. H. Brave Heart et al., 2005; Evans-Campbell, 2008; Whitbeck et al., 2004; Williams, 2018). All too often, these events involve genocide, enslavement, or decimation of marginalized factions of people.

M. Y. H. Brave Heart (2003, 2007) has identified the following symptoms as one example of a sort of historical trauma nosology among indigenous peoples of North America: depression, anxiety, isolation, loss of sleep, anger, discomfort around White people, shame, fear and distrust, loss of concentration, substance abuse, and violence and suicide. In other studies, evidence of generational trauma has been found in the children of Holocaust survivors (Gangi et al., 2009).

Wiseman et al. (2006), in their exploration of second-generation Holocaust survivors, have found that these offspring exhibit anger and guilt related to parental overprotectiveness, enmeshment, and expectations. The monumental losses suffered by Holocaust survivors dramatically influence their familial relationships, which often are characterized by an intense need to protect and maintain family cohesion as a survival strategy. Behaviors that are rooted in the trauma of a past violation are an ongoing influence in the actions of the present, and these even may be propagated by third-generation survivors (Scharf, 2007) and beyond. Sotero (2006) states that "a key feature of historical trauma theory is that the psychological and emotional consequences of the trauma experience are transmitted to subsequent generations through physiological, environmental and social [ecological] pathways resulting in an intergenerational cycle of trauma response" (p. 95).

We believe that it may be helpful to offer a real-world example, so that readers can understand the nature of the oppression described here. Although we look to the Hill District, located centrally in the city of Pittsburgh, Pennsylvania, as an apt example, we submit that the Hill shares demographic characteristics with trauma-affected, low-resource communities around the world; we offer field-based examples, about recent work in the Hill District, later in this chapter. The Hill has had a storied and challenging history, one that has been mixed with cultural and economic vibrancy, as well as external and internal factors influencing its decline in the 1960s and encroaching gentrification today. The Hill community is predominantly Black and African American, and historically, this population has experienced collective trauma(s) such as slavery, Jim Crow laws, and institutional racism. Historical trauma theory offers a path toward contextualizing current psychological and emotional distress, as articulated by the term "community trauma." In addition, current research has begun to link historical or transgenerational trauma with racial and ethnic health disparities (Atkinson et al., 2010; Sotero, 2006; Williams et al., 2003).

Sotero's (2006) model emerges from considering the subjugation of a population by a dominant group. Four elements must be present, as parts of the suppression, in order to qualify as subjugation: "(a) overwhelming physical and psychological violence, (b) segregation and/or displacement, (c) economic deprivation, and (d) cultural dispossession" (p. 99). From the primary generation that experienced the subjugation, future generations can be affected by the original trauma through various factors. These factors are by-products of extreme trauma experienced by the primary generation. Sotero states, "Extreme trauma may lead to subsequent impairments in the capacity for parenting. Physical and emotional trauma can impair genetic function and expression, which may in turn affect offspring genetically, through in-utero biological adaptations, or environmentally" (p. 99). In addition to such epigenetic changes, Sotero argues that future generations can experience vicarious traumatization through storytelling and oral traditions of the population. Sotero claims that historical trauma theory "creates an emotional and psychological release from blame and guilt about health status, empowers individuals and communities to address the root causes of poor health and allows for capacity building unique to culture, community and social structure" (p. 102).

Historical trauma theory can shed light on the possible underlying factors contributing to mental distress and mental health disparities in racial/ethnic minority populations. It is clear that the responses of individuals are related to the responses of their families, which are, in turn, influenced by the responses of the community as a whole. Although there is considerably more research to be done, we can view cultural trauma as a multisystemic influence that has long-term social manifestations across generations. Additionally, even though the focus of this discussion is on transgenerational and historical trauma, we would be remiss in not at least mentioning an additional strand in this discourse, namely, that of transgenerational resilience. In spite of experiencing horrendous trauma, across generations, affected groups of people have managed to survive and even thrive. This courageous resilience, in the face of egregious acts of violence and hatred, has been referenced in a nascent part of the literature as transgenerational resilience (e.g., Denham, 2008; Kirmayer et al., 2014) and begs further inquiry, along with transgenerational trauma. Due to the ramifications of historical trauma and the reality-based issues that arise in the lives of those affected, it is important to consider the need for situation-specific and culturally sensitive human services. The next section continues the thread from historical trauma theory to the developmental effects of trauma.

Posttraumatic Slave Syndrome

In addition to historical trauma theory, DeGruy's (2005) concept of "Posttraumatic Slave Syndrome" applies historical trauma theory to the Black and African American experience in the United States context. In DeGruy's (2005) *Post Traumatic Slave Syndrome: America's Legacy of Enduring Injury and Healing*, she provides an historical context for understanding the negative perceptions, images, and behaviors many Black and African Americans experience as a result of slavery. DeGruy traces the historical effects of American chattel slavery on Black and African Americans and how they have adapted their behaviors over the centuries in order to survive the effects of chattel slavery. She proposes the concept of Post Traumatic Slave Syndrome (PTSS) in order to conceptualize how the current lived experience of many African Americans is related to transgenerational adaptations linked to past traumas of slavery and ongoing oppression (p. 13). DeGruy defines PTSS as:

> A condition that exists when a population has experienced multigenerational trauma resulting from centuries of slavery and continues to experience oppression and institutionalized racism today. Added to this condition is a belief (real or imagined) that the benefits of the society in which they live are not accessible to them. This, then, is Post Traumatic Slave Syndrome:
> **M**ultigenerational trauma together with continued oppression and
> **A**bsence of opportunity to access the benefits available in the society leads to . . .
> **P**ost Traumatic Slave Syndrome. **M + A = P.** (p. 121)

Consequently, she argues that there are resulting common patterns of behaviors associated with PTSS. She identifies three categories: (a) vacant esteem; (b) ever present anger; and (c) racist socialization. The following paragraphs briefly describe the three categories.

Vacant esteem relates to a belief that an individual has little or no worth. This belief of having little or no worth has been influenced by three domains: society, community, and family. Society contributes to vacant esteem in a variety of ways from laws, institutions, and policies, as well as how African Americans are portrayed in the media. African Americans are disproportionally represented in the judicial system (M. Alexander, 2012). Racial bias and lethal force against Black and African Americans in policing is a systemic problem across the United States. To illustrate this point, in 2013, we note that a civil, nonviolent movement, with the hashtag #BlackLivesMatter, was formed after the acquittal of George Zimmerman in the shooting death of Trayvon Martin. The mission of #BlackLivesMatter has been to confront White supremacy by empowering local communities to intervene in violence targeted at Black communities by the state as well as by vigilantes (Black Lives Matter, 2020, "about" section).

#BlackLivesMatter has evolved since 2013 into a global network foundation and includes the United States, United Kingdom, and Canada. We witnessed, in the summer of 2020 in the United States, a tipping point to unwarranted police violence and systemic racism toward Blacks with the killing of George Floyd by a White police officer. George Floyd's death has symbolized the countless deaths of Black and African American individuals by police and the legacy of trauma inflicted by racially unjust systems, particularly racial profiling by police officers. In many ways, the #BlackLivesMatter movement has mitigated the uncritical reinforcement of vacant esteem. Vacant esteem arises and is influenced by the various systems (e.g., as denoted in the Bioecological Model) with which an individual interacts on a daily basis as well as by the historical context. As a result, vacant esteem can be passed down, through generations, in the form of parenting styles. #BlackLivesMatter had demonstrated that this, along with overall systemic racism, no longer is acceptable.

The next category associated with PTSS is "ever present anger," which DeGruy states is the most prominent behavior pattern related with PTSS. She suggests that the anger manifests from ongoing oppression by the dominant group, in which "goals are blocked"; this, then, may result in a fear of failure that often exists within Black and African American communities. An example that DeGruy points to, which she says has perpetuated "blocked goals," is the fallacy that Blacks and African Americans have been fully integrated into the greater society. The year 2020 has marked the 55th anniversary of "Bloody Sunday" and the march over the Edmund Pettus Bridge in Selma, Alabama. The protest (e.g., #BlackLivesMatter) for equality and justice for minority groups has only been partially realized, as evident by the disparities that exist in educational opportunities, healthcare, the judicial system, and bank lending practices in the United States, to name a few.

The last category is racist socialization, which DeGruy considers "the most insidious and pervasive symptom" of PTSS (p. 134). Racist socialization represents the social construction of a value system related to class and race/ethnicity, where "Whiteness" is superior to "Blackness." This is similar to Du Bois' (1903/1965) "double consciousness," which he articulates in *The Souls of Black Folk*. Du Bois suggests that not only do "Black folk" view themselves through their own Black identity, but they also view themselves or their community through White eyes. As a net result of the trauma from chattel slavery, residuals have been passed down through the generations, socializing Black and African Americans that they were inferior "physically, emotionally, spiritually, and intellectually" (DeGruy, 2005, p. 137). For many Black and African American communities, the residuals from transgenerational trauma associated with slavery and DeGruy's conceptualization of PTSS add another dimension and insight into the lived experience of community trauma.

Developmental Effects of Trauma

For the residents of low-resource, often marginalized communities of color that frequently are located in large urban areas, their trauma started when they were children and took on many forms of interpersonal traumas. Examples of these traumas include sexual abuse, physical and verbal violence inside or outside of the home, and being rejected or discriminated against because of skin color. The term "complex trauma" is used in the literature to describe the impact that multiple layers of interpersonal traumatic experiences can have on the development and identity formation of an individual (Courtois & Ford, 2013; Ford & Courtois, 2020). Complex trauma occurs when the stressor event is repeated over time and/or perpetrated by a family member or an authority figure; it usually begins in childhood or adolescence but also can occur in adulthood. Because these experiences usually occur within the child's primary caregiver system, it can affect the child's ability to regulate emotionally, feel safe, trust self and others, and make sense of what is happening to them. The effects of multiple traumatic experiences are related to multiple risk factors, which then can lead to long-term physical and behavioral health problems, as well as to negative coping mechanisms (Courtois & Ford, 2013; Ford & Courtois 2020). In addition to complex trauma relating to repeated individual victimization by primary caregivers, it also can exist within the context of the community. The following section further explores the role of attachment and the environment in this complex developmental cycle of maltreatment.

Role of Attachment and Environment

The effects of complex trauma are rooted in the nature of the attachment bonds that have formed between child and primary caregivers. Children who live in a secure and safe environment learn to trust their feelings and the world around them. Through the modeling of a primary caregiver, children learn increasingly more intricate vocabulary to describe emotions effectively. This learned emotional vocabulary and a trust in the primary caregiver's ability to restore a sense of control and safety, when a child is distressed, moderates against "trauma-induced terror" (van der Kolk, 2005). The opposite is true in an insecure environment and with primary attachments that have not established a sense of trust and safety in the child. Such children may be in extreme distress, existing in a situation in which no relief from the stress can be found, because either the primary caregiver is the source of the distress or is unable to model emotional regulation or an emotional vocabulary. This, in turn, fosters an environment in which the child lacks the ability to process, integrate, or categorize what is happening. If a child feels helpless and lacks any sense of stability or control, mechanisms of the primal brain can be triggered (i.e., fight/flight/freeze), and the child is not able to learn from the experience (van der Kolk, 2005, 2014).

The inability of the child to process, integrate, or categorize the stressor(s), along with the repetitious nature of complex trauma, can lead to a constant state of being in psychological and biological "survival" mode (Courtois & Ford, 2013). Over time, if the victimization continues or recurs, these survival reactions can be ingrained in the individual's personality as they develop. Survival can become the primary vehicle from which an individual conceptualizes their being in the world, affecting both personal relationships and the ability to self-regulate emotions. As a result of an inability to self-regulate and to maintain relationships, as well as being stuck in survivor mode, many survivors of complex trauma seek other coping mechanisms to self-soothe. Some of these coping mechanisms include alcohol and drug abuse, self-harm, and suicidality (Najavits, 2006; van der Kolk et al., 1991). Survivors of these early life traumas often struggle with anger, alienation, distrust, confusion, grief, low self-esteem, loneliness, shame, and self-loathing (Courtois & Ford, 2013). To examine the potential effects of negative childhood experiences further, the Adverse Childhood Experiences (ACE) study has provided needed context (Chapter 2 offers a brief description of the ACE study, and the reader can refer to the figure of the ACE Pyramid, presented there).

The Adverse Childhood Experiences Study

The ACE study (1995–1997) has been the largest study to date, with more than 17,000 participants, which has linked health risk behavior and disease in adulthood to exposure to emotional, physical, or sexual abuse, and household dysfunction during childhood (Felitti et al., 1998). The study found that nearly two-thirds of all respondents had at least one adverse childhood experience (occurring before the age of 18), and that 12% of the respondents had four or more adverse childhood experiences. The study also found a strong graded relationship to the amount of exposure to abuse or household dysfunction and multiple risk factors associated with some of the leading causes of death in adults. The ACE study found a significant relationship between adverse childhood experiences and alcoholism, drug abuse, sexual promiscuity, sexually transmitted diseases, intimate partner violence, obesity, physical inactivity, depression, suicide attempts, and smoking. Further, the more adverse childhood experiences reported, the more likely it is that a person may develop heart disease, cancer, diabetes, liver disease, stroke, and skeletal fractures.

The original ACE Pyramid graphic included the following, from the base to the top of the pyramid: Adverse Childhood Experiences; disrupted neurodevelopment; social, emotional, and cognitive impairment; adoption of health risk behaviors; disease, disability, and social problems; and early death (Centers for Disease Control and Prevention [CDC], 2020). However, over the last few years, the ACE Pyramid has been updated to include "social conditions/local context" and "generational embodiment/historical trauma" at the pyramid base, with the latter at the very bottom. These two blocks, positioned at the base of the pyramid, have underscored the impact that the environment/systems and generational trauma can have over the life-span of an individual. In addition, the ACE study has illustrated that adverse childhood experiences are more common than acknowledged; it shows the impact that these adverse experiences can have on physical and behavioral health later on in life, thus illuminating the need for culturally sensitive preventative interventions.

Community Trauma

In the research literature, community trauma often is associated with the impact that a particular event or events may have on a community. Some examples include chronic community violence, workplace and school violence, natural and manmade disaster, war, genocide, and terrorism (Herman, 1992/1997; Levers & Buck, 2012; Substance Abuse and Mental Health Services Administration [SAMHSA], 2017). Even though individual traumatic events happen within the context of a community, the term "community trauma" may refer to any form of violence that affects a number of people or an entire community. The World Health Organization (WHO) defines "violence" as "the intentional use of physical force or power, threatened or actual, against another person or against a group or community that results in or has a high likelihood of resulting in injury, death, psychological harm, maltreatment, or deprivation" (Krug et al., 2002, p. 5). This definition of violence is intentionally broad in scope, covering a wide range of violent acts toward an individual or a community, that go beyond typically defined outcomes of injury or death. This definition better illustrates the sometimes hidden acts of violence that the majority of those in our society do not experience or acknowledge, but that many in urban, ethnic/racial, minority communities experience on a daily basis (Alim et al., 2006; Breslau et al., 1998; Liebschutz et al., 2007). Some examples of these hidden acts of violence that may be experienced on a daily basis include racism, low SES, poverty, lack of adequate healthcare, and substandard educational opportunities. Community-based research conducted by Walsh (2015) suggests multidimensional origins that are caused not by one particular event, but rather by multiple contributing factors, including historical trauma that has been passed down through generations.

PUTTING IT ALL TOGETHER: TRAUMA-AFFECTED COMMUNITY

Over the last 20 years, the Substance Abuse and Mental Health Services Administration (SAMHSA, 2014) has been researching and working on developing a *Trauma-Informed Approach* that can be used across a variety of service sectors as a way to help resolve trauma-related issues. SAMHSA reports that trauma researchers, clinicians, and survivors suggest that non-integrated trauma-specific interventions are insufficient to improve treatment outcomes or healing for trauma survivors. Trauma-specific interventions that primarily are used in specialized clinical settings might only be effective for those who seek treatment, have access, and/or realize that their physical or mental distress may be related to a traumatic experience. As mentioned earlier in this chapter, we explore the Hill District, an area in central Pittsburgh, Pennsylvania, as an illustrative example of a trauma-affected community. Box 19.1 provides a description of the *Neighborhood Resilience Project*, which embodies the work of trauma-informed service provision in a trauma-affected community.

BOX 19.1

Case Illustration From the Field: Neighborhood Resilience Project

The *Neighborhood Resilience Project* (NRP) is a faith-based, nonprofit community agency, located in the Hill District of Pittsburgh, Pennsylvania. As informed by the lived experience of community trauma, at both individual and collective levels, NRP establishes and promotes resilient, healing, and healthy communities so that people can be healthy enough to sustain opportunities and to realize their potential. The NRP currently offers an array of psychosocial and medical services to residents of the Hill District, the Greater Pittsburgh area, and surrounding counties. Services include a free medical clinic in the Greater Pittsburgh area that also provides psychiatric services and trauma counseling, food and clothing programs for children and families, and a county-wide trauma response team that responds to homicides as a result of gun violence. This response includes trained trauma responders (primarily volunteers) who bring a mobile unit (fitted RV) to the affected site and remain as long as possible within the first 48 hours.

(continued)

The NRP works with neighborhoods, block-by-block, or the "micro-community," depending on the geography of the community, to assess the physical and behavioral health of residents as well as the social health of the block. Such assessments are a part of NRP's *Trauma Informed Community Development* (TICD) effort, which has gained national and international attention. TICD is a culturally sensitive and context-specific framework that uses grass-roots information from local stakeholders to conduct community-appropriate development. During the course of NRP's work in the Hill District and in response to demand, NRP now offers an annual *TICD Institute* that draws cohorts of community members from around the country whose agencies or groups are interested in using the TICD framework to advance their own aspirations in their home communities. By formalizing TICD into a national institute, other interested communities have had an opportunity to replicate the framework, with adaptation for local needs. Reports to date are that TICD replications have been successful across communities. NRP is also in the foundational stages of adapting TICD for use in school systems.

For many in the Hill District, trauma and trauma responses have become normalized in the community, which has contributed to non-help-seeking processes. Identifying *trauma-affected communities* is important as an extension of the current paradigm shift in the healthcare delivery system to a trauma-informed approach to development and community building. The following subsections elucidate a framework for working with a trauma-affected community; this framework is based upon our work and research in the Hill District and at the *Neighborhood Resilience Project*.

Environment as Risk or Protective Factor

Working from an ecological framework emphasizes the importance of identifying the protective and risk factors that interact within multiple environments and that influence the lived experience of community members, who have been affected by trauma, as well as of the community itself (e.g., Bronfenbrenner & Morris, 2006; Lynch & Cicchetti, 1998). In addition, recognizing and identifying the differences between life in affluent communities and life in minority or low-resource communities may lead to more divergent modes of thinking about trauma in the context of the community as a whole. The Reverend Paul Abernathy has stated that "Our community, our children are aware this [trauma] is happening. . . . Creating a worldview shaped by this trauma" (as cited in Walsh, 2015). This statement makes explicit the potential difference between the lived spaces of predominantly low-resourced neighborhoods and the lived space of predominantly high SES neighborhoods.

The framework for working in the Hill District emphasizes that the community's perceptions of trauma, or what "is" or "is not" happening in their respective neighborhoods, have a direct influence on how individuals in the community generate and sustain a worldview of either safety, security, and control, or a worldview devoid of them (Courtois & Ford, 2013; Singer, 2004; van der Kolk, 2005, 2014). The trauma literature is consistent in demonstrating the mitigating qualities that environments can have against various types of traumas, including how people make meaning from traumatic experiences; this, then, can facilitate those situations in which an individual feels safe and secure, has some degree of control, and develops healthy attachments (Park et al., 2008; Singer, 2004; van der Kolk, 2005, 2014). In addition, the indirect impact of residents "hearing about" (Horowitz et al., 1995) trauma or resilience can perpetuate views about their community as to whether or not the means are available in the community to keep the residents safe and secure.

Following Bronfenbrenner's (1979) bioecological model, Lynch and Cicchetti (1998) have proposed an ecological-transactional model in which an individual is "nested" within multiple levels or environments that have varying degrees of proximity to the individual. They have posited that transactions take place between the individual and multiple ecologies, and that these transactions are not unidirectional, but rather are bidirectional or multidirectional. This approach to viewing the individual as "nested" postulates that not only do multiple environments influence individual identity formation, but also that the individual can influence the environment. In other words, the relationship between the individual and their multiple environments is reciprocal; the ensuing dynamic is one of reciprocity, and this is useful in thinking about individual and community interactions. In addition, we typically think of inequity as an individual issue, but Radd et al. (2021) emphasize that the construct of inequity operates across historical, structural, and institutional dimensions, as well as spanning individual and interpersonal dimensions, depending upon the context. It would not be a theoretical leap, then, to imagine linking individuals' experiences of complex trauma or "compounded trauma" to a collective "identity of trauma" that influences and is influenced by multiple ecologies. In turn, this would require a paradigm shift, from focusing therapeutic interventions solely upon individuals to focusing interventions on the collective identity of trauma expressed in the community. This shift ultimately would direct the primary intentionality of interventions toward a more inclusive or expansive environment, engaging in a kind of *cultural therapeutics* (e.g., Romanyshyn, 2001).

Trauma-Affected Community: A Working Framework

As previously inferred in this chapter, many people are affected personally by the trauma that occurs within their communities and neighborhoods. We have proposed the following structure for understanding a trauma-affected community:

> A framework [is] used to illuminate the complex web of variables present in the environment that can influence identity and worldview formation founded on layers of victimization that exist in an individual and community context and that can be passed down through generations. This framework posits that community meaning-making has been influenced by multidimensional layering of traumas, which act as a conduit to the construction of a community and individual narrative based on negative views of the self and community, including lack of agency, "vacant esteem" (DeGruy, 2005), anger, isolation, and fragmented families and communities (Abernathy et al., 2019, p. 249).

The framework makes explicit the lived experience of traumas, as well as the ensuing meaning-making that emerges, within the context of the community. Such scaffolding illuminates the complex interwoven web of systemic issues and variables that may influence disparities in behavioral health treatment, urban/rural (re)development, and the overall well-being of the community. This framework highlights both the individual and collective experience of "suffering," which has the potential to influence negative meaning-making processes in the self, family, and ultimately in the community.

The framework highlights the centrality of the *culture*. The context for culture used in this framework alludes not only to the experiences of many in the African American community, but a community culture affected by multidimensional layering of traumas. These layers of traumas are interrelated between the individual and community as a shared experience and expression of each. Included in these layers of traumas are types of trauma, lived experiences, meaning-making, ACEs, social determinants, and the residuals from transgenerational or historical trauma. Community trauma, in this context, is not only a singular event or web of multiple events; community trauma can be conceptualized as a continuum of lived experiences of the past and present, which then informs current and future beliefs about one's potential and identity formation. An example of this would be DeGruy's (2005) PTSS. A participant from Walsh's (2015) study stated that "we are born into trauma, we die in trauma, and we live our lives in trauma . . . there is not an answer." The community's worldview has been influenced by the multidimensional layering of traumas, which can act as a conduit to the construction of a narrative that is based on negative views of the self. These negative views, as articulated in the prior definition of the framework, include the lack of agency, "vacant esteem" (DeGruy, 2005), anger, and fragmented families and communities. Ultimately, a trauma-affected community has an impact on the psychological and physical well-being of the individual and the community.

Walsh's (2015) study has suggested that the term "community trauma" does not fully capture the multidimensionality of trauma experiences in a trauma-affected community, which can influence not only the individual's subjective meaning (i.e., identity formation), but the community's as well. The term "community trauma" often has highlighted what is noticeable to the observer, such as chronic violence; however, it has not made explicit what are the more implicit pervasive experiences of many residents in a trauma-affected community. The framework, which has emerged from Walsh's inquiry, illuminates the complex web of variables present in the environment that can influence a worldview and identity formation founded on layers of victimization that exist on both individual and community levels and are passed down through generations.

Walsh's (2015) research findings have elucidated the connection between types of interpersonal traumas and environmental factors that have led to the idea of a "trauma-affected community" as described through the lived experience of key stakeholders. Walsh hypothesized that, due to the collective and overt nature of multiple types of traumas experienced across the life-span, capturing the lived experience of trauma in the Hill District was more fully understood from a community context. Individuals are "nested" within multiple ecologies, and if the social context does not provide access to essential resources for physiological and psychological needs, including safety and security, it can affect growth as well as the motivation for individuals to reach their full potential or to self-actualize (Lynch & Cicchetti, 1998; Maslow et al., 1970; Ryan & Deci, 2000). In low-resourced urban and rural environments, the lack of access to these essential resources or needs, mixed with the residuals from historical trauma, can contribute to the layering effect of traumas, resulting in a "collective traumatization" (Horowitz et al., 1995), or, more fully articulated, the idea of a trauma-affected community.

TRAUMA-INFORMED COMMUNITY DEVELOPMENT

The need for TICD emerged as a salient result in Walsh's (2015) community-based study in the Hill District. To mitigate the effects of trauma and to promote healing and recovery in trauma-affected communities, the construct of TICD was formalized, and the TICD model was constructed and assessed, as a part of the work of the NRP. The TICD framework uniquely combines five interrelated areas to produce a bio-behavioral change at the micro-community level. These five areas are comprised of the following: (a) bio-behavioral health community organizing; (b) community trauma and associated communal effects, which are distinct from the existing notion of trauma as an individually experienced phenomenon; (c) research strategies that prioritize the indigenous knowledge; (d) social, economic, cultural, and political capital building; and (e) micro-community as the primary unit of change and analysis, which is a new frame within community development research. Details about the TICD model are presented in Box 19.2.

BOX 19.2

Case Illustration From the Field: Trauma-Informed Community Development

Within a year of the first consultative workshop, the essential ingredients were put together to create the TICD framework. Through the direction of the Reverend Paul Abernathy, CEO of NRP, there were six major points that guided the development of TICD from the original

(continued)

research: (a) The plan uses a community-driven behavior health method, employing a holistic approach to well-being; (b) a medical safety net had already been provided through NRP's Free Health Center in the community, which addresses access issues; (c) NRP, as necessary, may act as a "proxy agency" (Bandura, 2001), thus providing a "safe place" for narrative sharing to begin and for *consciousness raising* to occur; (d) the community can begin to build and develop healthy micro-communities by using micro-community interventions (MCI) and housing co-ops; (e) the community can employ a trauma-informed approach to promote community development and community healing; and (f) the community can identify and nurture professionals from within the community, as well as to produce local paraprofessionals, in order to implement the strategy in culturally appropriate and culturally sensitive ways. TICD addresses stigma, chronic community violence, racism, negative social determinants, and transgenerational and historical trauma, as well as identifying and building upon existing protective factors and constructing new protective factors as needed. TICD redefines urban (re)development from viewing development as purely "brick and mortar" to an investment in "human development" (Abernathy et al., 2019).

As the community began to embrace the TICD model, critical community-based needs became more apparent and better defined. Walsh's (2015) original research continued, serving as a catalyst for ongoing monitoring and evaluation of services. The theoretical basis for TICD expanded, additional human resources developed to address community needs, and a major intervention evolved in order to further assess and meet community needs. These are discussed, briefly, in the subsections that follow.

Three Pillars of Trauma-Informed Community Development

The TICD framework states the following: "As informed by the lived experience of trauma, both personal and collective, TICD establishes and promotes resilient, healing communities so that people can be healthy enough to sustain opportunity and realize their potential" (Abernathy et al., 2019, p. 3). There are three pillars that have evolved over the last several years as the TICD framework has been refined: (a) community support, (b) health and well-being, and (c) leadership development. Many functions of the TICD framework brace these three pillars, but much of the work reinforcing the three pillars is carried out by the activity of the behavior health community organizers and within the scope of the micro-community interventions; these are detailed in the text that follows.

Behavior Health Community Organizer

For this strategy to be authentically community driven, the behavior health community organizers (BHCOs) needed to be selected from the local community—in this case, the Hill District. Key stakeholders reported that professionals and paraprofessionals needed to be able to "talk the talk and walk the walk," building rapport on the "streets." This would help to ensure that community members do not feel they are merely a part of another academic study, but rather that they are being offered authentic care and support. In addition, a BHCO who is from the neighborhood would build *trust* and improve *buy in* from the community. NRP and university partners worked with key stakeholders to develop a training program for the BHCO. The BHCO program has fostered community building, along with a sense of healing and recovery, and also has assisted in building micro-communities that have an understanding of health and well-being. The second component of the BHCO program has facilitated the establishment of micro-communities through block interventions or MCI.

Micro-Community Intervention

The BHCO serves as the organizer for the block interventions. The MCI aims to establish healthy micro-communities as a first step in defragmenting and reconnecting community members. MCIs employ a 10-step strength-based approach, focusing on human development. Some aspects of MCI include leadership development, well-being planning, place making, and reconnecting person and the community.

TICD seeks to redefine urban and rural community development by incorporating a trauma-informed approach. In the event of rural development in a trauma-affected community, the TICD framework is still applicable, as the MCI can pertain to a city block or a 30 square mile radius. The unit of measure is defined by the community utilizing the TICD framework. Urban communities with similar social and environmental characteristics as the Hill District are at risk for urban (re)development that is based solely on brick-and-mortar improvements. Traditional urban redevelopment often can lead to gentrification or re-gentrification of the neighborhood (Lees, 2008), rather than investing in human development and in healing trauma-affected communities. TICD is a community-driven approach to development and has the potential to heal the residual scars of historical traumas, reduce behavior health disparities in low-resourced populations, and build resilience.

CONCLUSION

In this chapter, we have explored the lived experience of community trauma from a cultural historical context. Historical trauma theory provides an understanding of *how* and *why* certain populations have a greater likelihood of disease and other disparities (Office of Disease Prevention and Health Promotion, 2020). Historical trauma theory traces the psychological and emotional consequences of a preceding oppressed or subjugated population's transmission to subsequent generations through bioecological pathways that can result in intergenerational trauma symptomology. We have explored the impact that psychosocial trauma can have developmentally (e.g., ACEs) as well as the role of attachment as a mitigating or aggravating factor (i.e., complex trauma). We have laid out a trauma-affected framework that expands upon the idea of community trauma to provide a fuller articulation of the elusive and layering nature of community trauma. Finally, we have offered a notable case study of a culturally sensitive community-based intervention, as inaugurated by the *Neighborhood Resilience Project*. TICD is a cultural therapeutic that targets the risk factors associated with trauma-affected communities, while at the same time strengthening protective factors at the individual and community levels, thereby influencing community resilience. We have concluded by offering a online list of practice-based resources.

ADDITIONAL RESOURCES

 SPRINGER PUBLISHING CONNECT™

A robust set of instructor resources designed to supplement this text is located at http://connect.springerpub.com/content/book/978-0-8261-5085-1. Qualifying instructors may request access by emailing textbook@springerpub.com.

PRACTICE-BASED RESOURCES AND REFERENCES

To view a list of resources and all the references, please visit connect.springerpub.com via the following url: http://connect.springerpub.com/content/book/978-0-8261-5085-1/part/part04/chapter/ch19

Mass Violence

KENYA JOHNS, TUMANI MALINGA, TAPOLOGO MAUNDENI, AND LISA LÓPEZ LEVERS

CHAPTER OVERVIEW

This chapter focuses on issues related to mass violence and the effects of mass violence on the populace, both in terms of proximal and distal locations of those affected. The increase of mass violence has caused global concern. The effects of mass violence events continue to traumatize those who are affected. This chapter offers insight to help understand the impacts of mass violence on survivors, families, communities, and society.

LEARNING OBJECTIVES

After reading this chapter, the reader should be able to:

1. Define mass violence;
2. Develop awareness about the prevalence of mass violence;
3. Identify specific types of mass violence;
4. Understand the kinds of traumatic responses that people may have in the face of a mass violence event; and,
5. Identify interventions that can help to support those who have experienced mass violence.

INTRODUCTION

Throughout history, there have been different rulers, kingdoms, dynasties, religious beliefs, and ways of living. Dating back to prehistoric times, there has been one constant that has linked all of these periods of history, times which have included Homo sapiens—better known as human beings—and that constant is violence. Humans have acted violently throughout history for various reasons; humans have used violence as a way to achieve power, to acquire wealth, to obtain leadership status, to assert dominance, and even as a form of protest. Although this list is not exhaustive, it illustrates how various societal mechanisms, throughout history, have perpetuated violence. Whether or not the calls for violence have been warranted, human acts of aggression have permutated in ways that sometimes seem to amplify violence, almost as if it were a language that has been a chosen form of expression for human beings.

Although humanity's history of violence spans eons, it was not until the early 20th century that we began to examine the impact of trauma on physical and emotional development, on culture in general, on our views about others, and even on the planet Earth. Violence is not a new problem; however, there is a growing concern regarding the prevalence of violence that has manifested throughout the last century and into the present (Gerlach, 2010; Savelsberg, 2015). With the development of man-made tools, such as guns, bombs, weapons of mass destruction, poisons, and so forth, there has been an increase in mass violence. This chapter explores the definition of mass violence, the prevalence of mass violence, the traumatic responses experienced after a mass violence event, and ways to support those who have experienced mass violence.

DEFINING MASS VIOLENCE

Mass violence is a term that encompasses a wide range of violent acts and events but that, at surface, gives no indication about the cause of or the motive to commit the violence (Adesola & Anyaduba, 2017; Cilliers, 2018; Parks et al., 2019). Gerlach (2006, 2010) argues that mass violence arises from complex processes within the society, stating that mass violence is "widespread violence against non-combatants, that is, outside of immediate fighting between military or paramilitary personnel, but reaching beyond mass killings" (Gerlach, 2006, p. 455). The Office for Victims of Crime and the American Red Cross offer the following definition of an act of mass violence: "an intentional violent crime . . . that results in physical, emotional, or psychological injury to a sufficiently large number of people and significantly increases the burden of victim assistance and compensation for the responding jurisdiction" (as cited in Substance Abuse and Mental Health Services Administration [SAMHSA], 2017, p. 3).

The World Health Assembly declared, in 1996, that violence is a major public health issue (Krug, Mercy et al., 2002). The World Health Organization (WHO) views violence as a universal challenge. The WHO further defines violence as the "intentional use of physical force or power, threatened or actual, against oneself, another person, or against a group or community, that either results in or has a high likelihood of resulting in injury, death, psychological harm, maldevelopment or deprivation" (WHO, 1996, cited in Krug, Mercy et al., 2002, p. 5). In the Foreword to the *World Report on Violence and Health* (Krug, Dahlberg et al., 2002), Mr. Nelson Mandela stated the following:

> The twentieth century will be remembered as a century marked by violence. It burdens us with its legacy of mass destruction, of violence inflicted on a scale never seen and never possible before in human history . . . the result of new technology in the service of ideologies of hate. ("Foreword," p. 1)

For many people, the thought of a mass violence event was once a foreign concept; however, there appears to be a shift or change in the ways that we think about and receive news regarding mass violence events. With mass violence events occurring more frequently, what once felt like an improbable occurrence now feels more plausible. In some ways, it almost seems as if a numbing process has taken hold; we feel "shocked" by each incident, but somehow we no longer seem "surprised." Use the self-reflection exercise in Box 20.1 to examine your suppositions.

BOX 20.1

Self-Reflection Exercise

When you think of mass violence, what do you think of? Take a minute to reflect on your own thoughts regarding mass violence:

- Did you become anxious?
- Did it have an impact on you (or not)?
- What kind of an impact?

Krug, Mercy et al. (2002) indicate that violence is the leading cause of death worldwide, claiming millions of victims annually. As previously indicated, violence that is committed by an individual or group of individuals, that is deliberate, and that happens across a large group or collective of people has come to be known as "mass violence." Garbarini and Adjemian (2015) argue that we can conceptualize mass violence in the following way:

> [as] a catch-all term referring to a host of crimes typically perpetrated in conjunction with one another, including murder, rape, torture, the brutal consequences of forced population transfer and resettlement, committed against non-state actors by a state or by a more-or-less organized group of other non-state actors. (p. 15)

Mass violence events also are defined as violent crimes that are committed with the intentional purpose of causing emotional, psychological, or physical harm to a large group of people. In this chapter, we use this definition of mass violence, with an emphasis on the public health concerns associated with mass violence. For the purpose of this chapter, we have reviewed the prevalence and impact of mass violence within the workplace, institutional settings, and university and campuses. This chapter illuminates the importance of developing a disaster plan and the implications for the counseling profession.

PREVALENCE AND IMPACT OF MASS VIOLENCE

Mass violence can happen anywhere and at any time. Within the last century, mass violence in public settings has occurred at an alarming rate; for example, the Gun Violence Archive (2021) has reported 109 mass shootings between January 1 and March 27, 2021. Figure 20.1 provides a

Figure 20.1

FBI: Quick Look

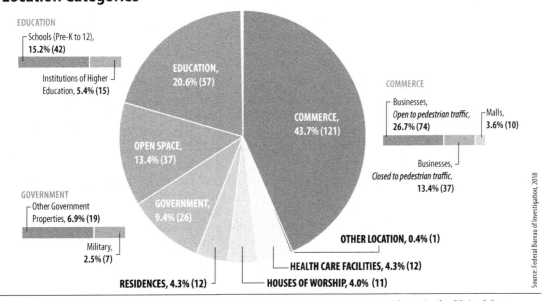

Quick Look: 277 Active Shooter Incidents in the United States Between 2000–2018
Location Categories

EDUCATION
Schools (Pre-K to 12), **15.2% (42)**
Institutions of Higher Education, **5.4% (15)**

EDUCATION, **20.6% (57)**

COMMERCE, **43.7% (121)**

COMMERCE
Businesses, *Open to pedestrian traffic,* **26.7% (74)** — Malls, **3.6% (10)**
Businesses, *Closed to pedestrian traffic,* **13.4% (37)**

OPEN SPACE, **13.4% (37)**

GOVERNMENT, **9.4% (26)**

GOVERNMENT
Other Government Properties, **6.9% (19)**
Military, **2.5% (7)**

OTHER LOCATION, **0.4% (1)**

HEALTH CARE FACILITIES, **4.3% (12)**

HOUSES OF WORSHIP, **4.0% (11)**

RESIDENCES, **4.3% (12)**

Source: Federal Bureau of Investigation, 2018

Source: Federal Bureau of Investigation. (2018). Quick look: 277 active shooter incidents in the United States from 2000 to 2018. U.S. Department of Justice. https://www.fbi.gov/about/partnerships/office-of-partner-engagement/active-shooter-incidents-graphic

breakdown of the mass violence events that have occurred in the United States of America between 2000 and 2018 (Federal Bureau of Investigation [FBI], 2018). Mass violence can emerge in the workplace, in institutional settings, at colleges and universities, and in public venues such as churches, bars, nightclubs, concert arenas, and malls. Although this list is not extensive, it provides some context for the prevalence of mass violence. Mass violence can happen anywhere, but it is preventable. In this section, we discuss the prevalence and impact of mass violence in the following subsections: Work Stress and Workplace Violence, Mass Violence in Institutional Settings, Mass Violence at Universities and Campus Shootings, Known Characteristics of a Mass Violence Perpetrator, and The Necessity of Having a Disaster Plan.

Work Stress and Workplace Violence

Engaging in a job and working is an essential part of life for most people. Working provides the financial security needed to sustain a viable living. Although working is essential and necessary for financial stability, it also can be stressful. If a person works 40 hours a week or more, the majority of the individual's time is spent at work. The amount of time devoted to work can create an imbalance of time in a person's life, particularly pertaining to other important and necessary aspects of living, thus causing increased stress. Due to the nature of the work, all varieties of workers may experience a myriad of emotions and reactions, which may lead to differing levels of stress.

Stress in the workplace is common. In fact, according to the results of stress-related research conducted by ComPsych (2019), most stressors experienced by American adults arise from workplace stress. For a large number of employees (61%), stress levels are high enough to cause them to feel fatigued and not in control (ComPsych, 2019). Key findings of the research indicate that 20% of workers miss more than 6 days of work annually, due to stress, and that 36% of employees identify "people problems" as causing the most stress at work (ComPsych, 2019). ComPsych's yearly surveys indicate that workplace stress varies for each individual. Workplace stress tends not to end at the completion of the workday, but rather to encroach into other areas of the worker's life. In other words, workplace stress can affect one's personal life as well as one's professional life. Workplace stress that is cumulative and not managed effectively can lead to workplace violence— not necessarily, but given the right combination of personal and environmental stressors, along with idiosyncratic characteristics and life circumstances of a particular individual, it might.

With workers experiencing an increase of stress within the workplace, the risk rises for the occurrence of violence. Workplace violence constitutes a physical, psychological, or emotional assault on a person that, in turn, causes mental or physical harm either intentionally or unintentionally. The Occupational Safety and Health Administration (OSHA, 2019) reported that more than two million workers a year experience workplace violence. Turner (2020) identifies four types of workplace violence. Type 1 is *criminal intent*. Criminal intent typically implies that someone who has no relationship with the business, or any of that business's employees, commits the act of violence; acts of terrorism and crime also belong in this category. An example of this is the 9/11 terrorist attacks, in which the terrorists hijacked the planes in order to commit other crimes. Type 2 involves the *customer/client*, in which a patron of the workplace commits the violent act. An example of the customer/client type is if a client attacks a counselor during a session. Type 3 is *worker on worker*, in which an employee is threatened, harassed, or physically harmed in the workplace by a past or present employee. For example, an ex-police officer, Christopher Dorner, was fired from his job and went back later to commit acts of violence against other police officers (Kelly, 2013). Type 4 is a *personal relationship*, in which the perpetrator has an association with an employee at the workplace and not the business. An example of this is the November 2018 Mercy Hospital shooting in Chicago, Illinois, in which a man murdered his ex-fiancée and two other people, who all worked at the hospital.

For the purpose of this section, we emphasize type 3, worker-on-worker workplace violence. This form of violence often is linked to workplace stress. Unbalanced workplace stress can lead to the development of poor social interactions, poor negative relationships with peers, poor production in work, poor mental and physical health, and poor personal relationship outcomes.

Not treating workplace stress can compound underlying stress that then can lead to poor work productivity, animosity, anxiety, depression, and even death (Murray et al., 2020). Although there is a need for more research regarding the correlation between workplace stress and mass violence, it is important to monitor it and to be cognizant of the effects of workplace stress on employees, in order to help prevent mass violence events within the workplace.

Mass Violence in Institutional Settings

Violence in institutional settings continues to grow (e.g., Cohen et al., 2014). At surface, this has some overlap with the previous section, in that an institution is a work setting for those who work there. Yet we discuss these institutional settings, here, as having the characteristic of being public or semi-public spaces (Parks et al., 2019), which serve distinct functions, and in which people are not expecting to experience violence while conducting routine activities, for example, shopping at a grocery store, attending a religious service, and listening to music at a concert. We report on several specific incidents in this section, all mass shootings and all relatively recent.

Harvest Music Festival, Las Vegas, Nevada (10/1/2017)

The Harvest Music Festival was one of the deadliest shootings in modern American history. The tragic event left 58 people murdered and more than 850 more injured. The event occurred during a country music festival on the Las Vegas, Nevada strip. The shooting occurred from a high-rise hotel by a lone assailant. This event catapulted fears from many regarding the increasing risk of being involved in a mass shooting. The criminal investigation was unable to identify a motive for this event, leaving many unanswered questions.

Tree of Life Synagogue, Pittsburgh, Pennsylvania (10/27/2018)

The Tree of Life Synagogue massacre was one of the deadliest mass shootings within the Jewish community in American history. The shooting left 11 people dead and six people wounded. The mass shooting occurred at a Jewish synagogue where members were preparing for a baby-naming ceremony. The mass shooting was completed by one individual, who was captured and charged with the murders. After law enforcement officials completed their investigation, it was determined that the mass shooting was inspired by hatred and was classified as a hate crime.

Christchurch, New Zealand Mosque Shootings (3/15/2019)

The Christchurch shooting occurred at two separate mosques in New Zealand, the Al Noor Mosque and the Linwood Islamic Centre. The murders left 51 killed and 40 injured. The initial event was live streamed on the Facebook platform, leaving the world to see this horrific event. The shooter was a lone assailant, who was linked to an alt-right hate group. The assailant was captured and sentenced to life in prison. This event added to the growing fear of safety while worshipping.

JC Kosher Supermarket, Jersey City, New Jersey (12/20/2019)

The JC Kosher Supermarket shooting occurred in Jersey City, New Jersey. The mass shooting left five people dead. Two assailants, who carried out the shooting, were killed during the mass shooting event. Because the shooting occurred at a kosher grocery store, it was investigated as a hate crime.

Multiple Spa Shootings, Atlanta, Georgia (3/16/2021)

On March 16, 2021, a series of mass shootings, which targeted the Asian American population, occurred in Atlanta, Georgia. The mass shootings took place at three separate spas in Atlanta, leaving eight people dead and one other person wounded. At the time of this book being written, it is inconclusive whether these heinous murders occurred as hate crimes or were due to other insidious motives of the lone assailant. At this time, the assailant was captured and charged with eight counts of murder.

King Soopers Supermarket, Boulder, Colorado (3/22/2021)

The King Soopers Supermarket shooting in Boulder, Colorado, is one of the most recent mass shootings as of the time of this writing. The King Soopers Supermarket shooting left 10 people dead and an unknown number of people physically injured. The event occurred when a lone assailant entered into a supermarket and opened fire on the patrons and on law enforcement. The investigation and motive for the shootings are still under review during the time of this chapter being written. The assailant was captured and charged with 10 counts of murder; the court procedures are ongoing.

Mass Violence at Universities and Campus Shootings

As an extension of the previous section, we continue the discussion of mass violence in an institutional setting, but in one that has some unique characteristics—that of the college campus. Unlike other types of institutional settings, in which people come and go freely and for differing reasons, in many ways universities share characteristics of both home and community. Students, and even some faculty members, live on campuses, as they would at home; similarly, while colleges are situated within a larger community, they share many aspects of a self-sufficient community.

Mass violence events may happen in any human-occupied space, including colleges and universities. In fact, we have seen a sharp rise of violence on college campuses (Voice of America, 2019). Between the years of 2010 and 2020, more than 50 mass violence events have occurred on a university or college campus worldwide (The Violence Project., 2020). Shahid and Duzor (2019) have reported the following:

> On the morning of Aug. 1, 1966, Charles Whitman, a former Marine, stepped out on the observation deck of the University of Texas Tower and aimed his Remington bolt-action rifle at his first victims on the campus below. More than an hour after the shooting began, 15 people were dead and 31 injured. Among those was Claire Wilson, the first target, who was shot in the stomach. Wilson, who was eight months pregnant at the time, lost her unborn child and spent several months recovering in the hospital. The massacre . . . wasn't the first mass shooting in modern U.S. history. But at the time, it was the deadliest, and marked a turning point in public awareness of mass shootings and shooters in the era of mass media.

The infamous Virginia Tech shooting, which unfortunately claimed the lives of 33 victims, including that of the perpetrator, was the deadliest college campus shooting in modern history. Seung-Hui Cho entered a residence hall on the campus of the Virginia Polytechnic University on the morning of April 16, 2007, where he shot and killed two students. Several hours later, Cho chained the doors of a classroom building and then opened fire on students and faculty members who were attending classes. By the end of that morning, 33 people were dead and another 17 were injured (Virginia Tech Review Panel, 2007). Since 2007, we have witnessed a surge in college and university campus shootings.

A recent campus shooting occurred at the University of North Carolina at Charlotte (Peterson & Densley, 2019) on April 30, 2019. The shooting originally left two people dead and four people injured. Although this latest school shooting is not technically a mass shooting, the event adds to the growing concern about mass shootings in public places. This shooting led to the arrest and conviction of the lone assailant. The assailant was sentenced to life imprisoned without the possibility of parole.

Although the prevalence of shootings at colleges and universities has increased in the last two decades, there is still a low probability that someone attending these institutions will be involved in a mass violence event. For a myriad of reasons, it is less likely for a mass violence event to occur on college and university campuses. One salient reason that this is less likely to happen is due to the policy frameworks at each institution. With the rise of campus shootings, there have been changes in policy on college campuses regarding firearm safety and monitoring on campuses. In addition, there has been more awareness across campuses, which has resulted in more people addressing their concerns to law enforcement to investigate. Also, these institutions have begun to create *disaster plans* in the event that a mass violence event does occur (Peterson et al., 2015; Weber et al., 2018).

Known Characteristics of a Mass Violence Perpetrator

Understandably, when an incident of mass violence occurs, widespread media coverage underscores the enormity of such events (Wormwood et al., 2019). Yet the incidents of mass violence remain relatively rare (Duwe, 2020). Because incidents are relatively rare, the need remains for collecting additional empirical evidence about the perpetrators of mass violence. The following common factors are identified in an American Psychiatric Association publication:

> Factors common among individuals who commit mass murder include extreme feelings of anger and revenge, the lack of an accomplice (when the perpetrator is an adult), feelings of social alienation, and planning well in advance of the offense. Many mass murderers do not plan to survive their own attacks and intend to commit suicide or to be killed by police after committing their assaults. However, in a detailed case study of five mass murderers who did survive, a number of common traits and historical factors were found. The subjects had all been bullied or isolated during childhood and subsequently became loners who felt despair over their social alienation. They demonstrated paranoid traits such as suspiciousness and grudge holding. Their worldview suggested a paranoid mindset; they believed others to be generally rejecting and uncaring. As a result, they spent a great deal of time feeling resentful and ruminating on past humiliations. The ruminations subsequently evolved into fantasies of violent revenge. (Knoll & Annas, 2016, pp. 84–85)

Perpetrators of mass violence certainly use multiple means to carry out their plans, but incidents of mass violence more typically involve guns (Peterson & Densley, 2019; Shahid & Duzor, 2019; The Violence Project. 2020; Voice of America [VOA], 2019). For this reason, we focus the discussion in the remaining part of this subsection on the known characteristics of mass shooters; this is emergent information, and thereby not intended to suggest the existence of a profile—as inferred previously, we do not yet have enough research-based information to formulate a definite perpetrator profile. Unfortunately, a prevalent stereotype of mass shooters as having a mental illness mischaracterizes and obscures the larger picture; a strong and enduring societal stereotype linking violence and mental illness simply is not supported by evidence (Levers, 2001). While some mass shooters may have a history of mental health issues, mental illness is not a singular causation (Shahid & Duzor, 2019). In the previously cited American Psychiatric Association publication, Knoll and Annas (2016) identify common misperceptions and evidence-based facts regarding mass shootings and mental illness. These are presented in Box 20.2.

BOX 20.2

From the Field

Common Misperceptions

- Mass shootings by people with serious mental illness represent the most significant relationship between gun violence and mental illness.

(continued)

- People with serious mental illness should be considered dangerous.
- Gun laws focusing on people with mental illness or with a psychiatric diagnosis can effectively prevent mass shootings.
- Gun laws focusing on people with mental illness or a psychiatric diagnosis are reasonable, even if they add to the stigma already associated with mental illness.

Evidence-Based Facts

- Mass shootings by people with serious mental illness represent less than 1% of all yearly gun-related homicides. In contrast, deaths by suicide using firearms account for the majority of yearly gun-related deaths.
- The overall contribution of people with serious mental illness to violent crimes is only about 3%. When these crimes are examined in detail, an even smaller percentage of them are found to involve firearms.
- Laws intended to reduce gun violence that focus on a population representing less than 3% of all gun violence will be extremely low yield, ineffective, and wasteful of scarce resources. Perpetrators of mass shootings are unlikely to have a history of involuntary psychiatric hospitalization. Thus, databases intended to restrict access to guns and established by guns laws that broadly target people with mental illness will not capture this group of individuals.
- Gun restriction laws focusing on people with mental illness perpetuate the myth that mental illness leads to violence, as well as the misperception that gun violence and mental illness are strongly linked. Stigma represents a major barrier to access and treatment of mental illness, which in turn increases the public health burden. (Knoll & Annas, 2016, pp. 81–82)

Once we deconstruct the myths and stereotypes that long have been associated with psychiatric disability and focus on facts and evidence, we begin to see some common characteristics that mass shooters seem to possess. According to The Violence Project (2020), most mass shooters have the following four characteristics in common:

- Early childhood trauma and exposure to violence at a young age
- An identifiable grievance or crisis point
- Have studied the actions of past shooters and seek validation for their methods and motives
- The means to carry out an attack (cited in Shahid & Duzor, 2019, "Mass Shooters (1966–2019)," p. 3)

It would seem that violence prevention and abatement programming, aimed at ending the various cycles of violence in our society, would be far more efficacious and fiscally responsible than continuing to support false narratives about mental illness being the cause of gun violence.

The Necessity of Having a Disaster Plan

Disaster plans are strategic frameworks designed to reduce the harmful and negative effects that occur when a mass violence event happens. Disaster plans represent action-based measures that aim to prevent or mitigate further harm; these practices serve as an action plan that can be carried out logically by first responders and other helpers called to the scene. Having a disaster plan in place helps to provide employees and staff with a blueprint for what to do if they are in a difficult and scary situation, such as a mass violence event. When a person is in a situation marked by high stress and fear, the disaster plan aids the individual in feeling more prepared; a well-crafted disaster plan also increases the likelihood of survival. Additionally, it provides a safe way to account for and locate all of the individuals who may be at risk. While all institutions' disaster plans are unique to their specific environments, the majority of plans include having an exit strategy, a rendezvous place, and a form of communication.

Previously, disaster plans focused on individuals waiting for law enforcement to arrive and to help them out of the situation; however, research has shown this to be ineffective (Federal Emergency Management Agency [FEMA], 2015). Disaster plans include getting out of the dangerous environment and to a safe location as soon as possible; a strong emphasis is rapid mobilization and movement to safety, and not waiting to do so. Having a disaster plan is essential.

TRAUMATIC RESPONSES AFTER A MASS VIOLENCE EVENT

The importance of deploying appropriate response mechanisms as immediately as possible, in the face of a mass violence event, cannot be overstated. During, immediately after, and in the hours and days that follow a mass violence event, effective professional interventions are imperative and can make the difference between a survivor's ability to cope and recover, versus reacting with continued anxiety and creating a greater potential for PTSD. This section focuses on the importance of post-violence debriefing along with the aftermath experiences of those most affected by the violence.

Post-Violence Debriefing

A critical need exists for conducting a post-violence debriefing after a mass shooting occurs. The post-violence debriefing helps to alert the public and law enforcement officials about what has occurred and how the shooting has been resolved. Reporting the accuracy of the mass shooting is integral to addressing the community and families that have been affected by the mass shooting. Debriefing helps by providing a sense of safety to communities and by decreasing the anxiety that people may be experiencing. Debriefing also provides an opportunity to develop a working alliance between law enforcement and citizens.

It is important to note that a post-violence debriefing should be conducted through multiple streams of communication, including text messaging, radio, TV broadcast, social media platforms, and all other available communications, in order to reach the most citizens. The debriefing should include ways to support those who have been affected by the mass shooting and those who are working to support the people affected. Research has found that the most useful debriefing strategies occur when support is provided within the first 24 to 72 hours after the event. The longer a person goes without support, the less likely it is that an intervention can be effective in minimizing long-term effects. Various ways to support those affected are discussed later in this chapter.

When developing a post-violence debriefing, it is important to use already-established community supports. Collaborating with known and familiar community agencies helps to increase recovery and to build resilience. Post-violence debriefing is a collaborative process that should make use of all of the available resources in the community.

Aftermath of Mass Violence

Mass violence affects individuals, families, communities, institutions, nations, and, given the preponderance of media and social media, the world. The impact of mass violence is felt not only by the individuals who suffer severe pain and loss of body parts or even loss of life, but also by other systems in the ecology within which the individuals interact. During the aftermath of mass violence, the plethora of situation-specific actors include the survivors, their family members, peers, those who witnessed the violence unfolding, the first responders, and hospital staff members dealing with injuries and casualties. Exposure to mass violence might result in anxiety, trauma, depression, and a variety of other mental health symptoms and disorders (de Zulueta, 2007; Murthy, 2007). Thompson et al. (2019) highlight the point that even excessive media exposure to mass violence can cause extreme distress among the viewers/consumers of news.

Mass violence exposes survivors and witnesses to psychologically traumatic events in ways that might disrupt their capacity to share the experience (Gobodo-Madikizela et al., 2014). Langer (1991) reports that traumatic experiences might take on a sense of timelessness, and that they can be relieved in various ways. The traumatic experiences, to which individuals and communities are exposed, may be worsened by the physical, social, and psychological strains of situations involving mass violence (Frazer et al., 2017; Hobfoll et al., 2007) along with the destruction of resources, services, and support which can deprive them of the needed support to cope with the trauma (Hobfoll, 1998). Furthermore, people may be affected by the lack of safety within the area where the mass violence occurred as well as by the loss of a sense of meaning (Hobfoll et al., 2007). The case of Jadyn, presented in Box 20.3, offers an example of how someone may be affected by mass violence.

BOX 20.3

Clinical Vignette: The Case of Jadyn

The client, Jadyn, is a 23-year-old African American male from Chicago, Illinois, who presented for treatment after surviving a mass shooting in the southside of Chicago. The mass shooting event happened while Jadyn was working at a local restaurant. The mass shooting occurred when two assailants with AR-15's drove down the busy street, opening fire on the patrons of the restaurant. The shooting left six people dead and four others injured, including Jadyn's best friend. Although Jadyn was not physically injured during the mass shooting, he expressed excessive worry and anxiety associated with thoughts about the shooting. He reported having nightmares that have caused him to lose sleep. He also has developed anxiety attacks when entering public spaces. He expressed feeling paranoid when leaving his house but also feeling alone due to not engaging with peers anymore.

Reflection Questions:

- What is the client experiencing?
- How has the client's traumatic experiences shaped his thinking?
- What would you do to support the client in recovery?

Because mass violence is unpredictable, survivors feel emotionally distressed; they might present with complaints like anxiety and trouble sleeping, among others, and the distress may be acted out in anger, fear, resentment, and aggression. Such symptoms might manifest weeks or months after the mass violence event occurs. As mass violence is a collectively experienced pain, the suffering and trauma that comes with it might be a barrier to cultural and communal bonds (Gobodo-Madikizela et al., 2014). It is therefore critical that victims and survivors develop some narratives around it, in order "to reconstruct a shattered self, find a voice, reclaim a sense of agency, and construct meaning from traumatic experience" (Gobodo-Madikizela et al., 2014, p. 86).

SUPPORTING THOSE WHO HAVE EXPERIENCED MASS VIOLENCE

Due to the psychological, social, emotional, and physical pain and suffering that mass violence inflicts upon families and communities, there is a need for early psychological intervention to respond to the traumatic event. Early intervention is defined as "any form of psychological intervention delivered within the first four weeks following a major incident or disaster" (Ritchie, 2003, p. 44). Ritchie further argues that the timing and the type of intervention necessitate consideration of several factors, such as:

- The type of event;
- The population affected, including family members, peers, and first responders;
- The environment of the recovery efforts; and,
- The actuality of whether responders are locals or from outside of the affected area.

There is also a need to consider the ways in which some groups will be more vulnerable than other groups. These include wounded victims and those who have lost loved ones in mass violence incidents, and those with psychiatric disorders, as their symptoms might become elevated in response to the mass violence event (Ritchie, 2003). In addition, Dyregrov and Regel (2012) suggest that guidelines need to be followed, in order to ensure that help is tailored to the individuals, families, and groups to whom professionals reach out. Dyregrov (2003) identified the following principles for responding to mass violence: immediacy, proximity, use of expectancy, and flexibility. Response to any mass violence crisis should be timely to the event and to the people affected. Dyregrov (2003) further indicates that several important factors be considered:

- Magnitude of the event: Mass-scale situations, disaster, terrorism or war versus one person event
- Duration of event: Single-event trauma versus cumulative trauma, exposure time
- Type of event: Accident, violence, death, other loss
- Type of exposure: survivor of direct life-threat, bystander, family member, helper, and so forth
- Place of exposure: home, work, street
- Immediate reactions and recovery environment
- Cause: human or natural
- Resources available to help
- Personality, personal history, cultural background, training, resources and social network
- Expressed need for assistance (Dyregrov, 2003, p. 18).

Based upon a scoping review of the relevant research literature, Richins et al. (2020) concluded that early interventions also "support emergency responders following exposure to trauma when these are tailored to the needs of the population, are supported by the host organization, and harness existing social cohesion and peer support processes within a team or unit" (p. 1). Richins et al. (2020) also emphasized the importance of evaluation of early interventions, along with the delivery of emergency response services. In the remaining parts of this section, we offer discussion about relevant neuroscience considerations, multicultural and social justice implications, trauma-informed treatment strategies, and counseling implications.

Relevant Neuroscience Considerations in Mass Violence Events

Recent research has examined the psychological impact that mass violence has on those directly and indirectly involved with the event. Research has shown that the neurological response to mass violence is person specific; however, we can assume that, for most individuals facing danger, the autonomic nervous system (ANS) will engage, with a fight-or-flight response likely. Fear is a strong motivator, and in the event of experiencing and witnessing mass violence, all of the neurobiological mechanisms described in Chapter 2 of this textbook are likely to be engaged. With the ANS engaged, the affected person's body, in a state of hyper arousal, may experience the release of glucose, rapid heartbeat, increased breathing due to lung dilation, increased blood pressure, increased alertness and sharper senses (due to more oxygen sent to the brain), muscular tension, increased perspiration, and a decrease in digestive activity. This sympathetic nervous system activity makes a fight-or-flight response more probable, and in the panic of trying to remove oneself from danger, the frightened person may not care about shoving another person out of the way. Conversely, if parasympathetic activity is engaged, the person may shut down or collapse in fear, even fainting in response to the danger.

Any individual who perceives themselves to be in extreme danger is susceptible to a wide range of responses, including but not limited to fear, depression, anxiety, posttraumatic stress disorder (PTSD), increased risk of a substance use concern, problems with sleep, and survivor's guilt. These responses can be exacerbated, depending on the trauma exposure, pre-disaster risk factors, and post-disaster environment. SAMHSA (2017) has categorized the mental and behavioral health responses into three categories:

Acute phase: In this phase, it is critical to develop support and treatment from mental health clinicians. Psychological First Aid (PFA) is the most effective strategy during this stage. In this acute phase, survivors experience the initial stage of shock, disbelief, and denial.

Intermediate phase: This phase includes psychological distress, such as anxiety, depression, fear, inability to focus, panic, sleep disturbances, and feeling the need to retaliate. Although this stage can cause psychological distress and feel harmful, this stage is normal.

Long-term phase: This is a critical phase in which a person begins to develop positive or negative coping strategies that will have an impact on their lives, long-term. In this phase, if the negative effects are not treated, they may manifest into illness or mental health crises.

Ongoing research continues to examine the persistence of mass violence events. As more longitudinal studies are conducted, more long-term impacts can be evaluated. It is important to understand that mass violence has an impact on everyone, collectively and individually. Although there may be shared experiences following a mass shooting, every person may experience these heinous acts differently, depending on a number of individual factors, including but not limited to previous exposure to violence, family history, individual resiliency, and the availability of treatment after the mass violence event.

Multicultural and Social Justice Implications of Mass Violence

It is important to acknowledge and address that mass violence events are documented differently in communities of color. One example of such differential interpretation and documentation is the "Kettling" of peaceful protesters in communities of color (Human Rights Watch, 2020). Gang violence or crimes that are committed in areas with high minority populations are not included in outcomes or treated as areas of mass violence events. In fact, among databases, there is not a clear definition regarding what constitutes a mass violence event (Booty et al., 2019), thus excluding communities that are experiencing gun violence at a disproportionate rate. It is imperative to address gun violence in communities of color, and to ensure that these communities are added to the mass violence count, in order to develop a complete understanding of the impacts that it has on all community members (Frazer et al., 2017).

In the previously cited American Psychiatric Association publication, Knoll and Annas (2016) have emphasized the importance of exploring salient sociocultural factors involved in mass shootings, not the least of which is the narcissism and entitlement often expressed by the perpetrators, both at individual and cultural levels. Knoll and Annas have suggested the following interventions:

- Policies and laws should focus on those individuals whose behaviors identify them as having increased risk for committing gun violence, rather than on broad categories such as mental illness or psychiatric diagnoses.
- Public health educational campaigns should emphasize the need for third-party reporting of intent or concerning warning behaviors to law enforcement.

▓ Institutions and communities should develop specialized forensic threat assessment teams to evaluate third-party reports of potential dangerousness.

▓ Resources should be increased to provide enhanced education, beginning in elementary school, with a focus on constructive coping skills for anger and conflict resolution, mental health, and mental wellness education. (Knoll & Annas, 2016, p. 99)

Trauma-Informed Treatment Strategies for Mass Violence Events

Mass violence continues to be explored, and treatment strategies continue to develop. For those who experience a mass violence event, the response will vary. Most survivors of mass violence events will not need additional support, beyond PFA. In fact, most survivors demonstrate resilience post-event. Early intervention outcomes should promote normal recovery, resiliency, and personal growth (Ritchie, 2003). As much as the focus is on the individual experiencing the trauma, it is critically important also to focus on the contextual component of the event (de Jong, n.d.). As illustrated by the bioecological framework, treatment or intervention can be offered at different levels, including the micro, meso, exo, and macro level systems (Bronfenbrenner, 1979, 1997; Bronfenbrenner & Morris, 1998; Bronfenbrenner et al., 1993). Involving all of the levels of the ecology ensures that all of those affected by mass violence, as well as those with whom they interact, can receive the necessary help (Frazer et al., 2017).

While most survivors develop resiliency, some may not. Further, in order to capture individual psychological vulnerability indicators, such as feeling safe in the present, being forced to move (de Jong et al., 2008), and experiencing a difficult recovery environment (Steel et al., 2009), strengths-based and somatic strategies are proposed. Similarly, Hobfoll et al. (2007) identified empirically supported intervention principles to guide and inform intervention for the survivors and witnesses of mass violence and other disasters. These include promoting the following: (a) a sense of safety, (b) calming, (c) a sense of self- and community efficacy, (d) connectedness, and (e) hope.

Another form of trauma-informed treatment is developing individualized plans that address the immediate needs of the survivor. Trauma-informed treatment focuses on addressing the traumatic event, that is, the mass violence event. PTSD treatment techniques have been found to be effective in addressing the longer-term concerns after a mass violence event. Therapy is a useful technique used to address the event, helping clients to learn skills, acknowledge the situation, and provide support. Eye Movement Desensitization and Reprocessing (EMDR) is a specialized therapeutic technique that is effective in helping to alleviate distress. For those who have severe PTSD symptoms, medication management is an option to help manage symptoms, as is acupuncture (Ding et al., 2020) and medical marijuana (Moss, 2018).

Counseling Implications for Responding to Mass Violence

Counselors play a pivotal role in addressing mass violence. Immediately following a mass violence event, counselors need to be present to assess the mental and physical needs of those involved as well as to assist the first responders. Counselors who are involved in traumatic events, such as mass violence events, should be trained in PFA. This foundational training provides insight into how to assess the situation, address the immediate needs, and be educated on the psychological impact of the event on those involved.

Counselors' assessments can help those involved in the event to navigate these experiences. Providing psychoeducation helps to increase the likelihood of a person affected by the event to develop resiliency. By offering their assistance, counselors can be among the first line of defense. Counselors help to provide effective coping strategies, consultations, support, and resources.

It is important for counselors to be aware of the impact that a mass violence event may have on their own mental health. Counselors have an ethical obligation to be cognizant of their own stress responses and the impact that this mass violence event may be having on them (Tarvydas et al., 2017). Counselors should monitor how much time they are spending at the trauma site, managing their own physical needs, such as food and rest.

CONCLUSION

Violence that is perpetrated by nongovernmental officials, and which is deliberate and happens across a large group or collective of people, is considered to be mass violence. Mass violence is a concern for us all, because it can happen anytime and anywhere. The insidious nature of mass violence is harmful, by definition. Although still rare, mass violence events have increased, exponentially, over the last century. Those who have lived through a mass violence event are at a higher risk of developing mental health concerns, such as PTSD, depression, or anxiety. Even those who have not lived through such an event personally, but have been exposed to the violence through the media, face the possibility of developing the same mental health concerns. It is important to address and to help minimize the potential for a mass violence event to occur. The goal is to not be reactive toward these atrocities, but rather to be proactive in preventing them from ever occurring.

ADDITIONAL RESOURCES

 A robust set of instructor resources designed to supplement this text is located at http://connect.springerpub.com/content/book/978-0-8261-5085-1. Qualifying instructors may request access by emailing textbook@springerpub.com.

PRACTICE-BASED RESOURCES AND REFERENCES

To view a list of resources and all the references, please visit connect.springerpub.com via the following url: http://connect.springerpub.com/content/book/978-0-8261-5085-1/part/part04/chapter/ch20

CHAPTER 21

School Violence and Trauma

AMY E. ALEXANDER AND LISA LÓPEZ LEVERS

CHAPTER OVERVIEW

This chapter examines the history and evolution of violence in schools and presents the various mental health and violence prevention theories and interventions that have developed and continue to emerge in the ever-changing landscape of the spillover of societal violence into spaces historically considered safe, such as American schools. This chapter delves into the discrepancies in response time and method, funding, and maintenance of follow-up in districts and communities that have fewer resources. Statistics regarding the occurrence of violence in public and private schools are presented, and strategies aimed at increasing safety are discussed. Brief and long-term counseling approaches are explored, and resources are offered online at Springer Connect.

LEARNING OBJECTIVES

After reading this chapter, the reader should be able to:

1. Understand preventative measures that schools can incorporate, in order to reduce violent acts in school and at school-sponsored events;
2. Identify specific ways an anti-violence culture can be established via district goals and programming into school communities;
3. List agencies that provide information and assistance to schools and communities directly affected by school violence;
4. Identify contributing factors to student and staff feelings of safety within schools and at school-related functions; and
5. Recognize community resources and partnerships that can be engaged within schools to build connections and strengthen relationships.

INTRODUCTION

While school violence often may be perceived as a mass shooting or hostage situation, in which extreme conditions require extreme actions, this typically is not the situation. Often, school violence is comprised of insidious acts such as bullying, harassment, and fighting that weigh on the collective psyche and set the atmosphere of a school community. This chapter addresses some of the ways in which events that are commonly considered the quotidian occurrences of contemporary 21st century school life affect the culture and trauma responses of not only students, but also of teachers and other school personnel, as well as of the surrounding communities. We consider how things have changed regarding school safety and protocol, in light of an increase in mass school shootings and school violence throughout the history of American public education. We also look at what constitutes best practice when considering school evacuation and disaster plans and aftercare of individuals and communities. These aims are accomplished in the following major sections of this chapter: Providing Context: School and Campus Population Numbers, Violence in American Educational Settings, School Environment, Weapons, Emergency and Disaster Planning. and School-Based Interventions, .

PROVIDING CONTEXT: SCHOOL AND CAMPUS POPULATION NUMBERS

In the fall of 2019, approximately 50.8 million students were enrolled in public schools in America. Another 5.8 million were enrolled in America's private schools (National Center for Education Statistics [NCES], 2020). The numbers for public school enrollment and attendance over the next decade are expected to increase to approximately 51.4 million (NCES, 2020). In the fall of 2019, there were 3.2 million public school teachers and 0.5 million teachers in private schools across America. With the addition of 19.9 million college students during that same period, there were over 70 million students in America. The number of college professors in American institutions of higher learning totaled approximately 1.5 million in 2017 (Institute of Education Services, National Center for Education Statistics, IES/NCES, 2020). Combining all of these groups together equals over 75 million people engaged in school settings in America every day. These numbers do not include university administrators or service workers such as those engaged in maintenance, food service, medical, and custodial duties. These numbers represent those who potentially could be affected, directly, by some form of school or campus violence each year in America. In the sections that follow, we flesh out the context for understanding school violence by looking at Violence in American Educational Settings, School Environment, Weapons, and Emergency and Disaster Planning.

VIOLENCE IN AMERICAN EDUCATIONAL SETTINGS

Violence in America is not new; we can identify numerous types of violence, including violence to control, violence to punish, and even violence to entertain. What is alarming about public school violence in particular is the mandatory, universal nature of the physical space. Because school attendance in America is compulsory, the ghoulish nature of any criminal or non-criminal act of violence committed in that setting is even more heinous. Certainly, school violence cannot be linked to one singular cause, as the complexity of our social fabric warrants more in-depth examinations of its roots as well as what sustains it. Even in an attempt to evaluate safer learning spaces for students and school employees, we must consider that there has been no period, in the history of America, in which parents and guardians could send their children to school with confidence in their safety and well-being (Midlarsky & Klain, 2005). Assurances simply have not existed that children never would suffer harm from violence by peers and teachers (Midlarsky & Klain, 2005). Considering the amount of time that learners spend in school and involved in school-related and school-sponsored activities, on average approximately 35 hours per week with 10 to 15 additional hours depending on extracurricular endeavors, parents and guardians should be able to have confidence in the societal systems that are in place and charged with keeping students safe.

Students are not the only demographic affected by school violence. There is a collective response to traumatic events within the entire school community, including teachers, administrators, parents and guardians, school counselors, school social workers, school psychologists, food service workers, bus drivers, custodians, maintenance workers, and security staff. We also must consider the neighborhood community and the greater geographical area. Most school districts employ a significant number of community residents, creating a kind of dual role of trauma response to violence that occurs in schools. This multilayered dynamic calls for a unique and well-thought-out approach to both interventions and postvention treatment.

School violence has other unique factors that have influenced its progression; this phenomenon actually began with the adults. *Teachers* are the originators of violence in schools. The focus on violence in schools typically has been on student behaviors, although "it is important to note that teachers also have long exhibited violent behavior" (Midlarsky & Klain, 2005, p. 46). In fact, the earliest recorded incidents of school violence have involved teacher-to-student violence, framed in what we often refer to as "corporal punishment" (Midlarsky & Klain, 2005, p. 46). Certainly, this form of school violence is not what first comes to mind when discussing violent acts in schools. However, we need to consider the history of human interaction within the school setting. It is necessary to parse out how we have arrived at our current perspective. As of 2005, only 27 states prohibited the use of corporal punishment in schools. Historically, the foundation of public schooling in America has been based on the Puritanical ideals of early colonists; therefore, a teacher's primary objective was to maintain class and societal order via physical discipline. It was believed that teachers were responsible for educating students to read the Word of God, in order to rescue their souls from evil and to ensure their eternal salvation. As society has evolved and become more religiously diverse, so has public education, and fortunately, violence in all forms is now unacceptable in most public learning spaces. Perhaps as we examine the proliferation of violence in schools, and attempt to explore treatment options for victims, we can glean some insights from history and use them to develop interventions that are more effective, along with devising preventative measures.

Where do school districts begin when attempting to establish or extend a climate and a culture of safety within the buildings themselves and at school-sponsored and school-related activities? Students spend most of their day in school. The physical space is where many eat breakfast, lunch, and dinner, in many cases. It is where they see their friends, establish relationships, study math, and learn how to be a good citizen. School provides the foundation for some of the most memorable, long-lasting relationships with peers, as well as with adults. It is where many Americans grow into themselves and learn who they are apart from their family of origin, religion, and established family cultural norms. American school systems play a substantial role in the life and culture of all Americans; therefore, we need to feel and be safe in those environments. How, then, do school officials create a safe school environment while protecting the individual and collective psyches of stakeholders?

SCHOOL ENVIRONMENT

In 2018, there was, on average, close to one mass shooting in the United States per day (Campisi, 2018). Guns killed or injured more than 2,700 people under the age of 18 by October of that year (Campisi, 2018). In many cases, these deaths and injuries have been associated with a school shooting (Musu et al., 2019). Wherever people gather, public places constitute potential targets, and architects and designers of schools should be ever mindful of the safety concerns and precautions necessary in providing the safest space possible for schoolchildren and staff. Hellman (2015) amplifies the importance of addressing school building safety "by incorporating the principles of crime prevention through environmental design" ("Principles of CPTED," p. 1). There is an obvious correlation between school violence and school environment. The way in which the value or perceived value of the physical space is addressed, along with the environment, culture, and attitudes regarding the idea of education and the people who occupy those spaces together, are key components that contribute to school environment. Both built environment and school climate will be discussed in the text that follows.

Physical Building

Consideration of the physical spaces and structures of school buildings are crucial to being able to prepare for safety. Many school officials deeply believe that the physical environment is critical in keeping schools safe and that there must be a balance between safety and a welcoming calmness in design and layout (Campisi, 2018). The level of care for the physical building also lends to a safer environment. Daniels and Haist (2012, p. 336) have pointed out that, "Buildings that are clean and well cared for generally have lower levels of violence than those that are dirty and cluttered." According to architectural designer Jenine Kotob, who has helped design multiple school building projects in Washington, DC, schools can be designed for safety without feeling cold or like prisons (cited in Cimino, 2018). According to architects who specialize in school design, safe schools should have plenty of both natural and artificial light. Lighted spaces discourage student misbehavior and victimization, as well as provide practical elements needed for hallways, classrooms, computer labs, and other learning spaces. Safe schools should have integrated alarms and a public address system that reaches classrooms, offices, and hallways; safe schools also should have fewer access points. Additionally, parking areas, traffic patterns, and open-space areas, such as playgrounds, sports fields and courts, and other open spaces, should be planned and laid out carefully.

School Climate

The school climate is equally as significant to the school environment as the physical building. School climate generally refers to the social-emotional atmosphere within a physical school structure as well as the attitudes and beliefs of the communities in which the schools geographically exist (Osher & Berg, 2017). Having partnerships with other community stakeholders is paramount to establishing and maintaining a safe and positive school climate. Local police departments can serve as key supporters of positive, safe school climates. When officers have a good relationship with a school, they are more likely to know the campus and individual building layout, safety protocols, the student body, and school staff. Knowing the unique needs of the school district, knowing the students' mindsets, and understanding how they think are intricacies that could be of assistance, should officers need to intervene in occurrences within the school buildings and at other school-related events and activities.

Cohen et al. (2009) have defined "school climate" as "the quality and character of school life" (p. 182). According to the National School Climate Center (n.d., "How Do We Define School Climate?", p. 1), "School climate is based on patterns of students', parents' and school personnel's experience of school life and reflects norms, goals, values, interpersonal relationships, teaching and learning practices, and organizational structures." Based upon a review of the available research on school safety at the time, Daniels and Bradley (2011) identified dimensions of the social-emotional climate that interrelate with a safe school environment. They asserted that safe schools and communities typically possess the following five factors:

- Skills instruction
- Expected student behaviors
- Engagement with the community
- Student self/other awareness
- Positive adult interactions

Skills instruction is applicable and beneficial to both learners and school employees. Learners receive instruction in such life skills as communication, decision-making, problem-solving, conflict resolution, cooperation, self-control, and interpersonal relating. School employees gain from training in crisis response, quality teaching pedagogy, and other forms of professional development (Daniels & Bradley, 2011). *Expected student behaviors* are those that students are supposed to exhibit while at school and in attendance at school-sponsored functions and activities, often with interventions by school employees. Such behaviors include checks on undesirable behavior, consistent and fair consequences, well-defined guidelines and rules that must be followed, heightened observation and increased supervision, intolerance of disrespectful behavior, establishment and enforcement of clear rules and boundaries, investigating all gossip and acting on it in a timely manner, physical safety, and effective leadership.

The third element related to school safety is *engagement with the community* (Daniels & Bradley, 2011). This component of school safety is key and requires the school to engage, interact, and integrate with the community and other stakeholders, and to recognize the importance of extracurricular activities to unite the community. Outside resources such as think tanks, local organizations, police, and even architectural firms also can be helpful in safeguarding school communities, but it is important to involve the community itself in the move to create a secure school. For example, a significant part of an architect's process can be participatory design, which allows all relevant voices to have the chance to contribute. For instance, teachers typically ask about things like classroom door hardware and other practical aspects of the physical space itself. If the approach to school safety is holistic, various stakeholders are invited to be seated at the discussion table, in order to provide differing insights. Working with community members also means involving students, who can serve as ambassadors to report potential threats, and consultants in creating safety protocol, or another set of "eyes and ears" capable of talking to school officers when they do not feel safe (Musu et al., 2019). Schools often overlook students in the process, yet the insights that they can provide are invaluable.

The fourth component, *student self/other awareness,* relies heavily on understanding one's own and others' emotions, as well as the tenets of social, emotional, and ethical learning, as much as possible. Finally, the fifth component is *positive interactions with adult stakeholders.* This critical piece includes adults displaying genuine warmth and authenticity toward students as well as maintaining interest in the whole learner; serving as positive role models; engaging consistently in equitable treatment for all learners; establishing and reinforcing trusting relationships; breaking the code of silence, including reframing common accusatory language; and treating all with dignity and respect. Additionally, this component entails nurturing connections and relationships with all learners, along with providing emotional and social safety and respecting diversity.

WEAPONS

In incidents of violence in American schools, more people tend to think of firearms or knives as the weapons most often used. Although there are other items that have been reported as being enlisted as weapons in schools, such as scissors, letter openers, and chairs, the most lethal are guns and knives. According to the National Center for Education Statistics:

> The percentage of students in grades 9 to 12 who reported being threatened or injured with a weapon on school property during the previous 12 months decreased from 9% in 2001 to 6% in 2017. The percentage also decreased between 2001 and 2017 for both male students (from 12% to 8%) and female students (from 7% to 4%). In each survey year from 2001 to 2017, a lower percentage of female students than of male students reported being threatened or injured with a weapon on school property. For instance, in 2017, approximately 4 percent of female students reported being threatened or injured with a weapon on school property, compared with 8 percent of male students. (NCES, 2019, "Indicator 4," p. 2)

With the proliferation of and easier access to firearms over the last several decades, school-aged youth are able to acquire guns more readily, whether legally or illegally. This more recent phenomenon further serves to complicate matters regarding school safety.

The previous 2017 statistics related to school violence reveal yet another aspect of the school violence discussion, that is, race/ethnicity and gender identity. In the same year, the percentage of students in grades 9 to 12 who reported being threatened or injured with a weapon on school property during the previous 12 months differed by race/ethnicity and grade level. Lower percentages of Asian American students (4%) and White students (5%) than of Black students (8%), students of two or more races (8%), and American Indian/Alaska Native students (14%) reported being threatened or injured with a weapon on school property (Musu et al., 2019). The percentage of Latinx students (6%) who reported being threatened or injured with a weapon on school property was lower than the percentages for African American students and American Indian/Alaska Native students. Lower percentages of 11th- and 12th-graders (5% each) than of 9th- and 10th-graders (7% each) reported being threatened or injured with a weapon on school property (Musu et al., 2019). Through various school surveys and commissions on violence in school, we also recognize that frequently students who bring weapons to school are responding to some sort of treatment they deem threatening, hurtful, or disrespectful in nature. Often, bringing weapons into the schools is a protective factor in the minds of those students who do it.

EMERGENCY AND DISASTER PLANNING

States have played a key role in the safety of schools. According to a *National Institute of Justice Report*, "States carry out a variety of activities to support school safety, including providing training, resources, and guidance to schools and school districts on topics that range from bullying to emergency operations planning" (Carlton et al., 2017, p. 2). However, the United States Government Accountability Office (USGAO, 2016) 2015 survey of 51 state educational agencies indicated that only 32 states required school districts to have an Emergency Operations Plan in place. According to the USGAO survey, a key strategy for schools—and even for businesses—to be able to respond effectively in an emergency entails having a specific plan for doing so. Typically referred to as an Emergency Operations Plan or EOP, this document outlines how a school will prepare for, respond to, and recover from an emergency. One of the earlier steps in developing an EOP is to form a planning committee that includes various school and community stakeholders. Such stakeholders might involve a school's administrators, teachers, counselors, social workers, psychologists, bus drivers, and security officers, as well as including community partners, like first responders, local emergency management staff, public health individuals, and the American Red Cross, as appropriate.

The designated team should establish a regular time to review, evaluate, and update the school EOP, at least every 2 years, and provide regular training on the school EOP to staff and students. Experts recommend that such a plan should describe contingencies for natural and human-made disasters, such as earthquakes, tornadoes, floods, fires, and chemical spills, as well as for other potential crises (Dorn et al., 2004; Ewton, 2014). The EOP also should include contingencies for acts of violence, including intruders and active shooters (Carlton et al., 2017).

One way to prepare for emergencies is to incorporate real-world scenarios into school safety training. These types of exercises facilitate participant discussions regarding emergency policies and procedures, and their roles and responsibilities before, during, and after an emergency scenario. This helps to improve performance during an actual incident (USGAO, 2016). Schools should reinforce training through drills and other exercises that are appropriate for the school's culture and community. Schools should conduct operations-based drills for staff and faculty along with developmentally appropriate trauma-informed drills for students, in order to test procedures and skills. Schools should mandate at least one operations-based exercise annually and include community partners along with school employees. Afterward, schools should construct an After-Action Report, along with an Improvement Plan, laying out the changes that were made and why (resources are provided online; see end of the chapter for access information). Issues related to the importance of emergency and disaster planning are discussed in the text that follows and detail the following concerns: Treating Students Exposed to Violence, Effects of Violence on Survivors, and Influences of Trauma Response to Violence in Schools.

Treating Students Exposed to Violence

The significance of the methods used to diagnose and treat individuals affected by school violence is of great consequence and should not be minimized during emergency and disaster planning. When trying to determine the most effective and appropriate treatments for children affected by school violence, clinicians should be well versed in childhood and adolescent developmental stages, as well as being aware of the lived experiences, ethnic and religious considerations, and stress and trauma responses of the specific individuals. With regard to adults affected by school violence, clinicians should be professionally competent and keenly aware of ethnic background, religious and spiritual beliefs, any cultural and gender role considerations of the specific survivors in selecting appropriate counseling methods, and theories to incorporate. As we entertain the implications of treatment, we must consider the effects of school violence on whole communities as well as on individuals, risk and protective factors of survivors and other stakeholders, internal and external conditions that have an impact on treatment, and school and community-based intervention and prevention approaches.

Effects of Violence on Survivors

The effects of traumatic events on humans of any ethnic or religious background, gender identity, or age are complex, reflecting human intricacies, diverse lived-experiences, individual trials, and a host of other factors that affect our human journey. Often when we experience trauma in a collective form, the healing processes differ from those that we would undergo as part of an individual journey. Ideas about how humans have internalized and processed trauma events have evolved over the years and continue to evolve. As discussed in Chapter 1, "An Introduction to Counseling Survivors of Trauma: Beginning to Understand the Historical and Psychosocial Implications of Trauma, Stress, Crisis, and Disaster," the *Diagnostic and Statistical Manual of Mental Disorders,* Third Edition (APA, 1980), was the first iteration of the publication to include trauma-related diagnostic criteria for posttraumatic stress disorder (PTSD). In subsequent versions of the manual, the definitions and criteria have expanded to include broader, more comprehensive scenarios and types of experiences, which extend to a more extensive swath of the population. These more inclusive criteria have resulted in a reduction of shame and embarrassment for those who might be apprehensive about seeking treatment for trauma related to school violence, thereby increasing the numbers of survivors who receive timely treatment and are able to begin the healing process.

In the interest of exploring how human development affects trauma responses, Bronfenbrenner's (1979) Bioecological Model of Human Development is enlightening. This model has posited the idea that human development and responses to trauma are influenced by more than our individual experiences, that they are interconnected with and affected by multiple social systems. Such an ecological-transactional perspective has allowed us to "situate the lived experiences of traumatized persons within the time and space of a relevant ecology in order to understand the trauma event as well as personal meaning making" (Levers, 2012, p. 7). According to Bronfenbrenner's (1979) ecological model, not only are our own lived experiences, cultures, religious beliefs, family traditions, and community connections indicative of how we respond to trauma, so is the chronological time frame, as well as the historical lens through which the event(s) has occurred. The most common responses that typically manifest, upon exposure to trauma, are anxiety and stress. Yet, those who experience trauma resulting from school violence are susceptible to adjustment, mood, sleep, and substance-related disorders as well. It then becomes important to explore how different manifestations of trauma emerge, depending on several internal and external factors present in survivors' lives, and how these factors influence responses to school violence.

Influences of Trauma Response to Violence in Schools

Generally speaking, schools are relatively safe spaces. Students are exposed to violence perpetration and victimization more frequently away from school property and events than they are at school (Ewton, 2014; Flannery et al., 2004). Despite this, students still report experiencing violence at school as witnesses more often than as victims; they also report experiencing violence in their neighborhoods and homes, depending on demographics, at a higher level than at school, even considering the high-profile school incidents of mass violence over the last 20 years (Musu et al., 2019). These factors, along with some additional considerations, influence how any individual may internalize traumatic events and what, if any, potential disorders may emerge as a result.

People, particularly younger children, who experience victimization from persistent violence suffer from higher levels of depression, anxiety, and self-doubt. Although there have not been vast amounts of research, historically, that focus on the impact of exposure to violence at school (Flannery et al., 2004), this area of research has expanded in recent years (e.g., National Institute of Justice, 2016). It further can be inferred that much of the existing research regarding violence and trauma reasonably can be applied to school violence as well. Differences in how individuals and groups process responses to violence depend on previous exposure, type of violence, whom the victim is, the victim's relationship to the perpetrator, developmental stage, any risk and protective factors present, and the perceived life threat. Risk and protective factors also are linked to cultural traditions and beliefs within some ethnic groups. Religious and spiritual beliefs, gender roles, value of familial ties, and strength of community connections are all potential risk or protective factors for victims of school violence, depending on the role they play in individuals' lives or collectively to a group.

Unique to the risk and protective factors related to school violence and trauma is the teacher-to-student ratio. Often, students feel physically safer in school spaces and are more likely to seek out adult help from school counselors, teachers, administrators, or other adult school personnel when there is sufficient staffing. The number of adults within a school building has a direct effect on the level and number of violent incidences that occur, thus influencing the intensity of the trauma response. Research also finds that the building size and design play a part in feelings of safety among students (Campisi, 2018; Carlton et al., 2017; Hellman, 2015). This, again, can influence trauma responses and the ability of an individual to heal, as safety concerns affect levels of anxiety and depression. The larger, more populous schools tend to record more violent incidents than smaller schools with fewer students to look after. Another possible risk factor, which operates within schools and is especially difficult to assess, is the lack of staff members who understand and respect cultural differences. A lack of understanding often is interpreted as a lack of empathy that might interfere with the ability of students and community members to move on from violent events within the school. The myriad factors that influence an individual's or group's trauma response to school violence are also indicators of what treatment interventions could work best in the healing process.

SCHOOL-BASED INTERVENTIONS

School personnel and outside consultants should be cognizant of the impact that exposure to school violence has on student achievement; academic interest and decline; behavior; relationships, particularly those formed and nurtured at school; and on overall mental health. Evaluations of survivors, perpetrators, and witnesses (adults as well as students) should be conducted to determine the level of intervention needed. Once triage is done, more specific treatment plans can be discussed and implemented. Intervention and treatment methods suggested to schools should address the particular needs of witnesses to school violence as well. Witnessing school violence such as fights, sexual assault, and threats also can have negative and severe repercussions, depending on the rates and persistence of exposure. While ethnicity may be a factor in developing and instituting specific culturally sensitive interventions for trauma that results from school violence, research shows that developmental processes, levels of academic achievement, and IQ play substantial roles in intervention outcomes (Flannery et al., 2004; Hellman, 2015). Treatment for the perpetrators or bullies also is paramount, as students who bully peers are shown to have been influenced by violence previously, whether as victims or witnesses (Estévez et al., 2009, p. 478). In this section, we explore the following intervention strategies: debriefing, long-term counseling interventions, and identifying the counseling implications of school violence and trauma.

Debriefing

Incidents of school shootings and hostage takings have become more prevalent in the last 20 years; however, there is still a lacuna of research regarding treatment for survivors exposed to such occurrences. Numerous studies have been conducted on trauma responses to other forms of single-incident violent events such as physical and sexual abuse. It is worth noting that survivors, particularly children, of any violent exposure who develop pathological responses to trauma tend to do so regardless of the type of violence or trauma experienced. Therefore, a number of interventions can be adapted to many types of traumatic exposure. There are two types of debriefing typically implemented with regard to violence exposure in schools: psychological debriefing and critical incident stress debriefing (CISD). Psychological debriefing is a single-session individual psychological intervention that involves reworking, reliving, or recalling the trauma and subsequent emotional reactions (Szumilas et al., 2010). It also can be applied to group formats, and "is designed to prevent negative psychological responses to the traumatic event" (Daniels & Haist, 2012, p. 341). Although CISD was designed for workers in high-risk occupations, such as police officers, disaster workers, and firefighters (Barboza, 2005), it has been adapted to use as a debriefing option in school violence incidents. Because of the sudden and unexpected nature of a critical incident, there are varying ideas about what types of events qualify as critical incidents.

Aucott and Soni (2016, p. 86) describe a critical incident, in part, as "a sudden and unexpected event that has the potential to overwhelm the coping mechanisms of a whole school or members of the school community." The aim of CISD is to reduce initial distress and to prevent the development of more severe psychological responses, including PTSD. The focus of CISD is threefold: (a) promoting emotional processing through allowing individuals to express reactions, (b) preparing individuals for possible experiences following a critical incident, and (c) identifying individuals who may require further intensive intervention (Mitchell & Everly, 1995, as cited in Aucott & Soni, 2016).

CISD is a psycho-educational approach that explores the cognitive and affective domains of an experience. Because CISD was not initially developed to be implemented in schools, there is little research either to support or to refute its effectiveness in a school setting. In the absence of empirical evidence, it is helpful to consider the underlying theoretical assumptions of CISD and the extent to which these would deem it an appropriate intervention to use with school staff. Therefore, literature from the general field of bereavement and loss has been drawn upon to give insight into the appropriateness of CISD in this context. Some advance the option of using the practical elements of CISD, such as teaching and re-entry, as they offer support in assisting participants to manage or cope with the critical incident. CISD also promotes a sense of control, encourages social support, and provides information regarding when and how to seek additional support (Morris & Block, 2012, as cited in Aucott & Soni, 2016). For example, support could be requested that equips survivors with additional knowledge and resources needed to help others who may seek their assistance (Aucott & Soni, 2016). It also is worth noting that debriefing of any sort is not therapy. Debriefing is intended to de-escalate any possible progression of symptoms, resulting from a violent exposure, which might spiral into more serious or pathological issues.

Long-Term Counseling Interventions

A certain number of survivors of school violence exposure incidents are likely to need more comprehensive therapy than just debriefing. There are varying options for such individuals, depending on the severity of any pathological indicators that emerge as a result of the event(s). We also need to consider the survivor's race and ethnicity, religious and spiritual needs, sexual orientation and identity, previous trauma experiences, other mental health concerns and diagnoses, and any additional lived experiences that might affect therapy. Schools can be systems that operate as unifiers and support within communities by providing "insulation" to children from violence, helping to minimize the effects, and teaching nonviolent methods of coping and behaving (Garner, 2014, p. 489). A contributing factor of recovery and maintenance after exposure to violence within schools is either to provide ongoing therapy within the school setting or to support out-of-school interventions.

Various counseling theories have been used with violence-exposed populations including play therapy, solution-focused brief therapy (SFBT), cognitive therapy (CT), rational emotive behavior therapy (REBT), and cognitive behavior therapy (CBT) (Daniels & Haist, 2012; Levers, 2012). Despite which form of therapeutic intervention is used with survivors of school violence, timely delivery of evidence-based treatment (EBT) with "trauma-related mental health sequelae is critical to prevent negative consequences of trauma exposure" (Dorsey et al., 2017). While there are multiple forms of CBT, a more commonly implemented version, when addressing child and adolescent violence exposure trauma, is trauma-focused cognitive behavioral therapy (TF-CBT). This form of therapy facilitates the involvement of parents and guardians in the process and includes some conjoint sessions (Dorsey et al., 2017). Most sessions are separate, incorporating the same therapeutic elements with parent/guardian and child. The elements include psychoeducation regarding violence exposure as trauma, PTSD coping skills, imaginal exposure, in vivo exposure, and safety skills training (Dorsey et al., 2017). Therapeutic elements such as parenting skills are added, eliminated, or limited, based on specific characteristics of the parent(s)/guardian(s) and child such as age and comorbidity. Children, in particular, who had overt exposure to elements of the trauma experience in TF-CBT, via talking about them or confronting triggers, experienced lower levels of fear associated with thinking and talking about their trauma experience (Dorsey et al., 2017).

Risk reduction through family therapy (RRFT) integrates TF-CBT and multisystemic therapy principles with other evidence-based interventions to address comorbid PTSD, substance abuse, and risky sexual behaviors. This form of treatment resulted in lower levels of substance abuse but not in risky sexual behaviors (Dorsey et al., 2017). Although used with only a small sample size, this form of treatment could be considered an option for school violence survivors who also are susceptible to comorbidity. In addition, some headway has been made regarding the use of individual CBT with parent involvement among culturally diverse children and adolescents, thus making it more desirable as a treatment option for those exposed to school violence and resulting trauma.

Cognitive behavioral interventions for trauma in schools (CBITS) is a form of group therapy that is implemented within the school facility and does not extensively include parent/guardian participation. Because CBITS occurs on school grounds and is comprised of other students of the same age range, teachers and other school personnel are included in the psychoeducational aspect of the process, which, in many ways, helps to form a cohesive school community and assists in strengthening the support system and the process of healing. This type of therapeutic process encourages participants to examine their thoughts, concurrent with the event, via a story-like construct called the trauma narrative, which can be written or drawn by the participants or dictated to an adult educator participant. After additional examination of the narrative by the student and educator, the child shares it with a parent or guardian to facilitate future awareness and communication. It is worth noting that CBITS has been tested with culturally and ethnically diverse populations from its inception, providing greater confidence regarding its effectiveness with youth beyond a White, middle-class population.

Jordan (2003) has developed a trauma and recovery model for those affected by a school shooting. She has termed such shootings as "catastrophic," indicating that the focus should be on behavior, cognitive dimensions, and the need to examine the psychological effects on the school, the students, and the needs of those affected. In analyzing the importance of this model, Shaughnessy et al. (2018, p. 7) have stated that, "Often the impact of a school shooting is not clearly understood and all too often the responses of those impacted are not extensively investigated or recognized or validated." As a relatively new phenomenon, school shootings often are misunderstood and not properly dealt with, and as is so often the case with psychological interventions, Jordan's model was based on a middle-class, White population and cannot necessarily be implemented successfully with more diverse populations (Daniels & Haist, 2012). Also emblematic of the knowledge gap regarding school violence exposure incidents, there is no prescriptive regarding perpetrators. To date, neither researchers nor clinicians has developed a comprehensive therapeutic intervention designed specifically to address the unique issues surrounding school shooting incidents.

EMDR generally incorporates coping skills, cognitive restructuring, imaginal exposure, and simultaneous bilateral sensory input (eye movement) and is individual in structure (Dorsey et al., 2017). EMDR has been regarded as similarly effective when compared to CBT. Individual integrated therapy for complex trauma (ITCT-A) amalgamates various theories such as attachment, developmental, family systems, and CBT within a complex trauma framework, which is defined by "cumulative poly-victimization" that is interpersonal in nature and involves "direct harm, exploitation, or neglect/abandonment by caregivers" (Dorsey et al., 2017, p. 13). Survivors who could benefit from this form of therapeutic intervention typically are considered to have more severe impairment issues and higher psychiatric comorbidity. While there are multiple forms of therapeutic intervention that are considered effective with those exposed to school violence, we remain mindful that all interventions should be geared toward the specific individual or group and should address culture and ethnicity, gender identification and sexual orientation, religious and spiritual issues, and lived experiences. Therapy is a personal experience and not something that can be implemented *en masse*, based on general commonalities.

A few additional therapeutic methods are worth mentioning, as they relate to exposure to school violence. These include individual client centered play therapy, groups creative expressive + CBT, and music therapy. The latter, music therapy, has been used to reduce anxiety, on both psychological and neurobiological levels; it is generally believed to support positive identity formation, and has been used by many ancient cultures for healing (McFerran & Wölfl, 2015).

Counseling Implications

Considerable evidence regarding the efficacy of psychosocial treatments for youths with mental health symptoms related to trauma exposure provides sufficient verification for CBT as the first-line treatment approach (Dorsey et al., 2017). However, the lacuna of research on therapeutic interventions appropriate for those who have experienced or will experience school violence exposure reflects the lack of professional options available to clinicians. The literature identifies some common elements across interventions and in the highest evidentiary levels of individual treatment options; these include a psychoeducational component, emotion regulation strategies, imaginal exposure, in vivo exposure, cognitive processing, and problem-solving (Dorsey et al., 2017).

Counselors and other mental health and education professionals should make themselves familiar with the signs and symptoms of traumatized youth and manifestations of pathology. Keeping in mind that the more prompt the intervention, the more likely students and other school community members with trauma due to violence exposure can recover, therapeutically speaking. The evidence supports a brief intervention for all and a follow-up assessment to determine who would benefit from treatment that is more comprehensive. The school-as-community has been shown to be a helpful perspective in recovery. The "insulation" that the school can provide as a significant piece of the therapeutic puzzle is helpful in reducing anxiety, depression, and other sequelae of violence exposure trauma. As the school is an integral part of culture and is essential to how societies function, it should be a safe space for all who enter its doors. Unfortunately, that is not the reality of our current existence. Therefore, we must prepare and educate ourselves as to how we react to any forms of violence that occur within school walls. Teacher-to-student violence, student-to-student violence, gun violence, sexual assault violence, bullying violence, and cyber violence are all unacceptable, and educators should be equipped with the proper tools to combat the internal and external factors that influence the onset of violent tendencies where possible. Support systems play an integral role in recovery, and schools provide a stable environment for students for an overwhelming amount of time. Not every student is afforded a safe and stable home environment, and for these students, their teachers, school counselors, food service workers, school bus drivers, administrators, and school resource officers play an even more significant role in everyday life and even more so in the recovery from violence exposure events. Box 21.1 offers a real-world illustration of violence which erupted at one high school; the event was highly publicized, locally, nationally, and even internationally. Box 21.1 is followed by a case analysis and then additional related information from the field in a subsequent box.

BOX 21.1

From the Field: High School Mass Stabbing

In April 2014, a 16-year-old sophomore stabbed and slashed 20 students and a security guard in an incident labeled as a mass stabbing in which 24 people (stabbings and other injuries) were counted among those injured (National Public Radio [NPR], 2014). After hearing of this incident at a nearby public high school, I heard from many of my students, who are demographically just about the polar opposite of those in the predominantly White, middle-class district where the mass stabbing occurred.

Many students with whom I had discussions about this incident, along with other notable instances of school violence, could not absorb how a high school student could attack fellow classmates at school. Many were more emotionally affected than they thought they would be, as they did not know the attacker personally nor any of the victims. Together, we were able to explore the idea of secondary trauma, make sense of our fears, and begin to comprehend how we are affected by trauma that seemingly is unrelated to us. These discussions helped us to understand better that we are all connected in ways that we might not realize until a trauma event occurs.

Reflection Questions:

- How might you begin to think about immediate student response to violence as this played out in the hallways?
- How might you begin to think about teacher response to violence in the present moment?
- How might you begin to conceptualize the chaos that would have been sparked by the initial and then the following stabbings?

Franklin Regional School District, where the event took place, is located in a municipality about 20 miles east of the city of Pittsburgh. The demographics on race breakdown are as follows: White 92% to 95%, African American 0.61% to 1.1%, Asian 3.28% to 5.0%, Native American 0.0% to 0.05%, Latinx of any race, 0.56% to 1.3% (Sperling's Best Places, n.d.). The racial demographics are included here to illustrate several points on school violence and our perception of it as well as to show the contrast between the district in which the first author of this chapter works and the district where the mass stabbing took place. Such data are germane in assessing the ability of some districts to respond to school violence in any form.

The preventative measures, the therapeutic and law enforcement interventions, and the ability to establish a safe school culture and environment are directly linked to the financial outlook of a community and school district. As with all other aspects of public education, the more affluent a district is, the better is its ability to be proactive in staving off acts of violence as well as to respond with sustained, quality response interventions. For purposes of illustration, we compare the district where the stabbings occurred, the Franklin Regional School District, with another nearby school district. The Penn Hills School District is located in the municipality of the same name, bordering the city of Pittsburgh to the east. Penn Hills is the second largest municipality in Allegheny County, Pennsylvania, smaller only than Pittsburgh. In stark contrast to Franklin Regional School District, the Penn Hills School District has a student population comprised of 70+% African American and another 2.5% to 3.0% of other ethnic minority students. The reader can recall the variations in services provided when race, gender, and economic status are considered, as these relate to the occurrence of and response to school violence, which vary significantly in comparison to districts that are more financially stable.

Fortunately, the Franklin Regional School District was able to enlist their many resources to help in responding to this tragic event. A few miles away, in the Penn Hills School District, as in most nearby districts and neighborhoods, learners and educators were shaken by the news of what happened at Franklin Regional High School. The incident opened up room for discussions and expressions of fear and some feelings of helplessness. While there is no conclusive data on the causes of school violence, "the level of economic development, as measured by the GDP (gross domestic product) per capita, is reported to be related to school violence" (Diagne, 2009, p. 138). Additionally, GDP has been found to be a major variable that significantly is associated with rates of school violence once national characteristics of schooling have been controlled for. Socioeconomic status (SES), as indicated by students who received free or reduced school meals and by the parents' occupation, also may be related to school violence. Numerous studies citing income inequality have found that countries, states, or neighborhoods that are less equal in wealth have higher rates of violent crime, including homicide. Therefore, it follows that school districts like Franklin Regional are more capable of responding to school violence in ways that are comprehensive and long-term, whether the violence occurs on their own property or in neighboring districts. In Box 21.2, the first author of this chapter discusses her response to the mass stabbing that occurred at the nearby school.

BOX 21.2

From the Field: A School Counselor's Response to School Violence

Much of what was expressed to me reflected a sense of disbelief. As a school counselor, I not only was responding to the fears and feelings of confusion and helplessness from students, but also from other educators, parents and guardians, community members, and a host of other stakeholders around this event. Feelings centered on the following concern: "We don't believe anything like this particular incident would occur in our spaces but, other forms of violence can and does." While our understandings of trauma continue to evolve, the evidence is pretty clear that distal trauma can and does have a serious impact. For example, most of us can think of where we were on September 11, 2001, when a terrorist attack took down the World Trade Center in New York City. Even people who were geographically distant from that area were likely to have been affected deeply by the occurrence. If individuals had no relative or other loved one lost to the events of that day, most still felt the pain and anguish of loss. The same is true of school violence; the fact that an incident did not occur in one's presence or own physical space does not eliminate the possible effects on those individuals or groups.

In the building in which I work, we were able to deconstruct and make meaning of our feelings of vulnerability related to the nearby school violence and then connect them to the real and perceived threats that we face daily and the stress and anxiety that they produce. Aware of

(continued)

risk factors and vulnerabilities, we leaned into the protective factors that we routinely experience, like a strong community and school presence. Mass shootings and stabbings, such as the ones that dominate news coverage, were not the source of my students' main fears. Rather, it was their lived experiences of community, neighborhood, and home violence that emerged as triggers in their quotidian lives.

Reflection Questions:

- If you were a school counselor working with the children described, how might you respond in the immediacy of the school violence?
- If you were a clinical mental health counselor to whom any of the previously described children were referred, how might you begin to think about a longer-term plan for ongoing counseling?
- If you were a marriage and family counselor, and the family of one of the previously described children came to you for counseling, how might you begin to think about addressing the counseling needs of the family?

While not much research exists on the full range of effects of various forms of school violence, other research strongly connects the everyday struggles of pervasive violence to higher incidences of anxiety, depression, inability to concentrate, addiction, predilection for adultification, and other sequelae of economic and cultural disadvantage and marginalization. Essentially, most students in urban and urban-like schools do not fear the mass shootings many associate with school violence in the 21st century. However, those occurrences may cause other trauma-related symptoms to emerge and affect schoolwork, the level of school violence that is acceptable to or normalized by learners as participants and bystanders, and other trauma-related symptoms.

Students have greater access to media and video from all over the world than ever before.

The chance that a majority of them will indeed bear witness to some form of school violence and its repercussions is extremely high. Within schools and their larger communities where violence occurs, everyone experiences manifestations of the trauma in differing ways, forms, and levels of intensity. It is imperative that we, as a nation and as citizens of the world, act preemptively and comprehensively, in all ways possible, to combat school violence in all forms, in all types of schools, and in every kind of manifestation. We need to protect our learners from the ramifications of experiencing such violence and from passing those manifestations on, into the future.

CONCLUSION

We live in a technology-driven society, and it is important to remember that, with the increase in the visibility of violent attacks on school properties, visuals can be sent around the world within moments, for all to see. In addition, interactions initiated via social media can be played out on school grounds, when those involved are gathered in a single physical space, thus increasing the number of possible altercations. In this sense, not only are the specific communities affected where such events take place, but people in other places around the world who are able to see the violence via technology may be as well. While technology may be positive in many cases, it also can increase the number of victims affected by a school violence event—an event that is hundreds or even thousands of miles away from where they actually live. This adds to the burden of school districts and employees of all schools to implement programs that address healthy ways of confronting anger and other feelings that could lead to violence.

As we attempt to develop more therapeutically appropriate interventions that are specific to school violence exposure trauma, we need to be mindful that distal trauma also can be an area for future examination. Additionally, multiple school plans and therapeutic interventions incorporate school counselors and other school staff into the treatment plan without any consideration that those school employees are also members of the school community and could very well be suffering from exposure to school violence events. We must consider the community make-up and norms, including socioeconomic status and ethnic and cultural traditions as well as any other aspects of the community that would have an impact on the types of therapies offered and implemented, in addition to the appropriate trauma- and event-specific interventions. Perhaps most significant in the quest to combat school violence, violence exposure, and the resulting trauma pathologies is comprehensive, district-specific, and appropriate plans to educate students and families about therapeutic interventions prior to violent events. If schools were able to prevent acts of violence and educate citizens about healthier means of dealing with feelings of anger, isolation, and fear, perhaps we would need fewer interventions on the other side of violence, because there would be fewer acts of violence.

ADDITIONAL RESOURCES

A robust set of instructor resources designed to supplement this text is located at http://connect.springerpub.com/content/book/978-0-8261-5085-1. Qualifying instructors may request access by emailing textbook@springerpub.com.

PRACTICE-BASED RESOURCES AND REFERENCES

To view a list of resources and all the references, please visit connect.springerpub.com via the following url: http://connect.springerpub.com/content/book/978-0-8261-5085-1/part/part04/chapter/ch21

CHAPTER 22

Natural Disasters and First Responder Mental Health

SCOTT L. TRACY

CHAPTER OVERVIEW

This chapter focuses on the counseling speciality of disaster mental health. Topics include a discussion of the science behind various natural disasters and the psychological effects experienced by the survivors. Also discussed are the stages of disaster recovery and counselor actions within each phase. Additionally, this chapter describes the unique lived experiences of first responders and ways that professional counselors can intervene to support the unique. behavioral health needs of rescue workers. Finally, the counselor's role in the COVID-19 pandemic is discussed.

LEARNING OBJECTIVES

After reading this chapter, the reader should be able to:

1. Describe the scientific processes associated with natural disasters;
2. Understand how categories of natural disasters have differing mental health implications for those affected;
3. Describe the stages of disaster recovery and counselor therapeutic actions for each stage;
4. Discuss the effects of the novel coronavirus pandemic on professional counseling;
5. List counseling techniques that can be implemented during a global pandemic response;
6. Differentiate between posttraumatic and cumulative stress reactions in first responders; and,
7. Discuss the unique psychological experiences of first responders and ways counselors can meet their behavioral health needs.

INTRODUCTION

Natural disasters can strike anywhere and at any time. Individuals, over their lifetimes, can expect to be affected by some sort of catastrophic event of nature. In fact, 2020 may be the most disastrous ever recorded in modern history. As of late 2020, the global pandemic created by the novel coronavirus took the lives of over 1.8 million people worldwide and over 348,000 in the United States alone (Johns Hopkins Corona Virus Research Center, 2020). Other pandemic end-of-year statistics are staggering. Worldwide, 84.1 million people contracted the highly infectious disease, with nearly one-quarter of those in the United States, which has experienced the highest death rate of any country by far. The economic impacts of shutdown and quarantine have devastated families and small businesses. Like most disasters, improvised populations and minorities suffered the greatest economic effects, which included unemployment, poor access to healthcare treatment, and higher infection rates. Nearly 14.4 million Americans became unemployed during the pandemic, matching levels not seen since the Great Depression (U.S. Bureau of Labor Statistics, 2020). It is estimated that one-third of the nation's small restaurants and entertainment venues may close permanently. The psychosocial effects are far reaching, and counselors have been at the frontline seeing record numbers of cases of traumatic stress created by the pandemic.

The pandemic only has added to the already occurring massive hurricanes, paralyzing blizzards, killer tornado outbreaks, and earthquakes that have wreaked havoc on every continent. There is general consensus among earth scientists that the effects of global warming may be responsible for the intensity of severe weather outbreaks that Earth has recently experienced (see Chapter 24, "A Confluence of Crises: Migration, Anthropogenic Climate Change, Mass Casualties, War, and Civil Unrest" for additional discussion regarding the effects of anthropogenic climate change). The scientific basis for climate change is well-established and natural disasters are on the rise (Tarvydus et al., 2017, 2018; Teahan et al., 2017). No one is immune and disadvantaged populations are most vulnerable. Professional counselors, more than ever before, have been called to duty to help survivors deal with the emotional consequences of disaster. In addition to providing service to the civilian population, counselors also are enlisted to help the emergency service clinicians who are on the front line of disaster response. These emergency clinicians (e.g., paramedics, fire fighters, and police officers) experience a deeply deleterious psychological toll as a result of their rescue efforts. The purpose of this chapter is to identify the nature of natural disasters and their impact on both civilian populations and emergency service clinicians. More importantly, this chapter aims to review the considerations of, actions by, and interventions for mental health professionals who are called to service during disaster events. These goals are realized through the discussions in the following sections: Types of Natural Disasters, Disaster Response System, and Counseling Implications. These main sections are followed by a summary of the chapter and an online list of relevant resources for students, clinicians, and instructors.

TYPES OF NATURAL DISASTERS

A *natural disaster* is defined as a catastrophic event of nature that creates a significant and often long-lasting change to the environment. Natural disasters can be categorized into several classes and are named by the etiological event (see Table 22.1). These categories include weather- and climate-related, earth movement-related, and biological/ecological-related disasters. It is important to note that this chapter does not directly discuss man-made disasters such as war, environmental pollution, and economic collapse, which also induce similar psychological sequelae, but warrant independent discussion separate from events of nature; the consequences of these man-made disasters are discussed in various chapters of this book.

Table 22.1

Disaster Events by Cause

Weather related	Hurricane, flood, tornadoes, severe thunderstorms, drought
Earth movement related	Earthquakes, tsunamis, volcanic eruptions
Biological/ecological related	Pandemic/disease, global warming, ecosystem destruction

It is important for counselors to understand the category types and likely events of natural disasters, so that they can better debrief both civilian and emergency service populations as they recover from horrific events. Disasters tend to have a regional probability of occurrence. For instance, towns located near a tectonic plate boundary may experience earthquakes, the American plains is known as "Tornado Alley" because of the preponderance of those storms in that region, and any ocean coast region may at some time see the effects of a tropical cyclone. Counselors need to become better informed about the regional disaster probability patterns of their practice area, so that they are able to respond better in times of crisis (Levers, 2020). The three categories of natural disaster are discussed in the remaining parts of this section: Weather-Related Disasters, Earth Movement-Related Disasters, and Biological/Ecological Disasters.

Weather-Related Disasters

Weather-related disasters are the most common types of catastrophic events. Hardly a week passes without breaking news of a hurricane, flood, blizzard, or tornado outbreak somewhere in America. Weather-related events are the product of a perpetual battle between warm air masses originating in the tropics, cold air masses stubbornly in place at the Earth's poles, and the collision between the two as a result of the planet's upper-level wind pattern, known as the jet stream. The bumping of these air masses at their boundaries creates instability in the atmosphere and becomes the breeding ground for storm systems.

Atmospheric storms can occur in various types. The most common type of atmospheric storm, and the leading cause of death from weather-related phenomena, is a thunderstorm. Thunderstorms originate from cells, or columns of rising warm air and sinking cold air. Lightning, hail, and heavy rain become the by-products of the storm's energy release. Cells that rise high into the atmosphere are termed super cell thunderstorms and can spawn tornadoes.

The single leading cause of weather-related deaths is from lightning strikes. However, flash flooding and wind damage can take human life and create significant structural damage to a region.

Tornadoes have been the scourge of the American Plains and the deep South throughout recorded history. These regions are prone to tornadoes because of their close proximity to the warm and cold air battle zones. Tornadoes develop most often in the spring and fall and frequently occur in outbreaks that can terrorize several states. Thanks to advanced atmospheric imagery, such as Doppler radar, severe thunderstorm and tornado warning systems have improved dramatically over the last two decades. As early as the 1960s, communities often received no warning of an incoming storm, and loss of life was enormous. However, with innovations in weather radar imagery and climate diagnostics, communities now can get warnings of severe storms as they form and then track the direction and intensity of their courses. The average person can expect to receive about a 12-minute window of warning before the arrival of a storm; however, outbreak regions can be identified days ahead of time. The problem is that people in the watch area need to monitor the weather forecast. Smartphones, for example, provide a great warning system mechanism; however, many folks in tornado alley cannot afford this type of technology. An overriding theme in natural disasters is that impoverished populations suffer the greatest impact. The poorest socioeconomic groups do not have the money to purchase warning technology, nor can they afford reinforced housing that is more resistant to damage from natural disasters. In essence, lives can be saved provided that people can afford it, which speaks to inequity issues in society, as much as it does weather and technology.

Despite better warning systems, since 2000, the *National Weather Service* has reported nearly 1,300 deaths from tornadoes in the United States, with 400 communities destroyed. In the spring of 2011, 505 people died in three states during two outbreaks. These atmospheric storms strike quickly and with devastating consequences. A family can lose their home and life possessions in minutes. Children and older adults present the highest risk for loss of life. Individuals who live in impoverished areas face the greatest economic impact, often because they live in unreinforced housing such as mobile trailer parks that offer little protection from storms. Twisters have a selective nature to their destruction. One home may be destroyed, whereas others on the same street are left untouched. Loss of life and injury reports have been reduced dramatically over the last 20 years, but the emotional effects of losing valuable possessions and the anxiety of starting life over, after the devastation, remain potent.

The largest type of atmospheric storm is a tropical cyclone, or a hurricane. Many American folktales surround these enormous storms. The *National Oceanic and Atmospheric Administration* ranks hurricanes as first among the disaster categories that can affect an entire region. Hurricane Katrina, which occurred in 2005, is listed as the single greatest natural disaster ever to affect the United States. Many other great hurricanes have made landfall on America's shore: Camille, Andrew, and the monster unnamed storm that destroyed Galveston, Texas, in 1900 are among these historic cyclones. Most disturbing is the frequency in the development of intense hurricanes. In addition to the global pandemic, 2020 will be recorded as the year with the most active tropical cyclones in Earth's history.

Hurricanes not only cause loss of life, but the massive flooding from a storm surge can submerge large areas of coastal land for months. A storm surge is the sudden rise of the ocean level that accompanies the approaching eye wall or center of the storm. The storm surge causes the greatest loss of life in hurricanes. Torrential rains and devastating winds can destroy the infrastructure of a region, shutting down power plants, water treatment facilities, and hospitals and making roads impassable. Once emergency personnel evacuate a region before the arrival of a hurricane, they often are unable to get back into the damaged area because of these infrastructure disruptions. This was the case in Hurricane Katrina, causing a several-day delay in the arrival of water, food, and medical supplies into the Gulf Coast region after landfall. Not only can the infrastructure of a region be affected, but the entire ecological environment can be altered after a great storm. The disappearance of marshes, beaches, and wildlife often occur and can disrupt the tropical ecosystem for decades. In many cases, the ecosystem is related to the economy. Beach towns are dependent upon the tourism industry. If the beach disappears, so do the tourists, thus further depleting the region's recovery resources. Not only could storm survivors lose their home to the disaster, but they may lose their jobs as well.

No part of America is free from the threat of flooding. Even the desert regions of the Southwest have seen devastation and loss of life from flash flooding. Flooding can occur from three sources. The first type occurs from prolonged rainfall over a region. The ground becomes saturated, and rainfall runoff fills lakes, streams, and rivers, which then rise over their banks. Along rivers, the area near the banks is called the flood plain.

The second origination of flooding occurs from snowpack melting and ice jamming. As the winter snowpack melts in the northern latitudes, mountain downslope movement of water can overtake a region's watershed, which acts as a natural drainage system. Damming can occur from debris and ice in the runoff streams and create rapid water rises along these streams and their tributaries. The heavy runoff can affect areas hundreds of miles from the actual melting ice and snow. Finally, flash flooding can develop quickly in an area that experiences heavy rainfall in a short time. Many factors predict flash flooding such as the ground saturation, runoff stream condition, terrain, and the amount of rainfall. Generally, rainfall amounts greater than 4 inches per hour can cause a flash flooding event. This type of torrential rain can occur in the late stages of a thunderstorm. Some regions may experience all three types of flooding. The city of Johnstown, Pennsylvania, was destroyed twice in the span of a century by a prolonged rainfall that caused a dam to break and a flash flood event from slow-moving thunderstorms.

Winter storms also constitute large scale disasters because of their ability to disable a region's infrastructure. Storms that produce heavy snowfall and ice may shut down roadways and snap trees and power lines, interrupting transit and turning off electrical supply for days at a time. The loss of power forces many citizens to endure cold, unheated homes. Again, the greatest impact typically is felt among impoverished populations and older adults. Under winter storm conditions, people often attempt to heat their homes using portable heaters that can create fires and cause dangerous levels of carbon monoxide gas to build in their homes. Initially, primary roadways such as interstate highways close. Secondary roads may remain snow-covered for days, preventing an entire population from having access to primary roads. Winter storms also slow rescue workers in their ability to respond to emergency situations.

Winter storms are typically a national event. During winter weather outbreaks in 2010 and 2011, which were particularly harsh, one-third of the nation was affected by four separate blizzard occurrences. The bitter cold that typically follows a winter storm may have a further blistering impact on a region's ability to cope with snow removal and rescue those trapped by the storm. Those living in substandard housing, who are homeless, and who are older adults are at most risk during winter emergencies.

Earth Movement-Related Disasters

The Earth's interior is a dynamic system. Earthquakes, tsunamis, and volcanoes are the products of this dynamic system. The surface of our planet sits on top of a layer known in geology as the crust. The Earth's crust is divided into two types, identified as either oceanic or continental. These layers are named because of the rocks that compose them. The oceanic rock, which contains the Earth's oceans, is lighter than the continental rock and tends to dive, or subduct, under the continents and near shorelines. The movement of these large plates of rock against one another is fueled by large convection currents of magma and heat originating from the Earth's interior. The battle between these large plates is mostly a stalemate but breaks or cracks can occur near the fringe areas of continental and oceanic plates. This entire process, known as *plate tectonics*, produces earth movements. Earthquakes, tsunamis, and volcanic eruptions occur because of these movements and have produced some of the greatest catastrophes in Earth's history. An earthquake occurs when a shift or break happens along a boundary or fault line. The San Andreas Fault in Southern California is one of the most famous of these fault lines. Large metropolitan centers have been built on or near many of the Earth's fault lines and subduction zones. The recipe for disaster has been made. Structural collapse and fires from broken gas lines represent the greatest land threat during an earthquake. This decade alone has seen massive death tolls in the hundreds of thousands from quakes in Haiti, Chile, China, and Japan.

When earthquakes occur in the ocean basin, large sea waves known as tsunamis can be formed. Twice in a 10-year span, the world watched in horror as these giant waves devastated the Indian Ocean basin (2004) and the Japanese coast (2011). These waves inundate coastal regions with giant, fast-moving walls of water. The height and speed of these waves act as a battering ram, destroying everything in their path. The water itself can be propelled miles inland, causing rapid flooding. There is no prewarning of an earthquake; however, because tsunamis occur after an earthquake, some advanced notice is possible, provided that people have access to the warning system. This lack of warning-system accessibility explained the massive loss of life in the Indian Ocean occurrence.

The intensity, or magnitude, of an earthquake is measured on a scale known as the *Richter scale*. The scale measures from 1 to 10. Earthquakes over a rating of seven are major, and those of nine or greater are catastrophic. There is a direct correlation between the magnitude of a quake and the damage it creates. It is important to note that a quake measured at five or six on the Richter scale can be devastating if it is centered in a populated area that lacks reinforced structures. Poorer sections of a region experience the greatest impact and loss of life because of this. As with weather-related disasters, impoverished populations suffer the greatest in an earth movement catastrophe.

As the rocks shift and return to a stalemate after an earthquake, smaller tremor activity, known as aftershocks, can occur. Many people initially have survived an earthquake, only to be trapped in a damaged building that finally collapses during one of these aftershocks. Aftershocks pose a significant threat to emergency responders during disaster rescue operations. These smaller quakes also provide a great mechanism for secondary traumatization among the survivors of a disaster.

Volcanoes are areas on the Earth where magma rises from deep under the crust and emerges onto the surface. Volcanoes can be contained in large mountains, such as Mount Saint Helens in Washington, or as flatter, more dome-shaped structures, such as the Hawaiian Islands. The large mountain volcanoes present a great risk for becoming a natural disaster. The city of Pompeii, Italy, was destroyed by the eruption of Mt. Vesuvius in 79 AD and has become one of the most famous volcanic eruptions in history. There was, however, another volcanic eruption that occurred in 1833 that caused a disaster of global proportion. The explosive eruption of Krakatoa sent a large ash cloud high into the Earth's atmosphere that was absorbed into global wind patterns. This large debris cloud reflected warming sunlight back into space, sending the entire planet into a mini ice age. Disease, severe weather outbreaks, and extreme cold weather wreaked havoc on our planet for several years. The eruption of this volcano was so large that the explosion was heard hundreds of miles away.

The scale of an Earth movement disaster can occur over very large areas. Travel into the region would be difficult at best. Roads, bridges, and highway systems would be destroyed. Multiple triage and crisis counseling centers would need to be established and maintained for extended time, while rescue and recovery operation continue and aftershocks subside.

Biological/Ecological Disasters

Every year our planet is threatened with a potential natural disaster of biblical proportion. This event is one of the largest health threats to any individual and the overall greatest threat to our species. It is a viral pandemic. The most common of these viruses is influenza, more commonly known as the flu. Over recorded history, the flu has taken more lives than all of Earth's wars combined. Prior to the advent of flu vaccines, major outbreaks became common and would shut down schools, businesses, and entire communities. For example, the 1917 to 1918 Spanish Flu Pandemic coincided with World War I (WWI) and actually took more lives than the war itself. Although the flu strain itself is generally not fatal, the secondary effects of dehydration, respiratory failure, and secondary infection can be lethal. Young children, older adults, and individuals with chronic illness are the most vulnerable. The Centers for Disease Control and Prevention (CDC) in Atlanta, Georgia, monitors influenza patterns and issues flu forecasts, much in the way that the National Weather Service predicts weather. The CDC maintains a stockpile of vaccines for the known strains of influenza and other contagious diseases and has an extensive infectious disease research unit that continuously develops new vaccines.

Epidemics occur when a viral strain affects a region. Pandemics occur when a strain spreads worldwide. Pandemics are much more serious and involve outbreaks that are global in nature. The great Bubonic Plague, also known as the "Black Plague," of the Middle Ages (c.1300 AD) caused an estimated 100 million deaths. This Black Plague may have reduced the planet's population by 50%. Humanity was on the verge of extinction. The novel (meaning new strain) coronavirus or COVID-19 is a current example of a pandemic. COVID is especially dangerous, because there was no existing vaccine and the disease attacked the respiratory system causing death by lung and heart failure. It is important for all individuals to receive an annual flu vaccination along with any other immunizations recommended by the CDC; this is especially imperative for counselors, because they work in close contact with others. Frequent hand washing and the use of antibacterial and antiviral soap are important in helping to prevent the spread of disease. During pandemics, social distancing and wearing a mask are proven interventions to mitigate the spread of disease and should be incorporated into a professional counselor's practice.

Collateral Effects of Disasters

The types of disasters mentioned previously can lead to a secondary disaster. For example, broken sewage lines in earthquakes and stagnant water in flooded areas become the breeding ground for germs. Poor hygiene among displaced survivors can cause various disease processes. Emergency medical personnel may require universal or other special precautions for counselors interacting in a disaster area. These precautions almost always are enforced in the morgue and

Table 22.2

Centers for Disease Control and Prevention Guidelines

During High-Risk Breakout Episodes	Telehealth Services Only Unless Event Is Crisis
During low to medium breakout episodes or for crisis intervention	1. Telehealth services for high-risk clients;
	2. Mask wearing by staff and clients;
	3. Plastic barriers in contact areas;
	4. Closed or socially distanced waiting room that maintains 6 feet of separation;
	5. Temperature and symptom checks for staff and clients prior to entering office;
	6. Frequent hand washing;
	7. Use of sanitizer solution on hands of staff and clients; and,
	8. Daily deep cleaning of facility.

medical treatment areas and include gowns, masks, and medical gloves. Counselors usually are briefed by healthcare clinicians on the greatest disease risk and the ways to minimize contact prior to going into these areas. With the onset of COVID and expanded CDC guidelines counselors need to become more acutely aware of disease prevention and how to incorporate those techniques in individual and group settings. Table 22.2 offers suggested CDC guidelines.

Ecological disasters can involve the food or life cycles of a region. The functions of ecosystems are based upon a natural balance of animals that prey upon one another and plant life that supports the animals and environment in which they live. Oil spills, such as the one that affected the Gulf Coast in 2011, or the 2019 Keystone Pipeline spill in North Dakota, destroy both animal and plant life by making the ecosystem uninhabitable for both. Humans may not notice the immediate effects of an ecosystem disaster; however, mental health professionals should be aware of the delayed emergence of ecosystem disasters and expect to engage in long-term counseling services in an affected region. Changes in the life cycle may take years to become permanent. As an example, previously rich fishing waters may become spoiled as the plant and animal life adapts to the ecosystem disaster. In human terms, an ecosystem disaster can knock a wealthy tourist town into a poverty-ridden ghost town. In most cases, ecosystem disasters are anything but natural and are created by man's need to conduct industrial manufacturing and pillage the natural resources of Earth's land and waters.

Our water is particularly vulnerable to an ecosystem disaster. Most people would think of an ocean oil spill as the most vivid type of ecosystem disaster, but we need only consider that 99% of Earth's water is unusable for human consumption. Most of our water is either filled with salt, as in the oceans; buried deep underground; or frozen in the polar ice caps. Humans exist on only 1% of the total water composition of Earth. Our fresh water supply is depleting, and if the trend is not reversed, this could have a serious impact on the time that humans have on this planet.

DISASTER RESPONSE SYSTEM

The disaster response system originated during post World War II America, as a way to prepare the American public for a response to nuclear attack. The war proved to be particularly devastating to large, underresourced civilian population centers in Europe and Asia. Known initially as *civil defense*, this government agency planned responses to large-scale disaster. The focus of civil defense surrounded what to do after a disaster strike and not on ways to mitigate or prevent a major emergency event. As the cold war ended, civil defense expanded its role and became a much broader government agency, now known as the Federal Emergency Management Agency, or FEMA. FEMA coordinates local, state, and federal responses to disasters of all types. Training, research, and prevention are core tenets of FEMA's role in the American government. A major focus of disaster response involves managing the psyche of the affected population and coordinating the needs of emergency clinicians called to duty in rescue and recovery operations. Current literature in the counseling arena describes phases of behavior and symptom patterns that affect individuals exposed to a natural disaster. Counseling interventions can be intimated to help individuals recover from devastating events. The study of the psychological effects of disaster and intervention strategies is known as disaster mental health (DMD) and is recognized by FEMA as a core response to any horrific event. This section elaborates upon the disaster response system by discussing the following relevant issues: The Psychological Effects of Disaster, Interventions, and Working With Emergency Clinicians.

The Psychological Effects of Disaster

Traumatic experiences from horrific disasters go beyond the human boundaries of age, culture, gender, or religion. The question is not "Can it happen?" but rather, "When will it happen?" Entire populations affected by a disaster can experience an intense release of emotions as a result of sudden, sad, and catastrophic events. Release of these emotions can cause various stress reactions. Medical literature has described these stress reactions as having an impact on both the physical and emotional well-being of an individual. Additional evidence also points toward the negative effects of frequent ongoing stressors, called "cumulative stress," in the weeks and months that follow a disaster. Traumatic experiences from natural disasters can be defined as occurring in two distinct phases, known as primary and secondary (or ongoing) traumatization. This section reviews relevant aspects of primary and secondary traumatization along with identifying the phases of disaster in psychological terms.

Primary Traumatization

Posttraumatic stress disorder (PTSD) is the most studied of the stress reactions and represents the most common result of primary, or initial ,traumatization by a catastrophic event (Everly, 1995). Detailed discussion of PTSD has been offered in previous chapters of this book, but it is worthy of revisiting specific details, because of the prevalence of PTSD among disaster victims.

In 1920, Sigmund Freud (1920/1956) published his book *Beyond the Pleasure Principle*, in which he addressed the topic of trauma The framework for traumatic response as described by Freud continues to influence the development of the diagnostic criteria for PTSD found in the ever evolving *Diagnostic and Statistical Manual of Mental Disorders*, now in its Fifth Edition (5th ed.; *DSM-5*; American Psychiatric Association, 2013). PTSD is now recognized as a multidimensional behavioral health disorder with complex symptomology (APA, 2013).

The lived experience of a natural disaster can cause immediate psychological distress, but the psychological consequences generally are transient (McFarlane, 1987). According to McFarlane, "In the early months, somatic complaints, PTSD and travel anxiety are frequently described. In the long term, however, depressive symptoms emerge. Many individuals with early difficulties rapidly improve while a few develop substantial long-term psychiatric problems" (p. 365). McFarlane suggested that early intervention and education on both the social and psychological impact of disaster may help to predict those who are at high risk for long-term problems. Numerous studies (Dyregrov, 1989; Hodgkinson & Stewart, 1991; Mitchell & Bray, 1990; Schnyder, 1997) concluded that prevention programs may also help to limit the high-risk group. Many surveys and studies, which ask recipients about their opinions surrounding the effectiveness of mental health services during disaster responses, have reported favorable findings (Robinson & Mitchell, 1993). For example, a 1997 study in Australia found that police and fire brigade workers rated professional mental health services as 95% effective, peer support services as 93% effective, and debriefing/defusing as 91% effective in helping them to cope with disaster response (Robinson, 1997). In that same study, 95% of respondents ($n = 755$, at a 60% response rate) supported the perceived importance of continuing counseling services for an extended period of time after a disaster. Knowledge about recovery from psychological trauma is growing. One aspect of recovery involves the importance of talking about one's experiences (van der Kolk & McFarlane, 1996). This belief infers that humans need to express their thoughts in some way. However, it has been suggested that people resist acknowledging, validating, and deliberating on those aspects of our existence that are emotionally difficult to comprehend (Tarvydus et al., 2017, 2018). Herman (1992) has asserted that, over time, an individual experiences waves of acknowledgment, followed by periods of denial of their experienced event. Herman has argued that the episodic nature of trauma requires continuous support for those exposed to it. Herman's beliefs have been integrated into contemporary treatment models.

Long-term outcomes after trauma are influenced by the nature of the posttrauma environment (Rapheal & Wilson, 1993). Repeated traumatization, such as aftershocks following an earthquake, adds an enduring traumatic stress response that is thought to synergize subsequent traumatic events (Levers, 2012, 2020). This means that lesser traumatic events can cause greater stress responses. As the individual experiences more and more traumatic events, as often occurs in the post-disaster recovery phase, the ability to cope becomes compromised. Rapheal and Wilson also recommend long-term support for those who experience disaster firsthand. Populations need continued system-based support services in helping them to deal with the emotions and cognitive distortions provoked by exposure to stressful events. Some observers see the role of mental health professionals as providers of vocabulary (Gist & Lubin, 1999). Counselors are able to offer labels for what individuals think and feel; in this way, mental health workers also can help survivors to normalize their emotional reactions.

Other factors that have an impact on the psychological response to disaster include the degree to which an individual perceives that events are uncontrollable versus preventable. Gist and Lubin (1999) suggest that individuals experience a faster return to normalcy when uncontrollable natural events such as a flash flood or hurricane strike occur. When horrible events occur that are man-made and perceived as preventable, psychological responses linger (Tomko, 2012; Tracy, 2006). Baum (1987) argued that victims of technological disasters are at greater risk for developing stress reactions because technology systems are assumed to be controllable; recent examples of this would be the nuclear radiation leaks in Russia and Japan and the Gulf of Mexico BP Oil Spill. Likewise, incompetence and failure of sociopolitical systems and political leaders in a disaster can increase the risk for stress reactions and psychological disorders. Tracy (2006) detailed the failures of FEMA during Hurricane Katrina recovery operations that resulted in inadequate medical and basic needs supplies for both storm survivors and rescue workers. This leadership failure resulted in deleterious psychological effects and hastened PTSD among first responders.

Secondary Traumatization

Jankoski (2002) conducted research that focused on the cost of caring; she stated that the "individuals who care for others often undergo a pain as a consequence of their exposure to others' traumatic material" (p. 11). Many other studies also have supported this claim of secondary or vicarious traumatization of emergency workers like emergency medical technicians, fire fighters, and law enforcement (Dyregrov & Mitchell, 1992; McCann & Pearlman, 1990; Raphael et al., 1984). This vicarious traumatization has occurred in emergency personnel after working with individuals who had undergone traumatic events. Likewise, relatives of survivors coming into a region to help loved ones clean up, utility workers, insurance adjusters, and members of the news media all can be victims of secondary traumatization.

Figley (1998) described a process called compassion fatigue in which traumatic symptoms can develop in individuals who are "empathetically engaged" with others who have experienced traumatic events. Figley listed two factors that have a causal relationship to compassion fatigue: "First, is that an exposure to another's traumatic experiences must occur; and second is an empathetic engagement with that individual must take place" (Figley, 1998, p. 7). The construct of compassion fatigue contends that trauma stress reactions are contagious and create effects in those individuals who work with psychological trauma victims. Dyregrov and Mitchell (1992) said that "the same traumatic stress symptoms that affect victims of psychological trauma also impact the professionals who work with them. These symptoms include sleep disturbances, flashbacks, nightmares, irritability, anxiety, and depression" (p. 51). Vicarious traumatization continues to be a concern for professionals during the recovery phase of a disaster.

Phases of Disaster in Psychological Terms

The sociological and psychological patterns of recovery occur in five specific stages (Farberow & Gordon, 1981). These patterns of behavior should dictate the types of interventions counselors use in helping individuals and communities to recover from a disaster. These five stages are:

- **Initial impact phase:** Patterns in the first phase include shock, fear, and extreme anxiety.
- **Heroic phase: This phase can last up to 1 week after the event and may occur in some cases before the initial impact phase. Disaster survivors reach out to one another in an attempt to save life and property and often involve extreme risk-taking or heroism involving altruistic actions.**
- **Honeymoon phase:** This phase may last from 2 weeks to 2 months. Survivors, and the community as a whole, develop a synergy from the outpouring of support and services that stream into a disaster area. A mood of optimism is prevalent and fueled by promises of relief from the government and service agencies.
- **Disillusionment phase:** Lasting from 2 months to a year or more, this phase is characterized by resentment, a sense of loss, and the development of an existential vacuum as government and relief agencies leave the region. The survivors often feel alone and abandoned, which may reactivate previous psychological trauma. This phase is often termed the "second disaster." Counselors need to be aware of the development of disillusionment and begin interventions that address traumatization and take care to provide reassurance.
- **Reconstruction phase:** Communities and individuals may remain in this phase for several years post disaster. A pattern of rebuilding and moving forward is prevalent as survivors achieve control of their reactions and personal problems related to the disaster.

These phases are labile and meant to identify general behavior patterns. It is important to note that individual responses vary and are based on many factors such as the health of the person's coping mechanisms, the presence of a support system, physical health, and other comorbid factors. It is useful to understand the behavioral patterns in order to establish an appropriate intervention strategy.

Interventions

Current interventions in DMH are based on a developmental three-stage model (UNODRR, 2009). Each stage in the model represents a different counseling intervention that matches victim behaviors along a temporal continuum of recovery. The model also uses a triage scheme, which helps to sort out individuals who are at high risk for the development of acute stress disorder (ASD) and PTSD while providing support to those who appear to be recovering adequately. The three stages of this model (see Table 22.3) are acute support, intermediate support, and ongoing treatment. Although specific timelines are given for each stage, it is important to understand the many variables that occur with each type of disaster and to know that no two disasters are ever alike. These variables are called temporal issues and must be considered by clinicians as they plan interventions. The three-stage model should be used as a guide rather than a dogmatic protocol. Hurricane Katrina is an example of the developmental nature of disasters. Many Gulf Coast residents were relieved as the outer edge of the hurricane passed, leaving their homes unharmed, only to be traumatized as the man-made levees failed, flooding their homes.

Table 22.3

Support Stages of Disaster Mental Health

Acute stage	1 week	Provide psychological first aid to survivors and perform triage.
Intermediate support	1 week to 1 month	Promote anxiety management and reduce stress. Perform triage and referral for ongoing support.
Ongoing support	1 month to 1 year or more	Provide diagnostic and long-term behavioral health services.

Table 22.4

Eight Steps of Psychological First Aid

Step 1	Make contact with survivors;
Step 2	Provide physical and emotional safety;
Step 3	Stabilize survivors' emotions through active listening, validation, and supportive statements;
Step 4	Gather information about survivors' immediate needs;
Step 5	Offer practical help to meet needs;
Step 6	Connect survivors with family, friends, and support systems such as the ARC;
Step 7	Provide psycho-educational information about stress reactions and reduction; and,
Step 8	Link survivors to collaborative services such as FEMA or a CMHA.

FEMA, Federal Emergency Management Agency.

Individuals who were recovering adequately, and perhaps were euphoric initially, were suddenly acute victims of a natural disaster (Rapheal & Wilson, 1993).

As a general procedural rule, behavior health specialists need to be aware of the setting they are entering and knowledgeable about the specific leadership, organizations, and policies already in place by the emergency management agencies. Many hazards are present near disaster areas, and hazards such as downed power lines, disease, flooding, threat of structure collapse, and fire may linger for weeks, post impact. Behavioral health clinicians always should follow the directions of the emergency management system that are in place. Depending on the scale of the disaster, the general command chain, known as the incident command system, follows a linear local, state, and FEMA structure. Large-scale and terrorist threats also may fall under the jurisdiction of military personnel. Order from chaos is the primary goal of emergency response organizations, as they begin the rescue operation phase of a disaster. Counselors need to understand that behavioral health issues may not be at the forefront of FEMA goals. It is important for counselors to support the incident command system as well as the leaders, who are experiencing a tremendous amount of rescue-work stress.

Stage 1: Acute Support

Acute support is the first stage and takes place immediately after the mass disaster. This treatment phase may last for up to 1 week. The counselor's goals in this initial stage are to establish contact with survivors, provide direct care, identify individuals who are at high risk for future psychological problems, and arrange for behavioral health follow-up. Many times, this type of intervention plan constitutes psychological first aid (PFA; Brymer et al., 2006). PFA focuses on managing the initial needs of survivors by providing support and resources to begin the recovery process and diminish acute stress reactions and posttraumatic stress. PFA often occurs within the disaster area, at shelters that have been established in churches, schools, or community centers. PFA promotes calm, connectedness, and hope through eight core counselor actions.

The eight steps of PFA are listed in Table 22.4.

PFA is a beginning tool that counselors can employ for use in a mass disaster. The primary result of PFA is establishing the linkages with other support systems that aid in the recovery process. Please see Box 22.1 for a clinical vignette in which to apply the PFA.

BOX 22.1

Clinical Vignette: Night Twister

Jorge is a 47-year-old Hispanic male, whom you meet at an evacuation shelter. Jorge is a single father who shares custody with his ex-wife in caring for their 13-year-old son, Jayna. Jorge's home was destroyed in the middle of the night by a large, destructive torna-do. Jorge tells you, "I feel like I am in a dream" and verbalizes his fear that he will never recover all that is lost. Jorge is unable to make contact with his ex-wife and Jayna. He also discovered that the store where he is employed has been destroyed. Jorge repeats that he had no warning and doesn't understand why his house was destroyed while others were untouched.

Conceptualization Questions:

1. What is Jorge's stage of disaster recovery?
2. What is Jorge's most immediate PFA needs?
3. Why does Jorge present as high risk for PTSD, and what can be done to reduce the effects of his traumatic stress?
4. What sociocultural issues need to be considered as counseling interventions progress into future stages of recovery?

Stage 2: Intermediate Support

Intermediate support is the second stage and takes place from 1 week to 1 month, post impact. The primary focus of treatment during this stage is to promote anxiety management and reduce stress, which may preclude an ASD. This is accomplished by the development of a therapeutic relationship using traditional client-centered theory and integrating cognitive-behavioral techniques to train survivors in anxiety management. Specific triage for ASD should occur and referrals made to behavioral health clinicians for intensive care when derealization, depersonalization, or flashbacks are present. There are five core treatment principles in the intermediate stage, and these are identified as follows:

1. Develop a strong working alliance with the survivor;
2. Collaborate with the client in the development of goals;
3. Provide empathy, friendship, and support;
4. Provide positive regard and acceptance; and,
5. Project an attitude of authenticity and genuineness.

Attention to the sociocultural dynamics of the survivors is critical during this stage and is best supported by the five steps just listed. Issues of privilege and dominance often emerge in survivors during this stage. The healer must be aware of their own personal beliefs and biases in order to support a trusting, collaborative therapeutic relationship.

Stage 3: Ongoing Treatment

The final stage typically occurs between 1 and 3 months but can last for years after the disaster impact. This stage focuses on individuals identified in stage 2 and provides more specific diagnostic and long-term behavioral health services. Specific goals in this stage are to offer a differential diagnosis and modify treatment based upon the clinical presentation. These diagnoses often involve anxiety, mood, and substance abuse disorders. Treatment often is carried out in a traditional mental health environment.

It is important to note that most individuals exposed to a natural disaster recover on their own and do not experience lasting psychological effects. Counselors always should focus on helping the survivors achieve safety and meet basic needs before providing other services. Professionals should make an effort to identify themselves as helpers and what their roles are in the disaster. It is important to help survivors gain accurate information about what is going on around them; this can be accomplished by providing practical and useful psychoeducation. Finally, helpers need to take care of themselves and know their limits. A wounded healer is of little use in DMH operations.

Working With Emergency Clinicians

It has been recognized for many years that emergency medical service (EMS) workers encounter psychologically stressful situations in the course of their jobs, especially those involving disaster and major emergency responses (Substance Use and Mental Health Services Administration [SAMHSA, 2018). The recent COVID pandemic has brought the world's emergency response systems to the breaking point, and the psychological health of our first responders with it. In his groundbreaking work on stress reactions among EMS personnel, Mitchell (1981) listed events that are likely to cause stress reactions in EMS responders. These events include emergencies involving the death of a coworker in the line of duty; death of a child; gruesome accidents; exposure to domestic violence; and natural disasters with widespread damage, injury, and death. Other scenarios, such as exposure to suicide and homicide crime scenes, terrorist attacks, and failed procedures by rescuers also have been attributed to causing stress reactions in emergency medical clinicians (Mitchell & Everly, 1996).

Medical literature has described these stress reactions as having an impact on both the physical and emotional well-being of rescue workers (Lawn et al., 2020;). In a 2002 study, conducted by McSwain (2003), nearly one-third of all EMS workers left their jobs within 3 years of hire for other occupations. The study also discovered that their workman's compensation insurance claims were three times higher than the average healthcare professional and that job dissatisfaction among emergency workers remained high. Some empirical evidence suggested that the negative effects of frequent ongoing stressors, also referred to as "cumulative stress," are possible reasons for attrition, illness, injury, and job dissatisfaction among EMS personnel (Mitchell & Bray, 1990). On average, natural disasters such as earthquakes, hurricanes, or tornadoes happen somewhere on the planet each day. What these horrific natural events have in common is the ability to affect many people at the same time but in different ways. Disaster workers can be both directly and indirectly affected by their work in these events. Lundin and Bodegård (1993) reported that the impact of the disaster on emergency workers is dependent upon several factors. First, the impact involves the harshness of the environment of the rescue operation. The harshness can be defined as the weather conditions, travel distance of the rescue teams, and the number of victims. Another aspect is the demography of the victims whom the disaster workers are trying to aid. Lundin and Bodegård suggest additional examples of this, including whether the victims have the same language and ethnic, religious, or cultural backgrounds; have the same interests; or are members of a shared occupational group, such as plant or office workers. Finally, McFarlane (1987) notes that "personal factors of the rescue workers such as maturity, level of education, amount of emergency service training, and earlier experiences in disaster response strongly influence the reactions of disaster workers" (p. 367).

EMS personnel deal with the sociocultural consequences of disaster at interpersonal levels. Not only do they experience the loss of life and physical disability of disaster victims, but the financial, interpersonal, and spiritual losses within the survivors (Raphael et al., 1984). As such, vicarious traumatization continues to be a concern for the rescue worker.

Previous Counseling Interventions for Emergency Personnel

A process to treat and prevent stress reactions, called critical incident stress debriefing (CISD), was introduced to emergency personnel by Mitchell in 1983. CISD became a widely accepted protocol for use by emergency service agencies such as law enforcement, fire departments, paramedical and rescue teams, and emergency department staff (Wilson, 1995). CISD evolved over time into a more comprehensive process involving a multicomponent work-based systems approach to helping EMS workers deal effectively with the traumatic and highly stressful components of their work. This evolved process was titled critical incident stress management (CISM; Mitchell & Everly, 1997). CISM was adopted in 2000 by the National Transportation and Highway Safety Administration (NTHSA, 2002) as the part of the national curriculum for emergency medical technicians and paramedics that deals with the stress reactions and the well-being of the EMS clinician. NTHSA, the federal agency that regulates EMS training in America, has made attempts at addressing PTSD and burnout among emergency health workers.

This process of CISM involves a team approach based upon a partnership of mental health professionals and a peer support group. The team helps the affected individual express their feelings toward a particular event or situation that had a strong emotional effect for the individual (Mitchell & Bray, 1990). CISM engages in an open discussion that relies on group support for helping participants overcome the stress brought about by a particular event (Mitchell & Everly, 1997).

The five core components of CISM are:

1. Early intervention treatments for EMS clinicians exposed to critical incidents;
2. Provision of psychosocial support to rescuers in need;
3. An opportunity for expression of thoughts and feelings;
4. Crisis education; and,
5. Assistance in the development of coping mechanisms.

Mitchell and Bray (1990) advise "that of all these components should be administered with cultural understanding and sensitivity" (p. 116). Furthermore, he describes that a disruption in one of these components can exacerbate stress reactions. Also, PTSD can create negative effects on the way caregivers perform their duty.

CISM programs consistently yield very positive comments in surveys and studies (Everly et al., 2000). Even studies that cited evidence of the lack of efficacy of CISM still reported high perceived helpfulness of the debriefing process by participants (Hytten & Hasle, 1989; Kenardy et al., 1996; Rogers, 1996). The American College of Emergency Physicians (ACEP; 2000) indicates that "CISM involves a partnership between mental health professionals and a peer support group of emergency workers. This partnership allows participants to express their feelings toward a particular situation that had a strong emotional effect and should be used as the mainstay for EMS provider wellness" (p. 62).

Although CISM has been identified as a process for the management of critical incident stress, it was not until recently that additional focus was placed on cumulative stress and its effects on EMS workers. CISM commonly is used in day-to-day impact incidents, but not for day-to-day low-impact incidents. Cumulative stress continues to be a significant problem for emergency workers, and we are seeing this play out during the COVID pandemic; unfortunately, it typically goes unaddressed. Better ways to support emergency workers from the long-term psychological effects of their job and a clearer understanding of the subculture of rescue work are needed.

The Culture of the Rescue Worker and Current Counseling Approaches

Paramedics, police officers, fire fighters, and other emergency workers know that they are the first to respond to horrific events on a daily basis. The reality of encountering extremely physically and emotionally traumatic situations, especially those involving disasters and major emergency responses, is an accepted part of the profession (Mitchell, 1981; Rapheal, 1977; Teahan et al., 2017). As a result, the first responders to medical emergencies and traumatic injury experience an intense, yet controlled release of emotions because of these catastrophic events. This unique experience helps to define the subculture of the emergency worker.

Mitchell and Bray (1990) outlined personality characteristics common to emergency service clinicians. Labeled as rescue personality traits, EMS personnel tend to be detail-oriented, set high performance standards, and be very dedicated. Additionally, rescuers are quick decision-makers and are action-oriented (see Table 22.5). Understanding the rescue personality is an important part of gaining entry into the subculture of emergency service clinicians.

Working in emergency service professions exposes an individual to significant suffering and pain. The types of pain being experienced by emergency workers in COVID response efforts are historic in context. Many EMS workers themselves had contracted and died from the COVID-19. Worldwide, rescuers have witnessed record call volumes, worked in cumbersome personal protective equipment that often was inadequate and in short supply, and held the hands of countless dying clients. First responders have experienced overwhelming complex emotions that include anxiety, depression, and mental and physical fatigue. Counseling interventions should focus on helping rescuers to understand their emotions and use that insight to help the victims who have called for their care (Tracy, 2006). EMS personnel need counseling models, which help them frame and control their emotions, rather than compiling a symptom inventory checklist of their physical and emotional reactions. Existential rather than cognitive and behavioral approaches may be advantageous for this specialized counseling population, especially when dealing with the complexity of emotions during COVID. Existential theory (ET) orientations provide a viable therapeutic system, because they help the emergency worker to verbalize, converse, question, and debate the horrific and stressful experiences they encounter. There are four key therapeutic issues in existential psychology: the search for meaning from life experiences, exploring feelings of isolation, developing an understanding of freedom, and the acceptance of death. EMS clinicians are faced with many of these issues at once. Focused listening and Socratic dialogue are the main techniques as the counselor listens for themes in the client's talk that reflect struggles with meaning and identity (Day, 2007). It is important to focus on the responder's need to make sense of the suffering that they have witnessed. Psychoeducation on self-care techniques should be incorporated into every session and may include healthy diet tips, exercise, sleep, hygiene, recreation activities, escape time, and meditation and mindfulness techniques. Frequent follow-up is important is reinforcing the self-care behaviors.

The main objective is to help the emergency workers restructure attitudes about themselves and their chaotic environment. This self-awareness and awareness of the environment can lead to positive new attitudes about the work. The ultimate outcome would be to help rescuers not become

Table 22.5

General Personality Traits of Emergency Service Clinicians

Thinking patterns:	Behavioral patterns:
Detail oriented	Action oriented
Obsessive	Quick decision-makers
Easily bored	Risk takers
Highly dedicated	Need to be in control
Need to be needed	High need for stimulation

trapped by past decisions, events, or patterns of behavior. It also allows workers to, in a safe and nonjudgmental environment, openly express their frustrations over system and leadership failures. First responders can share the many transgressions they have witnessed, especially against those citizens that are disadvantaged. Using the ET approaches would focus emergency workers on the importance of lifesaving work and help the rescuer define the meaning of their existence.

Mental health professionals need to work with families of emergency workers as well. Counseling and psychoeducational services should focus on assisting family members to gain insight into the stresses of emergency work and on helping their loved ones to employ effective coping strategies for the management of job-related stress. Most importantly, frequent referral and follow-up of EMS workers exposed to cumulative stress must occur.

Working with EMS personnel in essence is a counseling specialty. Training on cumulative stress and stress management, in general, must be an ongoing process during therapy sessions with rescue workers. Professional counselors should be aware of the specific stressors unique to rescue work and tailor counseling interventions to meet the needs of this special population. Finally, counseling theory grounded in ET can be a useful approach in helping EMS and their families make meaning out of human suffering (Box 22.2).

BOX 22.2

Clinical Vignette: Too Much and Not Enough

Madeline is a 32-year-old female and 8-year career paramedic who presents for counseling at the suggestion of her supervisor. Madeline has worked 12 days in a row during the pandemic state of emergency and has responded to nearly 60 emergency calls during that time. She reports difficulty falling asleep yet feels fatigued. Madeline states her appetite is poor and she can't concentrate at work. Madeline begins weeping in session and states the amount of death she has seen is too much for her to bear. She openly expresses anger on first responders not having enough PPE equipment. She states, "We knew the virus was coming but we were unprepared." Madeline now questions her desire to remain as a paramedic and states "What difference do I really make?"

Conceptualization Questions:

1. What are Madeline's existential issues and how can they be addressed in counseling?
2. What type(s) of stress reaction is Madeline experiencing?
3. How did system and leadership failure affect Madeline's ability to cope with the stress of disaster response?

COUNSELING IMPLICATIONS

DMH has many implications for counselors and really should be viewed as a counseling subspecialty. Mental health professionals, perhaps more so now than ever before, are likely to be called to duty to help populations affected by disaster. Global warming and the world-wide pandemic have forever changed humanity. Political system failures have worsened the effects of disasters, causing existential crisis in citizens and rescuers alike. It is important for professional counselors to understand the nature of the disaster and how to work with emergency service clinicians and the surviving population. The skills of triage and assessment are important counseling tools in disaster areas. Flexibility and adaptability are important. The work environment of a counselor changes during disasters. The tranquil office is moved to a school, church, or noisy community center. The office may become mobile and move from street to street as the rescue and recovery efforts progress. The COVID pandemic has necessitated that counselors provide telehealth services. In a disaster, counselors must be able to adapt their intervention approaches to meet the needs of the population as well as the demands of the environment, as dictated by the catastrophe. A thorough knowledge of the psychological effects of disaster is needed by all counselors. Counselors routinely should practice the skills of PFA. Professional counselors also should be aware of their changing role as the phases of disaster recovery progress.

Oftentimes, counselors themselves are victims—a tornado does not skip over a home, because there is a healer inside. Therefore, it is important to recognize that healers may be experiencing the same psychological effects as the population of a region. Counselor self-awareness is extremely important as the chaos of a disaster encompasses the counselor's environment. Response protocols usually dictate that counselors from other communities be used for psychological response efforts, but, as stated earlier in this chapter, infrastructure damage may delay the arrival of out-of-town helpers. In the event of regional disasters, many towns are affected, and the arrival of counselors is dependent upon their ability to gain entrance into the area from other parts of the country. This process may take many days to organize. These factors place counselors at high risk for secondary traumatization and other stress reactions. Counselor awareness and supervision are essential for clinicians functioning in a disaster area. Whenever possible, one experienced clinical supervisor should be identified to provide only supervision services. This supervisor should not participate in any other duties in the disaster response and should concentrate all of their efforts on helping the healers.

CONCLUSION

No one is immune to a natural disaster. Counselors can expect to be called to service several times during their career to help populations cope with the psychological consequences of a disaster. Counselors themselves often become a survivor of these events. It is important for healers to review disaster scenarios with emergency management agencies ahead of time.

Counselors need to learn and practice their roles in a disaster and to work as part of the emergency services team. All professional counselors should be aware of the stages of disaster response and be competent clinicians of PFA and triage. Counselors need to be aware of the cultural nature of disasters. The poor, older adults, and young children are at greatest risk for the development of psychological trauma from a disaster. Rescue personnel need immediate and long-term attention to help them deal with the psychological cost of caring. Specialized training and continuing education on DMH is a mandate for our profession and continues to emerge as our dynamic planet changes as a result of global warming. The question is not will we be called to service, but when.

ADDITIONAL RESOURCES

A robust set of instructor resources designed to supplement this text is located at http://connect.springerpub.com/content/book/978-0-8261-5085-1. Qualifying instructors may request access by emailing textbook@springerpub.com.

PRACTICE-BASED RESOURCES AND REFERENCES

To view a list of resources and all the references, please visit connect.springerpub.com via the following url: http://connect.springerpub.com/content/book/978-0-8261-5085-1/part/part04/chapter/ch22

CHAPTER 23

Genocide, War, and Political Violence

KIRRILY PELLS AND CHASTE UWIHOREYE

CHAPTER OVERVIEW

The distress of populations affected by genocide, war, and the specific phenomenon often referred to as "ethnic cleansing" and political violence is typically viewed through the lens of trauma and posttraumatic stress disorder (PTSD) (the word "war" is used in the rest of this chapter to refer specifically to "ethnic cleansing"). However, there have been increasing critiques of the assumed universal applicability of the trauma paradigm, from psychologists and psychiatrists, as well as anthropologists and sociologists, engaged with individuals and societies affected by mass violence. This chapter reviews how the specific characteristics of genocide, war, and political violence pose challenges to biomedical and Western psychological framings of trauma. It argues the need for greater attention to cultural context, intersecting structural oppressions, and social justice and considers how narrative- and arts-based tools, underpinned by principles drawn from multicultural and decolonial approaches, may assist in this endeavor.

LEARNING OBJECTIVES

After reading this chapter, the reader should be able to:

1. Explore the causes, manifestations, and consequences of mental distress for populations affected by genocide, war, and political violence;
2. Appraise critiques of biomedical and Western psychological framings of trauma, with a focus on the neglect of cultural specificity and structural oppressions, including colonialism and social justice;
3. Examine alternative approaches to working with populations affected by genocide, war, and political violence (in the country of origin and in exile), underpinned by principles drawn from multicultural and decolonial approaches to counseling; and,
4. Consider how the adoption and adaptation of narrative- and arts-based tools, within counseling practice, may aid greater sensitivity to cultural and power dynamics and foster meaning-making, empowerment, and calls for social justice.

This chapter is a revision of the chapter that appeared in the first edition of this textbook; Dr Karen Treisman co-authored the earlier version of this chapter, and we thank her for her original contribution.

INTRODUCTION AND CONTEXT

The evolution of trauma as a psychological concept is intimately connected with the shifting nature of warfare during the 20th century. The term "shell shock" was introduced to explain the trauma exhibited by soldiers following the first World War. Shell shock was understood as being due to soldiers' inner vulnerabilities being brought to the surface. This was challenged by research emanating from later conflicts, specifically Vietnam and the pioneering work of psychiatrist Robert Lifton (1973), which, along with research and advocacy from the movement to end violence against women, formed the basis for the diagnosis of PTSD and its inclusion within the *Diagnostic and Statistical Manual of Mental Disorders* (*DSM-III*) in 1980. In more recent years, the fallout from conflicts, and specifically genocide, war, and political violence, have continued to advance and challenge understandings of trauma, PTSD, and therapeutic approaches.

Counselors, social workers, psychologists, and psychiatrists engaging with individuals and societies affected by mass and political violence have become increasingly critical of attempts to apply narrow biomedical or biopsychological framings of trauma, particularly as found within the *DSM*, to diverse sociocultural contexts around the globe (Boothby et al., 2006; Bracken, 2002; Jones, 2004; Summerfield, 1999, 2001, 2002). This is not to deny that trauma has biological and psychological influences and manifestations, as explored elsewhere in this volume. However, this chapter suggests that there has been an overemphasis on intrapsychic functioning that is divorced from a consideration of "historical patterns of power, international politics and local patterns and languages of suffering" (Khan, 2017, p. 96). Drawing on scholarship from the fields of sociology and anthropology, as well as critical psychology, this chapter reviews how the specific characteristics and legacies of genocide, war, and political violence pose challenges to biomedical and Western psychological framings of trauma. It argues the need for greater attention to cultural context, intersecting structural oppressions, and social justice and considers how narrative- and arts-based tools, underpinned by principles drawn from multicultural and decolonial approaches, may assist counselors in working with survivors, whether in the country of origin, or with refugee and asylum-seeking populations in exile.

The chapter begins by exploring causes, manifestations, and consequences of mental distress for populations affected by genocide, war, and political violence before moving to sections focused on contextualizing trauma and meaning-making, structural oppressions and epistemic justice, and the politics of trauma. These major sections are followed by a summary conclusion of the chapter and a helpful, online list of resources for instructors, students, and clinicians.

MASS VIOLENCE AND MENTAL DISTRESS

This section provides a brief overview of how specific forms of mass violence, namely genocide, war, and political violence, are defined, along with illustrative examples, before turning to the effects on the lives of those who survive.

Genocide

Genocide is not a new phenomenon. From the campaign of Athens against Melos, through the crusades of the Knights Templar and Mongol conquests, to the decimation of the indigenous peoples of the Americas and Australia, the deliberate destruction of groups of people *because of who they are* is a constant refrain of human history (Chalk & Jonassohn, 1990; Levene, 2000). However, genocide as a concept was coined by a Polish lawyer, Raphäel Lemkin, in response to the systematic murder of six million Jews during the 1941 to 1945 Holocaust. The United Nations [UN] (1948) *Convention on the Prevention and Punishment of the Crime of Genocide* defines "genocide":

as any of a number of acts committed with the intent to destroy, in whole or in part, a national, ethnic, racial or religious group, as such:

1. Killing members of the group;
2. Causing serious bodily or mental harm to members of the group;
3. Deliberately inflicting on the group conditions of life calculated to bring about its physical destruction in whole or in part;
4. Imposing measures intended to prevent births within the group;
5. Forcibly transferring children of the group to another group. (UN, "Article 2," p. 1)

The term remains contested (M. Shaw, 2015). Some argue that it is too restrictive, by focusing on certain groups while not recognizing others, such as political groups (Hinton, 2002), whereas, others argue that the definition needs to evolve to address more recent acts of mass violence (Shaw, 2015). Consequently, there is disagreement over which events constitute genocide. There have been successful international prosecutions of genocide related to the 1994 Genocide Against the Tutsi (Rwanda) (see Box 23.1) and the 1995 Srebrenica genocide, where more than 8,000 Bosnian Muslim (Bosniak) men and boys were killed by Bosnian Serb forces in a designated U.N. safe area. Indictments for genocide also have been brought against members of the Khmer Rouge, who between 1975 and 1979 killed around two million political opponents, ethnic minorities, professionals, and intellectuals in Cambodia. The International Criminal Court has charged former Sudanese President Al Bashir with genocide, war crimes, and crimes against humanity in relation to the targeting of non-Arab civilians in Darfur (see Bloxham and Moses [2010] for a good overview of genocide across time and place). Box 23.1 offers a brief contextual discussion of the Rwandan genocide, in order to illustrate the need for culturally specific approaches in helping people to heal.

BOX 23.1

Tips From the Field

1994 Genocide Against the Tutsi: Cultural Approaches to Healing

The 1994 Genocide Against the Tutsi saw over one million, mainly Tutsi, systematically murdered in 100 days by an extremist, Hutu-led government (des Forges, 1999). This violence was the culmination of successive waves of violence, fueled by colonial divisionism by first German and later Belgian authorities. The colonial authorities reconstituted the social groups of Hutu, Tutsi, and Twa as ethnic groups, initially privileging the Tutsi monarchy, before power was handed to the Hutu majority with independence in 1962 (Prunier, 1995). Sexual violence was used systematically during the genocide, leading to a high HIV/AIDS prevalence rate among survivors, as well as children born of rape. An estimated 400,000 children were orphaned (Human Rights Watch [HRW], 2003). Thus, as Sinalo (2018, p. 31) observed, the genocide can be viewed as "a much more complex, chronic form of trauma" encompassing the structural violence of colonialism, neo-colonialism, authoritarianism, and patriarchy resulting in "the destruction of identity—that continues today."

Mental health infrastructure, resources, and personnel, both "traditional" and "modern," were destroyed during the genocide (Mukamana et al., 2019). Numerous surveys have been conducted to estimate the prevalence of PTSD and other mental disorders (Dyregrov et al., 2000; Munyandamutsa et al., 2012). However, the appropriateness and effectiveness of such "deficit-focused approaches" based on Western trauma paradigms have been questioned (Sinalo, 2018, p. 191). While manifestations of mental distress have been labelled as trauma

(continued)

and attempts have been made to find concepts within the Kinyarwanda language (e.g., *Ihaha-muka* is translated literally as breathless with fear and often is used synonymously with trauma [Taylor, 2017]). Rwandan psychologist Chaste Uwihoreye explains that this does not reflect the complexities of people's experiences, understandings, or processes of meaning-making (Den-borough & Uwihoreye, 2019). Uwihoreye notes that this views the mental distress as coming from within a person and is thus unaligned with Rwandan cultural worldviews, which frame mental distress as arising from interactions and events (Denborough & Uwihoreye, 2019).

Uwihoreye is pioneering an alternative approach, one which is deeply embedded in the Rwandan cultural context and informed by arts-based and narrative therapeutic approaches. For instance, Uwihoreye uses proverbs as a way to connect with individuals, to express stories, and to listen. In Rwanda, proverbs are "often used to express what a person has seen, heard, and experienced at the level of emotions, feelings, and states of mind, as well as to indicate to someone that they have been understood" (Bagilishya, 2000, p. 342). Proverbs can be used to elicit "a mode of expression used to recognize, confirm and participate in what the other is living on an emotional level" (Bagilishya, 2000, p. 342). Uwihoreye uses proverbs to describe a problem and separate it from an individual, for example: *ibuye ryagaragaye ntiba rikishe isuka* (meaning when you identify a stone in your field, this stone will never damage your hoe) and to acknowledge that the person is the expert of their pain. Arts-based methods are also used, such as drawing the pain and in identifying support networks.

Ethnic Cleansing

"Ethnic cleansing" is a form of war or mass violence and is a contested term, defined by the United Nations (1994) as "a purposeful policy designed by one ethnic or religious group to remove by violent and terror-inspiring means the civilian population of another ethnic or religious group from certain geographic areas" (p. 130). Critics have argued that it is an attempt to water down the Genocide Convention, which places the obligation on the international community to intervene in order to prevent its occurrence (Shaw, 2015). For example, there is considerable disagreement about the 1992 to 1995 "Bosnian War." Legally, the only part of the conflict deemed to be genocide is the 1995 Srebrenica massacre, whereas other cases before the UN-established International Criminal Tribunal for Yugoslavia have been ruled as ethnic cleansing, war crimes, and crimes against humanity rather than genocide. It was argued that it was not possible to demonstrate the "intention to destroy," despite massacres, systematic rape, the establishment of concentration camps, forced displacement, and the destruction of cultural heritage (Liberman, 2010). A more recent case of ethnic cleansing is the expulsion of over 900,000 Rohingya Muslims into Bangladesh from Myanmar since 2017, following the destruction of villages and the rape of women and girls (Human Rights Watch, 2017).

Political Violence

Political violence does not have a legal definition and is a very broad term encompassing: "a heterogeneous repertoire of actions oriented at inflicting physical, psychological, and symbolic damage to individuals and/or property with the intention of influencing various audiences for affecting or resisting political, social, and/or cultural change" (Bosi & Malthaner, 2015, p. 440). Actions include "attacks on property, bodily assaults, the planting of explosive devices, shooting attacks, kidnappings, hostage taking and the seizure of aircraft or ships, high profile assassinations, public self-immolation" as well as torture, forced disappearances, sexual slavery, or mass killings (Bosi & Malthaner, 2015, p. 440). Political violence can be enacted by state actors (e.g., government, police, or army), those working on behalf of the state (paramilitaries), or non-state actors. As Bosi and Malthaner (2015, p. 440) note, depending on the context, the actors involved, and who is speaking, "these radical forms of contentious politics may be called either terrorism or resistance." This is not to say that each label is equally valid in all cases, but rather to attend to the politicized nature of knowledge construction about events, experiences, and motivations.

Examples of political violence include the following: the tactics undertaken by the British and other colonial powers in subjugating populations (e.g., the brutal suppression of the Mau Mau uprising in Kenya in the 1950s); murder, extreme political repression, and/or disappearances of political opponents during dictatorships, such as under Mugabe in Zimbabwe (1987–2017) and Pinochet in Chile (1973–1990); apartheid in South Africa (1948-early 1990s); and, most recently, the police violence toward *Black Lives Matters* protesters in the United States (2020).

Legacies of Mass Violence

The psychological trauma paradigm, and specifically PTSD, has become the dominant lens through which the impact upon individuals of extreme violence of genocide, war, and political violence is viewed, not only by mental health professionals, but also by the media and more widely in popular, everyday usage, particularly within the Global North (Fassin & Rechtman, 2009). The symptomology of PTSD, as set out in the *Diagnostic and Statistical Manual of Mental Disorders* (5th ed.; *DSM-5*; American Psychiatric Association, 2013) is explored in-depth elsewhere in this volume (Chapters 1 and 2). In brief, PTSD is diagnosed when an individual (or a close relative or friend) directly experiences or witnesses actual or threatened death, serious injury, or sexual violence and experiences symptoms under four headings: re-experiencing the event, avoidance of reminders of the event, negative cognition and mood, and hyperarousal.

Notwithstanding the important insights that this framework has yielded in understanding and treating the impact of trauma on individuals, sociologists and anthropologists, along with mental health clinicians who have worked with survivors of mass violence, have suggested that the trauma paradigm fails to capture the experiences, perspectives, and legacies of survivors in a number of areas critical for the healing and re-building of lives (Boothby et al., 2006; Bracken, 2002; D. E. Hinton & Hinton, 2015; Jones, 2004; Khan, 2017; Summerfield, 1999, 2001, 2002).

First, genocide, war, and political violence are collective experiences, with individuals targeted because of their identity as a member of a group or collective. The social fabric is ripped apart, with the bonds between individual and community severed, thus suggesting a need to engage with the collective context and sociocultural processes of meaning-making.

Second, devastation is wrought not only on the psychological dimension of life, but also upon the physical (e.g., bodily injuries, malnutrition); material (e.g., destruction of homes and infrastructure); social (e.g., destruction or dislocation of familial and friendship networks and social institutions); and spiritual (A. L. Hinton, 2002, p. 12). "Trauma" is therefore ongoing, not just as a psychological construct, but also one firmly embedded in daily lives, relationships, and environments. Rather than an event or series of events, trauma is embedded in historical and contemporary structures of oppression. To facilitate processes of destruction, one "group" often constructs itself as superior and subjugates "the other" as inferior, the outsider, dangerous, and impure. For example, Nazi propaganda blamed the Jews for the economic depression in Germany and construed them as subhuman, in contrast to the pure Aryan race; the Nazis viewed the Jews as threatening to overrun the country. Likewise, during the early 1990s in Rwanda, Tutsi were portrayed as dishonest, as a threat to the country, and as cockroaches that needed to be exterminated. Repeated discrimination, dehumanization, and disempowerment can be compounded in the present, through asylum systems and nonreflexive psychological interventions.

Third, genocide and mass violence are inherently political acts, not just in their enactment, but in how they are responded to and remembered. Engaging with questions of politics, justice, and agency is therefore central when working with survivors of mass violence. This includes questions of whose knowledge and voices get heard and who is silenced. As Khan (2017, p. 100) questions: "How do people want to repair their own worlds compared with experts who speak on their behalf?" In the following sections we unpack each of these critiques in turn.

CONTEXTUALIZING TRAUMA AND MEANING-MAKING

Considerable debate has raged over the extent to which PTSD is a universal response to trauma. Critics have pointed to the specificity of the historical, cultural, and political contexts which have informed the diagnostic foundations of PTSD, namely calls for restitution for U.S. veterans who fought in Vietnam (1965–1975) (see Fassin & Rechtman, 2009; Young, 1995). In contrast, proponents have argued that the biological basis of symptoms, such as reexperiencing and arousal, suggest that PTSD does exist universally (Dyregrov et al., 2002; Marsella et al., 1996). In a review of studies, Hinton and Lewis-Fernández (2011) found substantial evidence of cross-cultural validity of the PTSD criteria (*DSM-IV*), but in a number of areas central to diagnosis, including avoidance/numbing, local interpretations of symptomatology, and the prevalence of somatic symptoms, more empirical research was required along with the need for re-working of criteria to increase cross-cultural applicability. While *DSM-5* has attempted a greater engagement with culture, with an appendix that includes cultural idioms of distress and cultural explanations of distress or perceived cases (Khan, 2017), cross-cultural applicability has not been developed, fully, in relation to PTSD.

While some symptoms at least may be found universally, the meanings given to the symptoms are shaped by a host of other factors, including history, culture, religion, politics, and personal life experiences (Bracken, 2002; Jones, 2004; Patel, 2003; Summerfield, 1999, 2004). This creates what Kleinman (1977) terms the "category fallacy." For example, nightmares are designated as a symptom of PTSD, yet it depends whether a given society regards nightmares as significant or problematic as to whether they may be reported (Bracken, 2002). Moreover, the ways in which the symptoms are interpreted may vary according to local ways of understanding and meaning-making. While in the Global North, in general, "medicalized ways of seeing have displaced religion as the source of everyday explanations for the vicissitudes of life and the vocabulary of distress," while in other societies, religious or cultural beliefs remain influential, with greater emphasis on the interconnections among mind, body, and spirit (Summerfield, 2004, p. 233).

A growing number of studies have sought not only to explore the cross-cultural validity of PTSD, but to examine the relationship with localized cultural idioms of distress (D. E. Hinton & Good, 2015a; Kirmayer et al., 2007). Idioms of distress are a "way of talking, or other forms of behavior shared with other people from the same culture (i.e., ethnicity, religion, community) used to express, communicate or comment on distress" (Kirmayer & Gómez-Carrillo, 2019, p. 8). For example, research conducted in Peru, following the political violence of the Shining Path (1980s–1990s), where 70,000 indigenous Andeans were killed by the guerilla movement and Peruvian military, found that while 25% of this population group exhibited PTSD symptoms, this did not fully capture expressions of distress and suffering. Instead, this suffering was better encapsulated by Quechua terms such as *pinsamientuwan* (roughly translated as worrying thoughts, worries), *ñakary* (suffering, especially collective suffering), and *llaki* (sorrow, sadness) (Pedersen et al., 2010). Therefore, any intervention requires an understanding of local knowledge and processes of meaning-making, as well as the recognition that suffering is often "both an interiorized and collective experience" (Khan, 2017, p. 23; Wilkinson & Kleinman, 2016).

Similarly, Wessells and Monteiro (2000) document a case of an Angolan orphanage, where the children exhibited typical clinical symptoms of trauma including nightmares, bedwetting, and concentration problems. The children believed a spirit was haunting the building, and so the Christian Children's Fund (CCF), now named ChildFund International, called on a local healer to perform a ritual for spiritual purification. Subsequently, the trauma symptoms diminished and the relationship between the children and adults improved. Consequently, Wessells and Monteiro (2000) argue that by developing a hybrid program that combines perspectives across cultural systems, a more holistic and context-specific understanding of healthy child development was gained ensuring the success of the project.

Clinical understandings of trauma and PTSD need to be contextualized socially and culturally, with the symptomology found in the *DSM-5* being only a "subset of symptoms associated with such syndromes" (D. E. Hinton & Good, 2015a, p. 14). Culture both shapes how traumatic events are understood and experienced and offers approaches to meaning-making and healing, particularly through cultural forms (as illustrated in Box 23.1), ritual practices, and religious traditions. While with any form of therapeutic work, it is important to ask critical questions about efficacy and not romanticize traditions that may reinforce unequal power relations or stigma (Wessells & Monteiro, 2000), there is increasing recognition of the importance of contextualizing psychiatry and psychology in ways that account for the interrelationships among the brain, lived experience, and the sociocultural world (Kirmayer et al., 2017).

STRUCTURAL OPPRESSIONS: PAST AND PRESENT

A second critique of the Western biomedical model of trauma and PTSD concerns how the traumatic event is conceptualized. The diagnosis of PTSD is unusual in that it is one of the few disorders in the *DSM-5* which specifies a cause, not just symptomology (Khan, 2017). Yet this cause is an extreme event, such as witnessing mass killings or experiencing sexual violence, which does not consider the "everyday" aspects of trauma (Sinalo, 2018). "Everyday," here, is meant in the sense of the routinized, '"nsidious" structural "conditions that enabled the traumatic abuse such as political oppression, racism or economic domination" to occur in the first place and which might compound distress in the aftermath of the event, including when engaging with health systems or psychological interventions (Craps, 2013, p. 24). Returning to the case study of Quechua-speaking communities in Peru, research has documented how idioms of distress are not only related to recent direct violence, but also to the structural and symbolic violence of poverty, racism, and inequality embedded in colonialism and enduring into the present, accompanied by concerns about modernity and globalization (Pedersen et al., 2010). Idioms of distress such as *ñakary* and *llaki* encapsulate suffering past, present, and anticipated, which have evolved over time to account for new meanings and attributions (Pedersen et al., 2010). Therefore, the concerns and priorities of survivors may not necessarily be "inwards, to their mental processes, but outwards to their devastated social world" (Summerfield, 1999, p. 1454).

Psychiatrist Jones (2004, p. 245) concluded from research in Bosnia-Herzegovina that children's lasting well-being did not correlate solely with the amount or length of violence to which the children had been exposed or with the ratings on PTSD scales. Instead, what mattered was "how personally disruptive the event had been: What had happened to their family and friends and the landscape in which they lived?" Consequently, she argues that "the main psychic injury of war is the disruption of those ties, the destruction of identity through the destruction of our social world" (Jones, 1995, p. 510). Continuity of the activities of daily life, such as going to school, can be influential in promoting well-being. In Sierra Leone, following the brutal civil war, Coulter (2009, p. 180) observed that while individuals did not forget what had happened to them and their families, "healing was conceived in terms of being able to procure a livelihood— to go to school, to trade, to get a job, to make a living—so that life could go on."

For those who remain in the countries where the atrocities were perpetrated, challenges are presented not only with the destruction of the physical and social landscape but also with living alongside those who perpetrated such atrocities (Pells, 2011). Das (2000) develops the notion of "poisonous knowledge" to describe this interaction between past and present. Das (2000, p. 208) argues that if it were "one's way of being-with-others" that "was brutally injured, then the past enters the present not necessarily as traumatic memory but as poisonous knowledge." Past events are not "present to consciousness as past events" but instead have come "to be incorporated through an individual's thoughts and actions into the temporal structure of relationships" (Das, 2000, p. 220). Past events are therefore ongoing, embedded in the structures and relations of daily life.

In contrast to the previous discussion, according to Patel (2003), those living in a new country may experience multiple losses, including:

> the loss of home, of homeland; the loss of health, of role, language and culture; the loss and separation from family, friends, compatriots; the loss of identity, dignity, purpose

and opportunity in life. The loss of hope . . .: the hope of justice, the hope of recognition, the hope of safety and protection, and the hope of a life without fear. (Patel, 2003, p. 18)

Mental distress can be compounded by ongoing structural oppressions. Patel (2003, p. 18) describes the effects of a combination of a "harsh (legal) asylum system, racism, detention, poverty, homelessness or very poor housing, difficulties in accessing health services, isolation and continued uncertainty"; such mental distress is reported by refugees as being "worse that the torture I suffered before." This leads to what Kleinman (2015, p. xiv) terms "the terrible irony of social suffering" as "those institutions created to cope with violence and its aftermath are also responsible for contributing to its intensification and bad outcome.

Moreover, the trauma discourse can medicalize and pathologize emotional and behavioral responses, which might be relatively common, given the circumstances (Jones, 2004; Wessells, 2006). For example, the desire for revenge toward killers has been reinterpreted as a sign of poor mental health (Summerfield, 2002). While it might not be considered as a "positive" emotion, it is understandable when individuals have lost family members during mass violence. In the UK, health workers are required to report individuals who are perceived to be vulnerable to radicalization under the counterterrorism "Prevent" policy. Terrorism is constructed as an irrational act, and thus falls under the remit of mental health services, resulting in "an individual's cognitive distortions, rather than their political demands, [and these] became the locus of intervention" disproportionately affecting individuals perceived to have been racialized as Muslim and impeding access to healthcare due to fears surrounding "Prevent" (Younis & Jadhav, 2020, p. 621).

In summary, structural inequities along political, economic, social, and cultural lines, at both the global and local level, drive and exacerbate mental distress (Khan, 2017; Wilkinson & Kleinman, 2016). This has led to calls to "decolonize" trauma counseling (Goodman, 2015); to adopt more expansive understandings of both "distress" and "healing," beyond a focus on the individual and the event; and to recognize and address external, ongoing sources of distress and how these are rooted in historical and current systemic oppressions, including transgenerational trauma. This requires engaging with considerations of politics and power, to which we now turn.

THE POLITICS OF TRAUMA

Genocide, war, and political violence are all political acts, and so working with survivors necessitates engaging with political questions, both within one's own work, as well as within a broader context. PTSD has been argued to function as a "political metaphor" (Fassin & Rechtman, 2009; Khan, 2017, p. 46), prescribing certain ways of being and acting, designating whom the legitimate victims are and reproducing relations of power, whether between counselor and survivor or in the realm of international political economy. This raises questions about how to address inequities and power relations in therapeutic work as well as in addressing the root causes of trauma in systemic social and political injustices (Martín-Baró, 1994).

Fassin and Rechtman (2009, p. xi) argue that "trauma has become a major signifier of our age" that is used politically to support certain claims, legitimate some forms of action, and undermine others. For example, "We are not mad, we are betrayed" was the response of a Bosnian refugee to researchers from a mental health project pilot (Summerfield, 2002, p. 1106). The refugee resented the "problem" being presented as a matter of individual illness rather than a collective, moral, and political issue. Although psychological interventions can assist survivors in coping with traumatic experiences, they rarely address the root of human rights violations and injustices and can become a smokescreen for a lack of political engagement (Summerfield, 2002). While neutrality is a key tenet of humanitarian intervention (an arena in which psychiatry and mental health has assumed an increased prominence), Jones (1998) argues that this can have adverse psychological and political consequences. This refers both to the individual therapist working on the ground as well as to organizations, donor agencies, and governmental departments in which the psychosocial approach is the selected mode of intervention.

The dangers of failing to consider politics and the balance of power within societies are exhibited in Argenti-Pillen's (2003) study of the "Cinnamon Garden culture." The "Cinnamon Garden culture" refers to the central Colombo location of many of the Sri Lankan mental health nongovernmental organizations (NGOs). Sri Lankan psychosocial workers translated trauma discourse into Sinhalese, finding equivalent concepts such as fear, terror, and violence. However, the psychosocial workers were part of the Colombo elite resulting in a "discursive distance" from the communities with whom they worked. Additionally, concepts were aligned with Orthodox Buddhism rather the heterogeneous practices of Sinhalese Buddhist villagers (Argenti-Pillen, 2003, p. 204). Consequently, Argenti-Pillen argues that the introduction of foreign concepts and their application exacerbated preexisting inequalities in Sri Lankan society. Therefore, with any intervention, professionals need to take the utmost care in first understanding local power dynamics and socially inscribed divisions, according to gender, race, class, religion, sexual orientation, and so on. Such issues relate to the politics of knowledge production, that is, whose knowledge counts and whose voice gets heard.

As noted previously, experiential knowledge and local ways of meaning-making may be discounted in favor of biomedical or biopsychological frameworks (Breslau, 2004; Patel, 2003). This can be fundamentally disempowering and may reproduce the power dynamics at play during the traumatic incident(s) in which survivors have limited or no control. Moreover, it constitutes a form of epistemic injustice. Fricker (2007, p. 44) defines "epistemic injustice" as occurring when "the subject is wronged in her capacity as a knower" which is "wronged therefore in a capacity essential to human value."

Alternative approaches have sought to create space for survivors to testify to their experiences and make demands for truth and justice. During the Guatemalan civil war (1960–1996), indigenous Mayan people were massacred by the army and paramilitaries. Following exhumations at Plan de Sánchez, in 1994, issues of truth, memory, and justice took tangible forms through community support groups, which involved truth-telling processes, in addition to the initiation of prosecutions of local military commissioners by NGOs. Sanford (2003, p. 242) argues that through combining "community recovery, the reintegration of agency, and a political project for seeking redress through the accretion of truth" it was possible to break "the binary that counterpoises justice and healing." By adapting the testimonial model from the individual to the community dimension, it can be possible for communities to challenge "structures of violence and lateral impunity" through the interaction between the local and national level (pp. 240–242). Similarly, in Rwanda, Sinalo (2018) documents the importance of creating space for genocide survivors to give testimonies and to participate in shaping public discourses. At the same time, testimony or public expression of past pain is not culturally acceptable in all societies. Again, care should be taken to understand sociocultural dynamics.

S. Shaw (2005) writes of the antipathy toward the Sierra Leonean Truth and Reconciliation Commission as "speaking of the violence—especially in public—was (and is) still viewed as encouraging its return, calling it forth when it is still very close and might at any moment erupt again . . .social forgetting is a refusal to reproduce the violence by talking about it publicly" (p. 9). Similarly, for those seeking asylum or for those who are refugees, the search for justice can be an important part of recovering a sense of agency and identity. As with the previous examples, this is a very individual choice. Whereas for some, speaking out is an important part of challenging injustices past and present, for others, addressing immediate needs such as housing and food, as well as concerns for personal security, may be paramount. Therapists can play an important role in supporting clients to connect with solidarity groups and in advocating for access to other services, such as housing, legal representation, education, and other health services (Patel, 2008).

Decolonizing trauma counseling therefore necessitates political literacy on the part of counselors, not only to understand the sociopolitical issues facing the individuals with whom they are working, but also to take an active role in the decolonization process (Goodman, 2015). This could include reviewing the policies and practices within institutions and organizations at a local, national, and international level to understand how policies may give rise to or accentuate trauma that has a disproportionate impact on certain marginalized groups and how resources are distributed (Goodman, 2015). Moreover, clinicians need to be reflexive of their own personal histories, assumptions, and practices in order not to sustain injustice and power inequalities within their own work (Jones, 1998; Martín-Baró, 1994).

TRAUMA-INFORMED PRACTICE AND IMPLICATIONS FOR COUNSELING

This section considers trauma-informed practice with survivors of genocide, war, and political violence, bearing in mind the critiques explored throughout this chapter. We begin by outlining frameworks, which have sought to bridge cultural and critical psychology, neuroscience, social sciences, and anthropology, and by identifying implications for integrating cultural and contextual factors into counseling practice, before turning to specific psychological tools within narrative- and arts-based approaches. Specialist training and supervision should be sought before working with trauma survivors. Well-meaning but ill-informed interventions can cause serious damage.

Cultural Humility and Social Justice

Bringing together psychological and anthropological perspectives, D. E. Hinton and Good (2015b) propose a holistic framework for working with trauma survivors of mass violence. Their framework is illustrated in Figure 23.1 and is composed of 11 dimensions for assessing trauma survivors.

The trauma survivor is positioned at the center, indicating the need for a person-centered approach, but one which is holistic and contextualized. The nature of the trauma experienced is crucial in understanding the impact and possible responses; for instance, the nature of the event (e.g., killing of family members, sexual violence), the symptoms induced, whether it was experienced as an individual, a group, intergenerationally, the type of loss (e.g., social, cultural, economic), and whether it was one-off, episodic, or chronic.

Figure 23.1

Eleven Dimensions for Assessing Trauma Survivors

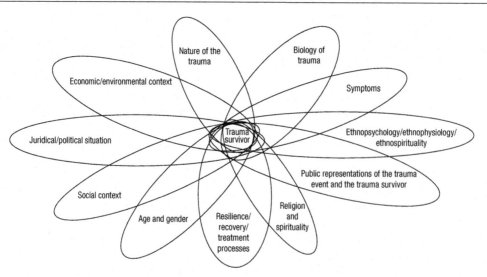

Source: Reproduced with permission from Hinton, D. E., & Good, B. (Eds.). (2015a). *Culture and PTSD: Trauma in global and historical perspective* (p. 51). University of Pennsylvania.

In understanding the impact on the individual, it is important to account for the biology of trauma, given the profound impact on the nervous and endocrine system (these issues are detailed in the chapters in the first section of this textbook) and that current stresses like poverty can compound symptoms. Symptoms include both those within the *DSM* as well as a much broader "traumatic symptom pool," which varies across cultures (D. E. Hinton & Good, 2015b, p. 59). Symptoms need to be interpreted in the local context, which can create "feedback loops," shaping which symptoms of trauma are more prevalent in any given context. Age and gender, which intersect with other inequalities such as race, class, sexual orientation, and so on, increase vulnerabilities to experiencing certain types of trauma (e.g., sexual violence among women); they also shape how trauma may have an impact on the individual and influence pathways to healing, such as barriers to seeking healthcare following sexual violence due to stigma.

Attending to the local context requires knowledge of ethnopsychology, ethnophysiology and ethnospirituality, which focus on how both the trauma and resultant symptoms are interpreted and experienced, including both idioms of distress and how these intersect with globally circulating discourses and approaches to trauma and PTSD. Religion or spirituality may be central here, and religious practices can provide remedies, in relation to complex bereavement, mourning, and rituals for the death of others. Public representation of the trauma event also has an impact on a survivor's sense of self and identity. For instance, if survivors are seen as weak or stigmatized because of their distress, this can construct and shape the ways in which survivors see themselves. Memorialization, commemoration practices, and the relationship between individual and collective memories may create opportunities for re-traumatization (e.g., if survivors are excluded or their narratives not heard) or for healing (D. E. Hinton & Hinton, 2015).

Approaches to therapeutic practices often are founded on a deficit approach, that is, what the individual is lacking or cannot do, rather than on strengths and sources of resilience, whether individual or collective in the recovery or treatment process. Interest has grown in the possibility of posttraumatic growth, whereby individuals may not only return to previous levels of functioning but may obtain new insights and strengths and participating in collective social action can play an important role (Goodman, 2015; Sinalo, 2018).

Processes of healing also may be shaped by a series of (or lack of) resources. First, social context: relationships and networks might have been disrupted due to death, displacement, or exile. Trauma can continue to reverberate through social structures and interactions, including intergenerationally, such as with increased rates of domestic violence and alcohol and drug abuse (D. E. Hinton & Good, 2015b, p. 84). Second, economic-environmental context: such as personal and familial safety, and access to housing, safe water, and food, without which traumatic symptoms such as anxiety may intensify. Impoverished groups typically have less access to healthcare and are more likely to suffer from physical and mental ill-health. Third, juridical/political situation: demands for redress and justice are often intertwined with survivors' journeys toward healing. Support is needed where survivors are called upon to testify and where justice mechanisms, such as trials, do not necessarily address local perceptions and realities, leading to resentment and revictimization.

Taken together, these perspectives enable counselors to consider the multiple factors that shape both trauma and the responses of survivors to their experiences, bridging the mind-body-world and the individual and collective. D. E. Hinton and Good (2015b) argue that this prevents any assessment from being decontextualized or abstracted and enables the counselor to identify key processes or areas for possible intervention. In the rest of the section, we turn to looking at additional considerations for trauma-informed practice.

Creating a Safe Environment

It is widely acknowledged that supporting trauma survivors practically and emotionally to feel safe and secure during counseling is of utmost importance. Depending on individual circumstances, it may be helpful to explore with survivors the possibility of finding a "safe place" that they can visit when dynamics in or out of therapy feel unsafe or overwhelming. This place can be a real or imagined place or space. The feelings, sounds, smells, and sensations associated with it need to be connected with and linked to a trigger word so that the person can self-soothe by going to this safe place; alternatively, the therapist can support or facilitate the survivor's connection with the safe place. Other grounding and self-soothing techniques should be in place, as well as buffering and building on the survivor's coping strategies and resources.

Attending to Power Dynamics and Reflexivity

Creating safety within therapeutic work extends beyond the cultural competence of the counselor, to adopting a systemic approach that considers the safety of systems, institutions, and clinical settings, while attending to power dynamics (Maercker et al., 2019). The therapeutic work itself may be reminiscent of aspects of the torture experience; for example, being alone in a closed room with a person who is positioned as a powerful/authoritative figure asking personal questions. Moreover, counselors could be perceived as representing various roles, including that of being a rescuer or savior to that of being an oppressor or persecutor. If the therapist is positioned as a rescuer, this might place the survivor in a position of victim or passive recipient. These issues around power are important to discuss in clinical supervision, as this type of work can provoke powerful transference and countertransference reactions.

Working With Interpreters

Interpreters may be required to ensure good communication and the creation of a safe space (Leanza et al., 2014; Tribe & Raval, 2003). Key issues worth considering include: (a) allowing additional session time, including the time to meet and build rapport with the interpreter; (b) examining roles and expectations; (c) discussing any observed nuances such as body language, gestures, and tone of voice (with reference to cultural knowledge); and (d) offering time to provide a debriefing experience for the interpreter.

The selection of an interpreter is a critical decision. Some people feel uncomfortable speaking with someone from their own community because of fears of confidentiality and/or of being judged, and this can be a barrier for openness. Other people may have specific preferences for interpreters with whom they would feel more comfortable, and these should be discussed. Unfortunately, many services are limited by a lack of resources, and therefore, choice is not an option. Also, there is often reliance on nonprofessional interpreters, which might affect the quality of the communication and raise confidentiality concerns (Maercker et al., 2019).

Impact of the Work

Healthcare professionals report profound psychological effects of the therapeutic work with refugee and asylum-seeking people (Rees et al., 2007). Counselors may experience changes in the way they perceive the world; may have feelings of anger, anxiety, and depression; and may encounter intrusive images (vicarious trauma), an overwhelming sense of responsibility, or even survivor guilt, depending on their own personal histories and contexts in which they are working (Sabin-Farrell & Turpin, 2003). Self-awareness and self-care are crucial, even more so when working in a post-conflict area with restricted resources and limited support networks.

Therapist's Position

Remaining "neutral" when working with refugee and asylum-seeking people is impossible, given the sociopolitical context (Tribe & Raval, 2003). In taking a nonneutral stance, the therapist clearly is opposing the atrocities experienced by the survivor. The survivor's experiences should be actively listened to and validated, and care needs to be taken to address the person as a whole individual and not to define the person by their traumatic experience and/or their immigration status. Providing a space in which the survivor can be held emotionally is crucial, one where the person is recognized, and their experiences are acknowledged. Additionally, it is essential to foster alternative ways to express (verbal and nonverbal) or name some of the unbearable experiences. This can support the survivor in meaning-making and serve to break the "conspiracy of silence" (Danieli, 1998) that often is experienced by survivors.

Psychological Approaches and Tools

In this section we consider narrative and arts-based tools for working with trauma survivors. While there are numerous tools available for counselors, we suggest that these approaches facilitate greater sensitivity to cultural context, encourage the decolonization of knowledge production, and have the potential to address social justice (though this is a work in progress and should not be assumed). This is by no means an inclusive summary; however, it is hoped that some of the breadth of options demonstrates the wide range of approaches available, to be creatively used and interwoven into existing multimodal therapies.

Selected therapies are discussed briefly in the following subsections: narrative therapy, tree of life technique, cultural genograms and life storybooks, testimonial psychotherapy, creative therapies, and bereavement work. A careful assessment and formulation is needed to ascertain the appropriateness of the type and time of these interventions, in order to ensure that the therapist is not adhering to a one-size-fits-all approach.

Narrative Therapy

Narrative therapy involves helping survivors to deconstruct and challenge their dominant stories and to create more empowering life narratives (White, 2000). Survivors' lives may seem full of problem-saturated stories and negative dominant discourses, such as of being "bad, damaged, and hopeless," which they then may internalize and thus self-stigmatize. Therefore, externalizing the problem, that is, seeing the problem as separate from the person, might support survivors to see that they are not the problem; the problem is the problem (White, 2004). Additionally, survivors can be supported in identifying unique outcomes or exceptions, which thicken the survivors' less told stories and may assist them in reconnecting with their strengths, skills, and values, as well as in providing an opportunity for them to reauthor their stories (Beaudoin, 2005). Narrative therapy acknowledges the connectedness of peoples' lives and builds on people's skills and sense of agency. Narrative therapy takes the stance that people always respond to trauma, and that these responses say something about what the person values or was preserving and protecting. For example, this can be supported through questions such as the following: What is this pain you feel a testimony to? What is it you hold precious that has been violated? What kind of life have you been fighting and struggling for?

Tree of Life Technique

This is a narrative therapy tool that originally was developed by Ncazelo Ncube, a Zimbabwean psychologist, for children who had been orphaned by HIV/AIDS. Since its origin, the tool has been extended to working with numerous age groups and in wide-reaching areas, including with those who have experienced trauma and loss. The Tree of Life enables people to strengthen their relationships with their own history, their culture, and the significant people in their lives.

In this technique, a tree is used as a metaphor to promote survivors' discussion about:

- The roots (origin of family name, country of birth, stories and songs from the past, and ancestors)
- The ground (everyday activities and the situation at present)
- The trunk (strengths, resiliencies, and skills)
- The branches (hopes, wishes, goals, and dreams)
- The leaves (people or pets—real, imagined—who have been important to the person)
- The fruits (the gifts people have been given, including both material and essential gifts of life such as love and kindness)

Often, these representations are in pictorial form, and people can express their ideas in whichever way they choose, including the use of objects, pictures, and paint. When the Tree of Life is done as a group, people can display all of their trees together, and in doing so, they can create a forest of trees, a community. This can support people in feeling part of something and listened to; then the group may choose to reflect and comment on what they have been struck by when reading other people's trees. The group then discusses the storms and dangers faced by trees; they can use this as a metaphor for thinking of ways of weathering through the storm and remembering the roots, leaves, and so forth. This process is usually completed with a certificate and ceremony.

The Tree of Life has been extended to work with different groups. For example, the principles of the tool were applied to the metaphor of a football pitch and were used with former child soldiers (Denborough, 2008). This technique has encouraged people to draw on their strengths, resiliencies, and narratives of the past, as well as to be part of a wider community. Another adaptation is the Kite of Life, which focuses on moving participants from intergenerational conflict to intergenerational alliance (Denborough, 2010).

Cultural Genograms and Life Storybooks

Cultural genograms have similar aims as those of the Tree of Life technique. A genogram is a pictorial representation of a family tree that goes beyond the factual detail by attending to themes, relational dynamics, and psychological factors while attending to cultural considerations (McGoldrick et al., 1999; Rigazio-DiGilio et al., 2005). The genogram is a way for the counselor to support the survivor in telling their life story. For example, when talking about overcoming hardship, the counselor may look at the genogram and inquire what hardships the survivor's grandmother or cousin may have experienced, or what the person thinks an aunt or husband might have thought of the hardship the survivor faced. This can be a sensitive way to explore other areas of difference such as spirituality, religion, cultural rituals, and race. Genograms can be complemented by other tools such as ecomaps, life storybooks, or timelines. These documents are a construction or reconstruction of an individual's life and involve the integration of internal processes with relationships and values within the family, as well as community within the cultural context (Cook-Cottone & Beck, 2007).

Testimonial Psychotherapy

It is important to support survivors in having their voices heard and encouraging them to feel that their voices are worth hearing; this ultimately can assist survivors with journeys of personal, as well as social action and change. One way that incorporates this stance, as well as embracing the storytelling culture of some communities, is through testimonial psychotherapy (Akinyela, 2005; Schwartz & Melzak, 2005). This therapy places justice as the therapeutic entry point (Agger et al., 2009). Testimonials allow the retelling of events to a therapist, who documents the narrative, and, through an interactive process of reviewing it with the survivor, produces a written testimony that acknowledges the experiences and provides vital documentation for political or personal purposes, transforming private pain into political or spiritual dignity (Agger & Jensen, 1990).

The testimonial process enables the victim to gain some distance from the event and to focus on different aspects of the story, such as on survival (Lustig et al., 2004). This can lead to essential and powerful meaning-making discoveries. Lustig et al. (2004) state the following:

> Testimonial therapy emphasizes an individual's personal resources by creating a written document for socio-political purposes, thereby engendering a sense of agency, and counteracting innate feelings of powerlessness and inferiority. Moreover, participants' control over the creation of the document, as well as their right to disseminate it, or keep it to themselves, contrasts sharply with the lack of influence over original events described in the testimony. (p. 34)

Creative Therapies

Creative therapies are based on the premise that art is healing and uses innovative means when working with people, including visual art, creative writing (including poetry), music, narradrama (Dunne, 2000), sociodrama (Kellerman, 2007), and dance/movement therapy (Gray, 2001; Harris, 2007). Using different media may be helpful in expressing the traumatic experiences while attending to multiple sensory processes, which is especially relevant as trauma can impair nonverbal domains of the body (van der Kolk, 1994). Additionally, using creative means can provide a contrary experience to that associated with trauma, thus facilitating distance, desensitization, processing of trauma memories (Kozlowska & Hanney, 2001), enhancing one's sense of control and authorship, stimulating the imagination, and facilitating the mind–body connection (Malchiodi, 2008). Furthermore, different ways of expressing oneself may resonate with those from communities where dance and music are culturally important means of storytelling.

Using creative means can facilitate connection. For example, in addition to verbally creating a safe place, the clinician and client may create a safe box, whereby the outside of the box can signify comforting and safe images, and the inside of the box can be used for objects and pictures that represent difficult feelings. Additionally, people can be encouraged to act, write a song or poem, dance, make a movement, or draw their life as a journey; others may find using dolls, puppets, and masks as powerful symbols for unexpressed feelings, and others may find writing a book about their experiences to be cathartic (Malchiodi, 2008).

Bereavement Work

Many survivors who have experienced mass violence and torture also have experienced multiple losses and bereavements (D. E. Hinton & Good, 2015b). Survivors may be uncertain of a family member's whereabouts or burial site, including the events leading to the killings. Bereavement work can be valuable, using a culturally appropriate medium and bearing in mind that ideas, beliefs, and rituals associated with death and the afterlife vary (Honwana, 1999). Useful techniques may include:

- writing a letter to the lost one/ones
- creating a memory box
- creating a remembrance mural or piece of artwork
- carrying out cultural or religious rituals or ceremonies
- discussing the stories, legacies, values, memories, and lessons that the person living can carry with them throughout life

Experiences of multiple losses must be taken into account throughout the therapeutic work, as the ending of therapy might be representative of these earlier losses and/or abandonment.

CONCLUSION

The existential horror of genocide, war, and political violence, and its enduring legacies for survivors, has been explored throughout this chapter. The extreme nature of the violence that has been experienced by individuals presents several challenges for clinicians above and beyond the usual therapeutic considerations. In addressing these challenges, we have advocated for the adoption of a broader framework than the purely psychological, illustrating how insights from sociology and anthropology can strengthen therapeutic work. This includes understanding sociocultural processes of meaning-making and systemic oppression, which shape idioms of distress and calls for justice. In practice, this requires a holistic framework, which addresses the needs of the individual, addressing the sociocultural, political, and environmental context, while also addressing the challenges of past, present, and future. These approaches also should focus on building upon individuals' strengths, resources, and values rather than pathologizing and medicalizing their experiences. The extreme nature of genocide, war, and political violence also accentuates the need for consideration of power dynamics, self-care, and transference and countertransference within the therapeutic relationship. Above all, it calls us to bear witness to gross human rights violations, to stand with those who have been abused, and to work with them to restore or create anew.

ADDITIONAL RESOURCES

A robust set of instructor resources designed to supplement this text is located at http://connect.springerpub.com/content/book/978-0-8261-5085-1. Qualifying instructors may request access by emailing textbook@springerpub.com.

PRACTICE-BASED RESOURCES AND REFERENCES

To view a list of resources and all the references, please visit connect.springerpub.com via the following url: http://connect.springerpub.com/content/book/978-0-8261-5085-1/part/part04/chapter/ch23

A Confluence of Crises: Migration, Anthropogenic Climate Change, Mass Casualties, War, and Civil Unrest

LISA LÓPEZ LEVERS AND NATALIE A. DROZDA

CHAPTER OVERVIEW

The purpose of this chapter is to explore the confluence of crisis issues that relates to migration, anthropogenic climate change, war, and civil unrest. Such a confluence of crises is complex and involves interrelated situations that may result in humanitarian emergencies and mass casualties. Events of the 21st century have made clear how critical it is for counselors and other helping professionals to understand the convergences of these very real human-behavior-driven dynamics and to intercede, as necessary, in ways that are productive. The major objective of this chapter is to elucidate this crucial contemporary issue of multiple intersecting crises and trauma events.

LEARNING OBJECTIVES

After reading this chapter, the reader should be able to:

1. Identify how intersecting mass crises and traumas affect individuals and communities;
2. Describe the dynamic interrelationships between and among crises and the influences that they have on one another;
3. Understand the nature of complex crises and the ecological effects that they have on individuals, from a holistic perspective; and,
4. Apply counseling techniques and public mental health strategies that are conducive to building both personal and community resilience and to assisting affected persons and communities in their recovery from complex crises.

INTRODUCTION AND CONTEXT

Traumatic events entail real or assumed threat, injury, or death to individuals, any of which may occur during a crisis. The term "crisis" often is embedded in the context of an individual experience—a crisis befalls one person or a family unit. However, crises also can happen on a much larger scale, in which even the helpers or first responders may be put into danger (Mathieu, 2012). These crises can be termed as complex humanitarian emergencies and may involve mass casualties. They can affect entire geographical areas and service sectors (e.g., water insecurity or drought due to climate change) or even, as in the case of a pandemic like COVID-19, the entire world (Ratha et al., 2020).

Unfortunately, there are often overlaps between and among crisis situations, with one exacerbating the effects of another. This is the essence of what is explored and explicated in this chapter. For example, climate change can lead to civil unrest due to a lack of essential resources for survival and a government's inability to respond effectively. This schism, in turn, can lead to war, which may cause unrest and famine, and then the famine may lead to subsequent migration. When mass trauma strikes, the same situation may affect people differently or not at all, because distribution of resources is not equal. Furthermore, as an example, the unprecedented circumstances resulting from a pandemic like COVID-19 have catapulted counselors and helpers around the world into the same or similar trauma experiences as prospective clients. Other relevant present-day comparisons to such circumstances are nearly impossible to conceptualize on such a massive scale. In this type of scenario, trauma counselors are faced with the need for personal healing and the imperative to provide professional help simultaneously; counselors dealing with the same life-altering situation as clients is a novel phenomenon for modern times.

This chapter explores issues pertaining to migration, anthropogenic climate change, war, and civil unrest as a confluence of crises, that is, as complex and interrelated situations that are likely to result in humanitarian emergencies and mass casualties. It is crucial that counselors and other helping professionals understand the intersections of these very real human-behavior-driven dynamics; therefore, a major aim of this chapter is to illuminate this critical contemporary issue of multiple intersections related to trauma and crises. Relevant research and suggestions for clinical practice are provided in this chapter to aid counselors in addressing the complex crisis situations that represent the interrelationships among these various, and sometimes seemingly disparate, crises. The confluence of complex crisis situations is discussed in the following sections: Complex Crises and Migration, Complex Crises and Anthropogenic Climate Change, Complex Crises and Mass Casualties, Complex Crises and War and Conflict, Relevance of Intersecting Trauma and Complex Crises, Complex Crises and Social Justice, and Counseling Implications of Complex Crises. These discussions are followed by a summary of their intersections as well as an online section presenting useful resources related to this topic.

COMPLEX CRISES AND MIGRATION

The interconnected issues of immigration and trauma, along with constructs and social dynamics that have parallel similarities to migration, are detailed in Chapter 17. However, the focus on migration, in the current chapter, reflects the complex intersection of migration with other forces, which can result in a set of complex crises. In this section, we explore how traumatic experiences can lead to leaving one's homeland, how trauma can occur during such a movement, the psychological effects of migration, and how migration intersects with other crises.

Leaving the Homeland

Migration is defined as traveling from one's home or familiar geographical location to a new place, for a multitude of reasons. Frequently this entails crossing large distances with the hope of better living circumstances. Levers and Hyatt-Burkhart (2012) have suggested the potential for many types of migration-related traumatic experiences, even under more ideal migration circumstances. Reaching a decision to leave one's homeland permanently, in and of itself, can be a stressful event—even when the purpose for relocation is for a desired outcome, such as employment or schooling. However, when people are forced to make such high-stakes decisions, in the face of potentially life-threatening situations like war, famine, water-scarcity, and other imperiling conditions, the imminent sense of danger may be overwhelming. Deciding to leave, perhaps with only the clothes on their backs, may push people further toward the brinks of despair and trauma that these types of volatile circumstances already create. See the case illustration in Box 24.1 for an example of why someone might be faced with making the decision to leave her homeland.

Complex crises and trauma certainly can lead people to choose to leave an area in mass numbers. As noted, reasons for a mass exodus may include war, poverty, climate change, civil unrest, and so forth, but unfortunately the trauma of the migration process itself often is overlooked, overshadowed by what people are trying to leave behind. In essence, the act of migration, in combination with the reasons for the migration, may create an exponential spiral of negative consequences and additional traumatic events. For example, during the last decade, we witnessed thousands of lives lost; migrants, fleeing their homelands due to a variety of complex crises, died trying to cross the Mediterranean Sea. Most were leaving the kinds of volatile situations that were previously described, but human ruthlessness also intersected with and contributed to these deaths; many of the migrants were exploited by those who monetized the need for emergency evacuation travel and sold transport on vessels known not to be seaworthy, while some other migrants became victims of human trafficking (Galos, 2017).

BOX 24.1

Case Illustration: Boipelo

Boipelo resides in a rural and remote area in an arid region of southern Africa, where she cares for her three children. After her partner was killed in a mining accident, she has even fewer resources to help sustain herself and her family, despite having other family members living in her village. With drinking water becoming more and more scarce, Boipelo is feeling a constant tension within herself and with the people around her, finding it hard to go about her daily responsibilities. The people in her community have been on edge for quite some time and have talked about leaving the area, but she is not sure how she could manage a long journey with three young children. There has been talk about neighboring groups coming to take what little resources this village still has. Feeling unsafe, with no time to grieve the loss of her partner, Boipelo faces a major life-altering decision with an uncertain future ahead of her. Does she make the decision to leave the only place she has ever known, to leave her rich culture and traditions? Alternatively, does she decide to stay and hope that her living circumstances will improve, even though the future looks bleak?

Reflection Questions

- What are some of the major issues that Boipelo faces, in both scenarios, of staying and of leaving?
- How do you think Boipelo is coping with her situation?
- What would be some adaptation mechanisms that Boipelo could enlist?
- How would you conceptualize Boipelo's situation if she came to discuss her circumstances with you?

Trauma During Migration

Trauma experienced prior to, during, and post migration can be detrimental to an individual's health and well-being (Clemens et al., 2020; Erazo, 2018; Hanna & Oliva, 2016; Larr & Neidell,

2016). These experiences may include, but are not limited to, experiencing violence as well as separation from family members. The latter garnered so much recent attention that the former president of the American Psychological Association (APA), Dr. Jessica Henderson Daniel, issued a statement asserting that separating families due to inadequate documentation is "needless and cruel," and "threatens the mental and physical health of both the children and their caregivers" (APA, 2018, "Statement of APA President," para. 2).

In response to family separation as a matter of policy, the United Nations (UN) began drafting the Global Compact for Safe, Orderly, and Regular Migration (Erazo, 2018; UN, 2018), which has outlined provisions for a smoother and safer migration experience. Objectives as well as actionable items related to pre, during, and post migration included the following: minimizing adverse drivers and structural factors that compel people to leave their country of origin, providing adequate and timely information at all stages of migration, addressing and reducing vulnerabilities in migration, facilitating fair and ethical recruitment and safeguarding conditions that ensure decent work, providing access to basic services for migrants, eliminating discrimination, and promoting fact-based public discourse to shape perceptions of migration (UN, 2018). This call to action has underscored how ubiquitous adverse experiences can be for migrants. The actionable items that were previously outlined can seem daunting, but are necessary because migrants' mental health is affected by the complex array of traumatic experiences that can befall them at any stage of migration (Levers & Hyatt-Burkhart, 2012).

Psychological Effects of Migration

The APA has espoused an ecological approach to explaining the effects of migration on an individual, meaning that the environment prior to, during, and after migration affects people—as no one exists without context, without a personal ecology (APA, 2012). This effect of migration on an individual can be framed as a "psychopathology of the crossing," which has entailed the relationship between mental health problems and the migration process, thus "shedding light on the multiplicity, complexity, and consequences of such traumas" (Cenat et al., 2020, p. 421). For example, traumatic consequences such as posttraumatic stress disorder (PTSD), anxiety, depression, deteriorating physical health, and the risk of deportation all contributed to the development of this psychopathology of crossing, or unique effects of migration stressors, for Haitian asylum seekers in Canada (Cenat et al., 2020).

Migrated individuals often experience a high prevalence of mental health problems and traumatic experiences, including personal/interpersonal, political, and labor-related (Knipscheer et al., 2009; Levers & Hyatt-Burkhart, 2012). The process of migration can be a long, dangerous, and arduous process, sometimes involving trekking many miles on foot. One such example includes Ethiopians leaving their home country for Saudi Arabia in the hopes of leaving poverty and political violence behind. Another example includes the "Lost Boys of Sudan," some 20,000 children forced to flee the civil war in 1987, making the dangerous 1,000-mile trek, on foot, to Ethiopia (International Rescue Committee, 2014). The road to be taken, with hopes for a better life, often is perilous and may include violence and exposure to the elements. It is not surprising, then, that migration-related stress is a strong predictor of depression (Fanfan et al., 2020). Pre-migration stress also influences this relationship, as it was shown in a Haitian sample of migrants that being present in Haiti during the 2010 earthquake had an amplifying effect on the relationship between migration-related stress and depression for Haitian immigrants in the United States (Fanfan et al., 2020). Even when migrants survive the journey, trials do not necessarily cease when the destination is reached.

The receiving community, into which migrants relocate, has an important influence on migrant mental health. Specifically, experiencing discrimination is directly associated with worsening mental health as evidenced by an increase in depression, anxiety, and posttraumatic stress symptoms (Lincoln et al., 2021). Indeed, the post-migration environment is a key factor related to well-being, correlating with quality of life for migrants (Zou et al., 2021). Not only do migrants have their individual experiences of the migration to process and integrate, but they also have to experience a new culture and its people, with concomitant issues that are likely to be different than those of their homeland and those to which they are accustomed.

Acculturation is the dynamic process of being exposed to a new culture and integrating into the culture, to varying degrees; however, acculturation is not without its challenges and subsequent stress (APA, 2012). Many migrants retain a cultural identity from their homeland, but this identity may clash with their new cultural surroundings. Aside from potentially not knowing the language, tensions between a collectivist and an individualistic cultural ethos can be felt. Additionally, children may feel as though their parents are ill-equipped to advise them in this new culture, and the children often assume a caregiver role of helping their parents with filing taxes, for example, as a sort of cultural ambassador—using skills that they may have picked up at school or had to learn on their own for survival. It was found that migrant adolescents, compared to host adolescents, had significantly more behavioral problems, but that these problems tended to taper off after about 2 years (Fang et al., 2020).

Confluences of Crises Leading to and Intersecting With Migration

Migration can be a voluntary act, such as when people migrate willingly for work; however, oftentimes people are compelled to relocate due to strong forces largely outside of their control. Fleeing religious persecution, civil unrest, war, degradation of the environment and subsequent resource scarcity, and climate change are among some of the reasons an individual or group of individuals may be forced to leave their homes of origin. Financial insecurity, at all points along the journey, also creates stress (Cenat et al., 2020). One of these circumstances alone may present substantial difficulties, but their intersections with traumatic experiences can compound into a complex crisis. For example, a World Bank report (Ratha et al., 2020) explores the intersection of the multiple crises associated with migration and COVID-19. The report states that "[t]he economic crisis induced by COVID-19 could be long, deep, and pervasive when viewed through a migration lens. Lockdowns, travel bans, and social distancing have brought global economic activities to a near standstill" (Ratha et al., 2020, p. viii).

Anthropogenic climate change causes drastic alterations in the environment and limits the resources that are available to people, which then can lead to tension and violence over those restricted resources. Thus, people may be led to environmentally motivated migration and termed "climatic refugees" (Cianconi et al., 2020, p. 11) or ecological migrants, illustrating how one crisis situation can lead to another (Fang et al., 2020). In the case of ecological migration, people are uprooted from their homes and the familiarity of life as they know it. In the next section, we focus on the complex crises and trauma that arise from anthropogenic climate change, or climate change spurred by the actions—or inactions—of humans.

COMPLEX CRISES AND ANTHROPOGENIC CLIMATE CHANGE

Anthropogenic climate change influences nearly every aspect of life on this planet, and it serves as a common link that is transforming our environment in radical ways, from dwindling glaciers and icecaps in the most remote parts of the world to rising water levels and "sinking cities," like New Orleans. Because the change is seemingly gradual, the effects may be easy for some to ignore or deny, at least currently, depending on their individual circumstances and geographical location, but these effects of climate change are pervasive and unlikely to stop or reverse without concerted attention and action.

Mann (2012, 2021) asserts the scientific fact of anthropogenic climate change, especially as underscored by the unprecedented number of weather events, including heat, heat waves, droughts, wildfires, super storms, and floods. The price tag for anthropogenic climate change is enormous; however, while the shift toward sustainable energy may be costly, the cost of *not* taking action will be far greater (Mann, 2021; U.S. Global Change Research Program, 2020). Dire consequences for human life already have become apparent for some, although they sometimes are disguised by or subsumed within other natural disasters or crises. In this section we provide a brief overview of climate change, as it relates to the topic of complex crises, and we examine the psychological effects of climate change and how it intersects with other crises.

Anthropogenic Climate Change

Life as we know it is made possible by the environment, which, by default, includes the climate, or vast array of meteorological elements such as temperature, atmospheric pressure, and rainfall, among others. According to NASA, climate change refers to long-term changes in the Earth's weather patterns that have widespread effects; such shifts are produced by natural warming as well as by human behavior (NASA, n.d). Empirical evidence overwhelmingly supports that human behavior has led to drastic changes in the Earth's weather patterns by means of carbon dioxide increases due to fossil fuel emissions, especially since the industrial era (Intergovernmental Panel on Climate Change [IPCC], 2014; Mann, 2012, 2021; Melillo et al., 2014; NASA, n.d.), hence the term "anthropogenic," or man-made, climate change. What is particularly frightening is that the current level of exploitation of the planet's natural resources may not produce effects that are felt immediately, but that are compounded over time (Levers & Drozda, 2018; Liu et al., 2007).

From an ecological perspective, "the reciprocal and transactional nature of the individual's effect on the environment, and vice versa, should not be minimized" (Levers & Drozda, 2018, p. 89). Levers and Drozda (2018) analyzed the existing social science literature related to anthropogenic climate change, and they emphasized the importance of a social science perspective in considering the perils of climate change. A major reason for emphasizing this is to develop a robust social science perspective, because if there is going to be any abatement of climate change effects, of necessity, it needs to involve human beings, and thus, it will require better understandings of human attitudes and human decision-making. In this way, humans are not separate from their environment; however, their actions influence the environment, and subsequently, changes in the environment influence humans. When we refer to climate change throughout this section, we are referring to the effects of the exacerbation of climate change by human behavior (anthropogenic climate change), while also acknowledging that there are natural warming trends, but that the rate at which change is occurring presently is greatly influenced by human behavior.

Climate change does not affect everyone equally, with economically disadvantaged people bearing the brunt of the stress (Parry et al., 2019; Stocker et al., 2013; UN, Climate Change, 2014). The deleterious effects of climate change are far-reaching, permeating beyond mere temperature shifts, to threaten agriculture, economy, ecosystems, way of life, individual physical and psychological well-being, and the very existence of some populations with limited access to resources (Bavel et al., 2020; Levers & Drozda, 2018). Water, for example, is a necessity for life to flourish. Botswana is among the countries most affected by water stress due to climate change (Boikanyo & Levers, 2017), which makes the situation for poor people in this country especially urgent. Water rationing may be a foreign concept to most people in the developed areas of the world, but it is an all too real experience for some individuals in arid countries like Botswana (Boikanyo & Levers, 2017). Rivers and dams have dried up, which may force people to make changes for which they do not have the resources. Whether people choose to stay or leave their home, the effects that climate change can have on an individual's mental health are troubling (APA, 2017).

Psychological Effects of Climate Change

A review of relevant literature in the behavioral and social sciences underscores the negative effects of climate change on human well-being and warns of the exacerbation of such consequences if human behavior continues along the same indiscriminate and destructive path (Levers & Drozda, 2018). Empirical evidence supports that environmental stressors produced by climate change threaten the psychological well-being of individuals through direct and indirect pathways, including the mental health of children and adolescents, jeopardizing their prospects for good physical health and a bright future (Bavel et al., 2020; Cianconi et al., 2020; Clemens et al., 2020; Hanna & Oliva, 2016; Howard et al., 2020; Kabir, 2018; Larr & Neidell, 2016; Obradovich et al., 2018). The threat to psychological well-being can include increased risk for psychological stress, depression, anxiety, addiction, posttraumatic stress, exacerbation of previous trauma, and even suicide (Howard et al., 2020; Kabir, 2018). For example, individuals from the hill-tracts region of Bangladesh indicated that alterations in the climate and their environment affected their ability to work, which in turn produced feelings of decreased self-worth (Kabir, 2018). When combined with other stressors and previous traumas, it was reported that the potential for suicidal ideation appeared to increase (Kabir, 2018). This particular linkage between climate change and detrimental psychological effects was observed anecdotally by health workers, though a direct causal relationship between climate change and suicidal ideation was not determined (Kabir, 2018).

For many, work is closely tied with survival, identity, fulfillment, and accomplishment—without it, despair may befall people. Similarly, a large-scale study of data from the United States found that people's mental health worsened with hotter temperatures, increased precipitation, and multiyear warming (APA, 2017; Obradovich et al., 2018). Researchers also found that exposure to tropical cyclones increased mental health issues (Obradovich et al., 2018). Researchers have reported that farmers and ranchers in the United States are feeling the effects of climate change via anxiety and distress (Howard et al., 2020). Because climate change has come with an increased incidence of extreme weather, the everyday lives of people are affected (Cianconi et al., 2020). This may be due to storms, droughts, flooding, decreased access to drinking water, heat waves, decreased air quality, fires, and the reemergence of diseases—all of which can influence psychological well-being (Cianconi et al., 2020).

The impact of climate change on mental health has become so evident that new terms have been generated to help describe it. These terms include "ecoanxiety," "ecoguilt," "ecological grief," and "solastalgia" (Cianconi et al., 2020). Issues related to climate change are complex, particularly because not everyone is affected equally nor at the same time, thereby not only making the effects difficult to measure, but also rendering the health risks to disadvantaged populations less visible to policy makers and researchers (Cianconi et al., 2020; Parry et al., 2019). For instance, people who are directly in contact with the land and deal with its resources recognize instantly how climate shifts are changing life, but people who are not an integral part of harvesting food, for example, may not feel the weight directly associated with shifts in the climate. When temperatures rise and resources that are needed for survival become scarce, it is not surprising that climate change directly and indirectly leads to a whole host of other issues.

Intersection of Climate Change With Other Crises

The environments in which people live can be taken for granted in terms of their stability. Climate change disrupts homeostasis for individuals and groups, threatening ways of life, safety, and survival. Disruption is a critical factor in understanding the impact of climate change in disaster scenarios and on communities and individuals; this, in turn, makes adaptation and resilience building crucial mechanisms for responding to climate-related disruption (Rodin, 2014). In this section we discuss how climate change is related to myriad changes in human behavior and the environment and how it contributes to complex crises.

Changes in the weather influence people's daily activities and also influence when crime is committed (Linning et al., 2017). Warmer temperatures are generally associated with increased human aggression as well as higher incidence of criminal behavior (Boikanyo & Levers, 2017; Brunsdon et al., 2009; Linning et al., 2017; Ranson, 2014). Data from the United States indicate that this increase pertains to all criminal behavior, such as theft and violence, and even rape and murder (Ranson, 2014). Simple seasonal change can affect crime rates, though researchers suggest that it may be useful to differentiate between types of crime (Linning et al., 2017). One can imagine, then, how more extreme and long-lasting changes can influence human behavior.

The factors leading to war and civil unrest are interconnected and complex, but regular and exacerbated climate change may amplify the effect of existing problems, make conflict more likely to occur, or serve as a catalyst for plans already set in place (Diaz & Trouet, 2014; Hicks & Maldonado, 2019; Mach et al., 2019). For example, those living in poverty are often less likely to have the resources necessary to adapt to climate change when compared to those in higher socioeconomic status brackets. When resources are scarce due to climate change, this may lead people to do things that they normally would not do for survival, or, as explicated in the previous section, they may choose or be forced to leave their homeland. While there certainly are nuances in the complex relationship between anthropogenic climate change and war and civil unrest, evidence suggests that even the more expected climate fluctuations and patterns, such as with the *El Nino—Southern Oscillation*, are strongly associated with conflict and civil unrest (Hicks & Maldonado, 2019), and that climate variability and change are linked to increased risk of armed conflict within countries (Mach et al., 2019). Not only is human behavior influenced by climate change, but physical health is as well.

Climate change effects are ubiquitous, influencing human physical health. One such example includes exacerbation of infectious disease conditions via air pollution (Patz et al., 2014). Furthermore, the fossil fuel emissions that lead to climate change are responsible for forming ozone and particulate matter in the air (Larr & Neidell, 2016). Such pollution can affect the heart and lungs of children, for example, and can lead to respiratory symptoms and aggravate asthma (Larr & Neidell, 2016). Serious pollution leads to and worsens health problems. Climate change also is one of the factors that can lead to more wide-scale health problems, including pandemics. According to Dr. Aaron Bernstein, the director of Harvard Chan C-CHANGE, treating climate change and global health policy as separate issues has been a gross oversight, citing the current biodiversity crisis, or mass extinction (Coronavirus and Climate Change, n.d). Many of the primary causes of climate change simultaneously increase the risk for pandemics; this can include deforestation, which forces animals to migrate to places that they otherwise may not have been, thus coming into contact with other animals and humans with whom they normally would not come into contact (Coronavirus and Climate Change, n.d). Thus, this complex forced migration increases the spread of germs and subsequently contributes directly and indirectly to mass loss of life.

COMPLEX CRISES AND MASS CASUALTIES

The interconnected issues of complex crises and mass violence are detailed in Chapter 20, "Mass Violence." However, the focus in the current chapter relates to mass casualties, in general, with discussion about two specific situations involving mass casualties, that of anthropogenic climate change and that of the most recent COVID-19 pandemic. Aspects of anthropogenic climate change may lead to situations of mass casualties. For example, an array of complex and interconnected issues has evolved into a wide-scale pandemic that continues to ravage life around the world. In this section, we discuss mass casualties that have resulted from anthropogenic climate change and those that have resulted from the COVID-19 pandemic.

Mass Casualties and Anthropogenic Climate Change

Climate change is listed among the top international threats (Poushter & Huang, 2019). Some fluctuations in the Earth's temperature and weather patterns, including warming, occur without human interference; however, as previously elucidated, human behavior has been instrumental to the exacerbation of some of these more extreme effects on our climate, having unprecedented consequences that threaten human life. For example, the heat wave of 2018 in Japan caused over one thousand people to lose their lives (Imada et al., 2019). Attribution science, or the branch of science that allows for investigating the influence of climate change on individual weather events, established that this heat wave could not have occurred without human-induced global warming, or anthropogenic climate change (Imada et al., 2019). Similarly, the Australian bush fires continue to endanger people and ecosystems, and attribution to anthropogenic climate change has been verified (van Oldenborgh et al., 2020). Climate change in general seems to remain an elusive concept, skirting accountability for loss of life, often overshadowed by the other crises that it leaves in its wake. However, direct examples of mass casualties linked to anthropogenic climate change exist, as in Japan and Australia, and this link no longer can be ignored or denied.

Mass Casualties and the COVID-19 Pandemic

An invisible killer has struck our planet. The novel coronavirus, SARS-CoV-2, or COVID-19, decimated the world population throughout 2020, with such a fury as modern times have never seen. In the first 3 months alone, nearly one million people were infected with the virus and 50,000 succumbed (National Institute of Allergy and Infectious Diseases, 2021). At the time of this writing in early 2021, over 2.24 million people have lost their lives to this relentless virus (Coronavirus World Map, 2021), although the reported numbers may actually underestimate the true loss of life. The weight of the loss is catastrophic, and the damage to the mental health of survivors is equally devastating.

Psychological Toll of COVID-19

Life has been forever altered as a result of this pandemic, dealing out many blows to the individual psyche. The collective stress and weight of the sheer numbers of those who have lost their lives to the virus is daunting, along with the shrinking of coping strategies available to people due to stay-at-home orders. According to PEW Research, four in ten American adults say they know someone who has been diagnosed with COVID-19, with African Americans being more likely to know someone who has been hospitalized or died from the virus (Kramer, 2020). In fact, data are already available that highlight the disproportionately higher COVID-19 cases and deaths in U.S. counties that have higher proportions of African American and Hispanic populations (Khanijahani, 2020). Recent data show that U.S. counties with a higher proportion of the population residing in racially or socioeconomically segregated census tracts had disproportionately higher COVID-19 deaths; the data further indicate that a reciprocal increase in the percentage of county residents living in racially and socioeconomically segregated areas has been associated with a much greater increase in COVID-19 deaths (Khanijahani & Tomassoni, 2021). Such health disparities naturally lead to behavioral health inequities as well. Compounded trauma and grief due to this pandemic include loss of jobs, loss of ways of life prior to the pandemic, isolation, and, of course, the loss of loved ones, friends, and family members. The health disparities that are intertwined throughout all of these important psychological issues also have forced us to acknowledge the degree to which social justice, or lack thereof, is a paramount factor of the pandemic.

Exacerbation of Stress

The toll of pandemic stress is vast and varied, including understandable fear and worry, changes in sleep or eating patterns, difficulty sleeping or concentrating, chronic health problems being aggravated, mental health declining, and increased substance use according to the Centers for Disease Control and Prevention (2020). Everyone responds differently to crises, and some people may respond more strongly to the circumstances brought about by COVID-19. These individuals can include but are not limited to children and teens, those with underlying medical conditions, healthcare workers, those in the food industry, people who are socially isolated or have mental health conditions, homeless individuals, and racial and ethnic minorities (CDC, 2020). When the present is uncertain and scary, and the future feels even less clear, it can be hard to cope with the massive loss of life on a global scale as well as an individual scale, not to mention livelihoods being destroyed. Young people and those financially affected by the pandemic are experiencing increased levels of psychological distress (Keeter, 2020). Because isolation is a risk factor for suicide, there is growing concern about rising suicide rates among teens and other young people. Many do not have the means to cope effectively.

Poverty and Lack of Resources

Poverty affects all aspects of life. When it comes to COVID-19, those in poverty may not have the opportunity to distance socially if they are living in an overcrowded space or in a studio apartment with another person. Needing to take public transportation to work can put people at increased risk, their jobs could be precariously hanging in the balance, or maybe they have lost jobs. Six months after the pandemic started, half of the people who reported job loss were still unemployed (Parker et al., 2020). Furthermore, the virus is expected to put an estimated 150 million people into extreme poverty in 2021, with the World Bank asserting that "the convergence of the COVID-19 pandemic with the pressures of conflict and climate change will put the goal of ending poverty by 2030 beyond reach without swift, significant and substantial policy action" (2020, *"Eight Out of 10 'New Poor' Will Be in Middle-Income Countries,"* para. 5). Understandably, tensions arise if people are operating within a system in which they do not agree with the decisions being made, such as being forced to close their businesses. Dire circumstances, poverty, and the lack of adequate resources push people toward conflict when their survival is on the line.

COMPLEX CRISES AND WAR AND CONFLICT

The interconnected issues of war and trauma are detailed in Chapters 23 and 25. However, the focus on war and its effects, in the current chapter, reflects the complex intersection of war and conflict situations with other forces, which can result in a set of complex crises. In this section, we briefly examine the effects of war, primarily the psychological toll, as well as the effects of civil unrest.

Effects of War

War harms on multiple levels; it harms us physically, psychologically, emotionally, socially, existentially, and spiritually. Regardless of how a person is involved in and affected by the violence that war entails, the instability, uncertainty, and fear associated with wartime permeates all parties involved. War exposure and armed conflict can increase mental health issues such as PTSD as well as overall psychological distress (Haer et al., 2021). Furthermore, depending on the particulars of the situation, war can influence social capital, or the structure and norms that hold a society together and connect people to one another (Haer et al., 2021). This has the potential, in drastic ways, to uproot the familiarity that is associated with people's daily lives, culture, and routines. Furthermore, psychological distress and PTSD are negatively associated with social capital—particularly involving interactions with other people and relying on others (Haer et al., 2021), highlighting the interconnectedness of these individual and societal issues.

It seems to be within our imagination to sense how wars can cause food and water scarcity, but it seems a bit more difficult for people to grasp how food and water insecurity can ignite war or civil unrest. Worsening climate change seems to be increasing the risk for violent conflict within countries (Mach et al., 2019). Bhatt (n.d., para. 2) reports, "Alarmingly, several studies suggest that climate change makes conflicts such as civil war or genocide more likely." Obviously, this complex issue includes an intricate set of interrelated and intersecting forces. It is not climate change alone that causes war or civil unrest; Bhatt (para. 2) refers to climate change as a "threat multiplier." It is the interaction of climate change with multiple risk factors like poverty, political upheavals, and crime that then amplifies the effects of climate change (Boikanyo & Levers, 2017; Levers & Drozda, 2018). Syria is a case in point, in which the adverse environmental effects of climate change sparked migration and eventually civil war (Bhatt, n.d.; Friedman, 2015). One of the earliest civil wars attributed to climate-induced origins was in Sudan, as documented in a thorough assessment by the United Nations Environment Programme (UNEP, 2007).

Effects of Civil Unrest

When people are in danger, are oppressed, or feel unheard or unprotected by a government charged with protecting them or acting in their best interest, people may organize in order to demonstrate their views, gain attention, and garner support. Tensions burn hot when there is disagreement over how people are treated, how tax money is spent, and how justice is served by police, legislators, and other authority figures. Precisely because of mounting tensions, acts of mass civil disobedience potentially, and sometimes easily, can turn into civil unrest and give way to mass violence. Examples of civil unrest can be seen internationally, nationally, regionally, and locally. In recent times alone, we have witnessed high levels of civil unrest, seemingly everywhere; some of these events are primarily politically motivated, but others involve complex crises that intersect with many of the issues under discussion here, like climate change.

When hostilities, justified or not, spill over into violence, public safety may be threatened and compromised; people may be harmed or even killed, and individuals may be traumatized. Mental health professionals are likely to become involved in multiple ways and at a number of levels. We may be asked for assistance with crisis intervention, with attending to the post-event psychosocial effects of trauma, and even with peace-building efforts to prevent further violence. Recent calls for police reform, for example, may bring a new wave of mental health professionals being called to respond to crisis situations and to address the psychosocial problems of people without adequate resources to fend for themselves. In other words, it is not an impossibility that mental health professionals may end up responding to situations to which police officers historically have been called, but which actually require mental health interventions. Counselors and other professional helpers need to possess the crisis intervention and trauma counseling skills that are being promoted throughout this textbook, in order to respond professionally and competently.

RELEVANCE OF INTERSECTING TRAUMA AND COMPLEX CRISES

It is critical that all mental health clinicians, public health clinicians, health policy implementers, and community planners begin to recognize how trauma and crises do not exist within a vacuum. Not only is an ecological perspective helpful, it is imperative, in order to understand the intersections of trauma and crises that form complex crises, as they continue to unfold in our world. We use this notion of intersection or convergence or confluence as a way of framing and understanding the exponential interconnectedness of trauma and multiple crises that often is overlooked. In this way, widening our field of vision helps us not to err by assuming that a crisis is occurring in isolation, when there clearly is a synergy with trauma and additional crises happening simultaneously. Rather, this allows us to enter into dialogues about creative and holistic solutions that can take into account multiple contributing factors within both local and global contexts, as needed. With the spirit of intersection in mind, as we discuss complex crises, we submit that the nature of each individual crisis not only overlaps and interacts with people's individual and social identities, but also overlaps and interacts with the nature of other crisis situations to form a complex crisis. In this section, we discuss complex crises in reference to recent neuroscience findings and to aspects of relevant mental health diagnoses.

Complex Crises and Neuroscience

The interconnected issues of recent neuroscience research findings and how the brain processes trauma are detailed in Chapters 2 and 4. However, the focus on brain science and the intricate interactions between the brain and trauma, in the current chapter, reflects the complex intersection of the other forces being discussed here with brain function, and how brain activity may contribute to a set of complex crises. Probably the most salient brain activity to consider, within the context of this discussion, is fear. When we perceive the threat of danger, during any crisis situation or trauma event, our autonomic nervous system engages; the parasympathetic nervous system may respond to fear by moving into freeze, or the sympathetic nervous system may respond to fear by moving into fight or flight. As discussed in greater detail in Chapters 2 and 4, Polyvagal Theory recently has informed our understandings about the implications of the vagus nerve during this engagement, and how the brain communicates with other organs in the body toward mobilization, social engagement, and immobilization (Porges, 2001, 2011).

Trauma directly affects the brain of both children and adults (Cassiers et al., 2018). Although specific traumas may influence an individual's system differently, chronic exposure to threatening conditions can have longstanding effects. The fight-or-flight reaction may be familiar, and when it comes to complex crisis, individuals' nervous systems may remain on overdrive for prolonged periods of time. However, recent and emerging research suggests an even more expansive explanation of how trauma can manifest in neurobiological changes in the body and resulting behavior, including social interactions and system shutdowns.

Interactions between people and the environment directly affect brain functioning, and subsequently which higher-order thinking processes and behaviors are available at any given time. Porges' (2011) Polyvagal Theory posits that the vagus nerve is a critical part of communication throughout the body and among the various organs, and so determines this level of functioning. The vagus nerve interacts with the autonomic nervous system (ANS), the system that controls bodily functions that are largely unconscious (we do not normally think about our breathing or heart beats while engaged in routine activities). At an unconscious level, bodily functions seem to be assessing: Is it OK to "rest and digest" (parasympathetic part of the ANS), or do I need to be on alert and prepare to react quickly (sympathetic part of the ANS)? It is the sympathetic nervous system that mobilizes us to fight or take flight when we perceive danger. Different parts of the vagus nerve serve different mechanisms. The dorsal branch controls the fight-or-flight and shutdown responses. These responses may involve muscle fatigue, dissociation, and changes to heart and lung functioning (Wagner, 2016). The ventral branch controls the social engagement system occurring above the diaphragm (Wagner, 2016).

There are three basic levels of functioning, according to Polyvagal Theory: being at ease, the fight-or-flight response, and partial or complete system shutdown. When we feel safe, we are able to engage socially with others, and myriad expressions are available to us (Porges, 2001, 2011, 2018). In this state, it is possible for us to communicate with other people in a reciprocal, comforting, and nourishing way. However, when we experience a trauma, our very chemical makeup is affected, and our ability to accurately interpret our surroundings may be impaired—we are more likely to see other people as threatening (Porges, 2018). Physical changes occur that alter access to higher levels of functioning, like perceptions and decision-making. When we are in danger or perceive the threat of danger, our access to clear, logical thinking is limited or shut off. We may be in a fight-or-flight state, and are thereby quick to react, or conversely, an involuntary nervous system response to shut down may be activated. Down to a neurobiological level, our bodies are screaming "danger!", even if the threat has long since passed. This "stuckness" is a hallmark of trauma and is integrally related to vagus nerve activity. The differences in functioning levels are the cornerstone of Polyvagal Theory. People who have experienced trauma in their lives often find it hard to feel safe and are likely operating at a level of functioning that inhibits them in some way, in terms of fight or flight or shutdown. The more primitive brain (brainstem structures) functions remain available when danger presents itself, with social systems playing less of a role and prosocial behaviors inactivated (Porges, 2001). Thus, Polyvagal Theory is instrumental in understanding mass trauma and complex crises: There is a biological basis for social behavior, whether prosocial or antisocial (Box 24.2), which necessitates holistic pathways to heal from trauma (Porges, 2001).

BOX 24.2

Case Illustration

To illustrate the integral effects of trauma on daily life, we might consider, for example, a person who has been living from paycheck to paycheck. This individual has been on high alert most of the time and in fear of losing their job because they are a single parent. The COVID-19 pandemic has hit, and they first have their hours cut at work, having to choose what bills get paid and forgoing many meals. The person then has learned that their employer needs to close the business, thus eliminating the person's job. With their brain in survival mode, they are not as communicative or close with their child anymore and are finding it increasingly hard to make daily decisions. More panicked by the family's escalating economic problems, the person becomes overwhelmed, even by seemingly simple tasks. Remember, crises for individuals can be complex and do not have to surround just isolated events—a person can be functioning in "crisis mode" for years, and the deleterious effects on the body become apparent.

Reflection Questions:

- How do we begin to frame the stress and anxiety levels presented by this client?
- How might we begin to frame immediate and shorter-term interventions?
- Are there any referrals that we might consider?
- How might we begin to frame the need for longer-term interventions?

To illustrate how trauma permeates multiple bodily systems, Kolacz et al. (2019) point out that gastrointestinal (GI) disorders and psychiatric disorders, including PTSD, frequently co-occur. In a synthesis of relevant studies, researchers highlight the neurobiological interconnection between GI functioning and socioemotional problems, triggered by acute and chronic threat states that influence the autonomic nervous system (Kolacz et al., 2019). Responses to threat alter sensory-motor processes and the feedback loops that keep the body in homeostasis (Kolacz et al., 2019). It may not be surprising that experiencing trauma can affect many areas of life.

Complex Crises and Relevant *Diagnostic and Statistical Manual of Mental Disorders*, Fifth Edition, Highlights

Although the current *Diagnostic and Statistical Manual of Mental Disorders* (5th ed.; *DSM-5*; *American Psychiatric Association, 2013*) does not include eco-anxiety, climate anxiety, or other related terms, an official diagnosis that describes these timely states or conditions may not be far off. The American Psychological Association acknowledges the effects of climate change on the psyche

(Clayton et al., 2017). Recent research has begun to highlight how climate change can exacerbate existing mental health symptoms as well as increases in "trauma and shock, post-traumatic stress disorder (PTSD), compounded stress, anxiety, substance abuse, and depression" (Clayton et al., 2017, p. 7). Among the diagnostic categories that necessarily are considered when working with a client who is experiencing, or has experienced, a situation of complex crises, perhaps some of the most important to appraise are PTSD, anxiety, depression, dissociation, and suicidality. It is beyond the scope of this chapter to provide detailed descriptions of these diagnostic categories; rather, the emphasis here is that the astute clinician needs to explore potential diagnoses within the context and parameters of the presenting set of complex crises, while also recognizing that anxiety and depression can appear as symptoms of underlying trauma.

COMPLEX CRISES AND SOCIAL JUSTICE

When community trauma strikes, movement away from ethnocentric monoculturalism and toward multicultural pluralism is needed even more than during usual circumstances. This shift entails the ability to see beyond our own worldview and acknowledge the worldviews and experiences of other people as valid. Epistemologically, multicultural pluralism means acknowledging that there is more than one way to behave in this world and more than one way to conceptualize culture. Shedding ethnocentric monoculturalism means shedding the blinders that narrow an individual's view to the point that they see only their own worldview as right and acceptable.

Social justice, or the idea that everyone should have equitable opportunities, protections, access to resources, and rights in society, is integrally related to experiences and discussions about mass trauma, which is discussed in greater detail in Chapter 20 of this textbook. Unprocessed intergenerational trauma is transmitted across time and space by way of implicit and explicit messages about certain groups of people, which influences oppression and marginalization of such groups (Charles, 2019), and we certainly continue to learn about the epigenetic transmission of the profound effects of intergenerational trauma. Because some beliefs, even unconscious beliefs and bias, are so deeply rooted, people may feel defensive and as though their very identities are being threatened when questioned or invited to enter into a dialogue. Poverty and lack of adequate resources, among various populations around the world, remain problematic and contribute to the multiplier factor of complex crises. Just as an example, one consequence of Western development that we rarely discuss is the economic disparity that has been created among people of color and in the geographic hemispheric south. We briefly discuss these important social justice issues in this section.

Multicultural Pluralism

In order for a society to exhibit multicultural pluralism, it must allow for the retention and expression of unique cultural and ethnic identities and perspectives. In the case of mass trauma, such inclusion of myriad voices and perspectives may look like the amelioration of different conceptualizations, interpretations, and healing processes from the traumatic event, series of events, or historical compounded trauma. Counselors are in an especially unique position to be able to encourage this retention and expression throughout the healing process. To aid counselors in this process, the term "multicultural pluralism" can be broken down. The word "pluralism" connotes a broader philosophical idea that multiple truths exists (Pedersen et al., 2018). When pluralism is coupled with multiculturalism, specific and often marginalized identity groups (e.g., cultural, religious, and racial identities) are embedded within the concept of multiple truths—highlighting how truth may be conceptualized differently within and between groups. Regardless of where a counselor practices, counseling from an affirming multicultural pluralistic framework is needed with the added recognition that the experience of mass trauma may be rooted deeply in many cultural and racial groups. It is critically important to acknowledge that multiple truths necessitate multiple paths to healing, and decolonizing this process begins with the embrace of multicultural pluralism.

Cultural Competence, Cultural Humility, and Beyond

Cultural competence and cultural humility have gained much attention, as the counseling profession strives to provide relevant and accessible services to diverse clients, but the two terms have sparked some debate and controversy over which may be more important. Both cultural competency and cultural humility invite the self-reflection of helping professionals, but some view cultural competency as unattainable, because becoming completely competent in cultures other than one's own typically is not possible (Greene-Moton & Minkler, 2020). Cultural humility specifically highlights the power imbalances, which need to be addressed and equalized, between groups of people (Greene-Moton & Minkler, 2020; Tervalon & Murray-García, 1998). Some may view the two terms to be in competition with one another, but the overlap between the two constructs is as apparent as the utility of both. Combining the terms has been suggested as a way to synergize the two constructs (Campinha-Bacote, 2019), thus promoting a paradigm shift that warrants the combined benefits of both cultural competence and cultural humility, so that these two important constructs are no longer viewed as fragmented and in opposition with one another.

Another recent driver in the discourse surrounding multicultural counseling is the imperative to decolonize counseling and psychological practices (e.g., Conwill, 2015; Gelberg & Poteet, 2018; Goodman, 2015; Shin, 2015; Smith & Chambers, 2015). Gelberg and Poteet (2018) identify issues of decolonization as "related to the harm that Euro-American contemporary psychology, research, social work, education, and counseling can impose on individuals who do not endorse the values of the dominant culture" (2018, p. 1). They further assert that "mental health professionals should be trained to recognize elements of their professional work that are based on biases that still reflect Euro-American colonization" (Gelberg & Poteet, 2018, p. 1). Such shifts in conceptualization allow for the interpretation that everyone is ever evolving, while underscoring the need to remain culturally aware (of self and others), in order to challenge systems and institutions that maintain and perpetuate the status quo of injustice. An example of this, in the context of complex crises, may encompass recognizing the injustices associated with poverty (Smith & Chambers, 2015) and then discerning the intersections of how people living in poverty are more likely to experience the negative consequences of climate change, and how this then can lead to complex crises and trauma (Intergovernmental Panel on Climate Change, 2014). In a very real sense, the intersections that we discuss throughout this chapter, as they pertain to complex crises, also embody *intersectionality*, as the term typically is used in the diversity literature (e.g., Crenshaw, 2008). Awareness of such dynamics, along with focused efforts in response, can assist counselors in bringing about a more equitable distribution of resources, power, opportunity, and access to education and healthcare.

COUNSELING IMPLICATIONS OF COMPLEX CRISES

Regardless of where in the world counselors practice, they are likely to encounter individuals who personally have been through some of the crises described in this chapter, or perhaps have family members who currently are experiencing or have experienced a large-scale crisis. Complex crises counseling places extreme and unique burdens on counselors, particularly if they are providing services while the trauma is ongoing. When working in an international context, an unstable political environment can even lead to aid workers being victims of theft, physically attacked, kidnapped, or even killed (Stoddard et al., 2014). And of course, as we saw in the U.S. National Capitol on January 6, 2021, first responders and police were killed and hurt by an unruly mob. In this section, we discuss some of the unique challenges for counselors working with complex crises, the importance of adaptation and sustainability, and the need for building resilience and using other community-based trauma-informed strategies.

Challenges of Working With Complex Crises

In a CDC publication, Nilles et al. (2020) describe unique challenges for humanitarian aid workers, highlighting safety and security concerns as well as mental health issues. Among the critical safety and security concerns identified for humanitarian aid workers are (a) exposure to the disaster or conflict environment that precipitated or sustained the crisis; (b) damaged or absent infrastructure, including sanitation facilities and living accommodations; and (c) high levels of insecurity (Nilles et al., 2020, "Unique Challenges for Humanitarian Aid Workers," para. 2). Among the important mental health issues identified for humanitarian aid workers are (a) stressful environments and (b) working long hours under adverse or extreme conditions (Nilles et al., 2020, "Unique Challenges for Humanitarian Aid Workers," para. 3). Similarly, the Substance Abuse and Mental Health Services Administration (SAMHSA, 2020) advises mental health approaches that align with the unique needs of populations experiencing various crises and the professionals who deliver those crisis services. Furthermore, unique ethical issues may arise when counselors find themselves functioning in a multicultural context, having to negotiate boundaries in new ways, interfacing with alternative healing modalities, and confronting ethical dilemmas not readily defined in current ethical standards (Tarvydas et al., 2017, 2018; Teahen et al., 2017). Notably, many of the current ethical standards referenced in the counseling profession may stem from a more Westernized notion of what helping professionals do and how they function within communities, thus illuminating the need for decolonization efforts, as previously discussed.

Another challenge involves the historical purview of all that involves a behavioral health perspective. Traditionally, mental health interventions have been equated with a focus on psychological concerns. But as soon as we adopt an ecological perspective of the individual's interface with society across all social systems, we begin to entertain a broader frame of reference regarding behavioral healthcare. For example, many health professionals are calling for the inclusion of a mental health point of view within the emerging discourse about anthropogenic climate change, as well as for health vulnerability assessments, in order to expand the conceptualization of health and wellness beyond the physiological (APA, 2017; Hayes & Poland, 2018). This of course relates to other health disparities in low-resource communities and the need for advocacy efforts concerning behavioral healthcare, especially within the context of complex crises. In fact, the trauma derived thereof is a collective experience, and helping individuals with trauma also aids in increasing social capital and healing societies at large (Haer et al., 2021).

Relative to complex crises, Porges' relatively recent Polyvagal Theory offers insights that are relevant to the interconnectedness of behavioral health and physiological health perspectives. Porges even has proposed a "fourth paradigm":

> Thus, it may be possible that creating states of calmness and exercising the neural regulation of brainstem structures may potentiate positive social behavior by stimulating and exercising the neural regulation of the social engagement system. This perspective or intervention paradigm, which focuses on biologically based behaviors, might be viewed as a fourth paradigm or approach to modify behavior in contrast to behavioral (i.e., learning theory-based), biochemical (i.e., pharmacological), and psychotherapeutic (i.e., including psychoanalysis and cognitive therapies) intervention strategies. (Porges, 2001, p. 142)

Adaptation and Sustainability

Planet Earth and all of her inhabitants are in crisis, in terms of anthropogenic climate change; human populations and societies are in turmoil, due to strife, warfare, inequity, and climate. We no longer can afford to think only about prevention, particularly in reference to climate change issues. We are in an era in which we must develop adaptation strategies in order to maintain any semblance of sustainability of life as we know it. In its *Global Sustainable Development Report*, the United Nations (2019) details the ways in which complex development issues have threatened the planet. While the need for building stronger communities, with an eye toward improved and more fluid adaptation (Rodin, 2014), has been apparent for some time, achieving sustainability is going to require transformational planning in order to address the effects of complex crises (Gates, 2021). Mental health professionals need to develop community-based strategies that can enable citizens to become aware of new and emerging challenges, learn how to respond, learn how to cope, learn how to adapt, and acquire new methods for sustainability. We have seen how trauma affects our very physiology and social behavior; this is why holistic and community-based interventions are so essential for adaptation and sustainable solutions to complex crises. We need to create systems that foster calm and promote prosocial behavior, so that we are responsive rather than reactive to our circumstances.

Building Resilience and Other Community-Based Trauma-Informed Strategies

Due to the collective nature of complex crises, it behooves us to think about the various relevant issues in terms of public health policies, which tend to prioritize prevention and strategic planning (Tarvydas et al., 2017; Terwindt et al., 2016). Of course, individual interventions are important, but even at the micro level, the efficacy of interventions needs to be monitored and evaluated in order to inform strategies and policies and then continue to enhance prevention efforts (Schmets et al., 2016). A great deal of care has been taken, throughout this textbook, to provide rich information about clinical models and how to assist individuals experiencing crisis and trauma. Of necessity, we focus primarily on trauma-informed community-based interventions here.

One very promising model is the Trauma-Informed Community Development (TICD) model, which is presented in Chapter 19; therefore, we only reiterate a brief description here, so as to bring TICD into the discourse about responding to complex crises. TICD is a research-based model that the Neighborhood Resilience Project (NRP), located in Pittsburgh, Pennsylvania, designed and developed to engage community residents in a low-resource community (Abernathy et al., 2019). TICD works with neighborhoods and communities, block-by-block or at the micro-community level, to assess the physical and behavioral health of residents as well as the social health of each block or micro-community. The stakeholder-centered assessments are an instrumental part of NRP's effort, which has gained national and international attention. TICD is a culturally sensitive and context-specific model that uses grass-roots information from local stakeholders to conduct community-appropriate development. In response to demand, NRP now offers an annual TICD Institute that draws cohorts of community professionals from around the country whose agencies are interested in replicating the TICD model in their home communities. Most recently, NRP has been working to initiate and extend the TICD model into local schools, with an aim toward building a school-based TICD model that could be adapted for use in other parts of the state, country, and world. The community-building aspects of TICD entail many efforts that focus on building and sustaining resilience within low-resource communities. The TICD model is robust and has the systemic elasticity to be used in complex crises situations.

Resilience is an essential aspect of crisis prevention, mitigation, and recovery. Human resilience is responsible for individuals remaining intact—physically, emotionally, existentially, spiritually—in spite of facing horrific experiences. Resilience allows us to cope with crisis, adapt, and recovery quickly. Levers and Drozda (2018) have examined issues associated with complex trauma, from an ecological framework, and encourage counselors to respond from their professional stance of client empathy, but to move beyond traditional empathy to an embrace of compassion as a means of intervention. Especially when considering coupled human and natural systems, human intervention is an essential cornerstone for maintaining resilience, or the "capability to retain similar structures and functioning after disturbances for continuous development" (Liu et al., 2007, p. 1515). Human action is necessary for systems to continue functioning, in general, but human action also is needed so that systems remain familiar (Levers & Drozda, 2018). In other words, any system has a threshold or breaking point, at which the stress placed upon the system simply is no longer sustainable. Human action then becomes essential, in order to revamp systems that perpetuate inequity and thus engender trauma.

Teahen et al. (2017) have pointed to the interconnections within complex crises and the urgency of disaster preparedness, discussing the proactive need for building and enhancing social-ecological resilience. Rodin's (2014) notion of a "resilience dividend" has amplified the need to lay groundwork for helping communities, which have experienced disruption due to disaster and complex crises, to transform into communities that self-regulate with resilience. Rodin, further, has emphasized the importance of prevention as a public health imperative in building resilient communities as a forward-thinking effort to stave off the worst effects of complex crisis. Likewise, Gates (2021) has promoted an optimistic agenda of multilayered planning aimed at avoiding further disaster. In the face of complex crises, we need to facilitate the "new normal" as one of resilience, particularly as it offers guidance for intervention, at multiple levels, and aims at mitigating the impacts of anthropogenic climate change and other complex crises (Teahen et al., 2017). Saul (2013) has identified the following four themes in community resilience and recovery:

- Emphasizing the importance of building community and enhancing social connectedness
- Facilitating the collective story telling of community experience and response
- Reestablishing the rhythms and routines of life and engaging in collective healing rituals
- Arriving at a positive vision of the future with renewed hope (pp. 105–106)

CONCLUSION

The call to conceptualize multiple crises as complex and interwoven is urgent. In this chapter we have offered numerous examples of the interplay between complex crises and how individuals and communities may be swept up by forces that are not necessarily under their control, but very well may be manageable, with adequate planning and prevention efforts in mind. It is imperative for counselors and other helping professionals to consider the intersections of multiple and complex crises, moving away from the notion of crises occurring in an acute, isolated, and time-bound manner and moving toward a more expansive understanding of complex crises as catalysts for individual and systemic complex trauma. We hope that this chapter has provided invitations for assisting with this new conceptualization as well as offerings for how to address and respond to a confluence of crises.

ADDITIONAL RESOURCES

A robust set of instructor resources designed to supplement this text is located at http://connect.springerpub.com/content/book/978-0-8261-5085-1. Qualifying instructors may request access by emailing textbook@springerpub.com.

PRACTICE-BASED RESOURCES AND REFERENCES

To view a list of resources and all the references, please visit connect.springerpub.com via the following url: http://connect.springerpub.com/content/book/978-0-8261-5085-1/part/part04/chapter/ch24

CHAPTER 25

The Impact of War on Military Veterans

ROBERT G. MOERING, ROGER P. BUCK, AND LISA LÓPEZ LEVERS

CHAPTER OVERVIEW

The purpose of this chapter is to explicate the impact that war has on members of the military. In describing the effects of war on combat veterans and the challenges posed for those who return from war, potential needs for relevant mental health services are made explicit. The chapter identifies practice implications and offers an online list of resources for professionals working with military veterans.

LEARNING OBJECTIVES

After reading this chapter, the reader should be able to:

1. Understand the diversity of populations within the military;
2. Develop awareness of the complexity of responses to war;
3. Learn ways to respond to the types of trauma that are experienced by veterans and to facilitate related recovery strategies;
4. Identify mechanisms for assisting with re-adaptation to civilian life and for building resilience among veterans; and,
5. Understand the counseling implications for working with veterans.

INTRODUCTION

This chapter focuses on the most salient factors that have an impact on military combatants and their experience of warfare. The circumstances and the environment associated with combat causes a set of complex and unique responses. Due to an immense diversity of experience, it is extremely difficult to identify all of the variables associated with human responses to warfare. This chapter is an *introduction* to the potential psychological jolts that war trauma has on the military combat veteran. There is a complex anatomy of human responses to war trauma to consider. Detailed in this chapter are five areas that reveal the complexity of this topic: (a) there are five major areas of research related to human responses to war trauma; (b) there are diverse populations of military personnel; (c) there are numerous and contrasting war experiences; (d) resilient individuals appear to adjust and reintegrate into daily society more easily; and (e) physiological brain structure changes occur in some veterans as a result of traumatic war experiences.

Readers will learn that post-trauma reactions are much more comprehensive than the label of anxiety disorder, and that traumatizing events affect the whole person. Physical adaptations, cognitive thought processes, emotional responses, behavioral changes, and subjective interpretations are all part of the psychological makeup of the person who experiences war trauma. Recovery, resilience, and reintegration are three major components in psychological adjustment following combat.

The devastating cost of warfare can be measured objectively through the number of lives lost, homes destroyed, damage to cities, agricultural carnage, and environmental destruction. The subjective and potentially devastating toll on the character of military combatants who experience the "sensory" reality of warfare is much more difficult to measure. Significant psychological, physical, emotional, and spiritual changes occur in individuals who experience traumatic war events. Permanent damage to a person's character does not have to occur following combat trauma. The purpose of this chapter is to identify the unique issues, problems, themes, and predictable human responses to military combat. This aim is accomplished through the discussions that appear in the major sections of the chapter that follow: (a) Historical Perspectives of Posttraumatic Stress Disorder (PTSD), (b) Psychosocial Context, (c) Complex Nature of Trauma Responses, (d) Treatment Modalities, and (e) Counseling Implications. These sections are followed by a summary of the chapter and an online-only list of relevant resources related to trauma and military veterans.

HISTORICAL PERSPECTIVES OF POSTTRAUMATIC STRESS DISORDER

Although the diagnosis of PTSD was not introduced formally until 1980, with the third edition of the *Diagnostic and Statistical Manual of Mental Disorders* (*DSM-III;* American Psychaitric Association [APA], 1980), the notion of an emotional response to combat trauma has been around for thousands of years. Greek historian Herodotus provided an account of combat stress in his writings about the Battle of Marathon, in 490 BCE (Marincola & De Selincourt, 2006). Hippocrates described soldiers who experienced nightmares about combat (Crocq & Crocq, 2000). Dr. Jacob Mendez Da Costa noted that many Civil War veterans suffered from physical issues (e.g., palpitations, constricted breathing, irritation, increased arousal, and other cardiac symptoms) not associated with any wounds; this became known, variably, as "soldier's heart" and "Da Costa syndrome" (Grinage, 2003). Capt. Charles Myers (Royal Army Medical Corps) documented incidences of soldiers who were experiencing a number of symptoms (e.g., anxiety, nightmares, tremors, impaired sight and hearing), which he described as "shell shock," because these symptoms began after being exposed to exploding shells on the battlefield (Alexander, 2010). The U.S. Department of the Army (1994), in World War II, identified "battle fatigue" as the successor to "shell shock," with symptoms similar to conditions previously identified (e.g., fatigue, anxiety, loss of concentration, depression, memory loss, decreased motivation, and other disturbances in physical functioning); the term "battle fatigue" subsequently was used until the aftermath of the Vietnam War.

Posttraumatic Stress Disorder

PTSD is significant in considering the effects of war on military personnel. As a diagnosis, PTSD gained widespread recognition in the aftermath of the Vietnam War, secondary to thousands of Vietnam veterans lining the halls of Veterans Affairs (VA) hospitals across the country (Dicks, 1990). Researchers became interested in learning about this new diagnosis, and in the early 1980s, Congress authorized the *Vietnam Veterans Readjustment Study* to determine the prevalence of PTSD in returning veterans as well as to identify problems with reintegration and adjustment, postdischarge (Kulka et al., 1990). According to Rosen et al. (2010), there have been over 12,000 studies in peer-reviewed journals related to PTSD.

Changing Criterion A

The *DSM-III* introduced PTSD, which was characterized as a cluster of symptoms, following a traumatic incident that most people would consider extreme or beyond normal. Traumatic stressors included rape, assault, combat, natural disasters, car accidents, airplane crashes, bombing, torture, and serious bodily injury. Without the traumatic events, as defined within Criterion A, a diagnosis of PTSD could not be made. In this sense, Criterion A served as the gatekeeper for the diagnosis of PTSD.

With the introduction of *DSM-IV* (APA, 1994), the emphasis in Criterion A shifted to components of the person's response to the specific traumatic event. In order to be diagnosed with PTSD, a person had to have experienced fear, helplessness, or horror in response to the trauma. Subsequently, in *DSM-5* (APA, 2013), Criterion A once again underwent revisions. In addition to having directly experienced the traumatic event or witnessed the traumatic event as it occurred to others, Criterion A included a category of having learned that the traumatic event occurred to a family member or close friend; it also established a category for individuals who repeatedly experienced exposure to aversive details of the traumatic events (e.g., first responders). The concept of having to experience fear, helplessness, or horror in response to the traumatic event was removed in *DSM-5*. Rosen et al. (2010) noted that research has continued to challenge the way we understand and subsequently treat PTSD. The changes in Criterion A, over time, have reflected the challenges and criticisms noted through research and debate over the years. It is unknown how PTSD will evolve, if at all, in the years to come; however, it is important for clinicians and researchers alike to continue to question what we know about PTSD, in order to ensure the validity of the diagnosis.

PSYCHOSOCIAL CONTEXT

Many male and female veterans of the U.S. military returning from the Vietnam War suffered from a problematic readjustment to civilian life (e.g., Buck, 1998; Ettedgui & Bridges, 1985; Evans & Sullivan, 1990; Everstine & Everstine, 1993; Figley, 1978; Goodwin, 1987; Herman, 1992; Sandecki, 1987; Strayer & Ellenhorn, 1975; van der Kolk, 1984, 1987, 1989; Williams, 1987). The unconventional warfare unique to Vietnam is thought to have caused an estimated 500,000 psychological casualties among soldiers, sailors, and airmen. Lack of popular support for the war in conjunction with war protests is considered a major contributor to problematic psychological adjustment of Vietnam veterans (Buck, 1998; Scott, 1993; Wilson, 1978).

With the appearance of PTSD in the *DSM-III* (APA, 1980) in 1980 came a change in focus. Psychological symptoms were first attributed to the traumatic events instead of individual weakness (Friedman, 2003). This new diagnosis recognized the potential for long-lasting psychological problems as a direct result of a specific trauma event or events (Fairbank et al., 1993). The uniqueness of PTSD is its direct link to an etiological stressor or trauma event (Breslau, 2002; Breslau et al., 1995). War is a traumatic event, and the predictable psychosocial responses and unique phases of adjustment are discussed in this chapter.

Understanding Psychosocial Responses to War

In 1983, a congressional mandate prompted further investigation of PTSD and other postwar psychological problems among Vietnam veterans. The National Vietnam Veterans' Readjustment Study (NVVRS) was conducted to obtain data identifying the prevalence of postwar psychological problems. The prevalence of PTSD among "Vietnam theater veterans" (veterans deployed to the war zone) was an estimated 15.2% (male) and 8.5% (female). Those individuals who had higher war zone exposure to the "sensory" reality of warfare had higher rates of PTSD at 35.8% (male) and 17.5% (female; Schlenger et al., 2002).

Table 25.1

Veterans Affairs/Department of Defense Classification System for Traumatic Brain Injury Severity

	Mild	Moderate	Severe
Glasgow Coma Scale	13–15	9–12	≤8
Loss of consciousness	0–30 min	30 min to 24 h	More than 24 h
Posttraumatic amnesia	Less than 24 h or none	More than 24 h - less than 1 week	More than 1 week
Alteration of consciousness/ Mental state	A moment up to 24 h	>24 h	>24 h

Source: Data from U.S. Department of Veterans Affairs & Department of Defense. (2016). *VA/DoD clinical practice guideline for the management of concussion—mild traumatic brain injury.* Report prepared by the Management of Concussion—Mild Traumatic Brain Injury Working Group. https://www.healthquality.va.gov/guidelines/rehab/mtbi/mtbicpgfullcpg50821816.pdf

More than 2.77 million U.S. troops were deployed in support of Operation Iraqi Freedom (OIF; Iraq) and Operation Enduring Freedom (OEF; Afghanistan), beginning as early as October 2001 (Wenger et al., 2018). The all-volunteer force experienced an unprecedented pace of deployments, including multiple deployments to combat with infrequent breaks between deployments (Belasco, 2007; Bruner, 2006; Hosek et al., 2006). There were more than 5.4 million deployments by those 2.77 million service members (Wenger et al., 2018). Fewer casualty rates (killed and wounded) for these deployments were due to advances in medical technology and the use of body armor (Regan, 2004; Warden, 2006).

Psychological and stress reactions have developed in soldiers because of the following factors: multiple deployments, dangers of combat as exemplified by improvised explosive devices (IEDs), and exposure to the uncertainties associated with nonconventional guerrilla warfare. There have been a range of estimates of mental health problems among OIF and OEF veterans over the years. In 2008, a RAND corporation monograph (Tanielian & Jaycox, 2008) indicated that of OIF and OEF veterans, 14% screened positive for PTSD, and 14% screened positive for major depression. Another 19% reported a probable traumatic brain injury (TBI) experience. In the 2017 VA Health Care Utilization report (Veterans Health Administration, 2017), OEF/OIF veterans made up approximately 10% of the more than 6.6 million veterans receiving care through the VA. Approximately 58% of the OEF/OIF veterans receiving care through the VA were noted to have been diagnosed with a mental disorder. PTSD, depression, and neurotic disorder accounted for approximately 38% of the mental disorders treated through the VA. The Defense and Veterans Brain Injury Center (DVBIC) indicate that over the 20-year period of 2000 to 2020, a total of 430,720 military veterans have experienced a TBI with the vast majority (nearly 355,000) being mild TBIs (as cited in U.S. Department of Veterans Affairs, 2021). Traumatic brain injury can be categorized broadly as penetrating or nonpenetrating, and as focal or diffuse. A penetrating injury occurs when an object pierces the skull and enters the brain tissue. A closed head injury (nonpenetrating injury) causes the brain to move within the skull and collide with the bone. A focal injury occurs when a specific area of the brain is injured, whereas a diffuse injury occurs over a large area of the brain. TBIs are classified as mild, moderate, or severe. The classification system used by the VA/DoD appears in Table 25.1.

Phases of Adjustment

As the military continues its rapid schedule of deployments, the ever-increasing psychological casualty statistics continue to reflect the physical, cognitive, emotional, behavioral, and spiritual (PCEBS) costs of warfare among our combat veterans. The immediate impact of the war may not be debilitating for many, but there is evidence that soldiers who witness horrific events are at risk for chronic mental health problems over their life-span (McFarlane, 2015; National Center for Posttraumatic Stress Disorder [NCPTSD] & Walter Reed Army Medical Center [WRAMC], 2004). PTSD symptoms are only some of the many manifestations of traumatic war experiences. An extensive library of related research is available online and explores such war experiences in detail (see U.S. Department of Veterans Affairs as well as NCPTSD in the online-only Resources section).

Symptom intensity, rate of recovery, and support needs for each veteran are all part of an elaborate and personally meaningful reintegration process that varies for each military veteran. Human traumatic response includes an intricate array of factors, and the complexities of human responses to military combat, relevant issues, and evidence-based practices are explored in the following section.

COMPLEX NATURE OF TRAUMA RESPONSES

Human beings respond to danger through a "complex, integrated system of reactions, encompassing both body and mind" according to Herman (1992). When attempting to assess the impact that crisis experiences have on the individual, the evaluator needs to consider three "interactive components" (Webb, 1991). According to Webb, the three components that determine individual responses to traumatic events are the following: (a) individual factors, (b) the nature of the crisis events, and (c) factors in the support system. Herman and Webb's early PTSD research provide an historical basis to organize and conceptualize more recent research findings.

There are five major research areas of human traumatic response to warfare: (a) Personal Characteristics of the Individual to Consider, (b) Psycho-Physiological and Other Somatic Factors to Consider, (c) Social Factors to Consider, (d) Characteristics of the Trauma Events to Consider, and (e) Treatment Modalities. These are discussed in the text that follows.

Personal Characteristics of the Individual to Consider

There are significant personal variables that determine an individual's responses to traumatic events, such as age, sex, cognitive level of function, moral and spiritual beliefs, previous trauma experiences, pre-crisis adjustment, cultural beliefs/background, and previous behavioral health issues (Buck, 1998; Janoff-Bulman, 1992; Herman, 1992; Webb, 1991). In fact, an individual's risk factors serve as a strong predictor of who develops PTSD and who does not (Rosen et al., 2010). While many risk factors of PTSD do not inform treatment of PTSD, Meyer et al. (2019) note that psychological inflexibility, which is the inability to shift mental or behavioral repertoires in accordance with varying situational demands, is a modifiable factor that can be targeted in treatment; psychological inflexibility may predict PTSD symptom severity.

Included within the factors under discussion here are subjective influences that are difficult to identify and categorize objectively. Students of trauma must recognize these subjective issues in order to gain a more comprehensive understanding of the human responses to traumatic war events. Three subjective existential issues are discussed in the following subsections: The Psychology of Warfare, Conceptualization of War, and Resistance to Killing.

The Psychology of Warfare

There is a myriad of psychological, economic, and social group theories that aim to explain why nations and human beings find it necessary to go to war (LeShan, 2002). Two major existential concepts related to the psychological response to warfare are examined here. First, LeShan argues that the manner in which nations and individuals conceptualize warfare should be studied as a way of understanding the underlying psychology of warfare. He believes that understanding how people conceptualize war leads to a deeper understanding of the function of war and the meaning that individuals and governments construct from participating in war. Second, Grossman (2009) suggests that there is a basic human resistance to killing another human being. To become more efficient in war and kill more of the enemy, contemporary military and police training methods differ from those used prior to the Korean War. Because of these training changes, soldiers of today are more likely to kill during combat than the soldiers in World War II and in previous wars. Grossman suggests that focusing on efficiency in killing has resulted in more severe psychological damage to the modern soldier. Both authors emphasize that the existential as well as the trauma-specific issues that arise are important. Sensory combat experiences must be processed and incorporated within the individual's perceptions and understandings of those objective events. LeShan and Grossman provide a framework for understanding the subjective interpretations that human beings make as a direct result of the objective experiences of war.

Conceptualization of War

LeShan (2002) suggests that the various psychological, economic, and social group theories of why nations and individuals allow themselves to get involved in war are limited in their views about the causes of warfare. He articulates the existence of a new conceptual framework that previously has been unavailable and unexplored. For the past 40 years, a new field of thought has developed that examines the diversity of how human beings perceive reality (LeShan, 2002). Perceptions of reality are altered when one nation goes to war with another. These perceptions do not necessarily represent the truth about the world and its structure; they are just perceptions. Perceptions that allow for warfare to develop are based on a bias or belief system that may or may not be accurate. To comprehend the full psychological motivation behind the behavior of warfare, LeShan asserts the centrality of basic human "drives," which potentially lead to the belief that war is the only way to resolve conflicting beliefs. In his book, *The Psychology of War*, LeShan explores human beings and the psychological tension of being a separate and unique individual, while simultaneously feeling the need to be accepted and to belong to a group.

LeShan (2002) refers to the Roman mystic, Plotinus, who suggests that we have an "amphibious nature" (LeShan, 2002, p. 27), and that we must find a strategy to integrate both the way of the one and the way of the many. War is one method in which human beings simultaneously can fill these fundamental needs. When a group/nation has the following three perceptions about the world and about another group/nation, then they have the necessary conditions to see war and violence as a viable option: (a) there is an enemy nation that is evil, and if they were destroyed, then the world would be a better place; (b) glory can be realized if action is taken against this evil enemy; and (c) everyone within the "tribe" must agree with this understanding about the evil enemy, or they are seen as a traitor to the group. If these three danger signs are present, then armed conflict may result.

What is created by the previous perceptions is a "mythic reality" of war, one in which a nation and its populace rally around a cause for the eradication of evil. This is what the nation perceives, but it is not at all what the soldier experiences. The combat soldier experiences the "sensory reality" of warfare. Initially, soldiers go into battle with the same mythic reality that is held by the larger populace, of which they are members. However, the soldier is faced with the visceral horrors of war; the senses are overwhelmed with the sights, sounds, smells, tastes, and touches of war. There is a crisis in perception, due to the incongruence associated with the mythic reality of war and the sensory experiences to which the soldier is subjected. There is a series of expectations or beliefs associated with the mythic reality. The soldier expects to engage an evil enemy and, along with their fellow soldiers, survive. When a soldier witnesses the death and suffering of fellow soldiers, it does not fit the expectations associated with the mythic reality.

The death or severe injury of a fellow soldier is seen as a violation of the mythic rules of war. Within the mythic reality, there are two sets of morals. Soldiers judge the killing and combat behavior of enemy soldiers as evil. Killing the evil enemy is acceptable, righteous, virtuous, and good. The more time a soldier spends in sensory combat, the more quickly the mythic reality begins to erode. Witnessing unconventional combatants such as women and children participating in the killing does not fit into the mythic reality of war. For U.S. military soldiers to kill women and children, even if it is in self-defense, takes its toll on the sensory perceptions of moral constructs associated with acceptable combat. When confronted with sensory warfare, soldiers begin to question why the country is at war, along with their own participation in the fighting and killing. Once a soldier is unable to maintain the mythic reality that the nation uses to justify the killing, then a "meaning" or "spiritual" crisis occurs, and the soldier can no longer justify their personal participation in killing, combat, and warfare.

The individual soldier's perception of the "evil enemy" is potentially transformed into recognizing that the people being killed are human beings. The "glory" of killing the evil enemy begins to fade, and the "sensory reality" (sights, sounds, smells, taste, and touch senses of death and destruction) begins to permeate the soldier's total awareness. Disenchantment replaces the mythical cause. Combat soldiers experience these changes in an environment of misunderstanding. Military planners and the nation's populace do not fully understand the sensory experiences of combat soldiers and the resulting shift in their perceptions. Because of this difference in perception, many combatants tend to isolate themselves both emotionally and physically. As a result, war's objective experiences begin to invade, wound, and transform the soldier's spirit and subjective understanding of self, others, and the world. These objective sensory experiences erode the "mythic beliefs," and the combat veteran struggles with understanding life events in an environment of self-imposed isolation.

Every human characteristic that the individual attributes to a sense of "self" must be reshaped in order to make sense out of seemingly senseless sensory experiences. The cognitive dissonance between the individual's sense of self and the actuality of the sensory experience can be illuminated, and thus better understood, by considering the personal characteristics presented in Box 25.1.

BOX 25.1

Clinical Insights: Personal Transitions

Human characteristics, involving the tensions between subjective- and objective-world experiences, include the following transitions:

- How the individual perceives personal power and control;
- Perceptions about the world and safety;
- How the mind organizes information;
- Alterations in the mind's total functioning;
- How an individual loves, relates, and connects intimately with others;
- What the individual believes about the world and about the self;
- Which values and ethical beliefs come into question;
- What is judged as good and evil;
- What is right and what is wrong; and,
- What is feared and what is loved, which becomes confusing.

It is important for the student of war trauma to realize that there is a deep personal transformation that soldiers go through as a result of the sensory experiences of warfare. This transformation cannot be explained fully by using just one label such as PTSD. Reactions to combat and war trauma are definitely a stress reaction to traumatic experiences, but it is potentially an identity and whole-person crisis, depending on a complex set of factors that is explained in the following section.

Resistance to Killing

Comprehending the human responses to war requires a fuller realization and understanding of the psychology behind the human capacity to create and conduct warfare, and, more specifically, the killing of another human being. In his book, *On Killing*, Lt. Col. Dave Grossman indicates that there is a significant psychological factor in most human beings, describing it as "an intense resistance to killing their fellow man. A resistance so strong that in many circumstances, soldiers on the battlefield will die before they can overcome it" (Grossman, 2009, p. 4). He refers to U.S. Army Brigadier General S. L. A. Marshall's experience and inquiry/questioning of World War II veterans and the fact that "only 15% to 20% would take any part with their weapons" (as cited in Grossman, 2009, p. 3). According to Grossman, the lack of enthusiasm for killing "causes soldiers to posture, submit, or flee, rather than fight; it represents a powerful psychological force on the battlefield; and it is a force that is discernible throughout the history of man" (Grossman, 2009, p. 29). He explains that "looking another human being in the eye, making an independent decision to kill him, and watching as he dies, due to your action, combine to form one of the most basic, important, primal, and potentially traumatic occurrences of war" (Grossman, 2009, p. 31). Marshall's research with World War II (WWII) veterans revealed that many soldiers fired in the general direction of the enemy, in an attempt to appear as if they were participating in killing enemy soldiers, and that most would not openly admit that they resisted the opportunity to kill the enemy.

Many soldiers during WWII openly volunteered to reload weapons for others, but the actual act of killing another human being was performed by approximately one-fifth of our U.S. combat soldiers (Marshall, as cited in Grossman, 2009). Those soldiers who fired weapons that were designed to kill from a distance such as mortar, rocket, cannon, or aircraft had a very high rate of participation, because they were not face to face with their enemy. So until the Korean and Vietnam wars, it is estimated that only about 20% of our military combat-experienced infantry veterans actually shot at and intended to kill enemy soldiers.

According to Grossman (2009), Marshall's findings largely have been ignored by the academic fields of psychology and psychiatry, but the U.S. Army has taken Marshall's discoveries seriously, and after the end of World War II, instituted several new training methods. Because of these training changes, various studies of Korean War veterans indicated a jump to a 55% firing rate, and in Vietnam, the firing rate increased to between 90% and 95%. The programming or conditioning methods used to train troops, which increased the firing rate for Vietnam War veterans, was classical and operant conditioning. Training methods included the following strategies: desensitization, conditioning, and denial defense mechanisms.

In the desensitization process, the idea of "killing" an enemy who is evil, different, and dehumanized begins as early as boot camp and continues throughout the training process. By dehumanizing the enemy and continuously making them appear evil, the soldier has little resistance to killing when the opportunity presents itself. Conditioning occurs with repeated practicing of "quick shoot" on a firing range that includes human-shaped targets. There is competition and also immediate gratification when the target falls or explodes. There is continuous reinforcement when the shooter is recognized by superiors and peers as an expert shooter. Expert shooters often graduate with honors from the training program and receive further reinforcement with other forms of personal recognition. Failure to complete the firing range activities results in delay of graduation and possible chastising by peers and superiors. There is extensive rehearsal, with nearly exacting battlefield conditions. Soldiers are taught to shoot reflexively and instantly as they "engage" the target. The word "engage" of course means to "kill" the enemy. The word "target" is used to represent the human enemy. This neutralizing, dehumanizing, and denial-based language originates in training but also carries over into combat. This nonspecific language becomes a part of combat. Soldiers have rehearsed shooting at "the target" so many times that when they actually shoot at a human being, they are just "engaging a target."

Psycho-Physiological and Other Somatic Factors to Consider

Significant investigations have been conducted regarding how the body responds to the extreme stresses that are associated with traumatic experiences; some of this research shows that the body's complex biochemistry becomes deregulated. Brain chemicals designed to protect us may become harmful due to the amount or dosage our body creates. The alertness of the brain, memory enhancement, and rapid heartbeat caused by increases in norepinephrine and epinephrine (adrenaline) benefit the human being as the fight-or-flight response to danger. Too high a level of these chemicals may cause learning and memory impairment and may induce confusion. The repeated infusion of excessive amounts of these chemicals appears to sensitize brain chemistry and results in increasing amounts of adrenaline release at lower stimulation thresholds. Emotional reactivity caused by the dysregulated nervous system results in hypersensitivity, exaggerated behavior responses, and more intense susceptibility to sensory triggers such as smells, sounds, and sights. This overabundance of chemicals potentially triggers a cinematic, even seizure-like, reliving of trauma referred to as a *flashback* (van der Kolk, 1984, 1987, 1989, 2014; Vasterling & Brewin, 2005). The negative effects of high levels of these chemicals may occur immediately following traumatic events and continue for a long time.

In addition to the chemical influences within the brain, there is also potential damage to the structure of the brain. Long-lasting damage to the hippocampus may occur, which is then linked to the development of short- and long-term memory. There is a significant 8% reduction in hippocampus size among military trauma victims ages 18 to 24 years (Bremner et al., 1995, 1997, 2002; Villarreal et al., 2002). In a related study of women with a history of childhood sexual abuse, there was a 12% decrease in left hippocampal volume (Bremner et al., 2003). Symptoms of PTSD are more pronounced for those individuals with a smaller hippocampus (Bremner, 2001; Gilbertson et al., 2002; Osuch et al., 2001; Shin, Orr, et al., 2004; Shin, Shin, et al., 2004). High cortisol levels have been linked to hippocampus shrinkage; as a result, high levels of cortisol, for longer and more chronic periods of exposure to danger, potentially produce more and longer-lasting damage to the brain. If the body attempts to compensate for this overuse of cortisol, and levels are over-reduced, the outcome could be brain-cell death in the dentate gyrus region of the hippocampus, where long-term memory and recall are created (Vasterling & Brewin, 2005). The potential symptoms that manifest as a result of this brain damage are fragmentary memories, amnesia, short-term memory lapses, verbal recall deficits, dissociation, and an inability to describe horrific experiences (Vasterling & Brewin, 2005; van der Kolk, 1984, 1987, 2014). These are just a few examples of brain chemistry alteration and structural brain changes due to chronic traumatic stress. In addition, recent insights drawn from Polyvagal Theory highlight the functions of the autonomic nervous system; Polyvagal Theory also illuminates the potential for impaired social engagement as an additional component of how trauma affects brain function, thus emphasizing the interrelationship between psycho-physiological and social factors (Porges, 2009, 2011).

Social Factors to Consider

A significant support strategy for recovery from traumatic experiences entails the social network available to combat veterans such as nuclear family, peers with shared experiences, supportive others, churches, school/educational institutions, personal friends, and extended family members. Military support systems are a unique population with variables significantly different than any other organization (Buck, 1998, 2012; LeShan, 2002; Tick, 2005, 2014; Wilson, 1978). Some of these unique circumstances are presented here so that the military trauma student recognizes the distinctive differences in this population of trauma victim.

An all-volunteer force has staffed the military since the end of the Vietnam War in 1973. In the 1990s and just prior to the war activities in the Middle East, the number of U.S. Army personnel reached an all-time low of 500,000 soldiers. The military of today is much more diverse than at any other time in U.S. history. For example, there are ethnic minorities ranging from 24% in the Air Force to 40% in the Army, and 16% of all active-duty military personnel are women. Over 50% of all military personnel are married, and 11% of those are married to other military service members (NCPTSD & WRAMC, 2004). Recent data show that in 2014, ethnic minorities constituted 22.6% of the total veteran population in the United States, and it is expected that by 2040, minorities are projected to make up 35.7% of all living veterans (U.S. Department of Veterans Affairs, 2017a). According to a publication by the Brookings Institution, "While the U.S. military today has never had a higher fraction of women, they remain just 16% of the total force" (Robinson & O'Hanlon, 2020).

Several different components exist within the five major military organizations of the Army, Navy, Marine Corps, Air Force, and Coast Guard. Because of the Global War on Terrorism (GWOT), many National Guard and Reserve units from all five branches of the military have been called to active combat duty multiple times. Several resources available on soldiers' home bases support regular military units and their families who often reside either on those bases or in the immediate area. Because of geographic distance, a military base does not routinely support reserve units. National Guard and Reservist's families are isolated from military supports while the service member is deployed. Deployed reservists and/or guardsmen often lose their jobs or experience financial loss when they return from combat. More detailed information related to deployment, family issues, and unit integrity are examined in *The Iraq War Clinician Guide*, Second Edition (NCPTSD & WRAMC, 2004) and should be reviewed by any professional who anticipates working with military war veterans.

Characteristics of the Trauma Events to Consider

There are many aspects of the specific traumatic event that may influence the response that an individual has to the event. The diversity of war and military experiences has a major impact on individual responses. For example, if the individual is exposed to a single traumatic event, the symptoms associated with this event are potentially less debilitating than chronic and long-term recurring events (Buck, 1998, 2012; Herman, 1992). The individual who experiences a single-event trauma may feel "not him/herself," while the chronic trauma victim may feel a total and irreversible loss in sense of "self" (Herman, 1992). If trauma is experienced in solitary, the individual may feel unprotected, alone, and abandoned; hence, the option of social supports, through a shared experience, may not be available to this person. There is also a direct correlation between the severity of loss and the number and intensity of symptoms that develop (Everstine & Everstine, 1993; Zimmerman et al., 2018).

Certainly, the loss and death of a family member or friend can intensify the trauma symptomatic response. Variables that determine how survivors react to death include the following: death due to misconduct or natural causes, age of the deceased, and circumstances related to the death. The most devastating psychological trauma occurs when the survivor believes that they contributed to death due to neglect, misconduct, or intent (Buck, 1998, 2012).

Other issues to consider relate to the nature of the trauma. These include the following factors: the proximity and level of exposure to the traumatic event; the presence of a loss in status, personal power, and control; and the loss of bodily function through physical injury or pain. During military operations, there are a multitude of differing experiences with which the individual soldier may be faced; these include pre-deployment, deployment, types of conflict, medical evacuation, psychological stresses and responses, psychiatric care needs, post-deployment, administrative discharges, and so forth (NCPTSD & WRAMC, 2004).

This subsection of the chapter focuses on the types of conflict that military combatants must endure and their psychological responses. Different experiences that occur in warfare include low-intensity combat, high-intensity combat, terrorist activities and guerilla warfare tactics, war zone stressors, moral injury considerations, other unique issues, and military sexual trauma. Human responses to these various experiences differ significantly.

Low-Intensity Combat

Low-intensity combat in a wartime or combat environment, where fear of death or injury is less imminent, often includes a chronic strain on the individual. The person is subjected to harsh living conditions, family separation, extremes of hot or cold, and long hours of being on duty with little to no respite. The combatant experiences isolation, minimal communication with family, boredom, and a chronic awareness of the potential dangers that exist in this environment. These human stressors often foster the development of mood and anxiety disorders, separation anxiety, and adjustment and personality crises. Preexisting conditions may be exacerbated by this level of combat. Development or recurrence of alcohol and drug abuse may occur, depending on availability of these substances.

High-Intensity Combat

Intensive combat includes emotional responses to combat experiences. These often are viewed in a multiphase trauma response continuum (NCPTSD & WRAMC, 2004), as described in the text that follows.

Immediate Phase

The immediate phase of response includes "normal" and predictable reactions to extreme stressors and would include disbelief, strong emotions, confusion, fear, and autonomic arousal and anxiety. Various forms of adjustment disorder or maladaptive traits often manifest during this phase due to the extreme nature and immediacy of combat. Any preexisting conditions may be exacerbated, such as depression, previous PTSD symptoms, and substance abuse. Additional issues related to nonconventional warfare such as biological agents and chemical warfare can add additional disruption in the life of a military combatant (DiGiovanni, 1999).

Delayed Phase

The delayed phase occurs following intense combat stressors and may result in unexplainable physical symptoms or other PTSD symptoms, followed by substance abuse. These symptoms might include persistent autonomic arousal characterized by somatic symptoms, intrusive recollections, irritability, apathy, persistent anger, dissociation, mourning, and social withdrawal (NCPTSD & WRAMC, 2004).

Chronic Phase

The chronic phase includes continued arousal and intrusive symptoms with infusion of existential questions and personal discovery. A mix of depression and anxiety or other mood disturbance often manifests during this phase. Substance abuse may become more entrenched, legal problems may emerge, and pervasive distrust of self and others often develops. Due, in part, to this lack of trust, many combat veterans avoid all reminders of the traumatic events and isolate themselves both physically and emotionally. In this phase, the individual is attempting to make sense out of senselessness and is assigning some form of meaning to the objective events that have been experienced (Buck, 1998, 2012; DiGiovanni, 1999; NCPTSD & WRAMC, 2004).

Terrorist Activities and Guerilla Warfare

The increase in hypervigilance and stress related to tactics of terror such as remotely detonated explosive devices, car bombings, and mortar and rocket attacks cause additional psychological stress for the individual. The fear and surprise associated with this kind of warfare takes a psychological toll on an individual's sense of power and control within their environment. A crisis of meaning and senselessness begins to invade the individual's sense of purpose for being in this environment. Enemy combatants often are not readily identifiable, as civilian women and children often participate in this type of warfare. Not having a clearly identifiable enemy, coupled with uncertainty and doubt as to personal power to keep self and fellow soldiers safe, causes the soldier to remain ever vigilant and on guard (NCPTSD & WRAMC, 2004).

War Zone Stressors

War-zone stressors do not solely develop from combat actions alone, but may also arise from various types of demands, stresses, and traumatizing events. Veterans complain about a lack of preparedness for their deployment or a lack of sufficient training for their deployment. They may note having the wrong equipment or broken-down equipment to complete their mission. These veterans are likely to note a greater feeling of helplessness and unpredictability in the war zone. Surveying the aftermath of combat operations may include seeing the remains of civilians, enemy forces, and U.S. or allied personnel. Veterans are likely to disclose seeing homes and whole villages destroyed and smelling the decaying bodies of humans and animals killed in action. Living conditions and overall work environment provide constant stress. Lack of creature comforts, inability to take a shower, uncomfortable climate, long workdays, and lack of privacy all take a toll on the individual. While deployed in a combat zone, service members are likely to report ongoing concerns about their families back home. Individuals who deploy as members of the National Guard or Reserves often leave higher-paying civilian jobs, which can put a strain on family finances and relationships. Service members who are single parents face an additional strain of placing their children with others and oftentimes missing out on key developmental moments in their children's lives (NCPTSD & WRAMC, 2004).

Moral Injury Considerations

According to Maltzahn (2020), "Moral Injury (MI) is a set of symptoms that revolve around questioning one's self, beliefs, life's meaning, and ideals causing intense guilt, shame, doubt, inferiority, or internal turmoil" (p. 17). MI results from exposure to a traumatic event that violates deeply held values and moral beliefs, which results in a number of emotions such as guilt, anger, and shame. It is the act of engaging in an activity that goes against one's underlying moral values and beliefs (e.g., "you don't kill women and children" or "thou shall not kill") that results in the injury to one's moral values and beliefs, which causes an emotional response such as anger, shame, or guilt. The notion that war fighters faced moral dilemmas is not new, but the advancement of guerilla warfare and terror tactics in urban areas has brought to the forefront the increased rate of such events. According to Farnsworth et al. (2014), about 25% of Army soldiers and Marines have encountered at least one situation in which they had to make a moral decision, and they were unsure how to act. Veterans experience emotionally painful emotions such as guilt, shame, anger, disgust, and contempt, which then must be repaired.

Other Unique Issues to Consider

U.S. military forces must follow rules of engagement, especially while fighting where civilian populations are present. To limit civilian casualties, the U.S. military command structure requires justification for each violent interaction with the enemy. All fighting incidences are subject to retrospective analysis by command leadership. Commanders often require post-action justification of violent action taken against an enemy. Many soldiers see this process as ridiculous and accusatory. If the combatant interprets the retrospective review in this manner, then the military commanders may appear uncaring, unreliable, and unsupportive. The combatant who feels betrayed by command often experiences more severe psychological symptom development (Grossman, 2009).

There are incidences in which U.S. military units mistakenly fire on their own personnel, resulting in injury and death. Incidents of "friendly fire" have occurred because of miscommunication, error, and confusion on the battlefield. Those who are responsible for such friendly fire incidences, as well as the victims of these mistakes, potentially suffer more negative perceptions about the war. It is very difficult for soldiers to make sense out of the war and its purpose when a military action or mistake costs the lives of fellow soldiers (Buck, 1998, 2012; Grossman, 2009; Tick, 2005, 2014).

Military Sexual Trauma

The U.S. Department of Veterans Affairs (VA, 2017b) uses the term "military sexual trauma (MST)," which is defined as "physical assault of a sexual nature, battery of a sexual nature, or sexual harassment which occurred while the veteran was serving on active duty or active duty for training" (38 U.S. Code Sec. 1720D). As reported in the *Iraq War Clinician Guide*, the Department of Defense (NCPTSD & WRAMC, 2004, p. 66) conducted a study in 1995 and found that the sexual harassment rate for women was 78%, and for men it was 38%. Sexual assault, both attempted and completed, was 6% for women and 1% for men. According to Barth et al. (2016), approximately 41% of women and 4% of men reported experiencing MST. The authors noted that 41% of women had experienced sexual harassment, and almost 4% of men had experienced sexual harassment. Other studies, conducted by the Veterans Administration and reported in the *Iraq War Clinician Guide*, indicate that female veterans reported sexual assault rates as high as 23%. Other studies (NCPTSD & WRAMC, 2004) suggest that the rates of sexual assault among active-duty military personnel are higher during wartime than peacetime. Barth et al. did not find an association between MST and deployment to a combat zone among women veterans; deployed men to a combat zone had lower risk of MST compared with nondeployed men. Sexual assault victims experience higher rates of lifetime PTSD symptoms. Trauma (PTSD) symptoms among male victims of sexual trauma last across the life-span at 65%, which is higher than combat-related PTSD, at 38.8%. Female victims of sexual assault have lifetime symptoms of PTSD at 46%. Sexual trauma occurs most often where the victim works or lives. In many cases, the victim must continue to live or work with the perpetrator or friends of the perpetrator. Potential impact on the victim includes the disruption of career goals, low performance evaluations, delayed promotions, continued contact with the perpetrator because of unit mission, and the need to maintain unit cohesion (NCPTSD & WRAMC, 2004).

Treatment Modalities

Before identifying the "best practice treatment methods" for military veterans, it is important to understand who is being treated. The need for accurate and comprehensive assessment cannot be overstressed when evaluating the individual's personal attributes (strengths/weaknesses) as well as the specifics of the traumatic event. Ethical practices, which include sensitivity to diversity and multicultural issues, must be used in the assessment, diagnosis, and mental health treatment of active-duty service members, veterans, and military families (Stebnicki, 2021).

It is important to assess the level and intensity of exposure, the type of experience, the duration of the experience, and the social supports that are already being provided or that may be available. It is extremely important to recognize the possibility of TBI caused by explosions, impact wounds, and other concussion-type experiences. The OEF and OIF campaigns have been identified as the TBI wars, and symptoms related to this type of injury can be temporarily or totally debilitating (Chemtob et al., 1998; Cifu et al., 2010).

According to Vaughn et al. (2014), the prevalence rate of PTSD and major depressive disorders among OEF/OIF veterans consistently has been higher, when compared to other generations of veterans; however, there has been a wide range of prevalence rates (1.6%–60%), according to a meta-analysis completed by Fulton et al. (2015). This range has been attributed to a number of factors including methodology, anonymity of reporting, method of diagnosing PTSD, military occupational specialty, and level of combat exposure. Military members may be reluctant to disclose PTSD-related symptoms out of fear of reprisal from peers and supervisors alike (Hogue et al., 2004). Fulton et al. concluded that the prevalence rate of PTSD in OEF/OIF veterans was 23%, which was lower than the 30% rate within the Vietnam veteran population (30%) but higher than the general population (8.7%). The environment often determines the subjective and somatic responses that an individual may have. For example, veterans of the OEF and OIF campaigns have been subjected to the following stressors: extended periods of constant stress; unavailability of any "safe zone"; constant exposure to danger (mortar/rocket attack and explosive devices planted along road and walkways); constant "hyperarousal"; a rigid, highly structured military environment; exposure to multiple types of terrorism; and an enemy not readily identifiable (women or children combatants). Because this type of environment requires constant hypervigilance, soldiers are often too exhausted to process war events, emotionally and psychologically, until they leave the battlefield.

Many soldiers report a hypnotic aspect to war and combat. Combat is perhaps the most exhilarating and energizing experience of a soldier's life. While witnessing and participating in multiple atrocities of warfare, they have experienced the excitement and thrill of combat. The ethical and spiritual incongruence of witnessing death and destruction, while simultaneously experiencing the physiological excitation of warfare, is difficult for many combat veterans to assimilate. They struggle with coming to terms with their own emotional responses of excitement in an environment in which they witnessed and felt the moral decay of a society through death and destruction (Grossman, 2009).

Another poignant actuality of war relates to psychiatric and psychological casualties and the presumption that they are caused by fear of death and injury. There is little evidence that fear of death is the cause of such casualties. More important variables that increase the soldier's symptom formation are the fears of letting others down or not being able to meet the expectations of combat (Grossman, 2009), along with the toll of autonomic nervous system responses to constant hypervigilance (Porges, 2009, 2011).

Many soldiers face the loss of a comrade, which is emotionally devastating and often leads to prolonged, unresolved grief, mourning, and anger. Survivor guilt is often intense, and veterans who blame themselves for the death of a comrade, due to their own inaction or erroneous action, are potentially at higher risk for psychological or psychiatric casualty, including increased risk of suicide (NCPTSD & WRAMC, 2004).

Treatment considerations for veterans are driven by the symptoms that are displayed and revealed through extensive assessment. The whole person is affected by traumatic events, and, as a result, the individual experiences PCEBS symptoms (physical, cognitive, emotional, behavioral, and spiritual). The symptoms displayed by returning veterans are detailed later, in the section entitled Counseling Implications.

Review of the primary treatment modalities that have extensive research bases include trauma-focused individual cognitive behavioral therapy, interpersonal group therapy, peer-support groups, family and couples counseling, pharmacological approaches, primary medical care, and integrated treatment for co-occurring mental illness and substance abuse (Department of Defense Task Force on Mental Health, 2007; Matsakis, 1994; President's New Freedom Commission on Mental Health, 2003). A recent U.S. Department of Veterans Affairs (2020) publication has identified the following trauma-focused psychotherapies as having the strongest evidence for use with veterans: prolonged exposure (PE), cognitive processing therapy (CPT), and Eye Movement Desensitization and Reprocessing (EMDR). This publication recommends other types of trauma-focused psychotherapy that also may be indicated for people with PTSD, including brief eclectic psychotherapy (BEP), narrative exposure therapy (NET), written narrative exposure, and specific cognitive behavioral therapies (CBTs) for veterans with PTSD.

There are emerging best practices and innovative therapies that are showing significant benefit for individuals with PTSD. The Veterans Health Administration has widely disseminated two empirically supported treatments for PTSD: CPT and PE (Karlin & Cross, 2014). According to Holder et al. (2020), veterans with certain comorbidities and clinical complexities (e.g., MST) were more likely to initiate treatment with CPT or PE, but those with certain comorbidities (e.g., pain disorder or depressive disorder) were more likely to have a delay in treatment of trauma.

Bodywork therapies have been explored, such as acupuncture, acupressure, and healing touch. Animal therapies such as equine therapy and pet therapy (e.g., psychiatric service dogs) are showing promise in helping PTSD clients to expand their social interaction and emotional healing. Expressive therapies allow clients to use various forms of nonverbal communication to express themselves creatively and to aid in recovery. Art therapy, sand tray therapy, music therapy, and drumming are just a few of these expressive therapies. Lifestyle and nature therapy techniques such as healthy lifestyle counseling, nutritional awareness, recreational activities, and connecting with nature and spiritual well-being are additional techniques used to augment traditional therapeutic interventions. Physical therapy and exercise that promotes overall wellness helps to realign mind, body, and spirit through activities such as yoga, physical therapy, personal training, soft-style martial arts like Tai-Chi, dance, and other movement therapies. Relaxation and stress reduction techniques also are useful and include biofeedback, guided imagery or visualization, and massage therapy.

Cranial electrotherapy stimulation (CES) is being prescribed more and more for both service members and veterans for the treatment of PTSD, depression, anxiety, insomnia, and chronic pain. Multiple studies (e.g., Hare et al., 2016; Kirsch et al., 2014; Platoni et al., 2019) have reported highly significant decreases in symptoms of the previously noted diagnoses. CES has been prescribed by the Department of Defense and the Veterans Affairs since the early 2000s; however, it was not until more recently that the utilization of CES to treat these conditions increased significantly. Electromedical Products International, Inc. (EPIi) has seen an increase from 2,791 devices delivered to service members or veterans in 2011 to 13,859 devices delivered in 2019 (Laura Alcaraz, EPIi sales representative, personal communication, June 18, 2020). This increase in CES utilization was likely the result of the Kirsch et al. study in 2014 that was based on just over 1,500 service members and veterans. CES was compared to several of the more common drugs used to treat depression, anxiety, PTSD, insomnia, and pain and was proven to be as effective or more effective than the medications without the side effects of the drugs (Kirsch et al., 2014). CES is a very effective tool that is safe to use and comes without the side effects of medications.

There are several medications approved by the Food and Drug Administration (FDA) for the treatment of PTSD. Traditional selective serotonin reuptake inhibitor (SSRI) medications such as Zoloft and Paxil have been widely used for years, but Ketamine was approved in 2019 for the treatment of treatment-resistant depression as well as PTSD. Ketamine acts like an antagonist to the NMDA receptor, a glutamate receptor and a major excitatory neurotransmitter in the brain that plays a large roll in PTSD.

Recovery

Early trauma research focused on two basic areas in an attempt to explain problematic psychological symptoms after exposure to traumatic events. First was the literature suggesting that people who developed problematic psychological symptoms had a predisposition or susceptibility to psychological breakdown (Ettedgui & Bridges, 1985; Worthington, 1977). Second was the opposing literature that focused on the analysis of the traumatic event as the appropriate predictor of problematic human response (Boulanger, 1986; Foy et al., 1987). Figure 25.1 illustrates how these opposing views align with the more holistic views of Buck (1998, 2012), Cohen (1993), and Webb (1991), who suggested that there are important personal traits and characteristics of the event that determine individual responses to traumatic events. The whole person is affected by traumatic experiences, and this interaction consists of internal and external variables. The internal variables include personal characteristics and the circumstances of the trauma. The external variables include personal support systems (e.g., family, friends, peers, school, and churches) and professional support and treatment services.

Figure 25.1

Four Central Dimensions of Recovery

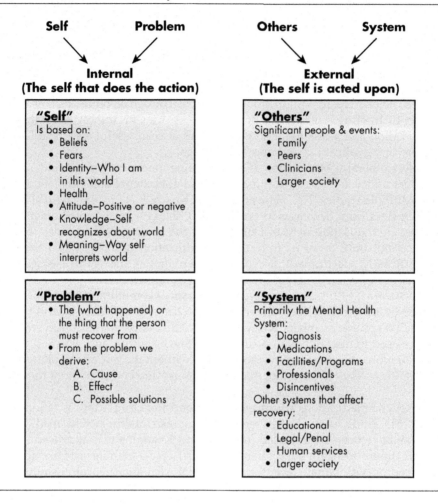

Self   Problem   Others   System

Internal
(The self that does the action)

External
(The self is acted upon)

"Self"
Is based on:
- Beliefs
- Fears
- Identity–Who I am in this world
- Health
- Attitude–Positive or negative
- Knowledge–Self recognizes about world
- Meaning–Way self interprets world

"Others"
Significant people & events:
- Family
- Peers
- Clinicians
- Larger society

"Problem"
- The (what happened) or the thing that the person must recover from
- From the problem we derive:
   A. Cause
   B. Effect
   C. Possible solutions

"System"
Primarily the Mental Health System:
- Diagnosis
- Medications
- Facilities/Programs
- Professionals
- Disincentives
Other systems that affect recovery:
- Educational
- Legal/Penal
- Human services
- Larger society

Variables for Recovery, Resiliency, and Reintegration

Recovery, resiliency, and reintegration are the three essential aspects of the military veteran's life-adjustment process that need to be considered by clinicians and students of military trauma. These three aspects are detailed in the following text.

Recovery Variables

Explaining the recovery process is perhaps best understood by identifying what an individual is attempting to recover. Buck (2012) proposed that the traumatized military veteran is trying to reestablish the following seven characteristics:

1. Recover a sense of personal "competency."
2. Recover a sense of personal "autonomy" (understand the "self" and how to relate to the world as a result of the changes to self).
3. Understand the impact of the objective traumatic experience as well as the subjective responses and symptom formation.

4. Recover a sense of intimacy and trust, enough to be vulnerable and flexible in intimate relationships with significant others.
5. "Trust" self and one's capacity for building trusting relationships with peers, coworkers, and society in general.
6. Develop a deep understanding about the trauma and the subjective interpretations about the meaning the experience has had on a sense of connection to the outside world.
7. Recover a positive personal identity, personality, and self-image, recognizing how each has been affected by traumatic events.

Resiliency Variables

Human beings are adaptable and have various innate strengths that can carry them through adversity and dangerous experiences. Like recovery, resiliency is best defined through the various indicators that demonstrate success in adjustment. The Army National Guard (ARNG, 2010) has developed a leader's guide for assessing and ensuring support for soldier resilience (*ARNG Leader's Guide: Soldier Resilience*). This guide provides extensive information on how to build resilience in the individual, the military unit, and the family during deployment. The following 12 indicators of resiliency are a comprehensive listing of concepts included in the *ARNG Leader's Guide* and have been skillfully compiled and summarized by the Ohio Department of Mental Health (2008) in their *Youth and Family Consensus Statement on Resiliency and Children's Mental Health*:

1. **Validation and valuing:** Appreciate life circumstances and life realities experienced
2. **Safety and basic needs:** Recognize and meet personal needs through personal strength and seeking supports as needed
3. **Sanctuary:** Identify a personal and protected space
4. **Justice:** Recognize that one has personal rights, voice, respect, and dignity. One needs to fight stigma and stereotype while making a commitment to self and others
5. **Competencies:** Recognize one's unique strengths, skills, talents, and abilities
6. **Self-wisdom:** As in recovery, recognize self as expert in one's own experiences and develop practical knowledge about coping/managing behavioral/emotional challenges
7. **Courage and confidence:** Personal courage and bravery to deal with life stressors
8. **Supportive connections:** Resiliency is nurtured by family, friends, peers, and professionals
9. **Expectations:** Maintain expectations that are reasonable and achievable and that maximize functioning and potential
10. **Participation:** People thrive when given opportunities to contribute, participate, and maintain positive involvement
11. **Hope and optimism:** Opportunities that challenge emotions often result in development of hope for a positive future
12. **Sense of meaning and joy:** Seek and find happiness, meaning, and joy in life events that bring satisfaction and quality to life

Reintegration Variables

Military veterans experience extensive training and preparation for the events that occur during time of war and in combat situations. During deployments and training exercises, military individuals are transformed into an elite fighting force whose mission is to overpower and destroy enemy forces. Changes have occurred within the veteran and in the family that must be assimilated. Being prepared for these changes is an important process, just as preparation for war is an important process. Military veterans with extensive traumatic experiences may have a more difficult time adjusting due to symptom formation. All military veterans potentially experience some need for reintegration training.

COUNSELING IMPLICATIONS

It is important for counselors and supportive others to recognize the PCEBS symptoms (physical, cognitive, emotional, behavioral, and spiritual) that manifest following traumatic events. Veterans and their families must realize that they may observe the veteran pacing, acting impulsively, walking aimlessly, distrusting others, being jumpy or startled by loud noises, spacing out, or having erratic movements that they did not have previous to deployment. It also is extremely important for veterans and their significant supporters to notice if there is an increased use of alcohol or drugs as a way of self-medicating for some of these symptoms.

How the veterans *feel*, both physically and emotionally, determines their success at reintegrating into family, work, college, or other civilian environments. Physical feelings such as muscle tension and pain, dizziness, headaches, grinding of teeth, stomach upset, chest pains, incessant thirst, fatigue, or fainting may all impact adjustment. Emotional feelings also will influence this adjustment process. Mood disturbances such as fear, panic, emptiness, sleep disturbance, uncertainty, anger/hostility, blame, grief, guilt, high anxiety, or flashback experiences all may be present within the combat veteran. Cognitive distortion such as intrusive thoughts, memory and concentration difficulties, recurring nightmares, confusion, preoccupation, self-blame, and distorted body image may interrupt the recovery process. These symptoms potentially cause relationship strain as well as personal isolation and withdrawal by the veteran. Many veterans report an extreme desire to connect intimately with others, but they often are reluctant because of lack of trust in self and others.

Trauma-Related Triggers

Triggers are usually external environmental sensory data such as sights, smells, sounds, tastes, or touch that stimulate an internal response. The internal response is usually an increased negative symptom, as listed previously, and is uncomfortable or disturbing for the individual. This sense of negativity is potentially interpreted subjectively as an indication that the person is "damaged" or "diminished" in some way because of the inability to control that reaction (Buck, 1998, 2012). Some typical triggers for combat veterans include the anniversary of the traumatic event, smells, loud noises, excessive stress, extreme guilt, feeling left out, work or school stress, relationship breakup, traffic, financial problems, being overly tired, sexual harassment, hearing others argue, being judged or criticized, spending too much time alone, and intimacy.

Making sense out of senseless life experiences is a truly monumental task for war zone veterans who have witnessed atrocity and loss of life of a comrade. A "crisis of faith" (Herman, 1992) may develop that potentially disrupts a trauma survivor's ability to create any positive meaning in life. Some of the *spiritual* responses experienced by many veterans include having anger at God; stopping attendance at religious services; experiencing emptiness or meaninglessness; feeling God has failed; questioning basic beliefs about self, the world, and God; and being angry or cynical toward clergy. Counseling professionals who are trauma-informed understand that these are "normal" responses to "abnormal" wartime events.

Healing Through Meaning

Ultimately, recovery from military and war zone traumatic events is an individual, personal, and private process that a soldier/veteran experiences. Veterans may not fully share themselves with others who do not understand the sensory reality of war. For many veterans, there is a lack of trust, a sense of personal damage, and alienation from others. Veterans typically desire to regain the capacity to connect intimately with others; however, their PCEBS symptoms interrupt their ability to do so. To "recover" from traumatic events, some veterans find meaning or make sense out of their war trauma through personal accounts of their experience. Telling their stories can provide significant cathartic relief for many veterans. Numerous examples of these narratives exist in the literature (e.g., Hedges, 2002; Kraft, 2007; Tick, 2005, 2014). Finding positive meaning in the face of traumatic events is a first step in the recovery process. Frankl (1955, 1963, 1978) warns that personal meaning derived through suffering must take place only when suffering is inescapable or unavoidable. Combat veterans experienced an environment in which suffering was unavoidable. It is essential that those who are recovering from traumatic events create a positive subjective interpretation and understanding of those traumatic life experiences. Through resiliency, as outlined previously in this chapter, military veterans may find positive meaning in their suffering. Trauma victims who are able to make sense of their experience and understand their reactions/symptoms are in the process of recovery (Buck, 1998, 2012; van der Kolk, 1984, 2014).

CONCLUSION

This chapter has examined a complex anatomy of war trauma and the unique issues, problems, and challenges that military veterans must address in their recovery process. Personal characteristics of the individual, specific variables related to the trauma event, and the availability of social supports interact to determine the degree of adjustment success following wartime experiences. Professionals who provide counseling services and other supports for military veterans must ensure that a comprehensive and accurate assessment of the various issues, problems, and challenges is conducted; at the same time, professionals must work toward a holistic understanding of the individual, as well as assuring that the individual's recovery and reintegration needs are met.

ADDITIONAL RESOURCES

| A robust set of instructor resources designed to supplement this text is located at http://connect.springerpub.com/content/book/978-0-8261-5085-1. Qualifying instructors may request access by emailing textbook@springerpub.com. |

PRACTICE-BASED RESOURCES AND REFERENCES

To view a list of resources and all the references, please visit connect.springerpub.com via the following url: http://connect.springerpub.com/content/book/978-0-8261-5085-1/part/part04/chapter/ch25

CHAPTER 26

Assessment in Psychological Trauma: Methods and Intervention

F. BARTON EVANS AND ALI KHADIVI

CHAPTER OVERVIEW

Psychological trauma is complex and sometimes difficult to understand, and its various manifestations can be challenging for the treating counselor. Psychological assessment and testing can provide the counselor with tools to hone clinical judgment and understanding of clients' trauma experiences beyond what is available in the counseling interview. After providing an overview of psychological assessment in general, we discuss the types of assessment methods available and provide specific instruments that can be of use in the assessment of psychological trauma. These methods include structured interviews, trauma-specific tests, and broad-based personality assessment tests, including self-report and performance-based methods. The chapter ends with a discussion of best practices in the psychological assessment of trauma along with recommendations for integrating assessment into counseling practice.

LEARNING OBJECTIVES

After reading this chapter, the reader should be able to:

1. Understand the value of standardized assessment in psychological trauma;
2. Identify major assessment methods when working with trauma-affected clients;
3. Describe the advantages and disadvantages of different methods for assessing trauma;
4. Understand the best practices for conducting psychological assessment; and,
5. Integrate psychological assessment methods into the practice of trauma counseling.

INTRODUCTION

The purpose of this chapter is to introduce the reader to the wide variety of available clinical psychological assessment methods that can aid the counselor in identifying and understanding the experience of the adult trauma victim. This chapter starts with a brief overview of psychological assessment in general. It will follow with a discussion of available psychological instruments for assessment of psychological trauma and its implication for counseling.

CONTEXT FOR ASSESSMENT

What Is Psychological Assessment?

For the purposes of this chapter, *psychological assessment* refers to the use of psychological tests in conjunction with a clinical interview to measure personality attributes, psychological symptoms, or cognitive functions with an eye toward developing hypotheses and predictions about the person's inner experience, interpersonal behavior, and performance. There are considerable advantages for counselors to incorporate psychological assessment into their clinical practice, either through consultation with an assessment professional or by receiving the education and training on how to administer, score, and interpret psychological assessment in a professionally ethical manner. Perhaps the major advantage is that psychological assessment is empirically grounded (see Kubiszyn et al., 2000; Meyer et al., 2001), providing objective information that considerably enhances the accuracy of clinical judgment.

Psychological assessment instruments include structured interview measures, self-report symptom-specific tests, multi-scale personality inventories, and performance-based personality tests. *Clinical interviews* are naturally at the heart of all mental health practice. They provide counselors with a powerful way to understand their client's history, interpersonal relationships, personal experience, and subjective reactions to these experiences and relationships. However, relying on unstructured clinical interviews alone has some important disadvantages, the first of which is that it runs the risk of missing important information. Additionally, as noted by Garb (1998) and R. Rogers (1995), all mental health professionals have their set of biases based on their own experience, education, and values. In contrast, psychological testing has a potential to improve accuracy and reliability of clinical judgments and reduce bias.

Structured interview-based measures are important psychological tests that systematically can assess signs and symptoms of psychological disorders. Sullivan's (1954) classic work, *The Psychiatric Interview*, skillfully introduced the idea of increasing reliability through a standard interview. With the advent of the *Structured Clinical Interview for DSM III (SCID-II, Ver. 1.0)* (Spitzer et al., 1990), the structured interview increasingly has become a gold standard for the most reliable diagnosis of mental disorder for research and clinical purposes.

Self-report symptom-specific tests are psychological assessment instruments, which include straightforward, face-valid instruments measuring a particular disorder or clinical phenomenon. They range from highly specific instruments (e.g., Beck Depression Inventory II [BDI-II]; Beck et al., 1996) and the Beck Anxiety Inventory (BAI; Beck, 1997) for depression and anxiety to comprehensive assessment measures for psychological sequelae of traumatic experiences (e.g., Briere's *Trauma Symptom Inventory-2* [TSI-2], 2011).

Among the most useful psychological assessment instruments are *personality tests*, which are designed to assess psychological symptoms broadly, as well as personality traits, behavioral predispositions, and inner experiences. Examples of personality tests include *multi-scale self-report tests*, that is, inventory-type, question-and-response tests, such as the Minnesota Multiphasic Personality Inventory-2 (MMPI-2; Butcher et al., 1989), Minnesota Multiphasic Personality Inventory-2-Restructured Form (MMPI-2-RF: Ben-Porath, 2011; Ben-Porath & Tellegen, 2008), and the Personality Assessment Inventory (PAI; Morey, 2007).

Additionally, *performance-based tests* like the *Rorschach Inkblot Method* (using either the Comprehensive System [CS; Exner, 2003; Weiner, 2003] or the Rorschach Performance Assessment System [R-PAS; Meyer et al., 2011] and *storytelling tests* (see Teglasi, 2010) such as the Thematic Apperception Test (TAT; Murray, 1943) are used to assess more subtle aspects of personality. The value of these comprehensive personality assessment measures is that they assess a wide variety of psychological states and personality traits, allowing the counselor to understand comorbid mental disorders and underlying personality issues better, as well as posttraumatic states.

Why Psychological Assessment for Posttraumatic States?

The context for assessing traumatic experience is broad, ranging from combat experiences to sexual assault, automotive accidents to life-threatening illness. Yet survivors of psychological trauma frequently express their experience in comprehensible ways that can be accurately assessed.

When a counselor first sees a person with psychological trauma, they are faced with a complex and daunting task. What is the nature of their trauma, and how severe was it? Who was the perpetrator—a stranger or someone the client counted on for protection? How long ago did it occur? Was the trauma a single episode or a series of repeated events over an extended period? What are the trauma victim's vulnerabilities and strengths? How has the inner experience and outer behavior manifested, both in terms of symptoms of psychopathology and disturbed interpersonal relations? These are but a few of the many issues and concerns that confront us when we enter the lives of individuals facing the impact of overwhelming, terrifying, horrific, and often incomprehensible life experiences. Psychological trauma is so profoundly destabilizing that it may be hard to imagine mistaking, overdiagnosing, or entirely ignoring it. Yet trauma disorders present in different and confusing ways, often with symptoms similar to other mental disorders, creating complex diagnostic and treatment challenges. To provide some groundwork for understanding the complexity of assessing psychological trauma, a brief description of trauma theory is presented here, along with implications for trauma assessment.

Prevalence studies of psychiatric clients show rates of trauma exposure that range from 60% to more than 80% (Bryer et al., 1987). Carlson's (1997) review concludes that counselors can expect at least 15% of their adult clients to have current or past trauma symptoms. As stated in the following text, presentations of psychological trauma can range from straightforward and clear to complex and disguised. As such, it is likely that counselors may be challenged with understanding clients with a wide variety of psychological trauma presentations. Therefore, counselors who become acquainted with a range of psychological assessment tools can increase their ability to understand and treat a wide range of trauma responses. When faced with this daunting task, psychological assessment methods can help quickly and reliably to provide a comprehensive view of the person and their struggles. In effect, as suggested by Finn and Tonsager (1997), psychological testing can serve as an "empathy magnifier."

In particular, there are two circumstances under which traumatized people come to the attention of counselors. First, individuals seek treatment following a clearly identified trauma such as a natural disaster, assault, rape, or life-threatening accident, illness, or injury. In these instances, the presenting psychological trauma is overt. Yet, posttraumatic stress disorder (PTSD) is only one of many possible ways in which traumatic experience presents itself (van der Kolk & McFarlane, 1996), and it not infrequently presents with comorbid mental disorders such as depression (Kessler et al., 1995). That is, a person may develop another psychiatric disorder in addition to the PTSD in response to the traumatic events. The psychological trauma also can activate a previously existing psychiatric disorder. For example, a person with a history of past panic disorder may re-experience panic attacks as a result of exposure to traumatic events. Further, the client may have past traumatic experiences that are activated by the current traumatic experience. Psychological assessment can shed light on the client's view of themselves, the ability to regulate emotions, interpersonal capacities, and coping mechanisms. In doing so, the counselor can better address the complexities of different trauma presentations in terms of symptoms, diagnosis, and, most importantly, effective treatment.

Second, counselors may see individuals with past psychological trauma, in which their trauma presentation is less obvious. In this instance, the clients may be unaware of the link between past traumatic experiences and their current suffering and symptoms and may not even see such experiences as relevant. For adult clients with past chronic childhood abuse and neglect, it is likely that traumatic dissociation has been used to cope with and survive the ordeal, which can limit clear memory of traumatic events and make it difficult for such clients to express their experiences in a coherent fashion. In such instances, psychological assessment, especially performance-based measures like the Rorschach or Adult Attachment Projective (Finn, 2011; George & Buchheim, 2014), can provide the counselor with the first indication of such buried trouble.

What Are the Faces of Trauma?

The word "trauma" is used increasingly in the common parlance as a word to indicate an unpleasant event, for example, "My girlfriend is giving me a lot of trauma these days about going out with the guys." Therefore, a more precise definition of psychological trauma is important. Unlike a distressing experience, the trauma response involves specific psychophysiological responses that are more extreme and enduring than the psychophysiology of distress (see Southwick et al., 2005). Such traumatic physiological reactions underlie the biphasic psychological response to trauma, which is the phasic alternation between intrusive (flashback/nightmares) and constrictive (avoidance/numbing) symptoms (van der Kolk & Ducey, 1984). Assessing the biphasic trauma response is critical in determining how to approach the client in treatment.

The best-known definition of the traumatic stressor is the stressor criteria used for PTSD described by the *Diagnostic and Statistical Manual of Mental Disorders* (5th ed.; *DSM-5*; American Psychiatric Association [APA], 2013). Criterion A-1 PTSD stressor criterion must include an "exposure to actual or threatened death, serious injury, or sexual violence." The *DSM-5* specifies that there are four different ways the person may be exposed to the traumatic events: (a) the person directly experiences the traumatic event(s); (b) the person witnesses the traumatic event(s) occurring to others; (c) the person learns that the traumatic event(s), which must be violent or accidental in nature, has occurred to a close friend or a family member; and (d) the person repeatedly experiences or is being exposed to extreme aversive details of traumatic event(s). Following traumatic exposure Criteria A, there are four symptom clusters: (a) intrusive symptoms, including re-experiencing the traumatic events; (b) persistent avoidance of any stimuli associated with the traumatic events; (c) negative alteration in mood and cognition, such as developing a persistent negative belief about oneself; and (d) marked alteration in arousal, such as becoming hypervigilant or having an exaggerated startle response. Finally, these symptoms must cause distress and/or social and emotional impairment.

The advantage of this definition is that it is relatively easy to quantify and therefore provides criteria that are reliable and researchable. The disadvantage is that it focuses on symptoms rather than experience and does not capture the terrible reality of protracted traumatic experience such as torture, domestic violence, and child abuse, where understanding the impact of captivity, degradation, and emotional abuse is critical.

A second, more liberal, and perhaps more satisfactory definition is found in the *International Classification of Diseases, Tenth Revision* (*ICD-10*; World Health Organization, 1992), which defines PTSD in the following way:

> [A] delayed and/or protracted response to a stressful event or situation (either short- or long-lasting) of an exceptionally threatening or catastrophic nature, which is likely to cause pervasive distress in almost anyone (e.g., natural or man-made disaster, combat, serious accident, witnessing the violent death of others, or being the victim of torture, terrorism, rape, or other crime) (World Health Organization, as cited in Houghton College, 1998, p. 1).

The three symptom clusters in the *ICD-10* are largely similar to those in the *DSM-IV*, instead of the four-factor symptom structure of *DSM-5* (see Zoellner et al., 2013 for a more comprehensive review of the change in the PTSD criteria in *DSM-5*). The *ICD-10* stressor definition is closer to the one in *DSM-III-R*, but was rejected for a more narrow definition in *DSM-IV* (and even more narrowly for *DSM-5*), because it was harder to quantify. The emphasis on a stressor that would cause pervasive distress in almost everyone provides a broader understanding of the power of events that are not strictly life threatening or integrity threatening (see M. J. Friedman et al., 2014, and van der Kolk, McFarlane, & Weisaeth, 1996, for two excellent comprehensive books on PTSD).

A third definition arises from the work of Herman (1992, 2015), who indicated that current PTSD diagnosis frequently does not capture the severe psychological harm from prolonged, repeated trauma and suggested a new diagnosis, complex PTSD, or disorders of extreme stress not otherwise specified (DESNOS), to describe the pervasive psychological and physiological effects of long-term trauma. The stressor criterion for diagnosis of complex PTSD is that the individual experienced a prolonged period (months to years) of total control by another. Six clusters of symptoms have been suggested for diagnosis of complex PTSD: (a) alterations in regulation of affect and impulses, (b) alterations in attention or consciousness, (c) alterations in self-perception, (d) alterations in relations with others, (e) somatization, and (f) alterations in systems of meaning (Pelcovitz et al., 1997). While *DSM-IV* field trials indicated that 92% of individuals with complex PTSD/DESNOS also met criteria for PTSD, complex PTSD was not added as a separate diagnosis (Roth et al., 1997). On the other hand, because of the different and more severe symptom pattern, assessment of complex PTSD is critical for determining special psychotherapeutic approaches. Herman (1992), Chu (1998), and Courtois and Ford (2009) offer more comprehensive discussions regarding the etiology, clinical phenomena, and treatment approaches of complex PTSD. Unfortunately, *DSM-5* did not add a diagnosis of complex PTSD, although extensive research (see Brewin et al., 2017) has been done to justify its inclusion in the forthcoming *ICD-11*.

In addition to these three specific diagnostic presentations of PTSD, other symptoms commonly found in individuals experiencing trauma include somatization, panic reactions, emotional lability, anxiety, agitation, depression, hopelessness, loss of life purpose, sleep problems, inability to self-soothe, and disturbances in thinking and reality testing. Symptoms of physiological dysregulation in chronic trauma and emotional lability can mask accurate diagnosis, because they are core symptoms in many other psychological disorders, such as bipolar disorder, panic disorder, and borderline personality disorder. Affective dysregulation can increase cognitive confusion, intrusions can be experienced on a cognitive level as hallucinatory flashbacks, and psychotic-like thinking has been observed in traumatized people who were previously clinically normal (Weisaeth, 1989), giving the impression of a psychotic disorder. Efforts to avoid re-experiencing traumatic memories may make traumatized clients appear withdrawn, uncooperative, and exhausted, causing difficulties connecting with them and complicating counselors' efforts to understand.

It is important to remember that not all individuals experiencing trauma show clinical signs and symptoms. There is no one-to-one relationship between an external trauma and the person's psychological response. Researchers estimate that only 25% to 30% of those exposed to trauma develop PTSD (Kessler et al., 1995; Ozer et al., 2003), although risk rates vary and depend on the kinds of stressors such as combat, rape, childhood abuse, or assault with a weapon. The studies indicate that women consistently show higher risk rates than men. However, many people spontaneously resolve the trauma and, in the process, may even develop greater coping skills (Solomon et al., 1988). Such findings underscore the importance of assessing individuals' strengths as well as vulnerabilities (Sullivan, 1954), further complicating the counselor's task.

PSYCHOLOGICAL ASSESSMENT METHODS, CONCERNS, AND PRACTICES

Several methods of psychological assessment are best indicated for use with survivors of trauma, and several important practice issues arise when considering relevant methods. These methods and associated issues and practices are discussed in the following sections: Clinical Interview, Trauma-Specific Scales, Personality Assessment Instruments, Performance-Based Tests, Feigning/Malingering, and Best Practices in Assessing Psychological Trauma.

Clinical Interview

The clinical interview is the most common psychological assessment strategy used by counselors, psychiatrists, social workers, psychiatric nurses, and psychologists alike. During interviews at the beginning of counseling, the counselor forms an initial opinion about the client's problems, subjective reactions to these problems, symptoms, diagnosis of mental disorder(s), and treatment strategy. Throughout the course of treatment, the counselor reassesses initial hypotheses about problems and alters the treatment course accordingly. Although the clinical interview is the core tool used for assessing and understanding the client, as stated earlier, all counselors are vulnerable to their biases and the limitations of understanding from a single source of data. G. A. Miller's (1956) classic article on the limits of our capacity to process information indicates that at any one time, we can hold seven pieces of information, plus or minus two. The implication for this psychological reality is that in order to deal with the complexity of psychological trauma, the counselor does well to operate from multiple information sources beyond a structured clinical interview. The assessment of symptoms and reactions to psychological trauma is aided by additional methods such as structured interviews. Four of the major structured interviews for the assessment of psychological trauma, along with several supporting methods, are described later. Although there are many others, it is beyond the scope of this chapter to be exhaustive.

Dimensional, Scale-Based Structured Interviews

When the presenting problem includes a clear description of a traumatic stressor, structured interviews of posttraumatic stress employing dimensional rather than categorical (presence/absence) rating scales can be invaluable in understanding the severity and nature of PTSD symptoms. Two examples of such interviews are the gold standard Clinician-Administered PTSD Scale for *DSM-5* (CAPS-5; Weathers et al., 2018; Weathers, Blake, et al., 2013) and the PTSD Symptom Scale-Interview Version (PSS-I-5, Foa & Capaldi, 2013).

Clinician-Administered PTSD Scale for DSM-5

Of all the structured interviews for PTSD, the CAPS-5 is the most comprehensive for assessing core and associated symptoms of PTSD. Weathers et al.'s (2001) literature review of more than 200 studies indicated impressive evidence of its reliability and validity. Several advantages of the CAPS over other structured interviews for PTSD are that it assesses the frequency and intensity of each symptom; has excellent prompt questions to elicit clinical examples; assesses both current and lifetime PTSD symptoms; and provides explicit, behaviorally anchored rating scales. The CAPS can be scored, providing both continuous and dichotomous scores with several scoring rules to assist the counselor (Weathers et al., 1999). The CAPS's primary disadvantage is its long assessment time of about 50 to 60 minutes. The Life Event's Checklist (LEC; Gray et al., 2004) is a brief, 17-item self-report measure designed to screen for potentially traumatic events in a respondent's lifetime. The LEC was developed concurrently with the CAPS and is administered before the CAPS.

PTSD Symptom Scale — Interview Version

When time is at a premium, PSS-I is a reasonable alternative. Studies indicate that the PSS-I is reliable and valid in civilian trauma survivors, making it a good instrument for most clients in the counselor's usual practice. In a comparison study with the CAPS (Foa & Tolin, 2000), the PSS-I performed about equally well in arriving at a diagnosis of PTSD, decreasing assessment time without sacrificing reliability or validity. On the other hand, what is gained in time savings is lost in providing a detailed rich description of the client's past and present psychological trauma.

Structured Interviews for Complex Posttraumatic Disorder and Dissociation

If the counselor has a practice involving adult victims of child abuse, the PTSD structured interviews mentioned earlier are likely not sufficient to assess the pervasive and complex psychological sequelae of complex PTSD. A groundbreaking study by Herman et al. (1989) found a strong association between a diagnosis of borderline personality disorder and a history of abuse in childhood, including physical abuse, sexual abuse, and witnessing serious domestic violence. This research was instrumental in developing the diagnosis formerly called DESNOS and now more commonly called complex PTSD.

Structured Interview for Disorders of Extreme Stress

As part of the field trials for *DSM-IV* (Roth et al., 1997), the aforementioned research team developed the Structured Interview for Disorders of Extreme Stress (SIDES; Pelcovitz et al., 1997), a validated structured interview assessment for complex posttraumatic stress, which subsequently was found to have considerable clinical utility (van der Kolk & Pelcovitz, 1999). The SIDES is a 45-item interview that consists of six subscales corresponding to the six complex PTSD symptom clusters. Like the CAPS, the SIDES measures current and lifetime presence of complex posttraumatic stress symptoms as well as symptom severity. In a recent study of individuals diagnosed with borderline personality disorder using the SIDES, McLean and Gallop (2003) concluded that "some women with a history of childhood sexual abuse may be extricated from the diagnosis of borderline personality disorder and subsumed under that of complex PTSD" (p. 371).

Dissociation and the Structured Interview for DSM-IV Dissociative Disorders-Revised

Dissociative responses and disorders (formerly called "multiple personality disorders") account for additional clinical phenomena closely associated with psychological trauma and its assessment. Dissociation is a state of fragmented consciousness involving amnesia, a sense of unreality, and a feeling of being disconnected from oneself or one's environment. Dissociation is a psychological process common to everyone, although in the extreme, it can become a severe disorder with fragmented identity states, previously and inaccurately referred to as "multiple personalities." Putnam (1997) estimated that most, if not all, dissociative disorders are caused by severe sexual, physical, and emotional abuse in childhood. Because of the complex and shifting affective and identity states in dissociative disorder, comprehensive evaluation provides the counselor with a significant advantage over the simple clinical interview.

One of the best methods for the comprehensive assessment of dissociative states and disorders is Steinberg's (1994) *Structured Clinical Interview for DSM-IV Dissociative Disorders-Revised* (SCID-D-R). Rigorously developed through the National Institute of Mental Health (NIMH) field trials, the SCID-D-R is a structured diagnostic interview that is specific to the assessment of *DSM-IV* dissociative disorders and acute stress disorder. It provides a careful and detailed decision tree approach, arriving at accurate *DSM-IV* diagnosis of Dissociative Amnesia, Depersonalization Disorder, Dissociative Disorder Not Otherwise Specified, Acute Stress Disorder, and Dissociative Trance Disorder. Perhaps of more importance to counselors, the SCID-D-R assesses a broad variety of posttraumatic dissociative symptoms that clients may not spontaneously share in unstructured interviews. Many dissociative clients have long learned that their dissociative experiences are treated by others as strange and bizarre and indeed some counselors may feel this way toward the clients as well. As a result, such clients have learned to avoid discussion, automatically, of these symptoms. Careful and empathic administration of the SCID-D-R can help dissociative clients better share their experiences and can reveal symptoms and psychological states that can be the focus of treatment intervention. Steinberg and Schnall's (2001) book is an approachable overview of dissociative disorder.

It is important to note that dissociative disorders underwent changes with *DSM*-5 to include certain possession-form phenomena and functional neurological symptoms. It is specific that transitions in identity may be observable by others or self-reported and that individuals with DID may have recurrent gaps in recall for everyday events and not just for traumatic experiences. Dissociative fugue is no longer a distinct diagnosis but is subsumed as a specifier with fugue under dissociative amnesia. Depersonalization disorder has been revised to include derealization, as both often co-occur. To date, there is no published update to the SCID-D-R, though Ross (2019) has an unpublished updated version of his Dissociative Disorders Interview Schedule.

Trauma-Specific Scales

The next set of assessment tools, for use with psychological trauma, is the *trauma-specific scales*, a group of self-report instruments that focuses specifically on the symptoms and phenomena of PTSD and psychological trauma. They range from instruments with high "face validity"—that is, instruments that assess specific symptoms of PTSD—to more subtle instruments, which include associated traumatic symptoms and experiences as well as, in some instances, validity scales. The advantages of trauma-specific scales include the following features: (a) they focus on specific psychological trauma symptoms and phenomena; (b) they provide ratings of symptom severity and frequency; and (c) they allow the counselor to select specific scales that best match specific populations, for example, sexual assault, combat trauma, and partner or domestic abuse. Such instruments allow the counselor to focus treatment on specific symptoms that are most distressing to the client. As mentioned earlier, there are variations in posttraumatic symptom presentation, that is, the biphasic response in which the client may have predominantly avoidant/numbing presentations; intrusive/flooding presentations; or, in some instances such as with torture victims, alternations between the two. For example, some trauma victims may so repress trauma memories that they do not have current intrusive symptoms. As Foa and Rothbaum (1998) report, rape victims with an avoidant presentation have poorer treatment outcomes generally than, and require a very different approach from, victims with active intrusive symptoms. Trauma-specific assessment tools can alert the counselor early on to the client's particular dilemmas, increasing the counselor's understanding of and empathy for the client and developing a more specific treatment approach.

Frequently Used Scales

Two commonly used PTSD-specific scales are the clinical version of the PTSD Checklist for *DSM-5* (PCL-5; Weathers, Litz, et al. (2013) and the Posttraumatic Stress Diagnostic Scale (PDS-5; Foa et al., 2016). These are described briefly in the following subsections.

PTSD Checklist-5
The PCL-5 is a brief, 20-item self-report measure of the 20 *DSM-5* symptoms of PTSD that assesses both symptoms and their severity. The PCL can be used for screening individuals for PTSD, diagnosing PTSD, and assessing symptom change during treatment. Blanchard et al.'s (1996) study of motor vehicle accident victims and sexual assault victims found a high correlation with the CAPS, concluding that the PCL is effective as a brief screening instrument for core symptoms of PTSD. Because of the high incidence of trauma victims among individuals presenting for psychotherapy, the PCL-5 also can be used as an important screening tool during intake with all clients. A problem with the PCL-5 is that it assesses only PTSD symptoms and not the specific trauma causing the symptoms. It assesses only severity of symptoms (i.e., "How much have you been bothered by each PTSD symptom?") but not frequency of symptoms (i.e., "How often have you experienced these symptoms?"). The PCL-5 asks about symptoms in the past month, so lifetime incidence is not assessed. The research on the initial version of the PCL (and very likely the PCL-5) even can be significant for individuals going through severe life events that do not specifically meet *DSM-IV* stressor criteria for PTSD (Robinson & Larson, 2010), making it a sensitive but not specific assessment instrument.

Posttraumatic Stress Diagnostic Scale for DSM-5
The PDS-5 is a 52-item self-report measure best used when assessing the severity of PTSD symptoms related to a single identified traumatic event. The PDS is one of only two among specific trauma self-report inventories to assess all of the *DSM-5* criteria for PTSD and can assist

in a clear, formal diagnosis. Further, it asks about the presence and frequency of symptoms in the past month, although other time frames can be used. Unlike the CAPS-5 and PCL-5, the PDS-5 does not ask about severity of PTSD symptoms. It does not assess for past traumatic events or their impact on the client's current life.

Assessing Combat-Related Trauma

Since the Vietnam War, and most recently Operation Enduring Freedom (Afghanistan) and Operation Iraqi Freedom, no survey of PTSD assessment would be complete without mention of the assessment of combat-related trauma. Since 1989, the U.S. Department of Veterans Affairs (USDVA, 2011) and its research and training arm, the National Center for PTSD (NCPTSD), have sought to understand better, and therefore better assess, the needs of veterans with military-related PTSD. Particularly, NCPTSD's Behavioral Science Division, headed by Dr. Terence Keane, has been the world's leader in the development and research of psychological assessment instruments for combat-related trauma. A core battery for the assessment of combat-related PTSD would include the following instruments: the Combat Exposure Scale (CES; Keane et al., 1989), the PTSD Checklist-Military (PCL-M; Bliese et al., 2008), and the Mississippi Scale for Combat-Related PTSD (M-PTSD; Keane et al., 1988).

Combat Exposure Scale
The CES is a seven-item self-report measure that assesses wartime combat stressors experienced by combatants. Respondents are asked to respond, based on their exposure to various combat situations, such as firing rounds at the enemy and being on dangerous duty. The CES is administered and scored easily, providing a classification for combat exposure that ranges from light to heavy and provides the counselor with information that the veteran may find difficult to describe fully.

PTSD Checklist-Military
The PCL-M is a military version of the PCL mentioned earlier, although it asks specifically about symptoms in response to stressful military experiences (Bliese et al., 2008). It is often used with active service members and veterans to gauge the presence and severity of symptoms of PTSD.

Mississippi Scale for Combat-Related PTSD
The M-PTSD is a 35-item self-report measure that assesses combat-related PTSD in veteran populations. Veterans rate how they feel about each item using a 5-point scale. These items are added together to provide an index of PTSD symptom severity, with cutoff scores for a probable PTSD diagnosis, for use primarily with veteran populations. Not only does it assess primary symptoms of PTSD, but it also taps features often associated with PTSD such as substance abuse, suicidality, and depression.

Disadvantages

While the trauma-specific self-report assessment methods mentioned earlier are very useful, these measures also have several notable disadvantages, which are shared in common with all other self-report assessment measures. Self-report measures depend on the clients' ability both to *understand* themselves sufficiently to respond accurately to the questions and to *be willing* to report what they experience. In the case with clients who are emotionally shut down, they may not realize and report symptoms that are obvious to others. Alternatively, other clients may carelessly respond or underreport or overreport symptoms and experiences on self-report measures for a variety of motivations such as compensation for injury or worries about who will see the clients' records if they report fully and honestly. These tendencies are known in assessment circles as *response styles*, that is, test-taking approaches that can bias or skew the interpretation of self-report measures.

Additional Inventories

Following the lead of major self-report inventories such as the MMPI-2 and PAI, Dr. John Briere has created several excellent, comprehensive trauma-specific self-report inventories, which not only measure traumatic experience comprehensively but also assess response style. The most widely used and best researched of his scales is the TSI-2 (Briere, 2011), which takes about 20 to 30 minutes to administer and is scored easily. Briere's TSI-2 includes validity scales that assess defensiveness (denial of difficulties) and symptom overendorsement (endorsement of atypical symptoms not common to PTSD). Additionally, the TSI-2 includes a validity scale for inconsistent, random reporting.

Trauma Symptom Inventory-2

Briere's TSI-2 is based on a well-conceptualized and well-researched understanding of traumatic phenomena and yields excellent information about the client's experiences and behaviors, which makes it exceptionally useful for framing empathic interventions. It surveys on both acute and chronic posttraumatic symptoms and experiences and has been widely used to assess the effects of sexual assault, domestic partner abuse, physical assault, combat experiences, major accidents, and natural disasters. In particular, the TSI-2 is an excellent instrument to use with adults subjected to childhood abuse and other early traumatic events. In addition to assessing common PTSD symptoms such as angry/irritable affect, intrusive symptoms, avoidance/numbing, and hyperarousal, the TSI-2 also assesses comorbid symptoms of both mood and cognitive distortions found in trauma-related depression, as well as dissociative symptoms. Further, this measure goes beyond the immediate posttraumatic symptoms and evaluates the long-term self-disturbance and interpersonal difficulties frequently found as a part of the chronic sequelae of earlier psychological trauma. The self-scales include sexual concerns (sexual dissatisfaction and distress), dysfunctional sexual behaviors (indiscriminate and self-harming sexual relations), impaired self-reference (identity confusion and poor self-care), and tension-reducing behavior (external ways of reducing inner tension such as suicidal threats, self-mutilation, and dysregulation of anger).

Dissociative Experience Scale II

No brief survey would be complete without mention of the Dissociative Experiences Scale II (DES II; Bernstein & Putnam, 1986), the widely used screening instrument for the frequency of dissociative experiences. As noted earlier, severe dissociative reactions are common in adult survivors of severe childhood trauma. Identification of these experiences is important, diagnostically and therapeutically, for treatment of such disorders as dissociative identity disorder. The DES is a brief self-report measure that assesses a continuum of dissociative experiences with normative data for normal, traumatized, and dissociative clients. It can be obtained online from the Sidran Institute at www.sidran.org.

Abusive Behavior Observation Checklist

The Abusive Behavior Observation Checklist (ABOC) is a powerful assessment measure for counselors working with both women and men who are the victims of domestic battery. Often, such individuals have extreme difficulty articulating their domestic abuse experience in interviews with even experienced counselors (see Dutton, 2000; Walker, 2000). Dutton's (2000) ABOC was developed to document the types and degree of interpersonal violence in domestic abuse such as physical, sexual, and psychological abuse, as well as victims' behavioral and cognitive adaptation to such abuse. The ABOC provides an exhaustive survey of the ways in which batterers abuse their spouses and spouses' adaptations to these abuses. Used together with the TSI, the ABOC provides an important avenue for battered spouses to share their traumatic experiences and effects on their functioning and view of themselves.

It should be noted that there are many trauma-specific self-report inventories for psychological trauma, although it is beyond the scope of this chapter to survey most of them. The reader is referred to two excellent books (Briere, 2004; Wilson & Keane, 2004) for a more detailed survey of psychometric issues as well as a wide variety of self-report trauma instruments for both adults and children.

Personality Assessment Instruments

Psychological trauma occurs within the context of the person and their personality. Individuals undergoing distressing life experiences may adapt in a variety of ways, depending on their past experiences and common patterns of response (Sullivan, 1953). While factors such as intensity of traumatic experience and a history of prior traumatic events clearly influence posttraumatic response (van der Kolk, 1987), M. W. Miller's (2004) review highlighted the intricate interplay between personality and the development and expression of PTSD. Personality assessment methods can be useful in helping to understand the impact of psychological trauma on the person, especially the long-term effects found in individuals with severe past trauma. As stated earlier, there are two kinds of personality assessment methods: *self-report tests* (formerly called "objective tests") and *performance-based tests* (formerly called "projective tests"). Meyer and Kurtz (2006) offer a helpful explanation of why this previous distinction did not accurately communicate the nature of these tests. As discussed in the following text, training for the use of the major personality tests requires a significant level of education, supervision, and experience, although in our opinions, it is well worth the effort.

Self-Report Tests

The most widely used and researched personality instrument is the MMPI-2. Based on the client's response to 567 True/False items, it yields 10 clinical scales and three primary validity scales, as well as literally hundreds of other scales. For the well-trained assessor, the MMPI-2 provides a rich palate of personality variables to understand the complexities of the client's personal functioning. Further, the strong actuarial base of the MMPI-2 deeply enhances the accuracy of clinical judgment with some psychologists, even arguing for the superiority of actuarial methods (see Grove, 2005). While it is beyond the scope of this chapter to discuss the psychometric properties of the MMPI-2, there are many excellent books on the MMPI-2, including A. F. Friedman et al. (2015) and Greene (2011), as well as on the MMPI-2-RF (Ben-Porath, 2011).

Understanding psychological trauma on the MMPI-2 can be a daunting task without adequate knowledge of how the instrument captures traumatic experience, and perhaps most importantly, how traumatic experience interacts with the individual's personality. It is important to remember that the MMPI-2 and its predecessor, the MMPI, were not developed with the assessment of psychological trauma in mind. Traditional interpretation of MMPI-2 clinical scales with trauma victims can be extremely misleading. A common code type (i.e., a configuration of significantly elevated clinical scales; see Greene, 2011) for traumatized individuals is a highly elevated 2-8/8-2, often with other scales elevated in the clinical range. The traditional interpretation for this configuration, especially when it is highly elevated, suggests an individual with serious and chronic psychopathology. Common diagnoses are bipolar disorder and schizoaffective disorder. Without careful analysis of subscales and supplementary scales, the traumatized individual with hallucinatory and dissociative flashbacks, vivid nightmares, and intrusive daydreams readily could be misdiagnosed with a psychotic disorder with severe depressive features, using standard interpretations on the MMPI-2.

One approach to the MMPI-2 has been to find a code type that definitively diagnoses PTSD. The results of this endeavor have been mixed and elusive, largely because the approach is nomothetic, that is, looking at group level findings. For example, Wilson and Walker (1990) found a 2-8/8-2 code type with an elevation on F to be the most common profile, whereas Lyons and Wheeler-Cox (1999) noted a 2-7-8 code type to be the most prominent. Glenn et al. (2002) found different predominate code types for Gulf War and Vietnam era veterans (1-8/8-1 and 2-8/8-2, respectively). Elhai et al. (2000) found that adult survivors of child sexual abuse and combat veterans were more similar than not on the MMPI-2. Griffith et al. (1997) found an 8-4 code type with women having histories of childhood sexual abuse, although scales 1, 2, 6, and 9 were elevated as well. Additionally, there have been several supplementary subscales developed to identify PTSD, the most enduring being the Keane PTSD Scale (Keane et al., 1984). The disadvantage of the PTSD subscales is that they were developed without specific PTSD items, and they do not include the specific symptoms common to PTSD.

Another approach to the MMPI-2 is Caldwell's (2001) adaptive approach, which focuses on how psychopathological behaviors measured by the test are positive adaptations to painful or overwhelming life experience. He stated that "[u]nderstanding all such behaviors as adaptive leads to a notable enhancement of empathy" (p. 1). Caldwell reframed several of the classic MMPI-2 scales, thus providing important insight into traumatic experiences. For example, his description of Scale 8 (Schizophrenia) emphasizes the mental confusion that frequently is attendant with early traumatic experiences. Caldwell elaborates,

> If, at an early age, your body was the object of someone's sexual gratification, someone who was cold to your distress or—worse yet—excited to greater sexual aggression by your pleadings that he or she stop, you end up deeply alienated and knowing yourself to be permanently damaged goods. (p. 13)

Such an approach is preferable for an individual-based (idiographic) interpretation of the MMPI-2, as it is ideally suited for giving feedback (Finn, 1994) and providing powerful assessment-based therapeutic intervention such as the therapeutic assessment (TA; Finn, 2007).

Another important and increasingly popular comprehensive self-report personality assessment instrument is the PAI (Morey, 2007). The PAI has fewer items and takes less time to complete than the MMPI-2. Instead of the *True or False* format of the MMPI-2, the PAI rates items on a 4-point scale, ranging from *false* to *very true*. It has 22 non-overlapping full scales, including four validity scales, 11 clinical scales, five treatment scales, and two interpersonal scales. The 11 clinical scales were developed to be consistent with current diagnoses in mind, making for an easier diagnostic description. The 11 clinical scales also contain conceptually derived subscales. Among the most useful of the clinical subscales is traumatic stress, which uses items more directly indicative of symptoms of PTSD.

Performance-Based Tests

As stated earlier, the performance-based (PB) personality assessment measures include what previously have been called projective tests. Through either storytelling methods, such as the TAT and the AAP (George & West, 2001), or inkblot methods, such as the Rorschach, PB personality tests are more open structured and elicit individuals' powerful inner narratives and emotional experience. Such instruments can allow the trauma victim a path to reveal inner experiences that are not readily available to conscious verbalization. Of these PB methods, the Rorschach is the most researched and best conceptualized.

In our opinion, the Rorschach is one of the most powerful personality assessments, when used by a sensitive examiner trained in the Rorschach comprehensive system (CS; Exner, 2003; R-PAS, Meyer et al., 2011), an empirically based method for administration, scoring, and interpretation. The advantage of the CS and R-PAS over other Rorschach methods is that interpretation is based on a very large body of literature, confirming the reliability and validity of the variables. Rorschach CS and R-PAS is therefore an idiographic instrument with normative data to assist in understanding the highly individualized results.

The Rorschach has been used extensively with individuals with psychological trauma, and the reader is referred to Armstrong and Kaser-Boyd (2003) and Kaser-Boyd and Evans (2007) for a comprehensive overview of its use. The CS has an important trauma indicator called the *Trauma Content Index* (TCI; Armstrong & Loewenstein, 1990), which has been used to help identify victims of sexual abuse (Kamphuis et al., 2000) and individuals with dissociative identity disorder (Brand et al., 2006). Recent work by Finn (2011) has hypothesized that the Rorschach and other PB measures in particular allow access to unconscious negative affect states and implicit models of the self that result from traumatic experience, especially early developmental trauma. He contrasts PB measures with self-report tests, which are more sensitive to explicit models of the self and to conscious affect states. Because an important dilemma in the treatment of victims of trauma is accessing their damaged view of themselves and easily triggered fear, the Rorschach and other PB tests hold a unique place in the assessment and treatment of individuals with psychological trauma.

Feigning/Malingering

No discussion regarding the assessment of psychological trauma would be complete without mentioning potential problems of feigning, which is defined as deliberate symptom exaggeration or fabrication. Psychological tests can measure feigning. Malingering is feigning for an external gain. Frueh et al. (2003) found up to 50% significant overreporting of symptoms among disability compensation seeking among veterans evaluated for PTSD. Rosen (2006) cautions that overreporting of PTSD in compensation cases is so common that it raises concern about inflating rates in the epidemiological PTSD database. While most individuals entering treatment for psychological trauma or for psychological problems eventually may find their root cause in traumatic experience, some individuals seek counseling, often on the advice of their attorneys, as a part of legal proceedings in which they are claiming PTSD as a consequence of an accident, personal injury, or disability claim.

The alert counselor is aware of this possibility and understands that there are important differences between clinical and forensic assessment (see Greenberg & Shuman, 1997). Many well-meaning counselors have been drawn into complex and contentious legal matters, making expert opinions without a proper basis, which is readily and successfully attacked by skillful defense attorneys. Such experiences often are painful and humiliating for the counselor and may lead to a loss of status in the professional community and even to malpractice suits. It is our advice that counselors always ask on intake whether the client is involved with or anticipates being involved with a legal matter related to their psychological state. If this is the case, we strongly advise developing a policy regarding the counselor's willingness to participate in such matters and only to become involved in such matters with extensive and rigorous training and supervision in forensic assessment.

Best Practices in Assessing Psychological Trauma

Having introduced the reader to the various kinds and benefits of assessment methods for psychological trauma, we would like to address the important issue of what constitutes best practices in psychological assessment and testing, especially the training necessary to engage in competent practice. Psychological assessment is a practice requiring special care because of the impact that it could have on clients' lives. As noted in the Society for Personality Assessment's (2006) "Standards for Education and Training in Psychological Assessment," unlike counseling or psychotherapy, where the counselor gets to know the client through many hours of interaction, psychological assessment may be a brief encounter in which mistakes can be magnified by misinterpretation. Further, psychological test reports usually become a part of clients' records, and mistakes may affect their entire lives. Additionally, psychological assessment can have a significant influence on important decisions about clients' lives, such as a need for hospitalization, assessment of dangerousness, custody of children, and employment situations. As such, inadequately trained psychological assessors can cause considerable emotional and personal damage.

Professional societies for psychology and counseling have provided important guidance on what constitutes ethical practice in psychological assessment. Some of the key resources are listed in the following texts:

- the American Psychological Association's *Guidelines for Test User Qualifications: An Executive Summary* (Turner et al., 2001),
- the *Standards for Qualifications of Test Users* (American Counseling Association, 2003),
- the *Responsibilities of Users of Standardized Tests* (Association for Assessment in Counseling, 2003), and
- the interdisciplinary *Standards for Educational and Psychological Testing* (American Educational Research Association, American Psychological Association, & National Council on Measurement in Education, 2014).

Knowledge of these guidelines and standards is necessary for any mental health professional wishing to engage in psychological assessment and testing. Unfortunately, these professional societies have not addressed what constitutes acceptable levels of education, training, and practice, leaving individuals who have not had a specific psychological assessment training sequence in graduate school with little place to turn for guidance. With this in mind, the Society for Personality Assessment (2006) promulgated a set of standards for education and training in psychological assessment to provide interdisciplinary guidance for mental health professionals in any jurisdiction with licensure permitting independent practice of psychological assessment. This document arose from the Society's concern about what it saw as an increasing number of individuals using psychological testing without proper knowledge of its complexities. The standards outline necessary courses, practicum, and supervisory experiences that can provide a basic education for adequate practice in psychological assessment. The standards also emphasize the important distinction between psychological appraisal and psychological assessment. The standards are publicly available on the Society's website, which is listed later in the online Resources section.

Three other topics regarding the adequate practice of psychological assessment are important to mention. First, as stated earlier, all individuals practicing psychological assessment should take into consideration the importance of response style in interpreting psychological tests, such as underreporting, overreporting, and inconsistent or confused reporting. Without some measure of response style, it is difficult to understand the true meaning of psychological test data. Second, the importance of a multimethod assessment (e.g., Erdberg, 2007; Meyer, 1996, 1997) cannot be overemphasized because of problems inherent in using only one test or one type of test, especially without at least one test with a measure of response style. Third, extreme caution should be used in relying solely on computer interpretive reports for interpretation of clients' problems. The direct use of computer interpretive statements in psychological assessment reports (often referred to as "plug and chug") is not an adequate practice. Greene (2011) reports research indicating that 15% to 20% of statements of MMPI-2 computer interpretative reports do not give an accurate interpretation of clients' psychopathology when additional scales and client history are taken into account. This is especially true with interpretation of the MMPI-2 with psychological trauma, in that computer interpretive reports are not trauma specific. As stated earlier, common code types for trauma victims give a very different picture, depending on whether psychological trauma is taken into consideration.

COUNSELING IMPLICATIONS

The issue of assessing survivors of trauma raises several implications for counselors. Perhaps most important is that careful assessment of psychological trauma can lead to clearer and more focused treatment interventions. Counselors are better able to assist their clients if they tailor their treatment to the problems in living that are troubling their clients. For example, focused assessment can let the counselor know if a client is struggling with intrusive experiences, upsetting their daily living, or if the client is emotionally shut down and socially detached because of a preponderance of numbing and avoidant symptoms. The client might be severely dissociated and disconnected in the treatment. Each of the psychological trauma presentations calls for a different treatment approach, and careful use of assessment instruments can assist the counselor in becoming more empathically linked to the client. Psychological assessment makes considerably more information available about the client's psychological functioning than the counselor can gain from unstructured clinical interviews alone.

Further, as Finn (2007) pointed out, psychological assessment is an empathy magnifier. Indeed, personalized, collaborative feedback using psychological assessment has been increasingly used as a powerful therapeutic and empirically valid treatment intervention in its own right. Models for integrating counseling with psychological assessment often are called collaborative assessment (see Fischer, 1985/1994) or Therapeutic Assessment (Finn, 2007). More detail about how this approach can be used in the treatment of psychological trauma can be found in the parallel chapter in the first edition of this book (see Evans, 2012).

Another important implication is that more powerful assessment instruments provide more incisive information about the trauma survivor. Whereas clinical interviews are the "meat and potatoes" of counseling practice, structured interviews and face-valid PTSD scales add greater specificity in assessing the client's dilemmas in living. More elaborate measures such as comprehensive PTSD scales and the TSI allow the counselor to see the client's difficulties in a more complex way, whereas personality assessment measures such as the MMPI-2 and the Rorschach allow the counselor a better understanding of how the individual's psychological trauma fits into the overall picture of the personality. As the counselor employs more powerful psychological assessment instruments, they have a greater responsibility to receive advanced training in these methods that perhaps were not part of the graduate training curriculum. Best Practices in Assessing Psychological Trauma was presented earlier in the chapter to provide guidance for the counselor desirous of advanced practice in the psychological assessment of trauma.

CONCLUSION

In closing, we have tried to present a brief overview of the importance and potential power of psychological assessment with victims of trauma. Apart from presenting the many useful methods of assessing psychological trauma, it is our hope that counselors reading this book will see ways in which assessment can enhance their practice by assisting in more accurate and focused ways to intervene with trauma victims. Working with the broken narrative of psychological trauma is complex and challenging, but ultimately highly rewarding, when the counselor can help trauma victims repair deeply damaged views of themselves and their relationships with others. While becoming proficient in psychological assessment may appear daunting at first, there is a large and responsive professional community to support this learning. We personally wish to extend an invitation for counselors to embrace this challenge.

ADDITIONAL RESOURCES

 A robust set of instructor resources designed to supplement this text is located at http://connect.springerpub.com/content/book/978-0-8261-5085-1. Qualifying instructors may request access by emailing textbook@springerpub.com.

PRACTICE-BASED RESOURCES AND REFERENCES

To view a list of resources and all the references, please visit connect.springerpub.com via the following url: http://connect.springerpub.com/content/book/978-0-8261-5085-1/part/part05/chapter/ch26

CHAPTER 27

Trauma, Crisis, and Disaster Interventions: Integrative Approaches to Therapy

LISA LÓPEZ LEVERS, JANE M. WEBBER, J. BARRY MASCARI, AND CAROL M. SMITH

CHAPTER OVERVIEW

This chapter focuses on integrative approaches to trauma therapy, crisis intervention, and disaster response. The purpose of the chapter is to identify and explain best practices for integrative mental health responses aimed at supporting survivors of trauma, crises, and disasters. While each unique situation requires a tailored response, this chapter describes the basic principles that apply to nearly all emergent, mass casualty, and traumatizing events.

LEARNING OBJECTIVES

After reading this chapter, the reader should be able to:

1. Select appropriate evidence-based psychotherapies which mitigate the effects of trauma;
2. Understand key integrative approaches to working with people who have experienced trauma;
3. Tailor salient integrative approaches to the therapeutic needs of clients affected by trauma, crisis, and disaster; and,
4. Describe counseling implications of integrative approaches to trauma, crisis, and disaster interventions.

INTRODUCTION

Before exploring the benefits of integrative approaches to treating individuals with trauma, a brief discussion to distinguish trauma, crises, and disasters can assist clinicians in planning treatment according to the needs of their clients. The term "trauma" refers to any experience that overwhelms a person's ability to cope *and* often is combined with a sense of helplessness, fear,

---

This chapter is dedicated to the memory of J. Barry Mascari, who contracted COVID-19 very early in the first wave of the pandemic in Spring of 2020. He was a devoted and profoundly gifted educator, counselor, author, mentor, and advocate in the field of professional counseling. He brought joy and compassion to every encounter, especially those involving his counseling-and-cappuccino sessions, and we will miss him for the rest of our lives.

and horror at what has happened (although helplessness, fear, and horror were removed from the 5th edition of the *Diagnostic and Statistical Manual* [5th ed.; DSM-5; American Psychiatric Association, 2013] as specific criteria for Acute Stress Disorder [ASAD] and Posttraumatic Stress Disorder [PTSD]). "Trauma," in some ways, is defined by the person experiencing it. For example, the death of a pet dog, while deeply sad and troubling, may not necessarily represent a traumatic experience for everyone. However, if the dog were a service animal for a person living with a disability, and if the dog's death happened in the line of duty, then the dog's death is almost certainly traumatic for its owner. "Trauma," then, is an overarching concept, and refers to any event that is negative, overwhelming, and has significant implications for a person's future. "Crisis" refers to an event that has the *potential* to turn into a trauma if a solution cannot be found or amelioration cannot be achieved. A crisis represents an event that overwhelms a person's immediate ability to cope and represents a threat to a person's ability to cope long term. By contrast, a trauma profoundly overwhelms a person's ability to cope, and over a longer time frame. Finally, "disaster" refers to a shared trauma that involves multiple people (usually many people) at the same time. Disasters can be natural, such as weather events, or human caused, such as large-scale accidents, crime, genocide, and terrorism, which overwhelm basic survival or safety needs and carry significant threat to human life (Webber & Mascari, 2018). Disasters, by definition, exemplify trauma and affect many people simultaneously. Crises can affect multiple people or an individual, and crises have the potential to become traumas, if solutions cannot be found quickly. Regardless of whether a situation constitutes a crisis, disaster, or trauma, integrative approaches to treatment represent the best practice of relevant mental healthcare. The recovery and therapeutic models for crises, disasters, or traumas have substantial overlap and, regardless of the type of precipitating event, foster improvement in mental health functioning.

Many contributors to the corpus of mental health theory, research, and practice literature regarding the effects of traumatic events, including crisis and disaster, have indicated that the best clinical models employ integrative therapies when counseling survivors of trauma (e.g., Bradshaw et al., 2011; Briere, 1997, 2002; Briere & Lanktree, 2013; Briere & Scott, 2014; Finkelstein et al., 2004; Foa et al., 2009; Killeen et al., 2015; Lanktree & Briere, 2017; Levers, 2012, 2020; Levers et al., 2012; Mahoney & Markel, 2016; Mattar & Frewen, 2020; van der Kolk, 2014; van der Kolk et al., 1996). Public health policy has focused on integrative healthcare for at least a decade (American Psychiatric Association [APA] & Academy of Psychosomatic Medicine [APM], 2016). It has incorporated behavioral health practices into medical services, including complementary and alternative medical practices (CAM; e.g., acupuncture, Tai Chi, yoga, medicinal herbs, mindfulness techniques, and so on). Integrated healthcare, in general, improves the healthcare experiences of individuals and their families by integrating mental healthcare with physical healthcare (Heath et al., 2013). An important national report (President's New Freedom Commission on Mental Health, 2003) has highlighted the need for increased coordination among primary care physicians, mental health clinicians, and other stakeholders, such as schools and community organizations, in order to improve treatment outcomes for those experiencing mental health issues (Levers & Hyatt-Burkhart, 2020). The framework for integrative healthcare offers important lessons for conceptualizing an integrative therapies approach to trauma, with significant implications for the treatment of PTSD.

Both the American Psychological Association (APA; 2017) and the U.S. Department of Veterans Affairs/U.S. Department of Defense (VA/DoD; 2017) published treatment guidelines for PTSD in 2017. The APA publication reported:

Following its detailed review and independent analysis of the findings of the systematic review, the APA Guideline Development Panel (GDP) strongly recommends the use of the following psychotherapies/interventions (all interventions that follow listed in alphabetical order) for adult patients with PTSD: cognitive behavioral therapy (CBT), cognitive processing therapy (CPT), cognitive therapy (CT), and prolonged exposure therapy (PE). The panel suggests the use of brief eclectic psychotherapy (BEP), Eye

Movement Desensitization and Reprocessing (EMDR), and narrative exposure therapy (NET). There is insufficient evidence to recommend for or against offering Seeking Safety (SS) or relaxation (RLX). For medications, the panel suggests offering the following (in alphabetical order): fluoxetine, paroxetine, sertraline, and venlafaxine. There is insufficient evidence to recommend for or against offering risperidone and topiramate. (APA, 2017, p. E-2)

The VA/DoD guidelines defined psychotherapy as "therapy that uses cognitive, emotional, or behavioral techniques to facilitate processing a traumatic experience and in which the trauma focus is a central component of the therapeutic process" (VA/DoD, 2017, p. 46). The VA/DoD guidelines advised the following:

The trauma-focused psychotherapies with the strongest evidence from clinical trials are Prolonged Exposure (PE), CPT, and Eye Movement Desensitization and Reprocessing (EMDR). These treatments have been tested in numerous clinical trials, in patients with complex presentations and comorbidities, compared to active control conditions, have long-term follow-up, and have been validated by research teams other than the developers. Other manualized protocols that have sufficient evidence to recommend use are: specific cognitive behavioral therapies for PTSD, Brief Eclectic Psychotherapy (BEP), Narrative Exposure Therapy (NET), and written narrative exposure. . . . There are other psychotherapies that meet the definition of trauma-focused treatment for which there is currently insufficient evidence to recommend for or against their use. (VA/DoD, 2017, pp. 46–47)

In a review of evidence-based psychotherapy interventions, Watkins et al. (2018) have emphasized that both of the previously cited guidelines overlap in their strong recommendations of the following psychological treatments: PE, CPT, and trauma-focused cognitive behavioral therapy (TF-CBT). It is essential for mental health professionals to use evidence-based practices. But because the experience of trauma is a complex phenomenon, and because the treatment of PTSD often requires multilayered and sometimes nuanced clinical responses, it is important to understand trauma counseling, crisis interventions, and disaster interventions within larger integrative healthcare frameworks. By understanding trauma-related service delivery in terms of a larger and scaffolded model, students and clinicians can more readily choose and combine therapies that make the most sense for individual client needs. This chapter outlines, briefly, key integrative approaches and highlights salient implications for counselors; these discussions are followed by a chapter summary and an online list of practical resources.

CLINICAL INTERVENTIONS AND INTEGRATIVE APPROACHES

While psychotherapists have been helping survivors of trauma to deal with the impacts of traumatic experiences for over a century, the emergence of the field of traumatology and the emphasis on treatment efficacy have developed more recently. Regarding trauma treatment, Briere and Scott (2014) have suggested the need for attachment-relational processes, combined with cognitive behavioral activities. They note the following:

The need for both relational and cognitive-behavioral interventions in the treatment of chronic and/or complex posttraumatic disturbance is not particularly surprising, especially when real-world clinical practice is examined. Probably all good trauma therapy is cognitive-behavioral, to the extent that it involves exploration of traumatic material (exposure) in a safe relationship (disparity) wherein the client is encouraged to feel and think about what happened to him or her (emotional and cognitive activation and processing). On the other hand, most effective therapy for complex trauma effects is also relational and "psychodynamic," involving the effects of activated attachment relationships and interpersonal processes. (Briere & Scott, 2014, p. 332)

Once considered anecdotal, or at the periphery of therapy otherwise focused on seemingly more salient presenting problems, the consideration of *trauma* is now recognized as a critical element in the therapeutic process. Trauma treatment should be contextualized and linked with specific targeted strategies within the mental healthcare system (Ko et al., 2008; Levers, 2020; Maercker & Hecker, 2016; Substance Abuse and Mental Health Services Administration [SAMHSA], 2014b; Sweeney et al., 2018). Although the notion of *trauma-sensitive* mental healthcare for clients with trauma histories has been a progressive step in providing adequate care, attention also must be paid to the overall systems in which clients are served.

Integrated approaches provide a more systemic structure for, and understanding of, matters pertaining to trauma, ensuring a greater likelihood that clients do not re-experience trauma and that they return for needed services. An important transformation has begun over the last several decades. We now see that service systems must be attuned to clients' traumatic experiences and that systems and clinicians need to shift from the institutional or medical model of care, which asks "What is wrong with you?" to a more relational model of care, which is grounded in the question "What has happened to you?" (Foderaro, cited in Bloom, 1994, p. 476). In this section, we offer discussions regarding Trauma-Informed and Trauma-Specific Care, Cognitive-Behavioral Therapy and Other Conjunctive Therapies, Eye Movement Desensitization and Reprocessing, Somatic Therapies, Observed and Experiential Integration, and Other Integrative Modalities.

Trauma-Informed and Trauma-Specific Care

Trauma-informed care represents a means to address trauma throughout a system of care (SAMHSA, 2014b). Hodas (2006, p. 32) states that "trauma informed care must begin with the provision of safety, both physical and emotional." Without the ability to feel safe in treatment, clients are unable to choose to change the way they make decisions, to consider new ideas, or to accept assistance from therapists and staff at treatment centers. Initially borne out of providing better care for children in service delivery systems, the principles of trauma-informed care apply and are used across treatment settings (SAMHSA, 2014b). As we learn more about traumatic events across the life-span, along with the lifelong effects of some trauma, it is increasingly evident that all care systems share the need and the responsibility for identifying and responding to trauma. MentalHealth.org (2015, "Known Trauma-Specific Interventions," p. 2) has identified the following trauma-specific interventions used extensively in public mental health system settings:

- Addiction and trauma recovery integration model (ATRIUM)
- Essence of being real
- Risking connection
- Sanctuary model
- Seeking safety
- Trauma, addictions, mental health, and recovery (TAMAR) model
- Trauma affect regulation: guide for education and therapy (TARGET)
- Trauma recovery and empowerment model (TREM and M-TREM)

The authors of this chapter do not intend to endorse any specific model of treatment; however, it is beneficial to explore particular models having many of the attributes of a trauma-informed system of care, as previously described. Therefore, although it is beyond the scope of this chapter to present detailed information about all forms of trauma-informed care, in this subsection, we offer a general description of trauma-informed care and a brief discussion of one example of trauma-informed care, the Sanctuary Model.

Trauma-Informed Care

As our understanding of the prevalence and significance of trauma has grown, the literature reflects, in more salient ways, the need to address the traumatized person in a more holistic fashion. Trauma-specific and trauma-informed practices are discussed frequently in the literature but are not always clearly delineated. For the purpose of this chapter, these terms are defined in the following ways: (a) trauma-specific therapy refers to the actual interventions, therapies, or treatment program designed to address traumatic events and concerns that have resulted from them; (b) trauma-informed models assess and structure all aspects of a treatment system to address how trauma may affect a client's interaction with a particular part of the system (Jennings, 2004; SAMHSA, 2014b).

Trauma-informed models of care are systemic by design. These approaches regard trauma as the primary precipitator leading many clients to seek counseling, and thus have focused on the traumatic experiences of clients. Jennings (2004) has offered the following systemic perspective:

The new system will be characterized by safety from physical harm and re-traumatization; an understanding of clients and their symptoms in the context of their life experiences and history, cultures, and their society; open and genuine collaboration between provider and consumer at all phases of the service delivery; an emphasis on skill building and acquisition rather than symptom management; an understanding of symptoms as attempts to cope; a view of trauma as a defining and organizing experience. (p. 15)

We can think of trauma-informed approaches as reflecting conformity to key principles rather than to a prescribed set of practices or procedures. Such principles apply across settings, even though the associated terminology and application may be specific to a particular setting. Similar to Jennings' (2004) perspective, cited previously, SAMHSA (2014b) has identified the key principles of a trauma-informed approach; these appear in Box 27.1.

BOX 27.1

From the Field: Key Principles of a Trauma-Informed Approach

A trauma-informed approach reflects adherence to six key principles rather than a prescribed set of practices or procedures. These principles may be generalizable across multiple types of settings, although terminology and application may be setting- or sector-specific.

- Safety
- Trustworthiness and transparency
- Peer support
- Collaboration and mutuality
- Empowerment, voice, and choice
- Cultural, historical, and gender issues (SAMHSA, 2014b, p. 10)

Creating a trauma-informed system of care requires each aspect of the system to be scrutinized and changed, so that it meets the needs of traumatized consumers (Levers, 2020; SAMHSA, 2014b). Appropriate training is an essential function in a trauma-informed service system. Providing adequate information about the pervasiveness of the psychological and neurobiological effects of trauma to program staff is essential if employees are expected to conceptualize the range of possible responses by their clients to activating stimuli. This training is equally important for all employees. Let us consider a receptionist who has no clinical training but interacts with clients as they enter the office and wait for appointments or visits. If a client becomes agitated at what appears to be nothing or reacts to something that seems inconsequential, a receptionist typically may become angry or upset because of what may appear to be a tantrum or other inappropriate behavior. Let us reconsider this same receptionist's ability to understand the client's reaction after receiving adequate instruction about the effects of trauma and how to respond within a trauma-informed system of care.

Organizational processes need to be adapted to reflect a more trauma-informed model of care (Levers, 2020; SAMHSA, 2014b). Policies and procedures must state that the organization follows trauma-informed practices. Hiring and selection practices should be based not only on education and on previous work experience, but they also need to include a candidate's knowledge and understanding of concepts and practices designed to support client wellness from a trauma-informed framework. Admission criteria, screening, and assessment directly need to reflect and address a client's history of trauma. This constitutes a significant paradigm shift, which places *trauma* as the central issue in a client's recovery, as opposed to antiquated models in which trauma is viewed as a secondary concern in treatment (Hodas, 2006; SAMHSA, 2014a; Sweeney et al., 2018). The need cannot be emphasized enough for trauma-specific treatments to be delivered by trained clinicians; this is a critical factor in supporting the recovery of the clients.

The Sanctuary Model

The Sanctuary Model (Bloom, 2005) was developed in an inpatient hospital setting providing acute care to adult survivors of childhood trauma. Although it is understood that clients who are traumatized often may respond to stimuli or triggers that are based on their traumatic histories, the Sanctuary Model also applies these concepts of trauma to organizations and institutions designed to work with traumatized populations as well as employees. The Sanctuary Model explores the parallel processes that may emerge among traumatized clients, staff, and organizations in an effort to manage the traumatic symptoms across all levels by creating a shared, more democratic community (Bloom, 2005). Bloom has identified the following seven main characteristics of a Sanctuary Model program:

- **Culture of Nonviolence:** Helping to build safety skills and a commitment to higher goals
- **Culture of Emotional Intelligence:** Helping to teach affect management skills
- **Culture of Inquiry and Social Learning:** Helping to build cognitive skills
- **Culture of Shared Governance:** Helping to create civic skills of self-control, self-discipline, and administration of healthy authority
- **Culture of Open Communication:** Helping to overcome barriers to healthy communication, reduce acting-out, enhance self-protective and self-correcting skills, and teach healthy boundaries
- **Culture of Social Responsibility:** Helping to rebuild social connection skills and establish healthy attachment relationships
- **Culture of Growth and Change:** Helping to restore hope, meaning, and purpose (Bloom, 2005, p. 71)

Programs like the Sanctuary Model allow organizations and staff to establish new norms. These new norms promote mutual respect and responsibility for all levels of the organizational structure, expectations for the manner in which consumers are treated, alternate strategies for managing negative and disruptive behaviors, and a structure for managing program violations. Creating a new norm of tolerance and understanding minimizes the possibility of an occurrence in which negative dynamics activate events that consequently result in traumatic responses. With such a norm, the focus shifts to treatment interventions as opposed to behavior management.

Cognitive Behavioral Therapy and Other Conjunctive Therapies

CBT long has been the treatment of choice for depression and anxiety-related symptoms (APA, 2017; Bryant et al., 1998; Dobson, 1989; Follette & Ruzek, 2006; Taylor, 2004; VA/DoD, 2017; Watkins et al., 2018). In relationship to trauma, the overarching goal of CBT is to help clients understand how certain thoughts, related to the traumatic event or trauma history, can cause associated stress and exacerbate trauma-related symptoms. Through CBT, clients can learn to identify negative thoughts about the world and about themselves that often make them feel at risk or even feel retraumatized. Through therapy, clients learn ways to replace such automatic negative thoughts with more accurate and less distressing thoughts.

A CBT approach can be used to reduce negative emotional and behavioral responses following traumatic events. The treatment is based, fundamentally, on learning and cognitive theories that address distorted beliefs and attributions related to the traumatic events experienced by an individual. Such treatment provides a supportive environment in which clients are encouraged to talk about their traumatic experiences. CBT also helps the individuals within a survivor's support system—those who have not been affected directly by the trauma—to cope effectively with their own emotional distress and to develop skills for supporting their loved ones.

One difficult task for clients who have been traumatized is to process the residual emotions after a traumatic event. Through CBT, the therapeutic relationship helps clients better manage their emotions. Through homework, clients learn to practice and apply skills from therapy in real life; these new skills can assist clients in dealing with feelings like anger, fear, sadness, frustration, and guilt.

Meta-analyses of the literature support the efficacy of CBT in combination with other therapeutic approaches, for example, exposure therapy (e.g., Institute of Medicine & Committee on Treatment of Posttraumatic Stress Disorder, 2008), EMDR (Seidler & Wagner, 2006), or dialectical behavior therapy (DBT). With its flexibility in and adaptability to other conditions, CBT is an integrative approach, which is used widely by many clinicians, and clearly is considered a best practice for aiding in the recovery process of traumatized clients (APA, 2017; Mahoney & Markel, 2016; VA/DoD, 2017). According to the National Center for Posttraumatic Stress Disorder (NCPTSD), CBT is the treatment of choice that is used for PTSD, and it is used almost exclusively for veterans through the Veterans Affairs healthcare systems (VA & DoD, 2010; VA/DoD, 2017); treating military veterans with PTSD is discussed in detail in Chapter 25, "The Impact of War on Military Veterans."

As an integrative approach, CBT includes several specific approaches for helping clients to deal with the aftermath of traumatic events. Although specific CBT-based strategies and techniques are identified and discussed in greater detail in Chapter 28, the following parts of this section offer brief overviews of several approaches commonly used in conjunction with CBT or as part of an overall integrative approach: exposure therapy, EMDR, and DBT.

Exposure Therapy

Exposure therapy aims to reduce or eliminate the fears that clients have associated with the traumatic event or have paired with their traumatic memories. Grohol (2016) provides the following characterization of exposure therapy:

> In PTSD, exposure therapy is intended to help the patient face and gain control of the fear and distress that was overwhelming in the trauma, and must be done very carefully in order not to re-traumatize the patient. In some cases, trauma memories or reminders can be confronted all at once ("flooding"), while for other individuals or traumas it is preferable to work gradually up to the most severe trauma by using relaxation techniques and either starting with less upsetting life stressors or by taking the trauma one piece at a time ("desensitization"). . . . A therapist works with the client to determine which method is best suited for the particular client and their trauma. (pp. 2–3)

The purpose of exposure therapy is to empower clients by using techniques to gain control of thoughts and feelings related to the trauma. By repeatedly talking about the event, therapeutic interventions allow clients to regain control over their emotions and eventually to abandon the feelings of helplessness that often accompany the aftermath of traumatic events. A frequent part of exposure therapy is "desensitization." According to Grohol (2016), this therapeutic technique allows clients to process less troubling memories before moving on to more severe or detailed aspects of the event. Conversely, exposure therapy also employs another technique that does not require gradual acquisition of control over one's emotions. Rather, therapists may employ the technique referred to as "flooding," whereby clients are asked to recall several memories at once, so that the learned response over time is not to feel overwhelmed. Although both techniques are helpful in the recovery process, training and supervision are required in order to practice either technique effectively. If done without training and adequate supervision, clinicians unwittingly and unintentionally may compromise the client's sense of safety, thereby placing the client at risk for being retraumatized.

Dialectical Behavior Therapy

With the integration of DBT as a treatment option for trauma survivors, clinicians are able to use a multifaceted approach toward empowering individuals via the client's own skill-building efforts and engagement in the therapeutic relationship. This integrative approach is ideal for managing the complexities of trauma; the literature supports the promotion of DBT as a best-practice approach for trauma recovery and as an essential tool for counselors working within the field of trauma.

DBT includes components of CBT; however, the emphasis in DBT is on the acceptance and validation of behaviors, as they exist in the "here and now." The foundational aspects of DBT lie in the integration of Eastern *mindfulness* practices, CBT, and Rogerian constructs (acceptance and validation, as they exist, in the moment). Therefore, for trauma survivors, behaviors are addressed as they exist in the present, and very little is relived or reexperienced as part of the past. For example, individuals who have suffered childhood abuse (sexual, physical, or emotional) often use maladaptive means to cope as adults. This can lead to self-injurious behaviors such as cutting, substance abuse, eating disorders, impulsivity, and other para-suicidal behaviors. Although many may view these behaviors as a defense mechanism or as a means for coping with traumatic revivification, others may view these behaviors as indicative of Axis II conditions, like borderline personality disorder (BPD). The implications for misdiagnosing a trauma-related response as something like BPD can be detrimental to a client and actually can lead to mistreatment.

The overarching goal of DBT is to increase skills for emotional regulation in clients who have suffered traumatic experiences. The skills taught through DBT target the maladaptive behaviors that are used to relieve the pain temporarily and that are caused by traumatic triggers in the environment. Four skill sets are taught in DBT: mindfulness, emotion regulation, distress tolerance, and interpersonal effectiveness (Linehan, 1993). Through these skill sets, clients can feel empowered to take control over their lives once again and to manage their emotions in more self-affirming ways. The techniques and advantages of this integrative approach are discussed in more depth in Chapter 28.

Eye Movement Desensitization and Reprocessing

Developed by Shapiro (1990) and Shapiro and Forrest (1997), EMDR is a method of psychotherapy that has been used widely in treating PTSD. Although EMDR has a cognition-focused dimension, it also focuses on bodily sensations and eye movement (Shapiro, 1990; Spates et al., 2009). Having some similarities to the other interventions discussed in the CBT part of this section, EMDR helps to reshape how a client views a traumatic event. In short, the dynamics surrounding EMDR involve thinking of or talking about memories, while concurrently focusing on other stimuli like eye movements, hand taps, or sounds. EMDR therapists guide the client in vividly, but safely, recalling distressing past experiences (desensitization) and gaining new understandings (reprocessing) of the events, the bodily and emotional feelings, and the thoughts and self-images associated with them (Shapiro & Forrest, 1997, 2001).

The "eye movement" aspect of EMDR involves the client moving their eyes in a back-and-forth (saccadic) manner while recalling the event(s). Building on Shapiro's (2001) earlier landmark work, many researchers have continued to explore the mechanisms and efficacy of EMDR (e.g., Beer, 2018; Charney et al., 2018; Forman-Hoffman et al., 2018). Initial observations by Shapiro and Forrest (1997) have revealed a reduction in PTSD symptoms by clients who have undergone the treatment; recent research supports Shapiro's earlier investigations, and a meta-analysis of the relevant literature has indicated that EMDR and CBT are equally efficacious (Seidler & Wagner, 2006). EMDR works with children and adults alike, who have suffered from various traumatic experiences (the use of EMDR is further discussed in Chapters 9 and 28.)

Somatic Therapies

Many types of somatic therapies address anxiety and mitigate the effects of trauma, and they are far too numerous to detail here. However, somatic therapy represents an important integrative approach to working with clients who have experienced trauma. Recent neurobiology discoveries have informed our understanding of trauma's impact on the body, as well as specifically on the brain, thus transforming trauma treatment to include not only top-down (cognitive) approaches but also bottom-up (somatic or body) approaches. Traditional talk therapy may lead to retraumatizing the client without carefully observing and monitoring the body's reactions. Talk therapy, by itself, does not resolve trauma; trauma survivors need a safe therapeutic relationship, along with emotional regulation skills, in order to tell the trauma story and to process it toward resolution. The bases for somatic therapies include "body awareness, body memory, and body resources as valuable adjuncts to trauma treatment" (Rothschild, 2017, p. xx).

Babette Rothschild placed the foundation for trauma treatment squarely on the body, as in her 2000 book *The Body Remembers* and the Volume 2 book of the same name (2017). Bessel van der Kolk (2014) reminds us that *The Body Keeps the Score*, insofar as trauma causes both emotion and somatic dysregulation; Levine (1997), in *Waking the Tiger*, cautions us that this is a challenging task. The scaffolding for somatic therapies is the body: scanning one's body and noticing feelings, pain, and movement, without judgment, and in the present moment rather than in the past.

Somatic therapies bypass retraumatization and facilitate the healthy resolution of trauma with or without retelling the trauma story. We now know that not all trauma survivors want or need to process their trauma story as a requirement for trauma resolution. Without the inclusion of body awareness, which involves noticing and observing bodily sensation along with learning emotion regulation skills, traditional talk therapy can lead inadvertently to retraumatization, even by the most well intended therapist, thus making clients worse. van der Kolk (2014) emphasizes that trauma counselors do not need to know the details of a client's trauma story; rather, they need to focus on the effects of the traumatic event.

Rothschild (2010, p. xi) reminds us that "the goal of trauma healing must be to relieve, not intensify, suffering." Trauma survivors need to be able to "brake," before accelerating and becoming overwhelmed, thus moving outside of the body's window of tolerance. Rothschild (2000) cautions therapists that "The purpose of hitting the brakes and dropping the level of arousal is not just to give a pause and a sense of safety. It also . . . enables the therapy to proceed at a reduced level of arousal (p. 115). Counselors using somatic therapies recognize that talk therapy does not work when the prefrontal cortex goes "off-line," due to stress, thereby having the potential to retraumatize survivors (Arnstena et al., 2015). Baranowsky and Gentry (2015) point out that "The treatment of traumatic stress, for many survivors, was as bad or worse than the symptoms they experienced. . . . It is no wonder many survivors during this period chose to keep their symptoms instead of enduring the rigors of this difficult treatment" (p. 152). In the remaining parts of this subsection, we discuss a few of the many somatic approaches.

Somatic Experiencing

Levine's (1997) best seller, *Waking the Tiger*, made somatic experiencing (SE) approaches accessible to the public, even enclosing a CD for readers to practice new skills. His trauma approach has been grounded in naturalistic observations of animals in the wild. He observed that when animals are hunted as prey but escape harm, they return to a normal state after the physical threat, and they rarely become traumatized. Thus, Levine's approach normalized trauma symptoms as a natural part of life and showed how trauma symptoms that result from dysregulation can be relieved by self-regulating changes in the autonomic nervous system. Levine observed the human body, twitching and trembling during the process of dissipating tension and excess energy, and called this process "pendulation," which encompasses movement between charging and discharging energy. This shifting, from positive orienting responses to defensive responses, has paralleled what Porges (2009a) terms as a shift from dorsal (the fight/flight response of the sympathetic nervous system) to ventral vagal responses, that is, social engagement and connected states. Levine's bottom up SIBAM model has incorporated five channels: sensation, image, behavior, affect, and meaning (or cognition), thus addressing trauma memories indirectly. By attending and listening to bodily sensations and somatic experiences, clients are able to track their felt experiences and heal.

Sensorimotor Psychotherapy

In the 1980s, Ogden (2017) developed sensorimotor psychotherapy and integrated talk therapy and top-down interventions with (bottom-up) somatic approaches. She observed and stabilized the critical space in the window of tolerance between hyper- and hypoarousal, in which clients could talk through microtracking, and she could read bodily movements that might be unfinished fragments of trauma movements. Ogden and the client monitored these "micromovements" to help the client stay in the current sensations, recognizing the need to "drop the emotion" or "drop the content." Through interventions using stillness, movement, and collapse, the client and therapist integrate the trauma into present and future life (Ogden, 2017; Ogden et al., 2006).

Forward Facing Therapy

As therapists continued to question the axiom that survivors must tell the trauma story to integrate the words and feelings of the trauma event and achieve resolution, Gentry applied this new knowledge to the approach that he termed "forward facing therapy." Gentry (2018) stated that "We do not need to excavate the past to eliminate triggers and forever free ourselves from the insidious effects of stress. . . . Instead, we can simply learn to *recognize* when we've been triggered and then *respond* by relaxing our bodies" (pp. 89–90). Gentry has focused on helping survivors learn skills to relax the body and live in the present.

Somatic Transformation

Informed by the interpersonal neurobiology of Porges (2009a, 2009b, 2011) and Schore (1994, 2009), somatic transformation is grounded in relational therapy and body-focused sensorimotor processing and is focused on the healing that transpires within the therapeutic relationship. Somatic transformation is grounded in six processes of natural human healing and feeling with the other person: embodiment, somatic awareness, somatic empathy, somatic inquiry, somatic interventions, and somatic reflection (Stanley, 2016). By employing these processes, therapists are able to assist clients in transforming the intense emotional experiences of the traumatic event. Somatic transformation involves holistic and profound change.

Observed and Experiential Integration

A newly articulated integrative model, originated by Audrey Cook (Bradshaw et al., 2011; Bradshaw et al., 2014), has emerged from Canada. The observed and experiential integration

(OEI) model incorporates present-focused experiential therapies with neurobiological, cognitive, affective, recall, enactment, and educational kinesiology therapies, among others. The model has some parallels with EMDR but differs in technical and procedural ways. A major aim of OEI is to bring the clients' traumatic issues to the surface, while restoring their ability to function and assisting them to regain a sense of control. The OEI model has been based on extensive research (Bradshaw et al., 2011; Bradshaw et al., 2014) and tens of thousands of hours of clinical observation. In addition to its success in treating PTSD, OEI also has been used successfully in resolving other anxiety-based disorders and addictions. Although the details of the model are far too technical to unpack in this chapter, it seems that OEI may be promising as an effective practice in resolving the sequelae of traumatic experiences.

Other Integrative Modalities

Additional integrative approaches exist but are too numerous for exhaustive inclusion here. Some of the related techniques and strategies—for example, brainspotting, the Comprehensive Resource Model (CRM), and narrative trauma therapy—are described in Chapter 28. However, several other integrative modalities deserve brief mention in the following subsections: Crisis- and Disaster-Focused Models, Substance Abuse-Focused Models, Herman's Recovery-Focused Model, and Briere's Self-Trauma Model. Short descriptions are offered in the following text.

Crisis- and Disaster-Focused Models

Yeager and Roberts (2003) have asserted the importance of clinicians being able to differentiate among the important constructs of stress, ASD, crisis episodes, trauma, and PTSD (the intersections of these constructs have been discussed in Chapters 2, 3, and 19). Several models of crisis and disaster intervention offer an integrative approach. For example, critical incident stress management (CISM is discussed in Chapter 22) is a comprehensive, integrative, multicomponent crisis intervention system (Mitchell & Everly, 1996). Roberts' (2002) assessment, crisis intervention, and trauma treatment (ACT) model, detailed in Chapter 3, offers an integrative intervention approach aimed at brief treatment and crisis intervention.

Substance Abuse-Focused Models

The relationship between interpersonal violence and substance abuse, especially as this affects women, has been well documented over the last several decades (e.g., Campbell, 2002; Felitti, 2002; Levers & Hawes, 1989; Liebschutz et al., 2002; Stuart et al., 2003). According to Finkelstein et al. (2004), "The prevalence of physical and sexual abuse among women in substance abuse treatment programs is estimated to range from 30% to more than 90%, depending on the definition of abuse and the specific target population" (p. 1). Extrapolating from the Substance Abuse and Mental Health Services Administration's (SAMHSA) Women With Co-occurring Disorders and Violence Study (WCDVS; Moses et al., 2004), which used four trauma-specific integrative models for substance abuse clients who also had trauma histories or exhibited PTSD symptoms, Finkelstein et al. (2004) reported on these four models and one additional model. The models are described briefly in the text that follows

1. The ATRIUM (Miller & Guidry, 2001) offers a 12-week bioecological curriculum, addressing the impact of trauma across physical, mental, and spiritual dimensions.
2. The Helping Women Recover (HWR; Covington, 2000) program provides a 17-session curriculum that addresses issues of self, relationships, sexuality, and spirituality.
3. Seeking safety (Najavits, 2002) is a present-focused model to facilitate safety and recovery and has been used in a wide variety of settings.
4. The Trauma Recovery and Empowerment Model (TREM; Harris et al., 1998) consists of multiple group interventions with traumatized women experiencing substance abuse or other

mental health problems and focuses on empowerment, trauma issues, and skill building. In addition to being integrative approaches, commonalities across these models include a focus on safety, the use of trauma-sensitive services, and an orientation toward trauma-informed care.

5. The Triad women's trauma model engages a four-phase, CBT-oriented group format. The Triad perspective is that complex disorders can arise from unaddressed trauma, and the primary treatment goal is to reduce trauma-related symptoms.

Herman's Recovery-Focused Model

Recovery-focused models of mental health therapy emphasize the client's potential for recovery or healing. Herman (1992/1997) has articulated an integrative recovery process, by which survivors of trauma heal from the negative consequences of their experiences. Herman's recovery model addresses what she has identified as the core experiences of trauma (Herman's theory is discussed more fully in Chapter 2) and employs the following three stages: establishing safety, reconstructing the trauma story, and reconnecting with ordinary life. Various compatible therapeutic approaches are incorporated to accomplish the recovery or healing process. The three stages that were identified by Herman (1992/1997) have proven to be compatible with strength-based, systemic, and resilience-producing approaches to resolving trauma (Levers, 2020; McEwen et al., 2015). They were prescient in their compatibility with emerging practices associated with Polyvagal Theory (Porges, 2009b, 2011).

Briere's Self-Trauma Model

Briere (1996, 1997, 2002) has developed an integrative model of treatment, the self-trauma model, which is based on trauma theory, CBT, and self-psychology. This model relies upon and employs a combination of psychoeducation, stress reduction, affect regulation training, cognitive interventions, emotional processing, improving identity problems, and facilitating relational functioning (Briere & Scott, 2014). The self-trauma model has been used with adults and is especially effective with adult clients who have experienced childhood trauma (the issue of adult survivors is discussed in Chapter 10, "Intimate Partner Violence"). The self-trauma model is also effective with children (Lanktree & Briere, 2017) and adolescents (Briere & Lanktree, 2013).

COUNSELING IMPLICATIONS

The major implication drawn from this discussion regards the contemporary clinical view that integrative approaches to trauma treatment represent the gold standard of care. As clinicians continue to work with trauma survivors, better understand the phenomenology of trauma, and become acutely more aware of issues of complex trauma, the need for multimodal and integrative therapies is more obvious. The very nature of traumatic events and their core experiences affect victims on multiple personal and systemic levels. The process of recovering and healing from trauma necessitates therapeutic interventions that are capable of addressing the victim's responses, simultaneously, on physical, cognitive, affective, and spiritual or existential levels. By considering the array of integrative approaches to trauma therapy and learning to use them effectively, we are better positioned to help the survivors of trauma who seek counseling from us.

CONCLUSION

This chapter has articulated the clinical relevance of integrative approaches to trauma. We have discussed several integrative interventions, including trauma-informed care, trauma-sensitive services, CBT, exposure therapy, EMDR, DBT, OEI, and somatic therapies. Additionally, we have examined several other integrative models, including crisis- and disaster-focused models, substance abuse-focused models, Herman's recovery-focused model, and Briere's self-trauma model. The major implication of this chapter is the agreement across clinical fields that integrative interventions constitute a best-practice approach to counseling survivors of trauma and those who have experienced crisis and disaster situations.

ADDITIONAL RESOURCES

 A robust set of instructor resources designed to supplement this text is located at http://connect.springerpub.com/content/book/978-0-8261-5085-1. Qualifying instructors may request access by emailing textbook@springerpub.com.

PRACTICE-BASED RESOURCES AND REFERENCES

To view a list of resources and all the references, please visit connect.springerpub.com via the following url: http://connect.springerpub.com/content/book/978-0-8261-5085-1/part/part05/chapter/ch27

Selected Strategies and Techniques for Counseling Survivors of Trauma in the Time of COVID-19

JANE M. WEBBER, CAROL M. SMITH, AND J. BARRY MASCARI

CHAPTER OVERVIEW

This chapter describes a range of techniques and strategies to facilitate trauma recovery. Included are examples from emotional, somatic, neurobiological, relational, and cognitive approaches to trauma-informed treatment. The chapter discusses techniques that are based on Herman's (1992/2015) three-phase model of safety/stabilization, working through, and reconnection, as well as integrative techniques based on a holistic approach to trauma recovery. These tools both empower survivors to self-regulate and to avoid retraumatization, with or without processing the trauma story through talk- or narrative therapy. Finally, individualized tools for addressing client and counselor self-care and self-regulation, shared trauma, and traumatic grief are discussed, with a special focus on trauma treatment during the global pandemic of COVID-19.

LEARNING OBJECTIVES

After reading this chapter, the reader should be able to:

1. Understand the types of techniques and strategies that clients and counselors can use in trauma-competent therapy;
2. Select client-appropriate tools and techniques for the phases of trauma treatment that best meet the client's needs including common techniques of self-awareness, mindfulness, breathwork, bodywork, self-regulation, resourcing, and expressive arts;
3. Identify individualized tools that avoid the potential for client retraumatization and facilitate healthy recovery with or without verbally processing the trauma narrative;
4. Integrate somatic and emotion co-regulation tools into cognitive, behavioral, and other conventional talk therapies that address client needs; and,
5. Practice counselor self-care using self-awareness, breathwork, bodywork, mindfulness, self-regulation, and resourcing tools, particularly with pandemic trauma, shared trauma, and pandemic traumatic grief.

This chapter is dedicated to the memory of J. Barry Mascari, who contracted COVID-19 very early in the first wave of the pandemic in Spring of 2020. He was a devoted and profoundly gifted educator, counselor, author, mentor, and advocate in the field of professional counseling. He brought joy and compassion to every encounter, especially those involving his counseling-and-cappuccino sessions, and we will miss him for the rest of our lives.

INTRODUCTION

With rapidly expanding knowledge about the brain and the autonomic nervous system, conventional talk therapies evolved to integrate new tools for safety and stabilization, self-regulation, empowerment, and recovery. Without first preparing clients with stabilizing and self-regulating techniques, trauma therapy unintentionally can retraumatize clients, leaving them feeling worse rather than better. Learning to monitor their own levels of distress and anxiety strengthens and empowers survivors to manage triggers and reactions for a healthier life. While the greatest emphasis in trauma treatment has been on processing the trauma narrative, not all survivors may want or need to go back to the details of the story.

The process of resolving trauma is a unique experience for each survivor that can overwhelm and retraumatize without careful monitoring and without emotion and somatic regulation tools. The choice of treatment and techniques should focus on the client's reactions to the traumatic event rather than retelling the trauma story (Porges, 2017; Rothschild, 2017; van der Kolk, 2014). Advances in neurobiological science have led to a paradigm shift in the course of trauma treatment, from formulaic talk therapy that fits the counselor's goals and approach, to individualized and integrated therapies with bodywork to fit the specific needs and goals of the client (see Chapter 27 ; Briere & Scott, 2012; Rothschild, 2000, 2017).

Once considered cathartic and necessary for trauma resolution, re-experiencing trauma is not necessarily therapeutic for all clients. In fact, telling and reliving the trauma story can be distinctly harmful. Clients should not be told that in order to feel better they must retell the story and that they need to reexperience emotional and physical pain. To reduce symptoms and prevent dissociation, van der Hart and Brown (1992) advocated for shifting the focus from catharsis to helping clients feel safe and remain calm. Safety and trust are the foundations of a strong therapeutic relationship. Likewise, the therapeutic relationship is the foundation of all treatment approaches, especially trauma therapy. Therefore, creating a safe, comforting, and resource-rich environment for survivors is essential for movement toward recovery. Yet traditional talk therapy treatment, causing emotional flooding for many survivors, seems to have followed the principle of no pain–no gain. Baranowsky and Gentry (2015b) emphasize this clinically relevant point in the following way:

> Until the early 1990s, the treatment of traumatic stress, for many survivors, was as bad or worse than the symptoms they experienced. . . . It is no wonder many survivors during this period chose to keep their symptoms instead of enduring the rigors of this difficult treatment. (p. 152)

ESSENTIAL ELEMENTS IN TRAUMA RECOVERY

Neurobiological research shows that the brain self-heals if the circumstances are set properly (Fernyhough, 2013). However, there is no one trauma treatment that works for all clients. Rothschild (2000) emphasized that multiple approaches and techniques are needed. In their landmark study, Hobfoll et al. (2007) identified five essential elements in trauma recovery: (a) a sense of safety, (b) calming, (c) self- and community-unity, (d) social connections, and (e) hope. These elements have influenced trauma treatment approaches and are considered the common factors of trauma recovery. Many current approaches have a prerequisite focus on developing a sense of safety, skills for self-regulation, and maintaining a relaxed and calm state prior to moving on to trauma processing. Similarly, van der Kolk (2014) outlined four steps that focus on calming and connecting: finding a way to calm, maintaining calm despite sensory reminders, being fully present and engaged in the moment with others, and not having secrets to oneself about past methods for survival.

In addition to symptom-specific techniques, trauma and posttraumatic stress disorder (PTSD) experts promote phase-specific treatment (Cloitre et al., 2011; Cloitre et al., 2012; Foa et al., 1999). Phase-specific techniques focus on one or more of the core phases of what frequently is illustrated as a trauma treatment pyramid, which includes the following: (a) safety and stabilization as the base, (b) processing or working through the traumatic event, and then (c) reconnection or reintegration (Herman, 1992/2015). Counselors intentionally emphasize the relational foundation of trauma therapy because it forms the base of the trauma treatment pyramid. The therapeutic relationship consists of a safe and secure environment, reciprocal engagement between the client and the counselor, and co-regulated emotional balance (Baranowsky & Gentry, 2015a, 2015b; Briere & Scott, 2012). Porges (2017) has emphasized the centrality of interpersonal connection and co-regulation in trauma recovery. Baranowsky and Gentry (2015b) have expanded the foundation of the pyramid to underscore the importance of establishing a strong trusting therapeutic relationship, as well as relaxation and self-regulation skills, before constructing and sharing any trauma narrative. Their trauma recovery pyramid consists of four stages: relationship building, psychoeducation and self-regulation, recovery and resolution, and posttraumatic resiliency building. In addition to the four stages, Gentry et al. (2017) have identified four "essential ingredients" or common elements: (a) cognitive restructuring with psychoeducation, (b) therapeutic relationship with the use of feedback-informed treatment, (c) self-regulation and relaxation, and (d) exposure or narrative.

In a survey of 50 trauma clinical experts, Cloitre et al. (2011) found that 84% endorsed phase-based or sequenced therapy as the most appropriate treatment approach. The first-line interventions that they identified included the following: (a) emotion regulation strategies, (b) narration of trauma memories as an exposure process, (c) cognitive restructuring, (d) anxiety and stress management, and (e) interpersonal skills development. The near consensus was that therapy works best in the context of a trusting relationship in which self-regulatory resources have been developed and strengthened before considering whether or how to process the story of a given traumatic event. In the next section—as body, mind, and integrated techniques are described and proposed for consideration—it is critical that counselors do not force the client to fit into the technique, but instead adjust the technique to fit the client.

BREATHWORK AND MINDFULNESS

The recognition that "trauma is in the nervous system not in the event" has refocused trauma interventions to shift from talk-only therapy to brain–body work (Levine & Kline, 2007, p. 4). Trauma treatment techniques have evolved toward integrating breathwork in body awareness, relaxation, and somatic and emotion regulation. Breathing is the single most effective somatic and emotion regulation tool and is an essential component of mindfulness. The most common therapeutic form of breathing as a trauma tool is diaphragmatic breathing, which also is called belly breathing. Counting breaths and lengthening exhalations activates the parasympathetic nervous system and enhances ventral vagal response, which facilitates social relationships and self-regulation (Dana, 2020). According to Schnur (2021), "breathing into the low belly stimulates the parasympathetic nervous system and massages the vagus nerve. It is the quickest way to return to a state of calm" ("Evidence-Based Breathing," para 2).

Breathing is more effective with a longer exhalation (Porges, 2017). This process directly links to the neurobiological impact of trauma. In one type of breathing, "4–7–8 breathing," individuals inhale for a count of 4, hold for a count of 7, and exhale for a count of 8. The exhalation with a count of 8 is twice as long as the inhalation with a count of 4. Trauma counselors integrate breathing, mindfulness, and meditation into Western counseling and trauma practices as a life-enhancing process that can reduce the survivor's level of hyperarousal and the intensity of reactions to triggers. For example, van der Kolk (as cited in Buczynski, 2020) begins a new trauma session with breathing:

One of the first things I do when I see people is I look at whether they are actually able to live within their rib cages. . . . I may spend the first hour with a new patient helping them to just open up their rib cage, and to breathe, because as long as that primitive part of someone's brain is all uptight, it's no use to do psychotherapy with them. (p. 1)

Survivors who feel uncomfortable or pressured with structured breathing techniques can breathe naturally, observe the feeling, and listen to their breath. Through mindful awareness, trauma survivors learn to observe and become more aware of their internal and external experiences without judgment (Kabat Zinn, 2005). Mindfulness increases the individual's ability to focus on the present moment, becoming aware of and accepting distress and triggers without judgment, thus helping to calm the mind and body naturally and reduce trauma symptoms (Pow & Cashwell, 2017; Thompson et al., 2011).

Mindfulness often is integrated with other techniques, such as bilateral movement, meditation, trauma-sensitive yoga, and enhanced breathwork. According to the International Society for Traumatic Stress Studies (ISTSS) Guidelines Committee (2018), mindfulness-based stress reduction (MBSR) helps "individuals experience traumatic-memories without significant distress by facilitating acceptance of them" (p. 27). In mindful meditation, the observing self becomes fully aware of feelings, physical sensations, expressions, and actions without judgment or analysis. This moment-by-moment experience reflects the existential practice of living in the human condition. Clients can practice mindfulness in sessions and use the technique to prevent or reduce distressed feelings and reactions outside the therapy session. Counselors often provide recordings for the client to use at home or at work, and several websites provide free recordings for mindfulness and guided imagery.

As an essential component of meditation, mindfulness intentionally focuses on being and observing oneself in the here and now (Kabat Zinn, 2005). For example, the counselor may guide the client with these guidelines: "As you inhale, say to yourself, 'Breathing in, I know that I am breathing in' or simply 'In.' As you exhale, say to yourself, 'Breathing out, I know that I am breathing out" or simply 'Out'" (Integrative Trauma Treatment, 2011). Each breath process ends with smiling, which relaxes the facial muscles, and thus contributes to relaxing body and mind. This intentional focus on a slowly breathing body in the here and now provides a calming and empowering alternative to fear-based thoughts about past traumas, while maintaining access to the prefrontal cortex in the counseling session. In essence, it lays the groundwork for cognitive restructuring (see Baranowsky & Gentry, 2015a). Counselors should model breathing techniques and teach clients how to observe and be mindful about their breathing. Observing one's own breathing—the physical movement, internal sounds, and rhythm—is a powerful, effective, and free calming technique, in which clients can say silently, "My body is filling with calm. . . . My body is releasing tension" (Brymer et al., 2006, p. 83).

BODY WORK AND SELF-REGULATION

For many years, the body was left out of talk therapy and trauma treatment. Posttraumatic symptoms were explained as adaptive coping responses to abnormal experiences, emphasizing that survivors were using the only resources that they had available to them at the time of the traumatic event. However, before addressing the trauma story, survivors need to develop new coping skills, with the counselor, to respond to stressors with bodily relaxation rather than with the hyperarousal that they used in the past; they need to learn to co-regulate, with the counselor, in sessions. "Somatic experiencing" (Levine, 2010) is a "bottom-up" tool that clients can use to become aware of and learn to manage stress in the body, especially when the thinking brain (top down) is off-line because of the affective overwhelm caused by recalling trauma. Integrating both bottom-up and top-down tools is the optimal strategy for survivors, in order to comprehend what is happening internally and to cope with traumatic distress.

Rothschild (2000) explained, "Emotions, though interpreted and named by the mind, are integrally an experience of the body" (p. 56). Learning body awareness and practicing self-regulation skills precedes using body work, the third phase of Gentry et al.'s (2017) four active ingredients (previously listed, in an earlier section). For example, clients can adopt an effective tactile grounding and anxiety-reducing technique by manipulating Play-Doh, relaxing both body and mind. Placing "hand over heart" or walking while intentionally swinging one's arms also reduces distress. Fisher (2019) combines small body movements into one integrated flowing movement as clients raise their arms to the sky, stretching the spine, then bringing both arms down into a butterfly hold over the heart, linking thumbs and tapping alternate sides of one's chest near the shoulders. Rothschild (2000) focused on safety, pacing, and calming tools and compared them to learning how to use the brakes before pressing the gas pedal. She further illuminated her metaphor in this way:

> The purpose of hitting the brakes and dropping the level of arousal is not just to give a pause and a sense of safety. It also enables the therapy to proceed at a reduced level of arousal. Without hitting the brakes, arousal will just build and build. (p. 113)

Other metaphors that illustrate the dangers of overarousal include a hissing pressure cooker, a pot boiling over, or a freshly shaken bottle of soda. Body awareness, self-monitoring, and calming strategies keep clients within the window of affective tolerance. Once the client moves outside that window of tolerance and becomes retraumatized, counselors need to apply specialized strategies to help them return to safety. Belleruth Naparstek recalls having to change her treatment when she pushed too quickly into the story and witnessed her client being retraumatized. She explained:

> I was consistently retraumatizing because I was doing what I was trained to do which is go for the painful material like a heat-seeking missile. And when you find it, it will come to the surface, and it will be a catharsis and all will be well. . . . I started teaching her self-regulation skills just to get her back to a place where she was before I started helping her. (PESI Inc., 2012, 24:12–25:48)

Bilateral Stimulation

A number of trauma treatment approaches, notably Eye Movement Desensitization and Reprocessing (EMDR) and resource tapping, integrate bilateral stimulation that results from rhythmic left-right movements crossing the midline to relax the body. "Crossing the midline" is essential for stimulation. Imagine a vertical line bisecting one's body from the top of the head to between both feet, separating the body into two equal sides. Using physical motions that cross the midline of the body creates equivalent neural firings that cross the corpus callosum (midline) of the brain. Intentionally *crossing the midline* facilitates interhemispheric coordination of neural firings in the brain, facilitating self-regulation. During EMDR sessions, bilateral movement promotes stimulation when clients use their eyes to follow the left-right, right-left, back-and-forth movements of the therapist's fingers or pointer. Walking also creates bilateral stimulation and can be further enhanced by swinging one arm forward and the other backward rhythmically.

Rather than stimulate the client, tapping each side of the body is a bilateral process that reduces distress and anxiety. The butterfly tap involves alternatively tapping the left shoulder with the right hand and the right shoulder with the left hand. In a sitting position, clients can alternately "lap tap" each thigh with the same side's hand: left thigh with the left hand and right thigh with the right hand. Tapping is best performed first by the counselor, to demonstrate the process, and then by the counselor and client each tapping their own body, as the counselor counts the taps aloud, for example "1 and 2 and 3 and . . . 30 and . . . " Each tapping set begins with a breath and also ends with a breath and a smile to increase calm.

Beyond the counselor's office, clients can calm themselves by: (a) alternately tapping each foot on the floor, (b) alternately squeezing one stress ball in the left hand and then another in the right hand, or (c) tapping the toes of each foot inside their shoes. Individuals breathe slowly, and rhythmically count silently or aloud as they tap. Butterfly hug tapping also provides clients with a sense of physical safety when treatment has accelerated too quickly. Clients cross their arms on their chest in the shape of a butterfly, gently tapping one shoulder with their opposite hand and then tapping the other side.

Using the "stress eraser" technique, individuals symbolically "erase" their distress and smooth out their breaths when breathing irregularly or rapidly (Webber & Mascari, 2012; Webber et al., 2018). With an open palm facing their forehead, the client moves their hand slowly from side to side, parallel to the forehead, nearly gently brushing the skin. Just as the hand-over-heart technique is calming, hand-over-forehead is also calming and grounding.

Likewise, the "windshield wipers" bilateral technique rhythmically slows down and calms the individual. For this movement, the client bends their elbows horizontally so that the tips of their fingers nearly touch, and their palms and arms are in a straight line parallel to and facing their body. The palms become the windshield, and the thumbs are the windshield wipers. The client moves their thumbs up and down as "wipers" wiping the "windshield" (created by the palm and the four other fingers). As the left thumb moves up the left palm "windshield," simultaneously the right thumb moves down the right palm's window, and vice versa. A second variation uses one windshield wiper at a time. First, the left thumb moves up and down the left palm as the windshield and then stops, and then the right thumb moves up and down the right palm windshield and then stops. Then the left, and the right again. As the client visually follows the left thumb and then the right thumb movements, the counselor can maintain a steady, slow pace saying a mantra—like "wipe away (left thumb) my stress (right thumb)" (Webber & Mascari, 2018, p. 30). These resource-tapping tools quickly facilitate calming, smooth out rhythmic breathing, and reduce anxiety (Parnell, 2008).

Body Distress Signals

A Subjective Units of Distress Scale (SUDS) provides a practical tool for clients learning how to monitor their levels of distress and is used widely in cognitive behavioral therapy (CBT) (Baranowsky & Gentry, 2015a, 2015b; Wolpe, 1969). Clients rate their discomfort using the SUD from 1 to 10, with 1 being "calm" and 10 being "highly distressed." During a session, periodic SUD monitoring alerts clients to increasing distress. The scale often is seen as a continuum of facial expressions from calm to most upsetting or as a feelings thermometer with readings from "no distress" to "highly distressed." Higher ratings indicate the need to make a shift quickly to using an anchor and calming techniques, as well as a need to slow the pace or stop processing the story.

Body Scan

Observing and listening to one's body is a mindfulness exercise that begins with noticing and observing the feet and toes, then moving up the body and observing each part. While moving slowly up the body during a personal body scan, the client becomes aware of where distress or pain is held in the body and where the body is calm. The client also can express sensations using words like "My body is calm here" or "My body is tense here." Practicing how to identify where distress is held in the body helps the client and counselor to know when to pause trauma talk and make a shift to calm those parts of the body before continuing.

Body Markers and Signals

In this technique, the counselor says, "On a paper outline of the body, mark the places where your body feels very stressed." When the level of arousal or distress increases too quickly in a session, and clients are unable to express their fear out loud, they can hold up one, two, or three fingers to signal the degree of distress to the counselor. Traffic light color cards (green, yellow, red) also signal the counselor to slow down or stop the storying process. When I (Jane) worked with a soccer player who had survived a serious accident, he felt more comfortable holding up a yellow (caution) card or red (violation) card to indicate his increasing level of distress or rapid movement toward overwhelm. Clients can signal with "thumbs up" (meaning OK) and "thumbs down" (not OK). Shaking the thumb back and forth signals the client is uncertain.

Bodyfulness

Clients not only need to learn how to become aware of any dysregulation in the body, but by observing muscle tension, they also can learn to shift down from sympathetic dominance to release the tension by relaxing muscles, particularly the pelvic muscles (Baranowsky & Gentry, 2015b), "Bodyfulness" conveys the resource that is more than merely noticing bodily distress; it also is learning to maintain a relaxed body throughout the day. As indicated by Baranowsky and Gentry,

> While "mindfulness" challenges the client to disengage from trying to control thoughts and just notice them while attempting to relax, the "bodyfulness" of self-regulation asks her or him to not attend to thoughts at all, but instead maintain an awareness and relaxation of their muscles. (Baranowsky & Gentry, 2015b, p. 165)

Grounding

When trauma clients become distressed or triggered internally by trauma memories, they rapidly can move outside the window of tolerance and dissociate. With intense flooding of memories and overwhelming feelings, clients may lose touch with the physical environment and their connection to the counselor. Immediate psychological first aid is called for when this happens. Grounding assists clients to move back into the present moment and reorient themselves to the counselor and the therapy room (Briere & Scott, 2012). Each element in the grounding sequence focuses on a different sense, such as sight, hearing, touch, smell, or taste. Box 28.1 offers an approach to grounding a distressed client.

BOX 28.1

Protocol for Client Grounding

The counselor checks in with the client about what is happening and how the client is experiencing it. Then the counselor can lead the client through the protocol by offering the following prompts:

- After a frightening experience, you can sometimes find yourself overwhelmed with emotions or unable to stop thinking about or imagining what happened. You can use a method called "grounding" to feel less overwhelmed. Grounding works by turning your attention from your thoughts back to the outside world. Here is what you do
- Sit in a comfortable position with your legs and arms uncrossed.
- Breathe in and out slowly and deeply.
- Look around you and name five nondistressing objects that you can see. For example, you could say, "I see the floor, I see a shoe, I see a table, I see a chair, I see a person."
- Breathe in and out slowly and deeply.
- Next, name five nondistressing sounds that you can hear. For example, "I hear a woman talking, I hear myself breathing, I hear a door close, I hear someone typing, I hear a cell phone ringing."

(continued)

- Breathe in and out slowly and deeply.
- Next, name five nondistressing things that you can feel. For example, "I can feel this wooden armrest with my hands, I can feel my toes inside my shoes, I can feel my back pressing against my chair, I can feel the blanket I am holding, I can feel my lips pressing together."
- Breathe in and out slowly and deeply. (Brymer et al., 2006, pp. 51–52).

The counselor and client also can count backward, 5–4–3–2–1, with the easier items to find, in the beginning of the exercise: "Name five things you see, four sounds you hear, three things you touch or feel with your body, two things you smell, and one thing you taste." Depending on the level of overwhelm, counselors can ask for only one or two items. Children and older adults may be more comfortable identifying items with a specific color. The counselor might ask the client to name "three things you see that are yellow, two things that are brown, one thing that is red." All of these are variations of grounding techniques, and clients can create their own versions of grounding for self-empowerment and self-expression.

Baranowsky and Gentry (2015b) describe a self-empowering grounding technique in which the counselor gives the client an object to feel, examine, and describe its texture. The counselor then gives four more objects to the client to examine. In the next step, the counselor asks the client to repeat the mindful procedure with one object they had heard, felt, and seen, and rate their current level of distress. In another approach to grounding called "earthing," the survivor connects kinesthetically to nature. For example, the person can walk barefooted, gather flowers or leaves, hold a stone, sit with the back touching a tree trunk, or wade in sand or shallow water. As the client moves back within the window of tolerance, walking reconnects the client and counselor through bilateral movement as well as grounding.

"Palm calm" is another bilateral movement and grounding technique for clients who are quickly losing touch with their present surroundings (Webber et al., 2008, 2018, p. 31). When the client feels overwhelmed, the counselor requests permission to try a helping exercise together. With arms stretched out forward and palms facing up, the counselor asks, "May I touch your palms with mine? Place your palms gently on my hands." With the client's palms face down on the counselor's palms that face up, the counselor gently moves the left hand upward and the right hand downward and rhythmically counts 1 and 2 and 3 and. . . . As in all grounding and bilateral techniques, counselor and client begin and end with a breath and a smile.

RESOURCING

Resourcing is an important component of trauma treatment that supports the day-to-day demands, triggers, and challenges that survivors face in order to cope between and beyond sessions. Survivors can use many of the techniques described in this chapter as resources between sessions and on their own path for recovery after counseling ends. According to Dana (2020), resourcing is "an action that moves your clients up the hierarchy toward ventral and, once there, helps them stay there" (p. 108). She reminds us that discovery of a new technique or resource and mastering its use are separate but necessary and connected processes for recovery. Dana also encourages that clients practice techniques on their own:

The therapy session is the time in your clients' week when they predictably experience co-regulation and connection to your ventral vagal state and can safely explore experiences of mobilization and collapse. The process of autonomic reorganization that starts in therapy is strengthened with practice between sessions. (pp. xxiii–xxiv)

Trauma survivors need multiple resources to manage emotion and somatic dysregulation outside of the therapy room and to maintain safety and social co-regulation. Clients learn to look for "glimmers" or micro-moments that build over time into a ventral vagal "glow" that strengthens the client's regulation. Resourcing follows the BASIC framework of (a) befriend, (b) attend, (c) shape, (d) integrate, and (e) connect (Dana, 2020). A resource can be a person, place, thing, or object, preferably from the client's own experience, that they can call on when their SUD (subjective units of distress) increases. Resources, like anchors, also include movements, such as yoga, chair yoga, drama, dance, hiking, walking, skipping, Tai Chi, and swimming, as well as tactile activities like knitting, crocheting, needlepoint, clay work, and finger painting.

Anchors

Anchors divert the survivor's attention from distressing thoughts and memories to a calming memory and image. Shifting the dialogue from the distressing experience to a calming and soothing one reduces the intensity of sympathetic system dominance. Thus, they feel supported with feelings and thoughts of safety and positivity of the anchor. Anchors also help survivors to "brake" before moving too fast with the traumatic story. The personal anchor can be called up easily as the counselor says, "Let's stop this for a moment. Tell me about your [anchor]."

"Safe places" are special protective anchors that provide bodily and emotional relief and lower hyperarousal. The best safe places are real (actual) spaces in the client's lived experience that evoke safe and happy feelings. Anchors can be a place or space (e.g., a room, a rocking chair, a house, castle, forest, or beach), an activity (e.g., gardening, floating, singing, or yoga), or a person or animal (e.g., grandfather, mother, teacher, pet). For example, yoga integrates intentional body movements with breathing and mindfulness as a bottom-up and top-down technique through bilateral communication between brain and body. Yoga also can be used as an anchor and performed to reduce bodily distress and intrusive thoughts and memories (Sullivan et al., 2018). Counselor and client practice bringing up the safe place when in the window of tolerance, so that it can be called up easily as needed. Caution should be taken as individuals with sexual or physical trauma may not have experienced an actual safe place in their history or lived experience. They may need to create a safe place with the counselor.

Psychoeducation and Virtual Resourcing

With the impact of the COVID-19 pandemic and its need for social distancing and isolation, self-help trauma recovery literature has expanded treatment access to the public, especially online. Examples include Rothschild's *8 Keys to Safe Trauma Recovery: Take-Charge Strategies to Empower Your Healing* and Fisher's *Transforming the Living Legacy of Trauma.* van der Kolk's (2014) book, *The Body Keeps the Score*, describes the neurobiology of trauma in everyday language and continues to be on the best-seller list. Internet-based counseling and resourcing has increased access to mental health services, especially during quarantines and virtual schooling. Internet counseling, supervision, mobile apps, and help lines have expanded services for individuals and families with trauma. Most federal and state trainings and services are now provided free online for both mental health professionals and the public (a sampling of these are listed in the online-only Resources section).

PROCESSING THE NARRATIVE

Constructing and processing the trauma story should begin only after the survivor and counselor have developed a safe therapeutic relationship, have practiced relaxation techniques to reduce distress, and have weighed the potential dangers of retraumatization. Current trauma resolution techniques also draw from existential, phenomenological, and neurobiological principles and worldviews; the survivor can choose to process the trauma story to resolution, or to bypass the story and choose coping techniques to promote recovery and a healthy future.

An important outcome of this re-storying process is to be able to tell the story as a normal historical memory and no longer as a traumatic memory, because "A traumatic memory cannot be adequately processed if its affective and sensory-motor elements remain isolated from the rest of the memory" (van der Kolk et al., 1996, p. 333). Moving the story toward trauma resolution requires physical (somatic), emotional (feeling), and thinking (cognitive) elements. In addition to conventional ways to write or record the narrative as chapters of a book or scenes in a drama, clients can choose an expressive or multisensory storying modality, such as drawing, photo board, sand tray, drama, illustrations, or music. Survivors initially may create a title with fearful words like "The Most Terrifying Event" and as they process events toward resolution; however, they later may revise the title to "My Journey of Survival and Hope." It is important for both counselor and client to monitor the stress level frequently, in order to pause or stop the story before overwhelm or retraumatization occur.

Clients can tell the story with or without words, and they can divide the narrative into timelines, chapters, or scenes (before the event, during the event, after the event). The narrative can be expressed in words, pictures, photos, sand tray scenes, illustrations, or other expressive modalities. Clients may choose to begin the story in a safe time period before the traumatic event, while others may prefer to begin at the end (the current moment in the session) where they know they are safe with the counselor and their family.

Storyboard

Graphic storyboards show the events through picture panels. Survivors often begin with the last part (recovery, being saved, or feeling safe) and then return to the first panel before the traumatic event. Filling in and processing the traumatic event panels may span several sessions, with time for breathing and calming exercises. Survivors may choose to draw each scene for the graphic storyboard, use pictures or photos from clip art, or express the events with abstract colors or figures (Baranowsky & Gentry, 2015a, 2015b; Webber & Mascari, 2012).

Timeline

As another example, the traumatic event can be depicted on a life-size timeline with yarn or rope on the floor that outlines a client's life story before, during, and after the traumatic event. Clients mark painful or negative events below the timeline with a symbol, such as a rock or stone. Positive events, as well as the client's supporters and helpers, are marked above the timeline with a positive, healing symbol, such as a flower, heart, or photograph. The counselor and client "walk" the timeline, pausing at the end, where a ball of yarn or rope holds a place for the future. As they video-record or photograph the timeline, clients acknowledge that the trauma is one of many events on their life's path, and that they have moved past it (Webber & Mascari, 2012).

Externalizing the Problem

Four narrative therapy principles and techniques promote empowerment and hope for recovery along with reducing traumatic distress. First, narrative trauma therapists remind their clients that they are not the problem. The "problem" (e.g., COVID-19, the sexual predator, anxiety) is the problem (White & Epston, 1990). Second, externalizing the problem and separating from the problem changes the client's relationship with the problem and affirms that they can empower themselves to distance themselves from the problem. Third, rather than focus on the problem and the past, the counselor asks clients about their wishes and dreams. Clients create their new preferred story and imagine what they would be doing when the problem is no longer controlling them. This empowerment reflects an emphasis on the present and future, much like the "miracle question" in brief solution-focused counseling. Fourth, the counselor and client look for "sparkling moments" or unique outcomes when the client was able to escape from the problem or the problem's power. Sparkling moments show parallels to "glimmers" in Polyvagal Theory and discovering exceptions in solution-focused counseling.

Slowing the Story

While some survivors do not want to address the story, others want to move quickly into the trauma details to gain physical and emotional relief, bypassing important steps toward learning emotion- and body-regulation skills to manage the process. The counselor affirms the client's desire but cautions about the dangers. A Substance Abuse and Mental Health Services Administration [SAMHSA] (2014) publication offers the following example:

> I understand this desire, but my concern for you at the moment is to help you establish a sense of safety and support before moving into the traumatic experiences. We want to avoid retraumatization, that means we want to establish resources that weren't available to you at the time of the trauma before delving into more content. (SAMHSA, 2014, p. 97)

Returning to the Window of Tolerance

When clients become overwhelmed quickly, they can slip outside of their window of tolerance without the ability or skills to return to the here and now. To help them move back into the present, counselors can shift from talk therapy (top down) to body approaches (bottom up), including movement, breathing, music, and exercise to re-engage clients slowly, by using their senses. Counselors use kinesthetic techniques to re-ground the client such as "Feel your feet on the floor," or "What sounds do you hear now?" These techniques shift clients' attention to their identified anchor and divert their thoughts to a safe place or person, thereby reducing the level of overwhelm.

Once clients move outside the window of tolerance, counselors need to take steps quickly to bring them back into safety. If a client is just outside the window of tolerance, the counselor should focus on reconnecting within the relationship. If the client cannot describe what is happening, Ogden checks for dissociation by asking, "Can you sense this moment?" (as cited in Buczynski, 2020, p. 5). The counselor can redirect the client by asking, "Look at me. Who am I?" or by saying, "You are in the here and now; you are not in your past experience."

To prevent dissociating and having more intense reactions, counselors and clients can walk together around the room and use grounding techniques to reconnect to their current surroundings. When clients can accept the present situation (even if they do not like it), the top-down (prefrontal cortex) and bottom-up (autonomic nervous system) responses are both back online, and clients are present and oriented in the here and now.

Crossing the Threshold

Asking a client to change locations (e.g., "Come; let's take a brief walk together" or "Come to this other room with me") intentionally guides the client across a threshold from one physical room to another. As the client crosses the threshold, the "doorway effect" may interfere with memory encoding in a therapeutic way, particularly if a client is overwhelmed by processing the narrative (Lawrence & Peterson, 2016; Pettijohn & Radvansky, 2018). Memories are encoded with reference to local boundaries (e.g., rooms, locations, doorways) and locations. Further, the invitation to join the counselor, by walking together, creates a brief social connection, as well as physical movement, and both foster new ways of thinking. Inviting a distressed client to another room or location also works in a crisis situation, by way of providing a literal time-and-space boundary or margin between the client and a crisis experience.

RECOVERY TECHNIQUES WITHOUT NARRATIVE PROCESSING

Telling and resolving the trauma story has been the cornerstone of traditional trauma treatment models, especially in cognitive-behavioral talk therapy. However, not all survivors want to process their trauma story out loud, especially those who question if they could bear more pain (by telling the story). "If I wanted to heal, I was told, I would have to confront my past and face down my traumatic memories. This process proved to be so terrifying and overwhelming for me that I fled therapy" (Gentry, 2016, p. 454). It is not necessary for clients to tell or retell their story in the therapeutic encounter in order to heal from traumatic experiences. Some clients find healing in telling the story to the counselor who bears compassionate witness and provides a shared sense of bearing or carrying the story. Other clients find telling the trauma story out loud unworkable, because they find it impossible to put the unspeakable into words, or because they do not want to reopen the psychological wound of the traumatic event, or for fear, shame, or other personal reasons. While traditional approaches to trauma therapy encourage telling the trauma story, it is not necessary for recovery.

Survivors should not be pressured to tell the trauma memory in order to recover and go on with their lives. They can choose trauma recovery now and learn to live safely and comfortably in their bodies; then, if they choose, they could process the trauma later. As clients become aware of the various options and timelines for treatment (which is the counselor's ethical responsibility to outline at the beginning of the therapeutic encounter), they can reduce their growing anxiety about feeling worse rather than better. They trust that the counselor will not push them until they are ready to take that step.

When survivors cannot process the trauma, they still need psychoeducation about trauma reactions; they need to learn skills for self-regulation, skills for coping with triggers, and resourcing techniques. According to Rothschild (2000, p. 78), "those clients who are not able to tolerate memory-oriented trauma treatment may still benefit from therapy geared to relieve symptoms, increase coping skills, and improve daily functioning." They need to learn (or relearn) when and how to breathe, how to stay connected to others, how to call up their safe place, and when to push the "pause button" (Snel, 2013, p. 11). Given the holistic nature of human experience, providing tools to relax one's body will create commensurate relief for the mind as well.

Whether the path involves recovery with or without trauma processing, the third phase of trauma recovery is essential. To move forward, survivors need to reconnect with family, friends, and community. White and Epston (1990) have encouraged survivors to share their recovery experience or trauma story with others, who would then affirm and validate the survivors. Rather than continue the secrecy, shame, and silence sanctioned by society for many traumatic events, sharing and connecting with others are healthy steps for recovery and ongoing resourcing, in order to move forward. The survivor's letters of gratitude to friends and supporters continue to foster the reconnection phase. Throughout the COVID-19 pandemic, for example, families have reconnected through social media and online videoconference get-togethers and have engaged in family rituals and events online: birthdays; religious, cultural, and civic holidays; and recovery from illness. Celebrations of life have taken place online for families and friends of those who died.

EXPRESSIVE TECHNIQUES

Multisensory storying modalities, such as art, sand tray, clay, music, drama, singing, and photography, facilitate the narrative process and open channels to the trauma story (Gallerani &

Dybicz, 2011; Gil, 2006; van der Kolk, 2014; van der Velden & Koops, 2005; Webber & Mascari, 2012). Expressive modalities also lead to creative ways to contain the trauma or overwhelming feelings toward the perpetrator during counseling sessions. Clients may feel safer when metaphorically or symbolically pushing or placing what is unsafe into metaphorical containers that hold the traumatic experience, feelings, or reactions. For example, one client sealed her trauma drawing in a large mailer, covered the surfaces with shipping tape, and stapled all the edges (Webber & Mascari, 2012). Another survivor selected miniature figures that represented the family members and friends who died and placed them together in a sand tray. A client who lost several family members to COVID-19 painted a small box white, wrote the names of each person in calligraphic style on the outside, and filled the box with mementos and photographs. The creation of symbolic containers empowers clients to decide what to do with representations of the traumatic events and any perpetrator(s) in a way that is safe and symbolically meaningful.

Sand Tray

Rather than write or tell their trauma story, survivors may prefer to draw or illustrate the events, or create a sand tray scene. Some trauma survivors literally cannot speak, but they often can express their experiences and feelings by creating a scene or story in sand, without words. Sand tray is a powerful therapeutic technique in which the individual creates a three-dimensional scene with miniature figures and objects in a tray filled with sand. Typical trays of modest size, for example, 9" × 13" aluminum baking pans, or larger trays, 2 feet by 3 feet, provide a container or "frame" in which to process a trauma. The tray is designed to be a safe, protected, and healing environment for counseling, and it can become a container for a traumatic experience or distress. The scene created in the tray often reflects clients' perceptions of their internal and external worlds. The counselor invites clients to look at the miniatures and select those that appeal to them and create a three-dimensional picture in the sand contained by the tray. Little direction is needed, except to "choose what you want to and place the figures in the sand as you wish" (adapted from Homeyer & Sweeney, 2016). Clients report that they feel drawn to certain figures and are surprised at the power of the sand tray experience in facilitating their disclosure of sensitive issues or trauma (Webber & Mascari, 2008). In my (Jane's) counseling experiences over five decades, clients with trauma are often surprised that they created a scene about their traumatic event when they had planned not to make the trauma known.

The counselor is fully present, attentive, and observing but does not verbally "track" the actions of the client, as would be done in play therapy. The counselor notices the client's development of the sand tray. Which figure is placed first? Does the creator engage the figures in action? Does the creator narrate the action or speak for the figures? What items did the creator move? Clients often feel empowered by the process and move people or objects, although they may not be aware that they changed the arrangement, thus changing the outcome. For example, one client was upset about what direction she would take with her life after her husband had died. In the middle of her tray, she placed a bridge. On one end of the bridge, she identified a box that represented the casket of her husband who had died. A figure representing the client stood on the other end of the bridge, and as the client spoke, she turned the bridge away from the casket toward an area of flowers and trees. The client was unaware she had moved the bridge, and, when the counselor described this change, she expressed gratitude that she had chosen a new direction in her life.

The client is the creator of the sand tray who is free to assign any name or meaning to a figure. Thus, the creator can make generic noncommercial figures like Lego or Playmobil, or any figure or object, into whomever or whatever the creator chooses. Counselors should neither assume what a figure represents nor label it on the client's behalf. The meaning of the tray comes wholly from the creator, not from the counselor. The clinical vignette in Box 28.2 illustrates the importance of this.

BOX 28.2

Clinical Vignette: Kara's Sand Tray

After the traumatic loss of a family member, the client may reconstruct the story, over time, in a way that restores relationships with family and friends and frees them to move forward. Often this process involves sand tray therapy with family members and children who find it is an expressive way of transforming their traumatic loss into a meaningful and manageable remembrance. After her father died in the World Trade Center disaster, Kara, a 4-year-old girl, attended weekend individual and family grief therapy sessions. She particularly liked working with figures in sand during her counseling sessions. Kara initially was hesitant to select and place objects in the sand tray. She started with tiny inanimate objects like miniature boxes, stones, and shells and grouped them in one corner, adding nothing else to the tray. Later, she added tiny trees and animals, often repeating scenes she had made earlier. Around 4 years later, when she was 8 years old, near the anniversary of September 11 and also her father's birthday, Kara selected a tree, an umbrella, and a picnic table and placed them in her tray, along with figures representing her mother, brother, and herself. When she could not find a birthday cake, she formed a cake and candles from clay. However, when she could not locate a barbeque grill in the collection of figures, she substituted a miniature chest in her tray, placing it carefully next to an empty chair. An intern who was assisting in the session admired the object, calling it a "treasure chest," and said that it must be filled with treasures and memories of her father. Kara was indignant and said the object was not a treasure chest; it was her father's barbeque grill for his birthday party. "Daddy always grilled hamburgers and hot dogs for his birthday." Kara wished that her mom would celebrate his birthday now. "Daddy misses his birthday party. We can't have it at home, because Mom cries so much. Happy birthday, Daddy."

Kara invited her mother and her brother to the sand tray room. She showed them her birthday party tray. They started to make scenes, and when they felt safe, the family shared stories of the father through sand trays. The sand tray process helped them to rebuild their lives and reestablish family rituals with new stories and old remembrances. (Adapted from Webber & Mascari, 2008, p. 3; Webber et al., 2010, pp. 15–16).

Survivors frequently select figures and objects that represent the traumatic event in some way (e.g., nurse, police, ambulance, or monster for the perpetrator). With the freedom to move figures around in the tray, creators can change the outcomes and meanings, and thereby develop a sense of mastery and empowerment over their traumatic experience (Gallerani & Dybicz, 2011; Gil, 2006). Sand tray therapy does not require verbal responses or processing, although clients often spontaneously describe their trays. In phenomenological and constructivist sand tray approaches, clients are the creators of their "world" and they provide insight into the tray. The meaning of the tray is that of the creator, not the counselor. When the three-dimensional scene is completed, the counselor asks permission to photograph the tray to chronicle the sand trays in the record for future sessions. Clients typically use their cell phones to photograph their trays, and some journal their experience or draw their tray. The sand tray is viewed as a "sacred" personal construction, and therefore, as a part of the creator. Thus, the scene is not dismantled until after the therapeutic session has ended, and the creator leaves the room. Weinrib (1983) explained, "to destroy a picture in the patient's presence would be to devalue a completed creation, to break the connection between the patient and his inner self and the unspoken connection to the therapist" (p. 14).

During the pandemic's quarantines and fear of contagion, there were few or no opportunities to do sand tray in person with a counselor. However, counselors created "go-bags" with figures, disposable trays, and plastic containers of play sand. Clients set up their laptop or cell phone so the counselor could observe them developing their sand tray scenes. Online sand tray sites are also useful when in-person sessions are unavailable (see https://onlinesandtray.com or http://ww1.simplysandtray.com or www.virtualsandtray.org).

Photo Storyboard

Sand tray and photo storyboards share similarities with multisensory expressions that often evoke disclosures and strong expressions of feelings. The photo storyboard is an intentional (not spontaneous) structured gallery of photographs reflecting the survivor's experiences in the trauma recovery process and easily can be done online using clip art and graphics. Clients can use Prezi or PowerPoint to express a story or event with the ability to change the story sequence and chapters around for new meanings and outcomes. The online storyboard, Prezi Make a Scene (see https://prezi.com/5efs69gf42zr/make-a-scene), and online virtual sand trays are not three-dimensional and lack the kinesthetic connection to the figures. However, the survivor still can create the trauma story, having a multisensory experience, with the power to re-story and change the outcome, and computer-savvy individuals might prefer this delivery.

TOOLS FOR VICARIOUS TRAUMATIZATION AND COMPASSION FATIGUE

Before ending this chapter, it is salient to address the effect of exposure to clients' trauma stories on the person of the counselor. The counselor's empathy and unconditional positive regard are essential elements for client recovery, and the client's trauma processing can affect the self of the counselor deeply. These qualities also represent the counselor's Achilles' heel. When providing trauma-informed therapy, counselors must be equipped with co-monitoring and co-regulating tools that are similar to what their clients use. Therefore, it is incumbent on ethical clinicians to monitor their own allostatic stress loads and to create intentional self-awareness and self-care practices, in order to manage and release the strain of bearing witness to so much traumatic material. Without self-care and prevention, the risk for clinical burnout and compassion fatigue significantly increases and ultimately can impair the professional (Baranowsky & Gentry, 2015b). Counselors and other mental health clinicians are wise to recognize that we, too, are human beings with human limitations, and that the same kinds of braking, dosing, containment, and stress-relief tools that we promote to our clients should be used in our own intentional plan of ongoing self-care (counselor self-care is discussed, in detail, in Chapter 31).

PANDEMIC TRAUMA

Despite the speed at which safe and effective vaccines have been developed and distributed, everyone, at the time of this writing, remains at risk for COVID-19. Thus, maintaining a sense of personal safety within the body, in therapeutic and family relationships, and in the community is a triple need and challenge. Survivors of trauma often perceive danger, even when it actually is not present; this dynamic has been intensified by COVID-19, especially as it is an invisible threat that can be present anywhere and at any time. Even with vaccinations, fear and dread continue to haunt us. Similar to other profound traumatic events of existential threat proportions, COVID-19 has been "a disruption so serious that it threatens our existence, shaking the foundation of who we are and who we once were" (Serlin & Cannon, 2004, p. 314). Shared trauma is an overriding concern, as counselors and mental health professionals also have been affected by the same fear and mass trauma as their clients. It is a distinct challenge to provide counseling during COVID-19, when both counselor and client share the same trauma of COVID-19. As a silent, invisible global pandemic, people cannot completely avoid COVID-19 by physically relocating or moving away. Even with frequent COVID testing and vaccinations, individuals do not know if they carry the virus, have transmitted it, or have contracted the virus from strangers, family members, or loved ones. Uncertainty, confusion, and fear lead to dread, chaos, inability to make plans, and competition for limited resources.

Many individuals have felt bereft of hope for a return to real, in-person, human connections. Victims of trauma eventually move out of the safety and intimacy of the therapeutic relationship to reintegrate into family and community life in phase three of the recovery process. Attempts to re-establish relationships continue to be fraught with fear and dread, even as social distancing regulations are relaxed. Myriad education and business closures, loss of jobs and resources, and unpredictable quarantines have exacerbated emotional and traumatic stress. Although the public health situation has begun to stabilize, remaining uncertainties continue to be sources of stress and anxiety for many people. Herman (1992/2015) has pointed out that "trauma isolates; the group re-creates a sense of belonging" (p. 246). Pandemic families and neighborhood groups have lived in cautious bubbles with a constant sense of fear of what cannot be seen. As protective rules loosen, small groups and families share in therapeutic and expressive experiences to reduce distress, to feel safer with others, and to shift to the ventral vagal system with expressive techniques including: sand tray, singing, and painting; movement like Tai Chi, drama, yoga, and dance; and mindfulness techniques like guided imagery and mindful minutes. Intertwined in the experience of traumatic isolation is the impact of illness and death from COVID-19. Those who have lost family members or friends during the time of COVID-19 shutdowns may have unresolved grief, particularly when separated from their loved ones in hospitals and rehabilitation centers.

Shared Trauma

The COVID-19 pandemic is a shared trauma that pushes all of us into uncharted waters. To cope, we return to the foundational principles of mental health to manage crises and distress and to adjust to this "new normal." Adding grief and sorrow, counselors need a new toolkit for both clients and themselves to weather continuing emotional and somatic assaults on the body and the brain; to refill depleted resilience reservoirs; and to find a path to rediscover hope, connection, and meaning. Particularly during intense COVID waves, individuals and families with pandemic traumatic grief were deprived of their normal group traditions and social, spiritual, and cultural tools to cope with illness and traumatic death. They were deprived of the normal and expected sources of soothing and comforting provided by group rituals for the deceased, such as last rites, wakes, sitting Shiva, funerals, religious and cultural ceremonies, and closure rituals of processions, burials, and memorials like celebrations of life. Some created virtual or Zoom substitutes to hold cultural and spiritual practices, but many others did not have the resources to do this.

Social Connectedness

Dana (2020) underscores the need for safety and social connections: "When we feel alone in the world we suffer. When that feeling of aloneness and isolation is chronic, medical and mental health risks multiply" (p. 27). Added to the fear and confusion of their upended world, individuals and families have been deeply affected by grief after illnesses or deaths of loved ones. The physical and emotional comfort and self-soothing with Play-Doh, sand tray, drawing, yoga, and movement can lower the somatic distress and provide some "glimmers" of calm. Body scans can identify areas of tension and pain, and while traumatic distress and grief can be intertwined in mass trauma, remaining in the present moment and not the past is vital. Expressions of gratitude can provide spiritual and emotional comfort and hope, despite the imposition of limits caused by COVID-19. For example, online photo boards and photo timelines provide virtual ways to celebrate the lives of victims and to hold their memories.

Polyvagal Theory asserts that social engagement is an essential human process (Porges, 2016); therefore, necessary accommodations during COVID-19 have been isolating and lonely for many people. The following sand tray group technique underscores the importance of co-regulation and social connections.

Selecting favorite miniatures that represent loved ones can bring family members together to reconnect during the pandemic. This circle-in-a-circle exercise promotes relationships and the sharing of feelings among family members. Gil (2006) suggests that the survivor invites family members to a group session. The survivor places a miniature that reflects who they are in the center of a smaller circle that is surrounded by a larger circle. Each family member selects a miniature that represents how they feel about the traumatic event and places it on the rim of the smaller circle. Each then chooses another figure that represents their relationship with the survivor, placing it on the outer circle. Thus, families can reduce the physical and emotional isolation and can co-regulate, through these representative symbols. In this way, they can repair lost or ruptured relationships.

In a wellness and "ventral vagal" state, people naturally seek out social connections. However, in the pandemic—a mass trauma currently without an endpoint—there is no clear point in time where people may feel safe enough to move away from a survival and protection norm and return to social engagement. Dana (2020) reminds us that "in a state of illness, the social engagement system retracts, responding to the physiological demand to attend to internal conditions" (p. 63). Moving from the sympathetic state to the ventral vagal state seems almost impossible with pandemic fear and grief that prevent a safe and open environment needed to reestablish social connections. Nevertheless, simple Polyvagal techniques help clients become aware of micro-moments or "glimmers" of safety and social connections. The glow of glimmers is reflected in such affirmations of community engagement as Italian families leaning out their windows and singing and auto parades past homes to celebrate birthdays. Dana uses a horizontal line to represent "the continuum between survival and social engagement" (p. 60). Clients mark multiple small steps they have taken on the continuum toward the other end to show clear awareness of subtle shifts of the autonomic nervous system. Rather than a dichotomous point of disconnection versus connection, clients mark their experiences along a social engagement scale, thus increasing awareness of their level of participation in the moment and monitoring the persons, places, and interactions in the ventral vagal state (p. 64). In essence, this teaches clients and counselors alike to move from an "either-or" to a "both-and" conceptualization of living in the ongoing context of COVID-19, and learning, nevertheless, to persist with resilience and hope.

CONCLUSION

Trauma treatment approaches have shifted from the traditional focus on retelling and resolving the trauma story using talk therapy to current integrated brain–body approaches grounded in emotion- and somatic-regulation techniques. Clients who do not want to revisit the details of their trauma can choose recovery and healthy living over trauma story resolution.

Processing the trauma story is fraught with dangers of retraumatization, requiring a tool kit of techniques for both client and counselor to remain within the affective window of tolerance. Core principles and practices across several treatment approaches and techniques focus on building safety, stabilization, emotion regulation, connections, and hope, especially during the isolation and mass trauma of the pandemic. Counselor and client co-regulate with unique combinations of interventions and techniques, especially bottom-up exercises and expressive techniques to promote relaxation, mindfulness, connections, and hope.

ADDITIONAL RESOURCES

PRACTICE-BASED RESOURCES AND REFERENCES

To view a list of resources and all the references, please visit connect.springerpub.com via the following url: http://connect.springerpub.com/content/book/978-0-8261-5085-1/part/part05/chapter/ch28

CHAPTER 29

Ethical Perspectives on Trauma Work

SARA P. JOHNSTON AND VILIA M. TARVYDAS

CHAPTER OVERVIEW

This chapter focuses on the ethical implications of trauma work. The chapter begins with a discussion of the five ethical principles and connects ethics to practice in trauma work. Next, the chapter defines and describes several key terms and concepts related to ethical practice, including wounded healers, compassion fatigue, ethical and moral behaviors, moral suffering, and self-care. The ethical implications of supervising counselors engaged in trauma work are described next, including the importance of addressing multicultural issues and intersectionality in practice. The crucial process of transforming from victim to survivor is described, as well as counselors' ethical obligations in that process. Finally, a number of resources, related to ethical practice in trauma work, is provided online.

LEARNING OBJECTIVES

After reading this chapter, the reader should be able to:

1. Name the five ethical principles and give examples of their application in trauma work;
2. Define the terms "wounded healer," "compassion fatigue," "ethical and moral behaviors," "moral suffering," and "self-care," and describe their importance to ethical practice in trauma work;
3. Discuss the role of supervision in trauma work;
4. Explain the ethical implications of multicultural sensitivity and intersectionality in trauma work, along with the role of counselors in promoting advocacy and social justice for marginalized populations affected by trauma;
5. Describe the process of transformation from victim to survivor and the counselor's ethical obligations in that process; and,
6. Identify resources related to the ethical practice of trauma work.

INTRODUCTION

In earlier chapters of this textbook, trauma was examined in depth and breadth: by context, type, and setting. All of the information conveys a clear message that trauma is inevitably a profound and complex experience—for survivors and responders alike. For counselors who seek to provide care in trauma and disaster situations, the ethical challenges are both profound and of a nature for which they may be ill-prepared. Sommers-Flanagan and Sommers-Flanagan (2008) articulated a basic truth about the stark ethical context of crisis work: "It has been said that the truest test of morality is how people behave when no one is looking and no one will know. The compelling human dimensions of crisis heighten every human emotion. The chaos of crisis obscures accountability" (p. 266).

Apart from its profundity and complexity, traumatic experience can be a source of excruciating pain and suffering to victims and survivors. Counselors involved in trauma work must attune to the taxing and daunting effects of trauma. In addition, counselors need to be aware of and confront ethical challenges and dilemmas that may seep into important facets of their lives. Ethics is an important aspect of competent counseling practice. Professionals in the field must strive to be fluent with the ethical codes of professional associations (e.g., the American Counseling Association [ACA], the American Psychological Association [APA], the National Association of Social Workers) and of other organizations that may provide additional ethical guidance in the specialized circumstance of trauma or disaster mental health counseling (see the discussion of the Green Cross's Standards of Self-Care and the American Red Cross's (2005) Code of Conduct at the conclusion of this chapter). Members of the various helping professions need to be knowledgeable of the ethics codes governing professional practice and integrate these codes into their professional lives. On a more sophisticated level, members are asked to model their ethical practices to clients, peers, and colleagues, living out what they promote and embrace.

This chapter facilitates mental health clinicians' awareness of traumatic situations that pose challenges to their ethical practice. This chapter also inspires professionals to reflect on and examine their helping intentions. This chapter culminates in the discussion of developing an ethical character consistent with trauma professionals' aspirations in their professional work in trauma. Specifically, the following eight topics will guide the process of discussion: (a) Understanding Ethical Principles in Trauma Practice, (b) Trauma and the Clinician, (c) Survivors as Consumers of Services, (d) Transformation From Victim to Survivor, (e) Survivor Input to Therapy and Recovery, (f) Survivor Mission, and (g) Counseling Implications. These major sections are followed by a summary of this chapter and an online list of useful resources. Cases of violation of ethics are illustrated in the latter part of this chapter.

Cottone et al. (2022) discuss two types of governance in ethical practice: mandatory and aspirational. Mandatory ethics functions at the most basic level, where counselors must attend to ethical standards and parameters of their practice through standards that are binding upon them by virtue of their memberships in an organization or holding of a credential (Cottone et al., 2022). The aspirational level of ethical governance is the more sophisticated level of practice, which voluntarily guides mental health clinicians to center on the welfare of clients and to act in the best interests of the entire helping profession (Cottone et al., 2022). Aspirational ethics is the level of practice characterized by professional helpers' indigenous character and attitudes as supplemented by advanced knowledge of ethical practices as informed by nonbinding ethical standards and professional knowledge. The level of aspirational ethical practice is pivotal in guiding professionals in making pertinent decisions in trauma work because limited mandatory guidance is available that applies specifically to work in this area of practice. As a result, it is imperative that trauma work professionals also become knowledgeable and adept in the use of a credible, scholarly ethical decision-making model that can bear public scrutiny. Many and diverse models exist, and clinicians are urged to develop a deep familiarity with the use of one suitable to their needs prior to becoming involved in the ethically charged, complex situations that trauma counseling entails. Because this important aspect of preparation for ethical trauma counseling is outside the scope of this chapter, readers are referred to the original work of some authorities who have published useful ethical decision-making models (Cottone, 2001; Garcia et al., 2004; Johnston & Tarvydas, 2019; Kitchener, 1984; Tarvydas & Johnston, 2018). Accordingly, discussions in this chapter will gravitate toward practice at a level above mandatory ethics.

Observing and living out the ethical codes are core elements of professionalism (Bernard & Goodyear, 2009). In effect, trauma helpers' hearts and minds are key factors that motivate counselors to observe and live out their professional practices. The mindset in this context relates to prudence. Cimperman (2005) summarized prudence as "the fruit of who we are at a given point in time as embodied relational agents" (p. 59). Aquinas (as cited in Cimperman, 2005) argued that prudence is legitimate logic toward one's actions. The "virtue of prudence," a value described by James Keenan, a theologian, accompanies fidelity, self-care, and justice (Cimperman, 2005). Prudence appears to be a fitting compass for counselors to navigate the ethical journey, safeguarding them from violating professional boundaries and inciting them to discern clients' best interests. Wholehearted commitment to service makes a remarkable contribution to professionalism, and it is not uncommon to hear that people are drawn to the counseling profession because of their burning desire to offer care and support to those who are in need. Their good natures inspire them to approach the counseling relationship with empathy, congruence, and unconditional positive regard (Rogers, 1975). These personal qualities are essential to ethical practice at the aspirational level, but if not properly harnessed they can also contribute to circumstances that compromise the ethical quality of service.

UNDERSTANDING ETHICAL PRINCIPLES IN TRAUMA PRACTICE

This chapter highlights understanding of trauma from the ethical perspective. The pillars of ethical guidelines, the traditional five moral principles identified by Kitchener (1984), are integrated into the examination of ethical dilemmas and challenges in trauma work. Understanding and reflecting on the five principles–autonomy, justice, beneficence, nonmaleficence, and fidelity–assist trauma helpers in navigating ethical conflicts that arise in counseling situations, including those faced in crisis and humanitarian interventions (Sommers-Flanagan, 2007).

Autonomy

Autonomy refers to "a right to self-determination of choice and freedom from the control of others" (Cottone et al., 2022, p. 88). Professional responsibility refers to professional helpers' commitment to clients and to the mental health profession (Cottone et al., 2022). In the aftermath of a traumatic event, a common feeling among victims is helplessness. The sudden and unpredictable way traumatic events unfold may cause clients to feel a loss of control over their lives. Clients may find it extremely difficult, if not impossible, to make decisions. They may tend to count on someone to speak and act on their behalf. Challenging as it may be, counselors must refer to clients' rights and freedom, and adhere to the profession's ethical codes that emphasize client informed choice (Tarvydas & Johnston, 2018). For immediate resolution to clients' pressing needs, it may seem pragmatic to furnish clients with some answers, and the initial phases of trauma work involve a great deal of practical assistance and assisting the client in reestablishing natural, supportive contact with valued others. Even the initial step of professionals clearly identifying themselves as a mental health professional who will be working with the survivor, making sure that the survivor who wishes to talk reestablishes a base level of control, and allows the survivor to—in some way—make a choice about what they choose to discuss, is vital.

The principle of autonomy in ethical practice places a clear focus on providing clients with proper informed consent and confidentiality, tasks that may be difficult, at best, in the conditions in which trauma and disaster mental health clinicians may find themselves. There may not be an office or private space in which to arrange for privacy, sessions may be on demand or spontaneous, record keeping may not be possible, or keeping records confidential may involve extraordinary efforts, and conditions may not allow for more structured interactions and explanations in a traditional sense. Counselors should ensure as far as they are able that they adhere to their ethical obligations by taking such measures as (a) identifying themselves clearly as a mental health professional, (b) providing a practical and abbreviated form of informed consent, (c) looking for and using as private a space as possible given the available surroundings, and (d) emphasizing and modeling keeping survivor information confidential with other workers and staff.

Sommers-Flanagan (2007) cautioned that counselors must not succumb to the disaster myths of the stunned or frozen victim, but rather must assume survivors' knowledge and competence to make their own choices. Counselors are responsible to ensure that survivors are given the encouragement, conditions, resources, and opportunity to understand and voluntarily consent to any decision affecting them. In this way, counselors must think and act in accordance with clients' well-being because clients are the ones who bear consequences of their decisions.

Counselors also can impair the immediate and longer-term autonomy of survivors if issues of control and empowerment are mishandled. For individuals who have experienced loss of control through trauma and disaster, the manner in which matters of autonomy are managed is likely to have profound therapeutic significance. The use of empowerment-oriented interventions is key to calling forth the necessary resiliency to potentiate healing from traumatic experiences. For this reason, counselors must honor the principle of autonomy by facilitating client decision-making that is in accordance with clients' own values, including sensitivity to issues of cultural diversity, social justice, and intersectionality (Levine & Breshears, 2019). These are discussed in more detail later on in the chapter. In sum, the principle of autonomy entails counselors practicing on both their mandatory and aspirational levels. Sommers-Flanagan (2007) offered some specific suggestions for ethical best practices that conform to the principle of autonomy in working with survivors of trauma (see Box 29.1).

BOX 29.1

Best Practices to Enhance the Autonomy of Trauma Survivors

1. Presume that survivors are capable of making decisions unless there is a specific pre-disaster or pretrauma condition that could suggest otherwise.
2. Think in terms of the types of decisions and match between the competency of the survivor to decide in that specific moment.
3. Think through how confidentiality issues might be handled in a disaster or trauma situation and inform survivors as appropriate; strive to ensure privacy of conversations and help survivors understand differences between confidential versus casual conversations.
4. Develop protocols of how informed consent will be obtained and include provisions for when survivors' decision-making capacities become impaired (e.g., use of substitute decision-makers who are most likely to know what the survivor may wish to decide for themselves).
5. Understand cultural dynamics that may reflect the survivors' differing ideas about who participates in decision-making.

Source: Adapted from Sommers-Flanagan, R. (2007). Ethical considerations in crisis and humanitarian interventions. *Ethics & Behavior, 17*(2), 187–202. https://doi.org/10 .1080/10508420701378123

Justice

Justice in the context of counseling refers to "fairness and equality in access to resources and treatment" (Cottone et al., 2022, p. 90). The principle of justice requires counselors to treat clients equally and impartially. The nature of disaster or trauma response assumes thoughtful allocation of services and resources to address the circumstances experienced by the survivors. It implies equal treatment of persons who are equal in status and resources, although this is rarely the case. The questions raised in the response to Hurricane Katrina in 2005 and in the response to the

COVID-19 pandemic in 2020 are illustrative of the power of issues related to fairness and justice, challenging both survivors', interveners', and society's assumptions about fairness. These are questions of distributive justice, or the model used to determine how scarce resources are allocated, which is particularly problematic for vulnerable persons (Hartley, 2012). This dynamic is especially salient in stages of disaster response beyond its initial phase in that as the crisis unfolds it often unmasks issues of unequal treatment of those of unequal status. It is important that counselors understand that the tendency to blame or avoid is a natural aspect of the stress response cycle for those in traumatic circumstances for workers and survivors, alike, and factor this possible reaction into their analysis of the situation. Counselors both must be aware of and sensitive to their own potential tendencies to place blame or to blame some survivors, and address others' reactions affecting survivors. Counselors must assist in advocacy efforts survivors may undertake or advocate on behalf of clients who are unable to self-advocate. Paradoxically, counselors must be mindful of a potential to alleviate the unfairness they observe through becoming unfair to others (Sommers-Flanagan, 2007). It is for these and other practical and sociopolitical considerations that the principle of neutrality despite worker disillusionment is ascribed to in the disaster responder community when the values of the intended beneficiaries conflict with those of the helping institutions.

On the individual level, experience of trauma might make people perceive that life is unfair. Very often trauma victims ask questions of meaning such as "Why me?" or "Why did this happen to me?" Counselors can assist clients as they move through the irrepressible "why" questions by listening to their search for meaning through exploring issues of fairness and equality through an existential or meaning-making framework (Dass-Brailsford, 2010). People's worldviews are changed, and they may perceive the world as unjust. In cases of murder or homicide, it might be difficult for surviving family members to see justice in society. It may aggravate pain or produce a re-traumatizing effect when counselors do not offer fair treatment to clients. Simple gestures such as scheduling appointments can precipitate clients' feeling of injustice. Counselors need to ponder the meanings of fairness and equality from clients' point of view. Care must be practiced when exploring with clients issues that are sensitive to justice, fairness, and equality. However, the professional traditions of trauma and disaster work include advocacy on behalf of the survivors if, after careful analysis, the individual is not receiving the services that are expected and intended by the service effort or agency.

Beneficence

Beneficence "involves a more active concept of contributing to the well-being of others" (Cottone et al., 2022, p. 89). In the context of trauma, the principle of beneficence requires counselors to develop sensitivity to clients' needs and serve clients in their best interests. Counselors must prioritize clients' concerns and issues rather than their own. Counselors' chief concern is their ability to help clients, rather than responding to their own feelings of anger, pity, or righteousness (Becker, 1985). They must respect clients and exhibit their support for the benefit of their clients. In addition, counselors must operate at their professional level of competency, and even in trauma or disaster situations, they must take care not to provide services outside of their scope of ability (Dailey & LaFauci Shutty, 2018). If asked to provide care in an emergency where no other care is available, counselors may do so until the incident is over and/or more skilled care is available. In doing so, they should use the applicable skills and training they do possess, while taking care that no harm is done to the survivor. With the increasing prevalence and awareness of traumatic events and disasters, it is important that counselors increase their specialized knowledge, training and experience of crisis, and trauma and disaster mental health counseling techniques to competently and ethically work with their clients (Webber & Mascari, 2009). Whether ever deployed to a disaster or involved in the acute treatment of a trauma survivor, counselors working in diverse types of community-based practices will be seeing an array of trauma survivors, whether they initially reveal these experiences or not. As a result, counselors must gain the knowledge, skills, and emotional capacity to work with clients on their posttraumatic growth and well-being.

Nonmaleficence

Nonmaleficence refers to the avoidance of behaviors that might create harm—intentionally or unintentionally (Cottone et al., 2022). Harm is a particularly sensitive matter to people who experienced trauma. Understandably, victims of trauma seem emotionally fragile, and counselors must demonstrate care and sensitivity to clients' emotions. It is fundamental that counselors seek to understand what harm means for clients. Also, they must learn about clients' cultural and spiritual values as these values are related to their thoughts and emotions. Counselors need to be vigilant of their words and actions that may be sources of affliction to clients. For instance, counselors must recognize that certain labels and terms can cause painful feelings for clients. Also, their insensitive probing can re-traumatize clients.

Counselors must refrain from practicing disaster response or trauma counseling beyond the extent of their competencies. For example, Figley (1995) has expressed concern that well-meaning counselors who are not appropriately trained might do more harm than good in their attempts to assist the many combat veterans who have posttraumatic stress disorders (PTSDs) that are reentering our communities at the present time. Another issue involving the ethical obligation of nonmaleficence: counselors should not pressure clients into engaging in unreliable or unproven treatments. Sommers-Flanagan and Sommers-Flanagan (2008) have placed special emphasis on the use of evidence-based interventions as a specific ethical requirement of crisis counseling. For example, specialized crisis interventions such as critical incident stress debriefing (Everly et al., 2005), may be undertaken only after a review of the evidence-based literature that examines its effectiveness, and only conducted under approved protocols, to avoid harming a client by a CISD intervention.

One of the difficulties in assuring that the trauma counselor's actions do not harm others involves carefully monitoring the frequent tendency of disaster and trauma professionals to form social or nonprofessional relationships with coworkers and survivors because of the especially intense emotional climate surrounding the experiences and the work they share. This climate interacts with the counselors', workers', and survivors' very human reactions to exposure to stress and trauma for reassurance and positive human contact. Yet, the survivor may be at their most vulnerable point, traditional boundaries are not clear, and the counselor–client power differential is at its height. It is for these and other compelling reasons that romantic or other intimate relationships with client–survivors, coworkers, and other parties to the trauma or disaster deployment or situation are not ethically appropriate during the period of service.

A final and overarching ethical concern involving nonmaleficence is that of not over-pathologizing survivors' reactions or prematurely diagnosing individuals who are exhibiting normal reactions to severely abnormal circumstances. Psychological triage may be performed with an initial psychological screening in disasters to assess psychological status of the person and provide information on who should be served next or in what manner. However, disaster and trauma counselors do not typically focus on assigning a diagnosis of mental illness in early stages of intervention, but rather work to provide assistance, support, and/or referrals for those experiencing the most extreme reactions, and to normalize and support strength-based or resilient disaster or trauma responses (Halpern & Tramontin, 2007). Such an approach avoids the possibility of future negative effects to the survivor by assigning an inaccurate or overly negative diagnosis to a person and exposing them to negative effects of stigmatization or erosion of sense of self-esteem, competence, and coping capability.

Fidelity

Fidelity is about keeping promise and commitment, and exemplifying honesty and loyalty (Cottone et al., 2022). This principle entails counselors to honor their words and to be true to their relationship with clients. In the aftermath of trauma, victims often relate their experiences to loss of control and to violations of trust. They lose a sense of their trust in others, self, and even their higher powers. As they see the world in a different light, they need help to reframe the notion of trust. Apart from facilitating clients to reestablish trust, counselors must be vigilant of their role in modeling trust. Counselors must practice genuineness and caution. Their words must be consistent with their actions, and experienced disaster and trauma counselors take particular care to promise only those things that they are certain that they can deliver, and to take extraordinary pains to assure that these obligations are met. By the same token, counselors must demonstrate trust in clients and encourage clients to keep their words, as it is crucial for them to learn to reestablish trust in themselves. Counselors' abilities to maintain proper boundaries with their clients and survivors, although related to the ethical principle of nonmaleficence as discussed earlier, also are integral to assisting the clients in reestablishing a sense that relationships are safe, stable, secure, and can be trusted even in the aftermath of tragedy and trauma. Disaster and trauma survivors are not in a position to protect themselves from exploitation, fraud, and incompetence, so the obligations of counselors to retain the objectivity and concern for the integrity of the client–survivor–counselor relationship assume added importance (Sommers-Flanagan, 2007).

TRAUMA AND THE CLINICIAN

It is apparent in the earlier discussion of the ethical principles that obligate the disaster and trauma counselor that ethical violations are more likely when counselors do not monitor and address their personal vulnerabilities through such steps as assessing their own motivations for helping and monitoring their levels of self-care and wellness (Cottone et al., 2022; Sommers-Flanagan, 2007). It would be ideal if wounded healers could use their own wounds as a source of healing (Nouwen, 1972). Some people have entered the counseling field as a result of their experience of suffering, which inspires them to help people alleviate pain and affliction. They believe that what they have gone through will help them understand their clients' agonies. No doubt, wounded counselors' experiences can be valuable and helpful. Yet, counselors must first become aware of their vulnerabilities and be prepared to manage them to enhance rather than detract from their capacities to help their clients. More important, they must recognize that trauma work, especially, can take a physical and emotional toll on them and erode their abilities to maintain appropriate levels of wellness and professional presence. More specifically, ethical counselors need to be mindful of projecting their own traumatic experience onto clients (McGee, 2005). ACA's *Code of Ethics* demands that counselors be aware of their impairments and be psychologically healthy and well for their work.

Paradoxically, empathy can be counselors' most profound gift as well as a burden. Counselors who offer empathy attempt to enter into clients' worlds. This empathic movement into the experiential and emotional world of clients can put counselors at high risk for developing secondary trauma or compassion fatigue (Shallcross, 2010). Ethical practice requires trauma counselors to become informed about the very specific risks of secondary trauma, to discern their risk of becoming "wounded healers," to explore effective and palatable means to deal with compassion fatigue, and to incorporate professional and personal self-care practices into their daily routines (Cottone et al., 2022; Sommers-Flanagan, 2007). Some of these issues are described at further length in the following text.

The Wounded Healer, Compassion Fatigue, and Self-Care

The personhood of the clinician is highly relevant when counseling survivors of trauma. For this reason, issues regarding the wounded healer, compassion fatigue, and self-care are examined in this section.

The Wounded Healer

One of the acquired skills of counselors is active listening. Simple as it may sound, it is taxing when counselors attempt to listen with the eyes and ears of their hearts to clients' account of traumatic experiences. The sight of wounds and damage and the sound of devastating cries flash vividly on counselors' mental movie screens. This devastating scenario may repeat as clients retell their stories, often accompanied by vivid displays of the emotions and traumatic circumstances they experienced. The impact can be magnified when counselors work with different clients on their debilitating experiences within an intense, brief period. Clients' predicaments incite counselors' empathic responses to enter mentally into the situation, and to take the risk of becoming psychologically injured themselves (Nouwen, 1972). How far and how deeply can counselors' involvement go? In circumstances when counselors' own traumatic issues are not yet resolved, countertransference is more likely to develop, exacerbating the level of risk to both counselor and client. Counselors must ensure that their unresolved issues do not induce harm to themselves, to clients, and to the therapeutic relationship, and accept that everyone has a susceptibility that may render them fragile to boundary crossing (Wicks, 2007). Refer to Chapters 30 and 31.

Compassion Fatigue

Figley (as cited in Sommer, 2008) describes compassion fatigue as the rippling effects of trauma that are experienced by both the primary survivors and people with whom they are in contact. Compassion fatigue is a term developed by traumatologist Charles Figley, describing the stress developed as a result of helping or being involved with people who experience trauma or extreme predicaments (Figley, 1995). Figley credited Joinson with using the term "compassion fatigue" to delineate burnout among nurses (as cited in Sommer, 2008). Sommer credited McCann and Pearlman with using the term "vicarious trauma." Chapter 30 is dedicated to the discussion of vicarious trauma whereby compassion fatigue will be explored and examined in a detailed fashion.

Peter Teahen has had decades of active national and international disaster response experience as president of the International Mass Fatalities Center, and with the American Red Cross (2020) and other national and international disaster response agencies. Teahen (2011) underscored the tremendous emotional and practical demands placed on disaster response workers, which expose them to greater risk for ongoing psychosocial difficulties. He placed the additional disaster worker-specific reactions and emotional responses within the context of the overall emotional phases of disaster recovery, originally described by Zunin and Myers (2000), that all participants in a disaster experience in the heroic, honeymoon, disillusionment, and reconstruction phases of disaster (Teahen, 2011). The range and seriousness of the demands and reactions experienced by disaster workers are portrayed in Table 29.1. These disaster worker reactions can be summarized into four emotional phases during a deployment cycle: the alarm, mobilization, action, and letdown phases. As a result of these demands, Teahen has strongly advocated that the needs of responders and their families must be prioritized along with the needs of the survivors and their families in any mass fatalities incident.

With regard to compassion fatigue in relation to ethical practice, trauma counselors are asked to pay attention to the effects of their levels of empathy on the internalization of their clients' traumas (Conrad & Kellar-Guenther, 2006). However, it is important to note that not all counselors experience compassion fatigue. Further, personal developmental levels of experience and other individual traits can protect or affect the individual emotional susceptibility of counselors (Stebnicki, 2008).

Wicks (2006) contended that trauma work precipitates another source of stress as counselors stand in the crossroad of ethical dilemma. For instance, counselors may be perplexed by different values that pose a challenge to their ethical concerns. For example, disaster counselors may be dismayed to witness a violent, angry reaction on the part of the local survivors against their insistence that a Red Cross hurricane evacuation shelter be set up without racial division. Such circumstances can be spiritually and emotionally draining for counselors. Another phenomenon that merits attention is selflessness. It is a poignant act when helpers wholeheartedly dedicate their efforts to helping others. Yet, selflessness can work against ethically sensitive practice,

Table 29.1

Disaster Worker Reactions by Emotional Phases of Disaster Recovery

Reactions of All Disaster Participants	Disaster Worker-Specific Experiences (Added to Reactions of All Participants)
Heroic Phase	
Shock	Stress of check-in and orientation
Fear	Frustration and anxiety to get started
Confusion	Once in action, inability to "let down" or rest
Adrenaline rush	Identification with victims
Heroic acts	Loyalty to fellow responders; living or dead
Coming together	
Honeymoon Phase	
Attendance to basic needs in a chaotic environment	Long hours for many days
Concerns about safety, food, and shelter	Constant exposure to clients and their losses
Unrealistic optimism about recovery	Thinking "but . . . I'm OK"
Community cohesion, sharing of resources, cooperation	
Denial of needs and emotional impact	
Disillusionment Phase	
Reality of impact	Overwhelmed by magnitude of losses
Realization of losses and work to be done	Pressures of community expectations and self-expectations
Procedures to get assistance are frustrating	Sleep deprivation and safety issues
Community politics emerge	Interpersonal and organization conflict
Grieving	Staff turnover
Health problems	
Family stress, domestic violence, substance abuse issues	
Reconstruction Phase	
Long phase of rebuilding financially, psychologically, physically, and spiritually	Left with follow-up
	Out-processing
Light at the end of the tunnel	Reorientation of thoughts to home and regular job
Begin to put disaster behind	"Let down," sense of loss, guilt of not doing enough
Renewed feeling of empowerment	
Posttraumatic stress disorder, depression, anxiety	
Return to predisaster activities	

Source: Adapted from Teahen, P. R. (2011). *Mass fatalities: Managing the community response.* Taylor Francis.

through overextension and a lack of self-care, which results in a counselor who is emotionally numb to her client's experience of her rape. Professional associations in person-centered disciplines, such as the ACA, APA, and the American Medical Association (AMA), require members to identify and guard against professional fatigue (Stebnicki, 2008). Competent and ethical healing efforts require healthy and well-grounded professionals (Stebnicki, 2008). Emotionally drained counselors are like an overdrawn bank account. Imagine the incredibly high bank charges that the account holder has to pay due to regular or prolonged overdrafts of more money than what is available. The role of counselor educators is to gauge harmful impact on counselors. Counselor educators and professional organization leaders can play a role in diminishing the harmful effects of many of these challenges to counselors through their efforts to provide relevant training for counselors to guard against possible harm to clients and counselors (Sommer, 2008). The addition of disaster and trauma-counseling educational standards by the Council for Accreditation for Counseling and Related Educational Programs (CACREP, 2016), in its educational program accreditation standards, is a very positive development that furthers this goal in counseling.

Self-Care

In addition to training, self-care is an approach that not only supports trauma counselors to cope with compassion or emotional fatigue, but also serves as a proactive means to prepare counselors for potential risk of injury. Counselors must learn about the meaning of self-care and incorporate personal and professional self-care into their life routines. Hamilton (2007) articulated that personal and professional self-care is the central means that helps counselors thwart compassion fatigue. Cottone et al. (2022) articulated that personal self-care skills include healthy personal habits, attention to relationships, recreational activities, relaxation and centeredness, and self-exploration and awareness. Some examples of personal self-care activities are physical exercise, massage therapy, balanced diet, sufficient sleep, movies, and concerts. Time spent on artwork, social events, and traveling are equally important. Professional self-care skills include continuing education, consultation and supervision, networking, and stress management strategies (Cottone et al., 2022). In addition, counselors must strive to balance workload and work hours, pace client meetings and the day to allow for breaks, integrate reflection into the day, and take time off for vacations. Understanding and complying with the ethics code suggest counselors' honesty to clients and themselves. Counselors' self-care behaviors are related to their work and their relationship with clients in a very elemental way.

Engaging in work that exceeds one's physical and emotional capacity is a disservice to clients. Seeing too many clients with devastating issues within a short period can lead to burnout and compassion fatigue. For counselors working at agencies where cases are assigned to them, it is both their responsibility and that of the organization to recognize the point when "enough is enough" (Bober & Regehr, 2005). Counselors have the ethical responsibility to advocate for their own health and functionality and to decline assigned workloads that they realize are beyond their limits. They can model self-care only when they are able to demonstrate to clients that they safeguard their own well-being (Welfel, 2005). It is also important that counselors do not deny stress. Knowing that stress is part of their lives, counselors must develop an accepting attitude toward it. Avoiding and limiting emotional fatigue in their own lives allow them to live out the passion in their work (Wicks, 2006). Chapter 31 contains more in-depth discussion on self-care, and readers should reflect upon the personal questions raised in Box 29.2 to better assess their current readiness for trauma and disaster work.

BOX 29.2

Tips From the Field

Questions for Personal Reflection Before Responding to Trauma or Disaster

1. Why am I interested in trauma or disaster response work?
2. How would my responding affect those around me?
3. What strengths do I bring as a responder?
4. What liabilities do I have as a responder?

(continued)

5. After personal reflection, what stage or type of trauma or disaster response best fits my unique profile of personal and professional characteristics, and still fulfills my healthy humanitarian impulses to help?
6. What activities, learning, or counseling do I need to undertake to either improve or maintain my capabilities to respond? Now? While engaged in response work?

Clinical Supervision

Clinical supervisors have their share of ethical responsibilities in trauma work. There is more scholarly interest in this area, and ACA and the National Board for Certified Counselors (NBCC, 1993) have established ethical guidelines for clinical supervisors that may guide their efforts with counselors in trauma-related work.

Association for Counselor Education and Supervision Guidelines

The Association for Counselor Education and Supervision (ACES, 1990) has established ethical guidelines for counseling supervisors, which specify that supervisors must administer ongoing assessment and evaluation of supervisees who must be aware of their personal and professional limitations that relate to their counseling efforts. Thus, supervisors are responsible for examining supervisees' competency and recommending relevant remedial assistance and service as needed.

National Board for Certified Counselors Code of Ethics for Approved Clinical Supervisors

The approved clinical supervisor code of ethics of the NBCC has listed several standards for clinical supervisors relevant to supervisory work in crisis and trauma counseling. For instance, supervisors are to arrange for training procedures with supervisees in connection with crisis management situations. Supervisors must intervene when supervisees are impaired and clients are at risk. In situations where supervisors notice that supervisees are incapable of providing adequate services, supervisors must avoid letting supervisees continue their work with clients.

Trauma-Sensitive Supervisors

It is imperative that supervisors incorporate trauma-sensitive supervision into their training. Supervisors of trauma counselors need to be vigilant of changes in counselors' behaviors and any extraordinary signs of stress or compassion fatigue (Sommer, 2008). For instance, supervisors must recognize when counselors are exhibiting problematic or changed patterns of substance use (Cross & Ashley, 2007). ACA has recognized the critical need to support counselors' personal and professional growth. In response to this need, clinical supervisors must pay attention to counselors' integration of self-care into their agendas. Supervisors also can lessen the chance of counselors developing compassion or emotional fatigue by using sound judgment when assigning traumatic cases to counselors, because counselors themselves may feel obligated to take on whatever cases are assigned by the supervisor or manager even when they are physically or emotionally exhausted. Supervisors too must practice self-care in order to serve as models for counselors. Technicalities and details of clinical supervision with regard to such need are further discussed in Chapter 32.

Multicultural Sensitivity

Sensitivity to multicultural perspectives is particularly germane to ethically competent counseling practice in trauma and disaster counseling. ACA's (2014) definition of counseling highlights diversity, which suggests counselors' sensitivity and respect for differences among individuals. People with traumatic experiences tend to develop their own culture, in addition to whatever pre-event diversity characteristics they may have. Their posttrauma perceptions of the world are different, and their levels of sensitivity to people and events are different. In brief, their beliefs, thoughts, feelings, and actions are characterized by their own culture. Considering trauma as a culture, counselors who are involved in overseas counseling work are simultaneously addressing a constellation of multicultural issues. Egan (2010) suggested the understanding of clients and their problem situations be viewed contextually. Cottone et al. (2022) cautioned counselors to be mindful of being culturally encapsulated. Cultural encapsulation refers to counselors' using their own socially constructed lens to view clients' experiences (Cottone et al., 2022).

First and foremost, counselors need to understand what trauma means for their clients. Counselors must develop sensitivity to understanding of clients' cultural background and current beliefs and values because these cultural nuances can have substantial impact on the way they respond to traumatic situations. Clients' cultural heritage also explains the meaning and types of support clients receive or do not receive from their families, friends, and communities. With regard to traumatic treatment, major ethical standards require that counselors be vigilant of their respect for autonomy of culturally different clients (Eagle, 2005). As stated earlier, counselors should not coerce clients to try to participate in any service or experience if they are reluctant to do so. Counselors must be sensitive to taboos or cultural traditions that deter clients from receiving treatments other than those consistent with their ethnic origins. For example, it would be culturally inappropriate for a conservative, traditional Muslim woman to have one-on-one counseling from a male counselor, no matter the dire nature of the circumstances. Likewise, counselors must be careful about making judgments of therapeutic treatments that are embraced by clients' ethnic culture. Also, counselors need to be gentle and culturally tactful when gathering information from clients about their traumatic experience. Cultural stigma attached to clients' ordeals may make it difficult, if not impossible, to verbalize what has happened.

In addition, having some knowledge about clients' religious beliefs is helpful to trauma counseling work. For instance, some cultures perceive suffering as something relating to one's spiritual path. Thus, counselors working with clients from different cultural backgrounds must develop sensitivity to the spiritual meaning clients assign to pain and suffering. Also, counselors must prepare their hearts and minds for exposures to a wide spectrum of agonies. In effect, counselors preparing themselves for trauma work in a foreign culture must endeavor to be culturally competent and be able to identify clients' capacity and means for healing (Shallcross, 2010). It would be ironic for ill-prepared counselors to receive comfort and solace from people who just experienced trauma, but much worse when counselors' disturbed reactions to trauma risk amplifying clients' afflictions.

Intersectionality

Intersectionality is a concept put forth by Black feminist scholars to reference the discrimination Black women experience in society. Over time, the term "intersectionality" has expanded to encompass an approach which recognizes that clients may belong to more than one minority group, based on their race/ethnicity, gender, disability status, religion, or other group with which they identify, and which informs their experiences. Counselors who take an intersectionality approach do so in recognition of the fact that clients' race/ethnicity, gender, disability status, age, and religion are not mutually exclusive or additive, but rather encompass the totality of their experiences, including systemic barriers such as discrimination (Levine & Breshears, 2019).

Ethical practice requires counselors to be competent in multicultural and social justice theories and techniques, as well as to possess an understanding of intersectionality. Clients who have experienced trauma or natural disaster may be a member of one or more marginalized groups (e.g., disability, gender, race/ethnicity) and counselors must understand the relationship between marginalized status and societal inequity, discrimination, and injustice.

In summary, counselors must be well equipped for trauma work in a culturally diverse place before beginning. Once in place, they must be open to learning from and relying on the assistance of the survivors themselves, cultural guides, and leaders in the cultural community with which they are working to assist them in more fully understanding the cultural context of their clients.

SURVIVORS AS CONSUMERS OF SERVICES

Trauma and suffering are common aspects of human life, and it is safe to assume that most adults have experienced or witnessed traumatic events in their lives. Survivors are people who have experienced and endured traumatic events. In the counseling domain, some clients have suffered trauma, and some of them have recovered from their suffering as a result of receiving counseling. Some might not have received therapeutic help; however, family and social support enabled them to function and return to regular routines. For others, the urgency of meeting their basic needs rendered them no time to focus on their suffering. By and by, these individuals all move from victims' to survivors' positions. In most cases, people who have not processed their traumatic ailment are not fully aware of their changed worldviews, beliefs, and behaviors. When they seek counseling later in life, their unresolved pain may surface somewhere in the process. Ethical practice requires counselors to heighten their sensitivity and awareness of clients' feelings, thoughts, and behaviors that may be associated with their clients' previous traumatic experiences. At this juncture, counselors must demonstrate their competency to assess clients' comfort level in dealing with their unresolved pain. In other words, counselors need to make sensible decisions with regard to clients' emotional capacity to confront pain and suffering.

Consumers of counseling services in trauma and crisis counseling come from different developmental stages; for example, some are children and young adolescents, and others are older adults. From an ethical point of view, counselors must receive training and cultivate skills appropriate for trauma work with specific populations; counselors must know how to address their unique needs. For example, it is helpful for them to know how children's responses to trauma differ from those of adults (Hosin, 2007). Are children more or less resilient to traumatic events? Also, counselors need to know which intervention approaches best suit children and how to apply them. Finally, counselors must ensure that these approaches are palatable to children with culturally different backgrounds.

TRANSFORMATION FROM VICTIM TO SURVIVOR

As stated earlier, feelings and interpretations of pain and suffering are unique among individuals. In other words, diversities of culture, belief, experience, and personality make a difference to people's experience of trauma. Correspondingly, the pace for people to transform from victims to survivors is something unique to the individual. It is not surprising to find some people staying in the victim's status for a very long period. Likewise, it is not astonishing to come across people who transition from victims to survivors in a matter of days. Ethically minded counselors must demonstrate prudence in making decisions to offer help to individuals who experience difficulty in transforming from victim to survivor. Realizing that transformation is a process, counselors may want to know where their clients stand along the transformation continuum and make careful judgments about the pace and manner with which clients move through this process.

Faith serves as the catalyst of change for some people. Therefore, it is helpful to explore with clients their religious beliefs. It is equally important to explore with clients some of the relevant existential aspects of the meaning they have assigned to their traumatic event or disaster experience. There are people whose traumatic experience inspires them to delve deeper into their purpose or meaning of life. For them, trauma brings new perspectives and meaning to life, and they may even view trauma as an opportunity of growth or transformation.

Although some trauma victims are able to rise above their predicaments, some may take a while to negotiate their emotions. Anger is another common emotion experienced by trauma victims and survivors. It is a legitimate feeling and healthy expression if it does not cause harm to anyone. Nevertheless, being angry as a result of trauma can consume a lot of energy. Ethical practice inspires mental health clinicians to explore with victims the source of their anger. It is important for these clinicians to work with victims to identify healthy coping mechanisms. Interestingly, some people are able to transfer anger into meaningful work (McGee, 2005). Counselors can encourage clients to express their anger, to let go of their negative energy, and to convert such energy into some positive sources. In the counseling field, it is not surprising to find that the helping intentions of some come from the source of anger. Their anger coupled with their sense of justice may be transformed into an ethical and helping spirit. Such a transformation process is cathartic, but it demands from sufferers a lot of courage and strength to negotiate with the painful truth and to confront feelings of loneliness, loss, and guilt. This profound experience provides them with a deeper understanding of the pain associated with this transformation. This is the opportunity for trauma helpers to intervene, facilitating clients to transform their agony into a source of ethical helping spirit. With reference to the discussion of aspirational ethics earlier in the chapter, such opportunity entails trauma helpers to practice the sophisticated level of ethics.

SURVIVOR INPUT TO THERAPY AND RECOVERY

It is possibly one of all counselors' most important ethical obligations to avoid nurturing client dependency or prolonging the counseling process when clients can stand on their own. The process of client transformation from victim to survivor is essential to this shift. Ethical counselors need to be aware of and understand this shift. Fritz Perls' theory of "homeostasis" illuminates the process of transformation whereby people who are traumatized, after going through some stages (such as receiving support from others, getting therapeutic help, or using personal resources), proceed from the stance of victims to survivors, and eventually arrive at the stage of healing. Perls (1973) argued that human living is about the constant play of balance and imbalance in the organism, which is connected to two goals: survival and growth. These goals explain people's strength to regain balance and to move on with their lives. Beyond survival and growth, some individuals are able to thrive as they persevere the experience of desolation, moving toward consolation. Such experience may become the driving force of their yearning to help others. Also, their sufferings may make them effective role models of trauma survivors as well as agents of change. Meanwhile, Taoist philosophy of the force of *yin and yang* aligns with the concept of homeostasis. *Yin* is the negative force and *yang* is the positive force. The uniqueness of individuals implies the different makeups of these two forces. These forces facilitate human beings to seek and maintain balance. Counselors can refer to these two schools of thought when working with trauma victims and survivors. Homeostasis and the forces of yin and yang exemplify the compelling flow of human adaptation, which is a source of strength and survival. In brief, counselors are responsible for helping clients identify and recognize their strengths, and strengths based on empowerment approaches to counseling are most effective in eliciting healing and recovery of survivors of trauma and disaster (Dass-Brailsford, 2007).

SURVIVOR MISSION

In the face of torment and life-threatening agonies, who can relate the experience they are going through to something as abstract sounding as a mission? Perhaps only martyrs can identify their suffering with their mission. Unfortunately, these people died, and the only things surviving in them are their spirits. Nonetheless, many trauma survivors eventually discover their meaning of suffering, and some invest their efforts in the helping professions. These survivors help people by providing emotional and spiritual support, by advocating on behalf of the victims, or by offering necessary food and household supplies.

One way in which this need for survivors to contribute to the increased well-being of others who experience trauma might be through participation in research studies. As scholarly interest in traumatology grows, it is becoming increasingly common in fields of mental health, education, and counseling that researchers invite people with traumatic experiences to participate in research studies. It is important that people in trauma-focused research exercise their ethical sensitivity when selecting participants, conducting surveys or interviews, analyzing, interpreting, and reporting information. In other words, the design, implementation, and summary of the research and findings must adhere to the principles of autonomy, justice, nonmaleficence, beneficence, fidelity, and truth (Newman et al., 2006), and careful consideration to the protection of vulnerable human subjects must be made. These issues are crucial to the work of researchers and institutional review boards (IRBs) at countless universities. Researchers must weigh the risks against the benefits of the research. In addition, sensitivity to and respect for cultural diversities must be part of the ethical concerns in trauma-related research. Sumathipala and Siribaddana (2005) spoke about trauma survivors who were prone to exploitation in their participation in international research studies cloaked in clinical care. The writers urged journal editors to be adamant about getting the endorsement from the country where research information is gathered. The writers also suggested researchers to refer to the "guidance for postdisaster research" (as cited in Sumathipala & Siribaddana, 2005) and acquire familiarity of the customs of the people and place where information and data are gathered and analyzed. Another group of potential research participants who deserve additional protection is children (Chu et al., 2008). There was no specific evidence that trauma-exposed children are more vulnerable to the possible costs of research than their nonexposed peers (Chu et al., 2008). Yet, it is important that trauma-focused researchers make relevant information transparent to parents and guardians.

COUNSELING IMPLICATIONS

This chapter does not close with a simple "conclusion," because it is really an opening to an enormous chest of ethical considerations that promotes advancement in counselors' work in the realm of trauma. The prevalence of suffering in contemporary society is the compelling reality that must be marked and attended to in every way possible (Cimperman, 2005). Traumatic occurrences have unfortunately become a sign of the times. Natural disasters, global pandemics, wars and other conflicts, inter-partner violence, and suicide are all on the rise. Approximately 50% of women and 60% of men will experience some form of trauma in their lives (National Center for PTSD, 2019). Therefore, it is crucial for counselors to perceive ethical concern and practice as processes and moral imperatives, rather than technical tasks.

Ethical Behaviors

Counselors study and take examinations to obtain the qualifications required to practice in the field. Some people are adept in writing examinations, although others are less skillful. When it comes to ethical practice, what do the examination scores indicate regarding counselors' ethical standing? Do counselors' high scores on ethical questions guarantee their ethical practice? One of the most challenging examinations of their ethical competency as counselors might be the examination of their ethical behavior in trauma and disaster counseling when accountability is obscured by the chaos of crisis (Sommers-Flanagan, 2007). As counselors think ahead to the day they retire, when they look back to their trauma work, it would be meaningful to reminisce over the experiences of being present for people when they are helpless and devastated. More importantly, examining past experiences and linking them to planning for future work helps counselors to sharpen their sensitivities and perspectives, as well as minimizing chances of regret. This crucial process is called "reflection." Reflection assists counselors in being proactive and ready for possible challenges. This proactive attitude resonates with Tarvydas et al.'s (2010) argument that a valuable code of ethics must be able "to anticipate emerging problems and issues" (p. 3), in addition to guiding counselors to make sound judgments and take ethical courses of action.

Moral Behaviors

Morality can be taught and caught. People learn about moral behaviors at home, in school, at work, and in society. Quite often, people observe others' practice of morality and recognize its importance to human lives. Complying with ethics demonstrates respect for one's profession, and practicing morality embodies a respect for self and others. For counselors, it would be ideal to incorporate the principles of autonomy, justice, fidelity, nonmaleficence, and beneficence into their everyday ways of living. Counselors should live out the ethics codes not because of their fear of violating jurisdictions, but because of their ardent desires to protect clients' well-being and to respect their profession. Counselors can begin by nurturing their ethical hearts and minds. Consider the case where a counselor tells a trauma victim that he cares about her because he is "doing his job." This counselor might be adept and diligent in observing rules and principles; however, his words might have led the client to think that he is doing what he needs to keep his job or maintain his work status. His words fail to convey genuine care and support to the client. People's behaviors are lived manifestations of their thoughts and feelings. Counselors who have not fully examined and aligned their ethical thinking processes with their feelings about their work and their skills may exhibit awkward and inconsistent behaviors under the duress of trauma counseling. Counselors' work with clients can be likened to a dance. In this dance, clients are sensitive to counselors' moral movements and ethical ideals and aspirations should be likened to the music that harmonizes intention with action, allowing the counselor and client to share in a respectful and dignified dance of recovery and celebration.

Moral Suffering in the Provision of Care During the COVID-19 Pandemic

As of this writing, the United States is nearly a year into what will likely be a multi-year global pandemic. Natural disasters, such as pandemics, cause social and economic disruption. The trauma of crises and their aftermath cause significant psychological distress, including depression, anxiety, grief, and hopelessness. The burdens are not shared equally, however, because disasters exacerbate existing structural inequalities. Marginalized populations experience more severe disruptions during the event and continue to experience them long after the crisis abates (Beaudoin, 2009). Pandemics in particular place enormous and long-lasting strains on healthcare infrastructure and related community services (Emanuel et al., 2020).

As the pandemic persists, counselors will work with clients who have experienced deep losses due to the pandemic. Counselors must be sensitive to the needs of clients who have experienced disproportionate effects from the pandemic, such as essential workers who are unable to work from home, racial/ethnic minorities at higher risk for serious complications from the virus, and families coping with disruptions to education and work. Some of these clients may be healthcare workers who are experiencing physical and psychological difficulties related to caring for COVID-19 clients in a healthcare system pushed to capacity by the pandemic. As COVID-19 spread around the world, anecdotal evidence emerged about the toll the pandemic has taken on healthcare clinicians, including working longer hours for extended periods of time; working while ill, as well as working while ill with COVID-19; lack of adequate personal protective equipment (PPE); concern that they, their clients, and their colleagues are not adequately protected from COVID-19, and that they may, in fact, be further spreading the virus; and the fear of carrying the virus home to their families on their clothes, shoes, and bodies. Many clinicians report that they have written a will due to their fear of contracting and dying from COVID-19 (Adams & Walls, 2020). Finally, pandemic-related triage plans and rationing of care have been put in place by healthcare systems, and supplies and care have been rationed in South Korea, the United Kingdom, Italy, and New York and other parts of the United States (Emmanuel et al., 2020; Wong, 2020).

Triage planning and rationing of care may create troubling ethical dilemmas for healthcare clinicians and first responders related to the ethical principles of beneficence, nonmaleficence, and justice. Earlier in the chapter, burnout and compassion fatigue were discussed in the context of providing counseling services to clients who have experienced trauma. Healthcare clinicians who have been asked to work long hours over an extended period of time with seriously ill and dying COVID-19 clients are certainly at risk for burnout and may exhibit physical and psychological symptoms such as exhaustion, depression, substance abuse, and suicidal ideation (Lagasse, 2020). They also may experience symptoms of compassion fatigue, such as a loss of empathy for the clients they are caring for (Figley, 1995). Healthcare clinicians who are asked to make decisions that are contrary to their morals and values, under a triage plan or rationing of care, are at risk for *moral suffering*, which is defined as "the anguish that caregivers experience in response to various forms of moral adversity, such as moral harms, wrongs or failures, or unrelieved moral stress, that in some way imperil integrity" (Rushton, 2018, pp. 12–13).

Moral suffering includes the intertwined concepts of "moral injury" and "moral distress." Moral injury encompasses situations that put a healthcare clinician into the position of knowing what needs to be done ethically and morally to provide care but being unable to provide that care due to restrictions or regulations beyond the clinician's control (Dean et al., 2019). The term includes any decisions or behaviors that require a clinician to perpetrate, fail to prevent, or bear witness to an action that violates a clinician's morals, ethics, and beliefs (Litz et al., 2009; Rushton, 2018). In the context of the pandemic, a clinician may face the ethical dilemma of following comfort protocols in allowing family to see their dying family member (beneficence) versus following COVID-19 protocols in allowing the person to die alone to protect the family, hospital staff, and the public from contracting the virus (nonmaleficence). Moral distress is the emotional response to experiences which require clinicians to make morally injurious decisions, such as guilt, shame, or horror, and which may result in a breakdown of trust in leadership and institutions (Bard & Bursztajn, 2020; Dean et al., 2019; Papazoglou & Chopko, 2017; Shay, 2014). Rushton asserts that addressing moral suffering requires both individual and systemic interventions.

Counselors have an ethical responsibility to be vigilant for the signs of burnout and to practice self-care to ensure that they are not practicing in an impaired state that may harm clients (Cottone et al., 2022). During the COVID-19 pandemic, counselors may have a further ethical responsibility to recognize the symptoms of burnout and compassion fatigue, as well as moral suffering, in their colleagues in the fields of nursing, respiratory therapy, medicine, and other health- and behavioral healthcare-related fields. They may also need to advocate for education, training, and counseling to address clinician burnout, compassion fatigue, and moral suffering. Counselors also must advocate for system change to address the systemic issues in the provision of healthcare which may lead to moral suffering as well as a breakdown of trust in leadership and institutions (Cottone et al., 2022; Nerlich et al., 2021).

CONCLUSION

The practice of trauma and disaster counseling is a highly meaningful one for both the counselor and client if the painful, complex, and ethically charged process is successfully navigated. This chapter has provided an understanding of the basic aspects of trauma from the ethical perspective. The importance of using a credible ethical decision-making model has been emphasized, and unique facets of the application of the five core ethical principles to trauma counseling practice were discussed. Understanding and reflecting upon the obligations entailed by the principles of autonomy, justice, beneficence, nonmaleficence, and fidelity allow counselors to better negotiate ethical dilemmas that arise in trauma contexts. The impact of trauma on the clinician, the wounded healer, and compassion fatigue have been considered as a way to develop important understandings of the challenges that are unique to trauma and disaster counseling. More specific ethical issues involved in clinical supervision, multicultural sensitivity, transformation of victim to survivor, and ethical practice implications of the COVID-19 pandemic were reviewed. Finally, an online list of resources for further ethical practice have been provided to the reader for further study.

ADDITIONAL RESOURCES

 A robust set of instructor resources designed to supplement this text is located at http://connect.springerpub.com/content/book/978-0-8261-5085-1. Qualifying instructors may request access by emailing textbook@springerpub.com.

PRACTICE-BASED RESOURCES AND REFERENCES

To view a list of resources and all the references, please visit connect.springerpub.com via the following url: http://connect.springerpub.com/content/book/978-0-8261-5085-1/part/part06/chapter/ch29

CHAPTER 30

Vicarious Traumatization

JO ANN JANKOSKI

CHAPTER OVERVIEW

This chapter focuses on a major occupational hazard associated with working in the human service field. The work exposure to traumatic material through compassionate listening, case reviews, working during a pandemic, responding to a fatality, delivering a death notification, and attending to acts of hate and terrorism and so much more requires an understanding of how each event has the potential to affect mental health workers in profound ways. There is a cost of caring, and human service professionals owe it to themselves—as well as to those for whom they work, to colleagues, and to loved ones—to learn about vicarious trauma and to understand how to intervene as needed, while creating healthy strategies for self-care.

LEARNING OBJECTIVES

After reading this chapter, the reader should be able to:

1. Discuss the four major concepts in the field of psychotraumatology;
2. Understand the personality theory that is integrated with vicarious trauma;
3. Identify and discuss signs and symptoms of vicarious trauma;
4. Develop awareness about ethical responsibility for self-care; and,
5. Name and discuss the Five Self-Capacities of Constructivist Self-Development Theory.

INTRODUCTION

We are living in a world we could not have anticipated at the beginning of this century. We knew or had heard about the 1918 Spanish Flu pandemic, polio, Ebola, the H1N1 flu, SARS, and other epidemics. Little did we know that we would be facing the COVID-19 public health crisis, with which we are faced as I write this. At this moment, each one of us is living through a traumatic event—the COVID-19 pandemic. We also are experiencing civil unrest, related to systemic racism, and political division, with an increase in hate incidents throughout the country. Along with readers, I have been making daily changes in both my personal and professional life.

Of all the different careers from which we could have chosen, why did we select the professional human services field? What was *our* thinking or reasoning when we chose to become a professional counselor, social worker, or other human service provider? Each one of

Figure 30.1

The Aspects of Listening

"TO LISTEN"

Ear

You
Eyes
Undivided
Attention

Heart

---

us was led by some motivation—wanting to make a difference in the world; advocating for others and promoting social justice issues; responding to emergencies; working in criminal justice; serving as a caseworker for children and adolescents; working with victims of domestic violence; helping returning soldiers; working with victims of physical, sexual, or drug and alcohol abuse; or working to prevent suicides. The list goes on.

I know that each one of us has made (or will make) a difference, but to what personal cost? Through our educational programs, we all receive the knowledge and skills necessary to care for others and to respond to their emotional needs; however, we receive very little, if any, training regarding care for ourselves.

Our master's programs prepare us with theories, research, interventions, practicums, and internships. One of the most important skills we are taught, and which we use on a daily basis, is active listening. In fact, the foundation of the human service profession *is* listening and our willingness to be present with the individuals whom we serve. An interesting side note here is the Chinese symbol for listening; notice that the symbol for "to listen" includes not only the "you" but also the person's ears, eyes, and heart along with undivided attention (Figure 30.1). Active listening, to be more specific, teaches "how to listen" so that we may fully understand the world in which our clients live.

What our master's programs often do not teach us is about the impact that trauma has, not on the victims we serve, but on us—the human service professionals. How well were we prepared for the emotional impact of listening, seeing, or responding to the human pain to which we must bear witness each day? How many times have we heard, "How do you do that every day?" or "I couldn't do what you do." How many of us have ever left work in the middle of a workday, screened our calls at home, or continued to think about one of our clients, wondering if they are okay? How likely might it be to become cynical about those we serve? These are all part of the "occupational hazards" we face for knowing, caring, and acknowledging the reality of trauma (Saakvitne & Pearlman, 1996).

THE FIELD OF PSYCHOTRAUMATOLOGY

Traumatic experiences are one of the few phenomena that have no boundaries, are not culturally specific, ignore age, are not prejudiced or biased, and are not gender specific. In reviewing the literature within the field of psychotraumatology, the *continuing* controversy about helping-induced trauma is not "Can it happen?" but rather, "What shall we call it?" (Stamm, 1997, 2009).

van der Kolk and McFarlane (1996) discussed trauma, as it has related to the history of the world:

> Experiencing trauma is an essential part of being human; history is written in blood. Although art and literature have always been preoccupied with how people cope with the inevitable tragedies of life, the large-scale scientific study of the effects of trauma on body and mind has had to wait till the latter part of this century. (p. 3)

In 1997, the former director of the National Center for Posttraumatic Stress Disorder (NCPTSD), Stamm, addressed the effects of trauma on those in helping roles. He said, "It is apparent that there is no routinely used term to designate exposure to another's traumatic material by virtue of one's role as a helper" (NCPTSD, 2007; Stamm, 1997, p. 1). There are four primary terms—countertransference (CT); compassionate fatigue (CF), later renamed secondary traumatic stress (STS); burnout; and vicarious trauma (VT)—which are most commonly used in an attempt to describe the impact of another's trauma on the helper; however, the debate over terminology continues. The primary focus of that debate is involved in describing the emotional toll of working in *high stress*, seemingly hopeless situations with people who suffer emotional pain (Corey et al., 2010; Figley, 1995; Maslach, 1982; McCann & Pearlman, 1990a, 1990b; Saakvitne & Pearlman, 1996).

THE FOUR CONCEPTS

We, as human service professionals, interact with traumatized individuals in our daily work; it is part of the routine, if unwritten, job description. The traumatized individuals with whom we work most often seek a safe environment—a therapeutic sanctuary—in which they eventually engage in an interpersonal relationship in order to move toward recovery so that the "stressful" experience is integrated within their ego structure in ways that are no longer disruptive of normal functioning or distressing to the individual (Herman, 1992). As in any therapeutic setting, the establishment of a trusting and safe environment is paramount; however, the helper is not an "outside observer." Rather, achieving empathy with one's client requires the ability to project oneself into the "phenomenological world being experienced by another person" (Wilson & Lindy, 1994, p. 7). This, indeed, affects the helper. The discussion remains: What shall we call this effect on the helper?

Countertransference

One of the terms often used to refer to the effects that another's trauma may have on the helper is "countertransference" (CT). This term originated with Freud in 1910 and traditionally has referred to "the reciprocal impact that the client and the therapist have on each other during the course of psychotherapy" (Wilson & Lindy, 1994, p. 9). Although Freud never clearly addressed his meaning of CT, he used the condition in a negative sense. Freud's two specific references to CT caution the clinician to "overcome" it (1910) and to keep it "in check" (1915). Freud's position on CT insinuated that the clinician's reaction was based on their own unresolved conflicts (Gorkin, 1987).

By the very nature of our humanness, we can become fascinated from hearing the horrific stories our clients have shared with us. Being human, we could become sexually aroused or excited or even curious about our clients' experiences (Davies & Frawley, 1994). Once this unconscious fascination is brought to the clinician's attention, they often experience feelings of shame, guilt, and/or shock (Neumann & Gamble, 1995).

Saakvitne (1990) introduced the term "container countertransference" to explain one form of CT experienced by some therapists. Clinicians are often asked to respond to a client's impaired capacity to manage and tolerate strong affect (Neumann & Gamble, 1995). The clinician may feel defeated when the client is unable to voice their inner experience or by the client's tendency to vacillate between controlling affect regulation and dramatic emotional abreactions. Caseworkers, therapists, and other professionals who work with the traumatized may encounter CT themes which, if left unaddressed, could affect the clinician in various ways. For example, some professionals may experience "rescue fantasies with intense preoccupation with their clients," "a strong need not to fail their clients," or a sense of "insecurity regarding one's own professional competency" (Neumann & Gamble, 1995, p. 342). Although container CT may explain some emotional problems that affect human service professionals, it does not address all helper issues.

Compassion Fatigue/Secondary Traumatic Stress

In an effort to address the stress experienced by human service professionals, Figley (1995) coined the phrase "compassion fatigue," later referred to as secondary traumatic stress (STS). Figley (1995, p. 10) stated that there is a "cost of caring"; that is, those individuals who care for others often undergo pain as a consequence of their exposure to others' traumatic material. Figley (1995, p. 12) defined STS as "the natural, consequent behaviors and emotions resulting from knowledge about a traumatizing event experienced by a significant other. It is the stress resulting from helping or wanting to help a traumatized or suffering person." In the latter part of the 20th century, a plethora of studies with references to secondary trauma were conducted. Those studies were primarily dedicated to the traumatization of crisis workers, firefighters, police, rescue workers, and emergency medical technicians and therapists (e.g., Horowitz et al., 1980; McCann & Pearlman, 1990b; Raphael et al., 1984; Weiss et al., 1985).

Figley (1999) stated that STS was a natural consequence of working with individuals who had undergone intensely stressful events, contending that STS developed as a result of two things—the clinician's exposure to the client's experiences and the clinician's empathetic engagement with the client. Figley (1995) proposed that family, friends, and professionals are vulnerable to developing traumatic stress symptoms from being empathetically engaged with victims of traumatic events. Other researchers of the late 20th century (e.g., Danieli, 1994; Dyregrov & Mitchell, 1992; Herman, 1988; McCann & Pearlman, 1990a, 1990b; McFarlane, 1986; Munroe, 1990; Pearlman & Saakvitne, 1995a; Pynoos & Eth, 1985; Stamm, 1997, 1999) also contended that traumatic stress symptoms were contagious, creating parallel effects in those who work with trauma victims.

Professionals who choose to work with individuals and their traumatic material undergo the same cluster of traumatic stress symptoms as do the victims of those traumatic events (Beaton & Murphy, 1995; Dyregrov & Mitchell, 1992; Figley, 1995; Horowitz, 1974; Pearlman & Saakvitne, 1995a; Sexton, 1999; Wilson & Lindy, 1994). The symptoms can include sleep disturbances, flashbacks, nightmares, irritability, anxiety, and a sense of loss of control. Trauma and its impact, frequency, and duration vary from person to person; the impact on the professional community is no different. There is an undeniable relationship among the longevity of a career, high caseloads, the intensity and repeated exposure to clients' traumatic material, and long hours to stress traumatic symptoms (Beaton & Murphy, 1995; Chrestman, 1999; Cornille & Meyers, 1999; Munroe, 1990; Pearlman, 1999).

Burnout

Along with the concepts of CT and secondary trauma, "burnout" is another idea that has been used to explain the influence of working with people. Burnout has a negative connotation attached to it. Initially, the term "burnout" referred to the consequences of prolonged drug abuse. Because of this, the concept of burnout is sometimes associated with individuals who are addicted to drugs. Freudenberger (1975) is given credit for introducing the term "burnout" in the human service realm. His model of burnout emphasized an individual psychology, whereas

Maslach (1982) studied burnout from a social-psychological perspective, with the focus on the connection between environmental and individual circumstances.

Maslach (1982), one of the first psychologists to perform research in the area of burnout, reported more than 30 definitions and descriptions of the term. She stated that burnout is a syndrome of emotional exhaustion, depersonalization, and reduced personal accomplishment that can occur among individuals who do "people work" of some kind. It is a response to the chronic emotional strain of dealing extensively with other human beings, particularly when they are troubled or having problems. (p. 3)

Vicarious Traumatization and the Constructivist Self-Development Theory

One does not need to be a professional to experience STS disorder. Family members, friends, coworkers, or any individual who hears, sees, or learns about the toll a traumatic event has on a victim can exhibit PTSD-like symptoms. Although CT, STS disorder, and burnout are significant concepts to assist us in understanding trauma and its impact, none of these concepts address how knowing about another's trauma, hearing about it, or seeing a traumatic event changes us as people.

We, as human service professionals, have chosen our area of specialization so that we may help others. But to what cost to the helpers? How do we make meaning out of the violence inflicted by other humans? What would cause someone to burn a child intentionally with a cigarette on the child's arm or face, shake a baby so violently that the child suffers cerebral hemorrhaging, or place a child on a hot stove to discipline the child? We, as helpers who empathically engage with our clients as they undertake their healing journeys, must be cognitively aware that we can become "hidden victims" in the healing process of others (Duckworth, 1991; Paton, 1989).

Figley (1985) conceptualized trauma as the response, rather than the stressor, related to a situation. He stated that trauma is an "emotional state of discomfort and stress resulting from memories of an extraordinary, catastrophic experience which shattered the survivor's sense of invulnerability to harm" (p. 35). McCann and Pearlman (1990a) went further and defined trauma as an individual's "psychological response" to a situation, adding that it can result in a "paralyzed, overwhelmed state, with immobilization, withdrawal, possible depersonalization, and evidence of disorganization" (p. 13).

McCann and Pearlman (1990a, 1990b) clearly stated that the concepts of burnout and CT are insufficient when trying to understand the impact of trauma work on clinicians. Instead, they proposed a new concept, vicarious traumatization (VT), to describe and articulate the repercussions of trauma and its consequences on therapists. VT, which was coined by Pearlman and Saakvitne, refers to the *transformation* that occurs in a therapist's persona and results from the therapist's empathic engagement with the exposure of another person's trauma material (Pearlman & Mac Ian, 1995; Pearlman & Saakvitne, 1995b). It must be remembered that VT can affect any individual in any walk of life; that is, the affected individual need not be a therapist. However, in this chapter, we focus on the impact of VT on therapists and other professional human service workers.

In the therapist, the trauma and its impact are marked by unique individual reactions to the client's experience and are determined by the meaning assigned to the trauma by the therapist. Stated another way, this means that the clinician's response is based on both personal characteristics, including cognitive schemas, and situational factors, such as the traumatic material presented by the client (Pearlman & Mac Ian, 1995; Pearlman & Saakvitne, 1995b).

The concept of VT itself is based on a theory developed by McCann and Pearlman, the constructivist self-development theory (CSDT), a "developmental, interpersonal theory explicating the impact of trauma on an individual's psychological development, adaptation, and identity" (Pearlman & Saakvitne, 1995b, p. 152). Hence, VT is an interactive approach to understanding the impact of trauma on the counselor, social worker, or human service professional and may allow for a more detailed understanding of the individual experiences of the professionals. McCann and Pearlman (1990a) stated that professionals working with individuals who experienced some type of trauma may experience some disruptive and agonizing emotional responses for weeks, months or years after a therapeutic session. This process is called "vicarious traumatization" (p. 133).

Prior to presenting their theory, McCann and Pearlman reviewed several leading theories—self-psychology (Kohut, 1977), social learning theory (Rotter, 1954), and developmental theory (Mahler et al., 1975). Although CSDT draws largely from developmental social cognition theories, McCann and Pearlman adopted several ideas from the preceding theories in an attempt to develop a comprehensive personality theory with a constructivist perspective.

> The major underlying premise of CSDT is that individuals possess an inherent capacity to construct their own personal realities as they interact with their environment. This constructivist position asserts that human beings actively create their representational models of the world" (McCann & Pearlman, 1990a, p. 6). Within CSDT, McCann and Pearlman (1990a, 1990b) focus on three psychological systems: (1) the self; (2) psychological needs; and (3) cognitive schemas. (p. 6)

Their propositions are in agreement with the findings of the following theorists—Rotter (1954; social learning theory); Kelly (1955; personal construct theory); Beck (1967; cognitive theory of depression); Piaget (1970, 1971; structural theory); Mancuso (1977; whose work synthesizes the work of Kelly and Piaget); Epstein (1980; cognitive-experiential self-theory); Mahoney (1981; cognitive constructivism); and Mahoney and Lyddon (1988; cognitive constructivism). Each of these theories focused on an individual's active participation in making sense of their life experiences through the development of cognitive structures (schemas).

Several conceptualizations, referring to the *self*, existed prior to McCann and Pearlman's work (e.g., Jung, 1960; Kohut, 1977). Several conceptualizations, referring to the *self*, existed prior to McCann and Pearlman's work (e.g., Jung, 1960; Kohut, 1977). More recently, however, McCann and Pearlman (1990a) described *self* as a theoretical concept used to define the psychological underpinnings of a person. Self is regarded as the uniqueness of a person used by the individual, through a reflective process, to interpret their own lived experiences; maintain healthy and positive self-esteem; establish healthy boundaries in all forms of relationships; and seek intimacy, trust, and interdependence.

There are five self-capacities within CSDT that allow an individual who has been traumatized to keep a constant sense of identity and self-esteem. The first category is denoted as *aspects of the self and their functions*; these regulate self-esteem and include the ability to tolerate strong affect, the ability to be alone without being lonely, the ability to calm oneself, and the ability to regulate self-loathing. The second category is labeled as *ego resources* and includes those items which regulate interactions with others—intelligence; introspection; willpower; initiative; empathy; awareness of psychological needs; and the ability to strive for personal growth, take perspective, foresee consequences, establish mature relations with others, establish healthy boundaries, and make self-protective judgments. The third category, *psychological needs*, refers to those items which motivate behaviors—frame of reference, safety, trust/dependency, esteem, independence, power, and intimacy. The fourth category, *cognitive schemas*, describes those characteristics that organize one's experiences of self and the world. Included in this area are beliefs, assumptions, and expectations related to psychological needs. The final category is called *memory and perceptions* and describes the narrative of one's experience, which includes the sensory, somatic, visual, affective, and behavioral reactions. This last category is the most disturbing capacity for therapists and the one that most often brings therapists to treatment (McCann & Pearlman, 1990a). These categories and their identifying markers are listed in Table 30.1.

The essential premise of CSDT is that human beings construct their own personal realities through the development of complex cognitive structures, which are used to interpret events. These cognitive structures are constantly evolving and become increasingly complicated as individuals interact with their environment (McCann & Pearlman, 1990b). These cognitive structures were described earlier as schemas by Piaget (1971) and include beliefs, assumptions, and expectations about self and world that enable individuals to make sense of their experiences.

Table 30.1

Five Self-Capacities of Constructivist Self-Development Theory

CSDT Category	Identifying Markers
Frame of reference	Identity, worldview, spirituality
Self-capacities	Affect, tolerance, interconnections with others, sense of *self* as viable
Ego resources	Self-awareness, skills, and interpersonal and self-protective skills
Psychological needs and cognitive schemas	Safety, self-esteem, trust, control, intimacy
Memory and perceptions	Narrative, memory, visual images, affective, sensory, interpersonal

CSDT, constructivist self-development theory.

Vicarious Trauma During a Pandemic

As I sit here in the fall of 2021, updating this chapter on vicarious trauma, the world is in the midst of the COVID-19 pandemic. I wonder, for all of us, how our life experiences have changed since the beginning of this pandemic. It has been 10 months since public awareness of the pandemic, over 700,000 Americans have died due to COVID-19 (as of late November 2021), and the number continues to rise. Were our outlooks on life changed by the onslaught of the virus? If our outlooks changed, what specific traumatic event(s)—personally, locally, nationally, or globally—affected us? Was isolation from family, friends, and colleagues the primary stimulus for that change? Did any one of us or someone we know lose their job because of the pandemic? Were any of us, a family member, a friend, or an acquaintance, food insecure, thus resulting in participation in one of the many food distributions? Did we have a child who needed to go to the hospital, where only one parent could be with them? Did we lose a significant person in our lives? Were we related, by family or friendship, to an older person living at a senior-care facility where visitors were not permitted? Did we know someone who died from the virus without family or friends to comfort them as they departed this life? Were any of us a frontline responder—nurse, doctor, mental health therapist, EMT? Did we and/or a family test positive for COVID-19? Are we still fighting the lingering side effect? Were any of us a student, teacher, or professor suddenly finding ourselves participating in remote learning? I received anecdotal reports from multiple individuals who shared information describing significant disruptions in their lives that align with McCann and Pearlman's (1990a) constructivist self-development theory.

A nurse shared with me that she questioned where God was in all this death, isolation, and loss; a teacher emphasized her "fear" of returning to the classroom—fear for herself and her students. A doctor stated that he no longer trusted the government or elected officials who asserted that we were prepared with enough supplies—PPEs, testing kits, ventilators—to battle the pandemic. He ended his tirade with "such BS!" and obviously was frustrated by the vacuum of leadership. An individual, whose loved one contracted the virus, was unable to be with him, needing to say goodbye over the phone.

An old catchphrase, "essential workers," came to be used in reference to mental health professionals, nurses, doctors, emergency medical service personnel, hospital social workers, grocery store employees, gas station attendants, garbage collectors, and others who worked to provide needed services. Had we not been essential workers prior at the outbreak? Are not all workers essential in a country such as ours?

Let us examine the five categories of CSDT as they relate to these observations. First, how has our *frame of reference* been affected? Do we question the role of "higher powers" in not eliminating this pandemic? Has our worldview changed, particularly with respect to the country in which the pandemic began? Are we fearful that we will contract the virus? Has our personal identity changed, because we no longer participate in society to the extent that we did prior to the spread of the virus?

What about our *self-capacities*? Have our interconnections with others and our sense of self changed? Have our *ego resources* changed? Do we still have the same views of our skills, especially the self-protective skills? Are they heightened? Are we as aware of them as we once were?

Do we feel safe? Do we trust? Do we believe that we have any control over the situation? Do we fear intimacy? Should we have shut down the country sooner? With orders to shelter in place and limit social outings, many people reported feeling disconnected, having no control in making decisions that were best for themselves, their families, or their careers. The question of trust came into many conversations: mistrusting elected officials; not being heard, valued, or respected; questioning whether, as a frontline worker, we were doing what was right. An essential worker yelled "Who do you trust?" The lack or delay of information from public health authorities, often due to poor coordination among health and government officials, unclear guidance and confusion about the reasons for quarantine, and perceived lack of transparency, have haunted many. These are all markers of *psychological needs and cognitive schemas*.

Regarding *memory and perceptions*, what visual images do we retain after viewing the news? Have our personal memories been altered? What sensory reactions do we hold onto because of the pandemic? How have we made sense of the pandemic? What beliefs or assumptions do we now have about living in a country where COVID-19 is running rampant? What new narratives have emerged about living through or learning from COVID-19?

Considering many of the questions posed, how might we conceptualize the case that is presented in Box 30.1? If we were to think about and discuss the questions posed at the end of the clinical vignette, how might we construct a strategy for assisting Victoria?

BOX 30.1

Clinical Vignette: What's Wrong With Me?

Victoria is a 37-year-old, with 18 years of being a nurse in the operating room. She was informed that all elective surgeries have been put on hold, and she was reassigned to work on one pre-designated COVID floor for 2 weeks, starting that Monday morning at 7:00. This temporary assignment is now into the fifth week, with Victoria working 16-hour shifts, 6 days a week. She reports early to work Monday feeling overwhelmed, and exhausted; she was overheard by a colleague saying "I can't do this anymore—too many deaths. God, where are you? I don't want to make any more calls to families informing them that their loved one is actively dying. Please no more." The director of nursing (DON) pulls Victoria aside, telling her to "pull yourself together, we have clients to attend to."

If you were a counselor or social worker on the floor, what could you do to support Victoria?
What could you say to Victoria?
What is Victoria dealing with?

The primary symptoms of vicarious traumatization such as loss of appetite, fatigue, physical decline, sleep disorders, irritability, inattention, numbness, fear, and despair are well recognized to be experienced by all individuals, at some point, due to some type of extreme distress. Frequently, these symptoms are accompanied by trauma responses and interpersonal conflicts that even compel some to commit suicide (Creighton et al., 2018).

During the COVID-19 outbreak, several frontline professionals committed suicide (Rosner & Sheehy, 2020). Included in this tragic category was a 49-year-old, with no prior mental health history, who headed the emergency department of a Manhattan hospital and a 23-year-old emergency medical responder. Unfortunately, these frontline workers were so busy taking care of their clients, no one took care of them.

Prior to the COVID-19 pandemic, Creighton et al. (2018) conducted a study of men who had committed suicide. Members of the research team met with family members and friends of the victims. Although the researchers were not subjects of the study, the research team leaders noted that the mental health of the frontline researchers was affected by their interactions with the survivors, particularly if the research team member had a personal history with suicide. Steps were taken to correct the effects observed in the members of the research team including the managers, interviewers, and even the transcribers. This leads to an important conclusion regarding those of us who work with victims—the need for personal and professional support to ameliorate the challenges faced by those in the mental health field who chose to work directly or remotely with victims. Aafjes-van Doorn et al. (2020) noted that this is particularly true among young therapists and those with less experience.

Therapists working with trauma victims may experience intrusive images and generate a heightened sense of vulnerability (Danieli, 1988; Figley, 1995; Haley, 1974; Herman, 1992; McCann & Pearlman, 1990a). Figley (1995) has stated that working with traumatized clients consists of "absorbing information that is about suffering" and that this process requires "absorbing the suffering as well" (p. 2). VT addresses the interplay between traumatic events, the therapist's cognitive schemas about self and the world, and their ability to adapt. This concept is *not* limited to trauma work. Professionals in all human service fields will experience personal and professional changes; the effects of VT are cumulative and may become permanent if not addressed. This is a direct result of the interaction of the traumatic material shared by the client and the personal attributes of the therapists (Pearlman & Mac Ian, 1995; Pearlman & Saakvitne, 1995a). The clinical vignette that is presented in Box 30.2 illustrates one scenario of a counselor coming to terms with her own self-realizations of VT.

BOX 30.2

Clinical Vignette: *Courage*

Malory, a master level mental health therapist, with 6 years of direct service working at an outpatient client, has seen an influx of cases with significant trauma histories. Her caseload has increased to 135 active clients. Malory has been suffering in silence, not wanting to disclose to anyone what she is experiencing; "I'm a therapist, I have to hold it all together! Who can I tell without passing judgement on me?" Malory realized that all of the "ugliness" is beginning to take an emotional toll on her, while interfering with her relationship with her significant other, as well as with the services she's providing to others.

Malory initially reflected inward, trying to identify what has changed. She could identify that she was experiencing intrusive images at night and disconnecting from others. She couldn't tolerate any type of violence, while at home she was refusing to answer the phone and experiencing sleep disturbances, just to name a few areas of concern. Malory decided to reach out to her supervisor to discuss her current caseload and her emotional state. Several weeks later, there was no change; in fact, she became more judgemental and critical toward everyone. Knowing herself well enough, along with acknowledging and honoring her ethical responsibility, Malory sought out a therapist.

This is an important "footnote" to students and clinicians in the helping professions. Remember every good therapist has a therapist. We are not "crazy" or "sick"; rather, we hurt from what we hear, see, and experience with each client and from the world around us.

There are various signs and symptoms of VT, which include those listed in Table 30.2. VT affects the way one acts and interacts with others at work, at home, and within the community.

Table 30.2

Vicarious Trauma: Signs and Symptoms

General Changes	Specific Changes
– No time or energy for oneself	– Disrupted frame of reference
– Disconnected from loved ones	– Changes in identity, worldview, spirituality
– Social withdrawal	– Diminished self-capacity
– Increased sensitivity to violence	– Impaired ego resources
– Cynicism	– Disrupted psychological needs and cognitive schemas
– General despair and hopelessness	– Intrusive images, depersonalization
– Nightmares	– Alterations to one's sensory experiences
– Screening phone calls	
– Sense of depression	
– Physical problems (e.g., aches, pain, lower GI disturbance)	

COUNSELING IMPLICATIONS

We live in a violent world where people of all racial identities, ethnic backgrounds, genders, ages, and sexual preferences can fall victim to some type of trauma—rape, vehicle accidents, casualty of war, racism, bullying, domestic violence, or sexual abuse. The list goes on. Recently, there has been an increase of victims seeking treatment from professionals to assist them in their journey of healing. But at what cost to the therapist, counselor, social worker, psychologist, school counselor, or other helper who serves witness to another individual's sustained horror?

VT has three different, but important, implications for the counseling field. First, the human service professions currently are fighting the ongoing battle of recruitment and retention. Administrators and supervisors must focus on the most important commodity within their agencies—their staffs. Here, the *staff* includes the professional staff, from administrators and supervisors to frontline workers; support staff, from those who answer the phones and type the reports to the individuals who maintain the physical facility; and ancillary individuals, such as foster parents who provide for displaced children.

I personally have served as a consultant with various human service agencies. They have reported low morale, high absenteeism, high turnover rates, and negative attitudinal changes, emotional displays, disclosures regarding changes in familial relationships, shared comments regarding imprinted memories of traumatic events, jaded and cynical attitudes concerning the provision of services, medical disturbances (e.g., higher levels of gastrointestinal pain and high blood pressure), depressive symptoms, and other similar complaints. Comments reported from the staff included: "I can't do this anymore; I can't get the pictures of that child out of my mind. I'm even afraid to pick up my own child." "That family has been in the system before. Why waste our time on them; they are not going to change." "I don't trust anyone anymore. This is not a safe world to live in." "I can't get the smell of burning flesh out of my head. I smell it everywhere."

To address these and similar issues, we must introduce the concept of VT in the human service professions. This includes any profession in which individuals work with people. VT has gone undetected, unrecognized, and unaddressed (Jankoski, 2002, 2010) and is the culprit affecting the human service system and the individuals who work throughout the system.

Agencies must offer forums for staff to discuss and share the difficulties of the job and the emotional toll it takes on everyone. They also must establish debriefing teams who can respond or debrief a staff person who may have experienced a traumatic event. A professional who worked in a mental health agency shared an exchange between herself and her supervisor: "I can't believe no one in my agency asked me if I was okay, after being verbally and physically assaulted by a client. My supervisor told me it was all part of the job, and I was supposed to 'move on!'"

Supervisors are important contributors who not only assist in the development of professionals but also have an ethical responsibility to check in with their supervisees to ensure that each one is mentally, emotionally, and physically well (issues related to supervision in trauma contexts are detailed in Chapter 32). Supervisors must be aware of the caseloads their supervisees are carrying and the type of clients they are serving. Organizations must provide a venue through which staff may process difficult situations and not view personnel as weak when they use that venue. Organizations also must offer training opportunities on VT, its signs and symptoms, and ways in which it may be ameliorated.

As vital as supervisors are, they often become so overwhelmed with administrative tasks that they never recognize the pain—mental, emotional, or physical—experienced by members of their staffs. The time has come for supervisors to examine the overall health of their staffs vigilantly and to assist those who need help in maintaining their well-being. Although VT is an "occupational hazard," we, as human service professionals, owe it to each other and those whom we love to not be damaged by the work we chose to do! If agencies/organizations stand back and do nothing, we will continue to experience the "revolving door syndrome," whereby we always are trying to fill vacancies within our organizations.

The second implication for the counseling field is *vicarious evil,* an invisible condition that has the potential of tearing away the fiber of one's soul. Unaware of its existence, it can reside in the wounded counselor, social worker, emergency medical technician, teacher, police officer, judge, nurse, doctor, soldier—anyone who deals with people on a daily basis.

The evil about which I am speaking is not the evil that is associated with serial killers and tyrannical dictators; rather, it is a different kind of evil—one that results in a personality change, in which one becomes jaded without realizing it—where we develop a protective shell around ourselves so that we cannot feel anything, where we become indifferent and lose our sense of hope, and where we wear invisible blinders so that we cannot see the evil that exists around us. Perhaps we can relate to this type of evil, as we think of examples of situations that have gone terribly wrong.

We may be tempted to "act" as if everything is fine; after all, we are the professionals who are supposed to have all the answers. However, we are not brick walls! We have thoughts, feelings, and opinions that must be honored. We, individually and as a profession, must acknowledge that vicarious evil exists. We can no longer ignore the emotional consequences of working with others. We must, as individuals, colleagues, and professionals, combat this complacency that we have regarding self-care, because by not doing so, we have the potential for causing harm, thus violating one of our core moral principles—do no harm.

This brings us to our third implication, the potential to harm our clients. This third implication is closely tied to the first two. If we do not recognize that we are suffering from VT; have no support in ameliorating it; become so jaded, detached, or cynical that we no longer empathize with our clients; or lose the sense of hope that so many of our clients need to hear, we are doing them a grave disservice. When we professionals become so overwhelmed by the ugliness of the world that we tend to not see the person who is sitting before us, we must take the action necessary to heal ourselves. We cannot allow our VT to further harm those whom we are professionally obliged to help.

ESTABLISHING RESOURCES

We have a "gift" for working with others, we give freely of ourselves, but are we aware of what is happening within us? Are others aware of the subtle changes within? "John, you have changed since you started working there" or "You're not the same person" are comments that have been shared by human service professionals. If we truly wanted to know the impact of our jobs on our own growing selves, then we need to ask the most important people in our lives: "What do you notice, if anything, that is different about me?" Will we be surprised by their responses? Are all human service professionals changed by their work? I believe that they are. How can we not be changed when we are choosing to sit with a person, listening to their struggles and pain?

Prevention and intervention for VT requires intentional and comprehensive effort on our part. VT is a process, not a one-time event; its effects are cumulative; and it is based on repeated exposure to another's emotional pain. Ignoring VT gradually may change our beliefs about ourselves and our worldview, and its effects can be permanent. With this said, VT and its effects can be modified! One of the most difficult resources to access for counselors, social workers, and other helpers is help for themselves. Each one of us tends to believe we can handle anything and everything, particularly when it is someone else's problem that we are trying to help them solve. Let us be honest—we have learned great skills in our graduate programs to take care of others, but we learned little regarding the care of ourselves. We are not weak; we are human beings responding to the everyday pain and loss of those we serve. Every good therapist needs a therapist; we are not crazy, we just hurt from the pain we hear and see in others (issues related to self-care are detailed in Chapter 31).

Self-care is an individualized process. Each clinician must identify what works for them. A good starting place for anyone is by taking the Professional Quality of Life: Compassion Satisfaction and Fatigue (ProQOL) Test Version 5 (2009) created by B. Hudnall Stamm. This self-inventory has 30 questions, which are answered by using a Likert-type scale. It is easy to score and will assist anyone along their journey of self-care. In addition to Stamm's ProQOL, there are several tools that have been established to assist us in finding a balance between work and emotional health. Constructing a personal self-care plan (PSCP; Norcross & Guy, 2007; Wolpow, 2011; Yassen, 1995) is one such tool that allows any individual to create a self-care plan. Initially, increasing one's awareness of the emotional toll of engaging regularly in those types of self-care activities—physical, emotional, cognitive, social, financial, and spiritual—also fosters the requisite resilience (Wolpow, 2011) that is necessary to cope with the emotional pain that we see on a daily basis. The PSCP addresses eight domains that guide counselors to look at ourselves honestly and to set achievable goals: physical exercise; nutrition and hydration; sleep and rest; assertiveness; centering and solitude; creativity, fun, and enjoyment; providing and receiving support; and the establishment of personal goals.

Srdanovic (2007) and Clemans (2004) introduced the ABCs (awareness, balance, and connection) of preventing VT. Awareness (A) involves becoming a reflective clinician, giving oneself permission to look within and to conduct a self-assessment to determine the effects of VT. Supervision, journaling, peer support, and soliciting feedback from family regarding what they are seeing and experiencing with their loved one are all ways in which the therapist can become a reflective clinician.

The clinician must determine what is important in their life. This includes making oneself a priority in one's own life and establishing health boundaries. This is all part of the balance (B) one must have in life. Connection (C) is important in anyone's life, particularly that of a therapist who is regularly exposed to others' trauma. In addition to family and friends, one must establish relationships with colleagues, because none of us can do this work alone (Box 30.3).

BOX 30.3

Tips From the Field: Insight Questions

QUESTION: What can you do to support a friend or colleague who is experiencing vicarious trauma?

POTENTIAL STRATEGIES: Reach out to them; talk with them about the current impact of work and caseloads; stress the importance of self-care as well as basic needs like eating,

(continued)

sleeping, and drinking water; stay connected; and encourage the person to discuss strategies for staying connected with loved ones, friends, and colleagues.

ADDITIONAL QUESTIONS: What can an organization do to address vicarious trauma in the workplace? What can supervisors do to address vicarious trauma in clinical supervision? How can we include family members, who's loved one may be experiencing vicarious trauma?

IMPORTANT NOTE: To understand trauma, we must overcome our natural reluctance to confront it; we must cultivate the courage to listen to the testimonies of survivors and helpers and to help them go on with their lives.

To lessen the shame and the isolation felt by clinicians and to increase their coping skills and retention, organizations need to consider providing open forums where VT can be openly discussed. Professionals leave the field because they feel "undervalued" (Jankoski, 2002, 2010). When workers feel "valued" by their administrators and supervisors, there is an increase of job satisfaction. Organizations can establish rapid response teams consisting of trained staff to be mobilized when needed to support other staff members who may have experienced a traumatic event—as defined by them. The goal is to keep the competent, well-trained staff within the organization. We are not robots. For an organization to ignore their staff members' emotional pain is to do them a serious injustice.

CONCLUSION

Professional counselors *will* change by virtue of the work that they have chosen to do—work with other individuals. The change may be positive, or it may be negative at different times during one's career—indeed, even at different times of the workday. We all have an ethical responsibility to our families, friends, colleagues, and clients to not be damaged by the work that we have chosen to do. As helpers, we have a special gift to be shared with many people, and every day we have an opportunity to make a difference—one person at a time. With this said, we must take care of ourselves—physically, emotionally, financially, and spiritually. Self-care is not an option; it is our personal and professional responsibility to address our own emotional pain. Each one of us, who is committed to making a difference in the lives of other individuals, is at risk of being affected by and of experiencing VT.

ADDITIONAL RESOURCES

A robust set of instructor resources designed to supplement this text is located at http://connect.springerpub.com/content/book/978-0-8261-5085-1. Qualifying instructors may request access by emailing textbook@springerpub.com.

PRACTICE-BASED RESOURCES AND REFERENCES

To view a list of resources and all the references, please visit connect.springerpub.com via the following url: http://connect.springerpub.com/content/book/978-0-8261-5085-1/part/part06/chapter/ch30

CHAPTER 31

Mindfulness-Based Self-Care for Counselors

SHANNON HODGES

CHAPTER OVERVIEW

Counselors and other therapists providing counseling to clients diagnosed with posttraumatic stress disorder (PTSD) may be at greater risk for developing secondary trauma, also called vicarious trauma. While PTSD had been the focus of much research in the counseling field, less emphasis has been placed on counselor self-care. This chapter focuses on the rationale for counselor self-care.

LEARNING OBJECTIVES

After reading this chapter, the reader should be able to answer the following questions:

1. Why are counselors and other therapists who treat PTSD clients at risk for developing secondary trauma?
2. What are three stress management tips that counselors can utilize?
3. How might the Professional Quality of Life Scale be helpful in charting counselor burnout?
4. How might reframing one's self-talk assist in managing stress and preventing burnout?

INTRODUCTION

Among the various mental health disciplines, the counseling profession is unique in that it was conceived with a strength-oriented wellness approach (Gladding, 2009; Levers, 2012; Myers et al., 2000; Witmer & Granello, 2005). Such an approach promotes a healthy and balanced life, not only for clients but also for counselors themselves. The intention of this chapter is to assist readers in maintaining a healthier, more balanced life as they proceed through practicum and internship. When working with trauma survivors, it is essential that counselors maintain a healthy lifestyle during their professional years (and well beyond, of course). An active self-care plan likely will mean a more effective counselor who will enjoy more productive years in the profession. Self-care is part of the American Counseling Association's (ACA) *Code of Ethics* as a buffer against professional impairment (Standard C.2.g) as is monitoring counselor effectiveness (Standard C.2.d). From my own anecdotal observations over the years, having witnessed many counselors' poor and marginal self-care, it is likely that adequate self-care is the most violated standard in the code of ethics. Therefore, as counselors assisting others in developing healthier lifestyles, it is essential that we practice what we teach.

As professional counselors, we may work with a variety of mental health professionals who *do not* practice what they teach regarding self-care. Unfortunately, far too many counselors and other mental health professionals struggle with addictions, codependence, anger management issues, dangerously inflated egos, and substandard ethical behavior that we would not want to emulate. Realistically, no one can expect counselors to have perfect dispositions, never get upset, or have a total lack of conflicts. Professional counselors must, however, learn to manage the challenges of our careers (not to mention life stress!). As a freshly minted counselor, I initially had much difficulty in managing the stress involved in working in a residential psychiatric facility that served adolescents. Consequently, I was so mentally and emotionally drained that I almost left the profession. Fortunately, through a colleague's encouragement, I was able to get the help I needed through counseling and making lifestyle changes. In similar fashion, I hope that this chapter provides some insights in recognizing stressors that accompany counseling a struggling population of clients. Perhaps more importantly, it is my hope that readers will be inspired to develop active self-care plans. Furthermore, it is worth mentioning that for some counselors, their supervisors and colleagues may provide more stress than the population they counsel! Workplace conflicts often are the primary reasons counselors leave their jobs, rather than a lack of professional knowledge or a difficult caseload (Bolles, 2015).

DEVELOPING A HEALTHY LIFESTYLE

There are many different pathways, plans, theories, approaches, books, journal articles, and other resources devoted to living a healthy and fulfilling life. The fact that so many authors, counselors, theologians, personal trainers, coaches, and others attempt to provide counseling, personal coaching, and information to manage stress and teach mindfulness, a balanced diet, exercise routine, and so forth, is indicative of just how stressful daily life has become in this postmodern age. As professional counselors, we are not strangers to the challenges of external demands. For graduate students, the practicum or internship experience placed atop family responsibilities, a job, academic work, and financial demands can create great stress in students' lives (Remley & Herlihy, 2016). The irony of life as a counselor is that while working to assist clients to live healthier, more fulfilling lives, the demands of the environment, combined with work and home-front demands, can potentially derail a counselor's own sense of harmony and balance. Somehow, counselors must learn to address this contradiction effectively and to develop healthy coping mechanisms. While every professional likely preaches better than they practice, developing healthy routines is essential for good physical, mental, and emotional health.

In this chapter devoted to self-care, I have created several self-reflection exercises. Self-reflection is a critical task not only for counselors but also for anyone in any occupation and is a process of examining oneself during times of difficulty or success. The ability to step back from an experience, however successful or disappointing, can be a key skill for personal success as a counselor. It is important to acknowledge that I likely have not created anything new in addressing the issues of healthy lifestyle or "wellness" in the counseling field (Myers et al., 2000), but it remains an essential message to emphasize. Also included are assessments on quality of life, burnout, and mindfulness. Regardless of how we decide to refer to managing stress, living a balanced life, and engaging in mindful living, we usually address the same common themes of how to live a fulfilling, meaningful, and healthy life. I also offer an online list of additional resources at the conclusion of this chapter for the reader's consideration.

One of the first topics to address is that of stress. Regardless of culture, age, occupation, and so forth, stress is simply an everyday unpleasant fact for everyone on the planet. Stress is an external change to which we are required to adjust our lives. Generally, we think of stress as being negative, such as the death of a loved one, unemployment, divorce, and other such challenges. Nevertheless, positive changes in our lives also can bring about stress. For example, getting married or partnered, moving across the country for a new job, buying a home, traveling overseas, making one's first professional conference presentation, and, of course, working as a counselor are all exciting experiences, but at the same time, they also can bring about new stressors that complicate our lives and have an impact on our mood, sleep, relationships, and work lives.

We can experience stress from three different sources: the environment, somatic experiences, and our thoughts (Davis et al., 2008). Environmental stressors might include conflicts in the workplace, harsh weather, pollution, overcrowding, impoverishment, and living in unsafe areas. Environmental stressors are the ones we commonly see played up in the media, such as the 2009 catastrophic oil leak off the coast of Louisiana, Hurricane Sandy in 2012, people living in poverty, and the trauma brought about by natural disasters such as recent wildfires in Australia, among others. Environmental concerns clearly illustrate the connection between harmony with the environment and a less stressful life, or the exact opposite. Other common forms of environmental stress might be difficulties with one's spouse/partner, roommates, colleagues at the office, and so forth.

The second source of stress is somatic, or how one's body interprets stress. High-paced work settings, poor diet, sleep disturbances, and addiction all stress the body. Our reactions to these external demands become triggered by a genetically programmed "fight–flight–freeze" response inherited from primitive ancestors who dealt daily with life-and-death issues. These genetic traits are passed down through the subsequent generations to assist people in their adaptation to environmental demands. Consequently, we all have, as part of our physiological system, the innate tendency to prepare the body to face the stressor or to flee from it. An adaptive example of "fighting" might be the coworker who requests to speak with the party with whom they are having conflicts. An example of *unhealthy* fighting would be the same coworker screaming obscenities at the other party. Adaptive "fleeing" is when someone takes a temporary break from the stressful event (say an argument with a spouse), then returns and requests to speak with the party with whom they are having the conflict. Unhealthy fleeing is when the hurt person says, "They don't bother me," when in fact nasty comments or disrespectful actions do in fact bother them (as they do everyone). Denial is a type of "unhealthy" fleeing. The critical factor here is "healthy" fighting and fleeing. The freeze response may occur when the fearful party cannot think of another response and stays put in the face of, say, verbal abuse.

The third source of stress derives from our cognitions. How we interpret or label stressful events will influence how well we resolve stress (Ellis, 2001). Essentially, what is the self-story being told regarding the challenges and frustrations that the person faces, and what is the evidence that this story is accurate? One of the ways our assumptions can add to stress is when we mistakenly interpret or distort messages. It would likely create stress, if, for example, someone were to interpret a supervisor's grimace to mean that they are upset and might fire the person. However, verifying this assumption might clear up the misunderstanding and significantly reduce stress levels. Remember, the supervisor's sour facial expressions, for example, may or may not have anything to do with a supervisee. So, do not overly interpret messages, but certainly investigate them. Alternatively, as the cognitive counselor might suggest, ask, "What's the evidence for this negative belief I hold?" Frequently, false beliefs enter our minds and cause us distress. As one of my colleagues is fond of saying, "I do not believe everything I think."

The Impact of Stress

Stress is difficult to define in a precise manner given the amount of subjectivity involved. Experiences that are stressful for some are pleasurable for others. For example, some people actually look forward to swimming with sharks while others (myself) are terrified at the prospect. We respond to stress in different ways: some people eat less when stressed, others overeat; some turn pale, whereas others blush; some use healthy coping skills, such as exercise and talking with friends, and others self-medicate with alcohol and other drugs. Table 31.1 lists some common signs of stress.

Table 31.1

Common Signs of Stress

1. Frequent headaches	14. Increased frustration
2. Disturbed sleep	15. Decreased appetite
3. Trembling of limbs	16. Depression and mood swings
4. Neckache, back pain, muscle spasms	17. Difficulty concentrating
5. Dizziness	18. Feeling overwhelmed
6. Sweating	19. Feeling worthless
7. Frequent colds	20. Suicidal thoughts
8. Stomach pain	21. Social anxiety
9. Constipation or diarrhea	22. Defensiveness
10. Hyperventilation	23. Reduces work efficiency
11. Frequent urination	24. Ongoing fatigue
12. Decreased sexual desire	25. Less optimistic
13. Excessive worry or anxiety	26. Elevated blood pressure and heart rate

Adapted from the American Institute of Stress. (n.d.). *Stress effects*. https://www.stress.org/stress-effects

Tips for Managing Stress

Stress is a reality in daily life, and one that we cannot completely eliminate. We can, however, manage the stress that comes into our lives. Box 31.1 has several tips for managing stress.

BOX 31.1

Tips From the Field: Managing Stress

Tip #1: Recognize stress and deal with it accordingly.

- Learn to say "no." This may take some practice. Know your limits and stay within them.
- Limit time with people you find toxic. Conversely, maximize your time with people you find affirming and supportive.
- Take a break from stressors. If traffic causes you unmanageable stress, take a different route or use alternative forms of transportation if possible (e.g., carpool, mass transit, cycling). If the daily news stresses you, take occasional breaks from reading the paper, online news, or watching TV.
- Refrain from overly discussing upsetting topics (there is a time and place for such discussions, just not too often). If discussing politics, religion, sex, or even sports causes you too much conflict, perhaps refrain from discussing them, at least with select people. If people try to engage you in arguments over these topics, simply inform them, "I don't discuss these topics."
- Prioritize your schedule. Make "to do" lists in order of what is most important. If there are unnecessary tasks, move them to the bottom of the list or eliminate them.

Tip #2: Be proactive.

- Find constructive ways to express your feelings instead of suppressing them. Practice expressing your feelings with a trustworthy friend and solicit feedback from that friend. This way you will be more prepared to do so during your practicum/internship.

(continued)

- Practice assertiveness and ask for what you need.
- Manage time effectively. Poor time management skills will lead to additional stress. Prioritize your workload, and this will help reduce your stress level.
- Be willing to compromise in conflicts. Do not make all the compromises but make the ones you can.

Tip #3: Reframing problems.
Reframing is a basic counseling technique. Here are some examples of how you might use reframing:

- Reframe personal conflicts as "growth opportunities," and seek to resolve them.
- Be realistic and let go of perfectionism. You are going to make mistakes during your practicum/internship. Make them and learn from them. Ask your supervisor for advice. Join the "recovering perfectionist" (RC) movement!
- Step back from a stress situation and ask, "How big an issue will this be in 6 months or a year?"
- On a regular basis, take time to reflect on the successes and blessings in your life. Challenging periods in life have a way of obliterating personal successes. So, take stock of your successes.

Tip #4: Accept what you cannot change and change what you can.
- **Control.** You cannot control other people. You can, however, manage your reactions to another's behavior and strategize effective ways to deal with challenging people. A potentially more effective approach is focusing more on your goal as opposed to people's behavior. Remember, you cannot control another person's behavior, but you can manage your own.
- **Get support.** Discussing concerns with close friends can be very helpful. For one thing, you realize that you are not alone; also, sharing a concern may provide an outside perspective that you might find useful.
- **Forgiveness.** No one is perfect and, with rare exception, other people are not out to make our lives miserable. Learning to forgive perceived slights can free you from negative energy. If you have trouble with forgiving others, counseling may be a viable option for you. Forgiveness often is more for the forgiver than the perceived transgressor.
- **Self-reflection.** What do I need to change about myself? You might ask a few trusted friends to help you with this. Do they see areas you could improve on? How could you improve on these areas? What would self-improvement look like?

Assessing and Preventing Compassion Fatigue and Burnout

Compassion fatigue and burnout are serious risks for counselors and counselors in training (the related issues of secondary and vicarious trauma are discussed, in detail, in Chapter 30). Compassion fatigue represents frustration, feelings of low energy, negative thoughts, workplace and home conflicts, and most symptoms of burnout (Stamm, 2005). Burnout is longer term and more serious. Burnout may be described as a state of physical, mental, and emotional exhaustion brought about by long-term stress (Carter, 2013). Potential warning signs of burnout might be:

1. **Chronic fatigue:** A sense of never feeling rested during the workday or weekends.
2. **Insomnia:** Stress has an impact on sleep quality. One may experience difficulty falling or staying asleep.
3. **Impaired concentration:** Feeling overwhelmed may compromise a counselor's ability to remember basic details typically recalled with little difficulty.

4. **Physical symptoms:** These may include shortness of breath, chest pains, gastrointestinal problems, dizziness, and headaches. Naturally, a medical professional should assess all of these.
5. **Increased illness:** Long-term stress may compromise the immune system, leaving an individual more susceptible to colds and the flu.
6. **Loss of appetite:** Food may no longer be appealing.
7. **Anxiety:** Anxiety may increase as a counselor moves from compassion fatigue to burnout. Panic attacks are a possibility.
8. **Depression:** One likely will feel sad initially, increasing in severity to ongoing depression. If sadness persists longer than a few days, the person should seek professional help.
9. **Anger:** As stress increases, momentary irritability may turn into angry outbursts (Carter, 2013).

The Professional Quality of Life Scale

The Professional Quality of Life Scale (ProQOL; Stamm, 2005) is the current version of the former Compassion Fatigue Test (Figley, 1995). Stamm (2005) modified the ProQOL in order to strengthen its psychometric properties as well as to reflect a preference for the more positive name of "professional quality of life." Essentially, he wanted the instrument to have more of a healthy assessment and instructional focus and utility. Stamm developed the ProQOL, with more than 1,000 participants, using items related to resilience (Stamm, 2005). The ProQOL now consists of three subscales: Compassion Satisfaction, Burnout, and Secondary Trauma. The ProQOL assesses quality of life as well as potential risk for burnout. Burnout risk is quantified as low, average, or high. The same scoring differentiation and cut-off scores also are used for the Compassion Satisfaction and the Secondary Trauma scales.

Stamm has made the ProQOL available in the public domain. The test may be freely copied, as long as (a) the author is credited, (b) no changes are made, and (c) it is not sold. Those interested in using the test should visit www.proqol.org to verify that the copy they are using is the most current version of the test. The ProQOL provides scores on three domains: (1) Secondary traumatic stress, (2) burnout, and (3) compassion satisfaction. Stamm (2005) has provided cut-off points for the three scales. Stamm recommends professionals periodically take the ProQOL to evaluate changes in the scales.

A Healthy Assets Ledger

Because counseling involves working with clients grappling with trauma, eating disorders, addiction, and major mental illness, developing a good self-care plan is essential for professional viability. To build on one's wellness practice, a counselor might consider the reflective questions in Box 31.2. These questions could be useful for purposes of self-exploration regarding personal, professional, and spiritual growth. The answers become a baseline for assessing ongoing emotional-spiritual-occupational-social balance in one's life.

BOX 31.2

Tips From the Field

Reflective Questions for Counselors to Consider
- How well developed and balanced are the personal, occupational, social, and spiritual (if appropriate) dimensions of your life?

(continued)

- Who do you say you are? Also, how does who you say you are compare to how others appear to view you? On the other hand, how great is the distance between who you really are and who you want to be? Be realistic but be honest about this "divide."
- How does this self-view correlate with how significant people in your life view you (you may wish to discuss this with relevant people in your life)?
- What is your most fulfilling time of the week? Why? If you feel a lack of fulfillment during your week, how could you create more meaning in your life?
- How would you describe this stage of your life?
- What issues and/or challenges are creating difficulty for you?
- How could you begin to lessen or better manage these challenges?
- What are your key strengths?
- What skills, hobbies, interests, and talents do you possess?
- What areas of your life would you like to explore? (**Note:** This could apply to personal relationships, travel, continuing education, career, or anything you deem important.)
- In what ways are you dependent on others?
- In what ways are you self-reliant?
- What conflicts are inhibiting your personal growth and professional effectiveness?
- How could you take steps to resolve these conflicts?

Regarding Major Successes and Failures in Your Life
- When you consider your major successes, what has worked well and why? What did your major successes teach you?
- Regarding your failures, what seemed to go wrong and why? What did your failures teach you?
- What could you do differently next time either to build on success or to ensure you did not fail in the next opportunity?

Another useful tool, reprinted in Box 31.3, is the Dimensions of a Healthy Lifestyle (DHL; Hodges, 2021, pp. 168–172, Exhibit 8.2). The DHL represents a self-monitoring system using scaling questions. This assessment technique provides a sense of where a counselor is located in the respective domains. The self-rating questions provide a constructive method of self-care. The questions are not a substitute to replace good personal, professional, and spiritual growth, but to serve and support wellness in these areas.

BOX 31.3

Tips From the Field

Dimensions of a Healthy Lifestyle

Spirituality/Religious Life

My spiritual/religious life provides a sense of purpose and helps me address major life challenges.

(**Note:** An alternate phrasing for nonspiritual/nonreligious people might be: "My sense of life meaning/purpose provides fulfillment and helps me address the challenges in my life.")

| 1 | 2 | 3 | 4 | 5 | 6 | 7 | 8 | 9 | 10 |

(1 = *No help at all*; 10 = *Strongly helps*)

If your score was less than five, how could you improve your situation?

(continued)

Personal Vision

"I have a clear vision in my personal, spiritual, and professional life."

1   2   3   4   5   6   7   8   9   10

(1 = *No vision*; 10 = *I have a clear vision*)

If you do not have a clear personal, spiritual, or professional vision, how could you develop one? Visioning is a key component to success in all these areas.

Self-Worth

"I feel worthwhile as a human being and have a strong sense of self-acceptance. Although I am not perfect, I feel generally good about myself."

1   2   3   4   5   6   7   8   9   10

(1 = *I am worthless*; 10 = *My self-worth is very strong*)

If you are experiencing low self-esteem, how could you begin to feel better about yourself? What actions could you take to begin to feel more self-confident?

Goal Setting

"I feel self-confident about setting and meeting goals and demands in my life."

1   2   3   4   5   6   7   8   9   10

(1 = *I lack confidence in my ability to meet demands and the goals I set*; 10 = *I feel very confident in setting, planning, and meeting goals and demands*)

If you lack clear goals in your life, how could you begin to create some clear goals?

Rational Thinking

"I believe I perceive my life and life situations in a rational manner. I seldom engage in overly negative thinking."

1   2   3   4   5   6   7   8   9   10

(1 = *I frequently engage in irrational thinking*; 10 = *I am very rational in my beliefs*)

If you have rated yourself as frequently engaging in irrational beliefs (e.g., "I am a loser," "I am worthless," "No one could ever love me"), how could you begin to think in a more rational manner? (Alternatively, if you are unsure as to whether your beliefs are rational, you might consider asking someone you trust for feedback.)

Emotional Understanding and Regulation

"I am in touch with my emotions and am able to express the full range of emotions appropriate to the situation. I also am not governed by my emotions."

1   2   3   4   5   6   7   8   9   10

(1 = *I am not able to regulate my emotions and often express emotions inappropriate to the situation*; 10 = *I am able to regulate my emotions and experience emotions appropriate to the situation*)

If you are not experiencing an appropriate range of emotions, or find yourself too often ruled by your emotions, how could you begin to change this? Remember, you will have "negative" emotions, so the task is to regulate them appropriately.

Resilience

"I am a resilient person, and able to analyze, synthesize, and make a plan to deal with challenges and projects that come my way."

1   2   3   4   5   6   7   8   9   10

(1 = *I do not feel resilient*; 10 = *I am very confident in my resiliency*)

(continued)

If you do not feel resilient (or you are not as resilient as you would like) or do not have the ability to resolve difficulties in your life, what could you do to begin to develop more resilience? (**Note:** If you feel stuck on strategizing with this component, perhaps begin by making a list of ways you feel resilient. Alternatively, ask someone who knows you well to list ways they see you as being resilient.)

Sense of Humor

"I possess a healthy, appropriate sense of humor that helps me deal with the stresses of life."

      1   2   3   4   5   6   7   8   9   10

    (1 = *I have no sense of humor*; 10 = *I have a healthy sense of humor*)

    If you do not feel your sense of humor is either strongly developed, appropriate, or provides an effective release of stress, what could you change to improve the situation?

Fitness or Recreation

"I have a regular weekly fitness/recreational routine that helps me stay physically and emotionally fit."

      1   2   3   4   5   6   7   8   9   10

    (1 = *I have no activity routine*; 10 = *I have an active physical/recreational routine*)

    If you do not have a regular weekly fitness routine, what could you do to change this? (Remember, you do not need to become a marathoner, competitive cyclist, swimmer, or dancer. It is simply about developing a regular routine of 20 minutes a day, at least 3 days a week.)

Healthy Diet

"I regularly eat a balanced diet, including healthy vegetables and fruits."

    (Note: Healthy is not meant to imply you *never* eat unhealthy foods because that is not realistic. In fact, sometimes it is good for the psyche to eat ice cream, cookies, and so forth. Just don't do it too often. Rather, it is about eating unhealthy food in moderation.)

      1   2   3   4   5   6   7   8   9   10

    (1 = *My diet is unbalanced and unhealthy*; 10 = *My diet is balanced and healthy*)

    If your diet is unhealthy (eating high-fat food, "junk" food, fast food too often), how could you begin to eat a healthier diet? (For in-depth help, you may wish to consult a dietician.)

Mindful Living

"I maintain a mindful lifestyle by not abusing alcohol or other drugs, by wearing a seat belt, having regular medical examinations, and by refraining from high-risk activities (e.g., casual sex, binge drinking, binge eating, restricting food)."

      1   2   3   4   5   6   7   8   9   10

    (1 = *I do not live a healthy, mindful life*; 10 = *I maintain a healthy, mindful lifestyle*)

    If you find you are not living a healthy, mindful life, what steps could you take to change this?

Managing Stress and Anxiety

"Through my diet, workout routine, friendships, and so forth, I have the ability to manage stress and anxiety. When I find I am unable to manage the stress and anxiety in my life, I check in with close friends and family or, if the need arises, I see a counselor."

      1   2   3   4   5   6   7   8   9   10

    (1 = *I am regularly unable to manage the stress and anxiety in my life*; 10 = *I am able to manage the stress and anxiety in my life*)

(continued)

If you find you regularly have difficulty managing the stress and anxiety in your life, how could you begin to manage that stress and anxiety better?

Sense of Self

"I feel that my self-identity is strong and well developed."

       1   2   3   4   5   6   7   8   9   10

(1 = *My sense of self is incongruent with who I am because I try too hard to be who others want me to be;* 10 = *My sense of self is very congruent with who I am*)

Some people struggle with their own identity for various reasons, such as enmeshment with family, codependence with a loved one, low self-esteem, and so forth. If you find you are struggling with an inability to develop your own identity, what are some options for exploration (i.e., options that would reduce your struggle or help you resolve your personal identity struggles)?

Connection to Family or Culture

"I feel a strong connection to my family or culture."

       1   2   3   4   5   6   7   8   9   10

(1 = *I feel no connection to my family or culture;* 10 = *I feel a strong and healthy connection to my family and culture*)

In the event you feel no connection to your family or culture, what would you say accounts for this? Also, how could you begin to make stronger connections to your family and culture?

Career/Vocational Development

"I feel a sense of satisfaction in the career I am pursuing" (e.g., mental health counselor, school counselor, rehabilitation counselor)

       1   2   3   4   5   6   7   8   9   10

(1 = *No satisfaction;* 10 = *Maximum satisfaction*)

If your chosen career does not provide personal challenge and satisfaction for you, what steps could you take to create more fulfillment and satisfaction? (Or, if you are unemployed, how could your job search become more fulfilling? Or, how could this period of unemployment be more productive?)

Hobbies

"My hobbies help me relax and provide a sense of enjoyment."

       1   2   3   4   5   6   7   8   9   10

(1 = *I have no hobbies or they provide no sense of enjoyment or relaxation;* 10 = *My hobbies are a pure joy*)

If you lack hobbies or outside interests from work, how could you create some fulfilling pursuits?

Social Life

"I have healthy relationships that provide me a sense of emotional connection and help make life more rewarding."

       1   2   3   4   5   6   7   8   9   10

(1 = *I have no significant relationships, they are shallow, or provide little in the way of emotional connection;* 10 = *I have healthy and fulfilling relationships and they are an important part of my life*)

(continued)

If you lack significant personal connections or your relationships do not provide you with a sense of emotional connection, how could you begin to address this? (On the other hand, how could you begin to create fulfilling relationships?)

Intimacy

"Intimacy, or love, is a central part of my life, and my relationship with my spouse/partner provides the grounding, intimacy, and close connection I need." (Note: Intimacy could involve sexual intimacy or even a close, nonsexual relationship).

1   2   3   4   5   6   7   8   9   10

(1 = *Intimacy is largely absent from my life*; 10 = *Intimacy is a large part of my life and provides me with great satisfaction*)

If intimacy seems absent from your life, or seems unhealthy or unfulfilling, what do you need to do to change this situation?

Questions Regarding Self-Care

Regarding these dimensions, which is your strongest? Weakest? How could you improve your strengths and build upon your weak areas? What action could you take to improve your self-care? What supports do you need to create a healthier lifestyle? If you are unsure how to create a healthy self-care lifestyle, whom could you ask for help (i.e., your doctor, counselor, a nutritionist, your spiritual leader, family member, friend)?

Additional Considerations for Managing Stress

Without question, managing stress likely will be as important to a viable, productive career as a counselor's skill. In addition to the previous Dimensions of Self-Care, Box 31.4 contains several stress management tips for consideration.

BOX 31.4

Tips From the Field: Setting Limits With Others

- Do you have difficulty saying "no" to other people? If so, how could you begin to say "no" when you know doing so is necessary? What makes setting limits difficult for you? Guilt? Fear? Something else? How could you begin to practice setting limits with others?
- What healthy risks can you undertake to enhance your personal and professional growth?
- When you think about the type of people who cause you stress, what is it that they do that is stressful for you? Okay, now that you have identified what is stressful about their behavior, how could you manage your stress level around them?

Developing Connections

- Would you want to make friends with someone like yourself? Why or why not? If "no," what might you wish to change?
- If you feel isolated, how could you begin to develop meaningful relationships?
- If you are in a marriage or partnership and you are not feeling fulfilled, how could you begin to create a greater sense of fulfillment in that relationship?
- If you are not in a relationship and would like to be, how could you begin to create such a relationship? (Or, what qualities would you like in a partner?)

(continued)

- Recall a difficult period in your life. How did you navigate your way through this time?
- How do you go about creating meaning in your life?
- Make a list of at least five skills you already possess that you can use to keep yourself well and fit.

Work and Career

- Are you pursuing your career of interest? Why or why not?
- Why did you choose to pursue counseling as a career? How happy are you thus far?
- What is your dream job or dream career? (Describe in some detail: title, location, and so on)
- How can you begin to create your dream job? What steps are necessary?
- Setting goals is important for success. What are your major goals for the next 5 years?
- In what ways have you changed since entering your graduate counseling program?

Mentoring

- Who are some people who have inspired you? *Note:* They need not necessarily be people you have met. For example, many have been inspired by the likes of Martin Luther King, Jr., Mahatma Gandhi, Mother Teresa, Dalai Lama, Stephen Hawking, and so forth, even though they have never met these people.
- Name five people and state how they have inspired you.
- Who are some people who share your hobbies and interests?
- Cite some organizations in which you are actively involved.
- List some people who share your spiritual beliefs (or who share your personal values).

The Importance of Meaning and Purpose in Life

Meaning in life is a concept of central importance to the human condition and has been studied across numerous disciplines (Schulenberg et al., 2011; Wong, 2012a, 2012b). Meaning in life has been a focal point of interest to theologians and philosophers for centuries, and more recently, the issue has become influential in the rapidly growing positive psychology movement (Schulenberg et al., 2011; Seligman, 2002; Sharma et al., 2017; Wong, 2012a). Meaning in life is positively correlated with happiness, well-being, resilience, coping skills, hope, self-esteem, and empowerment and inversely correlated with depression, PTSD, addiction, anxiety, and suicidality (Seligman, 2002; Wong, 2012a). People who perceive their lives as having meaning and purpose are more likely to be happier, healthier, less depressed, and less anxious. "The presence of meaning is an excellent marker of the good life" (Peterson & Park, 2012, p. 292).

While life meaning seems an important issue, the term is amorphous and often misunderstood (Heintzelman & King, 2014). A perusal of the bestseller lists, not to mention numerous workshops offered, suggest that the public is intensely interested in developing increased life meaning and purpose. While targeted as a necessity to emotional health, life meaning may be increasingly rare in a secularized society (Frankl, 1988; Wong, 2012a, 2012b). Thus, there is a dynamic tension between the hypothesis regarding the importance of meaning in life and research suggesting many people lack appropriate life meaning. Given the dynamic nature of a fast-paced, Western world, and the well-documented angst regarding 21st century college and graduate students' mental health needs (Mistler et al., 2012), meaning and purpose in life likely are critical necessities for emotional balance and well-being. Thus, assessing meaning in life in some type of objective manner could be very important for counselors in clinical work.

The Meaning in Life Questionnaire (MLQ) is a 10-item test assessing two dimensions of meaning in life on a seven-point scale from "Absolutely True" to "Absolutely Untrue" (Steger et al., 2006). The "Presence of Meaning" subscale measures the level of meaning in respondents' lives and the "Search for Meaning" subscale assesses respondents' levels of motivation to find or deepen life meaning. The MLQ has demonstrated validity and reliability in research on clinical and nonclinical populations (Schulenberg et al., 2011). The Meaning in Life Questionnaire assesses two dimensions of meaning in life using 10 items rated on a seven-point scale from "Absolutely True" to "Absolutely Untrue." The "Presence of Meaning" subscale measures the degree to which respondents feel their lives are meaningful. The "Search for Meaning" subscale measures how engaged and motivated respondents are in efforts to find meaning or deepen their understanding of meaning in their lives. The MLQ has excellent reliability, test-retest stability, stable factor structure, and convergence among informants. Presence of Meaning is positively related to well-being, intrinsic religiosity, extraversion, and agreeableness; it is negatively related to anxiety and depression. Search for Meaning is positively related to religious quest, rumination, past-negative and present-fatalistic time perspectives, negative affect, depression, and neuroticism; it is negatively related to future time perspective, closemindedness (dogmatism), and well-being. Presence relates, as expected, with personal growth self-appraisals and altruistic and spiritual behaviors as assessed through daily diaries. The MLQ does not have cut-off scores, like measures of psychological disorders might have. It is intended to measure meaning in life across the complete range of human functioning. The MLQ takes about 3 to 5 min to complete (it can be found at www.michaelfsteger.com/?page_id=13).

CONFLICT MANAGEMENT SKILLS

A big part of health and wellness involves managing conflict (Weinhold & Weinhold, 2009). As a future counselor, there will be many opportunities to help clients and fellow students identify, address, and manage conflict. Conflict between people is actually a very natural occurrence; yet, many people find conflict to be traumatic and stressful. Conflict need not be traumatic, however, and if managed and addressed, may provide the foundation for personal growth. The critical factor regarding conflict is that we acknowledge it, and then strategize on how to resolve it.

The first step in managing conflict is to admit that it exists. Because counseling can be demanding and stressful work, there will be many opportunities to work on developing competence in dealing with conflict. I have listed common assumptions about conflict, and then, a reframed response to these assumptions.

Assumption 1: "All conflict is bad and should be avoided."
Reframed response: Conflict is not necessarily "bad." Acknowledging and addressing conflict can be liberating and improve self-confidence.
Assumption 2: "Conflict is awful and terrible."
Reframed response: Conflict is neither "awful" nor "terrible," although refusing to admit to it or to address it can result in poor health. The trick is in learning to manage conflict. This requires revising one's self-talk, blood pressure, and exercising good emotional regulation (i.e., do not speak out of anger).
Assumption 3: "I simply can't deal with conflict."
Reframed response: Dealing with conflict is sometimes unpleasant for me. However, the more experienced I become at addressing conflicts, the more confident and effective I become at resolving them.
Assumption 4: "When I have conflicts, they always 'blow up' into something unmanageable, so it's just better to ignore them."
Reframed response: Sometimes my attempts at conflict resolution go awry and tempers can escalate. However, in many, if not most, cases, I am able to navigate conflict without causing further injury. It is helpful to remember the importance of good emotional regulation, revised self-talk, and monitoring blood pressure.

A critical factor, beyond admitting the existence of conflicts, is how we go about resolving them. Fortunately, people can improve their conflict resolution skills with practice. As my therapeutic orientation is cognitive behavioral, I believe that conflict resolution is grounded in childhood experiences of observing and participating in family conflicts. Our parents or guardians consciously or unconsciously modeled styles of conflict resolution, which we internalized and then repeated in our conflicts with siblings and peers. Some families are more functional at addressing conflict; children raised in functional homes will have an early advantage at conflict resolution. Children raised in less functional, dysfunctional, abusive, or neglectful homes are more likely to struggle with resolving conflict, as conflict either may represent danger or simply be denied.

Conflict Resolution Styles

Continuing along the line of managing stress, managing conflict is a key part of working in the mental health field. Because counselors and other professionals bring their own issues into the workplace, conflict is natural and expected. For consideration, several different conflict "personality" types are listed in the text that follows.

- **The Denier:** "Conflict? What conflict?" "Everything's just perfect."
- **The Minimizer:** "It's not anything to worry about." "No big deal."
- **The Overly Responsible Type:** "It's all my fault."
- **The Avoider:** "It's better to avoid conflict regardless of the cost."
- **The Aggressor:** "I have to get in people's face! That's how to resolve conflicts."
- **The Mindful Type:** "OK, there is a conflict. What steps can I take to resolve it?"

Counselors can examine the previously noted types of conflict and think about which type best fits how they generally behave when faced with conflict. No one will always choose only one type, but we can decide which of the conflict resolution styles most frequently describes our own approaches. Then we can think about which of these styles we would prefer.

The following questions address conflict resolution style and ways to modify it. Please see Box 31.5 for case illustrations in which you can apply these questions.

- Which of the mentioned conflict resolution style types usually describe the manner in which I deal with conflict?
- What do I fear about conflict? (or, What's the worst thing that could happen regarding conflict?)
- What types of conflict situations do I find most challenging?
- Who were my role models in learning how to address conflict?
- What are my strengths in resolving conflict?
- How effective is my style of conflict resolution?
- In what situations does my approach to resolving conflict work?
- In what situations does my approach to resolving conflict seem ineffective?
- What would I want to change about my style of conflict resolution?
- How could I begin to change my approach to conflict resolution?
- What is one small change I can make that will help me address conflict more effectively?
- My biggest challenge in improving my conflict resolution skills is _____.
- If we think of someone who seems effective in resolving conflict, what conflict resolution skills do they possess?
- What, in my professional training and background, assists me in resolving conflict?
- What types of conflict resolution work do I see myself performing in the future?
- What types of conflict resolution roles would be inconsistent with my future practice as a counselor?
- How would being skilled in conflict resolution assist me in becoming an effective counselor?

BOX 31.5

Case Illustration

Conflict Scenario One

You have just commenced your practicum. You get along very well with most of the staff and fellow graduate practicum students. However, after a few weeks, you discover another practicum student seems to be constantly belittling you (e.g., "You haven't learned much about counseling, have you?" "Your approach to counseling is all wrong."). You decide not to address the issue, hoping it will just resolve itself. Then, one of the other graduate students informs you the student in question is badmouthing you to the others.

How would you resolve this apparent conflict? What actions would be most constructive? What would healthy resolution look like? Now, if possible, role-play the scenario out with a classmate or friend. The more you practice resolving conflicts, the more skilled you will become at resolving them. You cannot force the other person to act professionally and respectfully, but you can behave both as a professional and with respect.

Conflict Scenario Two

You have completed practicum and are beginning the first internship at your placement. Your new supervisor seems very harsh with his criticism and is somewhat sarcastic during supervision sessions, making comments such as "This is subpar work!" and "I can't believe your last supervisor saw your work as worthy of passing practicum." Your supervisor discloses he really did not want to supervise you but felt compelled by the director of clinical services. Intimidated and discouraged, you soon discover yourself avoiding him, whenever you can, as weekly supervision arrives; your stomach is upset, and you feel very anxious. You realize this is an unhealthy situation and that you would like to switch supervisors, but you worry the answer will be "no" and that your supervisor may hold your actions against you. What steps might you take to deal with this conflict? Who might be a support for you in this challenging situation?

THE COUNSELING STUDENT AS CLIENT

Counseling work certainly can be very stressful, as clients bring in difficulties of their own, and there may be job conflicts with coworkers. As a graduate student in a counseling program, you have the added complication of coursework, along with seeing clients, balancing a home life, and numerous additional demands. Many counseling programs now mandate a few counseling sessions for their students. Counselors who have had the experience of being clients themselves may have a more complete understanding of the therapeutic process (Muller, 2016; Norcross et al., 1988). Putting yourself in the vulnerable position as a client also provides you the opportunity of experiencing the "other side" of the therapeutic experience and likely can help you develop more empathy for clients and their struggles.

I can state from experience that many counselors and other mental health professionals sometimes are reluctant to seek counseling services for themselves, out of their fear or arrogance, or simply being unaware of the extent of their personal issues. Self-care is a critical component of effective function for counselors and an issue addressed in the *ACA Code of Ethics* (Standard C.2.g). As a future professional counselor, graduate school is the optimal time to begin addressing your own mental health, to ensure that any personal concerns do not affect professional work. This is not to say a counselor must be a perfect human being; every counselor, no matter how successful and well adjusted, has some personal "baggage." Most importantly, counselors need to understand their personal issues and work to improve on them. After all, such is the nature of counseling work.

For a counselor considering that entering personal counseling might be a good idea, they should be aware that many counselors, psychologists, social workers, and other mental health professionals have already reached similar conclusions. Mahoney (1997) reported that 87% of mental health professionals surveyed admitted they had entered personal counseling at some point in their careers. Mental health professionals rated being a client as second to practical experience as the most important influence in their professional lives. A study of 500 counselors and psychologists revealed that 93% rated the experience from mildly positive to very positive (Baird et al., 1992). Other notable counseling professionals (e.g., Gladding, 2009) have posited personal counseling as a critical growth experience for counselor development. In fact, in the event that it has been a lengthy period since a counselor was a client, it is likely a good idea to seek counseling services as a routine mental health "checkup."

Pope and Tabachnick (1994) conducted a study of more than 800 psychologists, in which 84% admitted to having been in personal therapy. The most often-cited reasons for mental health professionals to seek counseling were (in descending order) depression; divorce or relationship difficulty; struggles with self-esteem; anxiety, or career, work, or study concerns; family of origin issues; loss; and stress (Pope & Tabachnick, 1994). Among those surveyed, 85% described the therapeutic experience as very or exceptionally helpful. What these and other studies suggest is that personal counseling can be very important for our own emotional health and personal growth. Furthermore, personal counseling helps counselors and other therapists remain healthy, and, in doing so, they likely are more effective at providing counseling. Furthermore, many counseling professionals have chosen to become helping professionals because of positive, life-transforming experiences, which they were able to process with greater clarity through their own personal counseling.

In addition to counseling, support groups can serve an important role for counselors and certainly for graduate students as well. I am not aware of counseling programs that require student participation in support groups, but it is a worthwhile concept, particularly given the stressful nature of graduate study, practicum and internship demands, and because the Council for Accreditation of Counseling and Related Educational Programs' (CACREP, 2016) standards essentially mandate preventing counselor impairment. In my own graduate counseling program, we were required to participate in an intensive growth experience for 3 days. I was a participant, both as a master's degree student and later as a group facilitator, as a part of my doctoral program. My experience in both groups was educational and very informative, especially related to the power that group experience has on individuals. However, my belief is that an ongoing support group would be more impactful regarding students' personal growth and development.

FINAL SUGGESTIONS FOR SELF-CARE

Blanchard et al. (1986), famous for the best-selling book *The One Minute Manager*, co-wrote a follow-up book titled *The One Minute Manager Gets Fit* in 1986. He was motivated to write this book after realizing that he was so consumed with chasing success that he forgot the most important thing: to keep his life in balance (Blanchard et al., 1986). He ate junk food, failed to work out, his weight ballooned, and his blood pressure rose to dangerously high levels (Blanchard et al., 1986). In the book, he listed the following directives as a means of assessing fitness level:

- I love my job (most of the time).
- I use safety precautions like wearing a seat belt in moving vehicles.
- I am within five pounds of my ideal weight.

- I know three methods to reduce stress that do not include the use of drugs or alcohol.
- I do not smoke.
- I sleep 6 to 8 h each night and wake up refreshed.
- I engage in regular physical activity at least three times per week (including sustained physical exertion for 20 to 30 min—for example, walking briskly, running, swimming, biking—plus strength and flexibility activities).
- I have seven or fewer alcoholic drinks a week.
- I know my blood pressure.
- I follow sensible eating habits (eat breakfast every day; limit salt, sugar, and [unhealthy] fats ... and eat adequate fiber and few snacks).
- I have a good social support system.
- I maintain a positive mental attitude. (p. 36)

The list contains many common-sense items, yet it is clear that many people, including some graduate students and professional counselors, struggle with a lot of them. Regular medical checkups, on an annual basis, also are highly recommended. Graduate students lacking health insurance should check with their campus health service, as student fees subsidize medical care. College health centers are significantly less expensive than off-campus clinicians are. Furthermore, as previously noted, good self-care is an ethical construct (Standard C.2.g); graduate counseling students would be wise to begin working on self-care development as immediately as possible. Professions at college and university counseling centers, student health centers, and clergy are in a good position to assist with this. Social support systems are critical for well-being as well. Students feeling isolated would be wise to check with a counselor or another of these aforementioned professionals. Support groups can be helpful, along with activities such as getting involved in a club or organization that is of interest (e.g., running club, meditation group, hiking club)

Assessing Your Stress

Stress is a major component of health-related issues and conditions related to anxiety, depression, and a number of somatic problems (Burns, 1993). The Perceived Stress Scale-4 (Box 31.6; Pss-4; Cohen et al., 1983) is a brief test to assess your stress level.

BOX 31.6

Tips From the Field

Perceived Stress Scale-4 (PSS-4)

Circle the number that best represents your stress level on each of the following questions:

1. In the last month, how often have you felt you were unable to control the important things in your life?
   Never (0)   Almost Never (1)   Sometimes (2) Fairly   Often (3)Very   Often (4)
2. In the last month, how often have you felt confident about your ability to handle your problems?
   Never (0)   Almost Never (1)   Sometimes (2)   Fairly Often (3)   Very Often (4)
3. In the last month, how often have you felt that things were going your way?
   Never (0)   Almost Never (1)   Sometimes (2)   Fairly Often (3)   Very Often (4)

(continued)

4. In the past month, how often have you felt difficulties were piling up so high that you could not resolve them?

Never (0)   Almost Never (1)   Sometimes (2)   Fairly Often (3)   Very Often (4)

Scoring for the Perceived Stress Scale 4 (PSS-4)

Questions 1 & 4	Questions 2 & 3
0 = Never	4 = Never
1 = Almost Never	3 = Almost Never
2 = Sometimes	2 = Sometimes
3 = Fairly Often	1 = Fairly Often
4 = Very Often	0 = Very Often
Lowest Score: 0	Highest Score: 16

Higher scores are correlated to feeling more stressed.

Self-Care: Your Owner's Manual on Well-Being

Self-care plans can provide a buffer against compassionate fatigue or burnout (Stamm, 2005). A sample self-care is provided in Box 31.7 for the reader's consideration.

BOX 31.7

Tips From the Field

A Sample Self-Care Plan

As described here and in the previous chapter, secondary trauma, compassion fatigue, and burnout are serious concerns for any counselor or counselor in training. Such maladies may be avoided, however, providing that a counselor has a good self-care plan. For a viable self-care plan, I recommend a minimum of seven dimensions: physical, emotional, cognitive, social, financial, spiritual care, and creative self-care. Naturally, there are individual variations to self-care plans, even within the seven dimensions recommended. The following is one example of how to construct a self-care plan.

   Author's Note: An active self-care plan is very helpful in managing the types of stress that counselors and counselors-in-training face. However, a self-care plan, while helpful in managing stress, is no guarantee against compassionate fatigue or burnout.

1. **Physical Self-Care Dimension:**
These are the activities that I regularly do in order to care for my body in healthy ways. Healthy examples may include regular exercise (e.g., jogging, yoga, Tai Chi, weight training), a balanced diet, abstinence from tobacco and alcohol (or moderate consumption), regular sleep, and annual physicals. In the space that follows, identify three activities you regularly engage in (or plan to engage in) to take care of your physical self:

A.
B.
C.

(continued)

2. **Emotional Self-Care Dimension:**
These are the healthy activities in which I engage in, so as to care for my emotional self. Examples may include daily or weekly journaling, counseling (if necessary), joining a support group, practicing healthy self-talk, positive affirmations, and so forth. In the space that follows, list three activities that you currently do or plan to engage in to care for your emotional self:

A.
B.
C.

3. **Cognitive Self-Care Dimension:**
Cognitive self-care includes activities that you undertake to engage your mind in a creative task. Cognitive self-care activities might include reading for pleasure, playing Scrabble, completing crossword puzzles, continuing education for your career (or future career), taking classes for enjoyment, learning a new skill, and so on. In the space that follows, list three cognitive self-care examples that you regularly engage in (or will engage in):

A.
B.
C.

4. **Social Self-Care Dimension:**
As humans are social creatures, it is important to maintain healthy relationships. Examples could include socializing with friends, family, and colleagues, joining clubs and organizations, going to plays or movies with a spouse/partner/friend, and so on. In the space that follows, identify three social self-care activities that you currently engage in (or will engage in) to care for your social self:

A.
B.
C.

5. **Financial Self-Care Dimension:**
Financial self-care includes how we spend and save money, as well as how we make responsible financial decisions (*this can be challenging as a graduate student on a fixed budget*). Examples include balancing the checking account, maintaining a healthy savings account, speaking with a financial planner regarding investments or future investments, attending a financial planning class, purchasing some of your clothes at Goodwill or the Salvation Army, and so forth. In the space that follows, identify three activities that you currently do or are planning to do for financial self-care.

A.
B.
C.

6. **Spiritual and Mindfulness Self-Care Dimension:**
Most people are spiritual beings in some manner. This may include membership in a faith-based community (e.g., church, mosque, temple), 12-step community, regular individual or group meditation, mindfulness practice, and so forth. **Author's Note**: A person may have no religious inclination but likely finds ways to incorporate meaning and purpose into their life. If you are not spiritually inclined, consider how meaning and purpose manifest in your life. In

(continued)

the space that follows, identify three spiritual/meaning activities you regularly engage in (or plan to engage in).

A.
B.
C.

7. **Creative Self-Care Dimension:**
Everyone is a creative person. Creativity does not require excellent talent and fame, but rather, you can identify simple ways to engage regularly in such pursuits. Creative expressions may include singing solo or in a choir; playing a musical instrument; writing poetry, prose, or music; creating any work or art; performing in community theatre; and so on. In the space that follows, cite three creative activities you regularly engage in (or will engage in).

A.
B.
C.

CONCLUSION

The practicum and internship experiences are intense; they can be very demanding, and occasionally create stress for graduate students. The good news is that survival rates are very high, and most students manage stressful times quite well. One should expect occasional times, however, of feeling overwhelmed or "stressed out." These times, though unpleasant, also provide some of the greatest opportunities. Counselors will have opportunities to practice the same stress management techniques and skills that they have been teaching clients. This is where self-reflection, reframing, meditation, prayer, exercise, friendships, and so forth, are so valuable and rewarding. Be aware of stress and anxiety levels and monitor them closely so as to remain physically and emotionally healthy. A burned-out counselor—one who tries to be everything to everyone—fails to set limits, lacks assertiveness, eats a poor diet, and may have few or no significant friendships; most importantly, the burned-out counselor is likely of limited value to theirr clients. So it helps to understand emotional and physical limitations and also to work to stay within those limitations. It is helpful to use self-assessments, such as the ones in this chapter, to assess stress levels, a healthy lifestyle, meaning in life, and other suggested practices to develop a self-care plan that is realistic and self-sustaining.

ADDITIONAL RESOURCES

 A robust set of instructor resources designed to supplement this text is located at http://connect.springerpub.com/content/book/978-0-8261-5085-1. Qualifying instructors may request access by emailing textbook@springerpub.com.

PRACTICE-BASED RESOURCES AND REFERENCES

To view a list of resources and all the references, please visit connect.springerpub.com via the following url: http://connect.springerpub.com/content/book/978-0-8261-5085-1/part/part06/chapter/ch31

CHAPTER 32

Trauma-Informed and Trauma-Specific Clinical Supervision

DEMOND E. BLEDSOE, ABEER ALI RASHEED,
FATEMAH S. ALGHAMDI, AND LISA LÓPEZ LEVERS

CHAPTER OVERVIEW

This chapter focuses on the importance of clinical supervisors having sufficient knowledge about trauma, stress, crisis, and disaster in order to supervise and mentor adequately. Supervisees are likely to bring complex cases into supervision, cases that involve multiple dimensions of crisis, stress, loss, grief, disaster, and trauma. For counselors serving traumatized clients, the potential for experiencing vicarious trauma increases. Supervisors need to possess the trauma-informed skills to offer relevant clinical supervision as well as to guide, mentor, and support supervisees on issues related to counselor self-care, in the face of dealing with stressful clinical scenarios.

LEARNING OBJECTIVES

After reading this chapter, the reader should be able to:

1. Develop a greater awareness of supervisory-relevant clinical theories concerning the neurobiological and psychosocial effects of trauma;
2. Apprehend the intersections of client trauma, stress, crisis, and disaster and how these might affect clinicians' concerns in supervision;
3. Understand supervisory intervention strategies aimed at mitigating the effects of client trauma on supervisees;
4. Learn to process the impact of trauma within the supervisory dyad;
5. Assist supervisees in increasing the effectiveness of the trauma-specific treatment, both with individual clients and within systems of care; and,
6. Develop awareness of the potential social justice issues concerning supervisees' clients as well as how clients' trauma experiences affect supervisees.

INTRODUCTION

The field of counseling has been growing and adapting to reflect the needs of the populations that it serves. Over the past 40 years, trauma counseling has seen a significant increase in the availability of research, resources, and training. The body of knowledge related to clinical supervision has followed closely on the heels of trauma counseling and has become more readily available. While the topics of trauma counseling and clinical supervision have begun to converge in ways that specifically support concerns related to trauma and associated dynamics, it has become apparent that clinical supervisors continue to need more information and more advanced skills, in order to address the trauma, stress, crisis, and disaster experienced by the clients of their supervisees.

Recent literature has begun to illuminate the critical need for trauma-informed supervision for counselors working with traumatized clients. However, the emphasis largely has focused on the potential for such counselors to experience vicarious trauma (e.g., Berger & Quiros, 2014; Ellis et al., 2019; Hayden et al., 2015; Jones & Branco, 2020; Jordan, 2018; Knight, 2018; Lonn & Haiyasoso, 2016; Rizkalla et al., 2021; Substance Abuse and Mental Health Services Administration [SAMHSA], 2014; Veach & Shilling, 2018). While this is an important and legitimate concern, and one that is addressed in this chapter, trauma-informed supervision needs to grow beyond attending to vicarious trauma. Given the current state of the world and the increasing demand for trauma-informed mental health services, especially for those needing trauma counseling, the arena of trauma-informed supervision for mental health clinicians treating trauma must evolve more robustly. An issue related to this emergent and developing area of trauma-informed supervision is the responsibility of preservice clinical programs to prepare and equip advanced clinicians with the necessary skills to supervise counselors treating trauma, stress, crisis, and disaster. Such accountability is requisite at this time (Ellis et al., 2019; Gaete et al., 2017).

The main purposes of this chapter are to elucidate how trauma is processed within the supervisory dyad and to highlight intervention strategies aimed at mitigating the effects of clients' trauma on clinicians so that they can increase the effectiveness of the treatment services being provided. In addition, this chapter emphasizes the need for clinical supervisors to understand contextual perspectives, as well as to incorporate a social justice framework into their selected model of supervision, in order to address the experiences of BIPOC (Black and Indigenous People of Color) clients and supervisees in relationship to their traumatic experiences (Dollarhide et al., 2021; Haans & Balke, 2018). The aims of this chapter are met in these major sections: Trauma and Supervision, Context and Supervision, and Clinical Implications of Trauma-Informed Supervision. These main sections are followed by a summary of the chapter and an online-only list of practice-based resources.

TRAUMA AND SUPERVISION

Supervision has been accepted for some time as an integral part of development for trainees and professionals alike; it also is a mandated part of most professional licenses and certifications for independent mental health clinicians. The increasing demands of a changing work environment have provided new and constantly changing needs within the supervisory relationship. Of primary current concern is the increasing volume of clients who have suffered severe and pervasive traumatic experiences throughout their lives; the number has escalated exponentially during recent times as people's mental health concerns have been amplified by the circumstances associated with the COVID-19 pandemic (e.g., Alghamdi, 2021). The groundbreaking Adverse Childhood Experiences Study (ACES) by Anda and Felitti (2003) continues to be the defining study that highlights the need for attention in the area of developmental and life-span trauma; recent advances in brain science have helped us, in remarkable ways, to understand the neurobiology of trauma. In this section, we discuss trauma-relevant aspects of supervision in the following subsections: Clinical Supervision, Polyvagal Theory From Counseling and Supervisory Perspectives, Vicarious Trauma and Secondary Traumatic Stress, and Trauma-Sensitive Supervision.

Clinical Supervision

Supervision is both an essential principle of the counseling field and a distinct intervention (Bernard & Goodyear, 2019; Falender & Shafranske, 2014; Falender et al., 2014). Far too often, professionals in the mental health field possess a unidimensional view of supervision, one that primarily or solely encompasses the routines of administrative supervision. While it is important to ensure that administrative details are addressed at all levels of organizational hierarchy, we clearly are not concerned so much with administrative supervision here. Rather, our focus is on clinical supervision and the vital role that trauma-informed clinical supervision plays in guiding and supporting clinicians who offer trauma-specific services—including those trauma-related services that attend to stress, crisis, and disaster, along with trauma.

Defining clinical supervision can be challenging because of the multiple dynamics of the supervisory process as well as the complexities of working with individuals who may possess differing perspectives (Falender, 2014). However, clinical supervision can be defined as an ongoing supportive learning process for clinicians at all levels to develop, enhance, monitor, and, when necessary, remediate professional functioning (Bernard & Goodyear, 2019). Ultimately, the goal of clinical supervision is to provide the most ethically sound and clinically competent service to the client in order to facilitate the achievement of the client's goals (Borders, 2014; Falender & Shafranske, 2014; Falender et al., 2014). Clinical supervision often is viewed as its own distinct specialty within the counseling profession, and has been gaining ground as an important facet of the overall counseling process. Viewed as a career-long process, clinical supervision has the potential to create immediate change as well as to create change that has lasting effects for supervisees and clients alike (Falender et al., 2004). Many clinicians identify clinical supervision as an integral component of their self-perceived efficacy as a counselor and as critical to their ability to mitigate the effects of emotional and job stress, thereby lowering the rate of burnout (Bransford, 2009; Gaete et al., 2017).

Of potential peril in the supervisory relationship is a tendency for the relationship to become authoritarian, with the supervisor regarded as the *expert* and the supervisee relegated to the role of *novice*, or somehow *lesser*, in terms of clinical skill, knowledge, and ability. Such a hierarchy can lead to a therapist's perceptions of the client changing without regard to a previous case conceptualization or to relevant dynamics of the counseling relationship (Holloway, 2016; Miehls, 2010). As these transitions occur, a therapist may repress feelings associated with the client due to a shift in focus or understanding of the case. This repression may increase stress and perhaps force the therapist not only to contain but also to cast aside these perceptions, without the ability to process or resolve the therapist's concerns or residual feelings. This is even more critical for a therapist who is encountering secondary stress reactions, as there seems to be an increased likelihood that the clinical viewpoint is less defined (Everall & Paulson, 2004; Soloski & Deitz, 2016) than in clinicians exhibiting a lower level of traumatic stress. This dynamic of secondary stress is addressed, in greater detail, later in this chapter.

Clinical supervision may be thought of as a reflective process by which issues discussed between the therapist and the client are recreated within the context of clinical supervision (Bernard & Goodyear, 2019; Miehls, 2010). This reflective process is necessary in developing a supervisory dyad that is supportive and that allows the clinician to manage personal feelings and emotions that may arise during the process of providing therapy to clients. In effective clinical supervisory relationships, authenticity and concepts of mutuality within the dyad can influence the counselor's relationships with clients in a parallel fashion (Miehls, 2010). The literature suggests that the effective clinical supervision relationship has a positive impact on client outcomes as well as on the learning and professional development of the supervisee (Beinart, 2014). It is important to note that, while we discuss the *supervisory dyad* (supervisor and supervisee), consistent with the professional literature on supervision, there are always three sets of concerns represented in supervision: those of the counselor, those of the supervisor, and, importantly, those of the client. The dynamics within the supervisor–supervisee dyad must never overshadow the concerns of the client.

Polyvagal Theory From Counseling and Supervisory Perspectives

An important recent development in traumatology, which has abundant implications for clinical supervision, relates to the neurobiological impact of traumatic events (Dana, 2018; Knight, 2018; Porges & Dana, 2018). Because we now understand the biology of trauma in much more detailed and profound ways, it is imperative for trauma-informed supervisors to be aware of recent brain science, particularly Porges' (2007, 2011) groundbreaking work in developing Polyvagal Theory (PVT). The name of this theory derives from the Latin "polus" meaning "many" and "vagal" meaning "nerve." The vagus nerve is the 10th cranial nerve and may be the most important nerve in the body that many of us never before knew about. Recent brain science and PVT are detailed in Chapters 2 and 4 of this textbook; however, it is essential, here, to make the connections between this corpus of relatively recent knowledge and what trauma-informed clinical supervisors need to understand in order to assist and guide counselors who provide trauma-specific services. Therefore, we need to explore this important part of the human anatomy, the brain, and its interface with the experience of trauma.

The human nervous system has two major parts: the central nervous system (CNS), which includes the brain and spinal cord, and the peripheral nervous system (PNS), which is divided into two branches, the somatic nervous system and the autonomic nervous system (ANS). The ANS controls the sympathetic nervous system (SNS) and parasympathetic nervous system (PNS). Our discussion here, regarding trauma-informed supervision and PVT, relates primarily to an understanding of the ANS. PVT (Porges, 2007, 2011) is derived from our most recent comprehensions of neuroscience; PVT has become instrumental for mental health professionals in understanding the effects of trauma, and by extension, in better understanding trauma-informed clinical counseling strategies and clinical supervision responses. PVT helps us in exploring the parasympathetic response within the ANS in relationship to clients who have a history of experiencing trauma. Furthermore, it is important to note the experiences and subsequent responses of the clients discussed during supervision are likely to mirror those of clinical supervisors or supervisees who are experiencing unresolved trauma. An understanding of PVT can assist clinical supervisors in grasping these dynamics and interpreting possible clinician countertransference in response to client trauma (Shubs, 2008).

Three ANS states are responsible for the regulation of responses and interactions: social engagement, mobilization, and immobilization. Each state has a set of attributes that are based upon the brain's perception of the events. This is important to note, as the actual events that lead to the traumatic reactions frequently are less significant than the person's perception of the events. Each individual perceives, interprets, and has their own distinct experience of the traumatic situation (Tehrani & Levers, 2016); this can be influenced strongly by the context in which the trauma occurred. In essence, the lived experience of trauma drives the immediate neural-level interpretation and expression of the event or events, and this, in turn, has further neurobiological implications.

When the body is in a safe state, or homeostasis, connections to others are possible, even facilitated. In this state, the SNS allows the body to access relationships with others, and to feel pleasure and emotional connections. The body is calm and relaxed and able to adapt to changing situations. When a person perceives a situation as unsafe, the body moves to a mobilized state in which the PNS engages and prepares for fight or flight. This pathway, comprised of the myelinated vagus nerve, prepares the body to endure a physical altercation or response in order to maintain safety (myelination of nerve cells enables faster transmission of neural information). Finally, the freeze or immobilized state is the body's attempt to return to homeostasis and balance. This is also a function of the PNS but flows along the unmyelinated (slower transmission) part of the vagus nerve.

Counselors and trainees need to know that individuals with unprocessed or unresolved traumatic experiences frequently vacillate between two states, as they manage their life stressors and relationships. These states are "mobilization," in which the SNS prepares for the fight or flight response, and "immobilization," in which the PNS shuts down and freezes one's ability to manage situations or interactions perceived as stressful or unsafe. Symptoms commonly experienced by those with traumatic experiences, and those which are likely to emerge as salient issues in a supervisory context, include dissociation, anger, sadness, depression, and hypervigilance (Tehrani & Levers, 2016). The symptoms and associated inability or unwillingness to engage in social connections can have a catastrophic effect on a person's quality of life and ability to experience happiness or reciprocal relationships (B. S. Austin, 2012; M. A. Austin et al., 2007; Dana, 2018). Additionally, traumatized individuals may detect danger in nondangerous situations by failing to read the socially responsive facial expressions of others. Therefore, they may experience anxiety, flashbacks, and somatic symptoms (Porges & Dana, 2018).

PVT has significant ramifications for counselors and the clinical supervision process. The therapeutic relationship between a counselor and a client places emphasis on the significant role of the social connection between them in order to heal trauma. In addition to the dysfunction and dysregulation potentially experienced by clients in their daily lives, clients turn to counselors to support their change and growth yet experience the same constrictions and constraints in forming meaningful and trusting relationships. This can cause the counseling dyad to become "stuck," marked by a lack of progress. Effective clinical supervision of trauma and trauma-associated issues, as informed by PVT, would encompass skill-based and developmental approaches aimed at helping the therapist to negotiate the therapeutic relationship and to navigate social connections with the client. Supported by trauma-informed supervision, counselors can develop pathways for healing during their sessions with clients, and this can begin with the therapist simply providing the client with cues that facilitate safety (Porges & Dana, 2018; Tehrani & Levers, 2016).

Vicarious Trauma and Secondary Traumatic Stress

It is essential for clinical supervisors to have a clear understanding of theories related to trauma therapy (Ellis et al., 2019; Etherington, 2000; Jones & Branco, 2020; Knight, 2018; Sommer, 2008; Sommer & Cox, 2005). The processes and treatment interventions for trauma-related concerns often are specific and encompass emotional, cognitive, and behavioral elements aimed at reducing the level of arousal, thereby facilitating more appropriate responses to stressful stimuli and situations. The recognition of traumatic stress symptoms in clinicians is an essential responsibility for clinical supervisors (Berger & Quiros, 2014; Etherington, 2000; Jordan, 2017). Early recognition of potential traumatic stress reactions or vicarious traumatization (VT) on the part of both supervisors and therapists can lead to requisite supervisory interventions that focus on providing the necessary support and guidance to assist the therapist in identifying issues that are emotionally taxing (vicarious trauma is discussed more fully in Chapter 30 of this book). Such acknowledgment can aid in identifying support systems and ways to reduce the negative aspects of the traumatic stress reaction; it also can ensure that treatment is being delivered to the client in an ethical and effective manner (Borders, 2014; Ellis et al., 2019). The validation and normalization of these reactions create an opportunity for the supervisee to navigate their experiences successfully (Knight, 2018). The clinical vignette presented in Box 32.1 illustrates the need for why a supervisor might address a counselor's potential VT.

BOX 32.1

Clinical Vignette: Bette Supervises Anthony

Anthony is an experienced licensed professional counselor, in private practice, who has a contract with the psychiatric unit of a local hospital. In cases involving suicide and other involuntary/court mandated hospitalizations, Anthony consults with the unit's clinical supervisor. Over the course of a holiday weekend, Anthony was called to the psychiatric unit to respond to five different cases, all involuntary hospitalizations that were court mandated and that included two people attempting suicide and three with florid psychotic symptoms. All five involved complex family dynamics and varying degrees of complex trauma. Each of the five required intensive

(continued)

immediate services, and Anthony averaged about 4 nonstop hours per case. Anthony's supervisor, Bette, scheduled a supervision session ahead of their normally scheduled supervision time, when she returned after the weekend and learned of Anthony's stressful cases.

Reflection Questions:

1. Imagine that you are Anthony. What kinds of clinical issues would you most want to discuss in supervision after such intensive consultations over the weekend?
2. Imagine that you are Bette. How would you begin to conceptualize Anthony's clinical experiences over the weekend? What kinds of supervisory issues might you raise?

Within the domain of counseling, the terms "secondary traumatic stress (STS) disorder" and "vicarious trauma (VT)" are used frequently and interchangeably; however, there are some distinct differences between these two concepts. STS is the empathic result of a therapist's exposure to another individual's traumatic incidents, hearing about them firsthand (Jones & Branco, 2020; Kirkinis et al., 2021). Primarily based in the expression of thoughts and behaviors, STS can have a rapid onset, and therapists experiencing STS may have symptoms often resembling those that meet the criteria for posttraumatic stress disorder (PTSD) (Etherington, 2000; Jones & Branco, 2020; Sommer, 2008). VT describes the cumulative effect on clinicians of working with the trauma experienced by others and may even precipitate changes in clinical personnel (SAMHSA, 2014). Trippany et al. (2004, p. 31) state that "[t]hese changes involve disruptions in the cognitive schemas of counselors' identity, memory system, and belief system." Trust, safety, control, esteem, and intimacy have been key areas associated with therapists' reactions to hearing the traumatic life stories of their clients (Jenkins & Baird, 2002; Lonn & Haiyasoso, 2016). Additionally, Knight (2018) identifies suspicion, pessimism, and powerlessness as constructs that may become entrenched in the counselor's worldview. The therapist's view of self, as well as their worldview, may be altered (Berger & Quiros, 2014; Bober & Regehr, 2006; Jordan, 2017) because of indirectly experiencing the trauma and resulting emotional responses described by clients. It is essential to remember that both VT and STS are occupational hazards and do not indicate pathology on the part of the therapist (Pearlman & Maclan, 1995; SAMHSA, 2014).

Although VT and STS are recognized as possible outcomes of repeated exposures to the traumatic experiences of the clients, there seems to be a discrepancy in the anecdotal reports of the prevalence of reactions in therapists and the actual presence of the conditions supported by empirical data (Elwood et al., 2011; Kadambi & Truscott, 2004). Research has not substantiated that the presence of STS or VT in clinicians, who primarily treat clients with severe trauma histories, occurs at a higher incidence than with clinicians who do not work primarily with trauma (Elwood et al., 2011). However, research does suggest that clinicians who work extensively with clients experiencing severe traumas tend to score higher on scales measuring VT and STS, although there is no increase in the scores reaching a clinically significant level (Bober & Regehr, 2006). Often thought to affect large numbers of clinicians, the instances of VT or STS may be overreported or may seem more prevalent, because the supervision of therapists encountering these symptoms may be intensive and frequent.

Another factor that cannot be ignored is the tendency for the presence of VT or STS in clinicians who themselves have a history of sexual or physical abuse or other psychological traumas that yet may be unresolved. Pearlman and Maclan (1995) found that therapists with personal trauma histories tended to score higher on scales designed to measure VT and STS than did therapists without personal trauma histories. This potentially may be one confounding factor in the results of a study of rape crisis counselors, which found that increased exposure to trauma was associated with increased supervision and may have accounted for what the researchers termed "trauma contagion" (Rizkalla et al., 2021).

Trauma-Sensitive Supervision

The concept of clinical supervision is one that increasingly has become accepted, even mandated, in the field of counseling over the past several decades and has developed into a distinct discipline. As the discipline continues to evolve, an iterative process has occurred, and distinct modalities or orientations have begun to appear. Trauma-sensitive supervision is one such modality and has gained ground in recent years, due to the prevalence of trauma in the population that is seeking counseling services. The integration of trauma theory with standard supervision theories arises from an intentional attempt to provide effective supervision that specifically relates to managing the effects of psychosocial trauma and that provides direct support for clinicians and indirect support for clients. Crunk and Barden (2017) argue for the use of integrated models for clinical supervision. They acknowledge that no one model appears to address the specific needs of all counselors or clinical supervisors, yet there are aspects from various models that support effective clinical supervision. They assert that there continues to be a lacuna in the professional literature concerning the need to find commonalities in supervision models or specific attributes increasing supervisory efficacy. This lacuna certainly applies to integrative models of trauma-informed supervision as well.

Providing adequate supervision for counselors working with clients who have experienced severe, persistent, and pervasive trauma is an ongoing dilemma for supervisors. Knight (2018) addresses the inevitability of indirect trauma that may occur in clinicians during the process of counseling. The emotional toll that clinicians experience often becomes a central theme in the supervisory process. Currently, no uniform documented process exists for providing supervision that fully supports clinicians as they work to improve the lives of clients with trauma histories. There are, however, some common factors and approaches, which have been identified as potentially equipping supervisors with the tools necessary to support the clinicians they supervise. One example of such common factors is what Gaete et al. (2017) reference as "orienting principles," which they identify as efficacy, responsiveness, and authenticity. The most critical of such orienting factors, relative to trauma-sensitive supervision, is the supervisor's own knowledge of trauma theory (Sommer, 2008). Miehls (2010) states that there are specific enactments or interactions that can occur between a client with a trauma history and a therapist, and that these same interactions then may occur between the clinician and the supervisor. This phenomenon in supervision is known as parallel process; it involves the client's transference and the counselor's countertransference, which the counselor then mirrors with the supervisor. A supervisor's understanding of trauma theory facilitates an acceptance of the clinician's countertransference reactions as well as allowing for an appropriate response that supports the clinician in professional development and working with the client. Trauma-sensitive supervision is based on understanding the constructs of parallel process and isomorphism (the systemic counterpart to parallel process), then pairing those constructs with trauma theory and applying interventions in a way that supports clinician development and client growth.

The most primary concern, when considering effective supervision for clinicians who work with trauma, has been ensuring that clinical supervision takes place frequently and consistently in a manner that adequately provides support for the therapists. Sommer and Cox (2005) noted in their study that counselors expressed concern over not receiving what they perceived as an adequate amount of supervision in order to feel competent and supported in their efforts to work with traumatized populations. Hanson et al. (2002) found that less than 33% of the sampled organizations provided supervision specifically designed to address concerns related to trauma in either the client or the clinician. Similarly, in her qualitative inquiry of the impact of VT on hundreds of state child welfare workers, Jankoski (2010) found that the workers felt great frustration regarding their limited opportunities for supervision.

The development of a strong supervisory relationship is a critical component for trauma-sensitive supervision (Sommer, 2008). This is highlighted by considering the importance of trust in the therapeutic relationship between client and clinician; it is trust, and an ensuing sense of safety, that enables clients to expose their most difficult feelings, concerns, inadequacies, and life events that have created psychological stress and anxiety. Without the presence of trust and respect, the process is inhibited, partially due to the emotional toll that may follow examinations of client trauma. An isomorphic or parallel process occurs in supervision (Bernard & Goodyear, 2019), in which the clinician must make a decision not only to share similar information but also must be willing to accept critical feedback and assessment. Bernard and Goodyear relate the processes of therapy such as joining, goal setting, challenging client realities, and possessing sensitivity to the same isomorphic principles in supervision. Furthermore, supervisors should use the same level of intentionality, which occurs in therapy, throughout the supervisory process (Bernard & Goodyear, 2019).

According to Miehls (2010), clinicians and supervisees tend to recreate enactments similar to those that occur in the course of the counseling relationship. Miehls states that in the supervisory relationship, these enactments are parallel to those that occur between the clinician and the client during the course of the treatment. An example of this is a scenario in which the client attempts to get the therapist to act in a manner similar to that of the client's abuser. Repeated and ongoing traumas may culminate in traumatic responses being less specific to the given situation and more ingrained and patterned, based on previous experiences (Berger & Quiros, 2014; Hodas, 2006). These traumatic responses lead to spontaneous enactments that pose unique opportunities for the clinician to reshape client expectations by providing positive, respectful, and nurturing responses—the kind of responses that the client could never expect from the abuser, as posed in the previous example. Analogous to the reshaping that occurs within the counseling relationship, supervisors have a similar opportunity to sculpt supervisee expectations by providing nurturing and supportive feedback. Just as the worldview of a client can evolve over the course of time, given a patterned set of responses that occur consistently within the confines of a relationship, the processes that occur within the supervisory relationship are parallel and provide a similar opportunity to change the clinician's worldview. Thus, the relationship between the supervisor and the supervisee becomes a critical factor in the process of change and growth for the supervisee. When this process occurs, the worldview of the clinician or the client, respectively, is reinforced and more likely to develop further, and into the future, in response to the positive and caring interactions.

The subjective experience of the relationship between the supervisor and supervisee can provide the experience necessary to create a relationship that is both genuine and authentic (Etherington, 2000; Tehrani & Levers, 2016) and that is able to foster growth and independence. Bennett (2008) suggests that when supervisors are more attuned to the attachment style and needs of the supervisee, a more secure bond may be formed, and this bond then can lead to a greater ability to repair any damage to the relationship that was done during therapy or supervision. Without the development of a secure relationship, the efforts of a therapist to assist a client may be viewed as threatening or overwhelming. The resulting use of defense mechanisms to ensure safety may hinder the therapeutic process (Pearlman & Courtois, 2005). A parallel process occurs during supervision when a supervisor attempts to address a clinical need; this can trigger a response of resistance (Bennett, 2008), and the resulting support that either is present or absent depends on the quality of the relationship in the supervisory dyad.

Another process likely to play out within the context of the supervisory dyad is dissociation, which is a typical response to traumatic situations (Hodas, 2006; Levers, 2020; Miehls, 2010). For clinicians working with clients who are survivors of trauma, dissociative symptoms may manifest as reports of intrusive imagery and may be present during supervision or counseling sessions (Levers, 2020; Sommer, 2008). Clinicians may notice disruptions outside of the workplace in their interpersonal relationships with family and friends (Etherington, 2000). There also may be changes in behavior that only can be noticed if the supervisor has a solid understanding of and relationship with the clinician (Miehls, 2010). Supervisory assessment for potential VT or STS reactions is crucial in clinician development and support. Frequent and ongoing assessment, specifically aimed at targeting changes in clinician behavior or the clinician's ability to process client concerns, can alert the supervisor to subtle changes outside the consciousness of the clinician. For many supervisors and clinicians alike, assessment is viewed narrowly as an administrative task for measuring competency and work performance, when in reality it should encompass multiple domains, including wellness and any other factor that helps or hinders the clinician's ability to provide treatment (Hayden et al., 2015).

Addressing the client-related dissociation that clinicians experience during the counseling or supervisory process must occur within the context of a supervisory relationship that is built on mutual respect and trust. Furthermore, clinicians must be provided a safe space and opportunity to discuss personal feelings freely, which may, on the surface, appear to be inappropriate for discussion in the professional arena. These discussions should include increasing the supervisee's self-awareness of the feelings that they experience during therapy sessions, imagery that is present, somatic sensations (Miehls, 2010), or feelings of anxiety that arise during specific conversations. Etherington (2009) suggests that supervisors help therapists to find meaning in their experiences. Similar to the processes of therapy, supervisors can encourage clinicians to explore their own personal or professional stories in hopes that they can better understand their responses to client narratives. This process permits the exploration of cognitive, behavioral, emotional, and neurobiological responses. It also may bring to light some of the unconscious responses present in the therapy sessions that are replicated during supervision.

Group clinical supervision may be an effective way to help therapists mitigate the effects of prolonged exposure to working with traumatized populations (Haans & Balke, 2018). As discussed previously, clinicians who score high on scales for VT or STS share a given set of responses to their experiences. Using group clinical supervision permits clinicians to normalize some of the feelings that they may be experiencing, takes the focus away from specific and individual difficulties, and allows for the discussion of common themes or experiences (Kitchiner et al., 2006). The normalization that occurs in groups, when clinicians share their feelings and experiences—those that result from dealing with the traumatic experiences of clients—allows clinicians to perceive their group-based supervision as perhaps more validating and supportive than in individual supervision (Trippany et al., 2004). Furthermore, Trippany et al. (2004) state that other constructs such as isolation, objectivity, and even compassion and empathy can be influenced by the support that a clinician experiences from peers, through informal supervision; however, this also can be applied to more formal group clinical supervision.

CONTEXT AND SUPERVISION

This chapter has focused, thus far, on the importance of the supervisory relationship as it relates to trauma-informed and trauma-specific counseling and supervision. However, we assert that the context, in which supervision is provided, may be as important as the relationship itself, especially as the context allows for or facilitates competent clinical supervision. In this section, we briefly discuss the importance of a systemic perspective and a social justice framework.

Systemic Perspective of Trauma-Informed Clinical Supervision

The SAMHSA (2014) recommends that trauma-informed care (TIC) be incorporated into behavioral health services at the institutional or organizational level. In this way, trauma-informed clinical supervision is one aspect of an entire systemic picture that supports and reinforces a trauma-informed approach. According to a SAMHSA publication, this is true in the following way:

> Ongoing supervision and consultation support the organizational message that TIC is the standard of practice. It normalizes secondary traumatization as a systemic issue (not the individual pathology of the counselor) and reinforces the need for counselor self-care to prevent and lessen the impact of secondary traumatization. Quality clinical supervision for direct care staff demonstrates the organization's commitment to implementing a fully integrated, trauma-informed system of care. (SAMHSA, 2014, p. 192)

In this sense, trauma-informed supervision is an integral part of TIC, and at the same time, this systemic approach to supervision drives essential clinical elements of the TIC system.

One commonly used theory of supervision is Bernard and Goodyear's (2019) discrimination model. It is both a competence-based and social-role model of supervision, and it well may be suited for providing a supervisory context within a TIC system (SAMHSA, 2014). The discrimination model addresses the counselor competencies of intervention (how the supervisee intervenes with clients and uses counseling strategies), conceptualization (how the supervisee understands clients' concerns), and personalization (the supervisee's personal style of counseling and any countertransference responses to clients' presentations). The discrimination model also focuses on the multiple roles of the supervisor as:

- Teacher (helping the supervisee to understand and further explore counseling strategies and interventions),
- Counselor (not as a personal counselor, but rather assisting the supervisee in pertinent clinical self-reflection as well as attending to process and relational dimensions of counseling), and
- Consultant (guiding the supervisee through the details of specific clinical conundrums). (Bernard & Goodyear, 2019)

A number of supervisory models exist, which rely upon systems theory and contextual perspectives as the bases for their conceptual frameworks. It is beyond the parameters of this chapter to offer a full account of supervision theory here. However, we offer a brief discussion of two supervision models that are systems and context based and that are adaptable to an alignment of supervision and trauma theories within the scope of supervision provision. Holloway's (2016) systems approach to supervision (SAS) is a multidimensional procedure that has emphasized how various clinical factors are incorporated into the supervisory process. The process itself is interactional and allows clinicians to focus on issues like trauma within the supervisory dyad. Ellis et al. (2019) have offered insight about supervisory practices aimed at addressing contextual trauma therapy. They have highlighted the exclusion of trauma treatment in a majority of mental health-related preservice training programs and advocate for linking trauma-based clinical supervision as a component of training programs.

Social Justice

The past decade has seen a rise in the recognition of the need for counselors to address the traumas that often are present in marginalized populations, within the United States as well as throughout the world. Additionally, awareness and understanding has increased in regard to the impact of social structures that frequently lead to traumatic experiences. Recent events, including the killings of George Floyd, Breonna Taylor, Ahmaud Arbery, Elijah McClain, and many more; the shootings at the Tree of Life Synagogue in Pittsburgh, Pennsylvania; and the shootings at the Emanuel AME Church in Charleston, South Carolina represent a few of the many situations that have added to a collective experience of trauma. Additionally, COVID-19 disproportionately has affected communities of color and other underserved communities, further disrupting access to adequate health and behavioral healthcare services as well as having trauma-related implications (Alghamdi, 2021; Loeb et al., 2021; Porges, 2020).

The integration of multicultural issues, diversity, and social justice in clinical supervision is essential to the process of effective clinical supervision (Haans & Balke, 2018; Nelson et al., 2015; H. P. Peters & Luke, 2021). Truly competent supervision always has required the clinical supervisor to initiate and engage in cultural discussions, encourage the use of culturally sensitive assessments and interventions, and evaluate the multicultural sensitivity and awareness of supervisees (Rasheed, 2015; Soheilian et al., 2014). These same considerations gain even greater clinical salience with the presence of trauma. According to Brown (2008, p. 3), "[a] psychotherapist's ability to understand how a trauma survivor's multiple identities and social contexts lend meaning to the experience of a trauma and the process of recovery comprises the central factor of culturally competent trauma practice." However, in order to infuse social justice into an effective trauma-related supervisory process, the clinical supervisor must model clinical competence, as well as demonstrate the trauma- and social justice-related competencies that are practiced within the supervisory dyad (Dollarhide et al., 2021).

Social justice in clinical supervision first requires the acknowledgement that disparities and inequalities are present. Social justice supervision requires counselors and supervisors not only to acknowledge and to address concerns presented by the client, but also to work actively to change the system that promotes the inequities and disparities that lead to poor outcomes and interfere with psychological development (Lee & Kelley-Petersen, 2018). Loeb et al. (2021) identified the need for mental health professionals to acknowledge, openly, the impact of hundreds of years of discrimination, racial injustices, and violence toward individuals, families, and communities of color that were perpetrated in the name of science and medicine. Specifically, they address the use of science to perpetuate the concept of White superiority over those who are non-White, the justification of a biological hierarchy in humans, and the victimization of marginalized communities in the name of science and medicine (Loeb et al., 2021). These same concepts apply to clinical supervision, and they alarmingly continue to remain relevant in our contemporary context.

Special attention must be paid to the relationship between the clinical supervisor and the supervisee. Dollarhide et al. (2021) suggested specific approaches to facilitate social justice within the supervisory dyad. Those approaches included the following elements: addressing the power dynamic, recognizing structural views, fostering relationships, and using developmental models. The presence of transference and countertransference may be rooted in the biases and stereotypes that are present in one or both members of the supervisory dyad (Hall & Spencer, 2017). The manner in which a member of the dyad interacts with the other member may be related to the member's personal history and experiences. An impaired interaction may serve as a significant impediment for the success of the supervisory relationship, especially in the case of a clinical supervisor who might exploit the power differential (Hall & Spencer, 2017).

The presence of a power differential is of particular interest, as it relates to trauma supervision. As discussed previously in this chapter, the one-up aspect of clinical supervision puts the supervisor in a position of authority over the therapist. For BIPOC counselors seeking supervision, this relationship can replicate the structures in place that have led to oppression and discrimination. It also may affect the perception of the working alliance from the perspective of the supervisee (Inman & Ladany, 2014). Hook et al. (2016; Hook et al., 2017) identified the concept of cultural humility as a significant factor in multicultural clinical supervision. They defined the term as a construct in which the clinical supervisor is able to maintain a viewpoint that is oriented toward the "other," the other being the supervisee (Hook et al., 2016). This is particularly relevant during instances in which the supervisee is from a nondominant group. Hook et al. (2016) proposed two overarching goals of cultural humility in supervision: (a) to be open to alternate beliefs and not to perceive one's own beliefs as superior and (b) to recognize the limitations of understanding the cultural background of the supervisee and the degree to which that background informs the practice of the supervisee.

In addition to the concerns previously addressed, the clinical supervisor must be acutely aware of the presence of trauma in the supervisee, specifically in relationship to the supervisee's experiences as a person of color or membership in another marginalized population. Clinical supervisors may benefit by considering the supervisee from an intersectional perspective. Clinicians perceive their clients through the personal lens of their own cultural, social, and institutional experiences; it is then important for supervisors to recognize that clinicians' experiences may influence their conceptualization of a case and the clinical interventions applied. Although the clinicians may have experienced oppression and discrimination, they may be unaware of the extent, impact, or ways in which their personal experiences shape their counseling (H. C. Peters, 2017). H. C. Peters (2017, p. 183) argues that due to the "nature of supervision, and the power and privilege supervisors hold, supervisors utilizing a lens grounded in multicultural complexity are required to make an ongoing investment in the experience, knowledge, and narratives that are emerging from the margins." This complexity must include investing in supporting trauma-informed counseling strategies that actually address the traumatic events that result from institutional inequities and marginalization.

CLINICAL IMPLICATIONS OF TRAUMA-INFORMED SUPERVISION

The discussions presented in this chapter have raised numerous clinical implications regarding the need for competent clinical supervision that intersects with the clinical needs of counselors who provide services to clients who have been traumatized—and by extension, also to clients who experience stress, crisis, and disaster. One very important implication concerns the issue of professional ethics. Just as the provision of clinical supervision is an ethical issue across the various mental health disciplines, the provision of competent trauma-informed clinical supervision to therapists who treat trauma also is a critical ethical issue (Tarvydas et al., 2017, 2018).

The process of supervision offers unique opportunities for learning and growth, both personally and professionally. This process is affected directly by the presence of trauma, by discrimination and oppression, and often by a lack of knowledge about the neurobiological processes of trauma. Special attention must be paid to the supervisory dyad in relationship to creating a safe place in which trauma, discrimination, or both can be acknowledged and addressed openly. The capability of clinical supervisors to develop a rapport and openness with their supervisees is paramount, as their ability to encourage growth and change is based upon the establishment and presence of a trusting relationship. The development of these relationships, particularly when the dyads are culturally dissimilar, must be predicated on the presence of cultural humility and mutual cultural respect. Developing a strong knowledge of trauma-related principles and techniques permits supervisors to support the expansion of their supervisees' ability to feel confident in treating clients with trauma histories; it further allows supervisors to address VT and STS reactions in the clinicians. Although the areas of trauma and clinical supervision have developed and evolved over the last several decades, the lack of their formally acknowledged interconnectedness has left a practice gap within the mental health professions. The integration of knowledge and skills from both areas is necessary, ethically and clinically, for trauma-informed clinical supervisors to continue to support clinicians effectively as they strive to provide quality trauma-informed counseling.

CONCLUSION

In this chapter, we have highlighted the importance of clinical supervision and the need to adopt trauma-informed supervisory models that address the important trauma-based concerns that counselors bring into supervision. We have introduced relevant aspects of clinical supervision that intersect with trauma-sensitive supervision, emphasizing critical perspectives that supervisors need to incorporate into their knowledge base, especially recent neurobiological research relating to the effects of trauma on the brain as well as the importance of understanding the impact of secondary traumatic stress and vicarious trauma. We have offered discussions about systemic perspectives of trauma-informed clinical supervision along with concerns about relevant social justice issues. We have identified the clinical implications regarding ways in which clinical supervision and trauma counseling intersect. It is essential, at this point in time, that the mental health professions endeavor to provide competent trauma-informed clinical supervision to therapists who deliver mental health services to clients who have experienced trauma, stress, crisis, or disaster events in their lives. Such adaptation is an issue of professional ethical practice.

ADDITIONAL RESOURCES

 A robust set of instructor resources designed to supplement this text is located at http://connect.springerpub.com/content/book/978-0-8261-5085-1. Qualifying instructors may request access by emailing textbook@springerpub.com.

PRACTICE-BASED RESOURCES AND REFERENCES

To view a list of resources and all the references, please visit connect.springerpub.com via the following url: http://connect.springerpub.com/content/book/978-0-8261-5085-1/part/part06/chapter/ch32

Conclusion: The Continued Need for Developing an Integrative Systemic Approach to Trauma, Stress, Crisis, and Disaster

LISA LÓPEZ LEVERS

CHAPTER OVERVIEW

This final chapter focuses on synthesizing the information about trauma, stress, crisis, and disaster presented in the previous 32 chapters of this textbook. As an extension of analyzing the counseling implications presented across all of the chapters of this book, Chapter 33 presents the details of an integrative systemic approach to trauma (ISAT) model, with the hope that it can expand upon and continue to construct the trauma scaffold described in the first four chapters of this textbook.

LEARNING OBJECTIVES

After reading this chapter, the reader should be able to:

1. Synthesize key clinical points about trauma, stress, crisis, and disaster, drawing from information provided in the previous 32 chapters of this textbook;
2. Understand the need for integrative approaches to trauma, stress, crisis, and disaster;
3. Identify the key elements of the ISAT model;
4. Develop a holistic awareness of the various approaches to and perspectives of trauma, stress, crisis, and disaster;
5. Become aware of the pedagogical and clinical supervisory issues germane to trauma, stress, crisis, and disaster; and,
6. Identify continuing research needs related to trauma, stress, crisis, and disaster.

INTRODUCTION

Until recently, just over the last couple of decades, many mental health-related educators and therapists seemingly have avoided intentional engagement with client trauma issues, perhaps daunted by the horrors experienced by many victims of trauma. However, in this age of high-technology immediacy, just as ordinary citizens of the planet, we are exposed, more frequently and with greater intensity, to the tragedies of other people. We no longer can deny the sometimes-unspeakable lived experiences of trauma, crisis, and disaster survivors. Throughout this textbook, the authors of various chapters have repeated that, to date, many single-theory clinical responses to client issues surrounding trauma have not been adequate. The professional literature is replete with such admonitions (e.g., American Psychiatric Association [APA] & Academy of Psychosomatic Medicine [APM], 2016; American Psychological Association, 2017; Bradshaw et al., 2014; Killen et al., 2015; Maercker & Hecker, 2016; Mahoney & Markel, 2016; Mattar & Frewen, 2020; Sweeney et al., 2018; Veterans Affairs & Department of Defense, 2017; Watkins et al., 2018). As students, instructors, supervisors, and clinicians, with our growing understandings of the multifaceted effects of trauma, we no longer can deny the reality of trauma-induced distress or the need for multimodal systemic and integrative approaches to helping survivors of trauma, stress, crisis, and disaster. This especially is true concerning advances in neurobiological research and our evolving comprehension of the effects of trauma on the brain; however, our psychotherapy-relevant responses to clients' trauma-related somatic concerns still need to be nested within larger and compatible psychosocial therapeutic frameworks.

As I have reread and reexamined the preceding 32 chapters of this textbook, I have noted many of the authors echoing what I consider to be relevant themes associated with counseling survivors of trauma. These themes offer some level of congruency among the various topics related to trauma, stress, crisis, and disaster as well as to how we categorize trauma and trauma-related events. The purpose of this chapter is to recap and to explicate some of the most salient implications for counseling, drawn from the chapters of this book, and to emphasize the need for an integrative systemic approach to trauma.

IMPLICATIONS FOR COUNSELING SURVIVORS OF TRAUMA, STRESS, CRISIS, AND DISASTER

Perhaps the most essential consideration in interventions that help survivors of trauma, stress, crisis, and disaster in their healing processes is the quality of the relationship between the therapist and the client. This seems so obvious, and yet it sometimes becomes woefully lost within treatment delivery systems that are not intentionally trauma informed (Substance Abuse and Mental Health Services Administration [SAMHSA], 2014, 2020). But paradoxically, although the dyadic relationship is paramount, the therapeutic alliance is not solely applicable to the client and the counselor; it also extends to the counselor's colleagues and to the service delivery system. The therapeutic dyad is nested within larger-but-still-relevant social units or systems; multiple influences, across any or all of these systems, may or may not be interlinked. Considering this as being parallel to the bioecological framework, the client and therapist are central, but their relationship is affected by perhaps countless other individuals and systems across multiple environments, over which the clinician and the client may have relatively little control. This is illustrated, very simplistically, in Figure 33.1.

1. The **clinical relationship**, of course, includes the client–clinician dyad, but it also includes any other more-or-less formal healing modalities in which the survivor may be involved, such as group therapy, a 12-step program, spiritual activities, and so forth. The emphasis of this dimension is on the traumatized client's ability to reestablish trusting relationships. However, *relationship* implies more than one person. Although the client is facing the aftermath of a trauma, stress, crisis, or disaster event, recognizing and treating trauma-related clinical features presented by the client constitutes an ecological transition for the therapist as well.

2. The **nexus of personal and treatment issues** includes matters associated with all of the actors who are involved in trauma treatment, as well as significant persons in the client's life who may affect treatment outcomes; this nexus also includes colleagues of the clinician, whose roles may have a direct impact on treatment (e.g., clinical supervisor, agency administrator). Similar to the representation of the individual in Bronfenbrenner's (1979, 1981, 1994)

Figure 33.1

Integrative Systemic Approach to Trauma (ISAT)

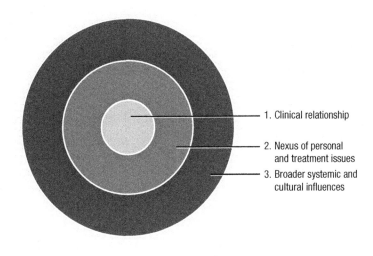

1. Clinical relationship
2. Nexus of personal and treatment issues
3. Broader systemic and cultural influences

bioecological model of human development, every personal aspect of the client remains relevant at this level of the model, including the client's neurobiological responses to trauma. The plethora of possible elements in this dimension are too numerous to detail here but include personal characteristics of the client and personal and professional characteristics and qualifications of the counselor, the treatment milieu, client lived experience, client triggers, informal client support systems, clinical supervision, other clinician support mechanisms, and so forth.

3. The **broader systemic and cultural influences** include the overall treatment system, funding mechanisms, and the mental health and other regulatory policies that exist at local, state, regional, national, and even global levels and that may have an ultimate effect on treatment outcome. This level also includes attitudinal and public health perspectives about who has access to healthcare, mental healthcare, and behavioral healthcare; lack of equity in access to any part(s) of the healthcare system obviously can affect clinical outcomes adversely.

These elements represent an ecological perspective of counseling survivors of trauma, what I am terming the "integrative systemic approach to trauma" (ISAT) model. The ISAT model offers a conceptual framework for aligning multiple levels of trauma response with what appear to be best-practice and best-milieu approaches. One promising study (Golfetto, 2017) has used the ISAT model as a part of the theoretical framework for exploring the perceptions of trauma-focused therapists mandated to use evidence-based practices (EBPs) when delivering sexual trauma interventions to clients. The major finding of the research indicated that, while experienced trauma clinicians respected and used EBPs, they preferred to operate from more flexible and integrative approaches to trauma counseling than the more prescriptive EPBs, alone, allowed.

The ISAT model assumes an overall understanding of the neurobiological effects of trauma along with a bioecological and systemic approach to counseling survivors of trauma, crisis, and disaster; it continually endeavors to construct and reconstruct integrative best-practice methods to assist clients' healing processes in trauma-informed environments. The model builds upon the trauma scaffold, discussed in the first four chapters of this book, and entails an iterative and recursive process of continuing to construct dynamic and integrative modes of response and recovery. Integral to this model is the attention paid to the trauma-associated lived experiences of survivors, to the trauma-specific training needs and the trauma-specific supervisory/support needs of therapists who work with traumatized clients, and to the degree to which the service-delivery system is sensitive to trauma and its related issues. Many of these features are identified and described in the various chapters of this textbook, and the work of refining this model is ongoing. The remaining parts of this section highlight the following themes that arise from the implications for counseling, which have been identified in the previous 32 chapters: (a) How We Understand and Approach Trauma, Stress, Crisis, and Disaster; (b) Social View and Systemic/Ecological Perspectives of Trauma; (c) Clinical Preparation; (d) Clinician-Related Characteristics/Attributes; (e) Client-Related Characteristics/Attributes; and (f) Research-Related Issues.

How We Understand and Approach Trauma, Stress, Crisis, and Disaster

Many of the authors of this textbook have emphasized the importance of an interdisciplinary approach to trauma treatment. Not exclusively viewed as the sole province of any one set of medical or social science professionals—including psychiatrists and other physicians, counselors, psychologists, social workers, teachers, nurses, pharmacists, and emergency first responders—the work of trauma recovery has been seen here as extending to additional professionals like anthropologists, sociologists, attorneys, judges, police officers, firemen, religious leaders, public health workers, and journalists who also may be intricately involved with our clients' trauma, stress, crisis, and disaster issues. However, regardless of discipline, the quality of the relationship between the trauma survivor and the therapist has been regarded as contributive to the success or failure of treatment.

Throughout this book, experiences of trauma have been framed as persistent across all levels of contemporary societies. In the various chapters of this book, authors have described best and promising practices associated with trauma counseling. A frequently expressed view has been that interventions need to incorporate multimodal, integrative, and systemic methods aimed at empowering survivors; many of the authors have expressed variations on the theme of "one size does *not* fit all," concerning trauma treatment. Most of the chapters have prioritized the relevance of attending to the neurobiological effects of trauma, stress, crisis, and disaster, along with contextual factors and cultural influences. Issues of prevention, multicultural considerations, historical/racial or transgenerational trauma, and the comorbidity of posttraumatic stress disorder (PTSD) with so many other conditions have been discussed variably across chapters. I particularly was taken by the sentiment, in so many of the chapters, that reflects Pearlman and Saakvitne's (1995) expression that the work of trauma therapy " is subversive work; we name and address society's shame" (p. 2). Indeed, acknowledging, facilitating expression of, and bearing witness to the lived experiences of trauma survivors often forces us to engage with the darkest dimensions of humanity, and this dynamic has been articulated, respectfully and humbly, throughout many of the chapters. Because the focus of this textbook has been on counseling survivors of trauma and the related constructs of stress, crisis, and disaster, it was beyond the scope of the book to address the circumstances and needs of perpetrators. However, a number of authors have noted that many perpetrators also have been victims of violence; thus, if we are going to have a public-health impact on interrupting and diminishing the cycle of violence, we need to develop effective treatment and prevention interventions for batterers, sexual predators, and other culprits of interpersonal and mass violence. Likewise, as we consider the effects of anthropogenic climate change and the relationship to trauma and disaster, corporate culpability and accountability also are issues that need to be explored more fully.

Social View and Systemic/Ecological Perspectives of Trauma

In several of the chapters in this textbook, authors have noted the lingering societal stigma, even today, regarding mental health treatment. The psychosocial needs of some groups, for example older adults, often are missed or undertreated. Primarily because of issues of stigma and inequity, mental health services are neither readily available nor realistically accessible to many groups of people. This includes clinical treatment for the effects of traumatic experiences, thereby constituting one facet of why issues of trauma extend to the arena of human rights and social justice.

Along with discussions regarding both the clinical and phenomenological features of trauma, several of the authors have commented on the notion of trauma as a socially constructed concept that has differing meanings in varying contexts. Some of the authors have noted the importance of counselors' worldviews when apprehending the effects of others' traumatic experiences. Several of the authors have discussed the impact of racial, historical, or transgenerational trauma on survivors.

Chapters throughout this textbook have embraced and expounded upon neurobiological and ecological conceptualizations of trauma, emphasizing the impact of traumatic events on individuals, on families, and on broader communities. Many of the authors have written about trauma from bioecological and transactional perspectives, signifying the importance of a systemic understanding of the impact of trauma; many of the discussions have illuminated the equity and social justice issues that intersect with and connect the neurobiological and the systemic. The various authors in this text have articulated the relevance of a range of counseling modalities, including integrative and trauma-informed approaches to trauma treatment.

Clinical Preparation

A major reason for developing this textbook was the lack of an effective tool for teaching a comprehensive graduate-level (or advanced undergraduate-level) human service course that addresses the various issues concerning trauma, stress, crisis, and disaster events. Endemic to this need is the reality that interest in such graduate or advanced training is a relatively recent phenomenon. Many of the authors of this book have asserted the unquestionable importance of adequate training in trauma-related issues and the need for advanced learning around adequate clinical supervision and other therapist-centered systemic support mechanisms—this includes preparing entry-level students to be receptive to clinical supervision as well as preparing advanced students to provide competent trauma-sensitive supervision. Most of the authors have advocated that preservice training related to trauma, stress, crisis, and disaster events be incorporated into master's-level social service academic programs; they also have highlighted the need for continuing education and in-service training in these areas. A number of the authors have espoused the idea that clinicians be trained in an integrated approach to trauma care. Several authors have suggested that preservice training is not sufficient, urging therapists to remain current with diagnostic and treatment issues by staying abreast of the most recent literature, reading peer-reviewed journals, and attending trainings and conferences concerning trauma. Throughout the textbook, authors have advocated that educators and clinical supervisors become proficient in understanding the clinical implications of the most recent neurobiological findings concerning the impact of trauma.

Across the chapters in this textbook, authors have reiterated the absolute necessity of adequate clinical supervision and support for therapists involved with trauma treatment. In the discussion surrounding the co-occurrence of trauma and addiction in Chapter 13, Wurzman has suggested that a treatment team or trauma-sensitive supervision group share in the responsibility of caring for complex and challenging clients. In Chapter 30, Jankoski has pointed to the need for supervisors working with trauma counselors to be knowledgeable about and sensitive to issues of trauma; she also has affirmed the supervisory duty of being actively aware of the content and severity of supervisees' caseloads. Finally, in Chapter 32, Bledsoe and colleagues have called for the social service professions to adopt more rigorous trauma-informed standards for and expectations of care and supervision, so that issues of trauma, stress, crisis, and disaster can be addressed more efficaciously and in a systemic fashion.

Clinician-Related Characteristics/Attributes

Across the various chapters, numerous authors have noted that the cost of caring is high in the trauma-, stress-, crisis-, and disaster-related situations described in this textbook; trauma counselors are at high risk for vicarious trauma and secondary traumatization. Therefore, most of the authors have emphasized strongly the importance of trauma therapists possessing keen self-reflection and self-care abilities. An underlying presumption, as highlighted by Johnson and Tarvydas in Chapter 29, has been that trauma counselors need to be ethical clinicians, taking seriously their ethical responsibility to self, to clients, and to constituent communities. Some of the authors here have indicated that counselors need to be in touch with their own histories of grief, loss, and trauma, as well as to be aware of the parallel process of feeling overwhelmed by client concerns. A number of the authors have stated that if a clinician has a history of trauma, this should be addressed in clinical supervision.

Throughout this text, the authors have expressed concern about the potential for therapists who are not adequately trained in trauma, stress, crisis, and disaster issues to harm their traumatized clients, emphasizing that, regardless of any other interaction, therapists must ensure that they do no harm to clients. Authors have asserted that trauma therapists need to have an adequate baseline of knowledge, including but not limited to the following:

- An understanding of the neurobiological impact of trauma, stress, crisis, and disaster on the autonomic nervous system;
- Knowledge of PTSD and trauma-related symptoms;
- An understanding of clients' triggers;
- Knowledge of assessment techniques;
- Knowledge of best-practice treatments; and,
- Knowledge of medication side effects and adverse drug reactions.

Authors consistently have identified and accentuated the following competencies of trauma counselors:

- Engaging with authenticity;
- Possessing empathy and compassion;
- Maintaining appropriate boundaries;
- Recognizing transference and the potential for countertransference, as well as engaging in clinical supervision to process countertransference;
- Being able to formulate intentional treatment strategies; and,
- Having a multisystemic, multidimensional understanding of trauma, stress, crisis, and disaster issues.

In several of the chapters, the authors have underscored the need for counselors to be aware of their own worldviews, so that they are not imposing their own values onto clients. Many of the authors have recommended that clinicians be sensitive to clients' contextual factors as well as to their unique experiences and backgrounds. In Chapter 17, Zeleke and Levers, and in Chapter 19, Walsh and colleagues have argued that clinicians need to take the cultural backgrounds of trauma survivors into consideration when designing treatment plans and selecting intervention techniques. Several authors have noted that therapists need to be aware of hate-motivated violence and to be prepared to address issues of aggression. In fact, Viehl and colleagues, in Chapter 18, have described the issue of gender-related hate crimes as an opportunity for service clinicians to act as agents of systemic change by advocating for social justice and human rights.

The contemporary service delivery system is more aware of trauma and its related issues than in the past; therefore, some of the authors have suggested that asking about a client's history of trauma should be considered a normalized line of inquiry now, as well as being a part of the routine intake process, across healthcare sectors. This may be an especially relevant issue, moving into the future, as so many people have experienced trauma, stress, crisis, and even disaster-level responses during the COVID-19 pandemic; these effects are likely to reverberate for many years. Various authors have identified the importance of clinicians *listening* to clients' narratives, rather than operating solely on canonical diagnostic tenets. Likewise, authors have advised that therapists need to take care not to use leading language with clients, concerning their trauma experiences, in order to ensure against potential iatrogenic effects.

In Chapter 22, relative to disaster work, Tracy has raised the importance of counselors knowing how to work, in tandem, with emergency service clinicians. Especially in situations of crisis and disaster, therapists may need to adapt, in unseemly situations, and treatment orientations may need to be adapted to a rapidly changing environment; in addition, the environmental situation may require mobile services. In Chapter 24, Levers and Drozda include the issues of anthropogenic climate change and mass casualties as parts of the trauma counseling discourse. In a number of chapters in Section IV of the textbook, authors have pointed out that, when responding to a disaster, therapists need to be prepared for the details associated with the specific disaster. Counselors need to be affiliated with an organization that is part of an official response structure, underscoring that a disaster clearly is not the time for "lone ranger" tactics, no matter how well intended. Finally, counselors need to understand the circumstances under which addressing immediate needs is essential, and thus psychotherapy is not appropriate in the moment.

Client-Related Characteristics/Attributes

One of the major implications for counseling, as expressed by the authors of this textbook, has been the necessity for therapists to help traumatized clients to feel safe and secure. When individuals experience traumatic events, their ability to trust in the world may shatter, life may feel fragmented and disconnected, and survivors of trauma may feel a sense of powerlessness. Although our diagnostic codes and treatment models may be based on objective criteria, we need to remember that our clients' responses to their lived experiences of traumatic events may be highly subjective. Although the lives of people affected by traumatic events may be *changed* permanently as a result of their traumatic experiences, they do not have to feel *damaged* permanently by these events. The core experiences of traumatic events affect victims on multiple physical, personal, and systemic levels; therefore, several of the authors have advocated employing a holistic perspective, engaging situations of trauma across the client's multiple dimensions of being, including physiological, psychosocial, cognitive, affective, and spiritual or existential. A common therapeutic aim expressed by many of the authors has emphasized the importance of therapists assisting clients to reconnect with self and others and to regain or develop a sense of empowerment and resilience.

Research-Related Issues

In many of the chapters in this textbook, authors have identified the need for more data-driven research in a variety of trauma-related areas. In general, authors have noted that additional research is necessary in order to refine current best-practice treatment modalities and to explicate the interactions between individual client needs and sociocultural context. Authors also have articulated several specific research needs. For example, in Chapters 1 and 2, Levers has identified the need for more research concerning pedagogical aspects of designing adequate preservice trauma curricula for academic programs as well as adequate in-service training for clinicians. In Chapter 6, Choate has asserted that future research should prioritize a multisystemic approach to the conceptualization of sexual violence. In Chapter 12, Mpofu has suggested the compelling need for more research about older adults' health resourcing and potential elder abuse. In Chapter 19, Walsh et al. have suggested more rigorous research concerning efficacious responses to community-based trauma and crisis. In Chapter 21, Alexander and Levers have addressed the need for more extensive applied research regarding school violence. In Chapter 26, Evans and Khadivi have asserted the need for more research that is specific to careful trauma-related psychological assessment practices.

THE NEED FOR AN INTEGRATIVE SYSTEMIC APPROACH TO TRAUMA

This textbook has been organized around the need for an instructional trauma scaffold, to assist students in beginning to comprehend the various dimensions of trauma, and to reflect the emerging perspective of an ISAT model. Like others in the field, I believe that it not only is important to acknowledge the necessity of approaching trauma treatment from multimodal and integrative perspectives, but that we also must be acutely aware of all neurobiological and systemic aspects of trauma care. In this case, both neurobiological and systemic aspects apply to individual trauma survivors as well as to the clinicians from whom they seek help and the organizations to which they go in an effort to heal. The ISAT model affirms the neurobiological, bioecological, systemic, and transactional perspectives of the individual's position within a family, community, society, and culture; it also presumes, much as with trauma-informed care, that the trauma care system needs to be much more aligned with client needs than ever before. Beyond system-of-care implications, ISAT views adequate trauma-related education and competent trauma-sensitive clinical supervision as essential aspects of a fluid system of trauma care.

The ISAT model promotes a keen and holistic understanding of the complexities of trauma counseling and supervision; it further emphasizes the systemic and reciprocal interrelationships among preservice training, counseling practice, in-service training, and supervision. This approach draws from the research, theory, and practice literatures, defining relevant constructs and offering a comprehensive and integrative conceptual model. Although addressing the pertinent diagnostic and treatment issues of trauma, stress, crisis, and disaster, the ISAT model has the potential for illuminating how various systems and multiple environments require an integrative and systemic approach when dealing with the complexities of trauma. This ecological model incorporates client, clinical, supervisory, consultative, administrative, organizational, societal, and cultural facets of service delivery; it offers a useful framework for conceptualizing a wholly integrative and systemic approach for helping the survivors of trauma to make meaning of their traumatic experiences and to heal.

CONCLUSION

In this chapter, I have examined the content of the previous 32 chapters of this textbook and have offered a brief analysis and synthesis of the trauma-related implications for counseling, as identified by the various authors. I have discussed the implications according to themes related to client- and profession-based issues. This discussion has illuminated the need for continued development of systemic approaches to trauma, stress, crisis, and disaster, as well as the need for a metasystemic framework for conceptualizing all aspects of trauma care, which I have advanced as the ISAT model.

ADDITIONAL RESOURCES

 A robust set of instructor resources designed to supplement this text is located at http://connect.springerpub.com/content/book/978-0-8261-5085-1. Qualifying instructors may request access by emailing textbook@springerpub.com.

PRACTICE-BASED RESOURCES AND REFERENCES

To view a list of resources and all the references, please visit connect.springerpub.com via the following url: http://connect.springerpub.com/content/book/978-0-8261-5085-1/part/part06/chapter/ch33

Index